OXFORD PICTURE DICTIONARY

SECOND EDITION

OPD

Jayme Adelson-Goldstein
Norma Shapiro

OXFORD
UNIVERSITY PRESS

198 Madison Avenue
New York, NY 10016 USA

Great Clarendon Street, Oxford OX2 6DP UK

Oxford University Press is a department of the University of Oxford.
It furthers the University's objective of excellence in research, scholarship,
and education by publishing worldwide in

Oxford New York

Auckland Cape Town Dar es Salaam Hong Kong Karachi
Kuala Lumpur Madrid Melbourne Mexico City Nairobi
New Delhi Shanghai Taipei Toronto

With offices in

Argentina Austria Brazil Chile Czech Republic France Greece
Guatemala Hungary Italy Japan Poland Portugal Singapore
South Korea Switzerland Thailand Turkey Ukraine Vietnam

OXFORD and OXFORD ENGLISH are registered trademarks of
Oxford University Press.

© Oxford University Press 2009

Library of Congress Cataloging-in-Publication Data

Adelson-Goldstein, Jayme.
  The Oxford picture dictionary. Monolingual /
Jayme Adelson-Goldstein and Norma Shapiro.– 2nd ed.
    p. cm.
  Includes index.
  ISBN-13: 978-0-19-474021-0

  1. Picture dictionaries, English. 2. English
language–Textbooks for foreign speakers.
I. Shapiro, Norma. II. Title.
PE1629.S52 2008
423'.1–dc22

2007041017

Database right Oxford University Press (maker)

Executive Publishing Manager: Stephanie Karras
Managing Editor: Sharon Sargent
Development Editors: Glenn Mathes II, Bruce Myint, Katie La Storia
Associate Development Editors: Olga Christopoulos, Hannah Ryu, Meredith Stoll
Design Manager: Maj-Britt Hagsted
Project Manager: Allison Harm
Senior Designers: Stacy Merlin, Michael Steinhofer
Designer: Jaclyn Smith
Senior Production Artist: Julie Armstrong
Production Layout Artist: Colleen Ho
Cover Design: Stacy Merlin
Senior Image Editor: Justine Eun
Image Editors: Robin Fadool, Fran Newman, Jenny Vainisi
Manufacturing Manager: Shanta Persaud
Manufacturing Controller: Faye Wang
Translated by: Techno-Graphics & Translations, Inc.

ISBN: 978 0 19 474021 0

Printed in China

10 9 8 7

This book is printed on paper from certified and well-managed sources.

The OPD team thanks the following artists for their storyboarding and sketches:
Cecilia Aranovich, Chris Brandt, Giacomo Ghiazza, Gary Goldstein, Gordan Kljucec,
Vincent Lucido, and Glenn Urieta

Illustrations by: Lori Anzalone: 13, 70-71, 76-77; Joe "Fearless" Arenella/Will Sumpter:
178; Argosy Publishing: 66-67 (call-outs), 98-99, 108-109, 112-113 (call-outs), 152, 178,
193, 194-195, 196, 197, 205; Barbara Bastian: 4, 15, 17, 20-21, 162 (map), 198, 216-217
(map), 220-221; Philip Batini/AA Reps: 50; Thomas Bayley/Sparks Literary Agency:
158-159; Sally Bensusen: 211, 214; Annie Bissett: 112; Peter Bollinger/Shannon
Associates: 14-15; Higgens Bond/Anita Grien: 226; Molly Borman-Pullman: 116, 117;
Jim Fanning/Ravenhill Represents: 80-81; Mike Gardner: 10, 12, 17, 22, 132, 114-115,
142-143, 174, 219, 228-229; Garth Glazier/AA Reps: 106, 118-119; Dennis Godfrey/
Mike Wepplo: 204; Steve Graham: 124-125, 224; Graphic Map & Chart Co.: 200-201,
202-203; Julia Green/Mendola Art: 225; Glenn Gustafson: 9, 27, 48, 76, 100, 101,
117, 132, 133, 136, 155, 161, 179, 196; Barbara Harmon: 212-213, 215; Ben Hasler/
NB Illustration: 94-95, 101, 148-149, 172, 182, 186-187; Betsy Hayes: 134, 138-139;
Matthew Holmes: 75; Stewart Holmes/Illustration Ltd.: 192; Janos Jantner/Beehive
Illustration: 5, 13, 82-83, 122-123, 130-131, 146-147, 164-165, 184, 185; Ken Joudrey/
Munro Campagna: 52, 68-69, 177, 208-209; Bob Kaganich/Deborah Wolfe: 10, 40-41,
121; Steve Karp: 230, 231; Mike Kasun/Munro Campagna: 218; Graham Kennedy:
27; Marcel Laverdet/AA Reps: 23; Jeffrey Lindberg: 33, 42-43, 92-93, 133, 160-161,
170-171, 176; Dennis Lyall/Artworks: 198; Chris Lyons:/Lindgren & Smith: 173, 191;
Alan Male/Artworks: 210, 211; Jeff Mangiat/Mendola Art: 53, 54, 55, 56, 57, 58, 59,
66-67; Adrian Mateescu/The Studio: 188-189, 232-233; Karen Minot: 28-29; Paul
Mirocha/The Wiley Group: 194, 216-217; Peter Miserendino/P.T. Pie Illustrations:
198; Lee Montgomery/Illustration Ltd.: 4; Roger Motzkus: 229; Laurie O'Keefe: 111,
216-217; Daniel O'Leary/Illustration Ltd.: 8-9, 26, 34-35, 78, 135, 136-137, 238; Vilma
Ortiz-Dillon: 16, 20-21, 60, 98-99, 100, 211; Terry Pazcko: 46-47, 144-145, 152, 180,
227; David Preiss/Munro Campagna: 5; Pronk & Associates: 192-193; Tony Randazzo/
AA Reps: 156, 234-235; Mike Renwick/Creative Eye: 126-127; Mark Riedy/Scott Hull
Associates: 48-49, 79, 140, 153; Jon Rogers/AA Reps: 112; Jeff Sanson/Schumann &
Co.: 84-85, 240-241; David Schweitzer/Munro Campagna: 162-163; Ben Shannon/
Magnet Reps: 11, 64-65, 90, 91, 96, 97, 166-167, 168-169, 179, 239; Reed Sprunger/
Jae Wagoner Artists Rep.: 18-19, 232-233; Studio Liddell/AA Reps: 27; Angelo Tillary:
108-109; Ralph Voltz/Deborah Wolfe: 50-51, 128-129, 141, 154, 175, 236-237;
Jeff Wack/Mendola Art: 24, 25, 86-87, 102-103, 134-135, 231; Brad Walker: 104-105,
150-151, 157, 206-207; Wendy Wassink: 110-111; John White/The Neis Group: 199;
Eric Wilkerson: 32, 138; Simon Williams/Illustration Ltd.: 2-3, 6-7, 30-31, 36, 38-39,
44-45, 72-73; Lee Woodgate/Eye Candy Illustration: 222-223; Andy Zito: 62-23; Craig
Zuckerman: 14, 88-89, 112-113, 120-121, 194-195.

Chapter icons designed by Von Glitschka/Scott Hull Associates

Cover Art by CUBE/Illustration Ltd (hummingbird, branch); Paul Mirocha/The Wiley
Group (cherry); Mark Riedy/Scott Hull Associates (stamp); 9 Surf Studios (lettering).

Studio photography for Oxford University Press done by Dennis Kitchen Studio: 37,
61, 72, 73, 74, 75, 95, 96, 100, 180, 181, 183, 226.

Stock Photography: Age FotoStock: 238 (flute; clarinet; bassoon; saxophone; violin; cello;
bass; guitar; trombone; trumpet; xylophone; harmonica); Comstock, 61 (window);
Morales, 221 (bat); Franco Pizzochero, 98 (cashmere); Thinkstock, 61 (sink); Alamy:
Corbis, 61 (table); Gary Crabbe, 220 (park ranger); The Associated Press: 198 (strike;
soldiers in trench); Joe Rosenthal, 198 (Iwo Jima); Neil Armstrong, 198 (Buzz Aldrin
on Moon); CORBIS: Philip Gould, 198 (Civil War); Photo Library, 220 (Yosemite Falls);
Danita Delimont: Greg Johnston, 220 (snorkeling); Jamie & Judy Wild, 220 (El Capitan);
Getty Images: 198 (Martin Luther King, Jr.); Amana Images, 61 (soapy plates), The
Granger Collection: 198 (Jazz Age); The Image Works: Kelly Spranger, 220 (sea turtle);
Inmagine: 238 (oboe; tuba; French horn; piano; drums; tambourine; accordion);
istockphoto: 61 (oven); 98 (silk); 99 (suede; lace; velvet); Jupiter Images: 61 (tiles); 98
(wool); 99 (corduroy); Foodpix, 98 (linen); Rob Melnychuk/Brand X Pictures, 61 (glass
shower door); Jupiter Unlimited: 220 (seagulls); 238 (electric keyboard); Comstock, 99
(denim); Mary Evans Picture Library: 198 (women in factory); NPS Photo: Peter Jones, 221
(Carlsbad Cavern entrance; tour; cavern; spelunker); OceanwideImages.com: Gary Bell,
220 (coral); Photo Edit, Inc: David Young-Wolff, 220 (trail); Picture History: 198 (Hiram
Rhodes); Robertstock: 198 (Great Depression); Punchstock: 98 (t-shirt), Robert Glusic,
31 (Monument Valley); Roland Corporation: 238 (organ); SuperStock: 99 (leather); 198
(Daniel Boone); Shutterstock: Marek Szumlas, 94 (watch); United States Mint: 126;
Veer: Brand X Pictures, 220 (deer); Photodisc, 220 (black bear); Yankee Fleet, Inc.: 220
(Fort Jefferson; Yankee Freedom Ferry), Emil von Maltitz/Lime Photo, 37 (baby carrier).

This second edition of
the Oxford Picture Dictionary
is lovingly dedicated to
the memory of Norma Shapiro.

Her ideas, her pictures, and
her stories continue to teach,
inspire, and delight.

Acknowledgments

The publisher and authors would like to acknowledge the following individuals for their invaluable feedback during the development of this program:

Dr. Macarena Aguilar, Cy-Fair College, Houston, TX

Joseph F. Anselme, Atlantic Technical Center, Coconut Creek, FL

Stacy Antonopoulos, Monterey Trail High School, Elk Grove, CA

Carol Antunano, The English Center, Miami, FL

Irma Arencibia, Thomas A. Edison School, Union City, NJ

Suzi Austin, Alexandria City Public School Adult Program, Alexandria, FL

Patricia S. Bell, Lake Technical Center, Eustis, FL

Jim Brice, San Diego Community College District, San Diego, CA

Phil Cackley, Arlington Education and Employment Program (REEP), Arlington, VA

Frieda Caldwell, Metropolitan Adult Education Program, San Jose, CA

Sandra Cancel, Robert Waters School, Union City, NJ

Anne Marie Caney, Chula Vista Adult School, Chula Vista, CA

Patricia Castro, Harvest English Institute, Newark, NJ

Paohui Lola Chen, Milpitas Adult School, Milpitas, CA

Lori Cisneros, Atlantic Vo-Tech, Ft. Lauderdale, FL

Joyce Clapp, Hayward Adult School, Hayward, CA

Stacy Clark, Arlington Education and Employment Program (REEP), Arlington, VA

Nancy B. Crowell, Southside Programs for Adults in Continuing Education, Prince George, VA

Doroti da Cunha, Hialeah-Miami Lakes Adult Education Center, Miami, FL

Paula Da Silva-Michelin, La Guardia Community College, Long Island City, NY

Cynthia L. Davies, Humble I.S.D., Humble, TX

Christopher Davis, Overfelt Adult Center, San Jose, CA

Beverly De Nicola, Capistrano Unified School District, San Juan Capistrano, CA

Beatriz Diaz, Miami-Dade County Public Schools, Miami, FL

Druci J. Diaz, Hillsborough County Public Schools, Tampa, FL

Marion Donahue, San Dieguito Adult School, Encinitas, CA

Nick Doorn, International Education Services, South Lyon, MI

Mercedes Douglass, Seminole Community College, Sanford, FL

Jenny Elliott, Montgomery College, Rockville, MD

Paige Endo, Mt. Diablo Adult Education, Concord, CA

Megan Ernst, Glendale Community College, Glendale, CA

Elizabeth Escobar, Robert Waters School, Union City, NJ

Joanne Everett, Dave Thomas Education Center, Pompano Beach, FL

Jennifer Fadden, Arlington Education and Employment Program (REEP), Arlington, VA

Judy Farron, Fort Myers Language Center, Fort Myers, FL

Sharyl Ferguson, Montwood High School, El Paso, TX

Dr. Monica Fishkin, University of Central Florida, Orlando, FL

Nancy Frampton, Reedley College, Reedley, CA

Lynn A. Freeland, San Dieguito Union High School District, Encinitas, CA

Cathy Gample, San Leandro Adult School, San Leandro, CA

Hillary Gardner, Center for Immigrant Education and Training, Long Island City, NY

Martha C. Giffen, Alhambra Unified School District, Alhambra, CA

Jill Gluck, Hollywood Community Adult School, Los Angeles, CA

Carolyn Grimaldi, LaGuardia Community College, Long Island City, NY

William Gruenholz, USD Adult School, Concord, CA

Sandra G. Gutierrez, Hialeah-Miami Lakes Adult Education Center, Miami, FL

Conte Gúzman-Hoffman, Triton College, River Grove, IL

Amanda Harllee, Palmetto High School, Palmetto, FL

Mercedes Hearn, Tampa Bay Technical Center, Tampa, FL

Robert Hearst, Truman College, Chicago, IL

Patty Heiser, University of Washington, Seattle, WA

Joyce Hettiger, Metropolitan Education District, San Jose, CA

Karen Hirsimaki, Napa Valley Adult School, Napa, CA

Marvina Hooper, Lake Technical Center, Eustis, FL

Katie Hurter, North Harris College, Houston, TX

Nuchamon James, Miami Dade College, Miami, FL

Linda Jennings, Montgomery College, Rockville, MD

Bonnie Boyd Johnson, Chapman Education Center, Garden Grove, CA

Fayne B. Johnson, Broward County Public Schools, Fort Lauderdale, FL

Stavroula Katseyeanis, Robert Waters School, Union City, NJ

Dale Keith, Broadbase Consulting, Inc. at Kidworks USA, Miami, FL

Blanche Kellawon, Bronx Community College, Bronx, NY

Mary Kernel, Migrant Education Regional Office, Northwest Educational Service District, Anacortes, WA

Karen Kipke, Antioch High School Freshman Academy, Antioch, TN

Jody Kirkwood, ABC Adult School, Cerritos, CA

Matthew Kogan, Evans Community Adult School, Los Angeles, CA

Ineza Kuceba, Renton Technical College, Renton, WA

John Kuntz, California State University, San Bernadino, San Bernadino, CA

Claudia Kupiec, DePaul University, Chicago, IL

E.C. Land, Southside Programs for Adult Continuing Education, Prince George, VA

Betty Lau, Franklin High School, Seattle, WA

Patt Lemonie, Thomas A. Edison School, Union City, NJ

Lia Lerner, Burbank Adult School, Burbank, CA

Krystyna Lett, Metropolitan Education District, San Jose, CA

Renata Lima, TALK International School of Languages, Fort Lauderdale, FL

Luz M. Lopez, Sweetwater Union High School District, Chula Vista, CA

Osmara Lopez, Bronx Community College, Bronx, NY

Heather Lozano, North Lake College, Irving, TX

Betty Lynch, Arlington Education and Employment Program (REEP), Arlington, VA

Meera Madan, REID Park Elementary School, Charlotte, NC

Ivanna Mann Thrower, Charlotte Mecklenburg Schools, Charlotte, NC

Michael R. Mason, Loma Vista Adult Center, Concord, CA

Holley Mayville, Charlotte Mecklenburg Schools, Charlotte, NC

Margaret McCabe, United Methodist Cooperative Ministries, Clearwater, FL

Todd McDonald, Hillsborough Adult Education, Tampa, FL

Nancy A. McKeand, ESL Consultant, St. Benedict, LA

Rebecca L. McLain, Gaston College, Dallas, NC

John M. Mendoza, Redlands Adult School, Redlands, CA

Bet Messmer, Santa Clara Adult Education Center, Santa Clara, CA

Christina Morales, BEGIN Managed Programs, New York, NY

Lisa Munoz, Metropolitan Education District, San Jose, CA

Mary Murphy-Clagett, Sweetwater Union High School District, Chula Vista, CA

Jonetta Myles, Rockdale County High School, Conyers, GA

Marwan Nabi, Troy High School, Fullerton, CA

Dr. Christine L. Nelsen, Salvation Army Community Center, Tampa, FL

Michael W. Newman, Arlington Education and Employment Program (REEP), Arlington, VA

Rehana Nusrat, Huntington Beach Adult School, Huntington Beach, CA

Cindy Oakley-Paulik, Embry-Riddle Aeronautical University, Daytona Beach, FL

Acknowledgments

Janet Ochi-Fontanott, Sweetwater Union High School District, Chula Vista, CA

Lorraine Pedretti, Metropolitan Education District, San Jose, CA

Isabel Pena, BE/ESL Programs, Garland, TX

Margaret Perry, Everett Public Schools, Everett, WA

Dale Pesmen, PhD, Chicago, IL

Cathleen Petersen, Chapman Education Center, Garden Grove, CA

Allison Pickering, Escondido Adult School, Escondido, CA

Ellen Quish, LaGuardia Community College, Long Island City, NY

Teresa Reen, Independence Adult Center, San Jose, CA

Kathleen Reynolds, Albany Park Community Center, Chicago, IL

Melba I. Rillen, Palmetto High School, Palmetto, FL

Lorraine Romero, Houston Community College, Houston, TX

Eric Rosenbaum, BEGIN Managed Programs, New York, NY

Blair Roy, Chapman Education Center, Garden Grove, CA

Arlene R. Schwartz, Broward Community Schools, Fort Lauderdale, FL

Geraldyne Blake Scott, Truman College, Chicago, IL

Sharada Sekar, Antioch High School Freshman Academy, Antioch, TN

Dr. Cheryl J. Serrano, Lynn University, Boca Raton, FL

Janet Setzekorn, United Methodist Cooperative Ministries, Clearwater, FL

Terry Shearer, EDUCALL Learning Services, Houston, TX

Elisabeth Sklar, Township High School District 113, Highland Park, IL

Robert Stein, BEGIN Managed Programs, New York, NY

Ruth Sutton, Township High School District 113, Highland Park, IL

Alisa Takeuchi, Chapman Education Center, Garden Grove, CA

Grace Tanaka, Santa Ana College School of Continuing Education, Santa Ana, CA

Annalisa Te, Overfelt Adult Center, San Jose, CA

Don Torluemke, South Bay Adult School, Redondo Beach, CA

Maliheh Vafai, Overfelt Adult Center, San Jose, CA

Tara Vasquez, Robert Waters School, Union City, NJ

Nina Velasco, Naples Language Center, Naples, FL

Theresa Warren, East Side Adult Center, San Jose, CA

Lucie Gates Watel, Truman College, Chicago, IL

Wendy Weil, Arnold Middle School, Cypress, TX

Patricia Weist, TALK International School of Languages, Fort Lauderdale, FL

Dr. Carole Lynn Weisz, Lehman College, Bronx, NY

Desiree Wesner, Robert Waters School, Union City, NJ

David Wexler, Napa Valley Adult School, Napa, CA

Cynthia Wiseman, Borough of Manhattan Community College, New York, NY

Debbie Cullinane Wood, Lincoln Education Center, Garden Grove, CA

Banu Yaylali, Miami Dade College, Miami, FL

Hongyan Zheng, Milpitas Adult Education, Milpitas, CA

Arlene Zivitz, ESOL Teacher, Jupiter, FL

The publisher, authors, and editors would like to thank the following people for their expertise in reviewing specific content areas:

Ross Feldberg, Tufts University, Medford, MA

William J. Hall, M.D. FACP/FRSM (UK), Cumberland Foreside, ME

Jill A. Horohoe, Arizona State University, Tempe, AZ

Phoebe B. Rouse, Louisiana State University, Baton Rouge, LA

Dr. Susan Rouse, Southern Wesleyan University, Central, SC

Dr. Ira M. Sheskin, University of Miami, Coral Gables, FL

Maiko Tomizawa, D.D.S., New York, NY

Table of Contents فهرست موضوعات

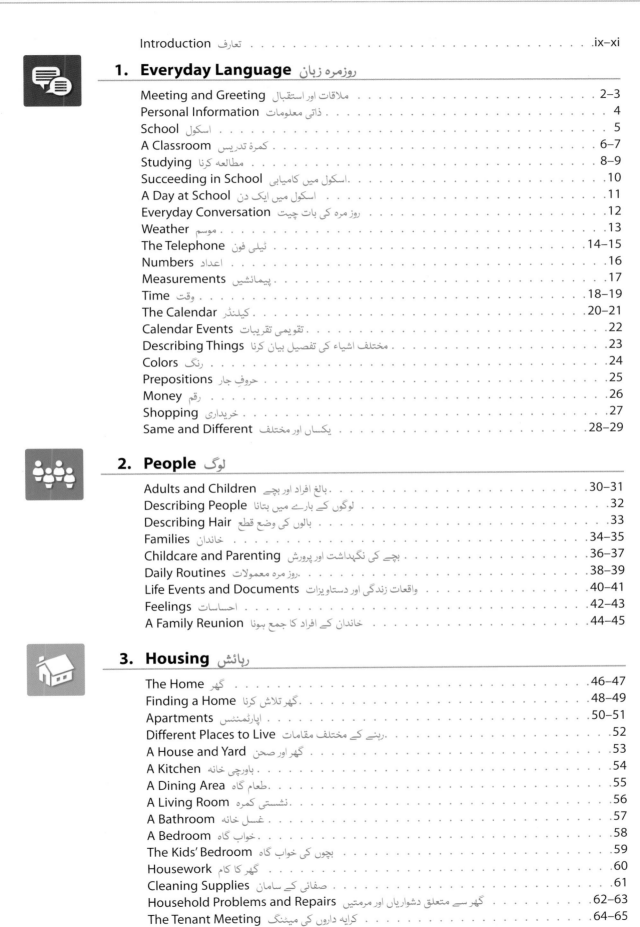

Introduction تعارف . . . . ix–xi

1. Everyday Language روزمرہ زبان

Meeting and Greeting ملاقات اور استقبال 2–3
Personal Information ذاتی معلومات 4
School اسکول 5
A Classroom کمرۂ تدریس 6–7
Studying مطالعہ کرنا 8–9
Succeeding in School اسکول میں کامیابی 10
A Day at School اسکول میں ایک دن 11
Everyday Conversation روز مرہ کی بات چیت 12
Weather موسم 13
The Telephone ٹیلی فون 14–15
Numbers اعداد 16
Measurements پیمائشیں 17
Time وقت 18–19
The Calendar کیلنڈر 20–21
Calendar Events تقویمی تقریبات 22
Describing Things مختلف اشیاء کی تفصیل بیان کرنا . . 23
Colors رنگ 24
Prepositions حروفِ جار 25
Money رقم 26
Shopping خریداری 27
Same and Different یکساں اور مختلف 28–29

2. People لوگ

Adults and Children بالغ افراد اور بچے 30–31
Describing People لوگوں کے بارے میں بتانا 32
Describing Hair بالوں کی وضع قطع 33
Families خاندان 34–35
Childcare and Parenting بچے کی نگہداشت اور پرورش . 36–37
Daily Routines روز مرہ معمولات 38–39
Life Events and Documents واقعات زندگی اور دستاویزات . 40–41
Feelings احساسات 42–43
A Family Reunion خاندان کے افراد کا جمع ہونا 44–45

3. Housing رہائش

The Home گھر 46–47
Finding a Home گھر تلاش کرنا 48–49
Apartments اپارٹمنٹس 50–51
Different Places to Live رہنے کے مختلف مقامات 52
A House and Yard گھر اور صحن 53
A Kitchen باورچی خانہ 54
A Dining Area طعام گاہ 55
A Living Room نشستی کمرہ 56
A Bathroom غسل خانہ 57
A Bedroom خواب گاہ 58
The Kids' Bedroom بچوں کی خواب گاہ 59
Housework گھر کا کام 60
Cleaning Supplies صفائی کے سامان 61
Household Problems and Repairs گھر سے متعلق دشواریاں اور مرمتیں . 62–63
The Tenant Meeting کرایہ داروں کی میٹنگ 64–65

Contents موضوعات

4. Food غذا

Back from the Market بازار سے واپسی 66–67
Fruit پھل 68
Vegetables سبزیاں 69
Meat and Poultry گوشت اور مرغ 70
Seafood and Deli سمندری غذائیں— دکان اور طعام خانہ 71
A Grocery Store کریانہ اسٹور 72–73
Containers and Packaging ڈبّے اور سامان رکھنے کے طریقے 74
Weights and Measurements وزن اور پیمائش 75
Food Preparation and Safety غذا کی تیاری اور حفاظت . . 76–77
Kitchen Utensils باورچی خانے کے برتن 78
Fast Food Restaurant جلدی سے تیار کھانے کا ریستوران . . 79
A Coffee Shop Menu کافی شاپ کا مینیو 80–81
A Restaurant ریستوران 82–83
The Farmers' Market کاشتکاروں کا بازار 84–85

5. Clothing لباس

Everyday Clothes روزمرہ کے کپڑے 86–87
Casual, Work, and Formal Clothes غیر رسمی، کام کے، اور رسمی کپڑے . . 88–89
Seasonal Clothing موسمی لباس 90
Underwear and Sleepwear زیر جامہ اور شب خوابی کا لباس . . . 91
Workplace Clothing کام کی جگہ کا لباس 92–93
Shoes and Accessories جوتے اور دیگر اضافی سامان 94–95
Describing Clothes کپڑوں کی تفصیل 96–97
Making Clothes کپڑے بنانا 98–99
Making Alterations کپڑوں میں ترمیم کرنا 100
Doing the Laundry کپڑے دھونا 101
A Garage Sale گیرج میں لگی دکان 102–103

6. Health صحت

The Body جسم 104–105
Inside and Outside the Body جسم کے اندر اور باہر . . . 106–107
Personal Hygiene ذاتی حفظان صحت اور صفائی 108–109
Symptoms and Injuries علامات اور چوٹیں 110
Illnesses and Medical Conditions بیماریاں اور صحتی خرابیاں . . . 111
A Pharmacy دوا خانہ 112–113
Taking Care of Your Health اپنی صحت کی دیکھ بھال کرنا . . 114–115
Medical Emergencies طبی ہنگامی حالات 116
First Aid فوری طبی امداد 117
Medical Care طبی نگہداشت 118
Dental Care دانتوں کی دیکھ بھال 119
Hospital اسپتال 120–121
A Health Fair صحت میلہ 122–123

7. Community سماج

Downtown شہر کا مرکز 124–125
City Streets شہر کی سڑکیں 126–127
An Intersection چورابا 128–129
A Mall بڑا بازار (مال) 130–131
The Bank بینک 132
The Library کتب خانہ 133
The Post Office ڈاک خانہ 134–135
Department of Motor Vehicles (DMV) موٹر گاڑیوں کا شعبہ (ڈی ایم وی) 136–137
Government and Military Service سرکاری اور فوجی ملازمت 138–139
Civic Rights and Responsibilities شہری حقوق اور ذمہ داریاں 140
The Legal System قانونی نظام 141
Crime جرم 142
Public Safety عوامی حفاظت 143
Emergencies and Natural Disasters ہنگامی حالات اور قدرتی آفات . . . 144–145
Emergency Procedures ہنگامی اقدامات 146–147
Community Cleanup کمیونٹی کی سطح پر صفائی 148–149

8. Transportation نقل و حمل

Basic Transportation بنیادی ذرائع نقل و حمل 150–151
Public Transportation عوامی ذرائع نقل و حمل 152
Prepositions of Motion حرکت سے متعلق حروف جار 153
Traffic Signs نقل و حمل سے متعلق علامات 154
Directions and Maps سمتیں اور نقشے 155
Cars and Trucks کاریں اور ٹرک 156
Buying and Maintaining a Car کار خریدنا اور اس کی دیکھ بھال کرنا . . . 157
Parts of a Car کار کے پرزے 158–159
An Airport ہوائی اڈہ 160–161
Taking a Trip کسی سفر پر جانا 162–163

9. Work کام

The Workplace کام کی جگہ 164–165
Jobs and Occupations A-C ملازمتیں اور پیشے اے - سی 166
Jobs and Occupations C-H ملازمتیں اور پیشے سی - ایچ 167
Jobs and Occupations H-P ملازمتیں اور پیشے ایچ - پی 168
Jobs and Occupations P-W ملازمتیں اور پیشے پی - ڈبلیو 169
Job Skills کام کی مہارتیں 170
Office Skills دفتری مہارتیں 171
Career Planning پیشے کی منصوبہ بندی 172
Job Search ملازمت کی تلاش 173
Interview Skills انٹرویو کی مہارتیں 174
A Factory فیکٹری 175
Landscaping and Gardening منظر کاری اور باغبانی 176
Farming and Ranching کاشتکاری اور مویشی بانی 177
Construction تعمیر 178
Job Safety کام کے دوران حفاظت 179
Tools and Building Supplies اوزار اور تعمیر کے سامان 180–181
An Office دفتر 182–183
A Hotel ہوٹل 184
Food Service کھانے کی خدمات 185
A Bad Day at Work دفتر میں ایک خراب دن 186–187

Contents موضوعات

10. Areas of Study مطالعے کے میدان

Schools and Subjects اسکول اور مضامین	188–189
English Composition انگریزی زبان کی تالیفی ترکیب	190–191
Mathematics ریاضی	192–193
Science سائنس	194–195
Computers کمپیوٹرز	196
The Internet انٹرنیٹ	197
U.S. History امریکی تاریخ	198
World History تاریخ عالم	199
North America and Central America شمالی امریکا اور وسطی امریکا	200–201
World Map دنیا کا نقشہ	202–203
Geography and Habitats جغرافیہ اور مقامات	204
The Universe کائنات	205
A Graduation گریجویشن کی ایک تقریب	206–207

11. Plants and Animals پیڑ پودے اور جانور

Nature Center قدرتی مرکز	208–209
Trees and Plants پیڑ اور پودے	210
Flowers پھول	211
Marine Life, Amphibians, and Reptiles سمندری زندگی، خشکی و پانی میں رہنے والے حیوانات اور سانپ اور چھپکلی کی نسل کے جانور	212–213
Birds, Insects, and Arachnids پرندے، کیڑے مکوڑے اور مفصل پایہ (چار جوڑی پیر والے کیڑے)	214
Domestic Animals and Rodents گھریلو جانور اور کترنے کے دانتوں والے جانور	215
Mammals تھن دار جانور	216–217
Energy and Conservation توانائی اور تحفظ	218–219
U.S. National Parks یو ایس نیشنل پارکس	220–221

12. Recreation تفریح

Places to Go اپنے شہر میں دیکھنے کے قابل مقامات	222–223
The Park and Playground پارک اور کھیل کے میدان	224
The Beach ساحل سمندر	225
Outdoor Recreation باہری تفریح	226
Winter and Water Sports سردی اور پانی کے کھیل	227
Individual Sports انفرادی کھیل کود	228
Team Sports جماعتی کھیل	229
Sports Verbs کھیل کود سے متعلق افعال	230
Sports Equipment کھیلوں کے آلات	231
Hobbies and Games پسندیدہ مشغلے اور کھیل	232–233
Electronics and Photography الیکٹرونکس اور فوٹوگرافی	234–235
Entertainment تفریح	236–237
Music موسیقی	238
Holidays تعطیلات	239
A Birthday Party ایک سالگرہ کی تقریب	240–241

Verb Guide فعل سے متعلق رہنمائی	242–244
How to Use the Index اشاریہ استعمال کرنے کا طریقہ	245
English Index انگریزی اشاریہ	246–281
Geographical Index جغرافیائی اشاریہ	282–284
Urdu Index اردو اشاریہ	285–304
Research Bibliography فہرست کتب	305

Teaching with the *Oxford Picture Dictionary* Program

The following general guidelines will help you prepare single and multilevel lessons using the OPD program. For step-by-step, topic-specific lesson plans, see *OPD Lesson Plans*.

1. Use Students' Needs to Identify Lesson Objectives

- Create communicative objectives based on your learners' needs assessments (*see OPD 2e Assessment Program*).
- Make sure objectives state what students will be able to do at the end of the lesson. For example: *Students will be able to respond to basic classroom commands and requests for classroom objects.* (pp. 6–7, A Classroom)
- For multilevel classes, identify a low-beginning, high-beginning, and low-intermediate objective for each topic.

2. Preview the Topic

Identify what your students already know about the topic.

- Ask general questions related to the topic.
- Have students list words they know from the topic.
- Ask questions about the picture(s) on the page.

3. Present the New Vocabulary

Research shows that it is best to present no more than 5–7 new words at a time. Here are a few presentation techniques:

- Say each new word and describe it within the context of the picture. Have volunteers act out verbs and verb sequences.
- Use Total Physical Response commands to build vocabulary comprehension.
- For long or unfamiliar word lists, introduce words by categories or select the words your students need most.
- Ask a series of questions to build comprehension and give students an opportunity to say the new words. Begin with *yes/no* questions: *Is #16 chalk?* Progress to *or* questions: *Is #16 chalk or a marker?* Finally, ask *Wh-* questions: *What can I use to write on this paper?*
- Focus on the words that students want to learn. Have them write 3–5 new words from each topic, along with meaning clues such as a drawing, translation, or sentence.

More vocabulary and **Grammar Point** sections provide additional presentation opportunities (see p. 5, School). For multilevel presentation ideas, see *OPD Lesson Plans*.

4. Check Comprehension

Make sure that students understand the target vocabulary. Here are two activities you can try:

- Say vocabulary words, and have students point to the correct items in their books. Walk around the room, checking if students are pointing to the correct pictures.
- Make true/false statements about the target vocabulary. Have students hold up two fingers for true, three for false.

5. Provide Guided and Communicative Practice

The exercise bands at the bottom of the topic pages provide a variety of guided and communicative practice opportunities and engage students' higher-level thinking.

6. Provide More Practice

OPD Second Edition offers a variety of components to facilitate vocabulary acquisition. Each of the print and electronic materials listed below offers suggestions and support for single and multilevel instruction.

OPD Lesson Plans Step-by-step multilevel lesson plans feature 3 CDs with multilevel listening, context-based pronunciation practice, and leveled reading practice. Includes multilevel teaching notes for *The OPD Reading Library*.

OPD Audio CDs or Audio Cassettes Each word in *OPD's* word list is recorded by topic.

Low-Beginning, High-Beginning, and Low-Intermediate Workbooks Guided practice for each page in *OPD* features linked visual contexts, realia, and listening practice.

Classic Classroom Activities A photocopiable resource of interactive multilevel activities, grammar practice, and communicative tasks.

The OPD Reading Library Readers include civics, academic content, and workplace themes.

Overhead Transparencies Vibrant transparencies help to focus students on the lesson.

OPD Presentation Software A multilevel interactive teaching tool using interactive whiteboard and LCD technology. Audio, animation, and video instructional support bring each dictionary topic to life.

The OPD CD-ROM An interactive learning tool featuring four-skill practice based on *OPD* topics.

Bilingual Editions *OPD* is available in numerous bilingual editions including Spanish, Chinese, Vietnamese, Arabic, Korean, and many more.

My hope is that OPD makes it easier for you to take your learners from comprehension to communication. Please share your thoughts with us as you make the book your own.

Jayme Adelson-Goldstein

Jayme Adelson-Goldstein

OPDteam.us@oup.com

Welcome to the
OPD SECOND EDITION

The second edition of the *Oxford Picture Dictionary* expands on the best aspects of the 1998 edition with:

- New artwork presenting words within meaningful, real-life contexts
- An updated word list to meet the needs of today's English language learners
- 4,000 English words and phrases, including 285 verbs
- 40 new topics with 12 intro pages and 12 story pages
- Unparalleled support for vocabulary teaching

Subtopics present the words in easy-to-learn "chunks."

Color coding and icons make it easy to navigate through *OPD*.

New art and rich contexts improve vocabulary acquisition.

Revised practice activities help students from low-beginning through low-intermediate levels.

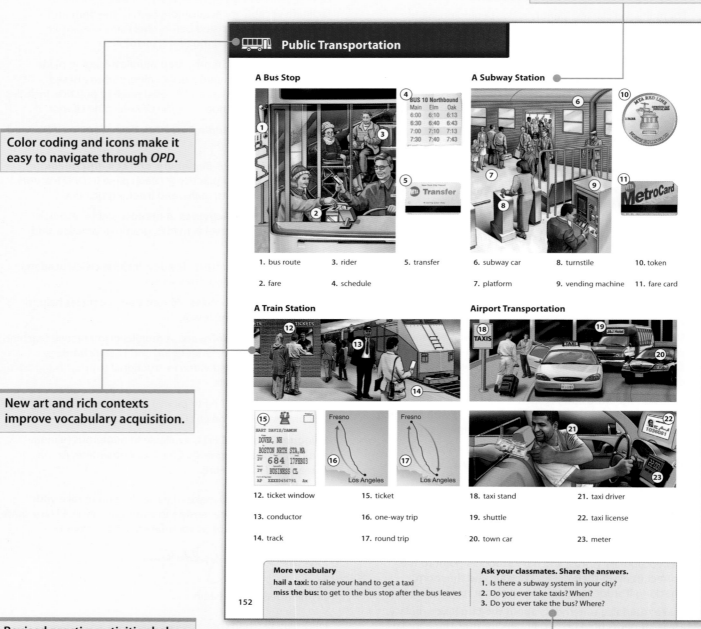

Public Transportation

A Bus Stop

BUS 10 Northbound

Main	Elm	Oak
6:00	6:10	6:13
6:30	6:40	6:43
7:00	7:10	7:13
7:30	7:40	7:43

MTA Transfer

1. bus route
2. fare
3. rider
4. schedule
5. transfer

A Subway Station

6. subway car
7. platform
8. turnstile
9. vending machine
10. token
11. fare card

A Train Station

HART DAVIS/DAMON
DOVER, NH
BOSTON NRTH STA, MA
2V 684 17FEB03
2V BUSINESS CL
AP XXXX0456791 Ax

Fresno / Los Angeles

Fresno / Los Angeles

12. ticket window
13. conductor
14. track
15. ticket
16. one-way trip
17. round trip

Airport Transportation

18. taxi stand
19. shuttle
20. town car
21. taxi driver
22. taxi license
23. meter

More vocabulary

hail a taxi: to raise your hand to get a taxi
miss the bus: to get to the bus stop after the bus leaves

Ask your classmates. Share the answers.

1. Is there a subway system in your city?
2. Do you ever take taxis? When?
3. Do you ever take the bus? Where?

152

Each intro page teaches key vocabulary items within the unit theme.

Practice activities make it easy to manage multilevel classrooms.

Pre-reading questions build students' previewing and predicting skills.

High-interest readings promote literacy skills.

Post-reading questions and role-play activities support critical thinking and encourage students to use the language they have learned.

The thematic word list previews words that students will encounter in the story.

A. **Say**, "Hello."
کہیئے، "ہیلو"۔

B. **Ask**, "How are you?"
پوچھیئے، "آپ کیسے ہیں؟"

C. **Introduce** yourself.
اپنا تعارف کرائیے۔

D. **Smile**.
مسکرائیے۔

E. **Hug**.
گلے ملیے۔

F. **Wave**.
ہاتھ ہلائیے۔

Hello.

Hi.

How are you?

Fine, thanks.

Hi. I'm Tom.

Hi, Tom. I'm Ana.

Tell your partner what to do. Take turns.

1. *Say,* "Hello."	4. *Shake hands.*
2. *Bow.*	5. *Wave.*
3. *Smile.*	6. *Say,* "Goodbye."

Dictate to your partner. Take turns.

A: *Write <u>smile</u>.*
B: *Is it spelled <u>s-m-i-l-e</u>?*
A: *Yes, that's right.*

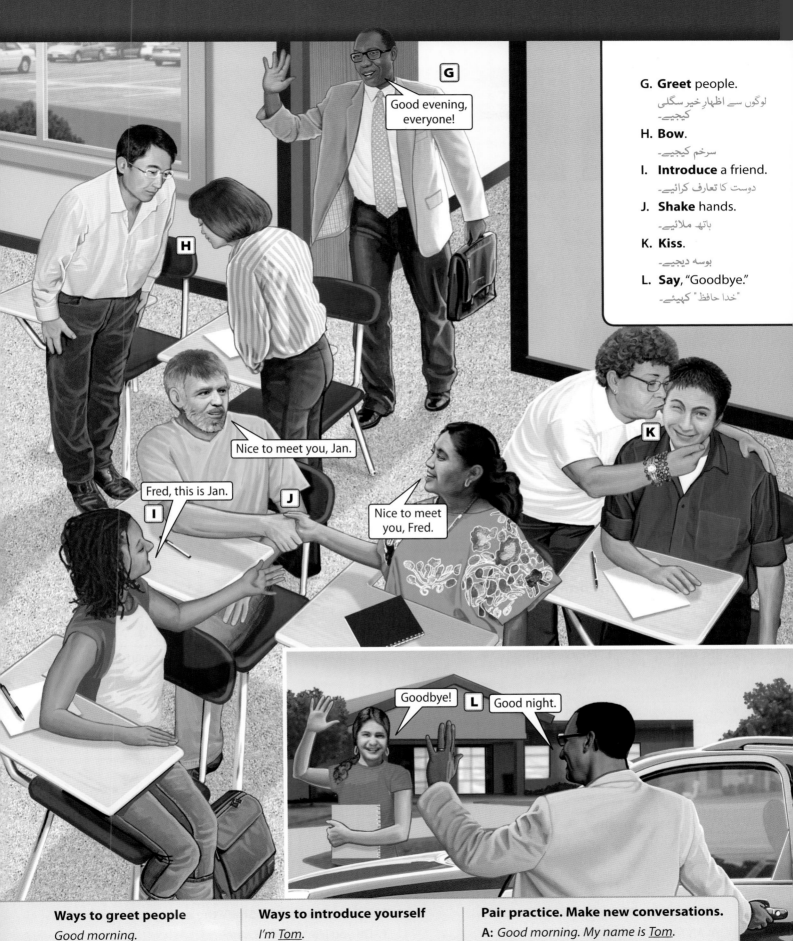

Ways to greet people

Good morning.
Good afternoon.
Good evening.

Ways to introduce yourself

I'm Tom.
My name is Tom.

Pair practice. Make new conversations.

A: *Good morning. My name is Tom.*
B: *Nice to meet you, Tom. I'm Sara.*
A: *Nice to meet you, Sara.*

3

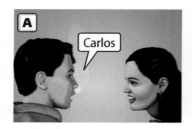

A. Say your name.

اپنا نام بتائیے۔

B. Spell your name.

اپنے نام کی ہجے کیجیے۔

C. Print your name.

اپنا نام بڑے حروف میں لکھیے۔

D. Sign your name.

اپنے نام کا دستخط کیجیے۔

Filling Out a Form فارم پُر کرنا

School Registration Form اسکول کا اندراج فارم

1. name:

نام:

2. first name	**3. middle initial**	**4. last name**	**5. address**	**6. apartment number**
پہلا نام	درمیانی نام کا پہلا حرف	آخری نام	پتہ	اپارٹمنٹ نمبر

7. city	**8. state**	**9. ZIP code**	**10. area code**	**11. phone number**
شہر	صوبہ	زپ کوڈ	علاقہ کا کوڈ	فون نمبر

12. cell phone number

سیل فون نمبر

13. date of birth (DOB)

تاریخ پیدائش (ڈی او بی)

14. place of birth

مقام پیدائش

15. Social Security number

سوشل سیکیوریٹی نمبر

16. sex:

جنس:

17. male ☐

مرد

18. female ☐

عورت

19. signature

دستخط

Pair practice. Make new conversations.

A: My first name is _Carlos_.

B: Please spell _Carlos_ for me.

A: _C-a-r-l-o-s_

Ask your classmates. Share the answers.

1. Do you like your first name?
2. Is your last name from your mother? father? husband?
3. What is your middle name?

Campus درسگاہ کا احاطہ

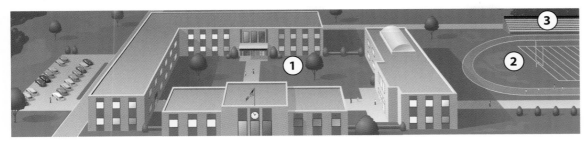

Administrators منتظمین

Around Campus درسگاہ کے احاطہ کے اطراف

1. quad
   چوگوشیہ
2. field
   میدان
3. bleachers
   کھیل کے میدان میں کھلی بیٹھنے کی جگہ
4. principal
   پرنسپل
5. assistant principal
   معاون پرنسپل
6. counselor
   صلاح کار
7. classroom
   کمرۂ تدریس
8. teacher
   استاد
9. restrooms
   بیت الخلاء
10. hallway
    راہداری
11. locker
    لاکر
12. main office
    مرکزی دفتر
13. clerk
    کلرک
14. cafeteria
    خود خدمت چائے کافی خانہ
15. computer lab
    کمپیوٹر تجربہ گاہ
16. teacher's aide
    استاد کا معاون
17. library
    کتب خانہ
18. auditorium
    جلسہ گاہ
19. gym
    ورزش گاہ
20. coach
    اتالیق
21. track
    مقابلہ کی دوڑ کا راستہ

More vocabulary

Students do not pay to go to a **public school.**
Students pay to go to a **private school.**
A church, mosque, or temple school is a **parochial school.**

Grammar Point: contractions of the verb *be*

He + is = He's   *He's a teacher.*
She + is = She's   *She's a counselor.*
They + are = They're   *They're students.*

5

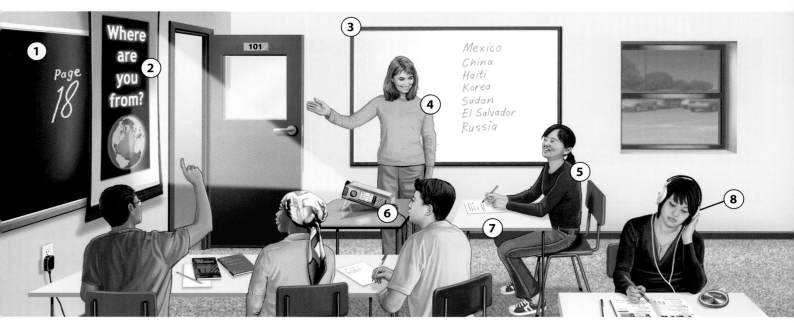

1. chalkboard
تختۂ سیاہ

3. whiteboard
تختۂ سفید

5. student
طالب علم

7. desk
ڈیسک

2. screen
اسکرین

4. teacher / instructor
استاد/معلم

6. LCD projector
ایل سی ڈی پروجیکٹر

8. headphones
ہیڈفونز / سرِ فون

A. Raise your hand.
اپنا ہاتھ **اٹھائیے۔**

B. Talk to the teacher.
استاد سے **بات کیجیے۔**

C. Listen to a CD.
کوئی سی ڈی **سنیے۔**

D. Stand up.
کھڑے ہو جائیے۔

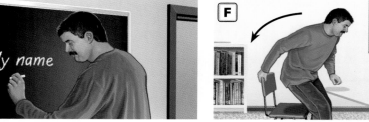

E. Write on the board.
بورڈ پر لکھیے۔

F. Sit down. / Take a seat.
بیٹھ جائیے۔ / نشست سنبھالیے۔

G. Open your book.
اپنی کتاب کھولیے۔

H. Close your book.
اپنی کتاب بند کیجیے۔

I. Pick up the pencil.
پنسل پکڑیے۔

J. Put down the pencil.
پنسل رکھ دیجیے۔

9. clock	**11. chair**	**13. alphabet**	**15. computer**
گھڑی	کرسی	حروف ہجاء	کمپیوٹر
10. bookcase	**12. map**	**14. bulletin board**	**16. overhead projector**
کتاب کی الماری	نقشہ	نوٹس لگانے والا تختہ	اوپری پروجیکٹر

17. dry erase marker	**21. (pencil) eraser**	**25. textbook**	**29. spiral notebook**
خشک مٹانے والا مارکر	ربر (پنسل مٹانے والا)	درسی کتاب	چھلے دار نوٹ بک
18. chalk	**22. pen**	**26. workbook**	**30. dictionary**
چاک	قلم	لکھنے کی کاپی	لغت
19. eraser	**23. pencil sharpener**	**27. 3-ring binder / notebook**	**31. picture dictionary**
مٹانے والا	پنسل تراش	3-کمانی دار جلد / نوٹ بک	تصویر والی لغت
20. pencil	**24. marker**	**28. notebook paper**	
پنسل	نشان زد کرنے والا	نوٹ بک پیپر	

Look at the picture.
Describe the classroom.

A: There's a chalkboard.
B: There are fifteen students.

Ask your classmates. Share the answers.
1. Do you like to raise your hand in class?
2. Do you like to listen to CDs in class?
3. Do you ever talk to the teacher?

Learning New Words نئے الفاظ سیکھنا

A. Look up the word.

لفظ کو دیکھیے۔

B. Read the definition.

اس کی تعریف پڑھیے۔

C. Translate the word.

لفظ کا ترجمہ کیجیے۔

D. Check the pronunciation.

تلفظ کی جانچ کیجیے۔

E. Copy the word.

لفظ کی نقل کیجیے۔

F. Draw a picture.

ایک تصویر بنائیے۔

Working with Your Classmates اپنے ہم جماعتوں کے ساتھ کام کرنا

G. Discuss a problem.

کسی مسئلہ پر گفتگو کیجیے۔

H. Brainstorm solutions / answers.

متفقہ غور و خوض کے بعد حل/جوابات۔

I. Work in a group.

جماعت میں کام کیجیے۔

J. Help a classmate.

کسی ہم جماعت کی مدد کیجیے۔

Working with a Partner کسی ساتھی کے ہمراہ کام کرنا

K. Ask a question.

کوئی سوال پوچھیے۔

L. Answer a question.

کسی سوال کا جواب دیجیے۔

M. Share a book.

کسی کتاب کو ملکر پڑھیے۔

N. Dictate a sentence.

کوئی جملہ بول کر لکھوائیے۔

Following Directions ہدایات پر عمل کرنا

O. **Fill in** the blank.
خالی جگہوں کو بھریے۔

P. **Choose** the correct answer.
صحیح جواب چنیے۔

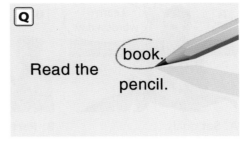

Q. **Circle** the answer.
جواب پر دائرہ بنائیے۔

R. **Cross out** the word.
لفظ کو کاٹ دیجیے۔

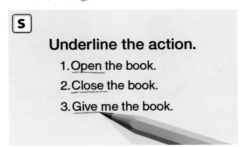

S. **Underline** the word.
لفظ کے نیچے خط کھینچیے۔

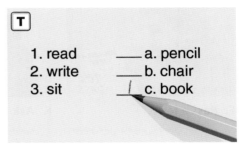

T. **Match** the items.
آئٹموں کو ملائیے۔

U. **Check** the correct boxes.
درست خانوں کی جانچ کیجیے۔

V. **Label** the picture.
تصویر پر لیبل لگائیے۔

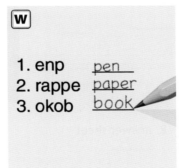

W. **Unscramble** the words.
حروف کو ترتیب دے کر لفظ بنائیے۔

X. **Put** the sentences in order.
جملوں کو ترتیب سے رکھیے۔

Y. **Take out** a piece of paper.
کاغذ کا ایک ٹکڑا نکالیے۔

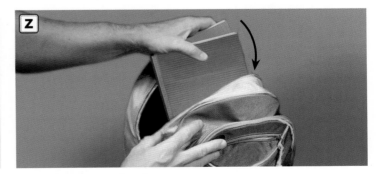

Z. **Put away** your books.
اپنی کتابیں مقررہ جگہ پر رکھیے۔

Ask your classmates. Share the answers.

1. Do you like to work in a group?
2. Do you ever share a book?
3. Do you like to answer questions?

Think about it. Discuss.

1. How can classmates help each other?
2. Why is it important to ask questions in class?
3. How can students check their pronunciation? Explain.

Ways to Succeed کامیابی کے طریقے

A. Set goals.
مقاصد کا تعین کیجیے۔

B. Participate in class.
کلاس میں شرکت کیجیے۔

C. Take notes.
وضاحتیں لکھیے۔

D. Study at home.
گھر پر مطالعہ کیجیے۔

E. Pass a test.
امتحان میں کامیابی حاصل کیجیے۔

F. Ask for help.
مدد طلب کیجیے۔

G. Make progress.
پیش رفت کیجیے۔

H. Get good grades.
اچھے درجات حاصل کیجیے۔

Taking a Test امتحان میں شریک ہونا

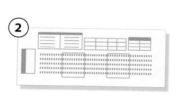

A	90%-100%	Outstanding
B	80%-89%	Very good
C	70%-79%	Satisfactory
D	60%-69%	Barely passing
F	0%-59%	Fail

1. test booklet
امتحان کی کاپی

2. answer sheet
جواب نامہ

3. score
نمبر

4. grades
درجات

I. Clear off your desk.
اپنی ڈیسک صاف کیجیے۔

J. Work on your own.
اپنے آپ کام کیجیے۔

K. Bubble in the answer.
جواب پر دائرہ بنائیے۔

L. Check your work.
اپنے کام کی جانچ کیجیے۔

M. Erase the mistake.
غلطیوں کو مٹائیے۔

N. Correct the mistake.
غلطیوں کو درست کیجیے۔

O. Hand in your test.
اپنے امتحان کی جوابی کاپی جمع کیجیے۔

A. Enter the room.
کمرے میں داخل ہوجائیے۔

B. Turn on the lights.
روشنیاں کھولیے۔

C. Walk to class.
کلاس کی طرف چلیے۔

D. Run to class.
کلاس کی طرف دوڑیے۔

E. Lift / Pick up the books.
کتابیں اٹھائیے / پکڑیے۔

F. Carry the books.
کتابیں لائیے۔

G. Deliver the books.
کتابیں پہنچائیے۔

H. Take a break.
ایک وقفہ لیجیے۔

I. Eat.
کھائیے۔

J. Drink.
پیجیے۔

K. Buy a snack.
ہلکا ناشتہ خریدیے۔

L. Have a conversation.
بات چیت کیجیے۔

M. Go back to class.
کلاس میں واپس جائیے۔

N. Throw away trash.
کوڑا کرکٹ پھینک دیجیے۔

O. Leave the room.
کمرے سے باہر جائیے۔

P. Turn off the lights.
روشنیاں بند کر دیجیے۔

Grammar Point: present continuous

Use **be** + verb + **ing**
He **is** walk**ing**. They **are** enter**ing**.
Note: He is runn**ing**. They are leav**ing**.

Look at the pictures.
Describe what is happening.

A: *They are <u>entering the room</u>.*
B: *He is <u>walking</u>.*

A. **start** a conversation
بات چیت شروع کیجیے

B. **make** small talk
عام گفتگو کیجیے

C. **compliment** someone
کسی کی تعریف کیجیے

D. **offer** something
کوئی چیز پیش کیجیے

E. **thank** someone
کسی کا شکریہ ادا کیجیے

F. **apologize**
معذرت کیجیے

G. **accept** an apology
معذرت قبول کیجیے

H. **invite** someone
کسی کو مدعو کیجیے

I. **accept** an invitation
دعوت نامہ قبول کیجیے

J. **decline** an invitation
دعوت نامہ قبول کرنے سے انکار کیجیے

K. **agree**
رضامندی ظاہر کیجیے

L. **disagree**
اختلاف کیجیے

M. **explain** something
کسی بات کی وضاحت کیجیے

N. **check** your understanding
اپنی فہم کی جانچ کیجیے

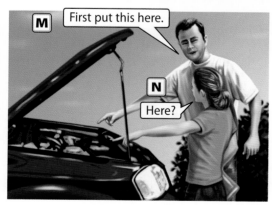

More vocabulary

request: to ask for something
accept a compliment: to thank someone for a compliment

Pair practice. Follow the directions.

1. Start a conversation with your partner.
2. Make small talk with your partner.
3. Compliment each other.

Temperature درجهٔ حرارت

1. Fahrenheit
فیرن ہائٹ
2. Celsius
سیلسیئس
3. hot
گرم
4. warm
نیم گرم
5. cool
ہلکا ٹھنڈا
6. cold
سرد
7. freezing
جمانے والی ٹھنڈک
8. degrees
ڈگریاں

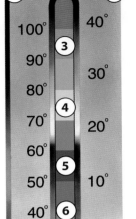

A Weather Map موسم کا نقشہ

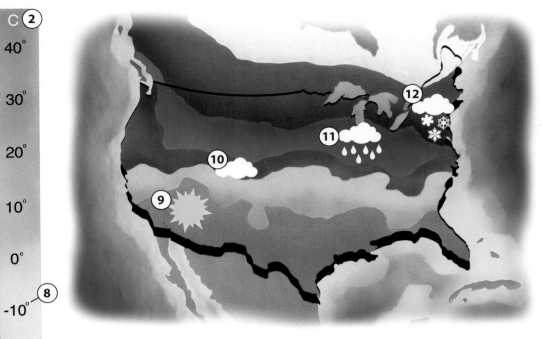

9. sunny / clear
دھوپ دار/کھلا ہوا
10. cloudy
ابر آلود
11. raining
بارش
12. snowing
برف باری

Weather Conditions موسم کی حالتیں

  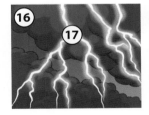  18

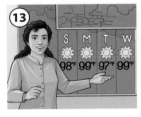   22

13. heat wave
گرمی کی لہر
14. smoggy
کہر آلود
15. humid
گرم اور مرطوب

16. thunderstorm
گرج کے ساتھ بارش
17. lightning
بجلی کا چمکنا
18. windy
تیز ہوا والا

19. dust storm
گرد کا طوفان
20. foggy
دھند آلود
21. hailstorm
ژالہ باری

22. icy
برفدار
23. snowstorm / blizzard
برف کا طوفان/ شدید ہوا کے
ساتھ برف کا طوفان

Ways to talk about the weather

It's <u>sunny</u> in <u>Dallas</u>.
What's the temperature?
It's <u>108</u>. They're having <u>a heat wave</u>.

Pair practice. Make new conversations.

A: *What's the weather like in <u>Chicago</u>?*
B: *It's <u>raining</u> and it's <u>cold</u>. It's <u>30</u> degrees.*

PARTS OF A PHONE

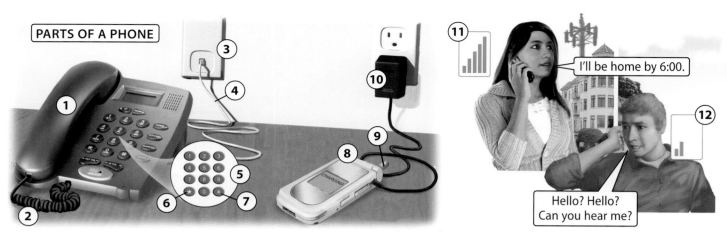

1. receiver / handset
چونگا / ہاتھ میں پکڑنے والا آلہ

2. cord
تار

3. phone jack
فون کا پلگ

4. phone line
فون لائن

5. key pad
تختۂ کلید

6. star key
ستارہ کلید

7. pound key
پاؤنڈ کے نشان کی کلید

8. cellular phone
بیٹری کا فون

9. antenna
اینٹینا

10. charger
چارجر

11. strong signal
طاقت ور سگنل

12. weak signal
کمزور سگنل

13. headset
سرِفون

14. wireless headset
بے تار سرِفون

15. calling card
پیش ادائیگی فون کارڈ

16. access number
نمبر رسائی

17. answering machine
جوابی مشین

18. voice message
صوتی پیغام

19. text message
متنی پیغام

20. Internet phone call
انٹرنیٹ فون کال

21. operator
آپریٹر

22. directory assistance
ڈائرکٹری مدد

23. automated phone system
خودکار فون نظام

24. cordless phone
بے تار فون

25. pay phone
پیش ادائیگی فون

26. TDD*
ٹی ڈی ڈی (بصری معذور لوگوں کا فون)

27. smart phone
اسمارٹ فون

Reading a Phone Bill فون بل پڑھنا

28. phone bill
فون بل

29. area code
علاقہ کا کوڈ

30. phone number
فون نمبر

31. local call
مقامی کال

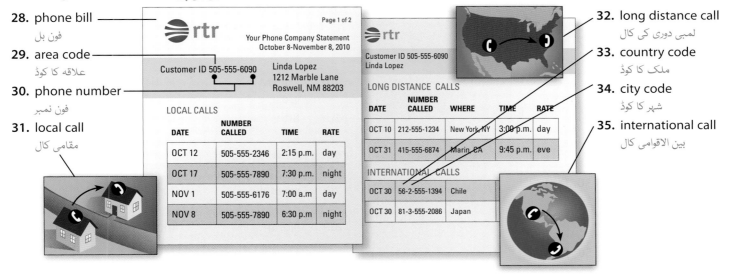

rtr
Page 1 of 2
Your Phone Company Statement
October 8–November 8, 2010

Customer ID 505-555-6090

Linda Lopez
1212 Marble Lane
Roswell, NM 88203

LOCAL CALLS

DATE	NUMBER CALLED	TIME	RATE
OCT 12	505-555-2346	2:15 p.m.	day
OCT 17	505-555-7890	7:30 p.m.	night
NOV 1	505-555-6176	7:00 a.m	day
NOV 8	505-555-7890	6:30 p.m	night

rtr

Customer ID 505-555-6090
Linda Lopez

LONG DISTANCE CALLS

DATE	NUMBER CALLED	WHERE	TIME	RATE
OCT 10	212-555-1234	New York, NY	3:00 p.m.	day
OCT 31	415-555-6874	Marin, CA	9:45 p.m.	eve

INTERNATIONAL CALLS

DATE	NUMBER CALLED	WHERE		
OCT 30	56-2-555-1394	Chile		
OCT 30	81-3-555-2086	Japan		

32. long distance call
لمبی دوری کی کال

33. country code
ملک کا کوڈ

34. city code
شہر کا کوڈ

35. international call
بین الاقوامی کال

Making a Phone Call فون کال کرنا

A. Dial the phone number.
فون نمبر ڈائل کیجیے۔

B. Press "send".
'ارسال کریں' دبائیے۔

C. Talk on the phone.
فون پر بات کیجیے۔

D. Hang up. / Press "end".
چونگا رکھ دیجیے۔ / 'خاتمہ' دبائیے۔

Making an Emergency Call ہنگامی کال کرنا

E. Dial 911.
۹۱۱ ڈائل کیجیے۔

This is Roy Chu.

F. Give your name.
اپنا نام بتائیے۔

There's a fire on 5th and Oak.

G. State the emergency.
ہنگامی صورت حال بیان کیجیے۔

Please stay on the line.

H. Stay on the line.
لائن پر موجود رہیے۔

*telecommunication device for the deaf

Cardinal Numbers بنیادی اعداد

0	zero	20	twenty
	۰ صفر		۲۰ بیس
1	one	21	twenty-one
	۱ ایک		۲۱ اکیس
2	two	22	twenty-two
	۲ دو		۲۲ بائیس
3	three	23	twenty-three
	۳ تین		۲۳ تیئیس
4	four	24	twenty-four
	۴ چار		۲۴ چوبیس
5	five	25	twenty-five
	۵ پانچ		۲۵ پچیس
6	six	30	thirty
	۶ چھ		۳۰ تیس
7	seven	40	forty
	۷ سات		۴۰ چالیس
8	eight	50	fifty
	۸ آٹھ		۵۰ پچاس
9	nine	60	sixty
	۹ نو		۶۰ سائٹھ
10	ten	70	seventy
	۱۰ دس		۷۰ ستر
11	eleven	80	eighty
	۱۱ گیارہ		۸۰ اسی
12	twelve	90	ninety
	۱۲ بارہ		۹۰ نوے
13	thirteen	100	one hundred
	۱۳ تیرہ		۱۰۰ ایک سو
14	fourteen	101	one hundred one
	۱۴ چودہ		۱۰۱ ایک سو ایک
15	fifteen	1,000	one thousand
	۱۵ پندرہ		۱۰۰۰ ایک ہزار
16	sixteen	10,000	ten thousand
	۱۶ سولہ		۱۰۰۰۰ دس ہزار
17	seventeen	100,000	one hundred thousand
	۱۷ سترہ		۱۰۰۰۰۰ ایک سو ہزار
18	eighteen	1,000,000	one million
	۱۸ اٹھارہ		۱۰۰۰۰۰۰ ایک ملین
19	nineteen	1,000,000,000	one billion
	۱۹ انیس		۱۰۰۰۰۰۰۰۰۰ ایک بلین

Ordinal Numbers ترتیبی اعداد

1st	first	16th	sixteenth
	پہلا		سولہواں
2nd	second	17th	seventeenth
	دوسرا		سترہواں
3rd	third	18th	eighteenth
	تیسرا		اٹھارہواں
4th	fourth	19th	nineteenth
	چوتھا		انیسواں
5th	fifth	20th	twentieth
	پانچواں		بیسواں
6th	sixth	21st	twenty-first
	چھٹا		اکیسواں
7th	seventh	30th	thirtieth
	ساتواں		تیسواں
8th	eighth	40th	fortieth
	آٹھواں		چالیسواں
9th	ninth	50th	fiftieth
	نواں		پچاسواں
10th	tenth	60th	sixtieth
	دسواں		سائٹھواں
11th	eleventh	70th	seventieth
	گیارہواں		سترواں
12th	twelfth	80th	eightieth
	بارہواں		اسی واں
13th	thirteenth	90th	ninetieth
	تیرہواں		نوے واں
14th	fourteenth	100th	one hundredth
	چودہواں		سوواں
15th	fifteenth	1,000th	one thousandth
	پندرہواں		ہزارواں

Roman Numerals رومن اعداد

I	= 1	VII	= 7	XXX	= 30
II	= 2	VIII	= 8	XL	= 40
III	= 3	IX	= 9	L	= 50
IV	= 4	X	= 10	C	= 100
V	= 5	XV	= 15	D	= 500
VI	= 6	XX	= 20	M	= 1,000

A $1 \div 4 = .25$

A. divide
تقسیم کیجیے

B 75% of 10 = 7.5

B. calculate
حساب لگائیے

C 2 inches

C. measure
ناپیے

D 1 mi. = 1.6 km

D. convert
تبدیل کیجیے

Fractions and Decimals کسرات اور اعشاریے

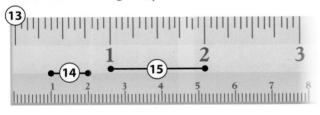

1. one whole
1 = 1.00
ایک مکمل

2. one half
1/2 = .5
نصف

3. one third
1/3 = .333
تہائی

4. one fourth
1/4 = .25
چوتھائی

5. one eighth
1/8 = .125
آٹھواں حصہ

Percents فیصد

6. calculator
کیلکولیٹر

7. decimal point
اعشاریہ

8 100 percent — 100%
9 75 percent — 75%
10 50 percent — 50%
11 25 percent — 25%
12 10 percent — 10%

0% 10% 20% 30% 40% 50% 60% 70% 80% 90% 100%

8. 100 percent
۱۰۰ فیصد

9. 75 percent
۷۵ فیصد

10. 50 percent
۵۰ فیصد

11. 25 percent
۲۵ فیصد

12. 10 percent
۱۰ فیصد

Measurement پیمائش

13. ruler
مسطر

14. centimeter [cm]
سینٹی میٹر [سی ایم]

15. inch [in.]
انچ [انچ]

Dimensions ابعاد

16. height
اونچائی

17. length
لمبائی

18. depth
گہرائی

19. width
چوڑائی

Equivalencies

12 inches = 1 foot

3 feet = 1 yard

1,760 yards = 1 mile

1 inch = 2.54 centimeters

1 yard = .91 meters

1 mile = 1.6 kilometers

Telling Time وقت بتانا

1. hour
گھنٹہ

2. minutes
منٹ

3. seconds
سیکنڈ

4. a.m.
دوپہر سے پہلے

5. p.m.
دوپہر بعد

6. 1:00
one o'clock
ایک بجے

7. 1:05
one-oh-five
five after one
ایک پانچ
ایک بج کر پانچ منٹ

8. 1:10
one-ten
ten after one
ایک دس
ایک بج کر دس منٹ

9. 1:15
one-fifteen
a quarter after one
ایک پندرہ
سوا بجے

10. 1:20
one-twenty
twenty after one
ایک بیس
ایک بج کر بیس منٹ

11. 1:30
one-thirty
half past one
ایک تیس
ڈیڑھ بجے

12. 1:40
one-forty
twenty to two
ایک چالیس
دو بجنے میں بیس منٹ

13. 1:45
one-forty-five
a quarter to two
ایک پینتالیس
پونے دو

Times of Day دن کے اوقات

14. sunrise
طلوع آفتاب

15. morning
صبح

16. noon
دوپہر

17. afternoon
دوپہر بعد

18. sunset
غروب آفتاب

19. evening
شام

20. night
رات

21. midnight
آدھی رات

Ways to talk about time

I wake up at 6:30 a.m.
I wake up at 6:30 in the morning.
I wake up at 6:30.

Pair practice. Make new conversations.

A: *What time do you wake up on weekdays?*
B: *At 6:30 a.m. How about you?*
A: *I wake up at 7:00.*

22. early
وقت سے پہلے

23. on time
بروقت

24. late
تاخیر سے

25. daylight saving time
دن کی روشنی کی بچت کا وقت

26. standard time
معیاری وقت

Time Zones وقت کے منطقے

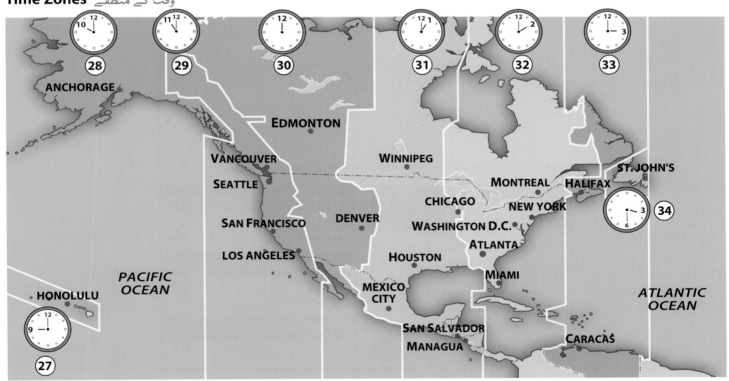

27. Hawaii-Aleutian time
ہوائی الوشیان وقت

28. Alaska time
الاسکا وقت

29. Pacific time
پیسیفک وقت

30. Mountain time
پہاڑی علاقوں کا معیاری وقت

31. Central time
مرکزی وقت

32. Eastern time
مشرقی وقت

33. Atlantic time
ائلانٹک وقت

34. Newfoundland time
نیوفاؤنڈلینڈ وقت

Ask your classmates. Share the answers.

1. When do you watch television? study? relax?
2. Do you like to stay up after midnight?
3. Do you like to wake up late on weekends?

Think about it. Discuss.

1. What is your favorite time of day? Why?
2. Do you think daylight saving time is a good idea? Why or why not?

1. date
تاریخ
2. day
دن
3. month
مہینہ
4. year
سال

5. today
آج
6. tomorrow
آئندہ کل
7. yesterday
گزشتہ کل

Days of the Week
ہفتے کے دن

8. Sunday
اتوار
9. Monday
پیر
10. Tuesday
منگل
11. Wednesday
بدھ
12. Thursday
جمعرات
13. Friday
جمعہ
14. Saturday
سنیچر

MAY

⑧ SUN	⑨ MON	⑩ TUE	⑪ WED	⑫ THU	⑬ FRI	⑭ SAT
1	2	3	4	5	6	7
8	9	10	11	12	13	14
15	16	17	18	19	20	21
22	23	24	25	26	27	28
29	30	31				

⑮
⑯
⑰

15. week
ہفتہ
16. weekdays
ہفتے کے دن
17. weekend
ختم ہفتہ

Frequency
تعدد

18. last week
گزشتہ ہفتے
19. this week
اس ہفتے
20. next week
اگلے ہفتے

SUN	MON	TUE	WED	THU	FRI	SAT
✓	✓	✓	✓	✓	✓	✓ ㉑

SUN	MON	TUE	WED	THU	FRI	SAT
	✓					㉒

SUN	MON	TUE	WED	THU	FRI	SAT
	✓		✓			㉓

SUN	MON	TUE	WED	THU	FRI	SAT
	✓	✓		✓		㉔

21. every day / daily
ہر روز/ روزانہ
22. once a week
ہفتے میں ایک بار
23. twice a week
ہفتے میں دو بار
24. three times a week
ہفتے میں تین بار

Ways to say the date
Today is May 10th. It's the tenth.
Yesterday was May 9th.
The party is on May 21st.

Pair practice. Make new conversations.
A: The test is on Friday, June 14th.
B: Did you say Friday, the fourteenth?
A: Yes, the fourteenth.

JAN (25)

SUN	MON	TUE	WED	THU	FRI	SAT
					1	2
3	4	5	6	7	8	9
10	11	12	13	14	15	16
17	18	19	20	21	22	23
24/31	25	26	27	28	29	30

FEB (26)

SUN	MON	TUE	WED	THU	FRI	SAT
	1	2	3	4	5	6
7	8	9	10	11	12	13
14	15	16	17	18	19	20
21	22	23	24	25	26	27
28						

MAR (27)

SUN	MON	TUE	WED	THU	FRI	SAT
	1	2	3	4	5	6
7	8	9	10	11	12	13
14	15	16	17	18	19	20
21	22	23	24	25	26	27
28	29	30	31			

APR (28)

SUN	MON	TUE	WED	THU	FRI	SAT
				1	2	3
4	5	6	7	8	9	10
11	12	13	14	15	16	17
18	19	20	21	22	23	24
25	26	27	28	29	30	

MAY (29)

SUN	MON	TUE	WED	THU	FRI	SAT
						1
2	3	4	5	6	7	8
9	10	11	12	13	14	15
16	17	18	19	20	21	22
23/30	24/31	25	26	27	28	29

JUN (30)

SUN	MON	TUE	WED	THU	FRI	SAT
		1	2	3	4	5
6	7	8	9	10	11	12
13	14	15	16	17	18	19
20	21	22	23	24	25	26
27	28	29	30			

JUL (31)

SUN	MON	TUE	WED	THU	FRI	SAT
				1	2	3
4	5	6	7	8	9	10
11	12	13	14	15	16	17
18	19	20	21	22	23	24
25	26	27	28	29	30	31

AUG (32)

SUN	MON	TUE	WED	THU	FRI	SAT
1	2	3	4	5	6	7
8	9	10	11	12	13	14
15	16	17	18	19	20	21
22	23	24	25	26	27	28
29	30	31				

SEP (33)

SUN	MON	TUE	WED	THU	FRI	SAT
			1	2	3	4
5	6	7	8	9	10	11
12	13	14	15	16	17	18
19	20	21	22	23	24	25
26	27	28	29	30		

OCT (34)

SUN	MON	TUE	WED	THU	FRI	SAT
					1	2
3	4	5	6	7	8	9
10	11	12	13	14	15	16
17	18	19	20	21	22	23
24/31	25	26	27	28	29	30

NOV (35)

SUN	MON	TUE	WED	THU	FRI	SAT
	1	2	3	4	5	6
7	8	9	10	11	12	13
14	15	16	17	18	19	20
21	22	23	24	25	26	27
28	29	30				

DEC (36)

SUN	MON	TUE	WED	THU	FRI	SAT
			1	2	3	4
5	6	7	8	9	10	11
12	13	14	15	16	17	18
19	20	21	22	23	24	25
26	27	28	29	30	31	

Months of the Year

سال کے مہینے

25. January
جنوری
26. February
فروری
27. March
مارچ
28. April
اپریل
29. May
مئی
30. June
جون
31. July
جولائی
32. August
اگست
33. September
ستمبر
34. October
اکتوبر
35. November
نومبر
36. December
دسمبر

Seasons

موسم

37. spring
بہار
38. summer
گرمی
39. fall / autumn
پت جھڑ / خزاں
40. winter
سردی

Dictate to your partner. Take turns.

A: *Write <u>Monday</u>.*
B: *Is it spelled <u>M-o-n-d-a-y</u>?*
A: *Yes, that's right.*

Ask your classmates. Share the answers.

1. What is your favorite day of the week? Why?
2. What is your busiest day of the week? Why?
3. What is your favorite season of the year? Why?

1. birthday
سالگرہ

2. wedding
شادی

3. anniversary
کسی گذشتہ واقعہ کی یاد کی تقریب

4. appointment
تقرری

5. parent-teacher conference
والدین استاد کی کانفرنس

6. vacation
تعطیل

7. religious holiday
مذبی تعطیل

8. legal holiday
قانونی تعطیل

Legal Holidays قانونی تعطیلات

9. New Year's Day
یومِ سالِ نو

10. Martin Luther King Jr. Day
یوم مارٹن لوتھر کنگ جونیئر

11. Presidents' Day
یوم صدر

12. Memorial Day
یوم یاد گار

13. Fourth of July /
Independence Day
چار جولائی / یومِ آزادی

14. Labor Day
یومِ محنت

15. Columbus Day
یومِ کولمبس

16. Veterans Day
یومِ جنگ دیدہ بزرگان

17. Thanksgiving
اظہار تشکر

18. Christmas
کرسمس

Pair practice. Make new conversations.

A: *When is your <u>birthday</u>?*
B: *It's on <u>January 31st</u>. How about you?*
A: *It's on <u>December 22nd</u>.*

Ask your classmates. Share the answers.

1. What are the legal holidays in your native country?
2. When is Labor Day in your native country?
3. When do you celebrate the New Year in your native country?

1. **little** hand
چھوٹا ہاتھ
2. **big** hand
بڑا ہاتھ

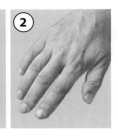  

13. **heavy** box
وزنی صندوق
14. **light** box
ہلکا صندوق

3. **fast** driver
تیز رفتار ڈرائیور
4. **slow** driver
سست رفتار ڈرائیور

15. **same** color
یکساں رنگ
16. **different** colors
مختلف رنگ

5. **hard** chair
سخت کرسی
6. **soft** chair
نرم کرسی

17. **good** dog
اچھا کتّا
18. **bad** dog
خراب کتّا

7. **thick** book
موٹی کتاب
8. **thin** book
پتلی کتاب

19. **expensive** ring
قیمتی انگوٹھی
20. **cheap** ring
سستی انگوٹھی

9. **full** glass
بھرا ہوا گلاس
10. **empty** glass
خالی گلاس

21. **beautiful** view
خوبصورت منظر
22. **ugly** view
بد صورت منظر

11. **noisy** children /
loud children
شور مچانے والے بچے /
چلّانے والے بچے
12. **quiet** children
خاموش بچے

   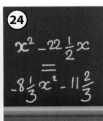

23. **easy** problem
آسان مسئلہ
24. **difficult** problem /
hard problem
مشکل مسئلہ / سخت
مسئلہ

On blackboard:
$1+1=2$

$x^2 - 22\tfrac{1}{2}x$
$=$
$-8\tfrac{1}{3}x^2 - 11\tfrac{2}{3}$

Ask your classmates. Share the answers.
1. Are you a slow driver or a fast driver?
2. Do you prefer a hard bed or a soft bed?
3. Do you like loud parties or quiet parties?

Use the new words.
Look at page 150–151. Describe the things you see.

A: _The street is hard._
B: _The truck is heavy._

Basic Colors بنیادی رنگ

1. red
سرخ

2. yellow
زرد

3. blue
نیلا

4. orange
نارنجی

5. green
سبز

6. purple
جامنی

7. pink
گلابی

8. violet
بنفشی

9. turquoise
فیروزی

10. dark blue
گہرا نیلا

11. light blue
ہلکا نیلا

12. bright blue
تیز نیلا

Neutral Colors ملے جُلے رنگ

13. black
سیاہ

14. white
سفید

15. gray
بھورا

16. cream / ivory
سفیدی مائل زرد / باٹھی دانت

17. brown
کتھئی

18. beige / tan
خاکستری / زردی آمیز بھورا رنگ

Ask your classmates. Share the answers.
1. What colors are you wearing today?
2. What colors do you like?
3. Is there a color you don't like? What is it?

Use the new words. Look at pages 86–87.
Take turns naming the colors you see.

A: *His shirt is blue.*
B: *Her shoes are white.*

1. The yellow sweaters are **on the left**.
   زرد سوئیٹر بائیں طرف ہیں۔

2. The purple sweaters are **in the middle**.
   جامنی سوئیٹر بیچ میں ہیں۔

3. The brown sweaters are **on the right**.
   کتھئی سوئیٹر داہنے طرف ہیں۔

4. The red sweaters are **above** the blue sweaters.
   سرخ سوئیٹر نیلے سوئیٹروں کے اوپر ہیں۔

5. The blue sweaters are **below** the red sweaters.
   نیلے سوئیٹر سرخ سوئیٹروں کے نیچے ہیں۔

6. The turquoise sweater is **in** the box.
   فیروزی سوئیٹر صندوق میں ہے۔

7. The white sweater is **in front of** the black sweater.
   سفید سوئیٹر سیاہ سوئیٹر کے سامنے ہے۔

8. The black sweater is **behind** the white sweater.
   سیاہ سوئیٹر سفید سوئیٹر کے پیچھے ہے۔

9. The orange sweater is **on** the gray sweater.
   نارنجی سوئیٹر بھورے سوئیٹر کے اوپر ہے۔

10. The violet sweater is **next to** the gray sweater.
    بنفشی سوئیٹر بھورے سوئیٹر کے بعد ہے۔

11. The gray sweater is **under** the orange sweater.
    بھورا سوئیٹر نارنجی سوئیٹر کے نیچے ہے۔

12. The green sweater is **between** the pink sweaters.
    سبز سوئیٹر گلابی سوئیٹروں کے درمیان ہے۔

More vocabulary

near: in the same area
far from: not near

Role play. Make new conversations.

A: *Excuse me. Where are the <u>red</u> sweaters?*
B: *They're <u>on the left</u>, <u>above</u> the <u>blue</u> sweaters.*
A: *Thanks very much.*

25

Coins سکے

1. $.01 = 1¢
a penny / 1 cent

ایک پینی / ۱ سنٹ

2. $.05 = 5¢
a nickel / 5 cents

ایک نکل / ۵ سنٹس

3. $.10 = 10¢
a dime / 10 cents

ایک ڈائم / ۱۰ سنٹس

4. $.25 = 25¢
a quarter / 25 cents

ایک کوارٹر / ۲۵ سنٹس

5. $.50 = 50¢
a half dollar

نصف ڈالر

6. $1.00
a dollar coin

ایک ڈالر کا سکہ

Bills نوٹ

7. $1.00
a dollar

ایک ڈالر

8. $5.00
five dollars

پانچ ڈالر

9. $10.00
ten dollars

دس ڈالر

10. $20.00
twenty dollars

بیس ڈالر

11. $50.00
fifty dollars

پچاس ڈالر

12. $100.00
one hundred dollars

ایک سو ڈالر

Do you have change for a dollar?

Yes, I do.

A. Get change.

کھلے پیسے حاصل کیجیے۔

Can I borrow a dollar?

Sure. Here you go.

B. Borrow money.

رقم اُدھار لیجیے۔

C. Lend money.

رقم اُدھار دیجیے۔

Thanks.

D. Pay back the money.

رقم واپس ادا کیجیے۔

Pair practice. Make new conversations.

A: *Do you have change for <u>a dollar</u>?*
B: *Sure. How about <u>two quarters</u> and <u>five dimes</u>?*
A: *Perfect!*

Think about it. Discuss.

1. Is it a good idea to lend money to a friend? Why or why not?
2. Is it better to carry a dollar or four quarters? Why?
3. Do you prefer dollar coins or dollar bills? Why?

Ways to Pay ادائیگی کے طریقے

A. pay cash
نقد ادائیگی کیجیے

B. use a credit card
کریڈٹ کارڈ استعمال کیجیے

C. use a debit card
ڈیبٹ کارڈ استعمال کیجیے

D. write a (personal) check
(ذاتی) چیک لکھیے

E. use a gift card
گفٹ کارڈ استعمال کیجیے

F. cash a traveler's check
ٹریولرز چیک بھنائیے

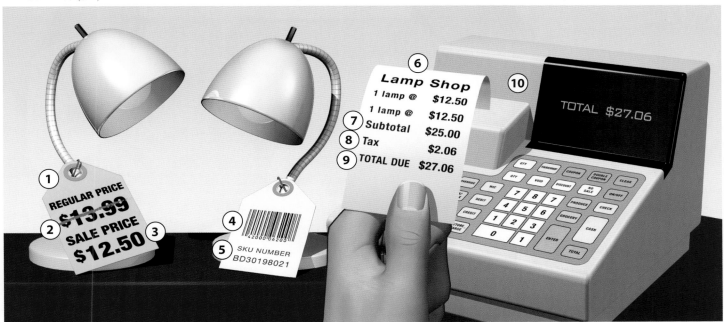

1. price tag	**3.** sale price	**5.** SKU number	**7.** price / cost	**9.** total
قیمت کا بلا	سستی فروخت کاری قیمت	ذخیرہ کاری فہرست اکائی نمبر	قیمت / لاگت	کل
2. regular price	**4.** bar code	**6.** receipt	**8.** sales tax	**10.** cash register
عام قیمت	بار کوڈ	رسید	سلیز ٹیکس	کیش رجسٹر

G. buy / pay for
خریدیے / قیمت ادا کیجیے

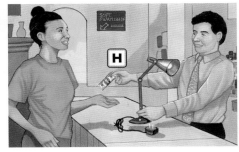

H. return
واپس کیجیے

I. exchange
تبادلہ کیجیے

1. twins
   جڑواں

2. sweater
   سوئیٹر

3. matching
   ملتا جلتا

4. disappointed
   مایوس

5. navy blue
   سمندری نیلا

6. happy
   خوش

A. **shop**
   خریدیے

B. **keep**
   رکھیے

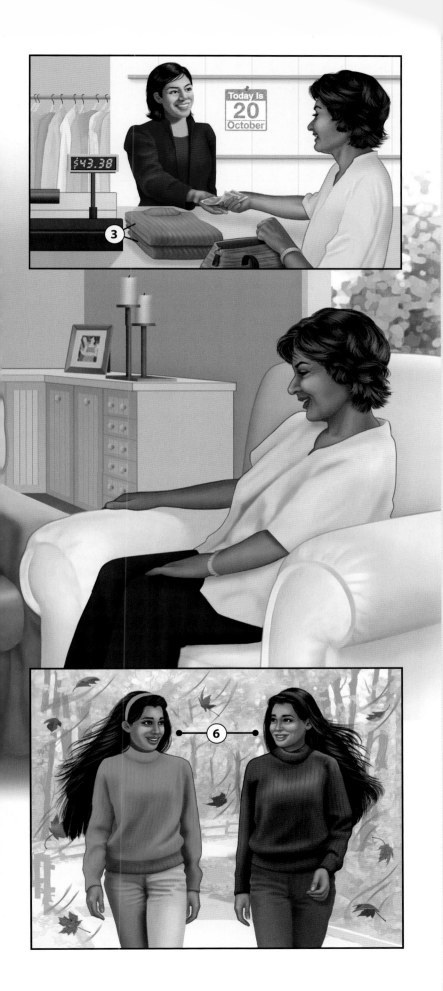

Look at the pictures.
What do you see?

Answer the questions.

1. Who is the woman shopping for?

2. Does she buy matching sweaters or different sweaters?

3. How does Anya feel about her green sweater? What does she do?

4. What does Manda do with her sweater?

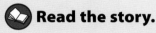 **Read the story.**

Same and Different

Mrs. Kumar likes to <u>shop</u> for her <u>twins</u>. Today she's looking at <u>sweaters</u>. There are many different colors on sale. Mrs. Kumar chooses two <u>matching</u> green sweaters.

The next day, Manda and Anya open their gifts. Manda likes the green sweater, but Anya is <u>disappointed</u>. Mrs. Kumar understands the problem. Anya wants to be different.

Manda <u>keeps</u> her sweater. But Anya goes to the store. She exchanges her green sweater for a <u>navy blue</u> sweater. It's an easy answer to Anya's problem. Now the twins can be warm, <u>happy</u>, and different.

Think about it.

1. Do you like to shop for other people? Why or why not?

2. Imagine you are Anya. Would you keep the sweater or exchange it? Why?

29

1. man
   مرد
2. woman
   عورت
3. women
   عورتیں
4. men
   ایک سے زیادہ مرد
5. senior citizen
   بزرگ شہری

Listen and point. Take turns.

A: *Point to a <u>woman</u>.*
B: *Point to a <u>senior citizen</u>.*
A: *Point to an <u>infant</u>.*

Dictate to your partner. Take turns.

A: *Write <u>woman</u>.*
B: *Is that spelled <u>w-o-m-a-n</u>?*
A: *Yes, that's right, <u>woman</u>.*

6. infant
نو زائیده بچه
7. baby
چھوٹا بچہ
8. toddler
چلنا شروع کرنے والا بچہ
9. 6-year-old boy
۶ سال کا بچہ
10. 10-year-old girl
۱۰ سال کی لڑکی
11. teenager / teen
۱۳ سے ۱۹ سال کی عمر کا
۱۳ سے ۱۹ سال کی عمر /

Ways to talk about age

1 month – 3 months old = **infant**	13 – 19 years old = **teenager**
18 months – 3 years old = **toddler**	18+ years old = **adult**
3 years old – 12 years old = **child**	62+ years old = **senior citizen**

Pair practice. Make new conversations.

A: *How old is Sandra?*
B: *She's thirteen years old.*
A: *Wow, she's a teenager now!*

31

Age عمر

1. young
نوجوان
2. middle-aged
درمیانی عمر کا
3. elderly
بزرگ

Height قد

4. tall
لمبا
5. average height
اوسط قد
6. short
پستہ قد

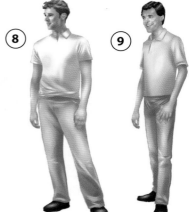

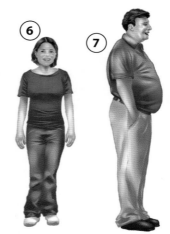

Weight وزن

7. heavy / fat
بھاری / موٹا
8. average weight
اوسط وزن
9. thin / slender
پتلا / دبلا

Disabilities معذوریاں

10. physically challenged
جسمانی طور پر معذور
11. sight impaired / blind
دیکھنے سے معذور / نابینا
12. hearing impaired / deaf
سننے سے معذور / بہرا

Prepositions of Motion p.153

Appearance ظاہری شکل

13. attractive
دلکش
14. cute
خوبصورت
15. pregnant
حاملہ
16. mole
تل
17. pierced ear
چھیدا ہوا کان
18. tattoo
جلد پر گودا ہوا نقش

Ways to describe people

He's a <u>heavy</u>, <u>young</u> man.
She's a <u>pregnant</u> woman with <u>a mole</u>.
He's <u>sight impaired</u>.

Use the new words. Look at pages 2–3.
Describe the people and point. Take turns.

A: *He's a <u>tall</u>, <u>thin</u>, <u>middle-aged</u> man.*
B: *She's a <u>short</u>, <u>average-weight</u> <u>young</u> woman.*

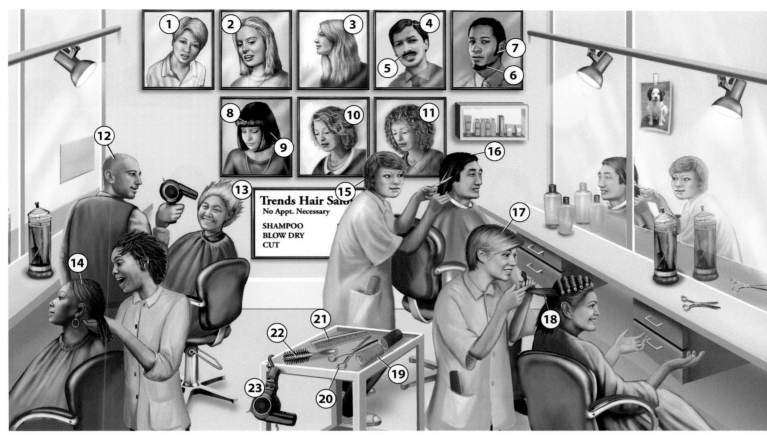

1. short hair
چھوٹے بال

2. shoulder-length hair
کندھے تک کے بال

3. long hair
لمبے بال

4. part
بالوں کی مانگ

5. mustache
مونچھ

6. beard
داڑھی

7. sideburns
قلمیں

8. bangs
پیشانی پر بالوں کی جھالر

9. straight hair
سیدھے بال

10. wavy hair
لہر دار بال

11. curly hair
گھنگھرالے بال

12. bald
گنجا

13. gray hair
بھورے بال

14. corn rows
مکئی کے دانوں کی طرح بنائے
گئے بال

15. red hair
سرخ بال

16. black hair
سیاہ بال

17. blond hair
سنہرے بال

18. brown hair
بھورے بال

19. rollers
بالوں میں گھونگر ڈالنے کے رولرز

20. scissors
قینچی

21. comb
کنگھا

22. brush
برش

23. blow dryer
بال سکھانے کا آلہ

Style Hair بالوں کی وضع بنائیے

A. cut hair
بالوں کو کاٹیے

B. perm hair
بالوں کو مستقل گھونگرالا بنائیے

C. set hair
بالوں کو ترتیب دیجیے

D. color hair / dye hair
بالوں کو رنگیے / خضاب لگائیے

Ways to talk about hair
Describe hair in this order: length, style, and then color.
She has <u>long</u>, <u>straight</u>, <u>brown</u> hair.

Role play. Talk to a stylist.
A: *I need a new hairstyle.*
B: *How about <u>short</u> and <u>straight</u>?*
A: *Great. Do you think I should <u>dye</u> it?*

1. grandmother
دادی،نانی

2. grandfather
دادا، نانا

3. mother
ماں

4. father
باپ

5. sister
بہن

6. brother
بھائی

7. aunt
چچی، ممانی، خالہ

8. uncle
چچا، ماموں، خالو

9. cousin
چچا زاد، خالہ زاد، ماموں زاد بھائی / بہن

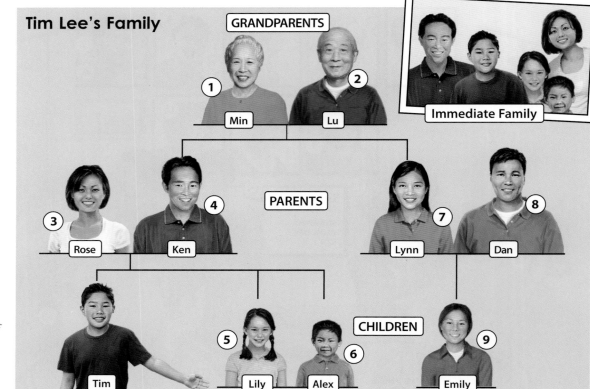

Tim Lee's Family

GRANDPARENTS

Immediate Family

PARENTS

CHILDREN

Min · Lu · Rose · Ken · Lynn · Dan · Tim · Lily · Alex · Emily

10. mother-in-law
ساس

11. father-in-law
سسر

12. wife
بیوی

13. husband
شوہر

14. daughter
بیٹی

15. son
بیٹا

16. sister-in-law
سالی

17. brother-in-law
بہنوئی / سالا

18. niece
بھانجی، بھتیجی

19. nephew
بھانجا، بھتیجا

Ana Garcia's Family

Extended Family

Eva · Sam · Ana · Tito · Marta · Carlos · Sara · Felix · Alice · Eddie

---

More vocabulary

Tim is Min and Lu's **grandson**.
Lily and Emily are Min and Lu's **granddaughters**.
Alex is Min's youngest **grandchild**.

Ana is Tito's **wife**.
Ana is Eva and Sam's **daughter-in-law**.
Carlos is Eva and Sam's **son-in-law**.

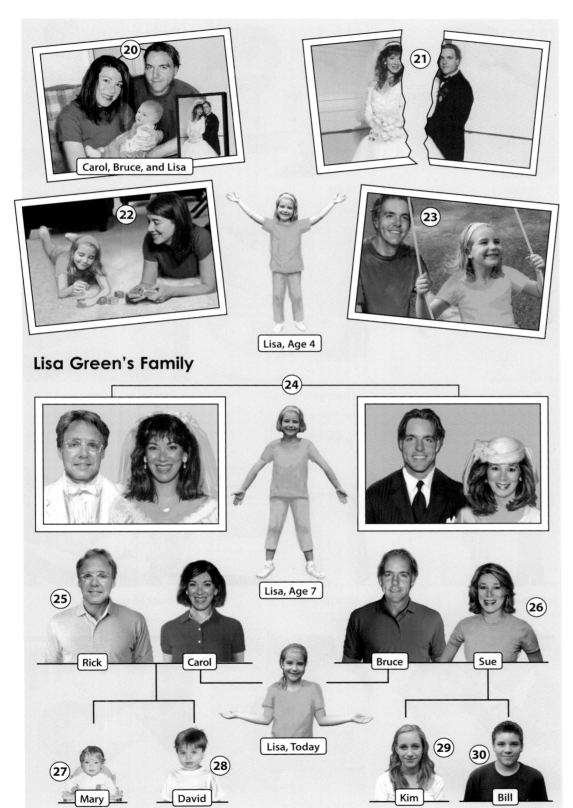

20. married couple
    شادی شده جوڑا
21. divorced couple
    طلاق شده جوڑا
22. single mother
    تنها ماں
23. single father
    تنها باپ

Carol, Bruce, and Lisa

Lisa, Age 4

Lisa Green's Family

24. remarried
    دوباره شادی شده
25. stepfather
    سوتیلا باپ
26. stepmother
    سوتیلی ماں
27. half sister
    مشترک ماں یا باپ والی بہن
28. half brother
    مشترک ماں یا باپ والا بھائی
29. stepsister
    سوتیلی بہن
30. stepbrother
    سوتیلا بھائی

Lisa, Age 7

Rick   Carol   Bruce   Sue

Lisa, Today

Mary   David   Kim   Bill

More vocabulary

Bruce is Carol's **former husband** or **ex-husband**.
Carol is Bruce's **former wife** or **ex-wife**.
Lisa is the **stepdaughter** of both Rick and Sue.

Look at the pictures.
Name the people.

A: *Who is Lisa's half sister?*
B: *Mary is. Who is Lisa's stepsister?*

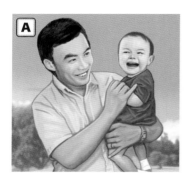

A. hold
گود میں لیجیے

B. nurse
دودھ پلائیے

C. feed
کھلائیے

D. rock
بانہوں میں جھلائیے

E. undress
بچے کے کپڑے اتاریئے

F. bathe
نہلائیے

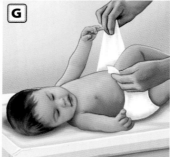

G. change a diaper
چڈی بدلیے

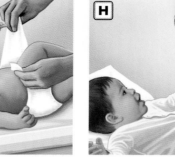

H. dress
کپڑے پہنائیے

I. comfort
تسلی دیجیے

Good job!

J. praise
تعریف کیجیے

No!

K. discipline
تادیب کیجیے

L. buckle up
بکسوا باندھیے

M. play with
ساتھ کھیلیے

N. read to
پڑھ کر سنائیے

O. sing a lullaby
کوئی لوری گائیے

P. kiss goodnight
شب بخیر کہتے ہوئے بوسہ دیجیے

Look at the pictures.
Describe what is happening.

A: She's <u>changing her baby's diaper</u>.
B: He's <u>kissing his son goodnight</u>.

Ask your classmates. Share the answers.
1. Do you like to take care of children?
2. Do you prefer to read to children or play with them?
3. Can you sing a lullaby? Which one?

1. bottle
بوتل

2. nipple
نپل

3. formula
بچے کی مخصوص غذا

4. baby food
بچے کی غذا

5. bib
گلو بند

6. high chair
اونچی کرسی

7. diaper pail
چڈی رکھنے کی بالٹی

8. cloth diaper
کپڑے کی چڈی

9. safety pins
سیفٹی پن

10. disposable diaper
ضائع کی جانے والی چڈی

11. training pants
تربیتی نیکر

12. potty seat
حاجتی سیٹ

13. baby lotion
بچوں کی مالش کا تیل

14. baby powder
بے بی پاؤڈر

15. wipes
خشک صاف کرنے والے رومال

16. baby bag
بے بی بیگ

17. baby carrier
بے بی کیریئر

18. stroller
بچوں کی دھکیلنے والی کرسی

19. car safety seat
کار کی حفاظتی سیٹ

20. carriage
گاڑی

21. rocking chair
جھولنے والی کرسی

22. nursery rhymes
نرسری گیت

23. teddy bear
ٹیڈی بیئر

24. pacifier
چسنی

25. teething ring
دانت نکلنے کے دوران منہ میں دبانے والا چھلا

26. rattle
جھنجھنا

27. night light
رات کی روشنی

Dictate to your partner. Take turns.

A: *Write pacifier.*
B: *Was that pacifier, p-a-c-i-f-i-e-r?*
A: *Yes, that's right.*

Think about it. Discuss.

1. How can parents discipline toddlers? teens?
2. What are some things you can say to praise a child?
3. Why are nursery rhymes important for young children?

37

A. wake up
جاگیے

B. get up
اٹھ جائیے

C. take a shower
فوارے سے نہائیے

D. get dressed
کپڑے پہنیے

E. eat breakfast
ناشتہ کیجیے

F. make lunch
دوپہر کا کھانا تیار کیجیے

G. take the children to school /
drop off the kids
بچوں کو اسکول لے جائیے /
بچوں کو اسکول چھوڑیے

H. take the bus to school
اسکول کی بس پکڑیے

I. drive to work / **go** to work
گاڑی سے کام پر جائیے / کام پر جائیے

J. go to class
کلاس میں جائیے

K. work
کام کیجیے

L. go to the grocery store
کریانہ اسٹور پر جائیے

M. pick up the kids
بچوں کو لائیے

N. leave work
کام سے واپس جائیے

Grammar Point: third person singular

For *he* and *she*, add **-s** or **-es** to the verb:

He *wakes* up.   He *watches* TV.

He *gets* up.   She *goes* to the store.

These verbs are different (irregular):

*Be: She **is** in school at 10:00 a.m.*

*Have: He **has** dinner at 6:30 p.m.*

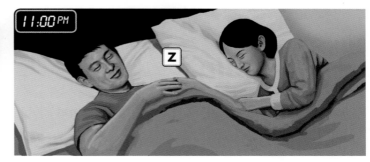

O. **clean** the house
گھر کی صفائی کیجیے

P. **exercise**
ورزش کیجیے

Q. **cook** dinner / **make** dinner
رات کا کھانا پکائیے / رات کا کھانا تیار کیجیے

R. **come** home / **get** home
گھر آئیے / گھر پہنچیے

S. **have** dinner / **eat** dinner
رات کا کھانا لیجیے / رات کا کھانا کھائیے

T. **do** homework
ہوم ورک کیجیے

U. **relax**
آرام کیجیے

V. **read** the paper
اخبار پڑھیے

W. **check** email
ای-میل دیکھیے

X. **watch** TV
ٹی وی دیکھیے

Y. **go** to bed
بستر پر لیٹ جائیے

Z. **go** to sleep
سو جائیے

Pair practice. Make new conversations.

A: *When does he go to work?*
B: *He goes to work at 8:00 a.m. When does she go to class?*
A: *She goes to class at 10:00 a.m.*

Ask your classmates. Share the answers.

1. Who cooks dinner in your family?
2. Who goes to the grocery store?
3. Who goes to work?

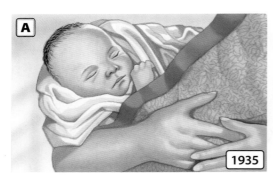

1935

A. be born
پیدائش

1940

B. start school
اسکول جانے کی ابتداء

DEPARTMENT OF IMMIGRATION

1950

C. immigrate
ایک ملک سے دوسرے ملک جانا

1953

D. graduate
تعلیم کی تکمیل

1953

E. learn to drive
گاڑی چلانا سیکھنا

1954

F. get a job
ملازمت حاصل کرنا

1954

G. become a citizen
شہریت کا حصول

1955

H. fall in love
کسی کو پسند کرنا

REGISTRO CIVIL
Acta de Nacimiento
MARTÍN PEREZ DE LÉON   B0983456
01-05-1935
Registro Civil
Acta de Nacimiento

1. birth certificate
تصدیق نامۂ پیدائش

PERMANENT RESIDENT CARD
PEREZ, MARTIN   A043398414
01-05-1935

2. Resident Alien card / green card
مقیم غیر ملکی کارڈ / گرین کارڈ

Los Angeles High School
Martin Perez

3. diploma
ڈپلوما

CALIFORNIA
DRIVER LICENSE
M06188
MARTIN PEREZ

4. driver's license
ڈرائیور لائسنس

SOCIAL SECURITY
987-65-4321
MARTIN PEREZ

5. Social Security card
سوشل سکیورٹی کارڈ

THE UNITED STATES OF AMERICA
CERTIFICATE OF NATURALIZATION
MARTIN PEREZ DE LEON

6. Certificate of Naturalization
غیر ملکی کی شہریت کا تصدیق نامہ

Grammar Point: past tense

start		immigrate	retire	
learn	+ed	graduate	die	+d
travel				

These verbs are different (irregular):

be – was	go – went	buy – bought
get – got	have – had	
become – became	fall – fell	

I. go to college
کالج جائیے

J. get engaged
منگنی کیجیے

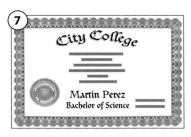

7. college degree
کالج کی سند

K. get married
شادی کیجیے

L. have a baby
بچہ پیدا کیجیے

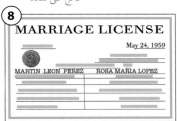

8. marriage license
شادی کا لائسنس

M. buy a home
گھر خریدیے

N. become a grandparent
دادا، دادی،نانا، نانی بنیئے

9. deed
معاہدہ

O. retire
سبکدوش ہو جائیے

P. travel
سفر کیجیے

10. passport
پاسپورٹ

Q. volunteer
رضاکارانہ خدمت کیجیے

R. die
موت

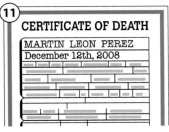

11. death certificate
موت کا تصدیق نامہ

More vocabulary

When a husband dies, his wife becomes a **widow**.
When a wife dies, her husband becomes a **widower**.

Ask your classmates. Share the answers.

1. When did you start school?
2. When did you get your first job?
3. Do you want to travel?

1. hot
گرم
2. thirsty
پیاسا
3. sleepy
اونگھتا ہوا
4. cold
ٹھنڈا
5. hungry
بھوکا
6. full / satisfied
پیٹ بھرا ہوا / مطمئن

7. disgusted
بیزار
8. calm
پُرسکون
9. uncomfortable
بے چین
10. nervous
گھبرایا ہوا

11. in pain
تکلیف کی حالت میں
12. sick
بیمار
13. worried
فکرمند
14. well
ٹھیک
15. relieved
مطمئن

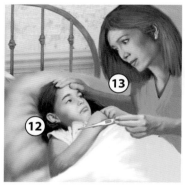

16. hurt
غمگین
17. lonely
تنہا
18. in love
عشق میں گرفتار

Pair practice. Make new conversations.

A: *How are you doing?*
B: *I'm <u>hungry</u>. How about you?*
A: *I'm <u>hungry</u> and <u>thirsty</u>, too!*

Use the new words.
Look at pages 40–41. Describe what each person is feeling.

A: *Martin is <u>excited</u>.*
B: *Martin's mother is <u>proud</u>.*

19. sad
أداس
20. homesick
گھر کی یاد میں رنجیدہ
21. proud
فخرمند

22. excited
پُرجوش
23. scared / afraid
ڈرا ہوا / خوف زدہ
24. embarrassed
شرمندہ

25. bored
اکتایا ہوا
26. confused
الجھن میں گرفتار
27. frustrated
مایوس

28. upset
پریشان
29. angry
ناراض

30. surprised
حیرت زدہ
31. happy
خوش
32. tired
تھکا ہوا

Ask your classmates. Share the answers.

1. Do you ever feel homesick?
2. What makes you feel frustrated?
3. Describe a time when you were very happy.

More vocabulary

exhausted: very tired
furious: very angry
humiliated: very embarrassed

overjoyed: very happy
starving: very hungry
terrified: very scared

43

LU FAMILY REUNION

1. banner	3. opinion	5. glad	A. **laugh**
جھنڈا	تبادلۂ خیال	مسرور	ہنسیے
2. baseball game	4. balloons	6. relatives	B. **misbehave**
بیس بال کا کھیل	غبارے	رشتے دار	غلط برتاؤ

I think large families are best.

Answer the questions.

1. How many relatives are there at this reunion?

2. How many children are there? Which children are misbehaving?

3. What are people doing at this reunion?

 Read the story.

A Family Reunion

Ben Lu has a lot of <u>relatives</u> and they're all at his house. Today is the Lu family reunion.

There is a lot of good food. There are also <u>balloons</u> and a <u>banner</u>. And this year there are four new babies!

People are having a good time at the reunion. Ben's grandfather and his aunt are talking about the <u>baseball game</u>. His cousins <u>are laughing</u>. His mother-in-law is giving her <u>opinion</u>. And many of the children <u>are misbehaving</u>.

Ben looks at his family and smiles. He loves his relatives, but he's <u>glad</u> the reunion is once a year.

Think about it.

1. Do you like to have large parties? Why or why not?

2. Imagine you see a little girl at a party. She's misbehaving. What do you do? What do you say?

45

1. roof
   چھت
2. bedroom
   خواب گاہ
3. door
   دروازہ
4. bathroom
   غسل خانہ
5. kitchen
   باورچی خانہ
6. floor
   فرش
7. dining area
   طعام گاہ

Listen and point. Take turns.

A: *Point to the kitchen.*
B: *Point to the living room.*
A: *Point to the basement.*

Dictate to your partner. Take turns.

A: *Write kitchen.*
B: *Was that k-i-t-c-h-e-n?*
A: *Yes, that's right, kitchen.*

8. attic
پرچھتی

9. kids' bedroom
بچوں کے سونے کا کمرہ

10. baby's room
چھوٹے بچے کا کمرہ

11. window
کھڑکی

12. living room
نشستی کمرہ

13. basement
تہہ خانہ

14. garage
موٹر گاڑی خانہ

Ways to give locations
I'm home.
I'm in the kitchen.
I'm on the roof.

Pair practice. Make new conversations.
A: *Where's the man?*
B: *He's in the attic. Where's the teenager?*
A: *She's in the laundry room.*

1. Internet listing
انٹرنیٹ سے تلاش

2. classified ad
زمرہ بند اشتہارات

Abbreviations

apt = apartment

bdrm = bedroom

ba = bathroom

kit = kitchen

yd = yard

util = utilities

incl = included

mo = month

furn = furnished

unfurn = unfurnished

mgr = manager

eves = evenings

3. furnished apartment
آراستہ اپارٹمنٹ

4. unfurnished apartment
غیر آراستہ اپارٹمنٹ

Gas   Water   Electricity   Phone   Cable   DSL

5. utilities
ضروری خدمات

Renting an Apartment اپارٹمنٹ کرایہ پر لینا

A. Call the manager.
مینیجر کو فون کیجیے۔

Are utilities included?

No, they aren't.

B. Ask about the features.
خصوصیات کے بارے میں دریافت کیجیے۔

C. Submit an application.
درخواست داخل کیجیے۔

D. Sign the rental agreement.
کرایہ داری معاہدے پر دستخط کیجیے۔

E. Pay the first and last month's rent.
پہلے اور آخری مہینہ کا کرایہ ادا کیجیے۔

F. Move in.
گھر میں منتقل ہو جائیے۔

More vocabulary

lease: a monthly or yearly rental agreement

redecorate: to change the paint and furniture in a home

move out: to pack and leave a home

Ask your classmates. Share the answers.

1. How did you find your home?

2. Do you like to paint or arrange furniture?

3. Does gas or electricity cost more for you?

Buying a House گھر خریدنا

G. Meet with a realtor.

کسی جائداد فروش سے ملاقات کیجیے۔

H. Look at houses.

گھروں کا معائنہ کیجیے۔

$$$$$

I. Make an offer.

کوئی پیش کش کیجیے۔

Congratulations!

J. Get a loan.

قرض لیجیے۔

K. Take ownership.

ملکیت حاصل کیجیے۔

L. Make a mortgage payment.

رہنی ادائیگی کیجیے۔

Moving In گھر میں منتقل ہونا

M. Pack.

سامان باندھیئے۔

N. Unpack.

سامان کھولیے۔

We have a new address.

O. Put the utilities in your name.

ضروری خدمات کو اپنے نام کرائیے۔

P. Paint.

گھر کی رنگائی کیجیے۔

Q. Arrange the furniture.

فرنیچر کو ترتیب سے رکھیے۔

Welcome!

R. Meet the neighbors.

پڑوسیوں سے ملیے۔

Ways to ask about a home's features

Are <u>utilities</u> included?
Is <u>the kitchen</u> large and sunny?
Are <u>the neighbors</u> quiet?

Role play. Talk to an apartment manager.

A: *Hi. I'm calling about <u>the apartment</u>.*
B: *OK. It's <u>unfurnished</u> and rent is $<u>800</u> a month.*
A: *Are utilities included?*

Fourth Floor

Third Floor

Second Floor

First Floor

1. **apartment building**
اپارٹمنٹ والی عمارت

2. **fire escape**
آگ لگنے پر بھاگنے کے لیے عقبی زینہ

3. **playground**
کھیل کا میدان

4. **roof garden**
چھت باغیچہ

Entrance داخلہ گاہ

5. **intercom / speaker**
صرف عمارت کے اندر کا فون / اسپیکر

6. **tenant**
کرایہ دار

7. **vacancy sign**
خالی ہونے کی علامت

8. **manager / superintendent**
مینیجر / سپرنٹنڈنٹ

Lobby لابی

9. **elevator**
لفٹ

10. **stairs / stairway**
زینے / زینے کا راستہ

11. **mailboxes**
ڈاک کی صندوقچیاں

Basement تہہ خانہ

LAUNDRY ROOM

RECREATION ROOM

GARAGE

12. **washer**
کپڑے دھونے والی مشین

13. **dryer**
کپڑے سُکھانے والی مشین

14. **big-screen TV**
بڑے اسکرین کا ٹی وی

15. **pool table**
اسنوکر کھیلنے کی میز

16. **security gate**
حفاظتی دروازہ

17. **storage locker**
اسٹوریج لاکر

18. **parking space**
گاڑی کھڑی کرنے کی جگہ

19. **security camera**
حفاظتی کیمرا

Grammar Point: _there is / there are_

singular: there is **plural:** there are
There is _a recreation room in the basement._
There are _mailboxes in the lobby._

Look at the pictures.
Describe the apartment building.

A: _There's <u>a pool table</u> in the recreation room._
B: _There are <u>parking spaces</u> in the garage._

APARTMENT COMPLEX

20. balcony
بالکنی

21. courtyard
آنگن

22. swimming pool
سوئمنگ پول

23. trash bin
کوڑا دان

24. alley
گلیارا

Hallway راہداری

25. emergency exit
ہنگامی دروازہ

26. trash chute
کوڑا شگاف

Rental Office دفتر امور کرایہ داری

27. landlord
مالک مکان

28. lease / rental agreement
پٹہ / معاہدۂ کرایہ داری

An Apartment Entryway اپارٹمنٹ میں داخلہ کا راستہ

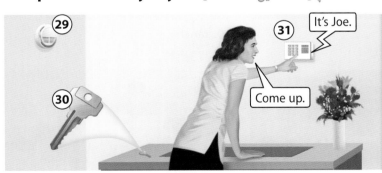

It's Joe.

Come up.

29. smoke detector
دھواں شناس آلہ

30. key
چابی

31. buzzer
برقی گھنٹی

32. peephole
جھانک کر دیکھنے والا سوراخ

33. door chain
دروازے کی زنجیر

34. dead-bolt lock
پوری طرح بند کرنے کا تالا

More vocabulary

upstairs: the floor(s) above you
downstairs: the floor(s) below you
fire exit: another name for emergency exit

Role play. Talk to a landlord.

A: Is there _a swimming pool_ in this _complex_?
B: Yes, there is. It's near _the courtyard_.
A: Is there…?

51

1. the city / an urban area
شہر / شہری علاقہ

2. the suburbs
مضافات

3. a small town / a village
چھوٹا قصبہ / ایک گاؤں

4. the country / a rural area
دیہات / دیہی علاقہ

5. condominium / condo
نجی ملکیت کے فلیٹوں کی عمارت / کونڈو

6. townhouse
شہر میں ایک دوسرے سے منسلک مکان

7. mobile home
چلتا پھرتا گھر / عارضی گھر

8. college dormitory / dorm
کالج کی مشترکہ اقامت گاہ / ڈورم

9. farm
زراعتی فارم مع رہائش

10. ranch
مویشی گاہ

11. senior housing
بزرگوں کی رہائش گاہ

12. nursing home
نرسنگ ہوم

13. shelter
افراد کے لیے مفت رہائش

More vocabulary

co-op: an apartment building owned by residents
duplex: a house divided into two homes
two-story house: a house with two floors

Think about it. Discuss.

1. What's good and bad about these places to live?
2. How are small towns different from cities?
3. How do shelters help people in need?

Front Yard and House سامنے کا صحن اور گھر

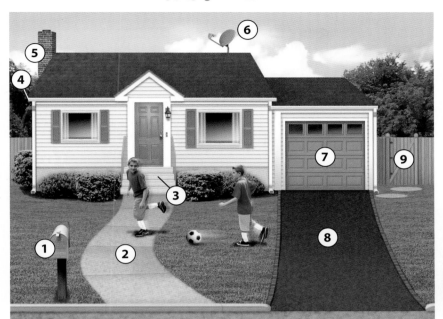

Front Porch سامنے کا پورچ

1. mailbox ڈاک کا صندوق	**4.** gutter پرنالہ	**7.** garage door گیرج کا دروازہ
2. front walk سامنے کی روش	**5.** chimney چمنی	**8.** driveway گاڑی لانے کا راستہ
3. steps سیڑھیاں	**6.** satellite dish سیٹیلائٹ طشتری	**9.** gate پھاٹک

10. storm door اضافی حفاظتی دروازہ	**13.** porch light پورچ کی روشنی
11. front door سامنے کا دروازہ	**14.** doorbell دروازے کی گھنٹی
12. doorknob دروازے کا لٹو	**15.** screen door پردہ نما دروازہ

Backyard عقبی صحن

16. patio آنگن	**19.** patio furniture آنگن کا فرنیچر	**22.** sprinkler پانی چھڑکنے کا آلہ	**25.** compost pile قدرتی کھاد کا ڈھیر	**A. take** a nap ہلکی نیند لیجیے
17. grill سینکنے والی بھٹی	**20.** flower bed پھولوں کی کیاری	**23.** hammock جالی دار جھولا	**26.** lawn سبزہ زار	**B. garden** باغ بانی کیجیے
18. sliding glass door کھسکانے والا شیشے کا دروازہ	**21.** hose پانی کا پائپ	**24.** garbage can کوڑے کی ٹوکری	**27.** vegetable garden سبزی باغ	

53

1. cabinet
کابینہ

2. shelf
الماری

3. paper towels
کاغذ کے رومال

4. sink
باورچی خانہ میں برتن دھونے کا حوض

5. dish rack
برتنوں کی کھلی الماری

6. toaster
ٹوسٹر

7. garbage disposal
کوڑے کی نکاسی

8. dishwasher
پلیٹیں دھونے کی مشین

9. refrigerator
ریفریجریٹر

10. freezer
جمانے والی مشین

11. coffeemaker
کافی بنانے والی مشین

12. blender
ملانے والی مشین

13. microwave
مائکروویو

14. electric can opener
برقی ڈبہ کھولنے کا آلہ

15. toaster oven
سینکنے والی بھٹی

16. pot
پتیلی

17. teakettle
چائے کی کیتلی

18. stove
اسٹوو

19. burner
برنر

20. oven
تنور

21. broiler
بھوننے کے لیے چولھے پر رکھی جانے والی جالی

22. counter
پیش تختہ

23. drawer
دراز

24. pan
کڑابہی

25. electric mixer
پھینٹنے کا برقی آلہ

26. food processor
کھانا بنانے میں مستعمل آلہ

27. cutting board
کاٹنے کا تختہ

28. mixing bowl
پھینٹنے کا پیالہ

Ways to talk about location using *on* and *in*

Use **on** for the counter, shelf, burner, stove, and cutting board. *It's **on** the counter.* Use **in** for the dishwasher, oven, sink, and drawer. *Put it **in** the sink.*

Pair practice. Make new conversations.

A: *Please move <u>the blender</u>.*
B: *Sure. Do you want it <u>in the cabinet</u>?*
A: *No, put it <u>on the counter</u>.*

1. dish / plate
قاب / پلیٹ

2. bowl
پیالہ

3. fork
کانٹا

4. knife
چھری

5. spoon
چمچہ

6. teacup
چائے کی پیالی

7. coffee mug
کافی کی پیالی

8. dining room chair
طعام گاہ کی کرسی

9. dining room table
طعام گاہ کی میز

10. napkin
زانو پوش

11. placemat
کھانے کی میز پر پلیٹ رکھنے کا تہ پوش

12. tablecloth
میز پوش

13. salt and pepper shakers
نمک اور کالی مرچ دانیاں

14. sugar bowl
چینی دان

15. creamer
کریم رکھنے کا جگ

16. teapot
چائے دانی

17. tray
سینی

18. light fixture
روشنی کی تنصیبات

19. fan
پنکھا

20. platter
طشت

21. serving bowl
یخنی شوربہ وغیرہ پیش کرنے
کا پیالہ

22. hutch
سامان رکھنے کی الماری

23. vase
گل دان

24. buffet
طعام خانے میں سامان رکھنے
کی الماری

Ways to make requests at the table

May I have the sugar bowl?
Would you pass the creamer, please?
Could I have a coffee mug?

Role play. Request items at the table.

A: *What do you need?*
B: *Could I have a coffee mug?*
A: *Certainly. And would you...*

55

1. **love seat**
   دو آدمیوں کے بیٹھنے کا صوفہ

2. **throw pillow**
   پھلو تکیہ

3. **basket**
   ٹوکری

4. **houseplant**
   اندر رکھنے والا پودا

5. **entertainment center**
   تفریحی مرکز

6. **TV (television)**
   ٹی وی (ٹیلی ویژن)

7. **DVD player**
   ڈی وی ڈی پلیئر

8. **stereo system**
   اسٹیریو سسٹم

9. **painting**
   ہاتھ سے بنائی تصویر

10. **wall**
    دیوار

11. **mantle**
    آتش دان کی دیوار

12. **fire screen**
    آتش دان سے بچاؤ کی جالی

13. **fireplace**
    آتش دان

14. **end table**
    کونے پر رکھنے کی تپائی

15. **floor lamp**
    معیاری لیمپ

16. **drapes**
    پردے

17. **window**
    کھڑکی

18. **sofa / couch**
    صوفہ / گدا

19. **coffee table**
    کافی کی میز

20. **candle**
    شمع

21. **candle holder**
    شمع دان

22. **armchair / easy chair**
    بتھے والی کرسی / آرام کرسی

23. **magazine holder**
    میگزین رکھنے کا بستہ

24. **carpet**
    قالین

Use the new words.
Look at pages 44–45. Name the things in the room.

A: *There's a TV.*
B: *There's a carpet.*

More vocabulary

light bulb: the light inside a lamp
lampshade: the part of the lamp that covers the light bulb
sofa cushions: the pillows that are part of the sofa

1. hamper
کپڑے رکھنے کی قبضہ دار بڑی باسکٹ

2. bathtub
نہانے کا ٹب

3. soap dish
صابن دانی

4. soap
صابن

5. rubber mat
ربر کی چٹائی

6. washcloth
نہانے کا کپڑا

7. drain
نالی

8. faucet
ٹونٹی

9. hot water
گرم پانی

10. cold water
ٹھنڈا پانی

11. grab bar
سہارے کا بتھا

12. tile
ٹائل

13. showerhead
شاور کا سرا

14. shower curtain
شاور کا پردہ

15. towel rack
تولیے ٹانگنے کی سلاخ

16. bath towel
نہانے کا تولیہ

17. hand towel
دستی تولیہ

18. mirror
آئینہ

19. toilet paper
طہارت کا کاغذ

20. toilet brush
بیت الخلاء صاف کرنے کا برش

21. toilet
بیت الخلاء

22. medicine cabinet
دوا کی الماری

23. toothbrush
دانت کا برش

24. toothbrush holder
دانتوں کا برش رکھنے کا برتن

25. sink
غسل خانے میں نصب تسلہ مع ٹونٹی

26. wastebasket
کوڑے کی ٹوکری

27. scale
ترازو

28. bath mat
غسل خانے کی چٹائی

More vocabulary

stall shower: a shower without a bathtub
half bath: a bathroom with no shower or tub
linen closet: a closet for towels and sheets

Ask your classmates. Share the answers.

1. Is your toothbrush on the sink or in the medicine cabinet?
2. Do you have a bathtub or a shower?
3. Do you have a shower curtain or a shower door?

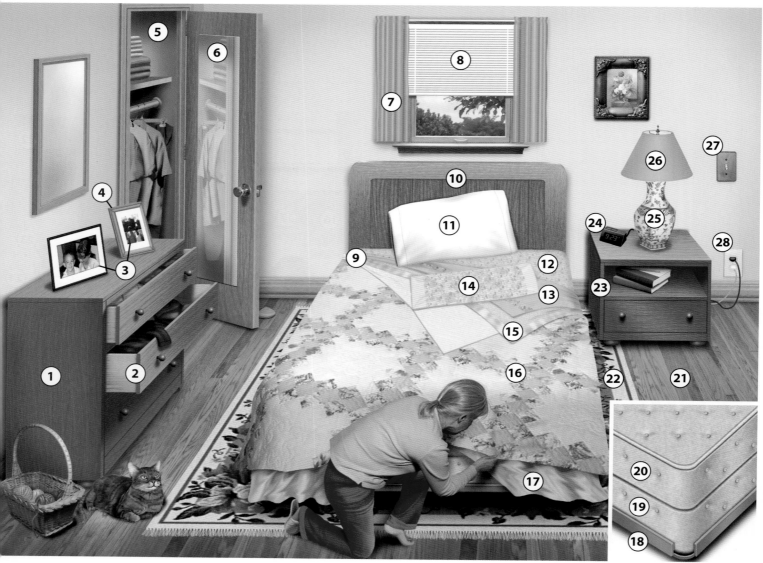

1. dresser / bureau
سنگارمیز / خانے دار الماری

2. drawer
دراز

3. photos
تصویریں

4. picture frame
تصویروں کا فریم

5. closet
الماری

6. full-length mirror
قد آدم آئینہ

7. curtains
پردے

8. mini-blinds
باہر سے اندر نہ دیکھ پانے والی چق

9. bed
بستر

10. headboard
سرہانہ

11. pillow
تکیہ

12. fitted sheet
پوری بچھی ہوئی چادر

13. flat sheet
ڈھیلی چادر

14. pillowcase
تکیے کا غلاف

15. blanket
کمبل

16. quilt
رضائی

17. dust ruffle
بستر سے فرش تک لٹکتی چادر

18. bed frame
بستر کا چوکھٹا

19. box spring
کنڈلی دار کمانیوں کے گدے والا بستر

20. mattress
گدا

21. wood floor
چوبی فرش

22. rug
قالین

23. night table / nightstand
سونے کے کمرے میں استعمال ہونے
والی میز / نائٹ اسٹینڈ

24. alarm clock
الارم گھڑی

25. lamp
لیمپ

26. lampshade
لیمپ کا ٹوپ

27. light switch
بجلی کا بٹن

28. outlet
برقی مخرج

Look at the pictures.
Describe the bedroom.

A: There's *a lamp* on *the nightstand*.
B: There's *a mirror* in *the closet*.

Ask your classmates. Share the answers.

1. Do you prefer a hard or a soft mattress?
2. Do you prefer mini-blinds or curtains?
3. How many pillows do you like on your bed?

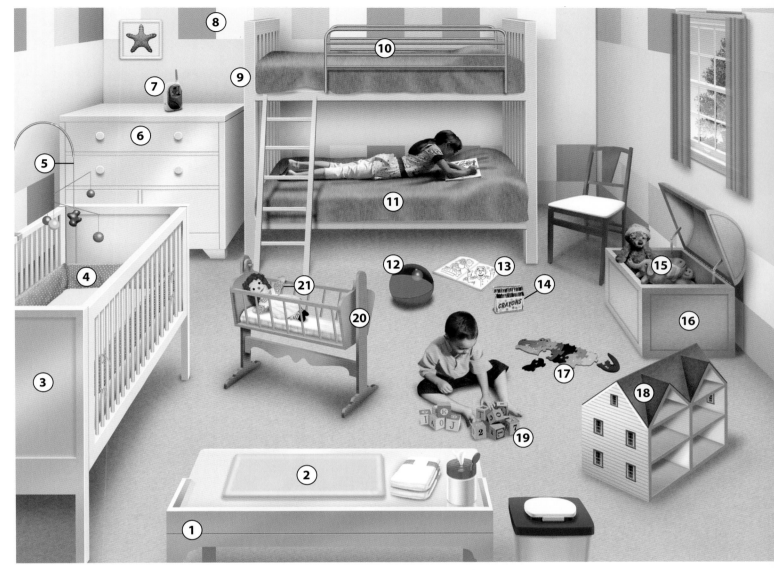

Furniture and Accessories فرنیچر اور لوازم

1. **changing table**
   کپڑے بدلنے کی میز
2. **changing pad**
   کپڑے بدلنے کا گدا
3. **crib**
   پالنا
4. **bumper pad**
   گرنے سے بچانے کے لیے گدے کی روک
5. **mobile**
   جھولتا ہوا کھلونا
6. **chest of drawers**
   درازوں والی الماری
7. **baby monitor**
   بچوں کی نگرانی کرنے والا آلہ
8. **wallpaper**
   دیواری کاغذ
9. **bunk beds**
   اوپر تلے بنے ہوئے بستر
10. **safety rail**
    حفاظتی ہتھے
11. **bedspread**
    پلنگ پوش

Toys and Games کھلونے اور کھیل

12. **ball**
    گیند
13. **coloring book**
    رنگ کرنے والی کتاب
14. **crayons**
    رنگین چاک یا موم بھری پنسلیں
15. **stuffed animals**
    روئی بھرے جانور
16. **toy chest**
    کھلونوں کی الماری
17. **puzzle**
    معمہ
18. **dollhouse**
    گڑیا گھر
19. **blocks**
    مکعب ٹکڑے
20. **cradle**
    جھولا
21. **doll**
    گڑیا

Pair practice. Make conversations.

A: *Where's the changing pad?*
B: *It's on the changing table.*

Think about it. Discuss.

1. Which toys help children learn? How?
2. Which toys are good for older and younger children?
3. What safety features does this room need? Why?

A. dust the furniture فرنیچر کی دھول جھاڑیے	**F. make** the bed بستر ٹھیک کیجیے	**K. scrub** the sink سنک کو رگڑیے	**P. change** the sheets چادریں تبدیل کیجیے
B. recycle the newspapers اخبارات کی بازتشکیل کیجیے	**G. put away** the toys کھلونوں کو دور رکھیے	**L. empty** the trash کوڑے دان کو خالی کیجیے	**Q. take out** the garbage کوڑا کرکٹ باہر لے جائیے
C. clean the oven تنور کی صفائی کیجیے	**H. vacuum** the carpet قالین کو خلا روب سے صاف کیجیے	**M. wash** the dishes پلیٹیں دھوئیے	
D. mop the floor فرش پونچھیے	**I. wash** the windows کھڑکیاں دھوئیے	**N. dry** the dishes پلیٹوں کو خشک کیجیے	
E. polish the furniture فرنیچر کی پالش کیجیے	**J. sweep** the floor فرش پونچھیے	**O. wipe** the counter کاؤنٹر کو پونچھیے	

Pair practice. Make new conversations.

A: *Let's clean this place. First, I'll <u>sweep the floor</u>.*
B: *I'll <u>mop the floor</u> when you finish.*

Ask your classmates. Share the answers.

1. Who does the housework in your home?
2. How often do you wash the windows?
3. When should kids start to do housework?

   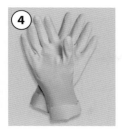  

1. **feather duster**
   پھول جھاڑو
2. **recycling bin**
   قابل بازتشکیل اشیاء کی ٹوکری
3. **oven cleaner**
   تنور کی صفائی کرنے والا
4. **rubber gloves**
   ربر کے دستانے
5. **steel-wool soap pads**
   اسٹیل کترن کے صفائی گدے
6. **sponge mop**
   اسپونج پونچھا
7. **bucket / pail**
   بالٹی / ڈول
8. **furniture polish**
   فرنیچر پالش

9. **rags**
   چیتھڑے
10. **vacuum cleaner**
    خلاء روب
11. **vacuum cleaner attachments**
    خلاء روب منسلکات
12. **vacuum cleaner bag**
    خلاء روب تھیلا
13. **stepladder**
    سیڑھی
14. **glass cleaner**
    شیشہ صافی
15. **squeegee**
    کھڑکیاں صاف کرنے کا ربر کا دستی آلہ
16. **broom**
    جھاڑو

17. **dustpan**
    کوڑا اٹھانے والا
18. **cleanser**
    صفائی کرنے والی محلول
19. **sponge**
    اسفنج
20. **scrub brush**
    رگڑنے والا برش
21. **dishwashing liquid**
    پلیٹ صاف کرنے والا محلول
22. **dish towel**
    پلیٹ میں رکھنے کا کاغذی رومال
23. **disinfectant wipes**
    جراثیم کش صفائی کرنے والا
24. **trash bags**
    کوڑا رکھنے کے تھیلے

Ways to ask for something

Please hand me the squeegee.
Can you get me the broom?
I need the sponge mop.

Pair practice. Make new conversations.

A: *Please hand me the sponge mop.*
B: *Here you go. Do you need the bucket?*
A: *Yes, please. Can you get me the rubber gloves, too?*

1. The water heater is **not working**.
   واٹر ہیٹر کام نہیں کر رہا ہے۔

2. The power is **out**.
   بجلی نہیں ہے۔

3. The roof is **leaking**.
   چھت رس رہی ہے۔

4. The tile is **cracked**.
   ٹائل چٹخی ہوئی ہے۔

5. The window is **broken**.
   کھڑکی ٹوٹی ہوئی ہے۔

6. The lock is **broken**.
   تالا ٹوٹا ہوا ہے۔

7. The steps are **broken**.
   قدمچے ٹوٹے ہوئے ہیں۔

8. roofer
   چھت مرمت کرنے والا

9. electrician
   بجلی مستری

10. repair person
    مرمت کرنے والا شخص

11. locksmith
    تالا بنانے والا شخص

12. carpenter
    بڑھئی

13. fuse box
    فیوز باکس

14. gas meter
    گیس میٹر

More vocabulary

fix: to repair something that is broken
pests: termites, fleas, rats, etc.
exterminate: to kill household pests

Pair practice. Make new conversations.

A: *The faucet is <u>leaking</u>.*
B: *Let's call <u>the plumber</u>. He can fix it.*

15. The furnace is **broken**.
بھٹی ٹوٹی ہوئی ہے۔

16. The pipes are **frozen**.
پائپ جم گئے ہیں۔

17. The faucet is **dripping**.
نل ٹپک رہا ہے۔

18. The sink is **overflowing**.
سنک سے پانی نکل رہا ہے۔

19. The toilet is **stopped up**.
بیت الخلاء اٹ گیا ہے۔

20. plumber
نل کار

21. exterminator
دافع دیمک وغیرہ

22. termites
دیمک

23. ants
چونٹیاں

24. bedbugs
کھنمل

25. fleas
پسّو

26. cockroaches / roaches
کاکروچ / روچ

27. rats
چوہے

28. mice*
چھچھوندر یا جنگلی چوہے

*Note: one mouse, two mice

Ways to ask about repairs

How much will this repair cost?
When can you begin?
How long will the repair take?

Role play. Talk to a repair person.

A: *Can you fix <u>the roof</u>?*
B: *Yes, but it will take <u>two weeks</u>.*
A: *How much will the repair cost?*

THE NEXT DAY…

LATER THAT EVENING…
- Use rec room for large parties
- No loud music on weeknights

1. roommates	3. music	5. noise	7. rules	9. invitation
کمرے کے ساتھی	موسیقی	شور و غل	ضابطے	دعوت نامہ
2. party	4. DJ	6. irritated	8. mess	A. **dance**
پارٹی	ڈی جے	جھنجلایا ہوا	کمرے میں بکھرا ہوا سامان	رقص کیجیے

THE NEXT SATURDAY...

Look at the pictures.
What do you see?

Answer the questions.

1. What happened in apartment 2B? How many people were there?

2. How did the neighbor feel? Why?

3. What rules did they write at the tenant meeting?

4. What did the roommates do after the tenant meeting?

📖 **Read the story.**

The Tenant Meeting

Sally Lopez and Tina Green are <u>roommates</u>. They live in apartment 2B. One night they had a big <u>party</u> with <u>music</u> and a <u>DJ</u>. There was a <u>mess</u> in the hallway. Their neighbors were very unhappy. Mr. Clark in 2A was very <u>irritated</u>. He hates <u>noise</u>!

The next day there was a tenant meeting. Everyone wanted <u>rules</u> about parties and loud music. The girls were very embarrassed.

After the meeting, the girls cleaned the mess in the hallway. Then they gave each neighbor an <u>invitation</u> to a new party. Everyone had a good time at the rec room party. Now the tenants have two new rules and a new place to <u>dance</u>.

Think about it.

1. What are the most important rules in an apartment building? Why?

2. Imagine you are the neighbor in 2A. What do you say to Tina and Sally?

1. fish
   مچھلی
2. meat
   گوشت
3. chicken
   مرغ
4. cheese
   پنیر
5. milk
   دودھ
6. butter
   مکھن
7. eggs
   انڈے
8. vegetables
   سبزیاں

Listen and point. Take turns.

A: *Point to the <u>vegetables</u>.*
B: *Point to the <u>bread</u>.*
A: *Point to the <u>fruit</u>.*

Pair Dictation

A: *Write <u>vegetables</u>.*
B: *Please spell <u>vegetables</u> for me.*
A: *V-e-g-e-t-a-b-l-e-s.*

9. fruit
پھل

10. rice
چاول

11. bread
روٹی

12. pasta
پاستا

13. grocery bag
کریانہ سامان کا تھیلا

14. shopping list
خریدے جانے والے سامان
کی فہرست

15. coupons
خریداری کی پرچیاں

✓ milk
✓ bread
✓ lettuce
✓ grapes

NO EXPIRATION DATE
Save $1.00
on 2 cans of Soup

NO EXPIRATION DATE
50¢ off
any Cereal

Granola
Cereal

Ways to talk about food.

Do we need <u>eggs</u>?
Do we have any <u>pasta</u>?
We have some <u>vegetables</u>, but we need <u>fruit</u>.

Role play. Talk about your shopping list.

A: *Do we need eggs?*
B: *No, we have some.*
A: *Do we have any...*

67

1. apples
سیب

2. bananas
کیلے

3. grapes
انگور

4. pears
ناشپاتی

5. oranges
سنترے

6. grapefruit
چکوترا

7. lemons
لیمو

8. limes
لائم

9. tangerines
نارنگی کی ایک قسم

10. peaches
آڑو

11. cherries
چیری

12. apricots
خوبانی

13. plums
آلو بخارے

14. strawberries
اسٹرابیریاں

15. raspberries
رس بھریاں

16. blueberries
نیلی بیریاں

17. blackberries
کالی بیریاں

18. watermelons
تربوز

19. melons
خربوزہ

20. papayas
پپیتا

21. mangoes
آم

22. kiwi
کیوی پھل

23. pineapples
انناس

24. coconuts
ناریل

25. raisins
کشمش

26. prunes
سکھایا ہوا آلو بخارہ

27. figs
انجیر

28. dates
کھجور

29. a bunch of bananas
کیلوں کا گچھا

30. **ripe** banana
پکے کیلے

31. **unripe** banana
کچے کیلے

32. **rotten** banana
سڑے کیلے

Pair practice. Make new conversations.

A: *What's your favorite fruit?*
B: *I like <u>apples</u>. Do you?*
A: *I prefer <u>bananas</u>.*

Ask your classmates. Share the answers.

1. Which fruit do you put in a fruit salad?
2. What kinds of fruit are common in your native country?
3. What kinds of fruit are in your kitchen right now?

1. lettuce
   کاہو کا سلاد

2. cabbage
   گوبھی

3. carrots
   گاجر

4. radishes
   مولی

5. beets
   چقندر

6. tomatoes
   ٹماٹر

7. bell peppers
   گول مرچ / گھنئی نما مرچ

8. string beans
   باقلا

9. celery
   کرفس، سلاد کے طور پر مستعمل

10. cucumbers
    کھیرا

11. spinach
    پالک

12. corn
    مکئی

13. broccoli
    پھول گوبھی کی ایک قسم

14. cauliflower
    پھول گوبھی

15. bok choy
    چینی گوبھی

16. turnips
    شلجم

17. potatoes
    آلو

18. sweet potatoes
    شکرقند

19. onions
    پیاز

20. green onions / scallions
    ہری پیاز / آل

21. peas
    مٹر

22. artichokes
    باٹھی چوک / سیب زمینی

23. eggplants
    بینگن

24. squash
    کدو کی ایک قسم

25. zucchini
    گھیاتوری

26. asparagus
    ہالون کا خوردنی ڈنٹھل

27. mushrooms
    سماروغ

28. parsley
    پودینہ، اجوائن خراسانی

29. chili peppers
    سرخ مرچ

30. garlic
    لہسن

31. a **bag of** lettuce
    سلاد کے پتوں کا تھیلا

32. a **head of** lettuce
    سلاد کے پتوں والا موٹا حصہ

Pair practice. Make new conversations.

A: *Do you eat* broccoli?
B: *Yes. I like most vegetables, but not* peppers.
A: *Really? Well, I don't like* cauliflower.

Ask your classmates. Share the answers.

1. Which vegetables do you eat raw? cooked?
2. Which vegetables do you put in a green salad?
3. Which vegetables are in your refrigerator right now?

69

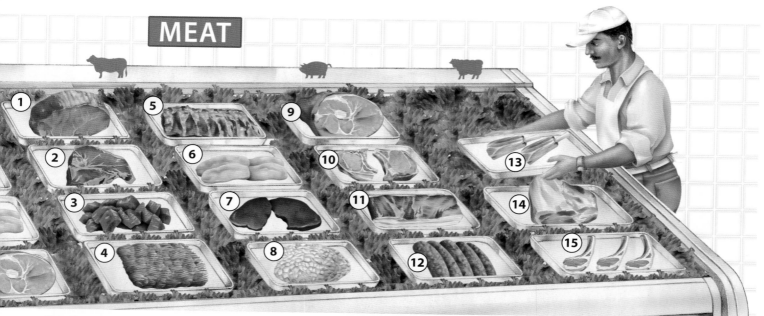

MEAT

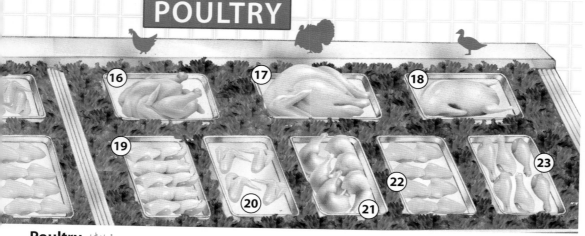

Beef گائے کا گوشت

1. roast
   بھنا ہوا
2. steak
   پسندے
3. stewing beef
   اسٹیو بنانے والا گائے کا گوشت
4. ground beef
   قیمہ

5. beef ribs
   گائے کی چاپ
6. veal cutlets
   بچھڑے کے گوشت کے پارچے
7. liver
   کلیجی
8. tripe
   جگالی کرنے والے جانور کا قابل
   خوردنی معدہ

Pork سور کا گوشت

9. ham
   ران کا گوشت
10. pork chops
    سور چاپ
11. bacon
    پشت یا پہلوؤں کا بنا ہوا گوشت
12. sausage
    آنت کے اندر قیمہ بھرا مسالے دار کیسہ

Lamb بھیڑ

13. lamb shanks
    بھیڑ کی ٹانگ کا نچلا حصہ
14. leg of lamb
    بھیڑ کی ٹانگ
15. lamb chops
    بھیڑ کی چاپ

POULTRY

Poultry مرغ انڈا

16. chicken
    چوزہ
17. turkey
    فیل مرغ

18. duck
    بطخ
19. breasts
    سینہ

20. wings
    بازو
21. legs
    ٹانگیں

22. thighs
    رانیں
23. drumsticks
    مرغ کی ٹانگیں

24. **raw** chicken
    کچا مرغ
25. **cooked** chicken
    پکا ہوا مرغ

More vocabulary

vegetarian: a person who doesn't eat meat
boneless: meat and poultry without bones
skinless: poultry without skin

Ask your classmates. Share the answers.

1. What kind of meat do you eat most often?
2. What kind of meat do you use in soups?
3. What part of the chicken do you like the most?

SEATFOOD

Fish مچھلی

1. trout
   ٹراوَٹ
2. catfish
   کیٹ فش
3. whole salmon
   سالم سالمن
4. salmon steak
   سالمن کے کباب
5. swordfish
   کنار مچھلی

6. halibut steak
   بیلی بٹ کے کباب
7. tuna
   ٹونا
8. cod
   کاڈ

Shellfish خول دار مچھلی

9. crab
   کیکڑا
10. lobster
    کیکٹ
11. shrimp
    جھینگا
12. scallops
    گھونگھا
13. mussels
    دوصمامی گھونگھا

14. oysters
    دو صمامی صدفہ
15. clams
    دومنہا صدفہ
16. **fresh** fish
    تازہ مچھلی
17. **frozen** fish
    برف میں جمی ہوئی مچھلی

DELI

18. white bread
    سفید روٹی
19. wheat bread
    گیہوں کی روٹی
20. rye bread
    رائی کی روٹی

21. roast beef
    بھنا ہوا گائے کا گوشت
22. corned beef
    نمکین بڑا گوشت
23. pastrami
    کوئلوں پر بھنا ہوا مسالے دار گوشت

24. salami
    مسالے دار قیمہ بھرا سموسہ
25. smoked turkey
    دھوئیں میں بھونا ہوا فیل مرغ
26. American cheese
    امریکی پنیر

27. Swiss cheese
    سوئنٹزرلینڈ کا پنیر
28. cheddar cheese
    چیڈر کا ٹھوس پنیر
29. mozzarella cheese
    اطالوی پنیر

Ways to order at the counter

I'd like some <u>roast beef</u>.
I'll have <u>a halibut steak</u> and some <u>shrimp</u>.
Could I get some <u>Swiss cheese</u>?

Pair practice. Make new conversations.

A: *What can I get for you?*
B: *<u>I'd like some roast beef</u>. How about a pound?*
A: *A pound of <u>roast beef</u> coming up!*

71

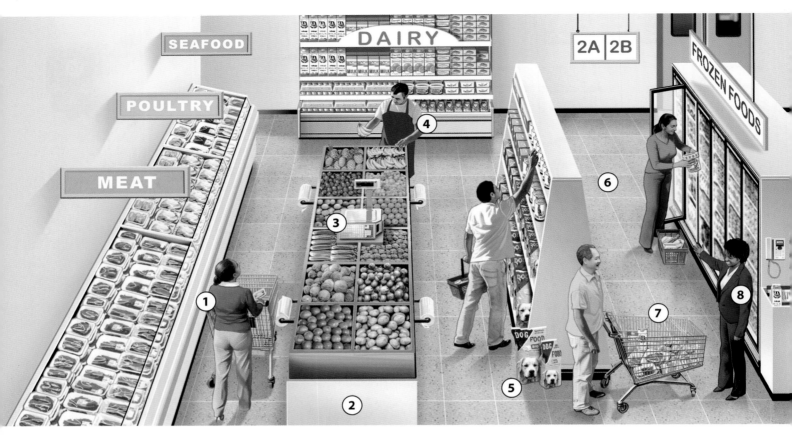

SEAFOOD

POULTRY

MEAT

DAIRY

2A | 2B

FROZEN FOODS

1. customer	**3.** scale	**5.** pet food	**7.** cart
گاہک	ترازو	پالتو جانوروں کا کھانا	پہیہ گاڑی
2. produce section	**4.** grocery clerk	**6.** aisle	**8.** manager
غذائی اجناس کا حصہ	کریانہ کلرک	راہداری	منتظم

Canned Foods
ڈبہ بند غذائیں

17. beans
پھلیاں

18. soup
شوربہ

19. tuna
ٹونا

Dairy
دودھ سے بنی غذائیں

20. margarine
نباتی تیلوں اور چربی کا مصنوعی مکھن

21. sour cream
کھٹی کریم

22. yogurt
دہی

Grocery Products
کریانہ کے سامان

23. aluminum foil
المونیم کی پنّی

24. plastic wrap
پلاسٹک سے بنا لپیٹنے والا لفافہ

25. plastic storage bags
پلاسٹک کا سامان رکھنے کا تھیلا

Frozen Foods
جمی ہوئی غذائیں

26. ice cream
آئس کریم

27. frozen vegetables
جمی ہوئی سبزیاں

28. frozen dinner
جما ہوا رات کا کھانا

Ways to ask for information in a grocery store

Excuse me, where are <u>the carrots</u>?
Can you please tell me where to find <u>the dog food</u>?
Do you have any <u>lamb chops</u> today?

Pair practice. Make conversations.

A: <u>*Can you please tell me where to find the dog food*</u>?
B: *Sure. It's in <u>aisle 1B</u>. Do you need anything else*?
A: *Yes, where are <u>the carrots</u>?*

BAKERY

Best Baked Goods

15 items or less

Cash for Bottles | Cash for Bottle

3A | 3B

SNACKS

9. **shopping basket**
خریداری کی ٹوکری

10. **self-checkout**
خود سامان کی جانچ کرنا

11. **line**
قطار

12. **checkstand**
حساب کرنے کا کاؤنٹر

13. **cashier**
خزانچی

14. **bagger**
تھیلے میں سامان رکھنے والا شخص

15. **cash register**
پیسے کا حساب لگانے کی مشین

16. **bottle return**
بوتل کی واپسی

WHOLE WHEAT — J&G — Franco's — Tasty Cola — Italian Roast — Baked not Fried! — YUM! CHOCOLATE

Baking Products
بیکری مصنوعات

29. **flour**
آٹا

30. **sugar**
چینی

31. **oil**
تیل

Beverages
مشروبات

32. **apple juice**
سیب کا رس

33. **coffee**
کافی

34. **soda / pop**
سوڈا / میٹھا مشروب

Snack Foods
ہلکے ناشتے کی غذائیں

35. **potato chips**
آلو کے قتلے

36. **nuts**
میوہ

37. **candy bar**
لمبی چاکلیٹ

Baked Goods
بیکری میں بنی اشیاء

38. **cookies**
بسکٹ

39. **cake**
کیک

40. **bagels**
گول چھلے دار روٹی

Ask your classmates. Share the answers.
1. What is your favorite grocery store?
2. Do you prefer to shop alone or with friends?
3. Which foods from your country are hard to find?

Think about it. Discuss.
1. Is it better to shop every day or once a week? Why?
2. Why do grocery stores put snacks near the checkstands?
3. What's good and what's bad about small grocery stores?

1. bottles
بوتلیں

2. jars
شیشیاں

3. cans
ٹن کے ڈبے

4. cartons
گتے کے ڈبے

5. containers
ڈبّے

6. boxes
صندوق

7. bags
تھیلے

8. packages
بند اشیا

9. six-packs
چھ عدد کے پیک

10. loaves
شکر کی ٹکیاں

11. rolls
لپٹی ہوئی اشیاء

12. tubes
ٹیوب

13. a bottle of water
پانی کی بوتل

14. a jar of jam
جام کی شیشی

15. a can of beans
پھلیوں کا ٹن کا ڈبہ

16. a carton of eggs
انڈوں کا کارٹن

17. a container of cottage cheese
دیسی پنیر کا ڈبہ

18. a box of cereal
اناج سے بنا ناشتے کا ڈبہ

19. a bag of flour
آٹے کا تھیلا

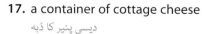
20. a package of cookies
بسکنوں کا پیکٹ

21. a six-pack of soda (pop)
چھ عدد سوڈا (میٹھا مشروب)

22. a loaf of bread
ڈبل روٹی کا ٹکڑا

23. a roll of paper towels
کاغذ کے رومالوں کا رول

24. a tube of toothpaste
ٹوتھ پیسٹ کا ٹیوب

Grammar Point: count and non-count

Some foods can be counted: *an apple, two apples.*
Some foods can't be counted: *some rice, some water.*
For non-count foods, count containers: *two bags of rice.*

Pair practice. Make conversations.

A: *How many* <u>boxes of cereal</u> *do we need?*
B: *We need* <u>two boxes</u>.

Weights and Measurements

A. Measure the ingredients.
اشیاء کو ناپیے۔

B. Weigh the food.
غذا کو تولیے۔

1 cup = 237 milliliters

C. Convert the measurements.
پیمائشوں کو تبدیل کیجیے۔

Liquid Measures رقیق پیمائشیں

1	2	3	4	5
1 fl. oz.	1 c.	1 pt.	1 qt.	1 gal.

Dry Measures خشک چیزوں کی پیمائشیں

6	7	8	9	10
1 tsp.	1 TBS.	1/4 c.	1/2 c.	1 c.

Weight وزن

11	12

1. a fluid ounce of milk
   ایک رقیق آونس دودھ
2. a cup of oil
   ایک پیالی تیل
3. a pint of frozen yogurt
   ایک پائنٹ جما ہوا دبی
4. a quart of milk
   ایک کوارٹ دودھ

5. a gallon of water
   ایک گیلن پانی
6. a teaspoon of salt
   ایک چائے کا چمچ بھر نمک
7. a tablespoon of sugar
   ایک چائے کا چمچ بھر چینی
8. a quarter cup of brown sugar
   ایک چوتھائی پیالی کھانڈ

9. a half cup of raisins
   آدھا پیالی کشمش
10. a cup of flour
    ایک پیالی آٹا
11. an ounce of cheese
    ایک آونس پنیر
12. a pound of roast beef
    ایک پاؤنڈ بھنا ہوا گائے کا گوشت

Equivalencies	
3 tsp. = 1 TBS.	2 c. = 1 pt.
2 TBS. = 1 fl. oz.	2 pt. = 1 qt.
8 fl. oz. = 1 c.	4 qt. = 1 gal.

Volume
1 fl. oz. = 30 ml
1 c. = 237 ml
1 pt. = .47 L
1 qt. = .95 L
1 gal. = 3.79 L

Weight
1 oz. = 28.35 grams (g)
1 lb. = 453.6 g
2.205 lbs. = 1 kilogram (kg)
1 lb. = 16 oz.

Food Safety   غذا کی حفاظت

A. **clean**
صاف کیجیے

B. **separate**
الگ کیجیے

C. **cook**
کھانا پکائیے

D. **chill**
ٹھنڈا کیجیے

A Clean counters!
20 SECONDS Wash your hands!

B Use separate cutting boards for vegetables and meat!

C Cook to the right temperature!

D Refrigerate leftovers quickly!

Ways to Serve Meat and Poultry   گوشت اور مرغ انڈا وغیرہ پیش کرنے کے طریقے

1. fried chicken
تلا ہوا مرغ

2. barbecued / grilled ribs
سینکی ہوئی / بھنی ہوئی چاپ

3. broiled steak
چولھے پر بھونا ہوا گوشت

4. roasted turkey
بھنا ہوا فیل مرغ

5. boiled ham
ابلی ہوئی سور کی ران کا گوشت

6. stir-fried beef
تلا ہوا گائے کا گوشت

Ways to Serve Eggs   انڈا پیش کرنے کے طریقے

7. scrambled eggs
پھینٹ کرتلے ہوئے انڈے

8. hardboiled eggs
پوری طرح ابلے ہوئے انڈے

9. poached eggs
ابلتے پانی میں پکائے گئے چھلے انڈے

10. eggs sunny-side up
ایک طرف سے تلے ہوئے انڈے

11. eggs over easy
دونوں طرف سے تلے ہوئے انڈے

12. omelet
آملیٹ

Role play. Make new conversations.

A: *How do you like your eggs?*
B: *I like them* <u>scrambled</u>. *And you?*
A: *I like them* <u>hardboiled</u>.

Ask your classmates. Share the answers.

1. Do you use separate cutting boards?
2. What is your favorite way to serve meat? poultry?
3. What are healthy ways of preparing meat? poultry?

Cheesy Tofu Vegetable Casserole پنیر دار ٹوفو (سویابین سے تیار کی گئی پینٹھی) سبزی کیسیرول

A. Preheat the oven.

تنور کو پہلے سے گرم کیجیے۔

B. Grease a baking pan.

سینکنے والے برتن میں ہلکا تیل لگائیے۔

C. Slice the tofu.

ٹوفو کے ٹکڑے کائیے۔

D. Steam the broccoli.

پھول گوبھی کو بھاپ دیجیے۔

E. Saute the mushrooms.

سماروغ روغن میں بھونیے۔

F. Spoon sauce on top.

اوپر چمچ سے چٹنی لگائیے۔

G. Grate the cheese.

پنیر کو کسیے۔

H. Bake.

سینکیے۔

Easy Chicken Soup آسان مرغ یخنی

I. Cut up the chicken.

مرغ کے ٹکڑے کیجیے۔

J. Dice the celery.

سلاد کے چوکور ٹکڑے کائیے۔

K. Peel the carrots.

گاجر چھیلیے۔

L. Chop the onions.

پیاز کے قتلے کیجیے۔

M. Boil the chicken.

مرغ کو ابالیے۔

N. Add the vegetables.

سبزیاں شامل کیجیے۔

O. Stir.

چلائیے۔

P. Simmer.

بلکی آنچ پر پکائیے۔

Quick and Easy Cake فوری اور آسان کیک

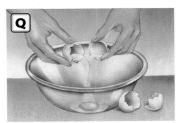

Q. Break 2 eggs into a microwave-safe bowl.

برقی تنور کے لیے محفوظ پیالے میں 2 انڈے توڑیے۔

R. Mix the ingredients.

اجزاء کو ملائیے۔

S. Beat the mixture.

اجزاء کے ملمے کو پھینٹیے۔

T. Microwave for 5 minutes.

۵ منٹ تک برقی تنور میں پکائیے۔

1. **can opener**
   ڈبہ کھولنے کا آلہ

2. **grater**
   ٹکڑے کرنے کا آلہ

3. **steamer**
   بھاپ سے پکانے والا برتن

4. **plastic storage container**
   ذخیرہ جمع کرنے کا پلاسٹک کا ڈبہ

5. **frying pan**
   تلنے کی کڑاہی

6. **pot**
   پتیلی

7. **ladle**
   کفگیر جیسا لمبا چمچہ

8. **double boiler**
   دو خانوں کا ابالنے والا ظرف

9. **wooden spoon**
   لکڑی کا چمچ

10. **casserole dish**
    ڈھکنے دار پکانے والی طشتری

11. **garlic press**
    لہسن پیسنے کا آلہ

12. **carving knife**
    کھرچنے کا چاقو

13. **roasting pan**
    بھوننے کا ظرف

14. **roasting rack**
    بھوننے کا سلاخوں دار خانہ

15. **vegetable peeler**
    سبزی چھیلنے کا آلہ

16. **paring knife**
    تراشنے /چھیلنے والا چاقو

17. **colander**
    سوراخ دار برتن

18. **kitchen timer**
    باورچی خانہ میں وقت شمار گھڑی

19. **spatula**
    کفچہ

20. **eggbeater**
    انڈا پھینٹنے کا آلہ

21. **whisk**
    پھینٹنے والا آلہ

22. **strainer**
    چھلنی

23. **tongs**
    چمٹی

24. **lid**
    ڈھکن

25. **saucepan**
    کھانا پکانے کا دستے دار برتن

26. **cake pan**
    کیک بنانے کا برتن

27. **cookie sheet**
    کوکی بنانے کی شیٹ

28. **pie pan**
    پیسٹری کی تہوں میں پھرنے والی
    ڈش تیار کرنے کا برتن

29. **pot holders**
    برتن رکھنے کی جگہ

30. **rolling pin**
    بیلن

31. **mixing bowl**
    ملانے والی قاب

Pair practice. Make new conversations.

A: *Please hand me <u>the whisk</u>.*
B: *Here's <u>the whisk</u>. Do you need anything else?*
A: *Yes, pass me <u>the casserole dish</u>.*

Use the new words.
Look at page 77. Name the kitchen utensils you see.

A: *Here's <u>a grater</u>.*
B: *This is <u>a mixing bowl</u>.*

1. **hamburger**
   نان کی تہہ میں لپٹا قیمہ کا تلا ہوا کباب

2. **french fries**
   تلے ہوئے آلو کے قتلے

3. **cheeseburger**
   نان کی تہہ میں لپٹا پنیر کا تلا ہوا کباب

4. **onion rings**
   پیاز چھلے

5. **chicken sandwich**
   مرغ سینڈوچ

6. **hot dog**
   ہاٹ ڈاگ (قیمے بھرے گول کلچے)

7. **nachos**
   مسالے اور پنیر کا مکئی کا کیک

8. **taco**
   ٹاکو (مکئی کی روٹی میں لپٹا ہوا قیمہ)

9. **burrito**
   لپٹی ہوئی شکم پور روٹی

10. **pizza**
    سبزیاں یا گوشت رکھ کر پکائی گئی موٹی روٹی

11. **soda**
    سوڈا

12. **iced tea**
    ٹھنڈی برف والی چائے

13. **ice-cream cone**
    آئس کریم کون

14. **milkshake**
    دودھ کا شربت یا لسّی

15. **donut**
    میٹھے آٹے کا پیڑا

16. **muffin**
    خمیری آٹے میں مکھن ملا کر تیار کیا گیا کیک

17. **counterperson**
    کاؤنٹر پر کھڑا شخص

18. **straw**
    پتلی نلکی

19. **plastic utensils**
    پلاسٹک کے برتن

20. **sugar substitute**
    چینی کے متبادلات

21. **ketchup**
    ٹماٹر سرکہ وغیرہ کی چٹنی

22. **mustard**
    رائی سے بنی چٹپٹی چٹنی

23. **mayonnaise**
    انڈے کی زردی، تیل اور سرکے سے تیار چٹنی

24. **salad bar**
    سلاد رکھنے کا بڑا ڈبہ

Grammar Point: yes/no questions (do)

Do you like hamburgers? Yes, I do.
Do you like nachos? No, I don't.

Think about it. Discuss.

1. Do you think that fast food is bad for people? Why or why not?
2. What fast foods do you have in your country?
3. Do you have a favorite fast food restaurant? Which one?

79

کافی شاپ کا مینیو

1. **bacon**
   سور کی پشت یا پٹھوں کا گوشت

2. **sausage**
   آنت کے اندر مسالے دار قیمہ بھر کر بنایا گیا کیسہ

3. **hash browns**
   چھلے آلو کی چاول وغیرہ کے ساتھ بنائی گئی غذا

4. **toast**
   سکا ہوا نان پاؤ

5. **English muffin**
   ہلکا بھورا گول کیک

6. **biscuits**
   بسکٹ

7. **pancakes**
   مخلوط اجزاء سے تیار کیک

8. **waffles**
   انڈے، آٹے، دودھ کا بنا کیک

9. **hot cereal**
   گرم دلیا

10. **grilled cheese sandwich**
    سکا ہوا پنیر سینڈوچ

11. **pickle**
    اچار

12. **club sandwich**
    تین تہوں والا سینڈوچ

13. **spinach salad**
    پالک سلاد

14. **chef's salad**
    پھلوں اور سبزیوں کا سلاد

15. **dinner salad**
    عشائیہ سلاد

16. **soup**
    یخنی

17. **rolls**
    ڈبل روٹی

18. **coleslaw**
    مسالے دار سلاد

19. **potato salad**
    آلو کی سلاد

20. **pasta salad**
    پاستا کی سلاد

21. **fruit salad**
    پھلوں کی سلاد

BREAKFAST SPECIAL
Served 6 a.m. to 11 a.m.

Two egg omelet with one side

LUNCH
Served 11 a.m. to 2 p.m.
All sandwiches come with soup or salad

SIDE SALADS

SALAD DRESSINGS

Thousand Island   Ranch

Italian   Blue Cheese

Ways to order from a menu

I'd like <u>a grilled cheese sandwich</u>.
I'll have <u>a bowl of tomato soup</u>.
Could I get <u>the chef's salad</u> with <u>ranch dressing</u>?

Pair practice. Make conversations.

A: <u>I'd like a grilled cheese sandwich, please</u>.
B: *Anything else for you?*
A: *Yes, I'll have <u>a bowl of tomato soup</u> with that.*

DINNER

DESSERTS

BEVERAGES

22. roast chicken
تندوری مرغ
23. mashed potatoes
آلو کا بھرتا
24. steak
پسندا
25. baked potato
بھنا ہوا آلو
26. spaghetti
لچھا سوئیاں
27. meatballs
کوفتے
28. garlic bread
لہسن ملی روٹی
29. grilled fish
سینکی ہوئی مچھلی
30. rice
چاول
31. meatloaf
پارچوں کی صورت میں بھنا قیمہ
32. steamed vegetables
بھاپ میں ابلی سبزیاں
33. layer cake
تہہ دار کیک
34. cheesecake
پنیر کیک
35. pie
پیسٹری کے لیے تیار کی گئی ڈش
36. mixed berries
مختلف اقسام کی بیریاں

37. coffee
کافی
38. decaf coffee
کیفین سے خالی کافی
39. tea
چائے
40. herbal tea
سبز چائے
41. cream
کریم
42. low-fat milk
کم چکنائی کا دودھ

Ask your classmates. Share the answers.

1. Do you prefer vegetable soup or chicken soup?
2. Do you prefer tea or coffee?
3. Which desserts on the menu do you like?

Role play. Order a dinner from the menu.

A: *Are you ready to order?*
B: *I think so. I'll have the roast chicken.*
A: *Would you also like…?*

81

1. **dining room**
   طعام گاہ

2. **hostess**
   خاتون میزبان

3. **high chair**
   بچے کی اونچی کرسی

4. **booth**
   علاحدہ گوشہ

5. **to-go box**
   سامان پیک کیے جانے والا بکس

6. **patron / diner**
   سرپرست / ریستوراں میں کھانے والا

7. **menu**
   فہرست

8. **server / waiter**
   خدمت کار / منتظر بیرا

A. **set** the table
میز آراستہ کیجیے

B. **seat** the customer
گاہک کو بٹھائیے

C. **pour** the water
پانی انڈیلیے

D. **order** from the menu
مینیو سے آرڈر دیجیے

E. **take** the order
آرڈر لیجیے

F. **serve** the meal
کھانا پیش کیجیے

G. **clear** / **bus** the dishes
پلیٹیں ہٹائیے / اٹھائیے

H. **carry** the tray
ٹرے لے جائیے

I. **pay** the check
بل ادا کیجیے

J. **leave** a tip
بخشش چھوڑ جائیے

More vocabulary

eat out: to go to a restaurant to eat
take out: to buy food at a restaurant and take it home to eat

Look at the pictures.
Describe what is happening.

A: *She's seating the customer.*
B: *He's taking the order.*

9. server / waitress
پیش کرنے والی خدمت کار خاتون

10. dessert tray
کھانے کے بعد پیش کی جانے والی
ڈش کی سینی

11. bread basket
روٹی کی ٹوکری

12. busser
مددگار بیرا

13. dish room
برتنوں کا کمرہ

14. dishwasher
برتن دھونے کی مشین

15. kitchen
باورچی خانہ

16. chef
باورچی

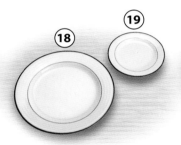

17. place setting
سامان درست جگہ رکھنا

18. dinner plate
کھانے کی بڑی قاب

19. bread-and-butter plate
روٹی اور مکھن کی قاب

20. salad plate
سلاد کی قاب

21. soup bowl
شوربے کا پیالہ

22. water glass
پانی کا گلاس

23. wine glass
شراب کا گلاس

24. cup
پیالی

25. saucer
پرچ

26. napkin
رومال

27. salad fork
سلاد کا کانٹا

28. dinner fork
عشائیہ کا کانٹا

29. steak knife
پسندے کی چھری

30. knife
چھری

31. teaspoon
چائے کا چمچ

32. soupspoon
شوربے کا چمچ

Pair practice. Make new conversations.

A: *Excuse me, this _spoon_ is dirty.*
B: *I'm so sorry. I'll get you a clean _spoon_ right away.*
A: *Thanks.*

Role play. Talk to a new busser.

A: *Do the _salad forks_ go on _the left_?*
B: *Yes. They go _next to the dinner forks_.*
A: *What about the…?*

83

1. live music
موسیقی

2. organic
نامیاتی

3. lemonade
لیموں کا شربت

4. sour
کھٹا

5. samples
نمونے

6. avocados
ناشپاتی سے مشابہ ایک وسط امریکی پھل

7. vendors
سامان بیچنے والے

8. sweets
مٹھائیاں

9. herbs
پھول پودے

A. count
گنتی کیجیے

CHIVES

DILL

PARSLEY

**Look at the pictures.
What do you see?**

Answer the questions.

1. How many vendors are at the market today?

2. Which vegetables are organic?

3. What are the children eating?

4. What is the woman counting? Why?

 Read the story.

The Farmers' Market

On Saturdays, the Novaks go to the farmers' market. They like to visit the <u>vendors</u>. Alex Novak always goes to the hot food stand for lunch. His children love to eat the fruit <u>samples</u>. Alex's father usually buys some <u>sweets</u> and <u>lemonade</u>. The lemonade is very <u>sour</u>.

Nina Novak likes to buy <u>organic</u> <u>herbs</u> and vegetables. Today, she is buying <u>avocados</u>. The market worker <u>counts</u> eight avocados. She gives Nina one more for free.

There are other things to do at the market. The Novaks like to listen to the <u>live music</u>. Sometimes they meet friends there. The farmers' market is a great place for families on a Saturday afternoon.

Think about it.

1. What's good or bad about shopping at a farmers' market?

2. Imagine you are at the farmers' market. What will you buy?

85

Everyday Clothes روزمرہ کے کپڑے

1. shirt
قمیض
2. jeans
جینس
3. dress
لباس
4. T-shirt
آدھی آستین کی قمیض
5. baseball cap
بیس بال ٹوپی
6. socks
موزے
7. athletic shoes
ورزش کے جوتے
A. **tie**
باندھیے

Listen and point. Take turns.

A: *Point to the dress.*
B: *Point to the T-shirt.*
A: *Point to the baseball cap.*

Dictate to your partner. Take turns.

A: *Write dress.*
B: *Is that spelled d-r-e-s-s?*
A: *Yes. That's right.*

ONE NIGHT ONLY

DOORS OPEN AT 8:00

8. blouse
زنانہ بالا پوش
9. handbag
دستی تھیلا
10. skirt
زنانہ کمر سے بندھنے والا لباس
11. suit
یک رنگی مردانہ / زنانہ لباس
12. slacks / pants
ڈھیلی ڈھالی / پتلون
13. shoes
جوتے
14. sweater
سوئیٹر
B. put on
پہنیے

Ways to compliment clothes

That's a pretty dress!
Those are great shoes!
I really like your baseball cap!

Role play. Compliment a friend.

A: *That's a pretty dress! Green is a great color on you.*
B: *Thanks! I really like your…*

Casual Clothes غیر رسمی کپڑے

1. cap
   ٹوپی

2. cardigan sweater
   لمبی آستینوں کا سامنے بٹن لگا سوئیٹر

3. pullover sweater
   سر سے پہنا جانے والا سوئیٹر

4. sports shirt
   کھیلنے کی قمیض

5. maternity dress
   زچگی کا لباس

6. overalls
   لبادے

7. knit top
   جالی دار قمیض

8. capris
   زنانہ چست گاؤدم پتلون

9. sandals
   سینڈل

Work Clothes کام کے کپڑے

10. uniform
    کام کے وقت کا مخصوص لباس

11. business suit
    رسمی لباس

12. tie
    ٹائی

13. briefcase
    چھوٹا بیگ

More vocabulary

three piece suit: matching jacket, vest, and slacks

outfit: clothes that look nice together

in fashion / in style: clothes that are popular now

Describe the people. Take turns.

A: *She's wearing a maternity dress.*

B: *He's wearing a uniform.*

Formal Clothes رسمی کپڑے

14. sports jacket / sports coat
کھلاڑیوں کی جیکٹ / کھلاڑیوں کا کوٹ

15. vest
صدری

16. bow tie
دبرے حلقے کی ٹائی

17. tuxedo
ضیافت کا لباس

18. evening gown
شام کی رسمی گاؤن

19. clutch bag
ہاتھ میں پکڑا جانے والا پرس

20. cocktail dress
شراب کی محفلوں میں شام کا ہلکا لباس

21. high heels
اونچی ایڑی کے جوتے

Exercise Wear ورزش کا لباس

22. sweatshirt / hoodie
پسینہ جذب کرنے والی / چھتر دار قمیض

23. sweatpants
پسینہ جذب کرنے والی پتلون

24. tank top
بغیر آستین کا بنیان

25. shorts
نیکر

Ask your classmates. Share the answers.

1. What's your favorite outfit?

2. Do you like to wear formal clothes? Why or why not?

3. Do you prefer to exercise in shorts or sweatpants?

Think about it. Discuss.

1. What jobs require formal clothes? Uniforms?

2. What's good and bad about wearing school uniforms?

3. What is your opinion of today's popular clothing?

89

1. hat	**5.** winter scarf
ٹوپ	سردی کا اسکارف
2. (over)coat	**6.** gloves
کپڑوں کے اوپر پہننے کا کوٹ	دستانے
3. headband	**7.** headwrap
سر پر باندھنے والی پٹی	سر پر لپیٹنے والا کپڑا
4. leather jacket	**8.** jacket
چمڑے کی جیکٹ	جیکٹ

9. parka	**13.** earmuffs
کھال کا بنا سر ڈھکنے والا کوٹ	کنٹوپ
10. mittens	**14.** down vest
دوہرا دستانہ، انگلیاں اور انگوٹھا الگ	نیچے تک کی صدری
11. ski hat	**15.** ski mask
اسکی کرنے کے دوران لگایا جانے والا ٹوپ	اسکی کرنے کے دوران لگایا جانے والا نقاب
12. leggings	**16.** down jacket
پنڈلیوں پر چڑھانے والی پوشش	لمبی جیکٹ

17. umbrella	**20.** rain boots
چھاتہ	برساتی بوٹ
18. raincoat	**21.** trench coat
برساتی	برساتی کوٹ
19. poncho	
کمبل نما جنوبی امریکی لباده	

22. swimming trunks	**25.** cover-up
تیراکی کا نیکر	تیراکی لباس کے اوپر پہنا جانے والا پوشش
23. straw hat	**26.** swimsuit / bathing suit
تنکوں کا بنا ٹوپ	تیراکی کا لباس / نہانے کا لباس
24. windbreaker	**27.** sunglasses
ہوا سے محفوظ کرنے والی جیکٹ	دھوپ کا چشمہ

Grammar Point: should

*It's raining. You **should** take an umbrella.*
*It's snowing. You **should** wear a scarf.*
*It's sunny. You **should** wear a straw hat.*

Pair practice. Make new conversations.

A: *It's snowing. You should wear a scarf.*
B: *Don't worry. I'm wearing my parka.*
A: *Good, and don't forget your mittens.*

Unisex Underwear
مرد اور عورت دونوں کے استعمال کا زیر جامہ

1. undershirt
زیریں قمیض

2. thermal undershirt
گرم زیریں قمیض

3. long underwear
لمبا زیر جامہ

Men's Underwear
مردانہ زیر جامہ

4. boxer shorts
مکے بازی کرنے کے دوران پہنا جانے والا نیکر

5. briefs
زیر جامے

6. athletic supporter / jockstrap
ورزشی لنگوٹ / مرد کھلاڑیوں کا حفاظتی بند

Unisex Socks
مرد اور عورت دونوں کے استعمال کے موزے

7. ankle socks
ٹخنوں تک کے موزے

8. crew socks
ٹخنوں کے اوپر تک کے موزے

9. dress socks
پنڈلیوں تک کے موزے

Women's Socks
زنانہ موزے

10. low-cut socks
ٹخنوں کے نیچے تک کے موزے

11. anklets
ٹخنوں تک کے موزے

12. knee highs
گھٹنوں تک کے موزے

Women's Underwear زنانہ زیر جامہ

13. (bikini) panties
(زنانہ جانگیہ) زیر جامہ

14. briefs / underpants
زیریں زیر جامہ / زیریں جانگیہ

15. body shaper / girdle
زنانہ زیر جامہ / کمر پٹکا

16. garter belt
پتلون کو سنبھالنے والی پٹی

17. stockings
زنانہ لمبی جراب

18. panty hose
موزوں کے ساتھ زنانہ چست پتلون

19. tights
چست لباس

20. bra
زنانہ انگیہ کا مخفف

21. camisole
کڑھا ہوا انگیہ

22. full slip
جلدی سے پہننے والا مکمل لباس

23. half slip
جلدی سے پہننے والا نصف لباس

Sleepwear شب خوابی کا لباس

24. pajamas
پاجامہ

25. nightgown
سوتے وقت کی گاؤن

26. slippers
چپل

27. blanket sleeper
سوتے وقت بچوں کا مکمل لباس

28. nightshirt
رات کی قمیض

29. robe
لبادہ

More vocabulary

lingerie: underwear or sleepwear for women
loungewear: very casual clothing for relaxing around the home

Ask your classmates. Share the answers.

1. What kind of socks are you wearing today?
2. What kind of sleepwear do you prefer?
3. Do you wear slippers at home?

91

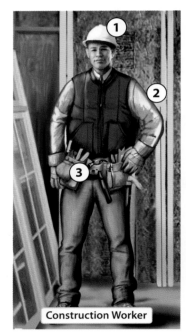

Construction Worker

Road Worker

Automotive Painter

Food Processor

1. hard hat
سخت ٹوپ

2. work shirt
کام کے دوران پہننے کی قمیض

3. tool belt
اوزار بیلٹ

4. Hi-Visibility safety vest
چمک دار حفاظتی پٹی

5. work pants
کام کے دوران پہننے کی پتلون

6. steel toe boots
لوہے کی ٹھوکر والا جوتا

7. ventilation mask
جالی دار خول

8. coveralls
پوری طرح ڈھکنے والا لباس

9. bump cap
حفاظتی ٹوپی

10. safety glasses
حفاظتی چشمے

11. apron
پیش بند

Manager

Salesperson

Farmworker

Ranch Hand

12. blazer
بلیزر

13. tie
ٹائی

14. polo shirt
پولو قمیض

15. name tag
نام کا بلّا

16. bandana
سربندھن

17. work gloves
کام کے دستانے

18. cowboy hat
چرواہے کا ٹوپ

19. jeans
موٹے سوتی کپڑے سے بنی چست پتلون

Pair practice. Make new conversations.

A: *What do <u>construction workers</u> wear to work?*
B: *They wear <u>hard hats</u> and <u>tool belts</u>.*
A: *What do <u>road workers</u> wear to work?*

Use the new words.
Look at pages 166–169. Name the workplace clothing you see.

A: *He's wearing <u>a hard hat</u>.*
B: *She's wearing <u>scrubs</u>.*

Security Guard

Emergency Worker

Counterperson

Chef

Line Cook

20. security shirt
حفاظتی دستہ کی قمیض

21. badge
علامتی بِلا

22. security pants
حفاظتی پتلون

23. helmet
سر کی حفاظتی ٹوپی

24. jumpsuit
پورے جسم کا ایک پارچہ لباس

25. hairnet
بالوں کی جالی

26. smock
ڈھیلا کُرتا

27. disposable gloves
قابل اتلاف دستانے

28. chef's hat
باورچی کی ٹوپی

29. chef's jacket
باورچی کی صدری

30. waist apron
کمر تک کا پیش بند

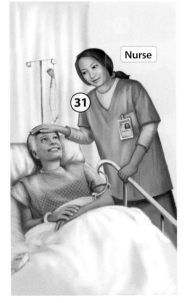

Nurse

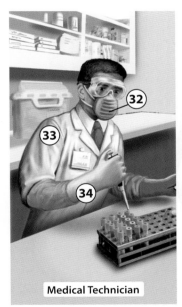

Medical Technician

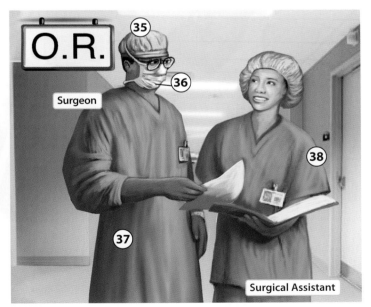

Surgeon

Surgical Assistant

31. scrubs
جراحت سے متعلق ڈاکٹر اور نرس
کے پہننے کا کوٹ

32. face mask
چہرے کا نقاب

33. lab coat
تجربہ گاہ میں پہنا جانے والا کوٹ

34. latex gloves
ربر کے دستانے

35. surgical scrub cap
جراحی کے دوران پہنی جانے والی ٹوپی

36. surgical mask
جراحی کے دوران لگانے والا نقاب

37. surgical gown
جراحی کے دوران پہننے جانے والا گاؤن

38. surgical scrubs
جراحی میں معاون کا کوٹ

Ask your classmates. Share the answers.

1. Which of these outfits would you like to wear?

2. Which of these items are in your closet?

3. Do you wear safety clothing at work? What kinds?

Think about it. Discuss.

1. What other jobs require helmets? disposable gloves?

2. Is it better to have a uniform or wear your own clothes at work? Why?

A. purchase
خریدیے

B. wait in line
قطار میں انتظار کیجیے

1. suspenders
دہرے تسمے

2. purses / handbags
بٹوے / دستی تھیلے

3. salesclerk
فروخت کار کلرک

4. customer
گاہک

5. display case
نمائش دان

6. belts
پیٹیاں

13. wallet
بٹوا

14. change purse / coin purse
ریزگاری / سکے رکھنے کا بٹوا

15. cell phone holder
سیل فون رکھنے کا خول

16. (wrist)watch
(دستی)گھڑی

17. shoulder bag
کندھوں پر لٹکانے والا تھیلا

18. backpack
کمر پر لٹکانے والا تھیلا

19. tote bag
بڑا تھیلا

20. belt buckle
پٹی کا بکسوا

21. sole
تلوا

22. heel
جوتے کی ایڑی

23. toe
جوتے کی اگلی ٹھوکر

24. shoelaces
جوتے کے فیتے

More vocabulary

gift: something you give or receive from friends or family for a special occasion

present: a gift

Grammar Point: object pronouns

My **sister** loves jewelry. I'll buy **her** a necklace.
My **dad** likes belts. I'll buy **him** a belt buckle.
My **friends** love scarves. I'll buy **them** scarves.

7. shoe department	**9.** bracelets	**11.** hats	**C.** **try on** shoes
جوتوں کا شعبہ	کڑے	ٹوپیاں	جوتے آزمائیے
8. jewelry department	**10.** necklaces	**12.** scarves	**D.** **assist** a customer
زیورات کا شعبہ	گلے کے ہار	مفلر	گاہک کی مدد کیجیے

25. high heels	**29.** oxfords	**33.** chain	**37.** clip-on earrings
اونچی ایڑی کے جوتے	آکسفرڈ طرز کے جوتے	زنجیر	کلپ سے لگائے جانے والی بالیاں
26. pumps	**30.** loafers	**34.** beads	**38.** pin
پر تکلف لباس کے ساتھ پہننے والے جوتے	بغیر تسمے کے جوتے	چھید والے دانے	پن
27. flats	**31.** hiking boots	**35.** locket	**39.** string of pearls
ہموار ایڑی کے جوتے	لمبی پیدل دوری طے کرنے کے جوتے	گلے میں لٹکانے کا زیور	موتیوں کی لڑی
28. boots	**32.** tennis shoes	**36.** pierced earrings	**40.** ring
پنڈلی تک کے جوتے	ٹینس کھیلنے کے جوتے	چھید کرکے لگانے والی بالیاں	انگوٹھی

Ways to talk about accessories

I need a hat to wear with this scarf.
I'd like earrings to go with the necklace.
Do you have a belt that would go with my shoes?

Role play. Talk to a salesperson.

A: *Do you have boots that would go with this skirt?*
B: *Let me see. How about these brown ones?*
A: *Perfect. I also need…*

95

Sizes سائز

1. extra small
غیر معمولی چھوٹا سائز

2. small
چھوٹا

3. medium
درمیانہ

4. large
بڑا

5. extra large
غیر معمولی بڑا

6. one-size-fits-all
ایک سائز سب کو فٹ ہونے والا

Styles اوضاع

7. **crewneck** sweater
بغیر کالر کا سوئیٹر

8. **V-neck** sweater
ل-شکل کی گردن والا سوئیٹر

9. **turtleneck** sweater
چست بڑے کالر والا سوئیٹر

10. **scoop neck** sweater
چوڑی گردن والا سوئیٹر

11. **sleeveless** shirt
بے آستین کی قمیض

12. **short-sleeved** shirt
چھوٹی-آستین والی قمیض

13. **3/4-sleeved** shirt
4\3-آستین والی قمیض

14. **long-sleeved** shirt
لمبی آستین والی قمیض

15. **mini**-skirt
بہت چھوٹا اسکرٹ

16. **short** skirt
چھوٹا اسکرٹ

17. **mid-length / calf-length** skirt
درمیانی لمبائی / پنڈلی تک کا اسکرٹ

18. **long** skirt
لمبا اسکرٹ

Patterns نمونے

19. solid
ہموار

20. striped
پٹی دار

21. polka-dotted
بوٹی دار

22. plaid
پچ رنگا یا چار خانے دار

23. print
چھینٹ

24. checked
خانے دار

25. floral
پھول پتی والا

26. paisley
خمیدہ تصویروں کے رنگین نقوش والا

Ask your classmates. Share the answers.

1. Do you prefer crewneck or V-neck sweaters?
2. Do you prefer checked or striped shirts?
3. Do you prefer short-sleeved or sleeveless shirts?

Role play. Talk to a salesperson.

A: *Excuse me. I'm looking for this <u>V-neck sweater</u> in <u>large</u>.*
B: *Here's a <u>large</u>. It's on sale for $<u>19.99</u>.*
A: *Wonderful! I'll take it. I'm also looking for…*

Comparing Clothing کپڑوں کا موازنہ

27. heavy jacket
موٹی جیکٹ

28. light jacket
ہلکی جیکٹ

29. tight pants
چست پتلون

30. loose / baggy pants
ڈھیلی / بیگی پتلون

31. low heels
کم ایڑی

32. high heels
زیادہ ایڑی

33. plain blouse
سادہ بالا پوش

34. fancy blouse
مرصّع بالا پوش

35. narrow tie
پتلی ٹائی

36. wide tie
چوڑی ٹائی

Clothing Problems کپڑوں کی خرابیاں

37. It's **too small**.
یہ بہت چھوٹا ہے۔

38. It's **too big**.
یہ بہت بڑا ہے۔

39. The zipper is **broken**.
زپر ٹوٹ گیا ہے۔

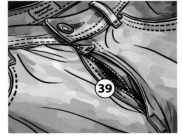

40. A button is **missing**.
ایک بٹن غائب ہے۔

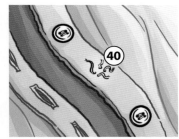

41. It's **ripped / torn**.
یہ اکھڑ / پھٹ گیا ہے۔

42. It's **stained**.
اس پر داغ ہے۔

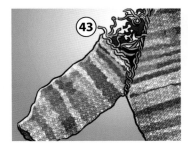

43. It's **unraveling**.
یہ ادھڑ رہا ہے

44. It's **too expensive**.
یہ بہت مہنگا ہے۔

More vocabulary

refund: money you get back when you return an item to the store
complaint: a statement that something is not right
customer service: the place customers go with their complaints

Role play. Return an item to a salesperson.

A: *Welcome to Shopmart. How may I help you?*
B: *This sweater is new, but it's unraveling.*
A: *I'm sorry. Would you like a refund?*

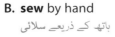
Types of Material کپڑوں کی اقسام

1. cotton
سوتی

2. linen
سن کے ریشے سے بنا ہوا

3. wool
اونی

4. cashmere
کشمیری نرم نفیس اون

5. silk
ریشمی

6. leather
چمڑا

A Garment Factory لباس ساز فیکٹری

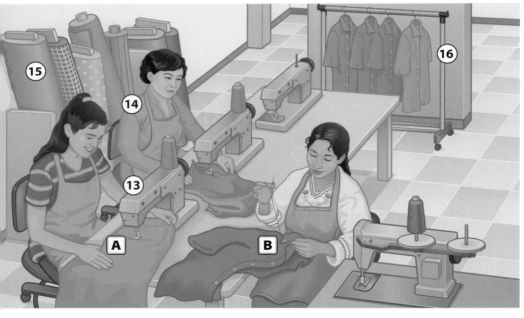

Parts of a Sewing Machine
سلائی مشین کے حصے

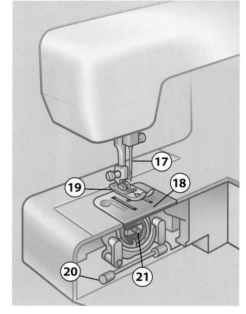

A. **sew** by machine
مشین کے ذریعے سلائی

B. **sew** by hand
ہاتھ کے ذریعے سلائی

13. sewing machine
سلائی مشین

14. sewing machine operator
سلائی مشین کا چلانے والا

15. bolt of fabric
کپڑے کا تھان

16. rack
الماری

17. needle
سوئی

18. needle plate
سوئی کی پلیٹ

19. presser foot
پاندان

20. feed dog / feed bar
دھاگہ پہنچانے کی چرخی / چھڑ

21. bobbin
دھاگہ لپیٹنے کی چرخی

More vocabulary

fashion designer: a person who makes original clothes
natural materials: cloth made from things that grow in nature
synthetic materials: cloth made by people, such as nylon

Use the new words.
Look at pages 86–87. Name the materials you see.

A: *That's denim.*
B: *That's leather.*

Types of Material کپڑوں کی اقسام

7. denim
نیلے رنگ کا موٹا پائندار کپڑا

8. suede
نرم چمڑے سے بنایا گیا

9. lace
روئی یا ریشم کے دھاگوں سے بنا

10. velvet
مخمل، اونی ریشوں والا

11. corduroy
دبیز سوتی ابھری دھاریوں کا کپڑا

12. nylon
نائلون

A Fabric Store کپڑوں کی دکان

Closures بند کرنے والی چیزیں

Trim تراشے

22. pattern
نمونہ

23. thread
دھاگہ

24. button
بٹن

25. zipper
بند کرنے والی چین

26. snap
بٹن کی جگہ کف آستین کو بند کرنے والا

27. hook and eye
بک اور پھندا

28. buckle
بکسوا

29. hook and loop fastener
بک اور ڈوری بند

30. ribbon
رِن

31. appliqué
منقش پارچہ کاری

32. beads
چھید کیے ہوئے دانے

33. sequins
ستارا

34. fringe
کناری

Ask your classmates. Share the answers.

1. Can you sew?
2. What's your favorite type of material?
3. How many types of material are you wearing today?

Think about it. Discuss.

1. Do most people make or buy clothes in your country?
2. Is it better to make or buy clothes? Why?
3. Which materials are best for formal clothes?

99

An Alterations Shop ترمیم کاری کی دکان

1. dressmaker
لباس ساز (درزی)

2. dressmaker's dummy
درزی کی دکان پر کپڑوں کے نمونے پہنانے کا پتلا

3. tailor
درزی

4. collar
کالر

5. waistband
کمر بند

6. sleeve
آستین

7. pocket
جیب

8. hem
گوٹ

9. cuff
آستین یا پانچوں کا سرا

Sewing Supplies سلائی کے سامان

10. needle
سوئی

11. thread
دھاگہ

12. (straight) pin
(سیدھی) پن

13. pin cushion
پن گدی

14. safety pin
تحفظی پن

15. thimble
انگشتانہ

16. pair of scissors
قینچی

17. tape measure
ناپنے والا فیتہ

18. seam ripper
بخیہ کھولنے والی آری

Alterations ترمیمات

A. **Lengthen** the pants.
پتلون کو لمبا کیجیے۔

B. **Shorten** the pants.
پتلون کو چھوٹا کیجیے۔

C. **Let out** the pants.
پتلون کو ڈھیلی کیجیے۔

D. **Take in** the pants.
پتلون کو تنگ کیجیے۔

Pair practice. Make new conversations.

A: *Would you hand me the thread?*
B: *OK. What are you going to do?*
A: *I'm going to take in these pants.*

Ask your classmates. Share the answers.

1. Is there an alterations shop near your home?
2. Do you ever go to a tailor or a dressmaker?
3. What sewing supplies do you have at home?

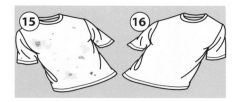

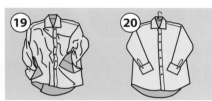

1. laundry
دھلنے والے کپڑے

2. laundry basket
دھلنے والے کپڑوں کی ٹوکری

3. washer
کپڑے دھونے کی مشین

4. dryer
کپڑے سکھانے کی مشین

5. dryer sheets
سکھانے والی پنیاں

6. fabric softener
کپڑا نرم کرنے والا محلول

7. bleach
میل ہٹانے والا محلول

8. laundry detergent
دھلائی میں استعمال ہونے والا میل کاٹ

9. clothesline
الگنی

10. clothespin
کپڑے لٹکانے کی چٹکیاں

11. hanger
کپڑے لٹکانے کی لکڑی یا لوہے کی پٹی

12. spray starch
چھڑکنے کا اسٹارچ

13. iron
استری

14. ironing board
استری تختہ

15. **dirty** T-shirt
میلی آدھی آستین کی قمیض

16. **clean** T-shirt
صاف آدھی آستین کی قمیض

17. **wet** shirt
بھیگی ہوئی قمیض

18. **dry** shirt
سوکھی قمیض

19. **wrinkled** shirt
سلوٹوں والی قمیض

20. **ironed** shirt
استری کی ہوئی قمیض

A. Sort the laundry.
دھلنے کے کپڑوں کو الگ الگ کیجیے۔

B. Add the detergent.
میل کاٹ ڈالیے۔

C. Load the washer.
دھونے والی مشین میں ڈالیے۔

D. Clean the lint trap.
پھنسا ہوا رواں صاف کیجیے۔

E. Unload the dryer.
سکھانے والی مشین سے کپڑے نکالیے۔

F. Fold the laundry.
دھلے کپڑے تہہ کیجیے۔

G. Iron the clothes.
کپڑوں پر استری کیجیے۔

H. Hang up the clothes.
کپڑوں کو ٹانگیے۔

wash in cold water

no bleach

line dry

dry clean only, do not wash

Pair practice. Make new conversations.

A: *I have to* sort the laundry. *Can you help?*
B: *Sure. Here's* the laundry basket.
A: *Thanks a lot!*

101

1. flyer
   دستی اشتہار

2. used clothing
   استعمال شدہ کپڑا

3. sticker
   چپکنے والا لیبل

4. folding card table
   تہہ کی جا سکنے والی میز

5. folding chair
   تہہ کی جا سکنے والی کرسی

6. clock radio
   گھڑی ریڈیو

7. VCR
   وی سی آر

A. **bargain**
   مول بھاؤ کیجیے

B. **browse**
   گھوم کر دیکھیے

**Look at the pictures.
What do you see?**

Answer the questions.

1. What kind of used clothing do you see?

2. What information is on the flyer?

3. Why are the stickers different colors?

4. How much is the clock radio? the VCR?

📖 **Read the story.**

A Garage Sale

Last Sunday, I had a garage sale. At 5:00 a.m., I put up <u>flyers</u> in my neighborhood. Next, I put price <u>stickers</u> on my <u>used clothing</u>, my <u>VCR</u>, and some other old things. At 7:00 a.m., I opened my <u>folding card table</u> and <u>folding chair</u>. Then I waited.

At 7:05 a.m., my first customer arrived. She asked, "How much is the sweatshirt?"

"Two dollars," I said.

She said, "It's stained. I can give you seventy-five cents." We <u>bargained</u> for a minute and she paid $1.00.

All day people came to <u>browse</u>, bargain, and buy. At 7:00 p.m., I had $85.00.

Now I know two things: Garage sales are hard work and nobody wants to buy an old <u>clock radio</u>!

Think about it.

1. Do you like to buy things at garage sales? Why or why not?

2. Imagine you want the VCR. How will you bargain for it?

1. head
   سر
2. hair
   بال
3. neck
   گردن
4. chest
   سینہ
5. back
   پیٹھ
6. nose
   ناک
7. mouth
   منہ
8. foot
   پیر

Listen and point. Take turns.

A: *Point to the chest.*

B: *Point to the neck.*

A: *Point to the mouth.*

Dictate to your partner. Take turns.

A: *Write hair.*

B: *Did you say hair?*

A: *That's right, h-a-i-r.*

9. leg
ٹانگ

10. toe
انگوٹھا

11. eye
آنکھ

12. ear
کان

13. shoulder
کندھا

14. arm
بانہہ

15. hand
ہاتھ

16. finger
انگلی

Grammar Point: imperatives

Please touch your right foot.
Put your hands on your feet.
Don't put your hands on your shoulders.

Pair practice. Take turns giving commands.

A: <u>Raise</u> your <u>arms</u>.
B: <u>Touch</u> your <u>feet</u>.
A: <u>Put</u> your <u>hand</u> on your <u>shoulder</u>.

105

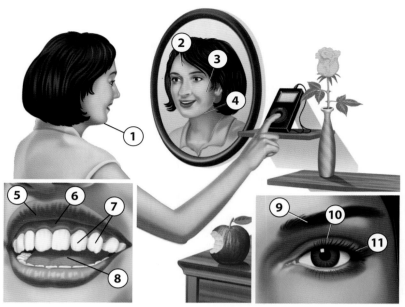

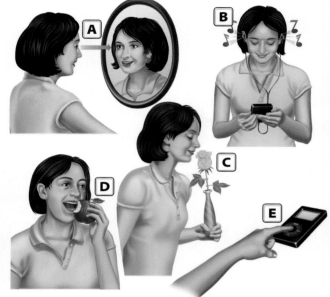

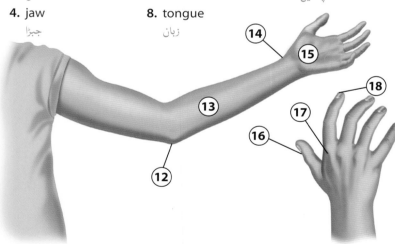

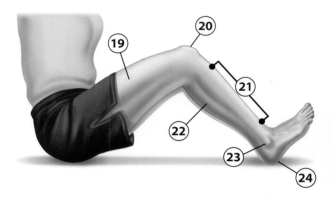

The Face
چہرہ

1. chin
ٹھوڑی
2. forehead
پیشانی
3. cheek
گال
4. jaw
جبڑا

The Mouth
منہ

5. lip
ہونٹ
6. gums
مسوڑھے
7. teeth
دانت
8. tongue
زبان

The Eye
آنکھ

9. eyebrow
بھویں
10. eyelid
پپوٹے
11. eyelashes
پلکیں

The Senses
حواس

A. see
دیکھنا
B. hear
سننا
C. smell
سونگھنا

D. taste
چکھنا
E. touch
چھونا

The Arm, Hand, and Fingers بانہہ، ہاتھ اور انگلیاں

12. elbow
کہنی
13. forearm
اگلی بانہہ
14. wrist
کلائی

15. palm
ہتھیلی
16. thumb
ہاتھ کا انگوٹھا

17. knuckle
انگلیوں کے جوڑ خصوصاً ہاتھ کے
18. fingernail
انگلی کے ناخن

The Leg and Foot ٹانگ اور پیر

19. thigh
ران
20. knee
گھٹنا
21. shin
پنڈلی کے اوپر کا حصہ

22. calf
پنڈلی
23. ankle
ٹخنہ
24. heel
ایڑی

More vocabulary

torso: the part of the body from the shoulders to the pelvis
limbs: arms and legs
toenail: the nail on your toe

Pair practice. Make new conversations.

A: Is your <u>arm</u> OK?
B: Yes, but now my <u>elbow</u> hurts.
A: I'm sorry to hear that.

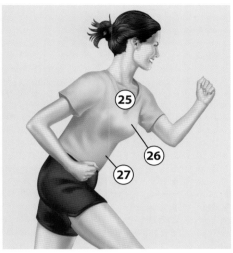
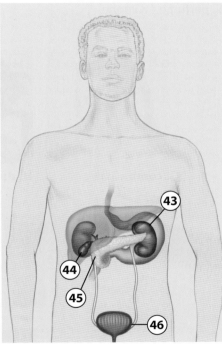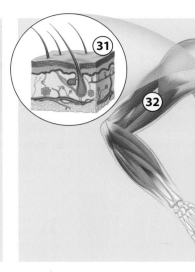
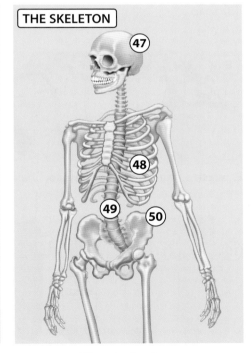

25. chest
سینہ
26. breast
چھاتی
27. abdomen
پیٹ

28. shoulder blade
کندھے کی ہڈی
29. lower back
پیٹھ کا نچلا حصہ
30. buttocks
کولھے

31. skin
جلد
32. muscle
گوشت
33. bone
ہڈی

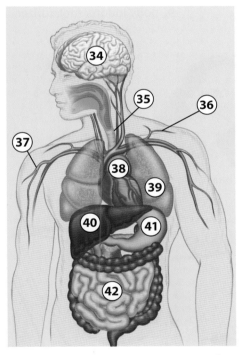
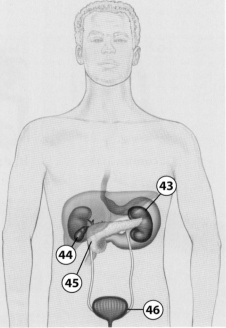

THE SKELETON

34. brain
دماغ
35. throat
گلا
36. artery
شریان
37. vein
ورید
38. heart
دل

39. lung
پھیپھڑا
40. liver
جگر
41. stomach
معدہ
42. intestines
آنتیں
43. kidney
گردہ

44. gallbladder
پت تھیلی
45. pancreas
لبلبۂ جگر
46. bladder
مثانہ
47. skull
کھوپڑی
48. rib cage
پسلیوں کا ڈھانچہ

49. spinal column
ریڑھ کی ہڈی
50. pelvis
پیڑو کا حصہ

Personal Hygiene

 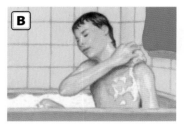  

A. take a shower

فوارے سے **نہائیے**

B. take a bath / **bathe**

غسل کیجیے / **نہائیے**

C. use deodorant

دافع بدبو استعمال کیجیے

D. put on sunscreen

دھوپ سے حفاظت کی کریم لگائیے

1. shower cap

شاور کے دوران لگانے کی ٹوپی

2. shower gel

شاور کے دوران استعمال کیا جانے والا جیل

3. soap

صابن

4. bath powder

نہانے کے بعد کا پاؤڈر

5. deodorant / antiperspirant

دافع بدبو / پسینہ روک پاؤڈر

6. perfume / cologne

عطر / خوشبو دار فرحت بخش محلول

7. sunscreen

دھوپ سے حفاظت کی کریم

8. sunblock

جلد کو دھوپ کی تمازت سے بچانے والا

9. body lotion / moisturizer

جسم پر ملنے والا لوشن / خشکی رفع کرنے والا

 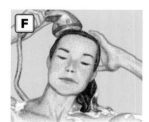 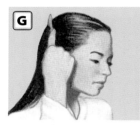  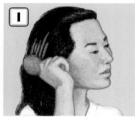

E. wash…hair

بالوں کو... دھوئیے

F. rinse…hair

بالوں پر... پانی ڈالیے

G. comb…hair

بالوں میں... کنگھا کیجیے

H. dry…hair

بالوں کو... سکھائیے

I. brush…hair

بالوں میں... برش کیجیے

10. shampoo

شیمپو

11. conditioner

بال ہموار کرنے والا مادہ

12. hair spray

بالوں کو جمانے والی پھوہار

13. comb

کنگھا

14. brush

برش

15. pick

کنگھی

16. hair gel

بالوں میں لگانے والا جیل

17. curling iron

بالوں کو گھنگرالے بنانے کا آلہ

18. blow dryer

گرم ہوا سے خشک کرنے کا آلہ

19. hair clip

بالوں میں لگانے کی کلپ

20. barrette

بالوں کو باندھ کر رکھنے کی بڑی کلپ

21. bobby pins

بالوں کو بکھرنے سے روکنے کی پنیں

More vocabulary

unscented: a product without perfume or scent
hypoallergenic: a product that is better for people with allergies

Think about it. Discuss.

1. Which personal hygiene products should someone use before a job interview?
2. What is the right age to start wearing makeup? Why?

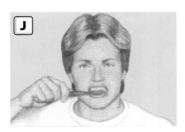

J. brush…teeth

دانت میں... برش کیجیے

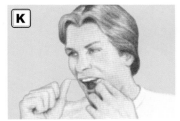

K. floss…teeth

دانت کو... لاس سے صاف کیجیے

L. gargle

غرارہ کیجیے

M. shave

داڑھی بنائیے

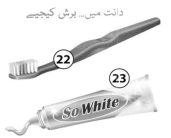

22. toothbrush

دانت صاف کرنے کا برش

23. toothpaste

ٹوتھ پیسٹ

24. dental floss

دانت صاف کرنے کا لاس

25. mouthwash

منہ صاف کرنے کا محلول

26. electric shaver

داڑھی بنانے کا برقی آلہ

27. razor

داڑھی بنانے کا محفوظ ریزر

28. razorblade

ریزر میں مستعمل بلیڈ

29. shaving cream

داڑھی بنانے کی کریم

30. aftershave

داڑھی بنانے کے بعد لگانے کا محلول

N. cut…nails

ناخن... کاٹیے

O. polish…nails

ناخنوں پر... پالش کیجیے

P. put on / apply

ملیے / لگائیے

Q. take off / remove

ہٹائیے / اتاریے

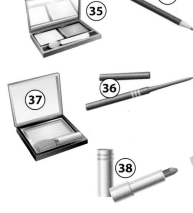

Makeup بناؤ سنگار

31. nail clipper

ناخن تراش

32. emery board

ناخن گھسنے کا آلہ

33. nail polish

ناخنوں پر لگانے کی پالش

34. eyebrow pencil

ابرو بنانے والی پنسل

35. eye shadow

آنکھوں کے گرد چھڑکنے والا پاؤڈر

36. eyeliner

آنکھوں کے گرد آرائشی لکیر بنانے والی پنسل

37. blush

چہرے پر سنگھار و آرائش والی پنسل

38. lipstick

ہونٹوں کی سُرخی

39. mascara

پلکوں کو رنگنے والا برش

40. foundation

سنگار کی بنیادی کریم

41. face powder

چہرے پر لگایا جانے والا پاؤڈر

42. makeup remover

سنگار مٹانے والا محلول

109

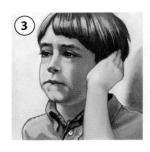

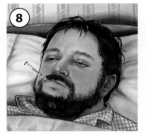

1. headache
   سردرد

2. toothache
   دانت درد

3. earache
   کان درد

4. stomachache
   پیٹ درد

5. backache
   کمر درد

6. sore throat
   گلے میں خراش

7. nasal congestion
   ناک میں جکڑن

8. fever / temperature
   بخار / حرارت

9. chills
   کپکپی

10. rash
    ددوڑے

A. **cough**
   کھانسنا

B. **sneeze**
   چھینکنا

C. **feel** dizzy
   سر چکرانا

D. **feel** nauseous
   ابکائی محسوس کرنا

E. **throw up / vomit**
   الٹی کرنا / قے کرنا

11. insect bite
    کیڑے کا کاٹنا

12. bruise
    چھل جانا

13. cut
    کٹنا

14. sunburn
    دھوپ میں جھلسنا

15. blister
    چھالا

16. swollen finger
    انگلی پر سوجن

17. bloody nose
    نکسیر

18. sprained ankle
    ٹخنے میں موچ

Look at the pictures.
Describe the symptoms and injuries.

A: *He has a backache*.
B: *She has a toothache*.

Think about it. Discuss.
1. What are some common cold symptoms?
2. What do you recommend for a stomachache?
3. What is the best way to stop a bloody nose?

Common Illnesses and Childhood Diseases عام بیماریاں اور بچپن کے امراض

1. cold
نزلہ

2. flu
زکام

3. ear infection
کان میں تعدیہ

4. strep throat
تعدیہ زدہ گلا

5. measles
خسرہ

6. chicken pox
چیچک

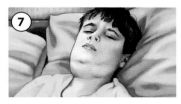

7. mumps
گل سوجا

8. allergies
الرجیاں

Serious Medical Conditions and Diseases صحتی شدید خرابیاں اور امراض

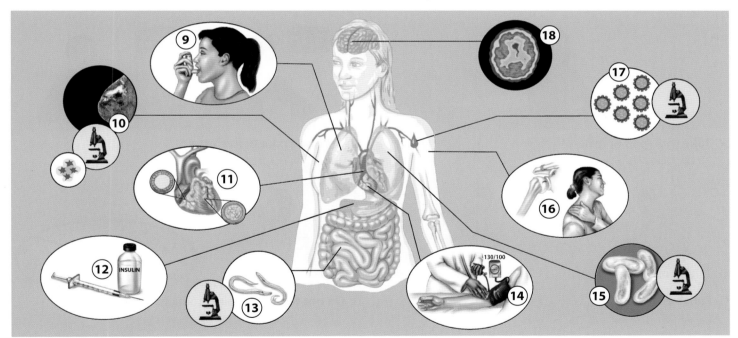

9. asthma
دمہ

10. cancer
سرطان

11. heart disease
دل کا مرض

12. diabetes
ذیابیطس

13. intestinal parasites
آنتوں کے طفیلی کیڑے

14. high blood pressure / hypertension
اونچے درجے کا دم الفشار / غیر معمولی فشار خون

15. TB (tuberculosis)
ٹی بی (تپ دق)

16. arthritis
گھٹیا

17. HIV (human immunodeficiency virus)
ایچ آئی وی (انسانی قوت مدافعت کم کرنے والا جرثومہ)

18. dementia
ازالۂ یادداشت

More vocabulary

AIDS (acquired immune deficiency syndrome): a medical condition that results from contracting the HIV virus
Alzheimer's disease: a disease that causes dementia

coronary disease: heart disease
infectious disease: a disease that is spread through air or water
influenza: flu

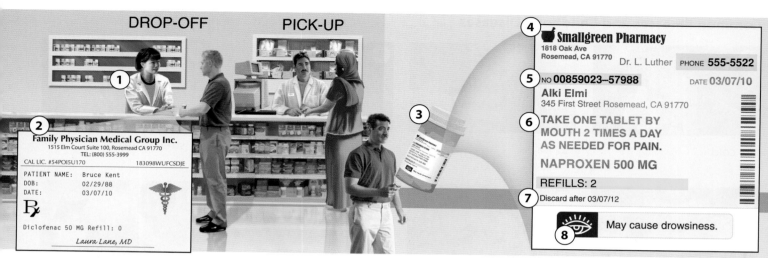

DROP-OFF   PICK-UP

Family Physician Medical Group Inc.
1515 Elm Court Suite 100, Rosemead CA 91770
TEL: (800) 555-3999
CAL LIC. #54POI5U170   183098WUFCSDJE

PATIENT NAME: Bruce Kent
DOB: 02/29/88
DATE: 03/07/10

℞

Diclofenac 50 MG Refill: 0

Laura Lane, MD

Smallgreen Pharmacy
1818 Oak Ave
Rosemead, CA 91770   Dr. L. Luther   PHONE **555-5522**

NO **00859023–57988**   DATE **03/07/10**

Alki Elmi
345 First Street Rosemead, CA 91770

**TAKE ONE TABLET BY
MOUTH 2 TIMES A DAY
AS NEEDED FOR PAIN.**

NAPROXEN 500 MG

REFILLS: 2

Discard after 03/07/12

👁 May cause drowsiness.

1. **pharmacist**
   دوا فروش

2. **prescription**
   دوا کا نسخہ

3. **prescription medication**
   تجویز کردہ دوا

4. **prescription label**
   نسخے کا لیبل

5. **prescription number**
   نسخے کا نمبر

6. **dosage**
   خوراک

7. **expiration date**
   تاریخ خاتمہ

8. **warning label**
   انتباہ کا لیبل

Medical Warnings طبی انتباہات

A. **Take** with food or milk.
غذا یا دودھ کے ساتھ استعمال کیجیے۔

B. **Take** one hour before eating.
کھانے سے ایک گھنٹہ پہلے استعمال کیجیے۔

C. **Finish** all medication.
تمام دوائیں ختم کیجیے۔

D. **Do not take** with dairy products.
دودھ سے بنی اشیاء کے ساتھ استعمال نہ کیجیے۔

E. **Do not drive or operate** heavy machinery.
بھاری مشینری پر کام مت کیجیے یا اسے مت چلائیے۔

F. **Do not drink** alcohol.
شراب نہ پیجیے۔

More vocabulary

prescribe medication: to write a prescription
fill prescriptions: to prepare medication for patients
pick up a prescription: to get prescription medication

Role play. Talk to the pharmacist.

A: *Hi. I need to pick up a prescription for Jones.*
B: *Here's your medication, Mr. Jones. Take these once a day with milk or food.*

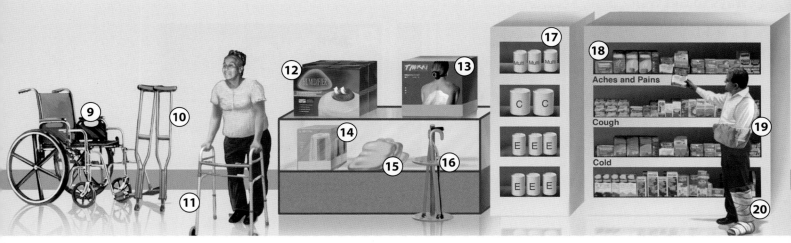

9. wheelchair
پہیہ کرسی

10. crutches
بیساکھیاں

11. walker
چلنے میں مدد کرنے والا

12. humidifier
ہوا میں نمی پیدا کرنے والا

13. heating pad
گرم کرنے کی گدی

14. air purifier
ہوا صاف کرنے والا

15. hot water bottle
گرم پانی کی بوتل

16. cane
کین (چھڑ)

17. vitamins
وئامن (حیاتین)

18. over-the-counter medication
کاؤنٹر پر ملنے والی دوائیں

19. sling
گل پٹی

20. cast
سانچا

Types of Medication دواؤں کی اقسام

21. pill
گولی

22. tablet
ٹکیہ

23. capsule
کیپسول

24. ointment
مرہم

25. cream
کریم

Over-the-Counter Medication معمولی خوردہ دوائیں

26. pain reliever
دافع درد دوا

27. cold tablets
نزلے کی ٹکیاں

28. antacid
دافع تیزابیت

29. cough syrup
کھانسی کا شربت

30. throat lozenges
گلا صاف کرنے والی گولیاں

31. eye drops
آنکھ میں ڈالنے کے قطرات

32. nasal spray
ناک میں چھڑکنے کی دوا

33. inhaler
سانس کے ذریعے سونگھنے والی دوائیں

Ways to talk about medication

Use *take* for pills, tablets, capsules, and cough syrup.
Use *apply* for ointments and creams.
Use *use* for drops, nasal sprays, and inhalers.

Ask your classmates. Share the answers.

1. What pharmacy do you go to?
2. Do you ever ask the pharmacist for advice?
3. Do you take any vitamins? Which ones?

Ways to Get Well   صحت یاب ہونے کے طریقے

A. Seek medical attention.

طبی مدد حاصل کیجیے۔

B. Get bed rest.

مکمل آرام کیجیے۔

C. Drink fluids.

رقیق اشیاء پیجیے۔

D. Take medicine.

دوا استعمال کیجیے۔

Ways to Stay Well   صحت مند رہنے کے طریقے

E. Stay fit.

چست اور پھرتیلے رہیے۔

F. Eat a healthy diet.

صحت مند غذا کھائیے۔

G. Don't smoke.

سگریٹ نوشی مت کیجیے۔

H. Have regular checkups.

پابندی سے معائنے کرائیے۔

I. Get immunized.

حفاظتی ٹیکے لگوائیے۔

J. Follow medical advice.

طبی مشورہ پر عمل کیجیے۔

Ms. Jones, you must stop smoking!

IMMUNIZATION SCHEDULE
Tetanus - Every 10 years
Flu Shot - Every year

More vocabulary

injection: medicine in a syringe that is put into the body
immunization / vaccination: an injection that stops serious diseases

Ask your classmates. Share the answers.

1. How do you stay fit?
2. What do you do when you're sick?
3. Which two foods are a part of your healthy diet?

Types of Health Problems صحت کے مسائل کی اقسام

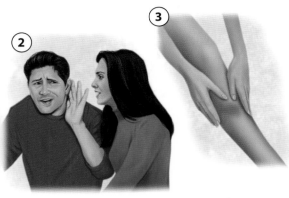

1. vision problems
آنکھ کی تکلیفیں

2. hearing loss
بہرہ پن

3. pain
درد

4. stress
تناؤ

5. depression
مایوسی

Help with Health Problems صحت کے مسائل میں مدد

6. optometrist
آنکھ کا نمبر جانچ کر عینک بنانے والا ماہر

7. glasses
چشمے

8. contact lenses
آنکھ کی پتلی پر لگانے والے عدسے

9. audiologist
ماہر سمعیات

10. hearing aid
سماعتی آلہ

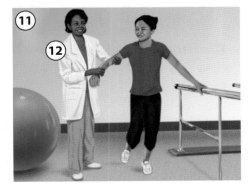

11. physical therapy
جسمانی معالجہ

12. physical therapist
جسمانی معالج

13. talk therapy
تکلمی معالجہ

14. therapist
معالج

15. support group
امدادی گروپ

Ways to ask about health problems

Are you <u>in pain</u>?
Are you having <u>vision problems</u>?
Are you experiencing <u>depression</u>?

Pair practice. Make new conversations.

A: *Do you know a good <u>optometrist</u>?*
B: *Why? <u>Are you having vision problems</u>?*
A: *Yes, I might need <u>glasses</u>.*

115

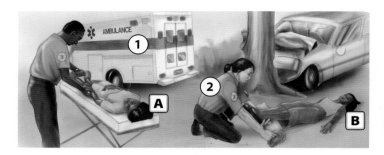

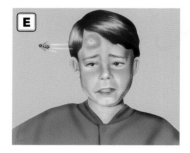

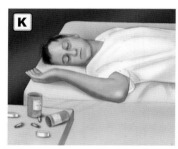
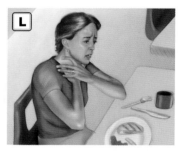

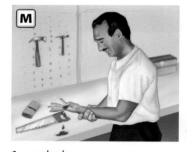

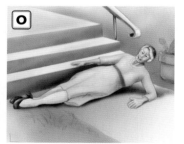

1. ambulance
   بیماروں کو لانے لے جانے والی گاڑی

2. paramedic
   نیم طبی کارکن

A. **be** unconscious
   بے ہوش ہونا

B. **be** in shock
   صدمے کی حالت میں ہونا

C. **be** injured / **be** hurt
   زخمی ہو جانا / چوٹ لگنا

D. **have** a heart attack
   دل کا دورہ پڑنا

E. **have** an allergic reaction
   کسی الرجی سے متاثر ہونا

F. **get** an electric shock
   بجلی کا جھٹکا لگنا

G. **get** frostbite
   برف کا شدید ٹھنڈا اثر ہونا

H. **burn** (your)self
   خود جل جانا

I. **drown**
   ڈوبنا

J. **swallow** poison
   زہر نگلنا

K. **overdose** on drugs
   دوا کی زیادہ خوراک لینا

L. **choke**
   سانس رکنا

M. **bleed**
   خون بہنا

N. **can't breathe**
   سانس نہ لے سکنا

O. **fall**
   گرنا

P. **break** a bone
   ہڈی ٹوٹ جانا

Grammar Point: past tense

For past tense add –ed:
burned, drowned, swallowed,
overdosed, choked

These verbs are different (irregular):

be – was, were   bleed – bled   fall – fell

have – had   can't – couldn't

get – got   break – broke

First Aid فوری طبی امداد

1. first aid kit
فوری طبی امداد کا بکسہ

2. first aid manual
فوری طبی امداد کا ہدایت نامہ

3. medical emergency bracelet
طبی ہنگامی حالت کا دست بند

Inside the Kit بکسے کے اندر

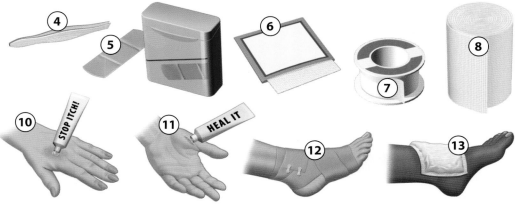  

4. tweezers
چمٹی

5. adhesive bandage
چپک دار پئی

6. sterile pad
جراثیم سے پاک گدی

7. sterile tape
جراثیم سے پاک پئی

8. gauze
جالی دار پئی

9. hydrogen peroxide
ہاڈروجن پراکسائڈ

10. antihistamine cream
نامیاتی مرکب یا الرجی مخالف کریم

11. antibacterial ointment
جراثیم کش مرہم

12. elastic bandage
لچکدار پئی

13. ice pack
برف کا پیک

14. splint
ٹوٹی ہوئی ہڈی کو جوڑ کر ملائے رکھنے والی پئی

First Aid Procedures فوری طبی امداد کے طریقے

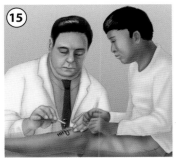 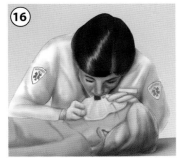 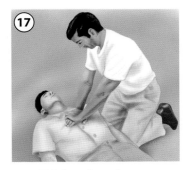 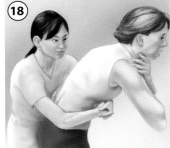

15. stitches
ٹانکے

16. rescue breathing
جان بچانے والی سانس پھنچانا

17. CPR (cardiopulmonary resuscitation)
سی پی آر (سینے پر دباؤ ڈال کر دل اور پھیپھڑوں کی حرکت بحال کرکے جان بچانا)

18. Heimlich maneuver
ہیملک طریقے سے سانس کی نلی کی رکاوٹ دور کرنا

Pair practice. Make new conversations.

A: *What do we need in the first aid kit?*
B: *We need <u>tweezers</u> and <u>gauze</u>.*
A: *I think we need <u>sterile tape</u>, too.*

Think about it. Discuss.

1. What are the three most important first aid items? Why?
2. Which first aid procedures should everyone know? Why?
3. What are some good places to keep a first aid kit?

117

In the Waiting Room انتظار گاہ میں

HEALTH FIRST
Name: Andre Zolmar
Group Number: 98765
Membership Number: 60756789

4
Health Form
Name: *Andre Zolmar*
Date of birth: *July 8, 1973*
Current symptoms: *stomachache*

Health History:

Childhood Diseases:
☑ chicken pox
☑ diphtheria
☑ rubella
☑ measles
☐ mumps
☐ other

Description of symptoms:

1. appointment
مقررہ وقت ملاقات

2. receptionist
استقبالیہ کار

3. health insurance card
صحت بیمہ کارڈ

4. health history form
طبی تفصیل کا فارم

In the Examining Room معائنہ گاہ میں

5. doctor
ڈاکٹر(معالج)

7. examination table
معائنے کی میز

9. blood pressure gauge
بلڈ پریشر پیما

11. thermometer
بخارپیما

6. patient
مریض

8. nurse
نرس

10. stethoscope
دل کی دھڑکن ناپنے کا آلہ

12. syringe
انجکشن لگانے کا آلہ

Medical Procedures طبی کارروائیاں

A. check…blood pressure
بلڈ پریشر... جانچیے

C. listen to…heart
دل کی دھڑکن... سنیے

E. examine…throat
گلے کا... معائنہ کیجیے

B. take…temperature
بخار... ناپیے

D. examine…eyes
آنکھوں کا... معائنہ کیجیے

F. draw…blood
خون... نکالیے

Grammar Point: future tense with *will* + verb

To show a future action, use *will* + verb.
The subject pronoun contraction of *will* is -*'ll*.
She **will draw** your blood. = She**'ll draw** your blood.

Role play. Talk to a medical receptionist.

A: Will the nurse <u>examine my eyes</u>?
B: No, but she'll <u>draw your blood</u>.
A: What will the doctor do?

Dentistry معالجۂ دندان

Orthodontics دانتوں اور جبڑوں کی خرابیوں کے علاج

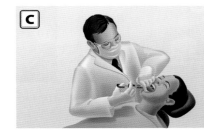

1. dentist
ماہر دندان

2. dental assistant
دندان سازی کا معاون

3. dental hygienist
دانتوں کی حفظانِ صحت کا ماہر

4. dental instruments
دانتوں کے اوزار

5. orthodontist
دانتوں اور جبڑوں کی خرابیوں کے علاج کا ماہر

6. braces
دانتوں کو صحیح حالت میں رکھنے کا تار

Dental Problems دانت کی بیماریاں

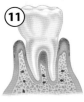

7. cavity / decay
کھوکھلا / سڑن

8. filling
بھرائی

9. crown
کراؤن (خول)

10. dentures
نقلی دانت

11. gum disease
مسوڑھے کے امراض

12. plaque
دانتوں پر جمنے والا جراثیم پرور میل

An Office Visit دفتر میں ایک ملاقات

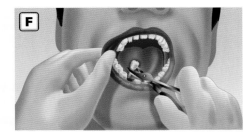

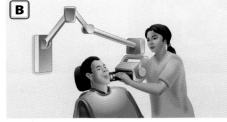

A. clean…teeth
دانت... صاف کرنا

B. take x-rays
ایکس-رے لینا

C. numb the mouth
منہ کو سن کرنا

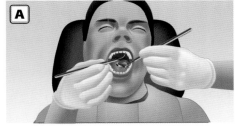

D. drill a tooth
دانت میں سوراخ کرنا

E. fill a cavity
کھوکھلا دانت بھرنا

F. pull a tooth
دانت اکھاڑنا

Ask your classmates. Share the answers.

1. Do you know someone with braces? Who?
2. Do dentists make you nervous? Why or why not?
3. How often do you go to the dentist?

Role play. Talk to a dentist.

A: *I think I have a cavity.*
B: *Let me take a look.*
A: *Will I need a filling?*

119

Medical Specialists طبی ماہرین

1. internist
داخلی طب کا ماہر

2. obstetrician
ماہر امراض نسواں

3. cardiologist
ماہر امراض قلب

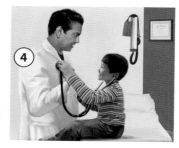

4. pediatrician
ماہر امراض اطفال

5. oncologist
ماہر سرطان

6. radiologist
شعاعی تشخیص کا ماہر

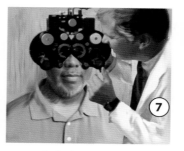

7. ophthalmologist
ماہر امراض چشم

8. psychiatrist
ماہر نفسیاتی امراض

Nursing Staff نرسنگ کا عملہ

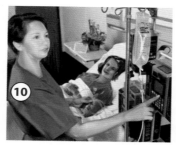

9. surgical nurse
جراحت معاون نرس

10. registered nurse (RN)
اندراج شدہ نرس (آر این)

11. licensed practical nurse (LPN)
لائسنس یافتہ پریکٹیکل نرس (ایل پی این)

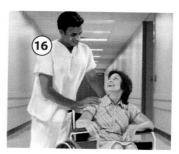

12. certified nursing assistant (CNA)
مستند نرسنگ معاون (سی این اے)

Hospital Staff اسپتال کا عملہ

13. administrator
منتظم

14. admissions clerk
داخلہ کلرک

15. dietician
ماہر غذائیات

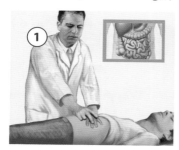

16. orderly
اسپتال کا مرد ملازم صفائی کرنے والا

More vocabulary

Gynecologists examine and treat women.
Nurse practitioners can give medical exams.
Nurse midwives deliver babies.

Chiropractors move the spine to improve health.
Orthopedists treat bone and joint problems.

A Hospital Room اسپتال کا ایک کمرہ

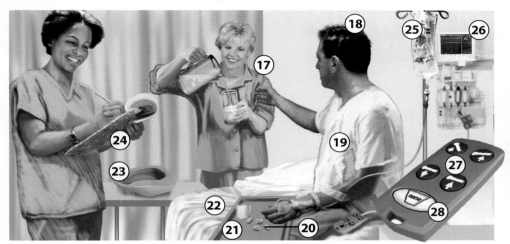

Lab تجربہ گاہ

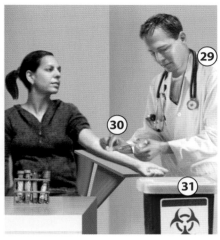

17. volunteer
رضاکار

18. patient
مریض

19. hospital gown
اسپتال کا گاؤن

20. medication
دوا دینا

21. bed table
بستر سے متصل میز

22. hospital bed
اسپتال کا بستر

23. bed pan
بستر کا سلفچی

24. medical chart
طبی جدول

25. IV (intravenous drip)
درون ورید (درون ورید دوا کا انجکشن)

26. vital signs monitor
اہم علامات کا نگراں

27. bed control
بستر کو صحیح حالت میں کرنے والا آلہ

28. call button
بلانے کا بٹن

29. phlebotomist
ورید پر نشتر لگانے والا

30. blood work / blood test
خون سے متعلق کام / خون کی جانچ

31. medical waste disposal
طبی فضلے کی نکاسی

Emergency Room Entrance
ہنگامی حالات کے کمرے میں داخلہ

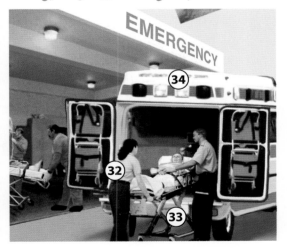

Operating Room
آپریشن کا کمرہ

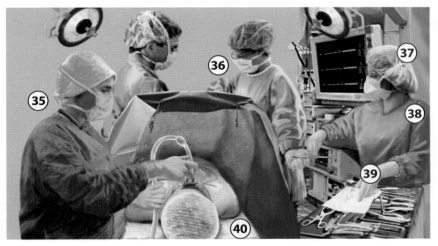

32. emergency medical technician (EMT)
ہنگامی طبی تکنیشین (ای ایم ٹی)

33. stretcher / gurney
مریض کو لانے لے جانے کا مخصوص ڈولا / گرنی

34. ambulance
مریض کو لانے لے جانے والی گاڑی

35. anesthesiologist
ماہر تخدیر (جراحت کے لیے بیہوش کرنے کا ماہر)

36. surgeon
جراح

37. surgical cap
جراحت کے دوران پہنی جانے والی ٹوپی

38. surgical gown
جراحت کے دوران پہنا جانے والا گاؤن

39. surgical gloves
جراحت کے دوران پہنے جانے والے دستانے

40. operating table
آپریشن کی میز

Dictate to your partner. Take turns.

A: *Write this sentence. She's a volunteer.*

B: *She's a what?*

A: *Volunteer. That's v-o-l-u-n-t-e-e-r.*

Role play. Ask about a doctor.

A: *I need to find a good surgeon.*

B: *Dr. Jones is a great surgeon. You should call him.*

A: *I will! Please give me his number.*

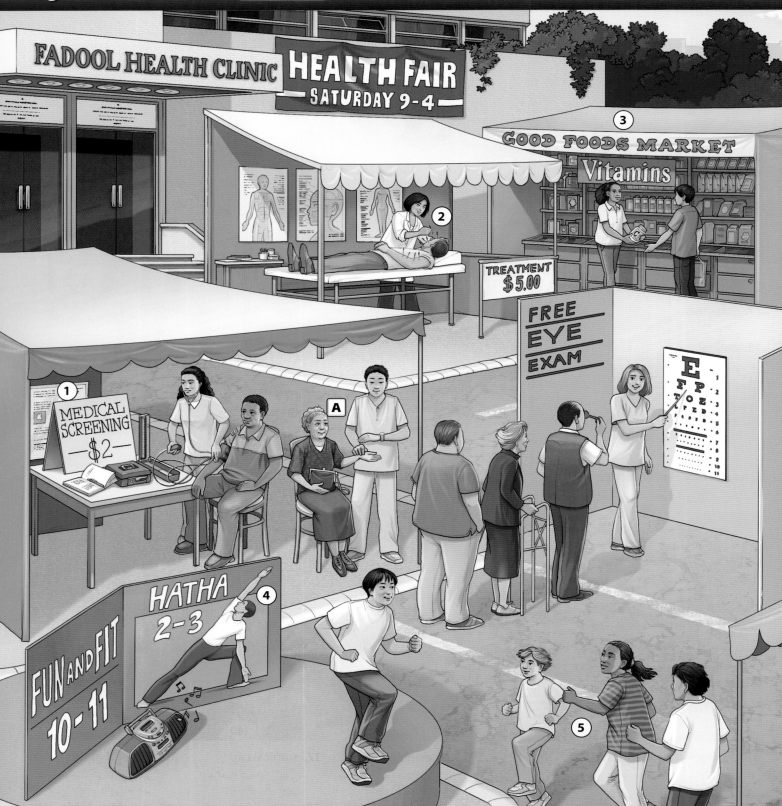

1. low-cost exam
کم قیمت جانچ

2. acupuncture
سوئیوں کے ذریعے چینی طریقۂ علاج

3. booth
عارضی دوکان

4. yoga
یوگا

5. aerobic exercise
جسم میں ہوا پہنچانے کے لیے کثرت

6. demonstration
مظاہرہ

7. sugar-free
بغیر چینی کی

8. nutrition label
تغذیہ کا لیبل

A. **check** ... pulse
نبض کی... جانچ کیجیے

B. **give** a lecture
لکچر دیجیے

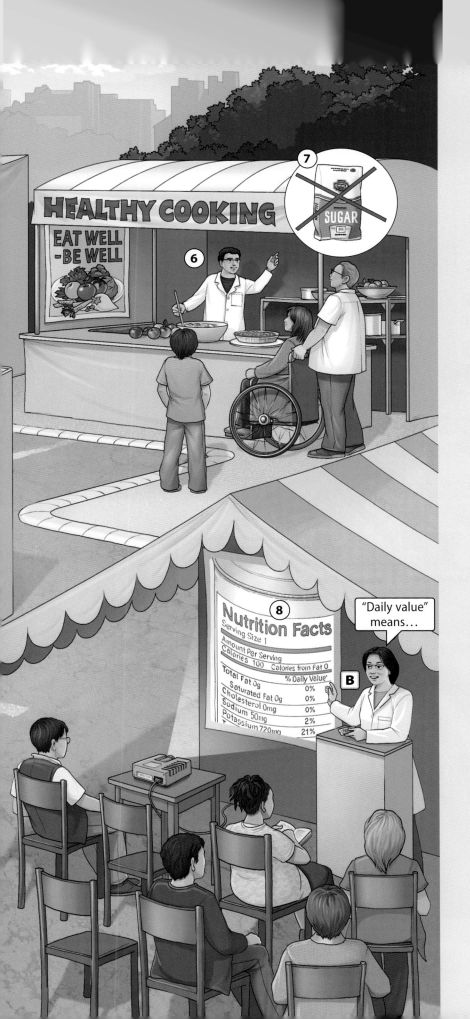

123

Look at the picture.
What do you see?

Answer the questions.

1. How many different booths are there at the health fair?

2. What kinds of exams and treatments can you get at the fair?

3. What kinds of lectures and demonstrations are there?

4. How much is an acupuncture treatment? a medical screening?

📖 Read the story.

A Health Fair

Once a month the Fadool Health Clinic has a health fair. You can get a <u>low-cost</u> medical <u>exam</u> at one <u>booth</u>. The nurses check your blood pressure and <u>check</u> your <u>pulse</u>. At another booth you can get a free eye exam. And an <u>acupuncture</u> treatment is only $5.00.

You can learn a lot at the fair. This month a doctor <u>is giving a lecture</u> on <u>nutrition labels</u>. There is also a <u>demonstration</u> on <u>sugar-free</u> cooking. You can learn to do <u>aerobic exercise</u> and <u>yoga</u>, too.

Do you want to get healthy and stay healthy? Then come to the Fadool Clinic Health Fair!

Think about it.

1. Which booths at this fair look interesting to you? Why?

2. Do you read nutrition labels? Why or why not?

Downtown

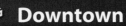شہر کا مرکز

1. parking garage
   گاڑیاں پارک کرنے کا گیرج

2. office building
   دفتر کی عمارت

3. hotel
   ہوٹل

4. Department of
   Motor Vehicles
   موٹر گاڑیوں کا شعبہ

5. bank
   بینک

6. police station
   تھانہ

7. bus station
   بس اڈّا

8. city hall
   بلدیہ دفاتر

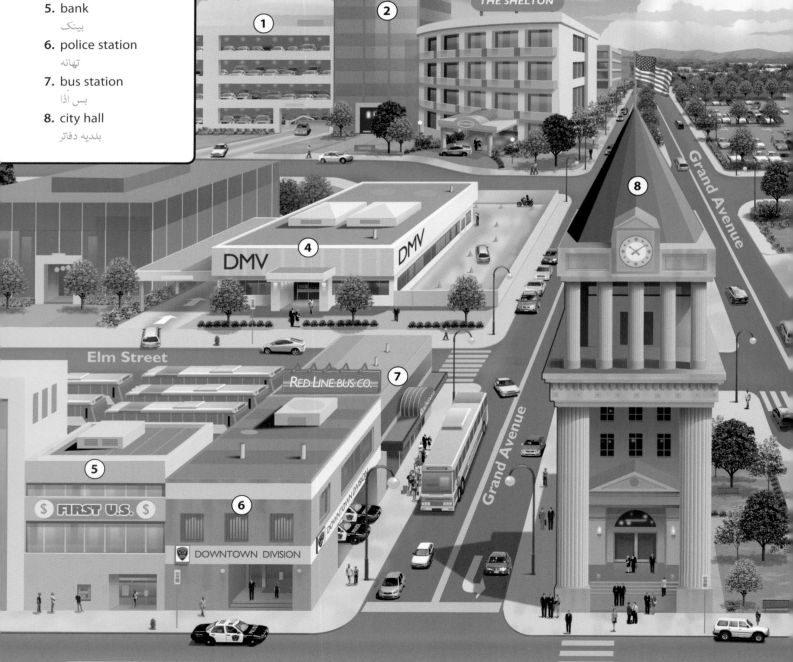

Listen and point. Take turns.

A: *Point to the bank.*
B: *Point to the hotel.*
A: *Point to the restaurant.*

Dictate to your partner. Take turns.

A: *Write bank.*
B: *Is that spelled b-a-n-k?*
A: *Yes, that's right.*

124

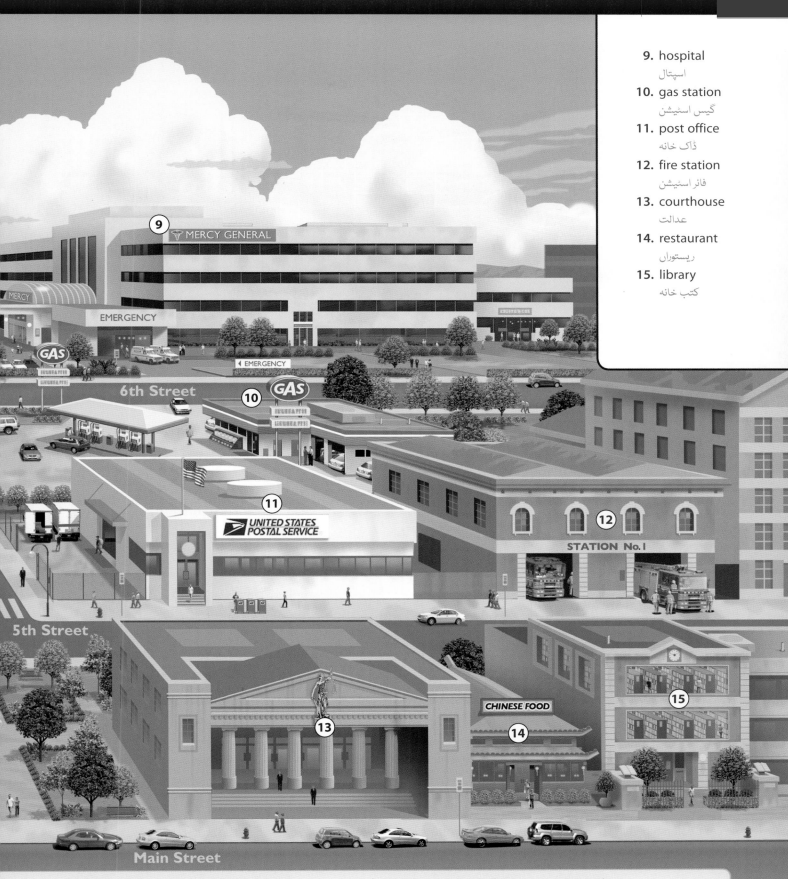

9. hospital
   اسپتال
10. gas station
    گیس اسٹیشن
11. post office
    ڈاک خانہ
12. fire station
    فائر اسٹیشن
13. courthouse
    عدالت
14. restaurant
    ریستوران
15. library
    کتب خانہ

Grammar Point: *in* and *at* with locations

Use *in* when you are inside the building. *I am in (inside) the bank.* Use *at* to describe your general location. *I am at the bank.*

Pair practice. Make new conversations.

A: *I'm in the <u>bank</u>. Where are you?*
B: *I'm at the <u>bank</u>, too, but I'm outside.*
A: *OK. I'll meet you there.*

125

شہر کی سڑکیں

1. stadium
اسٹیڈیم

2. construction site
تعمیراتی مقام

3. factory
فیکٹری

4. car dealership
کار کی تجارت

5. mosque
مسجد

6. movie theater
سنیما ہال

7. shopping mall
چھت پڑا ہوا بڑا بازار

8. furniture store
فرنیچر کی دکان

9. school
اسکول

10. gym
ورزش گاہ

11. coffee shop
کافی کی دکان

12. motel
موٹل، موٹر گاڑیوں سے سفر کرنے والوں کے لیے ہوٹل

Ways to state your destination using *to* and *to the*
Use **to** for schools, churches, and synagogues.
*I'm going **to** <u>school</u>.*
Use **to the** for all other locations. *I have to go **to the** <u>bakery</u>.*

Pair practice. Make new conversations.
A: *Where are you going today?*
B: *I'm going to <u>school</u>. How about you?*
A: *I have to go to the <u>bakery</u>.*

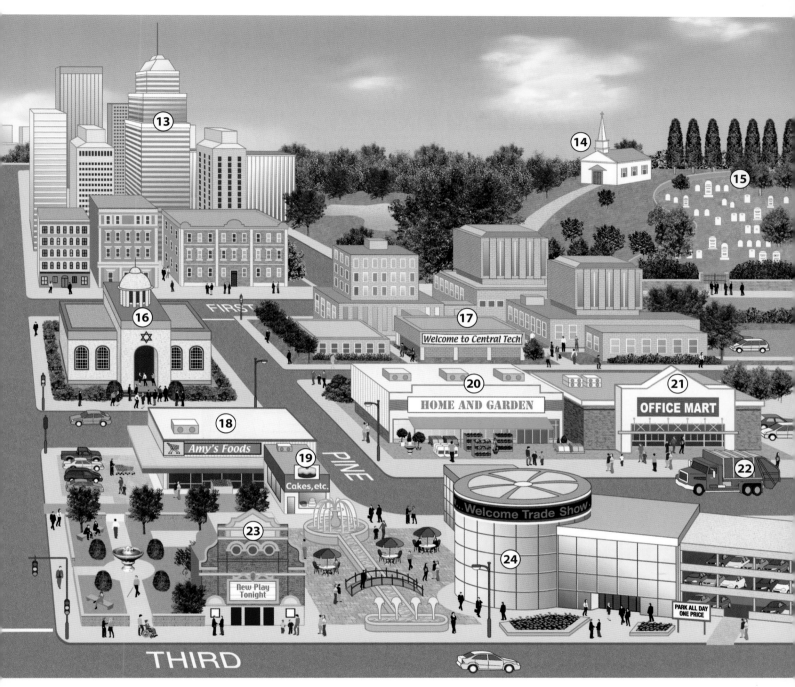

13. **skyscraper / high-rise**
کثیر منزلہ / فلک بوس عمارت

14. **church**
گرجا گھر

15. **cemetery**
قبرستان

16. **synagogue**
یہودی عبادت گاہ

17. **community college**
مقامی لوگوں کے لیے درسگاہ

18. **supermarket**
خردہ فروشی کی خود خدمتی دکان

19. **bakery**
بیکری

20. **home improvement store**
گھر کے آرائشی سامان کی دکان

21. **office supply store**
دفتری سامان کی فرہمی کی دکان

22. **garbage truck**
کوڑا اٹھانے والا ٹرک

23. **theater**
تھئیٹر

24. **convention center**
اجلاس کا مرکز

Ways to give locations

The mall is on 2nd Street.
The mall is on the corner of 2nd and Elm.
The mall is next to the movie theater.

Ask your classmates. Share the answers.

1. Where's your favorite coffee shop?
2. Where's your favorite supermarket?
3. Where's your favorite movie theater?

1. **laundromat**
   گابکوں کے لیے کپڑا دھلنے کی خود خدمت جگہ

2. **dry cleaners**
   ڈرائی کلینرز

3. **convenience store**
   زائد اوقات میں کھلنے والی بڑی دکان

4. **pharmacy**
   دواؤں کی دکان

5. **parking space**
   پارکنگ کی جگہ

6. **handicapped parking**
   معذوروں کی پارکنگ

7. **corner**
   کونا

8. **traffic light**
   ٹریفک لائٹ

9. **bus**
   بس

10. **fast food restaurant**
    جلدی سے تیار کھانے کا ریستوراں

11. **drive-thru window**
    گاڑی سے ہی خریداری کرنے کی کھڑکی

12. **newsstand**
    اخبار اور رسائل کی دکان

13. **mailbox**
    ڈاک صندوق

14. **pedestrian**
    پیدل چلنے والا

15. **crosswalk**
    سڑک پار کرنے کی جگہ

A. **cross** the street
   سڑک پار کیجیے

B. **wait for** the light
   روشنی کا انتظار کیجیے

C. **jaywalk**
   لاپرواہی سے سڑک پر چلنا

Pair practice. Make new conversations.

A: *I have a lot of errands to do today.*
B: *Me, too. First, I'm going to the laundromat.*
A: *I'll see you there after I stop at the copy center.*

Think about it. Discuss.

1. Which businesses are good to have in a neighborhood? Why?
2. Would you like to own a small business? If yes, what kind? If no, why not?

16. bus stop بس اسٹاپ	**22. bike** سائیکل	**28. cart** ٹھیلا
17. donut shop نان ختائی کی دکان	**23. pay phone** سکہ ڈال کر بات کرنے والا فون	**29. street vendor** خوانچہ فروش
18. copy center فوٹو کاپی کرنے کی دکان	**24. sidewalk** بغلی راستہ	**30. childcare center** مرکز نگہداشت اطفال
19. barbershop حجام کی دکان	**25. parking meter** گاڑی کھڑی کرنے کا خودکار میٹر	**D. ride** a bike سائیکل چلائیے
20. video store ویڈیو کی دکان	**26. street sign** سڑک پر لگی علامات	**E. park** the car کار پارک کیجیے
21. curb جنگلہ یا گھیرا	**27. fire hydrant** آگ بجھانے کے لیے پانی حاصل کرنے کا نلکا	**F. walk** a dog کتے کو ٹہلائیے

More vocabulary

neighborhood: the area close to your home
do errands: to make a short trip from your home to buy or pick up things

Ask your classmates. Share the answers.

1. What errands do you do every week?
2. What stores do you go to in your neighborhood?
3. What things can you buy from a street vendor?

1. **music store**
موسیقی کی دکان

2. **jewelry store**
زیورات کی دکان

3. **nail salon**
ناخن کی آرائش کا سیلون

4. **bookstore**
کتابوں کی دکان

5. **toy store**
کھلونے کی دکان

6. **pet store**
پالتو جانوروں کی دکان

7. **card store**
کارڈ و تحائف کی دکان

8. **florist**
گل فروش

9. **optician**
عینک ساز

10. **shoe store**
جوتے کی دکان

11. **play area**
کھیلنے کا علاقہ

12. **guest services**
مہمانوں کی خدمات

More vocabulary

beauty shop: hair salon

men's store: men's clothing store

gift shop: a store that sells t-shirts, mugs, and other small gifts

Pair practice. Make new conversations.

A: *Where is the florist?*

B: *It's on the first floor, next to the optician.*

13. department store
خرید و فروخت کی بڑی دکان
14. travel agency
سفر میں مدد کرنے والی ایجنسی
15. food court
کھانے کی دکانوں کا مجموعہ
16. ice cream shop
آئس کریم کی دکان

17. candy store
منہائی کی گولیوں اور ٹافیوں کی دکان
18. hair salon
بالوں کی آرائش کا سیلون
19. maternity store
زچگی کے سامان کی دکان
20. electronics store
الیکٹرونک اشیاء کی دکان

21. elevator
رافع مشین
22. cell phone kiosk
سیل فون کھوکھا
23. escalator
رواں یا متحرک زینہ
24. directory
ڈائرکٹری

Ways to talk about plans

Let's go to the <u>card store</u>.
I have to go to the <u>card store</u>.
I want to go to the <u>card store</u>.

Role play. Talk to a friend at the mall.

A: *Let's go to the <u>card store</u>. I need to buy <u>a card</u> for <u>Maggie's birthday</u>.*
B: *OK, but can we go to the <u>shoe store</u> next?*

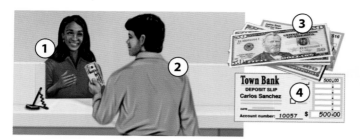

1. teller
نقدی لینے اور ادا کرنے پر مامور شخص

2. customer
گاہک

3. deposit
نقدی جمع کرنا

4. deposit slip
نقدی جمع کرنے کی پرچی

5. security guard
محافظ

6. vault
تجوری

7. safety deposit box
حفاظتی جمع کا صندوق

8. valuables
قیمتی اشیاء

Opening an Account کھاتہ کھولنا

9. account manager
اکاؤنٹ منیجر

10. passbook
پاس بک

11. savings account number
بچت کھاتے کا نمبر

12. check book
چیک بک

13. check
چیک

14. checking account number
زیادہ بار بینک سے پیسے نکالنے کا اکاؤنٹ نمبر

15. ATM card
خود کار ادائیگی مشین کارڈ

16. bank statement
بینک کا گوشوارہ

17. balance
بقایا رقم

A. Cash a check.
چیک بھنائیے۔

B. Make a deposit.
رقم جمع کیجیے۔

C. Bank online.
آن لائن بینک کاری کیجیے۔

The ATM (Automated Teller Machine) اے ٹی ایم (خود کار ادائیگی مشین)

D. Insert your ATM card.
اپنا اے ٹی ایم کارڈ داخل کیجیے۔

E. Enter your PIN.*
اپنا پن داخل کیجیے۔

F. Withdraw cash.
نقدی نکالیے۔

G. Remove your card.
اپنا کارڈ نکالیے۔

*PIN = personal identification number

A. get a library card
لائبریری کارڈ حاصل کیجیے

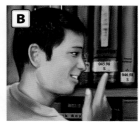

B. look for a book
کتاب تلاش کیجیے

C. check out a book
کتاب باہر لے جائیے

D. return a book
کتاب واپس کیجیے

E. pay a late fine
تاخیر کا جرمانہ ادا کیجیے

1. library clerk
لائبریری کلرک

2. circulation desk
کتابیں جاری اور وصول کرنے کا ڈیسک

3. library patron
لائبریری کا ممبر

4. periodicals
جرائد

5. magazine
رسالہ

6. newspaper
اخبار

7. headline
سرخی

8. atlas
ایٹلس

9. reference librarian
حوالہ جاتی لائبریرین

10. self-checkout
کتابوں کی خود جانچ کرانا

11. online catalog
کتابوں کی آن لائن فہرست

12. picture book
تصویروں والی کتاب

13. biography
سوانح حیات

14. title
عنوان

15. author
مصنف

16. novel
ناول

17. audiobook
آواز میں ریکارڈ کی گئی کتاب

18. videocassette
ویڈیو کیسٹ

19. DVD
ڈی وی ڈی

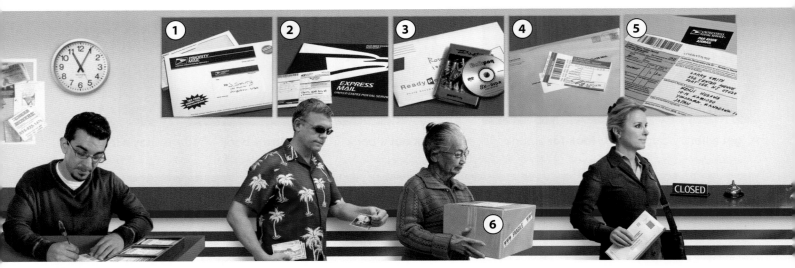

1. **Priority Mail**®
   ترجیحی ڈاک

2. **Express Mail**®
   تیز رفتار ڈاک

3. media mail
   میڈیا کی ڈاک

4. **Certified Mail**™
   اندراج شدہ ڈاک

5. airmail
   ہوائی ڈاک

6. ground post / parcel post
   زمینی ڈاک / پارسل ڈاک

13. letter
    خط

14. envelope
    لفافہ

15. greeting card
    تہنیتی کارڈ

16. post card
    پوسٹ کارڈ

17. package
    کسی شئے کا بند مجموعہ

18. book of stamps
    ٹکٹوں کی کتاب

19. postal forms
    ڈاک فارم

20. letter carrier
    مراسلہ بردار

21. return address
    جوابی پتہ

22. mailing address
    ڈاک کا پتہ

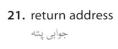

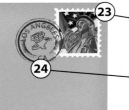

Sonya Enriquez
258 Quentin Avenue
Los Angeles, CA 90068-141

Cindy Lin
807 Glenn Drive
Charlotte, NC 28201

23. stamp
    ٹکٹ

24. postmark
    ڈاک کی مہر

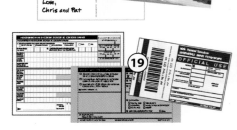

Ways to talk about sending mail

This letter has to get there tomorrow. (**Express Mail**®)
This letter has to arrive in two days. (**Priority Mail**®)
This letter can go in regular mail. (**First Class**)

Pair practice. Make new conversations.

A: Hi. *This letter has to get there tomorrow.*
B: *You can send it by Express Mail*®.
A: OK. *I need a book of stamps,* too.

7. postal clerk
ڈاک کلرک

8. scale
ترازو

9. post office box (PO box)
پوسٹ آفس باکس (پی او باکس)

10. automated postal center (APC)
خود کار ڈاک مرکز (اے پی سی)

11. stamp machine
ٹکٹ لگانے کی مشین

12. mailbox
ڈاک صندوق

Sending a Card کارڈ ارسال کرنا

A. **Write** a note in a card.
کارڈ میں وضاحت لکھیے۔

B. **Address** the envelope.
لفافے پر پتہ لکھیے۔

C. **Put on** a stamp.
ٹکٹ چپکائیے۔

D. **Mail** the card.
کارڈ ڈاک میں ڈالیے۔

E. **Deliver** the card.
کارڈ ڈاک بکس میں پہنچائیے۔

F. **Receive** the card.
کارڈ حاصل کیجیے۔

G. **Read** the card.
کارڈ پڑھیے۔

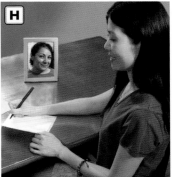

H. **Write** back.
جواب دیجیے۔

More vocabulary

overnight / next day mail: Express Mail®
postage: the cost to send mail
junk mail: mail you don't want

Think about it. Discuss.

1. What kind of mail do you send overnight?
2. Do you want to be a letter carrier? Why or why not?
3. Do you get junk mail? What do you do with it?

1. DMV handbook
موٹر گاڑیوں کے شعبہ کا کتابچہ

2. testing area
آزمائش کا علاقہ

3. DMV clerk
موٹر گاڑی شعبہ کا کلرک

4. photo
فوٹو

5. fingerprint
انگلی کا نشان

6. vision exam
نگاہ کا معائنہ

7. window
کھڑکی

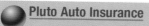

8. proof of insurance
بیمے کا ثبوت

9. driver's license
ڈرائیور لائسنس

10. expiration date
خاتمے کی تاریخ

11. driver's license number
ڈرائیور کا لائسنس نمبر

12. license plate
لائسنس پلیٹ

13. registration sticker / tag
اندراج کا اسٹکر / بلّا

More vocabulary

expire: a license is no good, or **expires**, after the expiration date
renew a license: to apply to keep a license before it expires
vanity plate: a more expensive, personal license plate

Ask your classmates. Share the answers.

1. How far is the DMV from your home?
2. Do you have a driver's license? If yes, when does it expire? If not, do you want one?

136

Getting Your First License اپنا پہلا لائسنس حاصل کرنا

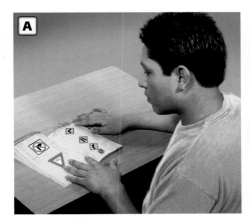

A. Study the handbook.

بینڈبک کا مطالعہ کیجیے۔

B. Take a driver education course.*

ڈرائیور تعلیمی نصاب میں داخلہ لیجیے۔

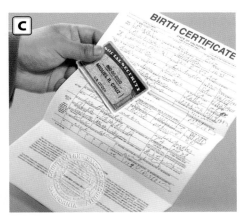

C. Show your identification.

اپنی شناخت دکھائیے۔

D. Pay the application fee.

درخواست فیس ادا کیجیے۔

E. Take a written test.

تحریری امتحان میں شرکت کیجیے۔

F. Get a learner's permit.

آموزگار اجازت نامہ حاصل کیجیے۔

G. Take a driver's training course.*

ڈرائیور کی تربیت کے نصاب میں داخلہ لیجیے۔

H. Pass a driving test.

ڈرائیونگ کا امتحان پاس کیجیے۔

I. Get your license.

اپنا لائسنس حاصل کیجیے۔

*Note: This is not required for drivers 18 and older.

Ways to request more information

What do I do next?
What's the next step?
Where do I go from here?

Role play. Talk to a DMV clerk.

A: *I want to apply for <u>a driver's license</u>.*
B: *Did you <u>study the handbook</u>?*
A: *Yes, I did. <u>What do I do next</u>?*

Federal Government وفاقی حکومت

Legislative Branch
قانون ساز برانچ

1. **U.S. Capitol**
   واشنگٹن کی وہ عمارت جہاں کانگریس کا اجلاس ہوتا ہے

2. **Congress**
   کانگریس

3. **House of Representatives**
   ایوان نمائندگان

4. **congressperson**
   کانگریس نمائندہ

5. **Senate**
   سینیٹ

6. **senator**
   سینیٹ کا ممبر

Executive Branch
ایگزیکیٹو برانچ

7. **White House**
   وہائٹ ہاؤس

8. **president**
   صدر

9. **vice president**
   نائب صدر

10. **Cabinet**
    کابینہ

Judicial Branch
عدلیہ برانچ

11. **Supreme Court**
    عدالت عظمیٰ

12. **justices**
    جج صاحبان

13. **chief justice**
    چیف جسٹس

The Military فوج

14. Army
بری فوج

15. Navy
بحریہ

16. Air Force
فضائیہ

17. Marines
بری و بحری فوج کا تربیت یافتہ کارکن

18. Coast Guard
کوسٹ گارڈ (ساحل محافظ)

19. National Guard
نیشنل گارڈ

State Government صوبائی حکومت

20. governor
گورنر

21. lieutenant governor
لفٹننٹ گورنر

22. state capital
صوبائی دار الحکومت

23. Legislature
قانون ساز ادارہ

24. assemblyperson
ممبر اسمبلی

25. state senator
صوبائی سینیٹ کا ممبر

City Government شہری حکومت

26. mayor
میئر

27. city council
شہری مجلس انتظامیہ

28. councilperson
رکن مجلس انتظامیہ

An Election انتخاب

A. **run for** office
عہدے کے لیے مقابلہ کیجیے

29. political campaign
سیاسی مہم

B. **debate**
بحث و مباحثہ کیجیے

30. opponent
مخالف امیدوار

C. **get elected**
منتخب ہوجائیے

31. election results
انتخاب کے نتائج

D. **serve**
خدمت کیجیے

32. elected official
منتخب عہدے دار

More vocabulary

term: the period of time an elected official serves
political party: a group of people with the same political goals

Think about it. Discuss.

1. Should everyone have to serve in the military? Why or why not?
2. Would you prefer to run for city council or mayor? Why?

139

Responsibilities ذمہ داریاں

A. vote
ووٹ دیجیے

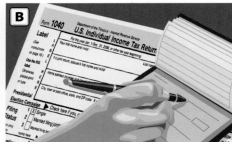

B. pay taxes
ٹیکس ادا کیجیے

C. obey the law
قانون کی تعمیل کیجیے

D. register with Selective Service*
سلیکٹؤ سروس میں اندراج کرائیے

E. serve on a jury
جیوری میں شمولیت کیجیے

F. be informed
باخبر رہیے

Citizenship Requirements شہریت کی شرائط

G. be 18 or older
۱۸ سال یا زیادہ عمر ہونا

H. live in the U.S. for 5 years
یو ایس میں ۵ سال یا زیادہ رہنا

I. take a citizenship test
شہریت سے متعلق امتحان دینا

Rights حقوق

1. peaceful assembly
پُر سکون اجتماع

2. free speech
تقریر کی آزادی

3. freedom of religion
مذہب کی آزادی

4. freedom of the press
پریس کی آزادی

5. fair trial
منصفانہ سماعت

*Note: All males 18 to 26 who live in the U.S. are required to register with Selective Service.

A. arrest a suspect
ملزم کو گرفتار کیجیے
1. police officer
پولس افسر
2. handcuffs
ہتھکڑی

B. hire a lawyer / **hire** an attorney
کسی وکیل / اٹارنی کی خدمات حاصل کیجیے
3. guard
پہرے دار
4. defense attorney
وکیل دفاع

C. appear in court
عدالت میں حاضری دیجیے
5. defendant
مدعا علیہ
6. judge
جج

D. stand trial
سماعت کا سامنا کیجیے
7. courtroom
کمرۂ عدالت
8. jury
جیوری
9. evidence
ثبوت
10. prosecuting attorney
وکیل استغاثہ
11. witness
گواہ
12. court reporter
پیش کار
13. bailiff
نظم اور نگرانی کا چھوٹا افسر

E. convict the defendant
مدعا علیہ کو قصوروار ثابت کیجیے
14. verdict*
فیصلہ

F. sentence the defendant
مدعا علیہ کو سزا سنائیے

G. go to jail / **go** to prison
جیل / قید خانے میں جائیے
15. convict / prisoner
سزا یافتہ / قیدی

H. be released
رہائی پائیے

*****Note:** There are two possible verdicts, "guilty" and "not guilty."

Look at the pictures.
Describe what happened.

A: *The police officer arrested a suspect.*
B: *He put handcuffs on him.*

Think about it. Discuss.
1. Would you want to serve on a jury? Why or why not?
2. Look at the crimes on page 142. What sentence would you give for each crime? Why?

1. vandalism
   غنڈہ گردی
2. burglary
   چوری

3. assault
   حملہ
4. gang violence
   گروہی تشدد

5. drunk driving
   نشے کی حالت میں گاڑی چلانا
6. illegal drugs
   غیر قانونی نشیلی دوائیں

7. arson
   آتش زنی
8. shoplifting
   اٹھائی گیری

9. identity theft
   شناخت کی چوری
10. victim
    مظلوم

11. mugging
    ریزنی
12. murder
    قتل
13. gun
    بندوق

More vocabulary

steal: to take money or things from someone illegally
commit a crime: to do something illegal
criminal: someone who does something illegal

Think about it. Discuss.

1. Is there too much crime on TV or in the movies? Explain.
2. How can communities help stop crime?

A. Walk with a friend.

کسی دوست کے ساتھ ٹھلیے۔

B. Stay on well-lit streets.

اچھی روشنی والی سڑک استعمال کیجیے۔

C. Conceal your PIN number.

اپنا پن نمبر چھپائیے۔

D. Protect your purse or wallet.

اپنے پرس یا بٹوے کی **حفاظت** کیجیے۔

E. Lock your doors.

اپنے دروازوں میں **تالا** لگائیے۔

F. Don't **open** your door to strangers.

اجنبیوں کو گھر میں نہ آنے دیجیے۔

G. Don't **drink** and **drive**.

شراب پی کر گاڑی نہ چلائیے۔

H. Shop on secure websites.

محفوظ ویب سائٹوں سے خریداری کیجیے۔

I. Be aware of your surroundings.

اپنے آس پاس سے باخبر رہیے۔

J. Report suspicious packages.

مشکوک پیکٹوں کی اطلاع دیجیے۔

K. Report crimes to the police.

پولس کو جرائم کی اطلاع دیجیے۔

L. Join a Neighborhood Watch.

"پڑوس پر نظر رکھنے والی جماعت" میں شمولیت کیجیے۔

More vocabulary

sober: not drunk

designated drivers: sober drivers who drive drunk people home safely

Ask your classmates. Share the answers.

1. Do you feel safe in your neighborhood?
2. Look at the pictures. Which of these things do you do?
3. What other things do you do to stay safe?

1. lost child
   گم شدہ بچہ

2. car accident
   کار کا حادثہ

3. airplane crash
   ہوائی جہاز کا حادثہ

4. explosion
   دھماکہ

5. earthquake
   زلزلہ

6. mudslide
   توده کهسکنا

7. forest fire
   جنگل میں آگ

8. fire
   آگ

9. firefighter
   آگ بجھانے والا فرد

10. fire truck
    آگ بجھانے والا ٹرک

Ways to report an emergency

First, give your name. *My name is Tim Johnson.*
Then, state the emergency and give the address.
There was a car accident at 219 Elm Street.

Role play. Call 911.

A: *911 Emergency Operator.*
B: *My name is Lisa Diaz. There is a fire at 323 Oak Street. Please hurry!*

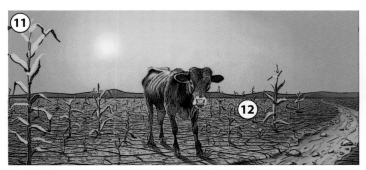

11. drought
خشک سالی

12. famine
قحط

13. blizzard
برفیلی ہواؤں کا طوفان

14. hurricane
آندھی

15. tornado
تیز آندھی

16. volcanic eruption
آتش فشاں کا پھٹ پڑنا

17. tidal wave / tsunami
مدوجزر کی لہر / سونامی

18. avalanche
پہاڑوں پر برف کا طوفان

19. flood
سیلاب

20. search and rescue team
تلاش اور بچاؤ کی ٹیم

Ask your classmates. Share the answers.

1. Which natural disaster worries you the most?

2. Which natural disaster worries you the least?

3. Which disasters are common in your local area?

Think about it. Discuss.

1. What organizations can help you in an emergency?

2. What are some ways to prepare for natural disasters?

3. Where would you go in an emergency?

145

Before an Emergency کسی ہنگامی حالت سے پہلے

A. **Plan** for an emergency.
ہنگامی حالت سے نبٹنے کا منصوبہ بنائیے۔

1. meeting place
ملنے کی جگہ

2. out-of-state contact
دور دراز کا رابطہ

3. escape route
بچ نکلنے کا راستہ

4. gas shut-off valve
گیس بند کرنے کا والو

5. evacuation route
انخلاء کا راستہ

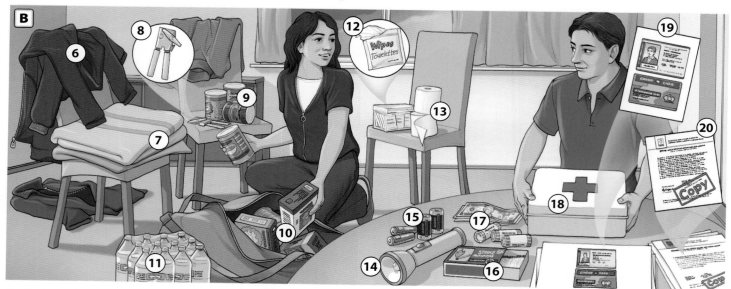

B. **Make** a disaster kit.
حفاظتی اشیاء کا بکسہ تیار کیجیے۔

6. warm clothes
گرم کپڑے

7. blankets
کمبل

8. can opener
ڈبہ کھولنے کا آلہ

9. canned food
ڈبہ بند غذا

10. packaged food
بند کیا ہوا غذا کا ڈبہ

11. bottled water
بوتل بند پانی

12. moist towelettes
بھیگے ہوئے چھوٹے تولیے

13. toilet paper
طہارت کا کاغذ

14. flashlight
ٹارچ

15. batteries
بیٹریاں

16. matches
ماچس

17. cash and coins
نقدی اور سکّے

18. first aid kit
فوری طبی امداد کا بکسہ

19. copies of ID and credit cards
شناخت اور کریڈٹ کارڈوں کی نقلیں

20. copies of important papers
اہم کاغذات کی نقلیں

Pair practice. Make new conversations.

A: *What do we need for our disaster kit?*
B: *We need _blankets_ and _matches_.*
A: *I think we also need _batteries_.*

Ask your classmates. Share the answers.

1. Who would you call first after an emergency?
2. Do you have escape and evacuation routes planned?
3. Are you a calm person in case of an emergency?

During an Emergency کسی ہنگامی حالت کے دوران

C. Watch the weather.
موسم کا مشاہدہ کیجیے۔

D. Pay attention to warnings.
انتباہات پر توجہ دیجیے۔

E. Remain calm.
پُرسکون رہیے۔

F. Follow directions.
ہدایات پر عمل کیجیے۔

G. Help people with disabilities.
معذوری سے متاثر لوگوں کی مدد کیجیے۔

H. Seek shelter.
پناہ تلاش کیجیے۔

I. Stay away from windows.
کھڑکیوں سے دور رہیے۔

J. Take cover.
آڑ میں رہیے۔

K. Evacuate the area.
علاقے سے لوگوں کو نکالیے۔

After an Emergency ہنگامی حالت کے بعد

L. Call out-of-state contacts.
دور دراز رابطوں کو فون کیجیے۔

M. Clean up debris.
ملبے کو صاف کیجیے۔

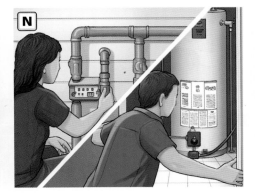

N. Inspect utilities.
استعمال کی چیزوں کا معائنہ کیجیے۔

Ways to say you're OK
I'm fine.
We're OK here.
Everything's under control.

Ways to say you need help
We need help.
Someone is hurt.
I'm injured. Please get help.

Role play. Prepare for an emergency.
A: They just issued *a hurricane* warning.
B: OK. We need to stay calm and follow directions.
A: What do we need to do first?

1. graffiti
اشتہار

2. litter
کوڑا کرکٹ

3. streetlight
سڑک کی روشنی

4. hardware store
ہارڈ وینئر اسٹور

5. petition
مقدمہ

A. **give** a speech
تقریر کیجیے

B. **applaud**
تعریف کیجیے

C. **change**
تبدیل کیجیے

Look at the pictures. What do you see?

Answer the questions.

1. What were the problems on Main Street?

2. What was the petition for?

3. Why did the city council applaud?

4. How did the people change the street?

📖 Read the story.

Community Cleanup

Marta Lopez has a donut shop on Main Street. One day she looked at her street and was very upset. She saw graffiti on her donut shop and the other stores. Litter was everywhere. All the streetlights were broken. Marta wanted to fix the lights and clean up the street.

Marta started a petition about the streetlights. Five hundred people signed it. Then she gave a speech to the city council. The council members voted to repair the streetlights. Everyone applauded. Marta was happy, but her work wasn't finished.

Next, Marta asked for volunteers to clean up Main Street. The hardware store manager gave the volunteers free paint. Marta gave them free donuts and coffee. The volunteers painted and cleaned. They changed Main Street. Now Main Street is beautiful and Marta is proud.

Think about it.

1. What are some problems in your community? How can people help?

2. Imagine you are Marta. What do you say in your speech to the city council?

1. car
کار

2. passenger
مسافر

3. taxi
ٹیکسی

4. motorcycle
موٹر سائیکل

5. street
سڑک

6. truck
ٹرک

7. train
ریل گاڑی

8. (air)plane
جہاز (ہوائی)

Listen and point. Take turns.

A: *Point to the motorcycle*.
B: *Point to the truck*.
A: *Point to the train*.

Dictate to your partner. Take turns.

A: *Write motorcycle*.
B: *Could you repeat that for me?*
A: *Motorcycle. M-o-t-o-r-c-y-c-l-e*.

9. helicopter
بیلی کاپٹر

10. airport
ہوائی اڈہ

11. subway station
زیر زمین اسٹیشن

12. subway
زیر زمین راستہ

13. bus stop
بس کا عارضی کھڑا کرنا

14. bus
بس

15. bicycle
دو پہیہ سائیکل

SUBWAY

Mario's ITALIAN DELI

Ways to talk about using transportation

Use **take** for buses, trains, subways, taxis, planes, and helicopters. Use **drive** for cars and trucks. Use **ride** for bicycles and motorcycles.

Pair practice. Make new conversations.

A: *How do you get to school?*
B: *I take the bus. How about you?*
A: *I ride a bicycle to school.*

151

A Bus Stop بس اسٹاپ

BUS 10 Northbound

Main	Elm	Oak
6:00	6:10	6:13
6:30	6:40	6:43
7:00	7:10	7:13
7:30	7:40	7:43

New York City Transit
Transfer
◀ Going your way

1. bus route
   بس کا راستہ
2. fare
   کرایہ
3. rider
   سواری کرنے والا
4. schedule
   نظام الاوقات
5. transfer
   منتقلی ٹکٹ

A Subway Station ایک زیر زمین اسٹیشن

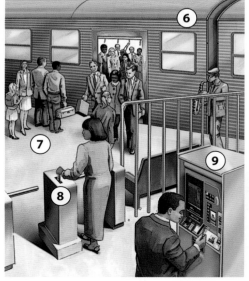

MTA RED LINE
OPENING DAY
JUNE 24, 2000
1 FARE
NORTH HOLLYWOOD

MetroCard

6. subway car
   زیر زمین چلنے والی گاڑی
7. platform
   پلیٹ فارم
8. turnstile
   صرف ایک شخص کے
   گذرنے کا خودکار دروازہ
9. vending machine
   خودکار ٹکٹ مشین
10. token
    ٹوکن
11. fare card
    کرایے کا کارڈ

A Train Station ریل گاڑی کا اسٹیشن

15. HART DAVIS/DAMON
From
DOVER, NH
To
BOSTON NRTH STA,MA
Carrier Train Date
2V 684 17FEB03
Accom Space/Car
2V BUSINESS CL
Form of Payment
AP XXXX0456791 Ax

16. Fresno → Los Angeles

17. Fresno → Los Angeles

12. ticket window
    ٹکٹ کھڑکی
13. conductor
    کنڈکٹر
14. track
    پٹری
15. ticket
    ٹکٹ
16. one-way trip
    یک طرفہ سفر
17. round trip
    دو طرفہ سفر

Airport Transportation ہوائی اڈے کے ذرائع نقل و حمل

TAXIS
TAXI
J&J Hotel

18. taxi stand
    ٹیکسی اسٹینڈ
19. shuttle
    آنے جانے والی بس
20. town car
    شہری استعمال کی چھوٹی کار
21. taxi driver
    ٹیکسی ڈرائیور
22. taxi license
    ٹیکسی لائسنس
23. meter
    گاڑی کے کرایہ کا میٹر

More vocabulary

hail a taxi: to raise your hand to get a taxi
miss the bus: to get to the bus stop after the bus leaves

Ask your classmates. Share the answers.

1. Is there a subway system in your city?
2. Do you ever take taxis? When?
3. Do you ever take the bus? Where?

A. go under the bridge
پل کے نیچے سے جائیے

B. go over the bridge
پل کے اوپر سے جائیے

C. walk up the steps
سیڑھیوں سے اوپر چڑھیے

D. walk down the steps
سیڑھیوں سے نیچے اتریے

E. get into the taxi
ٹیکسی کے اندر بیٹھیے

F. get out of the taxi
ٹیکسی سے باہر نکلیے

G. run across the street
سڑک کے آرپار دوڑیے

H. run around the corner
کونے کے اطراف دوڑیے

I. get on the highway
شاہراہ پر آئیے

J. get off the highway
شاہراہ سے نکلیے

K. drive through the tunnel
سرنگ سے گاڑی لے جائیے

Grammar Point: *into, out of, on, off*

Use *get into* for taxis and cars.
Use *get on* for buses, trains, planes, and highways.

Use *get out of* for taxis and cars.
Use *get off* for buses, trains, planes, and highways.

Traffic Signs

نقل و حمل سے متعلق علامات

1. stop
رُکیے

2. do not enter / wrong way
ادھر سے نہ جائیں / غلط راستہ

3. one way
یک طرفہ راستہ

4. speed limit
رفتار کی حد

5. U-turn OK
واپسی گھومنے کی اجازت

6. no outlet / dead end
باہر نکلنے کا راستہ نہیں / راستہ بند

7. right turn only
صرف دائیں طرف مڑ سکتے ہیں

8. no left turn
بائیں طرف مڑنا منع ہے

9. yield
دوسری گاڑی کو گزرنے دیجیے

10. merge
مدغم ٹریفک

11. no parking
گاڑی کھڑی کرنا منع ہے

12. handicapped parking
معذور افراد کے لیے پارکنگ

13. pedestrian crossing
پیدل چلنے والوں کا راستہ

14. railroad crossing
ریل کے راستے سے گزرنے والی سڑک

15. school crossing
اسکول کراسنگ

16. road work
سڑک پر کام ہو رہا ہے

17. U.S. route / highway marker
یو ایس شاہراہ / شاہراہ کا اشارہ

18. hospital
اسپتال

Pair practice. Make new conversations.

A: *Watch out! The sign says <u>no left turn</u>.*
B: *Sorry, I was looking at the <u>stop</u> sign.*
A: *That's OK. Just be careful!*

Ask your classmates. Share the answers.

1. How many traffic signs are on your street?
2. What's the speed limit on your street?
3. What traffic signs are the same in your native country?

Directions سمتیں

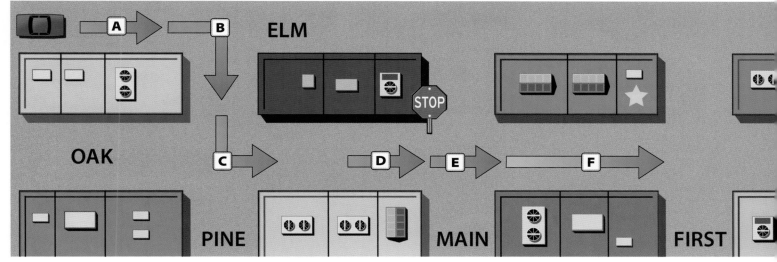

ELM

STOP

OAK

PINE   MAIN   FIRST

A. Go straight on Elm Street.
ایلم اسٹریٹ پر سیدھے جائیے۔

B. Turn right on Pine Street.
پائن اسٹریٹ پر دائنے مڑیے۔

C. Turn left on Oak Street.
اوک اسٹریٹ پربائیں مڑیے۔

D. Stop at the corner.
کونے پررکیے۔

E. Go past Main Street.
مین اسٹریٹ سے گذریے۔

F. Go one block to First Street.
فرسٹ اسٹریٹ تک ایک بلاک جائیے۔

Maps نقشے

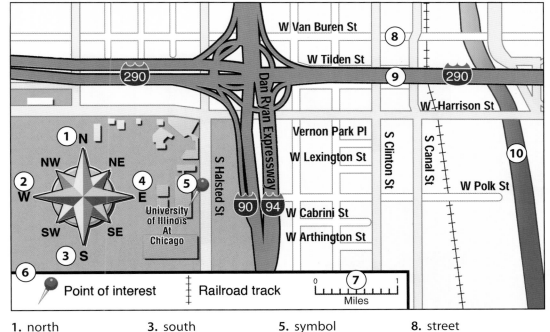

W Van Buren St
W Tilden St
290
Dan Ryan Expressway
W Harrison St
Vernon Park Pl
W Lexington St
S Clinton St
S Canal St
W Polk St
S Halsted St
90 94
W Cabrini St
W Arthington St
University of Illinois At Chicago

N
NW   NE
W   E
SW   SE
S

(1) (2) (3) (4) (5) (6) (7) (8) (9) (10)

📍 Point of interest   ┼ Railroad track   0 ___ 1 Miles

1. north شمال	3. south جنوب	5. symbol علامت	8. street سڑک
2. west مغرب	4. east مشرق	6. key کلید	9. highway شاہراہ
		7. scale پیمانہ	10. river ندی

11. GPS (global positioning system)
جی پی ایس (کرۂ جاتی مقام بندی نظام)

12. Internet map
انٹرنیٹ نقشہ

Role play. Ask for directions.

A: *I'm lost. I need to get to* <u>*Elm and Pine*</u>.
B: *Go* <u>*straight on Oak*</u> *and* <u>*make a right on Pine*</u>.
A: *Thanks so much.*

Ask your classmates. Share the answers.

1. How often do you use Internet maps? GPS? paper maps?
2. What was the last map you used? Why?

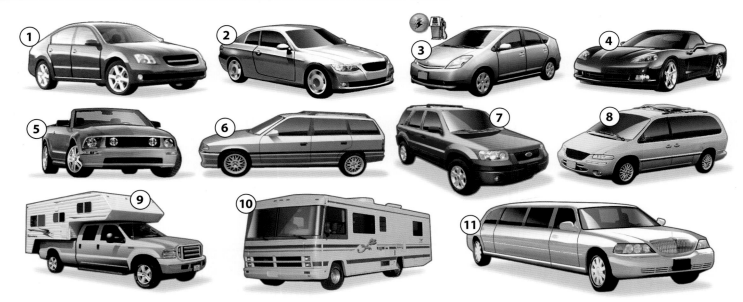

1. 4-door car / sedan
   ۴-دروازوں والی کار / سیڈان

2. 2-door car / coupe
   ۲-دروازوں والی کار / کوپے

3. hybrid
   مخلوط کار

4. sports car
   اسپورٹس کار

5. convertible
   قابل تبدیل

6. station wagon
   اسٹیشن ویگن

7. SUV (sport–utility vehicle)
   ایس یو وی (کھیلوں میں مستعمل گاڑی)

8. minivan
   چھوٹی وین

9. camper
   سفر کے لیے بڑی موٹر گاڑی

10. RV (recreational vehicle)
    آروی (آرائش و آسائش والی موٹر گاڑی)

11. limousine / limo
    پر تکلف گاڑی (لیمو)

12. pickup truck
    راستہ میں سے سامان اٹھانے والا ٹرک

13. cargo van
    کارگو وین

14. tow truck
    کھینچنے والا ٹرک

15. tractor trailer / semi
    ٹریکٹر ٹریلر / سیمی

16. cab
    گاڑی میں کرین ڈرائیور کی نشست والی جگہ

17. trailer
    کھینچ کر لے جانی جانے والی گاڑی

18. moving van
    مال بردار گاڑی

19. dump truck
    مال ادھر ادھر لے جانے والا ٹرک

20. tank truck
    ٹینک لے جانے والا ٹرک

21. school bus
    اسکول بس

Pair practice. Make new conversations.

A: *I have a new car!*
B: *Did you get a hybrid?*
A: *Yes, but I really wanted a sports car.*

More vocabulary

make: the name of the company that makes the car
model: the style of the car

Buying a Used Car پرانی کار خریدنا

A. Look at car ads.
کاروں کے اشتہارات دیکھیے۔

B. Ask the seller about the car.
بیچنے والے سے کار کے بارے میں پوچھیے۔

C. Take the car to a mechanic.
کار کو کسی مستری کے پاس لے جائیے۔

D. Negotiate a price.
قیمت طے کیجیے۔

E. Get the title from the seller.
بیچنے والے سے ملکیت کے کاغذات حاصل کیجیے۔

F. Register the car.
کار کا اندراج کرائیے۔

Taking Care of Your Car اپنی کار کی دیکھ بھال کرنا

G. Fill the tank with gas.
کار کے ٹینک میں گیس بھروائیے۔

H. Check the oil.
تیل کی جانچ کیجیے۔

I. Put in coolant.
دافع حرارت سیال ڈالیے۔

J. Go for a smog check.*
کار کو آلودگی کی جانچ کرانے لے جائیے۔

*smog check = emissions test

K. Replace the windshield wipers.
سامنے کے شیشہ پونچھ بدلیے۔

L. Fill the tires with air.
ٹائروں میں ہوا بھروائیے۔

Ways to request service

Please check the oil.
Could you fill the tank?
Put in coolant, please.

Think about it. Discuss.

1. What's good and bad about a used car?
2. Do you like to negotiate car prices? Why?
3. Do you know any good mechanics? Why are they good?

At the Dealer

بیچنے والے ڈیلر کے پاس

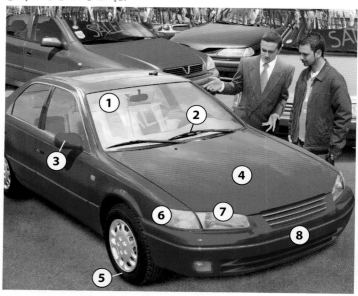

At the Mechanic

مستری کے پاس

1. **windshield**
   سامنے کا شیشہ

2. **windshield wipers**
   سامنے کے شیشے کے پونچھے

3. **sideview mirror**
   بغل کے منظر کا آئینہ

4. **hood**
   انجن کا خول

5. **tire**
   ٹائر

6. **turn signal**
   مڑنے کا اشارہ کرنے والی روشنیاں

7. **headlight**
   مرکزی روشنیاں

8. **bumper**
   ٹکر روک

9. **hubcap / wheel cover**
   کار کے پہیے کا ڈھکنا

10. **gas tank**
    پٹرول کی ٹنکی

11. **trunk**
    ڈکی

12. **license plate**
    نمبر کی پلیٹ

13. **tail light**
    پیچھے کی بتی

14. **brake light**
    بریک لگانے پر جلنے والی روشنی

15. **tail pipe**
    دھواں خارج کرنے والی نلکی

16. **muffler**
    موٹر کی خاموش گر نلکی

Under the Hood

انجن کے خول کے نیچے

Inside the Trunk

ڈکی کے اندر

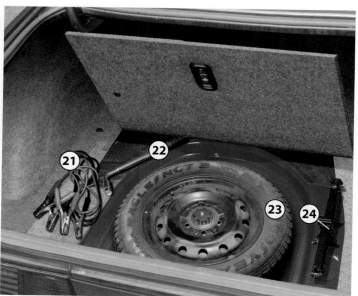

17. **fuel injection system**
    تیل پہنچانے والا نظام

18. **engine**
    انجن

19. **radiator**
    حرارت ربا

20. **battery**
    بیٹری

21. **jumper cables**
    عام طریقے کے علاوہ کسی اور طریقے
    سے گاڑی اسٹارٹ کرنے والا تار

22. **lug wrench**
    ڈھبریاں کھولنے کسنے کا اوزار

23. **spare tire**
    فاضل ٹائر

24. **jack**
    گاڑی اٹھانے والا آلہ

The Dashboard and Instrument Panel
گاڑی کے اگلے حصے میں گاڑی چلانے اور آلات وغیرہ رکھنے کا حصہ

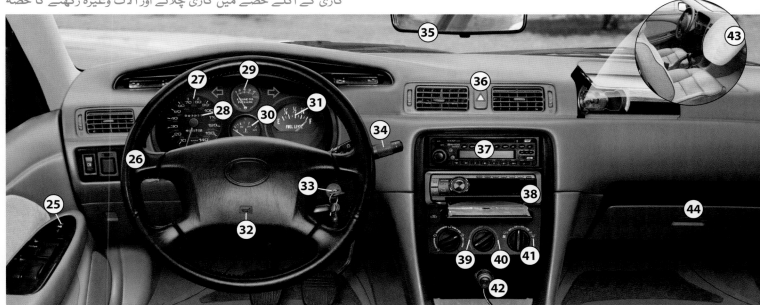

25. door lock	**30.** temperature gauge	**35.** rearview mirror	**40.** heater
دروازے کا تالا	حرارت پیما آلہ	عقبی منظر کا آئینہ	گرم کاری نظام
26. steering wheel	**31.** gas gauge	**36.** hazard lights	**41.** defroster
گاڑی چلانے یا موڑنے کا پہیہ	پیٹرول پیما آلہ	خطرے کی روشنیاں	برف پگھلانے والا نظام
27. speedometer	**32.** horn	**37.** radio	**42.** power outlet
رفتار پیما میٹر	بارن	ریڈیو	بجلی کا پلگ
28. odometer	**33.** ignition	**38.** CD player	**43.** air bag
فاصلہ پیما میٹر	گاڑی اسٹارٹ کرنا	سی ڈی پلیئر	حفاظتی غبارے
29. oil gauge	**34.** turn signal	**39.** air conditioner	**44.** glove compartment
تیل پیما آلہ	مڑنے کا اشارہ کرنے والی روشنی	ایئر کنڈیشنر	دستانے رکھنے کا خانہ

An Automatic Transmission
خودکار ٹرانسمشن

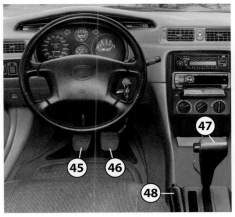

A Manual Transmission
دستی ٹرانسمشن

Inside the Car
کار کے اندر

45. brake pedal	**47.** gear shift	**49.** clutch	**51.** front seat	**53.** child safety seat
بریک لگانے والا پیڈل	گیئر بدلنے والا دستہ	کلچ	آگے کی سیٹ	بچے کی حفاظتی سیٹ
46. gas pedal / accelerator	**48.** hand brake	**50.** stick shift	**52.** seat belt	**54.** backseat
گیس پیڈل / رفتار بڑھانے والا پیڈل	ہاتھ سے لگانے والا بریک	گیئر اور کلچ کی دستی منتقلی	سیٹ پر باندھنے والی پٹی	پیچھے کی سیٹ

In the Airline Terminal ایئر لائن ٹرمنل کے اندر

At the Security Checkpoint
حفاظتی جانچ سے گزرنا

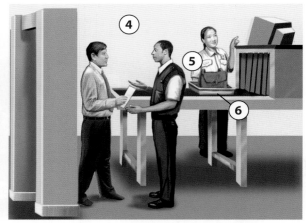

1. skycap
   ہوائی اڈے پر تعینات قلی

2. check-in kiosk
   آمد درج کرانے کی جگہ

3. ticket agent
   ٹکٹ جانچ کرنے والا

4. screening area
   جانچ کرنے کی جگہ

5. TSA* agent / security screener
   ٹی ایس اے ایجنٹ / حفاظتی جانچ کار

6. bin
   کوڑے دان

Taking a Flight پرواز پکڑنا

A. **Check in** electronically.
برقی طریقے سے اپنی آمد کی جانچ کرائیے۔

B. **Check** your bags.
اپنے تھیلوں کی جانچ کرائیے۔

C. **Show** your boarding pass and ID.
اپنا بورڈنگ پاس اور شناخت دکھائیے۔

D. **Go through** security.
حفاظتی جانچ سے گذریے۔

E. **Board** the plane.
ہوائی جہاز پر سوار ہو جائیے۔

F. **Find** your seat.
اپنی نشست تلاش کیجیے۔

G. **Stow** your carry-on bag.
ساتھ لے جانے والا تھیلا اوپر خانے میں رکھیے۔

H. **Fasten** your seat belt.
اپنی نشستی پٹی باندھیے۔

I. **Turn off** your cell phone.
اپنا سیل فون بند کر دیجیے۔

J. **Take off**. / **Leave**.
اڑان بھریے / روانہ ہو جائیے۔

K. **Land**. / **Arrive**.
اتریے / پہنچیے۔

L. **Claim** your baggage.
اپنے سامان کا مطالبہ کیجیے۔

* Transportation Security Administration

At the Gate پھاٹک پر

On the Airplane ہوائی جہاز پر

At Customs کسٹمز پر

7. arrival and departure monitors
آمد اور روانگی کے نگران

8. gate
پھاٹک

9. boarding area
بیٹھنے کی جگہ

10. cockpit
ہوائی جہاز میں پائلٹ کا کمرہ

11. pilot
ہوائی جہاز اڑانے والا

12. flight attendant
دوران اڑان معاون

13. overhead compartment
اوپر سامان رکھنے کے خانے

14. emergency exit
ہنگامی دروازہ

15. passenger
مسافر

16. declaration form
ظاہر کنندہ فارم

17. customs officer
کسٹمز افسر

18. luggage / bag
سامان / تھیلا

19. e-ticket
برقی ٹکٹ

20. boarding pass
داخلے کا پاس

21. tray table
سامان رکھنے کی میز

22. turbulence
موسم کی خرابی کی وجہ سے ہچکولے

23. baggage carousel
سامان لے جانے والی رواں پٹی

24. oxygen mask
آکسیجن کی نقاب

25. life vest
زندگی بچانے والی حفاظتی جیکٹ

26. emergency card
ایمرجنسی کارڈ

27. reclined seat
پیچھے جھکی ہوئی سیٹ

28. upright seat
سیدھی کھڑی سیٹ

29. on-time
بروقت

30. delayed flight
تاخیر سے آنے یا جانے والی پرواز

More vocabulary

departure time: the time the plane takes off
arrival time: the time the plane lands
direct flight: a trip with no stops

Pair practice. Make new conversations.

A: *Excuse me. Where do I <u>check in</u>?*
B: *At the <u>check-in kiosk</u>.*
A: *Thanks.*

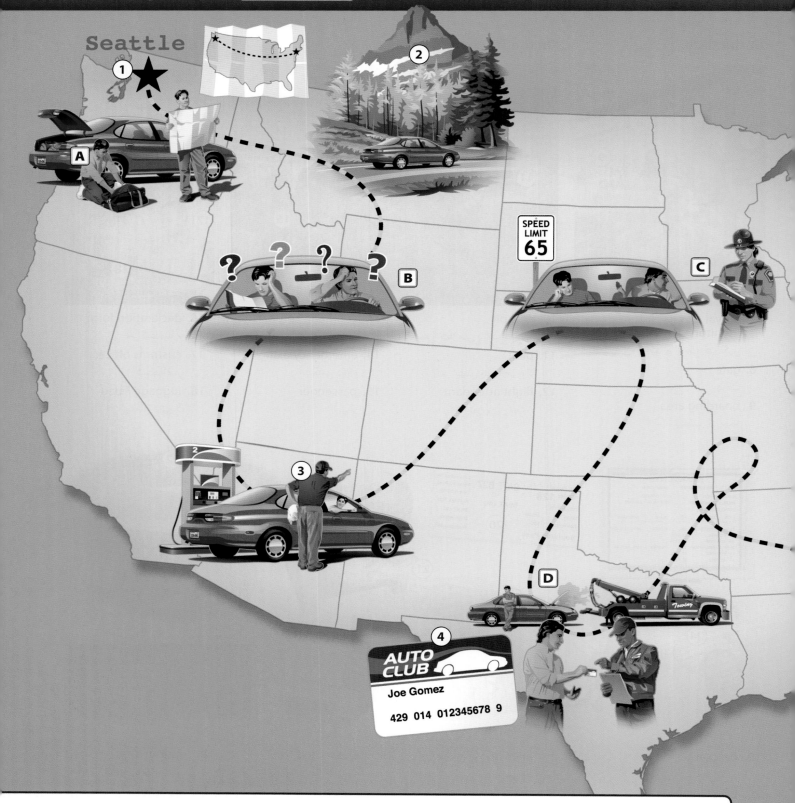

Seattle

SPEED LIMIT 65

AUTO CLUB

Joe Gomez

429 014 012345678 9

1. starting point
نقطۂ آغاز

2. scenery
قدرتی منظر

3. gas station attendant
گیس اسٹیشن معاون

4. auto club card
آٹو کلب کارڈ

5. destination
منزل

A. pack
سامان باندھیے

B. get lost
راستہ بھول جانا

C. get a speeding ticket
تیز رفتاری کا ٹکٹ لیجیے

D. break down
گاڑی میں خرابی

E. run out of gas
گیس ختم ہو گئی

F. have a flat tire
ٹائر کی ہوا نکل گئی

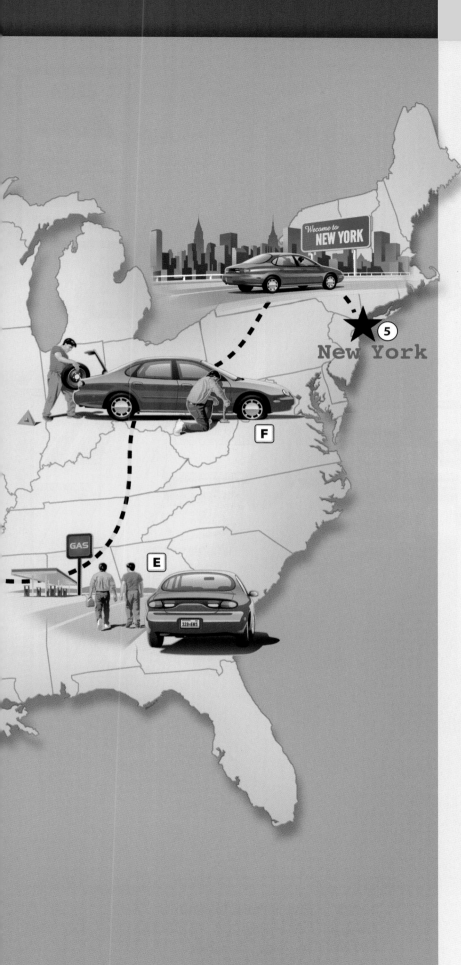

Look at the pictures. What do you see?

Answer the questions.

1. What are the young men's starting point and destination?

2. What do they see on their trip?

3. What kinds of problems do they have?

 Read the story.

A Road Trip

On July 7th Joe and Rob <u>packed</u> their bags for a road trip. Their <u>starting point</u> was Seattle. Their <u>destination</u> was New York City.

The young men saw beautiful <u>scenery</u> on their trip. But there were also problems. They <u>got lost</u>. Then, a <u>gas station attendant</u> gave them bad directions. Next, they <u>got a speeding ticket</u>. Joe was very upset. After that, their car <u>broke down</u>. Joe called a tow truck and used his <u>auto club card</u>.

The end of their trip was difficult, too. They <u>ran out of gas</u> and then they had a <u>flat tire</u>.

After 7,000 miles of problems, Joe and Rob arrived in New York City. They were happy, but tired. Next time, they're going to take the train.

Think about it.

1. What is the best way to travel across the U.S.? by car? by plane? by train? Why?

2. Imagine your car breaks down on the road. Who can you call? What can you do?

1. entrance
   داخله گاه
2. customer
   گاہک
3. office
   آفس
4. employer /
   boss
   آجر / مالک
5. receptionist
   استقبال کار
6. safety regulations
   حفاظتی ضابطے

Listen and point. Take turns.

A: Point to <u>the front entrance</u>.
B: Point to <u>the receptionist</u>.
A: Point to <u>the time clock</u>.

Dictate to your partner. Take turns.

A: *Can you spell <u>employer</u>?*
B: *I'm not sure. Is it <u>e-m-p-l-o-y-e-r</u>?*
A: *Yes, that's right.*

7. time clock
کارکنوں کے وقت کی اندراجی گھڑی

8. supervisor
نگرانی کرنے والا

9. employee
ملازم

10. payroll clerk
تنخواہ کلرک

11. pay stub
تنخواہ کی پرچی

12. wages
اجرتیں

13. deductions
کٹوتیاں

14. paycheck
تنخواہ کا چیک

Ways to talk about wages

I **earn** $250 a week.
He **makes** $7 an hour.
I'm **paid** $1,000 a month.

Role play. Talk to an employer.

A: Is everything correct on your paycheck?
B: No, it isn't. I make $250 a week, not $200.
A: Let's talk to the payroll clerk. Where is she?

165

1. accountant
محاسب

2. actor
اداکار

3. administrative assistant
معاون انتظامیہ

4. appliance repair person
آلات کی مرمت کا مستری

5. architect
نقشہ نویس

6. artist
فنکار

7. assembler
کل پرزے جوڑنے والا

8. auto mechanic
موٹر میکینک

9. babysitter
بچوں کی دیکھ بھال کرنے والی

10. baker
بیکر

11. business owner
کاروبار کا مالک

12. businessperson
تاجر

13. butcher
قصاب

14. carpenter
بڑھئی

15. cashier
خزانچی

16. childcare worker
نگہداشت اطفال کا کارکن

Ways to ask about someone's job

What's her job?
What does he do?
What kind of work do they do?

Pair practice. Make new conversations.

A: *What kind of work <u>does she</u> do?*
B: *<u>She's an accountant</u>. What <u>do they</u> do?*
A: *<u>They're actors</u>.*

17. commercial fisher
تجارتی ماہی گیر

18. computer software engineer
کمپیوٹر سافٹ ویئر انجینئر

19. computer technician
کمپیوٹر ٹیکنیشیئن

We have that shirt in red.

20. customer service representative
کمپیوٹر سروس نمائندہ

21. delivery person
پہنچانے والا شخص

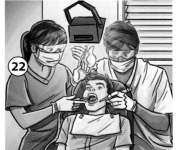

22. dental assistant
دانت کے ڈاکٹر کا معاون

23. dockworker
بندرگاہ پر کام کرنے والا

24. electronics repair person
الیکٹرونک سامانوں کا مستری

25. engineer
انجینئر

26. firefighter
آگ بجھانے والا

27. florist
گل فروش

28. gardener
مالی

29. garment worker
لباس ساز

30. graphic designer
کمپیوٹر پر تصویریں بنانے والا

31. hairdresser / hair stylist
بالوں کی آرائش کرنے والا / بالوں کی وضع بنانے والا

32. home health care aide
گھریلو نگہداشت صحت کا معاون

Ways to talk about jobs and occupations

Sue's a <u>garment worker</u>. She works **in** a factory.
Tom's <u>an engineer</u>. He works **for** <u>a large company</u>.
Ann's a <u>dental assistant</u>. She works **with** <u>a dentist</u>.

Role play. Talk about a friend's new job.

A: Does your friend like <u>his</u> new job?
B: Yes, <u>he</u> does. <u>He's a graphic designer</u>.
A: Does <u>he</u> work <u>in an office</u>?

33. homemaker
گھریلو

34. housekeeper
گھریلو معاملات کا انتظام کار

你好
He says, "Hi."

35. interpreter / translator
ترجمان / مترجم

36. lawyer
وکیل

37. machine operator
مشین آپریٹر

38. manicurist
ناخن کی آرائش کرنے والا

39. medical records technician
طبی ریکارڈ تکنیشئین

40. messenger / courier
پیغام بردار / کوریئر

41. model
نمونے پیش کرنے والے

42. mover
سامان منتقل کرنے والا

43. musician
موسیقار

44. nurse
نرس

45. occupational therapist
حرفتی معالج

46. (house) painter
(گھر کی) پتائی کرنے والا

47. physician assistant
ڈاکٹر کا معاون

48. police officer
پولس افسر

Grammar Point: past tense of *be*

I **was** a machine operator for 5 years.
She **was** a nurse for a year.
They **were** movers from 2003–2007.

Pair practice. Make new conversations.

A: *What was your first job?*
B: *I was a musician. How about you?*
A: *I was a messenger for a small company.*

168

49. postal worker
ڈاک کارکن

50. printer
طباعت کنندہ

51. receptionist
استقبال کرنے والی

52. reporter
خبر پہنچانے والا

53. retail clerk
خردہ فروش کلرک

54. sanitation worker
صفائی کارکن

55. security guard
چوکی دار

56. server
خدمت کار

Here are some programs that will help you.

57. social worker
سماجی کارکن

58. soldier
سپاہی

59. stock clerk
ذخیرہ کا انداز کرنے والا کلرک

Hello. I'm calling with a very special offer.

60. telemarketer
ٹیلیفون سے فروخت کاری کرنے والا

61. truck driver
ٹرک ڈرائیور

62. veterinarian
مویشی ڈاکٹر

63. welder
ٹانکا کار

Norma's Story

64. writer / author
مصنف / ادیب

Ask your classmates. Share the answers.
1. Which of these jobs could you do now?
2. What is one job you don't want to have?
3. Which jobs do you want to have?

Think about it. Discuss.
1. Which jobs need special training?
2. What kind of person makes a good interpreter? A good nurse? A good reporter? Why?

169

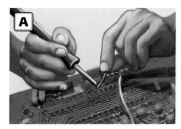

A. assemble components

پرزے جوڑیے

B. assist medical patients

طبی مریضوں کی مدد کیجیے

C. cook

کھانا پکائیے

D. do manual labor

مزدوری کیجیے

E. drive a truck

ٹرک چلائیے

F. fly a plane

ہوائی جہاز اڑائیے

G. make furniture

فرنیچر بنائیے

H. operate heavy machinery

بھاری مشینری چلائیے

I. program computers

کمپیوٹر پروگرام بنائیے

J. repair appliances

آلات کی مرمت کیجیے

K. sell cars

کاریں بیچیے

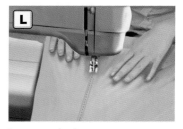

L. sew clothes

کپڑے سلیے

M. solve math problems

4% interest of 5K = x

ریاضی کے سوال حل کیجیے

N. speak another language

ПРИВЕТ

کوئی دوسری زبان بولیے

O. supervise people

لوگوں کی نگرانی کیجیے

P. take care of children

بچوں کی نگہداشت کیجیے

Q. teach

پڑھائیے

R. type

ٹائپ کیجیے

S. use a cash register

کیش رجسٹر استعمال کیجیے

T. wait on customers

گاہکوں سے صبر و تحمل کا اظہار کیجیے

Grammar Point: *can, can't*

I am a chef. I **can** cook.

I'm not a pilot. I **can't** fly a plane.

I **can't** speak French, but I **can** speak Spanish.

Role play. Talk to a job counselor.

A: *Tell me about your skills. Can you <u>type</u>?*

B: <u>*No, I can't*</u>, *but I <u>can use a cash register</u>.*

A: *OK. What other skills do you have?*

Customers need better service…

Let's meet at 2:00.
Sure.

Dear Mr. Smith…

Hello. ABC Company. How may I help you?

Please hold.

Mr. Perez, I'm transferring you.

Hello. This is Sue Jones. Please call me.
Message Pad
Call From: Ana Puerta
Tel: 555-1234
Message:
Please Call

This is Lee Tran. Please call me back.

Office Skills

دفتری مہارتیں

A. type a letter
خط ٹائپ کیجیے

B. enter data
متن داخل کیجیے

C. transcribe notes
وضاحت یادداشت کے طور پر
لکھیے

D. make copies
نقول بنائیے

E. collate papers
کاغذات کی ترتیب جانچیے

F. staple
اسٹیپل کیجیے

G. fax a document
کوئی دستاویز فیکس کیجیے

H. scan a document
کوئی دستاویز اسکین کیجیے

I. print a document
کوئی دستاویز چھاپیے

J. schedule a meeting
کسی میٹنگ کا وقت طے کیجیے

K. take dictation
املا لکھیے

L. organize materials
چیزوں کو منظم کیجیے

Telephone Skills

ٹیلیفون کی مہارتیں

M. greet the caller
کال کرنے والے کا استقبال کیجیے

N. put the caller on hold
کال کرنے والے کو انتظار کرنے
کے لیے کہیے

O. transfer the call
کال منتقل کیجیے

P. leave a message
کوئی پیغام چھوڑیے

Q. take a message
کوئی پیغام لیجیے

R. check messages
پیغامات کی جانچ کیجیے

Career Path پیشے کو اپنانے کا طریقہ

1. entry-level job
   داخلے کی سطح کی ملازمت

2. training
   تربیت

3. new job
   نئی ملازمت

4. promotion
   ترقی

Types of Job Training ملازمت سے متعلق تربیت کی اقسام

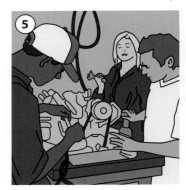

5. vocational training
   روزگاری تربیت

6. internship
   تربیتی ملازمت

7. on-the-job training
   دوران ملازمت تربیت

8. online course
   انٹرنیٹ کے ذریعے نصابی تربیت

Planning a Career پیشے کی منصوبہ بندی

9. resource center
   وسائل مرکز

10. career counselor
    پیشے سے متعلق صلاح کار

11. interest inventory
    دلچسپی کی فہرست

12. skill inventory
    ہنر کی فہرست

13. job fair
    ملازمت میلہ

14. recruiter
    تقر کار

Ways to talk about job training

I'm looking into <u>an online course</u>.
I'm interested in <u>on-the-job training</u>.
I want to sign up for <u>an internship</u>.

Ask your classmates. Share the answers.

1. What kind of job training are you interested in?
2. Would your rather learn English in an online course or in a classroom?

A. talk to friends / **network**
دوستوں سے بات کیجیے / نیٹ ورک بنائیے

B. look in the classifieds
زمرہ بند اشتہارات دیکھیے

C. look for help wanted signs
مدد مطلوب ہے کی علامات تلاش کیجیے

D. check Internet job sites
انٹرنیٹ کی ملازمتی سائٹیں دیکھیے

E. go to an employment agency
کسی روزگار ایجنسی میں جائیے

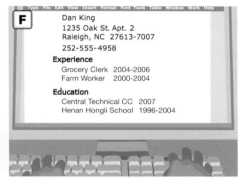

F. write a resume
اپنا کوائف نامہ لکھیے

G. write a cover letter
اس سے منسلک کیا جانے والا خط لکھیے

H. send in your resume and cover letter
اپنا کوائف نامہ اور خط ارسال کیجیے

I. set up an interview
انٹرویو مقرر کیجیے

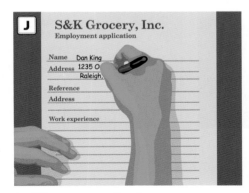

J. fill out an application
درخواست فارم بھریے

K. go on an interview
انٹرویو دیجیے

L. get hired
تقرری پائیے

A. Prepare for the interview.

انٹرویو کی تیاری کیجیے۔

B. Dress appropriately.

موزوں لباس پہنیے۔

C. Be neat.

صاف ستھرے بنیے۔

D. Bring your resume and ID.

اپنا کوائف نامہ اور شناخت لائیے۔

E. Don't be late.

تاخیر سے نہ پہنچیے۔

F. Be on time.

وقت پر پہنچیے۔

G. Turn off your cell phone.

اپنا سیل فون بند کر دیجیے۔

H. Greet the interviewer.

انٹرویو لینے والوں کا استقبال کیجیے۔

I. Shake hands.

مصافحہ کیجیے۔

J. Make eye contact.

آنکھیں ملائیے۔

K. Listen carefully.

غور سے سنیے۔

L. Talk about your experience.

اپنے تجربے کے بارے میں بات کیجیے۔

M. Ask questions.

سوالات پوچھیے۔

N. Thank the interviewer.

انٹرویو لینے والے کا شکریہ ادا کیجیے۔

O. Write a thank-you note.

شکریے کا نوٹ لکھیے۔

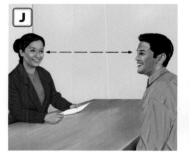

More vocabulary

benefits: health insurance, vacation pay, or other things the employer can offer an employee

inquire about benefits: ask about benefits

Think about it. Discuss.

1. How can you prepare for an interview?
2. Why is it important to make eye contact?
3. What kinds of questions should you ask?

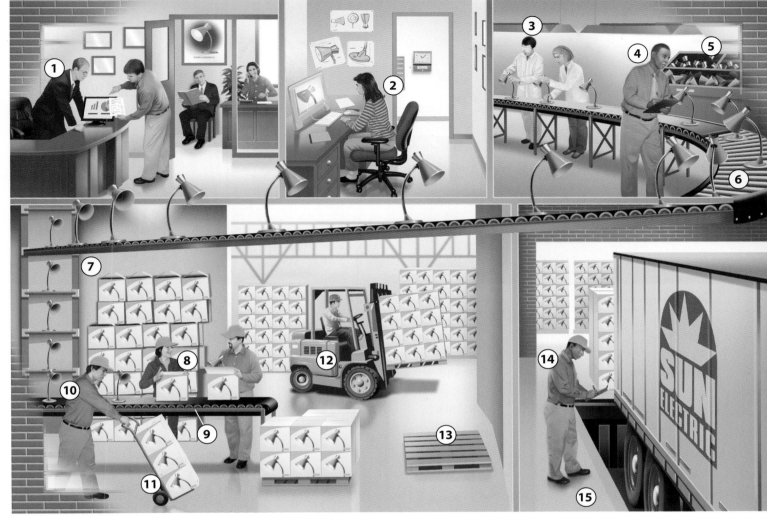

1. factory owner
   فیکٹری کا مالک

2. designer
   نمونے بنانے والا

3. factory worker
   فیکٹری کارکن

4. line supervisor
   کسی مخصوص کام کا منتظم

5. parts
   پرزے

6. assembly line
   پرزے جوڑنے والی لائن

7. warehouse
   گودام

8. packer
   پیک کرنے والا

9. conveyer belt
   سرکنے والی پٹی جو سامان پہنچاتی ہے

10. order puller
    ترتیب سے رکھنے والا

11. hand truck
    ہاتھ سے چلنے والا ٹھیلا

12. forklift
    دو شاخہ دار مال اٹھانے والی گاڑی

13. pallet
    سامان نقل پذیر تختہ

14. shipping clerk
    جہازرانی کا کلرک

15. loading dock
    مال لادنے کی گودی

A. **design**
نمونے تیار کیجیے

B. **manufacture**
فیکٹری میں تیار کیجیے

C. **assemble**
پرزے لگائیے

D. **ship**
لادیے

1. **gardening crew**
   باغبانی عملہ

2. **leaf blower**
   پتیاں اڑانے والا

3. **wheelbarrow**
   ایک پہیہ کی باغبانی کی گاڑی

4. **gardening crew leader**
   باغبانی عملے کا قائد

5. **landscape designer**
   منظرکاری کرنے والا

6. **lawn mower**
   گھاس کاٹنے کی مشین

7. **shovel**
   کھرپا

8. **rake**
   بیلچہ

9. **pruning shears**
   چھنٹائی قینچی

10. **trowel**
    کھرپی

11. **hedge clippers**
    جھاڑی کاٹنے کی قینچی

12. **weed whacker / weed eater**
    گھاس کاٹنے والا / گھاس ختم کرنے والا

A. **mow** the lawn
گھاس کاٹیے

B. **trim** the hedges
جھاڑیوں کو چھانٹیے

C. **rake** the leaves
پتیوں کو جمع کیجیے

D. **fertilize / feed** the plants
پودوں میں غذا / کھاد ڈالیے

E. **plant** a tree
درخت لگائیے

F. **water** the plants
پودوں میں پانی ڈالیے

G. **weed** the flower beds
کیاریوں میں سے خودرو گھاس چنیے

H. **install** a sprinkler system
پانی چھڑکنے کے نظام کو نصب کیجیے

Use the new words.
Look at page 53. Name what you can do in the yard.
A: I can <u>mow the lawn</u>.
B: I can <u>weed the flower bed</u>.

Ask your classmates. Share the answers.
1. Do you know someone who does landscaping? Who?
2. Do you enjoy gardening? Why or why not?
3. Which gardening activity is the hardest to do? Why?

Crops فصلیں

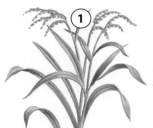

1. rice
چاول

2. wheat
گیہوں

3. soybeans
سویابین

4. corn
مکئی

5. alfalfa
الفالفا

6. cotton
روئی

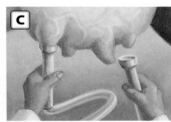

7. field
کھیت

12. farm equipment
کھیتی کے اوزار

17. corral
مویشی باڑا

22. rancher
مویشی بانی کرنے والا

8. farmworker
کھیت پر کام کرنے والا

13. farmer / grower
کاشتکار/اگانے والا

18. hay
بھوسہ

A. **plant**
پود لگائیے

9. tractor
ٹریکٹر

14. vegetable garden
سبزی باغ

19. fence
باڑھ

B. **harvest**
فصل کی کٹائی کیجیے

10. orchard
باغ

15. livestock
مویشی

20. hired hand
کرایہ پر رکھا گیا آدمی

C. **milk**
دودھ نکالیے

11. barn
اناج کوٹھی

16. vineyard
انگور کا باغ

21. cattle
مویشی

D. **feed**
چارا کھلائیے

177

1. construction worker تعمیراتی مزدور	**4.** scaffolding پاڑ لگانا	**7.** crane بھاری وزن اٹھانے والی مشین
2. ladder سیڑھی	**5.** cherry picker کرین یا لوگوں کو اوپر اٹھانے والی مشین	**8.** backhoe کھدائی کرنے کی مشین
3. I beam/girder آئی بیم / لوہے کا شہتیر	**6.** bulldozer بل ڈوزر	**9.** jackhammer / pneumatic drill پتھر پھوڑ برما / ہوا کے دباؤ سے سخت چٹان توڑنے کا برما

10. concrete کنکریٹ	**13.** trowel کرنی	**16.** window pane کھڑکی کا شیشہ	**19.** drywall خشک دیوار	**22.** shovel بیلچہ
11. tile ٹائل	**14.** insulation حرارت کا غیر موصل	**17.** wood / lumber لکڑی / لکڑ	**20.** shingles چھت کی پلیٹیں	**23.** sledgehammer گھمن
12. bricks اینٹیں	**15.** stucco سیمنٹ کا مسالہ	**18.** plywood پلائی وڈ	**21.** pickax کیل اکھاڑ کلہاڑی	

A. paint
رنگ کیجیے

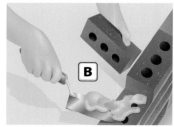

B. lay bricks
اینٹیں بچھائیے

C. install tile
ٹائل لگائیے

D. hammer
ٹھونکیے

Safety Hazards and Hazardous Materials حفاظتی خطرات اور خطرناک سامان

1. **careless worker**
   غیر محتاط کارکن

2. **careful worker**
   محتاط کارکن

3. **poisonous fumes**
   زہریلے دھوئیں

4. **broken equipment**
   ٹوٹے ہوئے اوزار

5. **frayed cord**
   گھسے ہوئے تار

6. **slippery floor**
   پھسلن دار فرش

7. **radioactive materials**
   تابکاری والے مواد

8. **flammable liquids**
   آگ پکڑنے والے سیالات

Safety Equipment حفاظتی آلات

9. **hard hat**
   سخت حفاظتی ٹوپی

10. **safety glasses**
    حفاظتی عینک

11. **safety goggles**
    حفاظتی دھوپ کے چشمے

12. **safety visor**
    حفاظتی نقاب

13. **respirator**
    تنفسی آلہ

14. **particle mask**
    ذرات سے بچاؤ کا نقاب

15. **ear plugs**
    کان میں لگانے کی ڈاٹ

16. **earmuffs**
    کان ڈھکنے کی جالی

17. **work gloves**
    کام کے دستانے

18. **back support belt**
    کمر کو سہارا دینے والی پٹی

19. **knee pads**
    گھٹنے کی گدیاں

20. **safety boots**
    حفاظتی بوٹ

21. **fire extinguisher**
    آگ بجھانے کا آلہ

22. **two-way radio**
    دو طرفہ ریڈیو

Tools and Building Supplies

اوزار اور تعمیر کے سامان

1. hammer
بتھوڑا

2. mallet
چوبی بتھوڑا

3. ax
کلہاڑی

4. handsaw
ہاتھ آرا

5. hacksaw
دھات کاٹنے کی آری

6. C-clamp
C نما شکنجہ

7. pliers
پلاس

8. electric drill
بجلی سے چلنے والی ڈرل

9. circular saw
گول آری

10. jigsaw
گول کاٹنے والی آری

11. power sander
مشینی ریگ مال

12. router
بجلی سے چلنے والا رندا

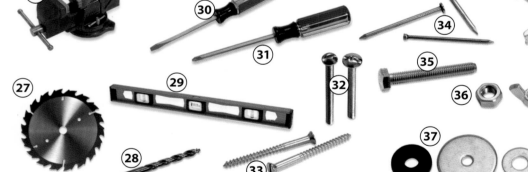

26. vise
شکنجہ

27. blade
بلیڈ

28. drill bit
سوراخ کرنے والی دھات کی چھڑی

29. level
افق پیما آلہ

30. screwdriver
پیچ کس

31. Phillips screwdriver
فلپس پیچ کس

32. machine screw
مشین کا پیچ

33. wood screw
لکڑی کا پیچ

34. nail
کیل

35. bolt
بولٹ

36. nut
ڈھبری

37. washer
واشر

38. toggle bolt
گل دار بولٹ

39. hook
ہک

40. eye hook
چھلے دار ہک

41. chain
زنجیر

Use the new words.
Look at pages 62–63. Name the tools you see.

A: *There's a hammer*.
B: *There's a pipe wrench*.

Ask your classmates. Share the answers.
1. Are you good with tools?
2. Which tools do you have at home?
3. Where can you shop for building supplies?

180

ELECTRICAL **PLUMBING** **LUMBER** **PAINT**

13. wire
تار

14. extension cord
توسیعی ڈوری

15. bungee cord
کھوکھلی ڈوری

16. yardstick
مسطر

17. pipe
پائپ

18. fittings
فٹنگز

19. 2 x 4 (two by four)
2 × 4 (دو ضرب چار)

20. particle board
لکڑی کے برادے سے بنا ہوا تختہ

21. spray gun
چھڑکنے والی مشین

22. paintbrush
رنگ کرنے کا برش

23. paint roller
پینٹ رولر

24. wood stain
لکڑی رنگنے کا برش

25. paint
رنگ

42. wire stripper
تار سے ربر ہٹانے کا آلہ

43. electrical tape
برقی تار پر لگانے کا ٹیپ

44. work light
بجلی کی فٹنگ کے دوران مستعمل بلب

45. tape measure
ناپنے کا ٹیپ

46. outlet cover
بجلی کے پلگ کا خول

47. pipe wrench
پائپ کسنے کا رینچ

48. adjustable wrench
ردوبدل کے قابل رینچ

49. duct tape
نلکی پر لگانے کا ٹیپ

50. plunger
دباؤ سے صاف کرنے کا آلہ

51. paint pan
رنگ کا برتن

52. scraper
کھرچنی

53. masking tape
چھپانے والا ٹیپ

54. drop cloth
رنگ وغیرہ سے بچانے کے بچھانے والا کپڑا

55. chisel
چھینی

56. sandpaper
ریگ مال

57. plane
رندا

Role play. Find an item in a building supply store.

A: *Where can I find <u>particle board</u>?*
B: *It's <u>on the back wall</u>, in the <u>lumber</u> section.*
A: *Great. And where <u>are the nails</u>?*

Think about it. Discuss.

1. Which tools are the most important to have? Why?
2. Which tools can be dangerous? Why?
3. Do you borrow tools from friends? Why or why not?

181

1. supply cabinet
سامان کی الماری

2. clerk
کلرک

3. janitor
صفائی اور دیکھ بھال کرنے والا

4. conference room
اجلاس کا کمرہ

5. executive
ایگزیکیٹو

6. presentation
پیشکش

7. cubicle
چھوٹا کمرہ

8. office manager
آفس منتظم

9. desk
ڈیسک

10. file clerk
فائل کلرک

11. file cabinet
فائل کی الماری

12. computer technician
کمپیوٹر تکنیشیئن

13. PBX
پی بی ایکس

14. receptionist
استقبال کار

15. reception area
استقبالیہ علاقہ

16. waiting area
انتظار گاہ

Ways to greet a receptionist

I'm here for a job interview.
I have a 9:00 a.m. appointment with Mr. Lee.
I'd like to leave a message for Mr. Lee.

Role play. Talk to a receptionist.

A: *Hello. How can I help you?*
B: *I'm here for a job interview with Mr. Lee.*
A: *OK. What is your name?*

Office Equipment دفتر کے آلات

17. computer
کمپیوٹر

18. inkjet printer
انک جیٹ پرنٹر

19. laser printer
لیزر پرنٹر

20. scanner
اسکینر

21. fax machine
فیکس مشین

22. paper cutter
کاغذ کائنے والی مشین

23. photocopier
فوٹو کاپیئر

24. paper shredder
کاغذ کی کترن کرنے والی مشین

25. calculator
کیلکولیٹر

26. electric pencil sharpener
الیکٹرک پنسل تراش

27. postal scale
ڈاک ترازو

Office Supplies دفتری سامان

28. stapler
اسٹیپلر

29. staples
اسٹیپلز

30. clear tape
شفاف ٹیپ

31. paper clip
پیپر کلپ

32. packing tape
پیکنگ ٹیپ

33. glue
گوند

34. rubber band
ربر بینڈ

35. pushpin
پش پن

36. correction fluid
تصحیح کار سیال

37. correction tape
تصحیح کار ٹیپ

38. legal pad
نوٹ بک

39. sticky notes
چپکدار نوٹ سلپ

40. mailer
میلر

41. mailing label
میلنگ لیبل

42. letterhead / stationery
سرِنامہ / اسٹیشنری

43. envelope
لفافہ

44. rotary card file
سرکنے والے کارڈ کی فائل

45. ink cartridge
انک کارٹرج

46. ink pad
انک پیڈ

47. stamp
مہر

48. appointment book
مقررہ ملاقات لکھنے کی کاپی

49. organizer
منصوبہ بندی کی نوٹ بک

50. file folder
فائل فولڈر

1. doorman
   دربان

2. revolving door
   گھومنے والا دروازہ

3. parking attendant
   پارکنگ چوکیدار

4. concierge
   کئی زبانیں جاننے والا، سامان، ڈاک،
   سفری سہولتوں کا منتظم

5. gift shop
   تحائف کی دکان

6. bell captain
   قلیوں کا نگران

7. bellhop
   قلی جو سامان کمرے تک پہنچاتا ہے

8. luggage cart
   سامان رکھنے کی پہیوں کی گاڑی

9. elevator
   لفٹ

10. guest
    مہمان

11. desk clerk
    ڈیسک کلرک

12. front desk
    فرنٹ ڈیسک

13. guest room
    گیسٹ روم

14. double bed
    ڈبل بیڈ

15. king-size bed
    بڑے سائز کا بیڈ

16. suite
    ہوٹل کا ایک جامع کمرہ

17. room service
    روم سروس

18. hallway
    راہداری

19. housekeeping cart
    سامان لانے لے جانے والی گاڑی

20. housekeeper
    گھر کی دیکھ بھال کرنے والا

21. pool service
    تیراکی کے پول کی دیکھ بھال

22. pool
    تیراکی کا پول

23. maintenance
    دیکھ بھال

24. gym
    ورزش گاہ

25. meeting room
    ملاقات کا کمرہ

26. ballroom
    رقص کا کمرہ

کھانے کی خدمات

A Restaurant Kitchen ریستوراں کا باورچی خانہ

1. **short-order cook**
جلد تیار ہونے والے کھانوں کا باورچی

2. **dishwasher**
برتن دھونے والا

3. **walk-in freezer**
سرد خانہ جس میں آنا جانا کر سکتے ہیں

4. **food preparation worker**
تیاری غذا کا کارکن

5. **storeroom**
ذخیرہ گاہ

6. **sous chef**
معاون باورچی

7. **head chef / executive chef**
سربراہ باورچی / ایگزیکیئو باورچی

Restaurant Dining ریستوراں طعام گاہ

8. **server**
خدمت کار

9. **diner**
کھانا کھانے والے

10. **buffet**
کھانے کی اشیاء رکھنے کا پیش تختہ

11. **maitre d'**
مہمانوں کی خدمت میں تعینات بیرا

12. **headwaiter**
بیروں کا سربراہ

13. **bus person**
برتنوں کو دھونے کے بعد ایک کونے میں میز تک پہنچانے والا

14. **banquet room**
ضیافت گاہ

15. **runner**
پیش تختہ سے کھانے کی میز تک کھانا لانے والا

16. **caterer**
کھانا فراہم کرنے والا

More vocabulary

line cook: short-order cook

wait staff: servers, headwaiters, and runners

Ask your classmates. Share the answers.

1. Have you ever worked in a hotel? What did you do?
2. What is the hardest job in a hotel?
3. Would you prefer to stay at a hotel in the city or in the country?

1. dangerous
خطرناک

2. clinic
مطب

3. budget
بجٹ

4. floor plan
عمارت کی کسی منزل کا نقشہ

5. contractor
ٹھیکیدار

6. electrical hazard
بجلی سے ہونے والا خطرہ

7. wiring
بجلی کے تار

8. bricklayer
معمار

A. **call in** sick
بیماری کی فون کال کیجیے

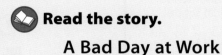
HEALTH CENTER

HARD HAT AREA

**Look at the picture.
What do you see?**

Answer the questions.

1. How many workers are there? How many are working?

2. Why did two workers call in sick?

3. What is dangerous at the construction site?

📖 **Read the story.**

A Bad Day at Work

Sam Lopez is the <u>contractor</u> for a new building. He makes the schedule and supervises the <u>budget</u>. He also solves problems. Today there are a lot of problems.

Two <u>bricklayers</u> <u>called in sick</u> this morning. Now Sam has only one bricklayer at work. One hour later, a construction worker fell. Now he has to go to the <u>clinic</u>. Sam always tells his workers to be careful. Construction work is <u>dangerous</u>. Sam's also worried because the new <u>wiring</u> is an <u>electrical hazard</u>.

Right now, the building owner is in Sam's office. Her new <u>floor plan</u> has 25 more offices. Sam has a headache. Maybe he needs to call in sick tomorrow.

Think about it.

1. What do you say when you can't come in to work? to school?

2. Imagine you are Sam. What do you tell the building owner? Why?

187

Schools and Subjects

اسکول اور مضامین

1. preschool /
   nursery school
   اسکول کی تیاری کی درسگاہ /
   نرسری اسکول

2. elementary school
   ابتدائی اسکول

3. middle school /
   junior high school
   مڈل اسکول / جونیر ہائی اسکول

4. high school
   ہائی اسکول

5. vocational school /
   technical school
   پیشہ ورانہ تربیتی اسکول /
   ٹیکنکل اسکول

6. community college
   مقامی لوگوں کے لیے درسگاہ

7. college / university
   کالج / یونیورسٹی

8. adult school
   بالغوں کا اسکول

Listen and point. Take turns.

A: *Point to the preschool.*
B: *Point to the high school.*
A: *Point to the adult school.*

Dictate to your partner. Take turns.

A: *Write preschool.*
B: *Is that p-r-e-s-c-h-o-o-l?*
A: *Yes. That's right.*

9. language arts
فنونِ زبان

10. math
ریاضی

11. science
سائنس

12. history
تاریخ

13. world languages
دنیا کی زبانیں

14. ESL / ESOL
انگریزی دیگر زبان بولنے والوں کی دوسری زبان / دوسری زبان کے طور پر انگریزی

15. arts
فنون

16. music
موسیقی

17. physical education
جسمانی تعلیم

Pair practice. Make new conversations.

A: I go to <u>community college</u>.
B: What subjects are you taking?
A: I'm taking <u>history</u> and <u>science</u>.

189

1

factory

1. word
لفظ

2

I worked in a factory.

2. sentence
جملہ

3

Little by little, work and success came to me. My first job wasn't good. I worked in a small factory. Now, I help manage two factories.

3. paragraph
پیراگراف

4

4. essay
مضمون

Parts of an Essay
مضمون کے اجزاء

5. title
عنوان

6. introduction
تعارف

7. body
عبارت

8. conclusion
اختتام

9. quotation
اقتباس

10. footnote
حاشیہ

Carlos Lopez
Eng. Comp.
10/21/10

5

Success in the U.S.

6 I came to Los Angeles from Mexico in 2006. I had no job, no friends, and no family here. I was homesick and scared, but I did not go home. I took English classes (always at night) and I studied hard. I believed in my future success!

7 More than 400,000 new immigrants come to the U.S every year. Most of us need to find work. During my first year here, my routine was the same: get up; look for work; go to class; go to bed. I had to take jobs with long hours and low pay. Often I had two or three jobs.

Little by little, work and success came to me. My first job wasn't good. I worked in a small factory. Now, I help manage two factories.

8 Hard work makes success possible. Henry David Thoreau said, "Men are born to succeed, not fail." My story shows that he was right. **9**

¹ U.S. Census **10**

Punctuation
رموزِ اوقاف

11. period .
وقفہ

12. question mark ?
سوالیہ نشان

13. exclamation mark !
علامتِ استعجاب

14. comma ,
کاما

15. quotation marks " "
علامات اقتباس

16. apostrophe '
علامت اعراب جو اضافت
تملیکی کے طور پر آتی ہے

17. colon :
کولن

18. semicolon ;
عبارت میں وقفہ کا نشان

19. parentheses ( )
قوسین (بریکٹ)

20. hyphen -
علامت ربط و الحاق

Writing Rules لکھنے کے ضابطے

A

Carlos
Mexico
Los Angeles

A. **Capitalize** names.
ناموں کو بڑے حروف میں لکھیے۔

B

Hard work makes success possible.

B. **Capitalize** the first letter in a sentence.
کسی جملے کا پہلا حرف بڑا لکھیے۔

C

I was homesick and scared, but I did not go home.

C. **Use** punctuation.
رموزِ اوقاف استعمال کیجیے۔

D

I came to Los Angeles from Mexico in 2006. I had no job, no friends, and no family here. I was homesick and scared, but I did not go home. I took English classes (always at night) and I studied hard. I believed in my future success!

D. **Indent** the first sentence in a paragraph.
پیراگراف کے پہلے جملے کا کنارہ خالی چھوڑیے۔

Ways to ask for suggestions on your compositions

What do you think of this title?
Is this paragraph OK? Is the punctuation correct?
Do you have any suggestions for the conclusion?

Pair practice. Make new conversations.

A: *What do you think of this title?*
B: *I think you need to revise it.*
A: *Thanks. Do you have any more suggestions?*

190

The Writing Process لکھنے کا عمل

PREWRITING

Writing assignment - Due 10/3
Write an essay about
your first year in the U.S.

my life … hmmm…
what can I say…
I have one week…

E. Think about the assignment.
تفویض کے بارے میں سوچیے۔

factory
work
2 jobs
ESL
1st year
2006
friends
no family
lonely

F. Brainstorm ideas.
خیالات پر غور و خوض کیجیے۔

I. Mexico to Los Angeles
A. No family
1. Homesick
2. Scared
B. No job
II. Daily routine
A. Job search
B. ESL class
1. Friends
III. Success

G. Organize your ideas.
اپنے خیالات کو منظم کیجیے۔

WRITING AND REVISING

I came to
Los Angeles
from Mexico
in 2006…

H. Write a first draft.
پہلا مسودہ لکھیے۔

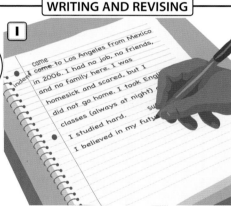

I came to Los Angeles from Mexico
in 2006. I had no job, no friends,
and no family here. I was
homesick and scared, but I
did not go home. I took English
classes (always at night)
I studied hard.   su
I believed in my futu

I. Edit. / Proofread.
ترمیم کیجیے / اوراق کی تصحیح کیجیے۔

came to Los Angeles fi
I came to Los An
in 2006. I had no
no family here. I
scared, but I di
English classes
I studied ha
I beli

J. Revise. / Rewrite.
دہرائیے / دوبارہ لکھیے۔

SHARING AND RESPONDING

OCTOBER 1

I like the part
about your
daily routine.

K. Get feedback.
جوابی معلومات حاصل کیجیے۔

L. Write a final draft.
آخری مسودہ لکھیے۔

OCTOBER 3

M. Turn in your paper.
اپنے مسودے کو واپس کیجیے۔

Ask your classmates. Share the answers.
1. Do you like to write essays?
2. Which part of the writing process do you like best? least?

Think about it. Discuss.
1. In which jobs are writing skills important?
2. What tools can help you edit your writing?
3. What are some good subjects for essays?

191

Integers اعداد صحیح

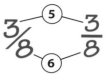

$$....-4\ -3\ -2\ -1\ \ 0\ \ 1\ \ 2\ \ 3\ \ 4 ...$$

1. negative integers
   منفی اعداد صحیح
2. positive integers
   مثبت اعداد صحیح

Fractions کسریں

3. 1, 3, 5, 7, 9, 11 ...
4. 2, 4, 6, 8, 10 ...

$\frac{3}{8}$ $\frac{3}{8}$

3. odd numbers
   طاق اعداد
4. even numbers
   جفت اعداد

5. numerator
   شمار کنندہ
6. denominator
   نسب نما

Math Operations ریاضی کے اعمال

A. **add**
جوڑنا

B. **subtract**
گھٹانا

C. **multiply**
ضرب دینا

D. **divide**
تقسیم کرنا

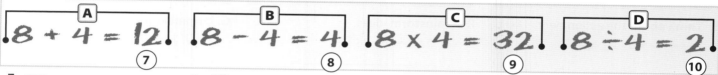

A: $8 + 4 = 12$
B: $8 - 4 = 4$
C: $8 \times 4 = 32$
D: $8 \div 4 = 2$

7. sum
   حاصل جمع
8. difference
   فرق
9. product
   حاصل ضرب
10. quotient
    حاصل تقسیم

A Math Problem ریاضی کا ایک مسئلہ

(11)
Tom is 10 years older than Kim. Next year he will be twice as old as Kim. How old is Tom this year?

(12)
x = Kim's age now
$x + 10$ = Tom's age now
$x + 1$ = Kim's age next year
$2(x + 1)$ = Tom's age next year

$x + 10 + 1 = 2(x + 1)$
$x + 11 = 2x + 2$
$11 - 2 = 2x - x$ (13)

(14) **$x = 9$, Kim is 9, Tom is 19**

(15)
horizontal axis

vertical axis

11. word problem
    لفظ کا مسئلہ
12. variable
    متغیر
13. equation
    مساوات
14. solution
    حل
15. graph
    گراف

Types of Math ریاضی کی قسمیں

(16) How much are they?

x = the sale price
x = 79.00 - .40 (79.00)
x = $47.40

16. algebra
    الجبرا

(17) How many do I need?

area of path = 24 square ft.
area of brick = 2 square ft.
24/2 = 12 bricks

17. geometry
    اقلیدس

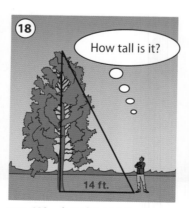

(18) How tall is it?

14 ft.

$\tan 63°$ = height / 14 feet
height = 14 feet ($\tan 63°$)
height $\simeq$ 27.48 feet

18. trigonometry
    علم مثلث

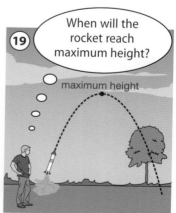

(19) When will the rocket reach maximum height?

maximum height

$s(t) = -\frac{1}{2} gt^2 + V_0 t + h$
$s'(t) = -gt + V_0 = 0$
$t = V_0 / g$

19. calculus
    طریق احصاء

Lines خطوط

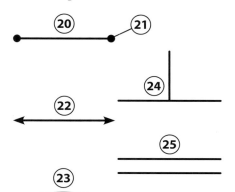

Angles زاویے

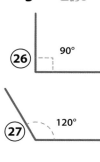

90°

120°

20°

Shapes شکلیں

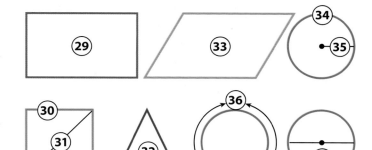

20. line segment
قطعۂ خط

21. endpoint
نقطۂ انتہا

22. straight line
خط مستقیم

23. curved line
خط منحنی

24. perpendicular lines
عمودی خطوط

25. parallel lines
متوازی خطوط

26. right angle / 90° angle
زاویۂ قائمہ / 90 ڈگری کا زاویہ

27. obtuse angle
زاویہ منفرجہ 90 ڈگری سے زیادہ

28. acute angle
زاویۂ 90 ڈگری سے کم

29. rectangle
مستطیل

30. square
مربع

31. diagonal
آڑا

32. triangle
مثلث، تکونہ

33. parallelogram
متوازی الاضلاع

34. circle
دائرہ

35. radius
نصف قطر

36. circumference
محیط

37. diameter
قطر

Geometric Solids
اقلیدسی ٹھوس شکلیں

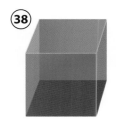
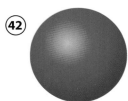

Measuring Area and Volume
رقبہ اور مقدار کی پیمائش

$\ell \times w = $ area

$6 \times f = $ surface area

w

ℓ

38. cube
مکعب

39. pyramid
ہرم (ابرام)

40. cone
مخروط

43. perimeter
احاطہ

44. face
سامنے کا رخ

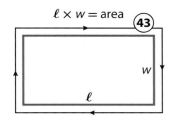
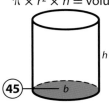
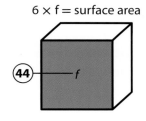
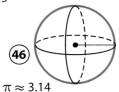

$\pi \times r^2 \times h = $ volume

$\frac{4}{3} \times \pi \times r^3 = $ volume

h

b

$\pi \approx 3.14$

41. cylinder
اسطوانہ، بیلن

42. sphere
کرہ، گولا

45. base
تلی

46. pi
دائرے کے محیط اور قطر کے تناسب
کی علامت

Ask your classmates. Share the answers.

1. Are you good at math?
2. Which types of math are easy for you?
3. Which types of math are difficult for you?

Think about it. Discuss.

1. What's the best way to learn mathematics?
2. How can you find the area of your classroom?
3. Which jobs use math? Which don't?

Biology حیاتیات

1. organisms
   جسم نامیے

2. biologist
   ماہر حیاتیات

3. slide
   خوردبینی معائنہ کے لیے کسی شئے کو رکھنے کا شیشہ

4. cell
   خلیہ

5. cell wall
   دیوار خلیہ

6. cell membrane
   خلیے کی جھلی

7. nucleus
   مرکزہ (ایک خلوی عضو)

8. chromosome
   مرکزہ میں ریشہ نما ساخت

9. cytoplasm
   خلومایہ / مرکزہ اور خلیہ کی جھلی کے درمیان مادہ

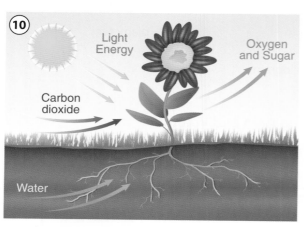

10. photosynthesis
    نوری تالیف

11. habitat
    مسکن

12. vertebrates
    ریڑھ والے جانور

13. invertebrates
    بغیر ریڑھ والے جانور

A Microscope خوردبین

14. eyepiece
    چشمیہ

15. revolving nosepiece
    خوردبین کے گھومنے والے عدسے

16. objective
    دبانے کا عدسہ

17. stage
    خوردبین کی تختی

18. diaphragm
    عدسے کے سوراخ کو چھوٹا بڑا کرنے کا پرزہ

19. light source
    روشنی کا ماخذ

20. base
    بنیاد

21. stage clips
    خوردبین تختی کے کلپ

22. fine adjustment knob
    خوردبینی عمل کے دوران باریک بین ردوبدل کرنے کا پرزہ

23. arm
    بتھا

24. coarse adjustment knob
    عام ردوبدل کرنے کا پرزہ

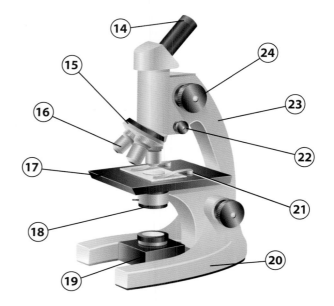

Chemistry کیمیا

25. chemist
کیمیاگر

26. periodic table
کیمیائی عناصر کی دوری جدول

27. molecule
سالمہ

28. atom
جوہر، کسی کیمیائی عنصر کا اقل ترین جز

29. nucleus
مرکزہ

30. electron
منفی بار کا حامل برقیہ

Physics طبیعات

31. proton
ثابت تحت جوہری ذرہ

32. neutron
تحت جوہری ذرہ

33. physicist
ماہرِ طبیعیات

34. formula
فارمولا

35. prism
طیف

36. magnet
مقناطیس

A Science Lab ایک سائنسی تجربہ گاہ

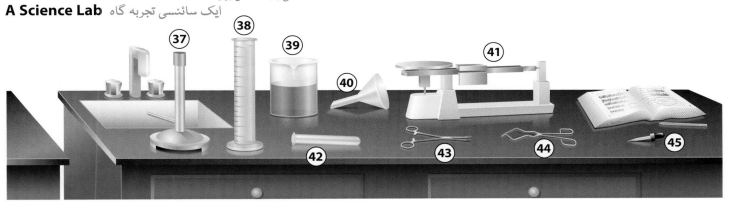

37. Bunsen burner
بنسن کا لیمپ

38. graduated cylinder
درجہ بند سلنڈر

39. beaker
بیکر

40. funnel
قیف

41. balance / scale
ترازو / پیمانہ

42. test tube
جانچ کی نلی

43. forceps
چمٹی جیسا آلہ

44. crucible tongs
کھالی پکڑنے والی چمٹی

45. dropper
قطرہ قطرہ سیال ٹپکانے کا پرزہ

An Experiment ایک تجربہ

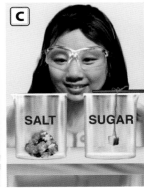

A. State a hypothesis.
کوئی نظریہ بیان کیجیے۔

B. Do an experiment.
کوئی تجربہ انجام دیجیے۔

C. Observe.
مشاہدہ کیجیے۔

D. Record the results.
نتائج کو ریکارڈ کیجیے۔

E. Draw a conclusion.
کوئی رائے قائم کیجیے۔

Desktop Computer ڈیسک ٹاپ کمپیوٹر

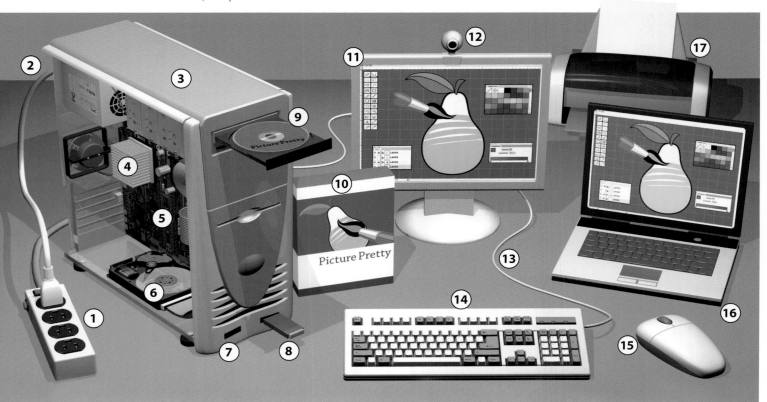

1. surge protector
برقی رو میں اچانک اضافے کو روکنے والا

2. power cord
برقی لائن سے جوڑنے والا تار

3. tower
ٹاور (بکس جس میں اہم پرزے ہوتے ہیں)

4. microprocessor / CPU
مائکرو پروسیسر (مربوط برقی دور) / سی پی یو (مرکزی عامل اکائی)

5. motherboard
مدربورڈ (برقی دوری نظام کا مجموعہ)

6. hard drive
بارڈ ڈرائیو (زیادہ معلومات کا ذخیرہ کرنے والی مقناطیسی قرص)

7. USB port
یو ایس بی پورٹ

8. flash drive
فلیش ڈرائیو

9. DVD and CD-ROM drive
ڈی وی ڈی اور سی ڈی روم ڈرائیو

10. software
سافٹ ویئر (کمپیوٹر چلانے والے پروگرام)

11. monitor /screen
مانیٹر / اسکرین

12. webcam
ویب کیمرہ

13. cable
تار

14. keyboard
تختہ کلید

15. mouse
ماؤز

16. laptop
لیپ ٹاپ (چھوٹا کمپیوٹر)

17. printer
پرنٹر (چھاپنے والا آلہ)

Keyboarding تختہٗ کلید کا استعمال

A. type
ٹائپ کیجیے

B. select
منتخب کیجیے

C. delete
حذف کیجیے

D. go to the next line
اگلی سطر پر جائیے

Navigating a Webpage ویب صفحے میں تلاش کرنے کے لیے اسے دیکھنا

1. **menu bar**
   فہرستی پٹی

2. **back button**
   پیچھے جانے کا بٹن

3. **forward button**
   آگے جانے کا بٹن

4. **URL / website address**
   یو آر ایل / ویب سائٹ کا پتہ

5. **search box**
   تلاش کرنے کا خانہ

6. **search engine**
   تلاش میں مدد کرنے والی ویب سائٹیں (سرچ انجن)

7. **tab**
   ٹیب

8. **drop-down menu**
   نیچے گر کر دکھائی دینے والی فہرست

9. **pop-up ad**
   خود کار طور پر اچانک سامنے آنے والے اشتہار

10. **links**
    ربط

11. **video player**
    ویڈیو پلیئر

12. **pointer**
    اشارہ کنندہ

13. **text box**
    متن کا خانہ

14. **cursor**
    کرسر

15. **scroll bar**
    اسکرال بار (صفحے کو اِدھر اُدھر یا اوپر نیچے حرکت دینے کے لیے)

Logging on and Sending Email لاگنگ آن اور ای میل ارسال کرنا

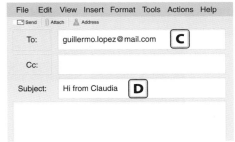

A. **type** your password
   اپنا لفظ شناخت ٹائپ کیجیے

B. **click** "sign in"
   "سائن اِن" پر کلک کیجیے

C. **address** the email
   ای میل کا پتہ لکھیے

D. **type** the subject
   موضوع ٹائپ کیجیے

E. **type** the message
   پیغام ٹائپ کیجیے

F. **check** your spelling
   اپنی ہجے کی جانچ کیجیے

G. **attach** a picture
   کوئی تصویر منسلک کیجیے

H. **attach** a file
   کوئی فائل منسلک کیجیے

I. **send** the email
   ای میل ارسال کیجیے

197

Colonial Period نوآبادیاتی دور

1. thirteen colonies
تیرہ کالونیاں

2. colonists
استعماریت پسند

3. Native Americans
قدیم امریکی باشندے

4. slave
غلام

5. Declaration of Independence
اعلان آزادی

6. First Continental Congress
پہلی براعظمی کانگریس

7. founders
بانیان

8. Revolutionary War
انقلابی جنگ

9. redcoat
برطانوی سپاہی

10. minuteman
امریکی انقلاب کے زمانے کا فوجی رضاکار

11. first president
پہلا صدر

12. Constitution
آئین

13. Bill of Rights
حقوق کا بل (بل آف رائٹس)

Western Expansion
1803 – 1893

Civil War
1861 – 1865

World War I
1914 – 1918

Jazz Age
1920 – 1929

World War II
1941 – 1945

Civil Rights Movement
1954 – 1972

Information Age
1959 – now

1800   1850   1900   1950   2000 →

Industrial Revolution
1793 – 1908

1st African American senator: H. Revels
Reconstruction
1865 – 1877

Progressivism
1889 – 1916

Great Depression
1929 – 1941

Cold War
1945 – 1989

Space Age
1958 – now

Global Age
1994 – now

Civilizations تہذیبیں

Pyramids — Parthenon
Times Square

Caesar
Qin Shi Huang

King Henry VIII
Queen Elizabeth I

Juarez

Mussolini

Churchill

1. ancient
   قدیم
2. modern
   جدید

3. emperor
   شہنشاہ
4. monarch
   حکمران

5. president
   صدر
6. dictator
   مطلق العنان

7. prime minister
   وزیر اعظم

Historical Terms تاریخی اصطلاحات

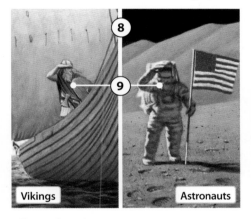
Vikings — Astronauts

8. exploration
   تلاش و جستجو
9. explorer
   متلاشی

10. war
    جنگ
11. army
    فوج

12. immigration
    ترک وطن
13. immigrant
    تارک وطن

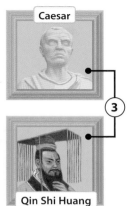
Mozart — Duke Ellington

Susan B. Anthony — César Chávez

Edison — Camarena

14. composer
    موسیقی ترتیب دینے والا
15. composition
    موسیقی کی ترتیب دینا

16. political movement
    سیاسی تحریک
17. activist
    انقلاب پسند

18. inventor
    مؤجد
19. invention
    ایجاد

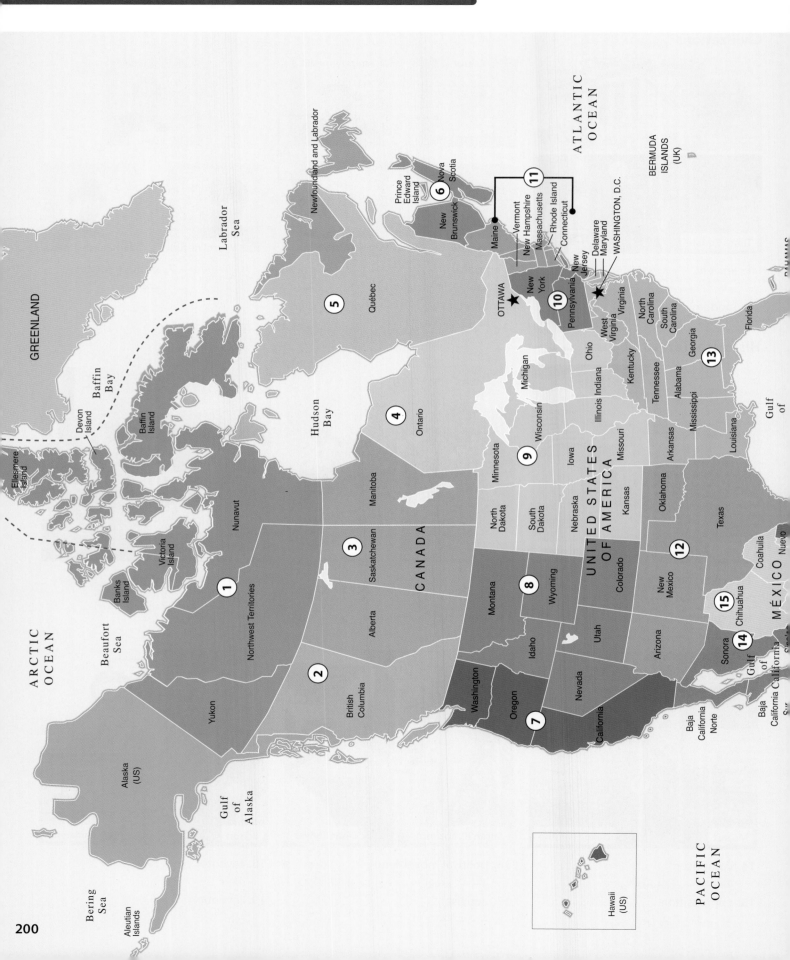

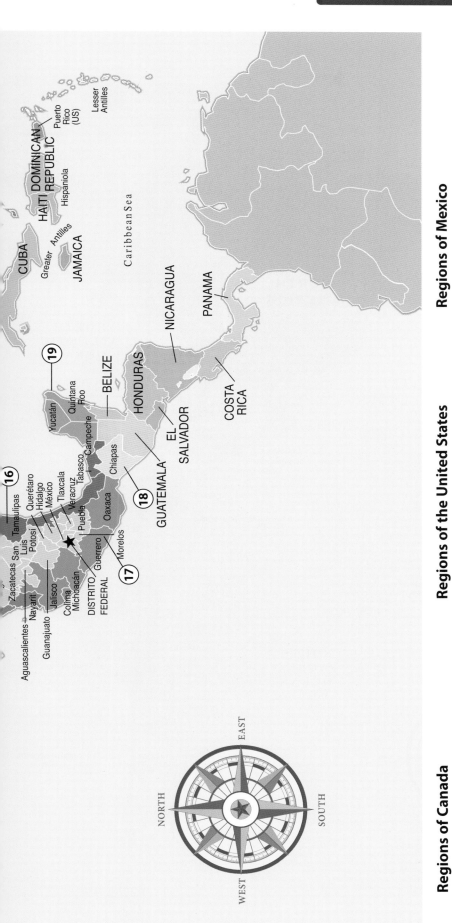

Greater Antilles
Lesser Antilles
Puerto Rico (US)
Hispaniola
DOMINICAN REPUBLIC
HAITI
CUBA
JAMAICA
Caribbean Sea
NICARAGUA
PANAMA
BELIZE
Yucatán
Quintana Roo
Campeche
HONDURAS
Tabasco
Veracruz
Chiapas
Oaxaca
Puebla
Tlaxcala
México
Hidalgo
Querétaro
EL SALVADOR
GUATEMALA
COSTA RICA
Morelos
Guerrero
DISTRITO FEDERAL
Michoacán
Colima
Jalisco
Nayarit
Zacatecas
San Luis Potosí
Tamaulipas
Aguascalientes
Guanajuato

16 **17** **18** **19**

EAST
NORTH
SOUTH
WEST

Regions of Canada
کناڈا کے خطے

1. Northern Canada
   شمالی کناڈا

2. British Columbia
   برٹش کولمبیا

3. The Prairie Provinces
   پریری کی ریاستیں

4. Ontario
   آنٹیریو

5. Québec
   کیوبیک

6. The Maritime Provinces
   میری ٹائم ریاستیں

Regions of the United States
ریاستہائے متحدہ کے خطے

7. The Pacific States / the West Coast
    بحر الکاہلی ریاستیں / جنوبی ساحل

8. The Rocky Mountain States
    روکی ماؤنٹین ریاستیں

9. The Midwest
    وسطی مغربی

10. The Mid-Atlantic States
     وسط اوقیانوسی ریاستیں

11. New England
     نیو انگلینڈ

12. The Southwest
     جنوبی مغربی

13. The Southeast / the South
     جنوبی مشرق / جنوب

Regions of Mexico
میکسیکو کے علاقے

14. The Pacific Northwest
     بحرالکاہلی شمال مغرب

15. The Plateau of Mexico
     میکسیکو کا پٹھار

16. The Gulf Coastal Plain
     خلیج ساحلی میدان

17. The Southern Uplands
     جنوبی اوپچ میدان

18. The Chiapas Highlands
     چیاپاس پہاڑیاں

19. The Yucatan Peninsula
     یوکاتان جزیرہ نما

Continents
براعظم

1. **North America**
   جنوبی امریکا
2. **South America**
   شمالی امریکا
3. **Europe**
   یورپ
4. **Asia**
   ایشیا
5. **Africa**
   افریقہ
6. **Australia**
   آسٹریلیا
7. **Antarctica**
   انارکٹکا

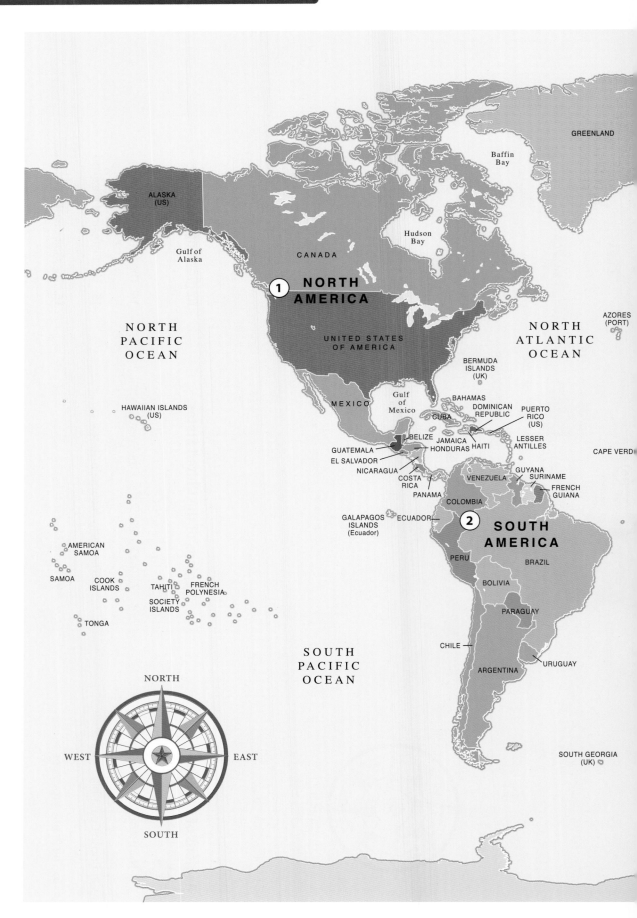

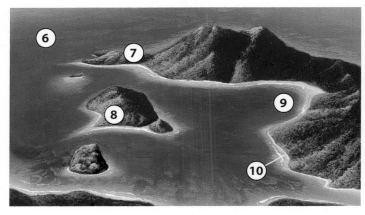

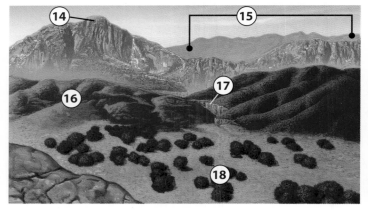

1. **rain forest**
   بارانی جنگل

2. **waterfall**
   چشمہ

3. **river**
   ندی

4. **desert**
   ریگستان

5. **sand dune**
   ریت کا تودہ

6. **ocean**
   سمندر

7. **peninsula**
   جزیرہ نما

8. **island**
   جزیرہ

9. **bay**
   خلیج

10. **beach**
    ساحلِ سمندر

11. **forest**
    جنگل

12. **shore**
    دریا کا کنارہ

13. **lake**
    جھیل

14. **mountain peak**
    پہاڑ کی چوٹی

15. **mountain range**
    پہاڑی سلسلہ

16. **hills**
    پہاڑیاں

17. **canyon**
    ندی کے ذریعے بنائی گئی کھائی

18. **valley**
    وادی

19. **plains**
    میدان

20. **meadow**
    چراہ گاہ

21. **pond**
    تالاب

More vocabulary

a body of water: a river, lake, or ocean
stream / creek: a very small river

Ask your classmates. Share the answers.

1. Would you rather live near a river or a lake?
2. Would you rather travel through a forest or a desert?
3. How often do you go to the beach or the shore?

The Solar System and the Planets نظام شمسی اور سیارے

Sun

1 2 3 4 5 6 7 8

Asteroid Belt

Orbit

1. Mercury عطارو	**3. Earth** زمین	**5. Jupiter** مشتری	**7. Uranus** یورینس
2. Venus زہرہ	**4. Mars** مریخ	**6. Saturn** زحل	**8. Neptune** نیپچون

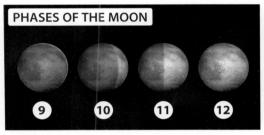

PHASES OF THE MOON

9 10 11 12

SPACE

15 14 13

16

9. new moon نیا چاند	**11. quarter moon** چوتھائی چاند	**13. star** ستارہ	**15. galaxy** کہکشاں
10. crescent moon بلال	**12. full moon** پورا چاند	**14. constellation** ستاروں کا جھرمٹ	**16. solar eclipse** سورج گرہن

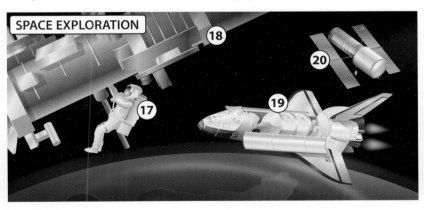

SPACE EXPLORATION

17 18 19 20

ASTRONOMY

21 22 23 24

17. astronaut خلا باز	**19. space shuttle** خلائی گاڑی	**21. observatory** رصدگاہ	**23. telescope** دوربین
18. space station خلائی اسٹیشن	**20. satellite** مصنوعی سیارہ	**22. astronomer** ماہر فلکیات	**24. comet** دمدار ستارہ

More vocabulary

solar eclipse: when the moon is between the earth and the sun
Big Dipper: a famous part of the constellation Ursa Major
Sirius: the brightest star in the night sky

Ask your classmates. Share the answers.

1. How do you feel when you look at the night sky?
2. Can you name one or more constellations?
3. Do you want to travel in space?

MySpot.Edu | Help | SignOut

Home | Search | Invite | Mail |

All Adelia's photos

I loved Art History.

My last economics lesson

Marching Band is great!

The photographer was upset.

We look good!

I get my diploma.

Dad and his digital camera

1. photographer
فوٹو گرافر

2. funny photo
غیر سنجیدہ تصویر

3. serious photo
سنجیدہ فوٹو

4. guest speaker
مہمان مقرر

5. podium
منبر پر مقرر کے سامنے لمبا بکسہ

6. ceremony
تقریب

7. cap
ٹوپی

8. gown
گاؤن

A. **take** a picture
تصویر لیجیے

B. **cry**
چیخیے

C. **celebrate**
جشن منائیے

People	Comments	
Sara	**June 29th 8:19 p.m.** Great pictures! What a day!	Delete
Zannie baby	**June 30th 10 a.m.** Love the funny photo.	Delete

I'm behind the mayor.

We're all very happy.

Look at the pictures.
What do you see?

Answer the questions.

1. How many people are wearing caps and gowns?

2. How many people are being funny? How many are being serious?

3. Who is standing at the podium?

4. Why are the graduates throwing their caps in the air?

 Read the story.

A Graduation

Look at these great photos on my web page! The first three are from my favorite classes, but the other pictures are from graduation day.

There are two pictures of my classmates in <u>caps</u> and <u>gowns</u>. In the first picture, we're laughing and the <u>photographer</u> is upset. In the second photo, we're serious. I like the <u>serious photo</u>, but I love the <u>funny photo</u>!

There's also a picture of our <u>guest speaker</u>, the mayor. She is standing at the <u>podium</u>. Next, you can see me at the graduation <u>ceremony</u>. My dad wanted to <u>take a picture</u> of me with my diploma. That's my mom next to him. She <u>cries</u> when she's happy.

After the ceremony, everyone was happy, but no one cried. We wanted to <u>celebrate</u> and we did!

Think about it.

1. What kinds of ceremonies are important for children? for teens? for adults?

2. Imagine you are the guest speaker at a graduation. What will you say to the graduates?

Nature Center قدرتی مرکز

1. trees
   درخت
2. soil
   مٹی
3. path
   راستہ
4. bird
   چڑیا
5. plants
   پودے
6. rock
   چٹان
7. flowers
   پھول

OAK **WILLOW** **ELM**

PLANT SALE 50% OFF

$7.

Listen and point. Take turns.

A: *Point to the trees.*
B: *Point to a bird.*
A: *Point to the flowers.*

Dictate to your partner. Take turns.

A: *Write it's a tree.*
B: *Let me check that. I-t-'s -a- t-r-e-e?*
A: *Yes, that's right.*

8. sun
سورج

9. sky
آسمان

10. mammals
تھن دار جانور

11. insects
کیڑے مکوڑے

12. nest
گھونسلا

13. water
پانی

14. fish
مچھلی

Ways to talk about nature

Look at the sky! Isn't it beautiful?
Did you see the fish / insects?
It's / They're so interesting.

Pair practice. Make new conversations.

A: *Do you know the name of that yellow flower?*
B: *I think it's a sunflower.*
A: *Oh, and what about that blue bird?*

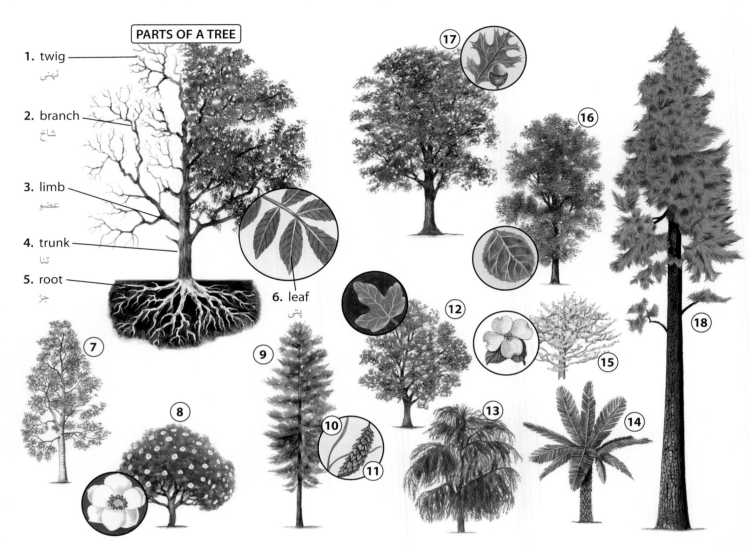

PARTS OF A TREE

1. twig
ٹہنی

2. branch
شاخ

3. limb
عضو

4. trunk
تنا

5. root
جڑ

6. leaf
پتی

7. birch بھوج پتر	**10.** needle سوئی نما پتی	**13.** willow بید یا بیدِ مجنوں	**16.** elm شجربق
8. magnolia زرد چکتے پھولوں کا درخت میگنولیہ	**11.** pinecone چیڑ کا پھل	**14.** palm پام	**17.** oak اوک
9. pine چیڑ	**12.** maple میپل	**15.** dogwood جنگلی کندر	**18.** redwood امریکی سرخ لکڑی کا پیڑ

Plants پودے

19. holly راج درخت ہولی	**21.** cactus ناگ پھنی	**23.** poison sumac زہریلا سماق	**25.** poison ivy زہریلا آئی وی
20. berries بیری	**22.** vine انگور	**24.** poison oak زہریلا اوک	

Parts of a Flower پھول کے اجزاء

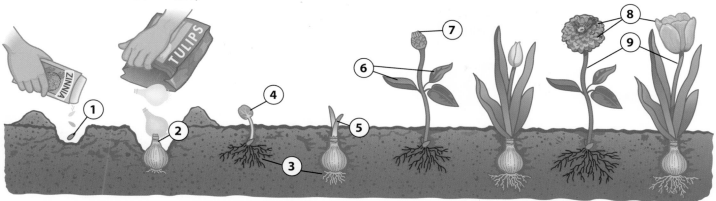

1. **seed**
   بیج

2. **bulb**
   گانٹھ

3. **roots**
   جڑ

4. **seedling**
   انکھوا

5. **shoot**
   کونپل

6. **leaves**
   پتیاں

7. **bud**
   کلی

8. **petals**
   پنکھڑیاں

9. **stems**
   تنے

10. **sunflower**
    سورج مکھی

11. **tulip**
    لالہ

12. **hibiscus**
    گڑہل

13. **marigold**
    گیندا

14. **daisy**
    ڈیزی

15. **rose**
    گلاب

16. **iris**
    سوسن

17. **crocus**
    زعفران

18. **gardenia**
    گارڈینیا

19. **orchid**
    آرچڈ

20. **carnation**
    گل لحمی

21. **chrysanthemum**
    گل داؤدی

22. **jasmine**
    یاسمین

23. **violet**
    بنفشہ

24. **poinsettia**
    زرد پھول اور گلابی پتیوں کی ایک جھاڑی

25. **daffodil**
    جنس نرگسی کا ذرا بڑا پیلے
    پھولوں کا پودا

26. **lily**
    نرگس

27. **houseplant**
    گھریلو پودا

28. **bouquet**
    گل دستہ

29. **thorn**
    کانٹا

Sea Animals سمندری حیوانات

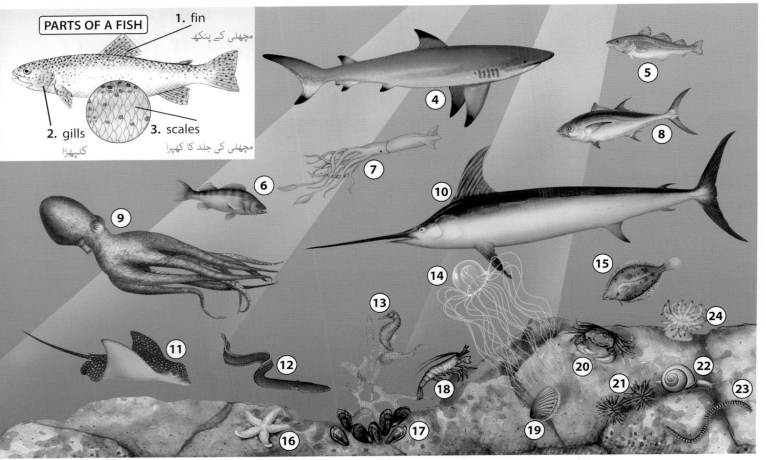

PARTS OF A FISH

1. fin
مچھلی کے پنکھ

2. gills
گلپھڑا

3. scales
مچھلی کی جلد کا کھپرا

4. shark شارک مچھلی / کلب البحر	**8. tuna** تونا مچھلی	**13. seahorse** گھوڑا مچھلی	**17. mussel** دوصمامی گھونگھا	**22. snail** گھونگھا کی ایک قسم
5. cod کاڈ مچھلی	**9. octopus** آکٹوپس / آٹھ پایہ صوفہ	**14. jellyfish** جیلی نما جسم کا سمندری مرجانی جانور	**18. shrimp** دس پاؤں والا جھینگا	**23. worm** لمبا پتلا رینگنے والا جانور
6. bass عام کانٹے دار مچھلی / خار ماہی	**10. swordfish** کنار مچھلی / سیاف	**15. flounder** چپٹی خوردنی / فلاؤنڈر مچھلی	**19. scallop** گھونگھا	**24. sea anemone** کوئی سمندری مرجانی حیویہ
7. squid لمبا آٹھ سر پایہ صدفہ	**11. ray** رائیہ مچھلی	**16. starfish** ستارہ مچھلی	**20. crab** کیکڑا	
	12. eel بام / سانپ نما مچھلی		**21. sea urchin** سمندری ارچن	

Amphibians خشکی اور پانی میں رہنے والے جانور

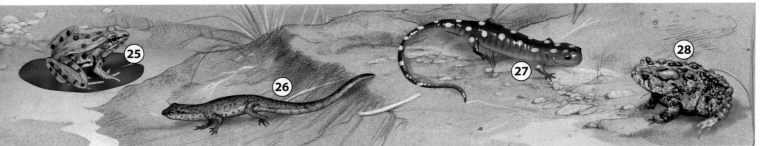

25. frog مینڈک	**26. newt** نیوٹ	**27. salamander** سالمنڈر	**28. toad** ٹوڈ (مینڈک کی ایک قسم)

سمندری زندگی، خشکی و پانی میں رہنے والے حیوانات اور سانپ اور چھپکلی کی نسل کے جانور

Sea Mammals سمندری تھن دار جانور

29. whale	**31.** dolphin	**33.** sea lion	**35.** sea otter
وہیل	ڈولفن	بحر الکاہل میں پایا جانے والا بحری شیر	اود بلاؤ
30. porpoise	**32.** walrus	**34.** seal	
وہیل کی نسل کا جانور	شمالی قطبی علاقہ کا فیل البحر	سیل	

Reptiles سانپ اور چھپکلی کی نسل کے رینگنے والے جانور

36. alligator	**38.** rattlesnake	**40.** lizard	**42.** tortoise
گھڑیال	زہریلا کھڑ کھڑ یا سانپ / مارزنگی	چھپکلی	پاتر
37. crocodile	**39.** garter snake	**41.** cobra	**43.** turtle
مگرمچھ	لمبی پٹیوں والا شمالی امریکی سانپ	ناگ	کچھوا

Birds, Insects, and Arachnids

پرندے، کیڑے مکوڑے اور مفصل پایہ
(چار جوڑی پیر والے کیڑے)

PARTS OF A BIRD

1. wing
بازو / پنکھ

2. claw
پنجہ

3. beak / bill
چونچ / پتلی چونچ

4. feather
پَر

5. owl اُلّو	**8.** woodpecker کٹھ پھوڑ / بڈ بڈ	**11.** penguin پنگوئن / بطریق	**14.** peacock مور
6. blue jay نیلی بہت شور مچانے والی یورپی چڑیا	**9.** eagle باز / عقاب	**12.** duck بطخ	**15.** pigeon کبوتر
7. sparrow گوریا	**10.** hummingbird مرمر پرندہ / شکرخوار	**13.** goose ہنس / بطخ خاندان کے آبی پرندے	**16.** robin کستوری

Insects and Arachnids کیڑے مکوڑے اور مفصل پایہ

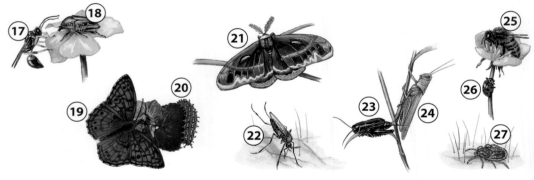

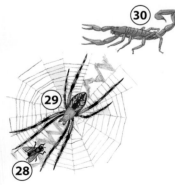

17. wasp بھڑ / تتیا	**21.** moth بھونرا / پتنگا	**25.** honeybee شہد کی مکھی	**29.** spider مکڑی
18. beetle تل چنا	**22.** mosquito مچھر	**26.** ladybug چتی دار بھونرا	**30.** scorpion بچھو
19. butterfly تتلی	**23.** cricket جھینگر	**27.** tick چیچڑی	
20. caterpillar تتلی کا رینگنے والا بچہ	**24.** grasshopper ٹڈی	**28.** fly مکھی	

Farm Animals کاشت کے جانور

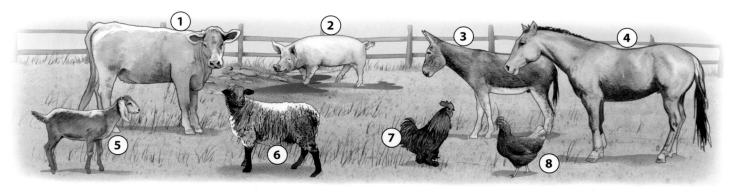

1. cow
گائے

2. pig
سور

3. donkey
گدھا

4. horse
گھوڑا

5. goat
بکری

6. sheep
بھیڑ

7. rooster
گھریلو مرغا

8. hen
مرغی

Pets پالتو جانور

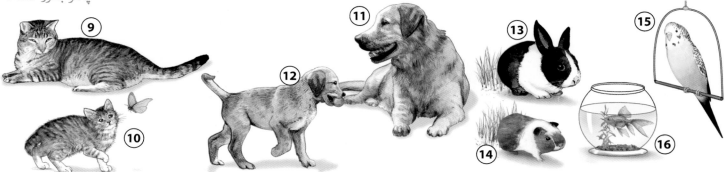

9. cat
بلّی

10. kitten
بلّی کا بچہ

11. dog
کتّا

12. puppy
پلّا

13. rabbit
خرگوش

14. guinea pig
گنی پگ / پالتو چوہا

15. parakeet
پیراکیٹ / لمبی دم والا طوطا

16. goldfish
گولڈ فش / سیم مابی

Rodents کترنے کے دانتوں والے جانور

17. rat
چوہا

18. mouse
جنگلی چوہا

19. gopher
شمالی امریکہ کا پھولے کلوں کا چوہا

20. chipmunk
چپ منک (زمینی گلہری)

21. squirrel
گلہری

22. prairie dog
پریری کتّا (کتّے کی سی آواز والا)

More vocabulary

domesticated: animals that work for and / or live with people

wild: animals that live away from people

Ask your classmates. Share the answers.

1. Have you worked with farm animals? Which ones?
2. Are you afraid of rodents? Which ones?
3. Do you have a pet? What kind?

1. moose
موز

2. mountain lion
پہاڑی شیر

3. coyote
کویوٹ

4. opossum
اوپوسم

5. wolf
بھیڑیا

6. buffalo / bison
بھینس / بائیسن

7. bat
چمگادڑ

8. armadillo
آرماڈلو

9. beaver
بیور

10. porcupine
سیہی

11. bear
ریچھ

12. skunk
اسکنک

13. raccoon
ریکون

14. deer
برن

15. fox
لومڑی

16. antlers
بارہ سنگھوں کی شاخ

17. hooves
کھر

18. whiskers
گل مچھے

19. coat / fur
بالوں والی بابری جلد / فر

20. paw
پنجہ

21. horn
سینگ

22. tail
دُم

23. quill
سیہی کا کانٹا

216

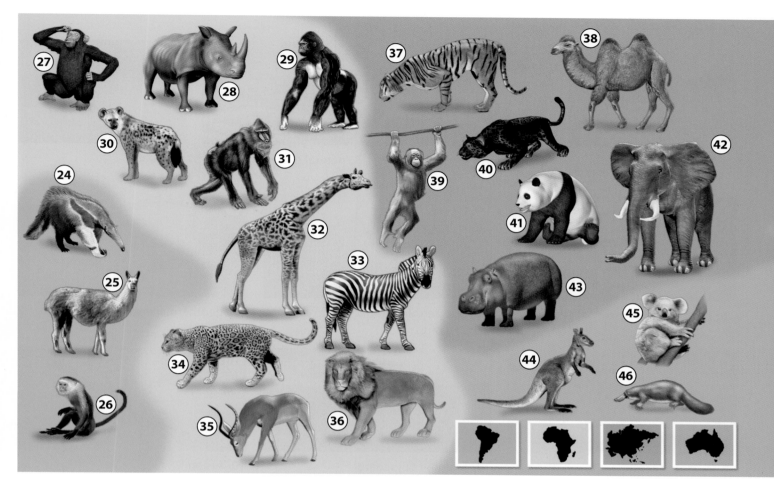

24. anteater	29. gorilla	34. leopard	39. orangutan	44. kangaroo
چيونٹی خور	گوريلا	تيندوا	اورنگٹان	کنگارو
25. llama	30. hyena	35. antelope	40. panther	45. koala
لاما	لکڑبگھا	باره سنگھا	کالا چيتا	کوالا
26. monkey	31. baboon	36. lion	41. panda	46. platypus
بندر	ببون	شيرِببر	پانڈا	پليئی پس
27. chimpanzee	32. giraffe	37. tiger	42. elephant	
چمپنزی	جراف	باگھ	باتھی	
28. rhinoceros	33. zebra	38. camel	43. hippopotamus	
گينڈا	زيبرا	اونٹ	دريائی گھوڑا	

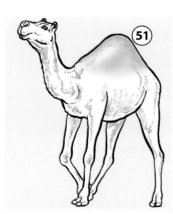

47. trunk	48. tusk	49. mane	50. pouch	51. hump
سونڈ	باتھی دانت	شير کی ايال	تھيلی	کوبان

217

Energy Sources توانائی کے ذرائع

1. solar energy
شمسی توانائی

2. wind power
ہوائی طاقت

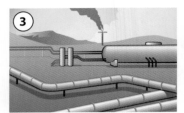
3. natural gas
قدرتی گیس

4. coal
کوئلہ

5. hydroelectric power
پانی سے پیدا کی ہوئی بجلی

6. oil / petroleum
تیل / پٹرولیم

7. geothermal energy
زمینی حرارت کی توانائی

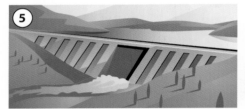
8. nuclear energy
نیوکلیائی توانائی

9. biomass / bioenergy
حیاتیاتی تجمع / حیاتیاتی توانائی

10. fusion
اختلاط

Pollution آلودگی

11. air pollution / smog
ہوائی آلودگی / دھند

12. hazardous waste
خطرناک فضلہ

13. acid rain
تیزابی بارش

14. water pollution
آبی آلودگی

15. radiation
تابکاری

16. pesticide poisoning
کیڑا مار دواؤں کے زہریلے اثرات

17. oil spill
تیل کا رساؤ

Ask your classmates. Share the answers.
1. What types of things do you recycle?
2. What types of energy sources are in your area?
3. What types of pollution do you worry about?

Think about it. Discuss.
1. How can you save energy in the summer? winter?
2. What are some other ways that people can conserve energy or prevent pollution?

Ways to Conserve Energy and Resources توانائی اور وسائل کو محفوظ رکھنے کے طریقے

A. reduce trash
کوڑا کرکٹ کم کیجیے

B. reuse shopping bags
خریداری تھیلیوں کو دوبارہ استعمال کیجیے

C. recycle
بازگردانی کیجیے

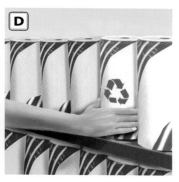

D. buy recycled products
بازگردانی کیے گئے سامان خریدیے

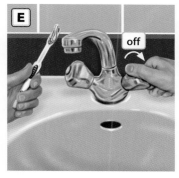

E. save water
پانی بچائیے

F. fix leaky faucets
رستے ہوئے نلوں کو ٹھیک کیجیے

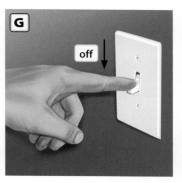

G. turn off lights
روشنی بلب بند کر دیجیے

H. use energy-efficient bulbs
بجلی بچانے والے بلب استعمال کیجیے

I. carpool
گاڑی کو مشترک طور پر استعمال کیجیے

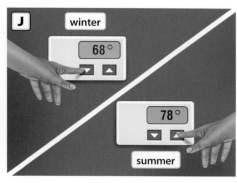

J. adjust the thermostat
تھرموسنیٹ ایڈجسٹ کیجیے

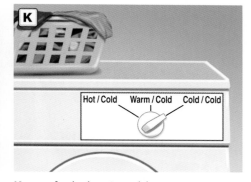

K. wash clothes in cold water
کپڑے ٹھنڈے پانی سے دھوئیے

L. don't litter
فضلہ ادھر ادھر نہ پھیلائیے

M. compost food scraps
بچے ہوئے کھانے سے کھاد بنائیے

N. plant a tree
درخت لگائیے

Yosemite
NATIONAL PARK

Dry Tortugas
NATIONAL PARK

Half Dome

Fort Jefferson

1

2

4

3

5

1. landmarks	3. wildlife	5. coral	7. caverns
ابم علامات	جنگلی زندگی	مونگا	اندھیری بڑی غار
2. park ranger	4. ferry	6. cave	A. **take** a tour
پارک رینجر	کشتی	غار	سفر کیجیے

220

CARLSBAD CAVERNS

NATIONAL PARK

6

7

A

Answer the questions.

1. How many U.S. landmarks are in the pictures?
2. What kinds of wildlife do you see?
3. What can you do at Carlsbad Caverns?

Read the story.

U.S. National Parks

More than 200 million people visit U.S. National Parks every year. These parks protect the <u>wildlife</u> and <u>landmarks</u> of the United States. Each park is different, and each one is beautiful.

At Yosemite, in California, you can take a nature walk with a <u>park ranger</u>. You'll see waterfalls, redwoods, and deer there.

In south Florida, you can take a <u>ferry</u> to Dry Tortugas. It's great to snorkel around the park's <u>coral</u> islands.

There are 113 <u>caves</u> at Carlsbad <u>Caverns</u> in New Mexico. The deepest cave is 830 feet below the desert! You can <u>take a tour</u> of these beautiful caverns.

There are 391 national parks to see. Go online for information about a park near you.

Think about it.

1. Why are national parks important?
2. Imagine you are a park ranger at a national park. Give your classmates a tour of the landmarks and wildlife.

221

اپنے شہر میں دیکھنے کے قابل مقامات

1. zoo
چڑیا گھر

2. movies
سنیما

3. botanical garden
نباتاتی باغ

4. bowling alley
باؤلنگ کھیلنے کی جگہ

5. rock concert
راک کنسرٹ

6. swap meet /
flea market
مبادلہ بازار / پرانی اشیاء کا بازار

7. aquarium
زندہ آبی جانوروں و پودوں کی
نمائش

| File | Edit | View | History | Bookmarks | Tools |

Places to Go in Our City

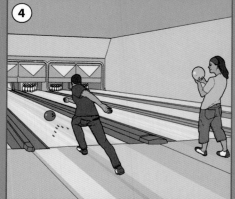

Listen and point. Take turns.

A: *Point to the zoo.*
B: *Point to the flea market.*
A: *Point to the rock concert.*

Dictate to your partner. Take turns.

A: *Write these words: zoo, movies, aquarium.*
B: *Zoo, movies, and what?*
A: *Aquarium.*

Search

8. play
کھیل / ڈرامہ
9. art museum
عجائب خانۂ فن
10. amusement park
تفریحی پارک
11. opera
اوپیرا
12. nightclub
ڈسکو کلب
13. county fair
کاؤنٹی میله
14. classical concert
کلاسیکی موسیقی کی محفل

BACH FESTIVAL

Ways to make plans using *Let's go*

***Let's go** to the amusement park tomorrow.*
***Let's go** to the opera on Saturday.*
***Let's go** to the movies tonight.*

Pair practice. Make new conversations.

A: *Let's go to the zoo this afternoon.*
B: *OK. And let's go to the movies tonight.*
A: *That sounds like a good plan.*

223

1. **ball field**
   گیند کھیلنے کا میدان

2. **cyclist**
   سائیکل سوار

3. **bike path**
   سائیکل چلانے کا راستہ

4. **jump rope**
   رسّہ کودنے والی رسّی

5. **fountain**
   فوارہ

6. **tennis court**
   ٹینس کا کورٹ

7. **skateboard**
   اسکیٹ بورڈ

8. **picnic table**
   پکنک کی میز

9. **water fountain**
   پانی کا فوارہ

10. **bench**
    بنچ

11. **swings**
    جھولے

12. **tricycle**
    تین پہیہ سائیکل

13. **slide**
    سلائڈ

14. **climbing apparatus**
    چڑھنے والے اوزار

15. **sandbox**
    سینڈ باکس

16. **seesaw**
    سلامی دار ڈھانچہ

A. pull the wagon
ویگن کو کھینچیے

B. push the swing
جھولے کو دھکّا دیجیے

C. climb the bars
بلیوں پر چڑھیے

D. picnic / have a picnic
پکنک منائیے / پکنک پر جائیے

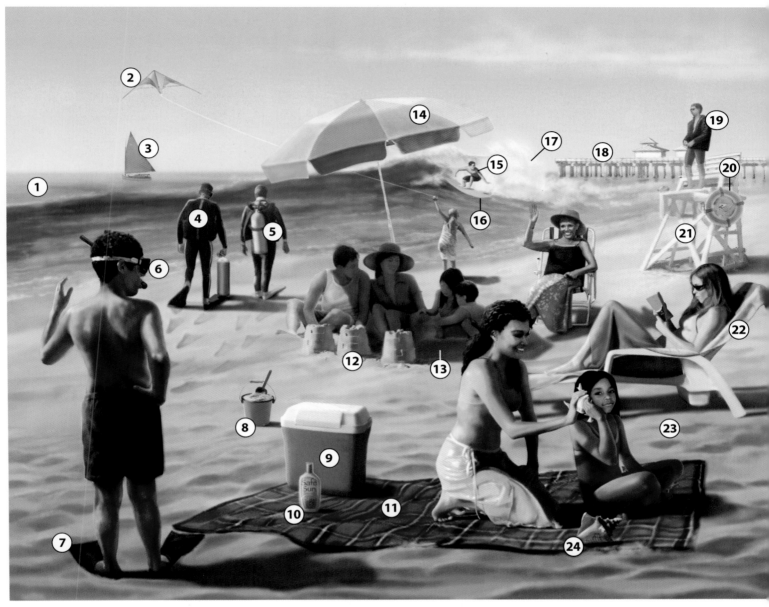

1. ocean / water
سمندر / پانی

2. kite
پتنگ

3. sailboat
پتواری کشتی

4. wet suit
پانی کا لباس

5. scuba tank
پانی کے اندر سانس لینے کا ٹینک

6. diving mask
ڈُبکی لگاتے وقت پہننے والی نقاب

7. fins
مچھلی کے بازو جیسے پر

8. pail / bucket
ڈول / بالٹی

9. cooler
ٹھنڈا رکھنے والا

10. sunscreen / sunblock
دھوپ سے بچنے کے لیے اسکرین / محلول

11. blanket
کمبل

12. sand castle
ریت محل

13. shade
سائبان

14. beach umbrella
ساحلی چھتری

15. surfer
موجوں پر تیرنے والا

16. surfboard
موجوں پر تیرنے کے لیے لکڑی کا تختہ

17. wave
لہر

18. pier
گھاٹ

19. lifeguard
زندگی بچانے والا محافظ

20. lifesaving device
زندگی بچانے والے آلات

21. lifeguard station
زندگی بچانے والے محافظوں کا اسٹیشن

22. beach chair
ساحلی کرسی

23. sand
ریت

24. seashell
سمندری سیپ

More vocabulary

seaweed: a plant that grows in the ocean
tide: the level of the ocean. The tide goes in and out every 12 hours.

Ask your classmates. Share the answers.

1. Do you like to go to the beach?
2. Are there famous beaches in your native country?
3. Do you prefer to be on the sand or in the water?

225

1. boating
   کشتی رانی
2. rafting
   بجرا چلانا
3. canoeing
   چھوٹی کشتی چلانا
4. fishing
   مچھلی پکڑنا
5. camping
   خیمہ لگانا
6. backpacking
   پیٹھ پر سامان لادنا
7. hiking
   پیدل چلنا
8. mountain biking
   پہاڑ پر سائیکل چلانا
9. horseback riding
   گھوڑ سواری

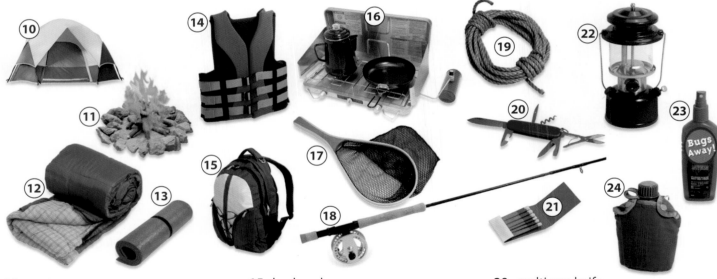

10. tent
    خیمہ
11. campfire
    رات میں تمبو کے باہر جلائی گئی آگ
12. sleeping bag
    سونے والے تھیلے
13. foam pad
    ربر کا گدا
14. life vest
    حفاظتی صدری
15. backpack
    کمر پر لادنے والا تھیلا
16. camping stove
    تمبو میں استعمال ہونے والا اسٹوو
17. fishing net
    مچھلی پکڑنے کا جال
18. fishing pole
    مچھلی پکڑنے کی چھڑ
19. rope
    رسی
20. multi-use knife
    کئی کاموں والا چاقو
21. matches
    ماچس
22. lantern
    لالٹین
23. insect repellent
    کیڑوں کو دور رکھنے والا مادہ
24. canteen
    کینٹین

1. downhill skiing
پہاڑ سے نیچے کی طرف اسکیئنگ

2. snowboarding
سنو بورڈنگ

3. cross-country skiing
دیہاتی علاقے میں اسکیئنگ

4. ice skating
آئس اسکیئنگ

5. figure skating
فیگر اسکیئنگ

6. sledding
برف پر بغیر پہیوں کی گاڑی سے پھسلنا

7. waterskiing
وائٹر اسکیئنگ

8. sailing
کشتی رانی

9. surfing
سرفنگ

10. windsurfing
ونڈ سرفنگ

11. snorkeling
زیرِ آب تیرنا

12. scuba diving
سانس لینے کے آلہ کی مدد سے غوطہ لگانا

More vocabulary

speed skating: racing while ice skating
windsurfing: sailboarding

Ask your classmates. Share the answers.

1. Which of these sports do you like?
2. Which of these sports would you like to learn?
3. Which of these sports is the most fun to watch?

227

1. archery
تیر اندازی

2. billiards / pool
بلیرڈز / پول

3. bowling
گیند بازی

4. boxing
مکے بازی

5. cycling / biking
سائیکل چلانا / بائیسکل چلانا

6. badminton
بیڈمنٹن

7. fencing
تلوار بازی

8. golf
گولف

9. gymnastics
جسمانی کرتب بازی

10. inline skating
ان لائن اسکیٹنگ

11. martial arts
مارشل آرٹس

12. racquetball
ریکٹ بال

13. skateboarding
اسکیٹنگ بورڈنگ

14. table tennis
ٹیبل ٹینس

15. tennis
ٹینس

16. weightlifting
وزن اٹھانا

17. wrestling
کشتی

18. track and field
دوڑ اور دیگر میدانی کھیل

19. horse racing
گھڑ دوڑ

Pair practice. Make new conversations.

A: *What sports do you like?*
B: *I like bowling. What do you like?*
A: *I like gymnastics.*

Think about it. Discuss.

1. Why do people like to watch sports?
2. Which sports can be dangerous?
3. Why do people do dangerous sports?

1. score
اسکور

2. coach
کھیلوں کا اطالیق

3. team
ٹیم

4. fan
کھیل دیکھنے کا شوقین

5. player
کھلاڑی

6. official / referee
افسر / ریفری

7. basketball court
باسکٹ بال کورٹ

8. basketball
باسکٹ بال

9. baseball
بیس بال

10. softball
سافٹ بال

11. football
فٹ بال

12. soccer
ساکر (فٹ بال)

13. ice hockey
برف کے میدان کا ہاکی کا کھیل

14. volleyball
والی بال

15. water polo
واٹر پولو

More Vocabulary

win: to have the best score
lose: the opposite of win
tie: to have the same score

captain: the team leader
umpire: the name of the referee in baseball
Little League: a baseball and softball program for children

A. **pitch**
بلّے کی طرف گیند پھینکیے

B. **hit**
ضرب لگائیے

C. **throw**
پھینکیے

D. **catch**
گیند پکڑیے

E. **kick**
ٹھوکر لگائیے

F. **tackle**
گیند کو سنبھالتے ہوئے آگے بڑھیے

G. **pass**
گیند دوسرے کو دیجیے

H. **shoot**
نشانہ لگائیے

I. **jump**
اچھلیے

J. **dribble**
گیند کو دوسرے کھلاڑی سے بچاتے ہوئے آگے بڑھیے

K. **dive**
پانی میں چھلانگ لگائیے

L. **swim**
تیرئیے

M. **stretch**
پھیلائیے

N. **exercise / work out**
ورزش کیجیے / محنت کیجیے

O. **bend**
جھکیے

P. **serve**
گیند سے کھیل شروع کیجیے

Q. **swing**
(گولف میں) زور کی ضرب لگائیے

R. **start**
شروع کیجیے

S. **race**
دوڑ لگائیے

T. **finish**
ختم کیجیے

U. **skate**
اسکیٹ کیجیے

V. **ski**
اسکی کیجیے

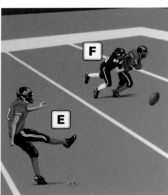

Use the new words.
Look on page 229. Name the actions you see.

A: He's _throwing_.
B: She's _jumping_.

Ways to talk about your sports skills

I can _throw_, but I can't _catch_.
I _swim_ well, but I don't _dive_ well.
I'm good at _skating_, but I'm terrible at _skiing_.

1. golf club
   گولف کلب

2. tennis racket
   ٹینس کا ریکٹ

3. volleyball
   والی بال

4. basketball
   باسکٹ بال

5. bowling ball
   پھینکنے والی بال

6. bow
   کمان

7. target
   نشانہ

8. arrow
   تیر

9. ice skates
   برف پر چلنے والے جوتے

10. inline skates
    ان لائن اسکیٹس

11. hockey stick
    ہاکی اسٹک

12. soccer ball
    ساکر بال (فٹ بال)

13. shin guards
    ساق بند

14. baseball bat
    بیس بال بلّا

15. catcher's mask
    بلّے باز کے پیچھے کھڑے کھلاڑی کی نقاب

16. uniform
    کھیل کا لباس

17. glove
    دستانہ

18. baseball
    بیس بال

19. football helmet
    فٹ بال ہیلمٹ

20. shoulder pads
    کندھے کی گدی

21. football
    فٹ بال

22. weights
    وزن

23. snowboard
    برف رانی والا تختہ

24. skis
    برف رانی والے لمبے نکیلے تختے

25. ski poles
    برف رانی کے ہاتھ سے استعمال کرنے والے ڈنڈے

26. ski boots
    اسکی بوٹ

27. flying disc*
    اڑانے والی تشتری

* **Note:** one brand is Frisbee®, of Wham-O, Inc.

Use the new words.
Look at pages 228–229. Name the sports equipment you see.

A: *Those are ice skates.*
B: *That's a football.*

Ask your classmates. Share the answers.

1. Do you own any sports equipment? What kind?
2. What do you want to buy at this store?
3. Where is the best place to buy sports equipment?

231

پسندیدہ مشغلے اور کھیل

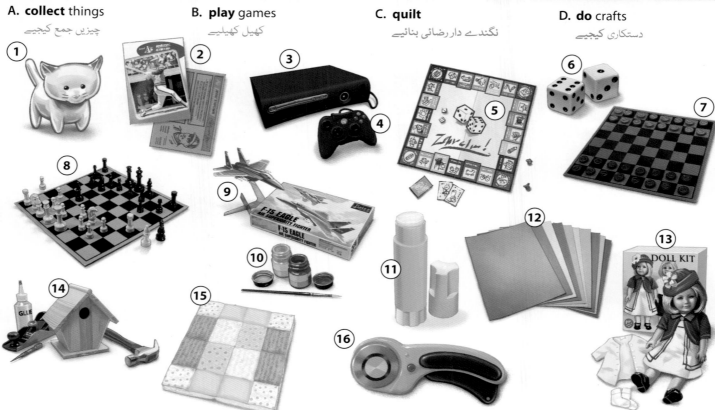

A. collect things
چیزیں جمع کیجیے

B. play games
کھیل کھیلیے

C. quilt
نگندے دار رضائی بنائیے

D. do crafts
دستکاری کیجیے

1. figurine
چھوٹی مورت

2. baseball cards
بیس بال کارڈ

3. video game console
ویڈیو گیم کھیلنے کا تختہ

4. video game control
ویڈیو گیم کنٹرول

5. board game
بورڈ گیم

6. dice
پانسہ

7. checkers
ڈرافٹس کا کھیل

8. chess
شطرنج

9. model kit
کوئی نمونہ بنانے والا ساز و سامان

10. acrylic paint
ایکریلک رنگ

11. glue stick
گوند اسٹک

12. construction paper
تعمیر کرنے والا رنگ برنگا کاغذ

13. doll making kit
گڑیا بنانے کا ساز و سامان

14. woodworking kit
لکڑی کے کام کا ساز و سامان

15. quilt block
رضائی بنانے کا بلاک

16. rotary cutter
کائنے والی چرخی

Grammar Point: *How often do you play cards?*

*I play **all the time**. (every day)*
*I play **sometimes**. (once a month)*
*I **never** play. (0 times)*

Pair practice. Make new conversations.

A: *How often do you do your hobbies?*
B: *I play games all the time. I love chess.*
A: *Really? I never play chess.*

E. paint
رنگائی کیجیے

F. knit
بنائی کیجیے

G. pretend
تماشہ کیجیے

H. play cards
تاش کھیلیے

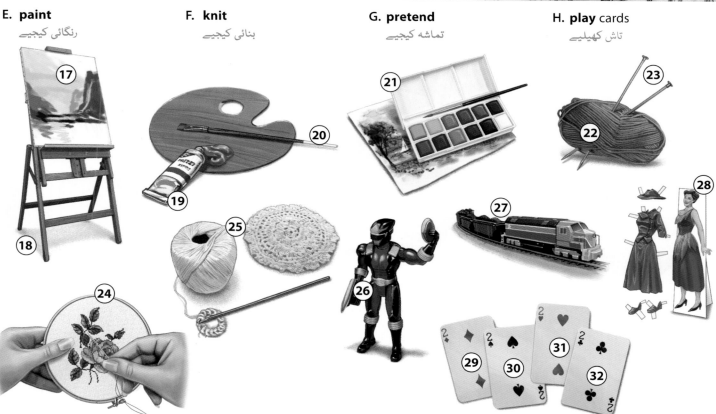

17. canvas
تصویر بنانے کا موٹا کپڑا

18. easel
ڈھانچہ

19. oil paint
تیل سے بنائے گئے رنگ

20. paintbrush
رنگائی کرنے والا برش

21. watercolor
آبی رنگ

22. yarn
اون

23. knitting needles
بنائی کی سلائیاں

24. embroidery
کڑھائی

25. crocheting
کروشیا

26. action figure
حرکی کھلونا

27. model trains
ریل گاڑی کا نمونے

28. paper dolls
کاغذ کی گڑیاں

29. diamonds
اینٹ کے پتوں کا سلسلہ

30. spades
حکم کے پتوں کا سلسلہ

31. hearts
پان کے پتوں کا سلسلہ

32. clubs
پھول کے پتوں کا سلسلہ

Ways to talk about hobbies and games

*This <u>board game</u> is **interesting**. It makes me think.*
*That <u>video game</u> is **boring**. Nothing happens.*
*I love to <u>play cards</u>. It's **fun** to play with my friends.*

Ask your classmates. Share the answers.

1. Do you collect anything? What?
2. Which games do you like to play?
3. What hobbies did you have as a child?

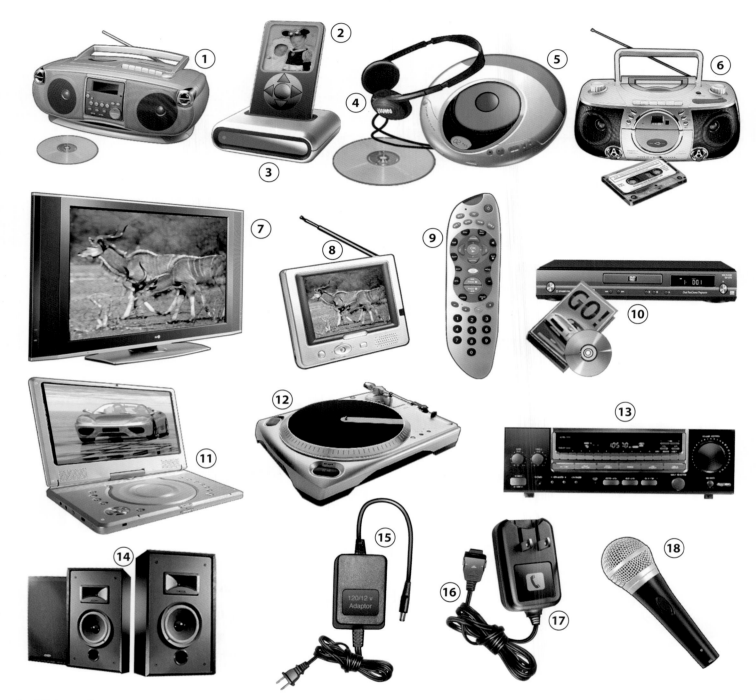

1. CD boombox
   پورٹیبل سی ڈی اسٹیریو

2. MP3 player
   ایم پی تھری پلیئر

3. dock
   ڈاک

4. headphones
   ہیڈفونز

5. personal CD player
   ذاتی سی ڈی پلیئر

6. portable cassette player
   چھوٹا کیسٹ پلیئر

7. flat screen TV / flat panel TV
   بالکل چپنے اسکرین کا ٹی وی / چپٹے پردے کا ٹی وی

8. portable TV
   چھوٹا ٹی وی

9. universal remote
   متعدد افعال کے لیے ریموٹ

10. DVD player
    ڈی وی ڈی پلیئر

11. portable DVD player
    چھوٹا ڈی وی ڈی پلیئر

12. turntable
    ٹرن ٹیبل

13. tuner
    ٹیونر

14. speakers
    اسپیکرز

15. adapter
    اڈاپٹر

16. plug
    پلگ

17. charger
    چارجر

18. microphone
    مائکروفون

19. digital camera
عددی (ڈیجیٹل) کیمرا

20. memory card
حافظہ (میموری) کارڈ

21. film camera / 35 mm camera
فلم کیمرا / ۳۵ ایم ایم کیمرا

22. film
فلم

23. zoom lens
چھوٹا بڑا کرنے والا عدسہ

24. camcorder
پورٹیبل ویڈیو کیمرہ

25. tripod
تین ڈنڈوں کا اسٹینڈ

26. battery pack
بیٹری پیک

27. battery charger
بیٹری چارجر

28. camera case
کیمرہ رکھنے کا خول

29. LCD projector
ایل سی ڈی پروجیکٹر

30. screen
پردہ

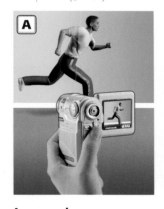

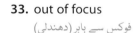

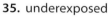

31. photo album
فوٹو البم

32. digital photo album
عددی (ڈیجیٹل) فوٹو البم

33. out of focus
فوکس سے باہر (دھندلی)

34. overexposed
زیادہ دیر تک روشنی پڑنے والی تصویر

35. underexposed
تھوڑی دیر تک روشنی پڑنے والی تصویر

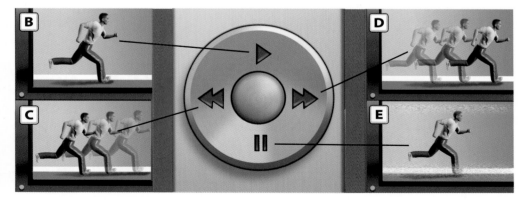

A. record
ریکارڈ کریں

B. play
چلائیں

C. rewind
پیچھے گھمائیں

D. fast forward
آگے بڑھائیں

E. pause
موقوف کریں

Types of TV Programs ٹی وی پروگرام کی قسمیں

1. news program
خبروں کے پروگرام

2. sitcom (situation comedy)
مزاحیہ صورت حال کا ڈرامہ

3. cartoon
کارٹون

4. talk show
گفتگو و مباحثے کے پروگرام

5. soap opera
لمبے چلنے والے (سیریل) پروگرام

6. reality show
حقیقی پروگرام

7. nature program
قدرتی مناظر کے پروگرام

8. game show
لاٹری وغیرہ سے متعلق پروگرام

9. children's program
بچوں کے پروگرام

10. shopping program
خرید و فروخت کے پروگرام

11. sports program
کھیلوں کے پروگرام

12. drama
ڈرامہ

236

Types of Movies فلموں کی قسمیں

13. comedy
طربیہ / کامیڈی

14. tragedy
المیہ / ٹریجڈی

15. western
تاریخی اعتبار سے قدیم مغربی
امریکی انداز کی فلمیں

16. romance
رومانی

17. horror story
ڈراؤنی کہانی

18. science fiction story
سائنسی تخیلی کہانی

19. action story / adventure story
تیز طرار کہانی/مہم جوئی کی کہانی

20. mystery / suspense
حیرت ناک / پر اسرار واقعات

Types of Music موسیقی کی قسمیں

21. classical
کلاسیکی

22. blues
دکھ بھری موسیقی

23. rock
جھوم جھوم کر گانا بجانا

24. jazz
امریکی حبشی نژاد باشندوں کا گانا

25. pop
پاپ

26. hip hop
ہپ ہاپ

27. country
دیہی

28. R&B / soul
آر و بی/ سول

29. folk
جماعتی

30. gospel
مذہبی / مسیحی

31. reggae
غرب الہندی موسیقی

32. world music
عالمی موسیقی

A. **play** an instrument
کوئی ساز بجائیے

B. **sing** a song
کوئی گانا گائیے

C. **conduct** an orchestra
آرکسٹرا کو ہدایت دیجیے

D. **be** in a rock band
راک بینڈ میں شمولیت کیجیے

Woodwinds ووڈونڈز (منہ سے بجانے والے لکڑی کے ساز)

1. flute
   بانسری
2. clarinet
   ایک نے کی نفیری
3. oboe
   نرسلوں والا الفوزہ
4. bassoon
   دوہری بانسری
5. saxophone
   پھونک کر بجانے والا نفیری کی طرز کا ساز

Strings تار والے ساز

6. violin
   وائلن / بیلا
7. cello
   وائلن کی قسم کا ایک کھرج ساز
8. bass
   باس / وائلن کی قسموں میں سب سے کمترسر نکالنے والا ساز
9. guitar
   گٹار

Brass پیتل والے ساز

10. trombone
    ترم
11. trumpet / horn
    ترم / نفیر کنڈلی دار ساز
12. tuba
    بھونپو نما باجا
13. French horn
    برنجی کنڈلی دار ساز

Percussion ضرب سے بجانے والے

14. piano
    بڑا کلیدی تختوں پر کلیدوں سے بجایا جانے والا ساز
15. xylophone
    چوبی سنتور
16. drums
    ڈھول / تاشہ
17. tambourine
    طنبورین

Other Instruments دیگر آلات

18. electric keyboard
    برقی تختہ کلید
19. accordion
    تہ ہو جانے والا اور پھونک کر بجایا جانے والا ساز
20. organ
    دستی آلہ موسیقی
21. harmonica
    ہارمونیکا (بڑے سائز کا دھونکنی والا باجا)

1. parade
پریڈ

2. float
عرشۂ جلوس

3. confetti
رنگین کاغذ کے ٹکڑے

4. couple
جوڑا

5. card
کارڈ

6. heart
دل کی روایتی علامت

7. fireworks
پٹاخے

8. flag
جھنڈا

9. mask
نقاب

10. jack-o'-lantern
کدوکے خول میں چھید کرکے بنائی
انسانی شکل

11. costume
مخصوص لباس

12. candy
کینڈی / ٹافی

13. feast
دعوت

14. turkey
فیل مرغ

15. ornament
زیور

16. Christmas tree
کرسمس کا پیڑ

17. candy cane
کینڈی کا ڈبہ

18. string lights
لڑی دار روشنیاں

*Thanksgiving is on the fourth Thursday in November.

239

1. decorations
   سجاوٹیں

2. deck
   چبوترہ

3. present / gift
   تحفہ / ہدیہ

A. **videotape**
   ویڈیو ٹیپ بنائیے

B. **make** a wish
   خواہش کا اظہار کیجیے

C. **blow out**
   شمع بجھائیے

D. **hide**
   چھپائیے

E. **bring**
   لائیے

F. **wrap**
   لپیٹیے

Happy Birthday!

Look at the picture.
What do you see?

Answer the questions.

1. What kinds of decorations do you see?
2. What are people doing at this birthday party?
3. What wish did the teenager make?
4. How many presents did people bring?

Read the story.

A Birthday Party

Today is Lou and Gani Bombata's birthday barbecue. There are <u>decorations</u> around the backyard, and food and drinks on the <u>deck</u>. There are also <u>presents</u>. Everyone in the Bombata family likes to <u>bring</u> presents.

Right now, it's time for cake. Gani <u>is blowing out</u> the candles, and Lou <u>is making a wish</u>. Lou's mom wants to <u>videotape</u> everyone, but she can't find Lou's brother, Todd. Todd hates to sing, so he always <u>hides</u> for the birthday song.

Lou's sister, Amaka, has to <u>wrap</u> some <u>gifts</u>. She doesn't want Lou to see. Amaka isn't worried. She knows her family loves to sing. She can put her gifts on the present table before they finish the first song.

Think about it.

1. What wish do you think Gani made?
2. What kinds of presents do you give to relatives? What kinds of presents can you give to friends or co-workers?

Verb Guide

Verbs in English are either regular or irregular in the past tense and past participle forms.

Regular Verbs

The regular verbs below are marked 1, 2, 3, or 4 according to four different spelling patterns. (See page 244 for the irregular verbs which do not follow any of these patterns.)

Spelling Patterns for the Past and the Past Participle	Example	
1. Add -ed to the end of the verb.	**ASK**	**ASKED**
2. Add -d to the end of the verb.	**LIVE**	**LIVED**
3. Double the final consonant and add -ed to the end of the verb.	**DROP**	**DROPPED**
4. Drop the final y and add -ied to the end of the verb.	**CRY**	**CRIED**

The Oxford Picture Dictionary List of Regular Verbs

accept (1)
add (1)
address (1)
adjust (1)
agree (2)
answer (1)
apologize (2)
appear (1)
applaud (1)
apply (4)
arrange (2)
arrest (1)
arrive (2)
ask (1)
assemble (2)
assist (1)
attach (1)
bake (2)
bank (1)
bargain (1)
bathe (2)
board (1)
boil (1)
borrow (1)
bow (1)
brainstorm (1)
breathe (2)
browse (2)
brush (1)
bubble (2)
buckle (2)
burn (1)
bus (1)
calculate (2)
call (1)
capitalize (2)
carpool (1)

carry (4)
cash (1)
celebrate (2)
change (2)
check (1)
chill (1)
choke (2)
chop (3)
circle (2)
claim (1)
clean (1)
clear (1)
click (1)
climb (1)
close (2)
collate (2)
collect (1)
color (1)
comb (1)
comfort (1)
commit (3)
compliment (1)
compost (1)
conceal (1)
conduct (1)
convert (1)
convict (1)
cook (1)
copy (4)
correct (1)
cough (1)
count (1)
cross (1)
cry (4)
dance (2)
debate (2)
decline (2)

delete (2)
deliver (1)
design (1)
dial (1)
dice (2)
dictate (2)
die (2)
disagree (2)
discipline (2)
discuss (1)
dive (2)
divide (2)
dress (1)
dribble (2)
drill (1)
drop (3)
drown (1)
dry (4)
dust (1)
dye (2)
edit (1)
empty (4)
enter (1)
erase (2)
evacuate (2)
examine (2)
exchange (2)
exercise (2)
expire (2)
explain (1)
exterminate (2)
fasten (1)
fast forward (1)
fax (1)
fertilize (2)
fill (1)
finish (1)

fix (1)
floss (1)
fold (1)
follow (1)
garden (1)
gargle (2)
graduate (2)
grate (2)
grease (2)
greet (1)
hail (1)
hammer (1)
hand (1)
harvest (1)
help (1)
hire (2)
hug (3)
immigrate (2)
indent (1)
inquire (2)
insert (1)
inspect (1)
install (1)
introduce (2)
invite (2)
iron (1)
jaywalk (1)
join (1)
jump (1)
kick (1)
kiss (1)
knit (3)
label (1)
land (1)
laugh (1)
learn (1)
lengthen (1)

lift (1)
listen (1)
litter (1)
live (2)
load (1)
lock (1)
look (1)
mail (1)
manufacture (2)
match (1)
measure (2)
microwave (2)
milk (1)
misbehave (2)
miss (1)
mix (1)
mop (3)
move (2)
mow (1)
multiply (4)
negotiate (2)
network (1)
numb (1)
nurse (2)
obey (1)
observe (2)
offer (1)
open (1)
operate (2)
order (1)
organize (2)
overdose (2)
pack (1)
paint (1)
park (1)
participate (2)
pass (1)
pause (2)
peel (1)
perm (1)
pick (1)

pitch (1)
plan (3)
plant (1)
play (1)
polish (1)
pour (1)
praise (2)
preheat (1)
prepare (2)
prescribe (2)
press (1)
pretend (1)
print (1)
program (3)
protect (1)
pull (1)
purchase (2)
push (1)
quilt (1)
race (2)
raise (2)
rake (2)
receive (2)
record (1)
recycle (2)
redecorate (2)
reduce (2)
register (1)
relax (1)
remain (1)
remove (2)
renew (1)
repair (1)
replace (2)
report (1)
request (1)
retire (2)
return (1)
reuse (2)
revise (2)
rinse (2)

rock (1)
sauté (1)
save (2)
scan (3)
schedule (2)
scrub (3)
seat (1)
select (1)
sentence (2)
separate (2)
serve (2)
share (2)
shave (2)
ship (3)
shop (3)
shorten (1)
sign (1)
simmer (1)
skate (2)
ski (1)
slice (2)
smell (1)
smile (2)
smoke (2)
sneeze (2)
solve (2)
sort (1)
spell (1)
spoon (1)
staple (2)
start (1)
state (2)
stay (1)
steam (1)
stir (3)
stop (3)
stow (1)
stretch (1)
study (4)
submit (3)
subtract (1)

supervise (2)
swallow (1)
tackle (2)
talk (1)
taste (2)
thank (1)
tie (2)
touch (1)
transcribe (2)
transfer (3)
translate (2)
travel (1)
trim (3)
try (4)
turn (1)
type (2)
underline (2)
undress (1)
unload (1)
unpack (1)
unscramble (2)
use (2)
vacuum (1)
videotape (2)
volunteer (1)
vomit (1)
vote (2)
wait (1)
walk (1)
wash (1)
watch (1)
water (1)
wave (2)
weed (1)
weigh (1)
wipe (2)
work (1)
wrap (3)

Irregular Verbs

These verbs have irregular endings in the past and/or the past participle.

The Oxford Picture Dictionary List of Irregular Verbs

simple	past	past participle	simple	past	past participle
be	was	been	make	made	made
beat	beat	beaten	meet	met	met
become	became	become	pay	paid	paid
bend	bent	bent	picnic	picnicked	picnicked
bleed	bled	bled	proofread	proofread	proofread
blow	blew	blown	put	put	put
break	broke	broken	read	read	read
bring	brought	brought	rewind	rewound	rewound
buy	bought	bought	rewrite	rewrote	rewritten
catch	caught	caught	ride	rode	ridden
choose	chose	chosen	run	ran	run
come	came	come	say	said	said
cut	cut	cut	see	saw	seen
do	did	done	seek	sought	sought
draw	drew	drawn	sell	sold	sold
drink	drank	drunk	send	sent	sent
drive	drove	driven	set	set	set
eat	ate	eaten	sew	sewed	sewn
fall	fell	fallen	shake	shook	shaken
feed	fed	fed	shoot	shot	shot
feel	felt	felt	show	showed	shown
find	found	found	sing	sang	sung
fly	flew	flown	sit	sat	sat
get	got	gotten	speak	spoke	spoken
give	gave	given	stand	stood	stood
go	went	gone	steal	stole	stolen
hang	hung	hung	sweep	swept	swept
have	had	had	swim	swam	swum
hear	heard	heard	swing	swung	swung
hide	hid	hidden	take	took	taken
hit	hit	hit	teach	taught	taught
hold	held	held	think	thought	thought
keep	kept	kept	throw	threw	thrown
lay	laid	laid	wake	woke	woken
leave	left	left	withdraw	withdrew	withdrawn
lend	lent	lent	write	wrote	written
let	let	let			

Index

Index Key

Font
bold type = verbs or verb phrases (example: **catch**)
ordinary type = all other parts of speech (example: baseball)
ALL CAPS = unit titles (example: MATHEMATICS)
Initial caps = subunit titles (example: Equivalencies)

Symbols
✦ = word found in exercise band at bottom of page

Numbers/Letters
first number in **bold** type = page on which word appears
second number, or letter, following number in **bold** type = item number on page
(examples: cool [ko͞ol] **13**-5 means that the word *cool* is item number 5 on page 13;
across [ə krös/] **153**–G means that the word *across* is item G on page 153).

Pronunciation Guide

The index includes a pronunciation guide for all the words and phrases illustrated in the book. This guide uses symbols commonly found in dictionaries for native speakers. These symbols, unlike those used in pronunciation systems such as the International Phonetic Alphabet, tend to use English spelling patterns and so should help you to become more aware of the connections between written English and spoken English.

Consonants

[b] as in back [băk]
[ch] as in cheek [chēk]
[d] as in date [dāt]
[dh] as in this [dhĭs]
[f] as in face [fās]
[g] as in gas [găs]
[h] as in half [hăf]
[j] as in jam [jăm]

[k] as in key [kē]
[l] as in leaf [lēf]
[m] as in match [măch]
[n] as in neck [nĕk]
[ng] as in ring [rĭng]
[p] as in park [pärk]
[r] as in rice [rīs]
[s] as in sand [sănd]

[sh] as in shoe [sho͞o]
[t] as in tape [tāp]
[th] as in three [thrē]
[v] as in vine [vīn]
[w] as in wait [wāt]
[y] as in yams [yămz]
[z] as in zoo [zo͞o]
[zh] as in measure [mĕzhər]

Vowels

[ā] as in bake [bāk]
[ă] as in back [băk]
[ä] as in car [kär] or box [bäks]
[ē] as in beat [bēt]
[ĕ] as in bed [bĕd]
[ë] as in bear [bër]

[ī] as in line [līn]
[ĭ] as in lip [lĭp]
[ï] as in near [nïr]
[ō] as in cold [kōld]
[ö] as in short [shört] or claw [klö]
[o͞o] as in cool [ko͞ol]

[o͝o] as in cook [ko͝ok]
[ow] as in cow [kow]
[oy] as in boy [boy]
[ŭ] as in cut [kŭt]
[ü] as in curb [kürb]
[ə] as in above [ə bŭv/]

All the pronunciation symbols used are alphabetical except for the schwa [ə]. The schwa is the most frequent vowel sound in English. If you use the schwa appropriately in unstressed syllables, your pronunciation will sound more natural.

Vowels before [r] are shown with the symbol [¨] to call attention to the special quality that vowels have before [r]. (Note that the symbols [ä] and [ö] are also used for vowels not followed by [r], as in *box* or *claw*.) You should listen carefully to native speakers to discover how these vowels actually sound.

Stress
This index follows the system for marking stress used in many dictionaries for native speakers.
1. Stress is not marked if a word consisting of a single syllable occurs by itself.
2. Where stress is marked, two levels are distinguished:
a bold accent [/] is placed after each syllable with primary (or strong) stress, a light accent [/] is placed after each syllable with secondary (or weaker) stress. In phrases and other combinations of words, stress is indicated for each word as it would be pronounced within the whole phrase.

Syllable Boundaries
Syllable boundaries are indicated by a single space or by a stress mark.

Note: The pronunciations shown in this index are based on patterns of American English. There has been no attempt to represent all of the varieties of American English. Students should listen to native speakers to hear how the language actually sounds in a particular region.

Abbreviations [ə brē′vē ā′shənz] **48**
abdomen [ăb′də mən] **107**–27
about [ə bowt′] **48**–B, **174**–L, **191**–E
above [ə bŭv′] **25**–4
accelerator [ĭk sĕl′ə rā′tər] **159**–46
accept [ĭk sĕpt′] **12**–G, **12**–I, **12** ✦
access number [ăk′sĕs′ nŭm′bər] **14**–16
Accessories [ĭk sĕs′ə rēz] **59, 94–95**
accident [ăk′sə dənt] **144**–2
accordion [ə kör′dē ən] **238**–19
account [ə kownt′] **132**–11, **132**–14
    account manager [ə kownt′ măn′ə jər] **132**–9
Account [ə kownt′] **132**
accountant [ə kown′tənt] **166**–1
ache [āk]
    backache [băk′āk′] **110**–5
    earache [ïr′āk′] **110**–3
    headache [hĕd′āk′] **110**–1
    stomachache [stŭm′ək āk′] **110**–4
    toothache [tōōth′āk′] **110**–2
acid rain [ăs′əd rān′] **218**–13
across [ə krös′] **153**–G
acrylic paint [ə krĭl′ĭk pānt] **232**–10
action [ăk′shən]
    action figure [ăk′shən fĭg′yər] **233**–26
    action story [ăk′shən stör′ē] **237**–19
activist [ăk′tə vĭst] **199**–17
actor [ăk′tər] **166**–2
acupuncture [ăk′yə pŭngk′chər] **122**–2
acute angle [ə kyōōt′ ăng′gəl] **193**–28
ad [ăd] **48**–2, **197**–9
adapter [ə dăp′tər] **234**–15
add [ăd] **77**–N, **101**–B, **192**–A
address [ə drĕs′, ă′drĕs] **4**–5
    mailing address [mā′lĭng ə drĕs′, –ă′drĕs] **134**–22
    return address [rĭ tŭrn′ ə drĕs′, –ă′drĕs] **134**–21
    website address [wĕb′sīt ə drĕs′, –ă′drĕs] **197**–4
address [ə drĕs′] **135**–B, **197**–C
adhesive bandage [ad hē′sĭv băn′dĭj] **117**–5
adjust [ə jŭst′] **219**–J
    adjustable wrench [ə jŭs′tə bəl rĕnch′] **181**–48
    adjustment [ə jŭst′mənt] **194**–23, **194**–24
administrative assistant
    [əd mĭn′ə strā′tĭv ə sĭs′tənt] **166**–3
administrator [əd mĭn′ə strā′tər] **120**–13
Administrators [əd mĭn′ə strā′tərz] **5**
admissions clerk [əd mĭ′shənz klŭrk′] **120**–14
ADULTS AND CHILDREN [ə dŭlts′ en chĭl′ drən] **30–31**
adult school [ə dŭlt′ skōōl′, ăd′ŭlt–] **188**–8
adventure story [əd vĕn′chər stör′ē] **237**–19
aerobic exercise [ə rō′bĭk ĕk′sər sīz′] **122**–5
afraid [ə frād′] **43**–23
after [ăf′tər]
    afternoon [ăf′tər nōōn′] **18**–17
    aftershave [ăf′tər shāv′] **109**–30
    five after one [fīv′ ăf′tər wŭn′] **18**–7
    quarter after one [kwör′tər ăf′tər wŭn′] **18**–9
    ten after one [tĕn′ ăf′tər wŭn′] **18**–8
    twenty after one [twĕn′tē ăf′tər wŭn′] **18**–10
After an Emergency [ăf′tər ən ĭ mŭr′jən sē] **147**
Age [āj] **32**
agency [ā′jən sē] **131**–14

agent [ā′jənt] **160**–3, **160**–5
agree [ə grē′] **12**–K
agreement [ə grē′mənt] **51**–28
aid [ād]
    first aid kit [fürst′ ād′ kĭt′] **117**–1, **146**–18
    first aid manual [fürst′ ād′ măn′yōō əl] **117**–2
    hearing aid [hïr′ĭng ād′] **115**–10
aide [ād] **167**–32
AIDS (acquired immune deficiency syndrome) [ādz] /
    [ə kwī′rd ĭ myōōn′ də fĭ′shən sē sĭn′drōm] **111** ✦
air [ër]
    air bag [ër′ băg′] **159**–43
    air conditioner [ër′ kən dĭsh′ə nər] **159**–39
    Air Force [ër′ förs′] **138**–16
    airmail [ër′māl′] **134**–5
    airplane [ër′plān′] **150**–8
    airplane crash [ër′plān′ krăsh′] **144**–3
    air pollution [ër′ pə lōō′shən] **218**–11
    airport [ër′pört′] **151**–10
    air purifier [ër′ pyōōr′ə fī ər] **113**–14
Airline Terminal [ër′līn′ tür′mə nəl] **160**
Airplane [ër′plān′] **161**
AIRPORT [ër′pört′] **160–161**
Airport Transportation
    [ër′pört′ trăns′pər tā′shən] **152**
aisle [īl] **72**–6
alarm clock [ə lärm′ kläk′] **58**–24
Alaska time [ə lăs′kə tīm′] **19**–28
album [ăl′bəm] **235**–31, **235**–32
alfalfa [ăl făl′fə] **177**–5
algebra [ăl′jə brə] **192**–16
allergic reaction [ə lür′jĭk rē ăk′shən] **116**–E
allergies [ăl′ər jēz] **111**–8
alley [ăl′ē] **51**–24, **222**–4
alligator [ăl′ə gā′tər] **213**–36
alphabet [ăl′fə bĕt′] **7**–13
Alterations [öl′tə rā′shənz] **100**
ALTERATIONS [öl′tə rā′shənz] **100**
Alteration Shop [öl′tə rā′shən shäp′] **100**
aluminum foil [ə lōō′mə nəm foyl′] **72**–23
Alzheimer's disease [älts′hī mərz dĭ zēz′, älts–] **111** ✦
a.m. [ā′ĕm′] **18**–4
ambulance [ăm′byə ləns] **116**–1, **121**–34
AMERICA [ə mĕr′ə kə] **200–201**
American cheese [ə mĕr′ə kən chēz′] **71**–26
Americans [ə mĕr′ə kənz] **198**–3
Amphibians [ăm fĭb′ē ənz] **212**
AMPHIBIANS [ăm fĭb′ē ənz] **212–213**
amusement park [ə myōōz′mənt pärk′] **223**–10
ancient [ān′shənt] **199**–1
anemone [ə nĕ′mə nē] **212**–24
anesthesiologist [ă′nəs thē′zē ŏ′lə jĭst] **121**–35
angle [ăng′gəl] **193**–26, **193**–27, **193**–28
Angles [ăng′gəlz] **193**
angry [ăng′grē] **43**–29
animals [ăn′ə məlz] **59**–15
Animals [ăn′ə məlz] **212, 215**
ANIMALS [ăn′ə məlz] **215**
ankle [ăng′kəl] **106**–23, **110**–18
    ankle socks [ăng′kəl säks′] **91**–7
anklets [ăngk′ləts′] **91**–11
anniversary [ăn′ə vür′sə rē] **22**–3

answer [ăn′sər] **8**–L
answering machine [ăn′sə rĭng mə shēn′] **14**–17
answer sheet [ăn′sər shēt′] **10**–2
antacid [ănt ăs′əd] **113**–28
anteater [ănt′ē′tər] **217**–24
antelope [ăn′tə lōp′] **217**–35
antenna [ăn tĕ′nə] **14**–9
antibacterial ointment
    [ăn′tē băk tïr′ē əl oynt′mənt] **117**–10
antihistamine cream [ăn′tī hĭs′tə mēn krēm′] **117**–11
antiperspirant [ăn′tē pürs′pə rənt] **108**–5
antlers [ănt′lərz] **216**–16
ants [ăntz] **63**–23
apartment [ə pärt′mənt] **48**–3, **48**–4
    apartment building [ə pärt′mənt bĭl′dĭng] **50**–1
    apartment number [ə pärt′mənt nŭm′bər] **4**–6
Apartment [ə pärt′mənt] **48**
Apartment Complex [ə pärt′mənt käm′plĕx] **51**
Apartment Entryway [ə pärt′mənt ĕn′trē wā′] **51**
APARTMENTS [ə pärt′məntz] **50–51**
APC (automated postal center) [ā′pē′sē′] /
    [ö′tə māt ĭd pōs′təl–sĕn′tər] **135**–10
apologize [ə päl′ə jīz′] **12**–F
apostrophe [ə päs′trə fē] **190**–16
apparatus [ăp′ə rā′təs] **224**–14
appear [ə pïr′] **141**–C
Appearance [ə pïr′əns] **32**
applaud [ə plöd′] **148**–B
apples [ăp′əlz] **68**–1
    apple juice [ăp′əl jōōs′] **73**–32
appliance repair person
    [ə plī′əns rĭ për′ pür′sən] **166**–4
appliqué [ăp′lə kā′] **99**–31
apply [ə plī′] **109**–P
appointment [ə poynt′mənt] **22**–4, **118**–1
    appointment book [ə poynt′mənt bŏŏk′] **183**–48
apricots [ăp′rə käts′] **68**–12
April [ā′prəl] **21**–28
apron [ā′prən] **92**–11, **93**–30
aquarium [ə kwër′ əm] **222**–7
Arachnids [ə răk′nĭdz′] **214**
ARACHNIDS [ə răk′nĭdz′] **214**
archery [är′chə rē] **228**–1
architect [är′kə tĕkt′] **166**–5
area [ër′ē ə]
    area code [ër′ē ə kōd′] **4**–10, **15**–29
    boarding area [bör′dĭng ër′ē ə] **161**–9
    dining area [dī′nĭng ër′ē ə] **46**–7
    play area [plā′ ër′ē ə] **130**–11
    reception area [rĭ sĕp′shən ër′ē ə] **182**–5
    rural area [rŏŏr′ əl ër′ē ə] **52**–4
    screening area [skrē′nĭng ër′ē ə] **160**–4
    testing area [tĕs′tĭng ër′ē ə] **136**–2
    urban area [ür′bən ër′ē ə] **52**–1
AREA [ër′ē ə] **55**
Area and Volume [ër′ē ə ən văl′yəm, –yōōm] **193**
arm [ärm] **105**–14, **194**–15
    armchair [ärm′chër′] **56**–22
    armadillo [är′mə dĭl′ō] **216**–8
Arm, Hand, and Fingers [ärm′ hănd′ ən fĭng′gərz] **106**
Army [är′mē] **138**–14, **199**–11
around [ə rownd′] **153**–H

Around Campus [ə rownd/ kăm/pəs] **5**
arrange [ə rānj/] **49**–Q
arrest [ə rĕst/] **141**–A
arrival [ə rī/vəl] **161**–7, **161** ✦
arrive [ə rīv/] **160**–K
arrow [ăr/ō] **231**–8
arson [är/sən] **142**–7
artery [är/tə rē] **107**–36
arthritis [är thrī/təs] **111**–16
artichokes [är/tə chōks/] **69**–22
artist [är/tĭst] **166**–6
arts [ärts] **189**–9, **189**–15, **228**–11
    art museum [ärt/ myōō zē/əm] **223**–9
ask [ăsk] **2**–B
    ask about [ăsk/ ə bowt/] **48**–B, **157**–B
    ask for [ăsk/ för/] **10**–F
    ask questions [ăsk/ kwĕs/chənz] **8**–K, **174**–M
asparagus [ə spĕr/ə gəs] **69**–26
assault [ə sölt/] **142**–3
assemble [ə sĕm/bəl] **170**–A, **175**–C
assembler [ə sĕm/blər] **166**–7
assembly [ə sĕm/blē/] **140**–1
    assembly line [ə sĕm/blē līn/] **175**–6
    assemblyperson [ə sĕm/blē pür/sən] **139**–24
assist [ə sĭst/] **95**–D, **170**–B
assistance [ə sĭs/təns] **14**–22
assistant [ə sĭs/tənt]
    administrative assistant
        [əd mĭn/ ə strā/ tĭv ə sĭs/tənt] **166**–3
    assistant principal [ə sĭs/tənt prĭn/sə pəl] **5**–5
    certified nursing assistant (CNA) [sür/tə fīd/
        nür/sĭng ə sĭs/tənt] / [sē/ĕn/ā/] **120**–12
    dental assistant [dĕn/təl ə sĭs/tənt] **119**–2, **167**–22
    physician assistant [fə zĭ/shən ə sĭs/tənt] **168**–47
Assistant [ə sĭs/tənt] **93**
asthma [ăz/mə] **111**–9
astronaut [ăs/trə nöt/] **205**–17
astronomer [ə strä/nə mər] **205**–22
Astronomy [ə strä/nə mē] **205**
At Customs [ăt/ kŭs/təmz] **161**
athletic [ăth lĕt/ĭk]
    athletic shoes [ăth lĕt/ĭk shōōz/] **86**–7
    athletic supporter [ăth lĕt/ĭk sə pör/tər] **91**–6
Atlantic time [ət lăn/tĭk tīm/] **19**–33
atlas [ăt/ləs] **133**–8
ATM (Automated Teller Machine) [ā/tē/ĕm/] /
    [ö/tə mät ĭd tĕ/lər mə shēn/] **132**
ATM card [ā/tē/ĕm/ kärd/] **132**–15
atom [ăt/əm] **195**–28
attach [ə tăch/] **197**–G, **197**–H
attachments [ə tăch/mənts] **61**–11
attack [ə tăk/] **116**–D
attendant [ə tĕn/dənt] **161**–12, **162**–3, **184**–3
At the Dealer [ăt/ dhə dē/lər] **158**
At the Gate [ăt/ dhə gāt/] **161**
At the Mechanic [ăt/ dhə mə kăn/ĭk] **158**
At the Security Checkpoint
    [ăt/ dhə sə kyōō/ rə tē/ chĕk/ poynt/] **160**
attic [ăt/ĭk] **47**–7
attorney [ə tür/nē] **141**–4, **141**–10
attractive [ə trăk/tĭv] **32**–13
audiobook [ö/dē ō bōōk/] **133**–17

audiologist [ö dē ä/lə jĭst] **115**–9
auditorium [ö/də tör/ē əm] **5**–18
August [ö/gəst] **21**–32
aunt [ănt] **34**–7
author [ö/thər] **133**–15, **169**–64
auto [ö/tō]
    auto club card [ö/tō klŭb/ kärd/] **162**–4
    auto mechanic [ö/tō mə kăn/ĭk] **166**–8
automated [ö/tə mät ĭd]
    automated phone system
        [ö/tə mät ĭd fōn/ sĭs/təm] **14**–23
    automated postal center (APC)
        [ö/tə mät ĭd pōs/təl sĕn/tər] / [ā/pē/sē/] **135**–10
Automated Teller Machine
    [ö/tə mät ĭd tĕl/ər mə shēn/] **132**
Automatic Transmission
    [ö tə mät/ĭk tränz mĭ/shən] **159**
Automotive Painter [ö tə mōt/ĭv pān/tər] **92**
autumn [ö/təm] **21**–39
avalanche [ăv/ə lănch/] **145**–18
average [ăv/rĭj]
    average height [ăv/rĭj hīt/] **32**–5
    average weight [ăv/rĭj wāt/] **32**–8
avocados [ä/və kä/dōz, ăv/ə–] **84**–6
ax [ăks] **180**–3
baboon [bă bōōn/] **217**–31
baby [bā/bē] **31**–7
    baby bag [bā/bē băg/] **37**–16
    baby carrier [bā/bē kă/rē/ər] **37**–17
    baby food [bā/bē fōōd/] **37**–4
    baby lotion [bā/bē lō/shən] **37**–13
    baby monitor [bā/bē män/ə tər] **59**–7
    baby powder [bā/bē pow/dər] **37**–14
    babysitter [bā/bē sĭt/ər] **166**–9
    baby's room [bā/bēz/ rōōm/] **47**–10
back [băk] **104**–5
    backache [băk/āk/] **110**–5
    back button [băk/ bŭt/n] **197**–2
    backhoe [băk/hō/] **178**–8
    backpack [băk/păk/] **94**–18, **226**–15
    backpacking [băk/păk/ĭng] **226**–6
    backseat [băk/sēt/] **159**–54
    back support belt [băk/ sə pört/ bĕlt/] **179**–18
    go back [gō/ băk/] **11**–M
    horseback riding [hörs/băk/ rī/dĭng] **226**–9
    lower back [lō/ər băk/] **107**–29
    pay back [pā/ băk/] **26**–D
Backyard [băk/yärd/] **53**
BACK FROM THE MARKET
    [băk/ frəm dhə mär/kət] **66**–67
bacon [bā/kən] **70**–11, **80**–1
bad [băd] **23**–18
BAD DAY AT WORK [băd/ dā/ ăt würk/] **186**–187
badge [băj] **93**–21
badminton [băd/mĭn tən] **228**–6
bag [băg] **69**–31, **74**–7, **74**–19, **161**–18
    air bag [ĕr/ băg/] **159**–43
    baby bag [bā/bē băg/] **37**–16
    clutch bag [klŭch/ băg/] **89**–19
    grocery bag [grōs/rē băg/] **67**–13
    handbag [hănd/ băg/] **87**–9, **94**–2
    plastic storage bags [plăs/tĭk stör/ĭj băgz/] **72**–25

    shoulder bag [shōl/dər băg/] **94**–17
    sleeping bag [slē/pĭng băg/] **226**–12
    totebag [tōt/ băg/] **94**–19
    trash bags [trăsh/ băgz/] **61**–24
    vacuum cleaner bag
        [văk/yōōm klē/nər băg/] **61**–12
bagels [bā/gəlz] **73**–40
baggage [băg/ĭj]
    baggage carousel [băg/ĭj kăr/ə sĕl/] **161**–23
bagger [băg/ər] **73**–14
baggy [băg/ē] **97**–30
bailiff [bā/lĭf] **141**–13
bake [bāk] **77**–H
Baked Goods [bākt/ gōōdz/] **73**
baked potato [bākt/ pə tā/tō] **81**–25
baker [bā/kər] **166**–10
bakery [bā/kə rē] **127**–19
Baking Products [bā/kĭng prăd/ŭkts] **73**
balance [băl/əns] **132**–17, **195**–41
balcony [băl/kə nē] **51**–20
bald [böld] **33**–12
ball [böl] **59**–12, **231**–5, **231**–12
    ball field [böl/ fēld/] **224**–1
    ballroom [böl/rōōm/] **184**–26
    baseball [bās/böl/] **231**–18, **231**–14
    basketball [băs/kət böl/] **229**–8, **231**–4
    basketball court [băs/kət böl/ kört/] **229**–7
    football [fŏŏt/böl/] **229**–11, **231**–21
    meatballs [mēt/bölz/] **81**–27
    racquetball [răk/ət böl/] **228**–12
    softball [söft/böl/] **229**–10
    volleyball [väl/ē böl/] **229**–14, **231**–3
balloons [bə lōōnz/] **44**–4
bananas [bə nän/əz] **68**–2
band [bănd] **183**–34
    headband [hĕd/bănd/] **90**–3
    waistband [wāst/bănd/] **100**–5
bandage [băn/dĭj] **117**–5, **117**–12
bandana [băn dä/nə] **92**–16
bangs [băngz] **33**–8
bank [băngk] **124**–5
    bank statement [băngk/ stāt/mənt] **132**–16
bank online [băngk/ än līn/] **132**–C
BANK [băngk] **132**
banner [băn/ər] **44**–1
banquet room [băng/kwət rōōm/] **185**–14
bar [bär]
    bar code [bär/ kōd/] **27**–4
    candy bar [kăn/dē bär/] **73**–37
    grab bar [grăb/ bär/] **57**–9
    menu bar [mĕn/yōō bär/] **197**–1
    salad bar [săl/əd bär/] **79**–24
    scroll bar [skrōl/ bär/] **197**–15
barbecued ribs [bär/bĭ kyōō/d rĭbz/] **76**–2
barbershop [bär/bər shäp/] **129**–19
bargain [bär/gən] **102**–A
barn [bärn] **177**–11
barrette [bə rĕt/] **108**–20
base [bās] **193**–45, **194**–20
baseball [bās/böl/] **229**–9, **231**–18
    baseball bat [bās/böl/ băt/] **231**–14
    baseball cap [bās/böl/ kăp/] **86**–5

baseball cards [bās/böl/ kärds/] **232**–2
baseball game [bās/böl/ gām/] **44**–2
basement [bās/mənt] **47**–13
Basement [bās/mənt] **50**
Basic Colors [bā/sĭk kŭ/lərz] **24**
BASIC TRANSPORTATION
   [bā/sĭk trănz/pər tā/shən] **150**–**151**
basket [bās/kət] **56**–3
  basketball [bās/kət böl/] **229**–8, **231**–4
  basketball court [bās/kət böl kört/] **229**–7
  bread basket [brĕd/ bās/kət] **83**–11
  laundry basket [lön/drē bās/kət] **101**–2
  shopping basket [shäp/ĭng bās/kət] **73**–9
  wastebasket [wāst/bās/kət] **57**–26
bass [bās] **212**–6, [bās] **238**–8
bassoon [bə sōōn/] **238**–4
bat [băt] **216**–7, **231**–14
bath [băth]
  bath mat [băth/ măt/] **57**–28
  bath powder [băth/ pow/dər] **108**–4
  bathroom [băth/rōōm/] **46**–4
  bath towel [băth/ tow/əl] **57**–13
  bathtub [băth/tŭb/] **57**–2
  half bath [hăf/ băth/] **57** ✦
bathe [bādh] **36**–F, **108**–B
bathing suit [bā/dhĭng sōōt/] **90**–26
BATHROOM [băth/rōōm/] **57**
battery / batteries [băt/ə rē] / [băt/ə rēz]
  146–15, **158**–20
  battery charger [băt/ə rē chär/jər] **235**–27
  battery pack [băt/ə rē păk/] **235**–26
bay [bā] **204**–9
be [bē]
  be aware [bē ə wër/] **143**–I
  be born [bē börn/] **40**–A
  be 18 or older [bē ā/tēn/ ör öld/ər] **140**–G
  be hurt [bē hürt/] **116**–C
  be informed [bē ĭn förmd/] **140**–F
  be injured [bē ĭn/jərd] **116**–C
  be in shock [bē ĭn shäk/] **116**–B
  be neat [bē nēt/] **174**–C
  be on time [bē ön tīm/] **174**–F
  be released [bē rĭ lēst/] **141**–H
  be in a rock band [bē ĭn ə räk/ bănd/] **238**–D
  be unconscious [bē ŭn kän/shəs] **116**–A
  don't be late [dönt/ bē lāt/] **174**–D
beach [bēch] **204**–10
  beach chair [bēch/ chër/] **225**–22
  beach umbrella [bēch/ ŭm brĕl/ə] **225**–14
BEACH [bēch] **225**
beads [bēdz] **95**–34, **99**–32
beak [bēk] **214**–3
beaker [bē/kər] **195**–39
beam [bēm] **178**–3
beans [bēnz] **69**–8, **72**–17
  soybeans [soy/bēnz/] **177**–3
bear [bër] **37**–23, **216**–11
beard [bërd] **33**–6
beat [bēt] **77**–S
beater [bē/tər]
  eggbeater [ĕg/bē/tər] **78**–20
beautiful [byōō/tə fəl] **23**–21

beauty shop [byōō/tē shäp/] **130** ✦
beaver [bē/vər] **216**–9
become [bē kŭm/] **40**–G, **41**–N
bed [bĕd] **58**–9
  bedbugs [bĕd/bŭgz/] **63**–24
  bed control [bĕd/ kən tröl/] **121**–27
  bed frame [bĕd/ frām/] **58**–18
  bed pan [bĕd/ păn/] **121**–23
  bedroom [bĕd/rōōm/] **46**–2
  bedspread [bĕd/sprĕd/] **59**–11
  bed table [bĕd/ tā/bəl] **121**–21
  bunk beds [bŭnk/ bĕdz/] **59**–9
  double bed [dŭb/əl bĕd/] **184**–14
  flower bed [flow/ər bĕd/] **53**–20
  hospital bed [häs/pĭ tl bĕd/] **121**–22
  kids' bedroom [kĭdz/ bĕd/rōōm/] **47**–9
  king-size bed [kĭng/sīz/ bĕd/] **184**–15
BEDROOM [bĕd/rōōm/] **58, 59**
bee [bē]
  honeybee [hŭn/ē bē/] **214**–25
beef [bēf]
  beef ribs [bēf/ rĭbz/] **70**–5
  corned beef [körnd/ bēf/] **71**–22
  ground beef [grownd/ bēf/] **70**–4
  roast beef [rōst/ bēf/] **71**–21
  stewing beef [stōō/ĭng bēf/] **70**–3
  stir-fried beef [stür/frīd/ bēf/] **76**–6
Beef [bēf] **70**
beetle [bēt/l] **214**–18
beets [bēts] **69**–5
Before an Emergency [bĭ för/ ən ĭ mür/ jən sē] **146**
behind [bĭ hīnd/] **25**–8
beige [bāzh] **24**–18
bell [bĕl]
  bell captain [bĕl/ kăp/tən] **184**–6
  bellhop [bĕl/häp/] **184**–7
  bell peppers [bĕl/ pĕp/ərz] **69**–7
  doorbell [dör/bĕl/] **53**–14
below [bĭ lō/] **25**–5
belts [bĕlts] **94**–6
  back support belt [băk/ sə pört/ bĕlt/] **179**–18
  belt buckle [bĕlt/ bŭk/əl] **94**–20
  conveyor belt [kən vā/ər bĕlt/] **175**–9
  garter belt [gär/tər bĕlt/] **91**–16
  seat belt [sēt/ bĕlt/] **159**–52
  tool belt [tōōl/ bĕlt/] **92**–3
bench [bĕnch] **224**–10
bend [bĕnd] **230**–O
benefits [bĕn/ə fĭts] **174** ✦
berries [bĕr/ēz] **210**–20
  blackberries [blăk/bĕr/ēz] **68**–17
  blueberries [blōō/bĕr/ēz] **68**–16
  mixed berries [mĭkst/ bĕr/ēz] **81**–36
  raspberries [răz/bĕr/ēz] **68**–15
  strawberries [strö/bĕr/ēz] **68**–14
between [bĭ twēn/] **25**–12
Beverages [bĕv/rə jəz] **73, 81**
bib [bĭb] **37**–5
bicycle / bike [bī/sĭ kəl] / [bīk] **129**–22, **151**–15
big [bĭg] **23**–2, **97**–38
  Big Dipper [bĭg/ dĭ/pər] **205** ✦
  big-screen TV [bĭg/skrēn/ tē/vē/] **50**–15

bike / bicycle [bīk] / [bī/sĭ kəl] **129**–22, **151**–15
  bike path [bīk/ păth/] **224**–3
biking [bī/kĭng] **226**–8, **228**–5
bikini panties [bə kē/nē păn/tēz] **91**–13
bill [bĭl] **214**–3
Bill [bĭl] **15**
billiards [bĭl/yərdz] **228**–2
Bill of Rights [bĭl/ əv rīts/] **198**–10
Bills [bĭlz] **26**
bin [bĭn] **51**–23, **61**–2, **160**–6
bioenergy [bī/ō ĕn/ər jē] **218**–9
biography [bī ä/grə fē] **133**–15
biologist [bī ä/lə jĭst] **194**–2
Biology [bī ä/lə jē] **194**
biomass [bī/ō mäs/] **218**–9
birch [bürch] **210**–7
bird [bürd] **208**–4
Bird [bürd] **214**
BIRDS, INSECTS, AND ARACHNIDS
   [bürdz/ ĭn/sĕkts ən ə răk/nĭdz] **214**
birth [bürth]
  birth certificate [bürth/ sər tĭf/ə kət] **40**–1
  birthday [bürth/dā/] **22**–1
BIRTHDAY PARTY [bürth/dā/ pär/tē] **240**–**241**
biscuits [bĭs/kəts] **80**–6
bison [bī/sən] **216**–6
bit [bĭt] **180**–28
bite [bīt] **110**–11
black [blăk] **24**–13
  blackberries [blăk/bĕr/ēz] **68**–17
  black hair [blăk/ hër/] **33**–16
bladder [blăd/ər] **107**–46
blade [blād] **107**–28, **109**–28, **180**–27
blankets [blăng/kəts] **58**–15, **146**–7, **225**–11
  blanket sleeper [blăng/kət slē/pər] **91**–27
blazer [blā/zər] **92**–12
bleach [blēch] **101**–7
bleachers [blē/chərz] **5**–3
bleed [blēd] **116**–M
blender [blĕn/dər] **54**–12
blind [blīnd] **32**–11
blister [blĭs/tər] **110**–15
blizzard [blĭz/ərd] **13**–23, **145**–13
blocks [blăks] **59**–19
  quilt block [kwĭlt/ blăk/] **232**–15
  sunblock [sŭn/blăk/] **108**–8, **225**–10
blond hair [bländ/ hër/] **33**–17
blood [blŭd] **111**–14
  blood pressure gauge [blŭd/ prĕsh/ər gäj/] **118**–9
  blood test [blŭd/ tĕst/] **121**–30
  blood work [blŭd/ würk/] **121**–30
  bloody nose [blŭd/ē nōz/] **110**–17
blouse [blows] **87**–8
blow dryer [blō/ drī/ər] **33**–23, **108**–18
blower [blō/ər] **176**–2
blow out [blō/ owt/] **240**–C
blue [blōō] **24**–3
  blueberries [blōō/bĕr/ēz] **68**–16
  blue jay [blōō/ jā/] **214**–6
  bright blue [brīt/ blōō/] **24**–12
  dark blue [därk/ blōō/] **24**–10
  light blue [lĭt/ blōō/] **24**–11
  navy blue [nā/vē blōō/] **28**–5

blues [blōōz] **237**–22
blush [blŭsh] **109**–37
board [bōrd]
    board game [bōrd/ gàm/] **232**–5
    bulletin board [bŏŏl/ə tn bōrd/] **7**–14
    chalkboard [chök/bōrd/] **6**–1
    cutting board [kŭt/ĭng bōrd/] **54**–27
    emery board [ĕm/ə rē bōrd/, ĕm/rē–] **109**–32
    headboard [hĕd/bōrd/] **58**–10
    ironing board [ī/ər nĭng bōrd/] **101**–14
    motherboard [mŭdh/ər bōrd/] **196**–5
    particle board [pär/tə kəl bōrd/] **181**–20
    skateboard [skāt/bōrd/] **224**–7
    snowboard [snō/bōrd/] **231**–23
    surfboard [sürf/bōrd/] **225**–16
    whiteboard [wīt/bōrd/] **6**–3
board [bōrd] **160**–E
boarding [bōr/dĭng]
    boarding area [bōr/dĭng ër/ē ə] **161**–9
    boarding pass [bōr/dĭng păs/] **161**–20
    sailboarding [sāl/bōr/dĭng] **227** ✦
    skateboarding [skāt/bōr/dĭng] **228**–13
    snowboarding [snō/bōr/dĭng] **227**–2
boat [bōt]
    sailboat [sāl/bōt/] **225**–3
boating [bō/tĭng] **226**–1
bobbin [bä/bĭn] **98**–21
bobby pins [bäb/ē pĭnz/] **108**–21
body [bäd/ē] **190**–7
    body lotion [bäd/ē lō/shən] **108**–9
    body of water [bäd/ē əv wö/tər] **204** ✦
    body shaper [bäd/ē/ shā/pər] **91**–15
BODY [bäd/ē] **104**–105, **106**–107
boil [boyl] **77**–M
boiled ham [boyld/ hăm/] **76**–5
boiler [boy/lər] **78**–8
bok choy [bäk/ choy/] **69**–15
bolt [bōlt] **51**–34, **180**–35, **180**–38
    bolt of fabric [bōlt/ əv făb/rĭk] **98**–15
bone [bōn] **107**–33, **116**–P
    boneless [bōn/ləs] **70** ✦
book [bŏŏk]
    appointment book [ə poynt/mənt bŏŏk/] **183**–48
    audiobook [ö/dē ō bŏŏk/] **133**–17
    bookkeeper [bŏŏk/ kē/pər] **175**–2
    book of stamps [bŏŏk/ əv stămps/] **134**–18
    bookcase [bŏŏk/ kās/] **7**–10
    bookstore [bŏŏk/ stōr/] **130**–4
    check book [chĕk/ bŏŏk/] **132**–12
    coloring book [kŭl/ə rĭng bŏŏk/] **59**–13
    DMV handbook [dē/ĕm/vē/ hănd/bŏŏk/] **136**–1
    notebook [nōt/bŏŏk/] **7**–27
    passbook [păs/bŏŏk/] **132**–10
    picture book [pĭk/chər bŏŏk/] **133**–12
    spiral notebook [spī/rəl nōt/bŏŏk/] **7**–29
    test booklet [tĕst/ bŏŏk/lət] **10**–1
    textbook [tĕkst/bŏŏk/, tĕks/–] **7**–25
    workbook [würk/bŏŏk/] **7**–26
boombox [bōōm/bäks/] **234**–1
booth [bōōth] **82**–4, **122**–3

boots [bōōts] **95**–28
    hiking boots [hī/kĭng bōōts/] **95**–31
    rain boots [răn/ bōōts/] **90**–20
    safety boots [sāf/tē bōōts/] **179**–20
    ski boots [skē/ bōōts/] **231**–26
    steel toe boots [stēl/ tō/ bōōts/] **92**–6
bored [bōrd] **43**–25
borrow [bär/ō, bör/ō] **26**–B
boss [bäs] **164**–4
botanical garden [bə tăn/ĭ kəl gär/dn] **222**–3
bottle [bät/l] **37**–1, **74**–1, **74**–13
    bottle return [bät/l rĭ türn/] **73**–16
    hot water bottle [hät/ wö/tər bät/l] **113**–15
bottled water [bät/ld wö/tər] **146**–11
bouquet [bō kā/, bōō–] **211**–28
bow [bō] **231**–6
    bow tie [bō/ tī/] **89**–16
bow [bow] **3**–H
bowl [bōl] **55**–2
    mixing bowl [mĭks/ĭng bōl/] **54**–28, **78**–31
    serving bowl [sürv/ĭng bōl/] **55**–21
    soup bowl [sōōp/ bōl/] **83**–21
    sugar bowl [shŏŏg/ər bōl/] **55**–14
bowling [bō/lĭng] **228**–3
    bowling alley [bō/lĭng ăl/ē] **222**–4
    bowling ball [bō/lĭng bōl/] **231**–5
box / boxes [bäks/, bäks/ĭz] **74**–6, **74**–18
    box spring [bäks/ sprĭng/] **58**–19
    CD boombox [sē/dē/ bōōm/bäks/] **234**–1
    fuse box [fyōōz/ bäks/] **62**–13
    mailboxes [māl/bäk/səz] **50**–11, **128**–13
    post office box (PO box)
        [pōst/ ö/fəs bäks/] / [pē/ō bäks/] **135**–9
    safety deposit box [sāf/tē dĭ päz/ət bäks/] **132**–7
    sandbox [sănd/bäks/] **224**–15
    search box [sürch/ bäks/] **197**–5
    text box [tĕkst/ bäks/] **197**–13
    to-go box [tə gō/ bäks/] **82**–5
boxer shorts [bäk/sər shörts/] **91**–4
boxing [bäks/ĭng] **228**–4
boy [boy] **31**–9
bra [brä] **91**–20
bracelets [brās/ləts] **95**–9, **117**–3
braces [brā/səz] **119**–6
brain [brān] **107**–34
brainstorm [brān/störm/] **8**–H, **191**–F
brake [brāk] **159**–48
    brake light [brāk/ līt/] **158**–14
    brake pedal [brāk/ pĕd/l] **159**–45
branch [brănch] **210**–2
Branch [brănch] **138**
Brass [brăs] **238**
bread [brĕd] **67**–11
    bread-and-butter plate [brĕd/ n bŭt/ər plāt/] **83**–19
    bread basket [brĕd/ băs/kət] **83**–11
    garlic bread [gär/lĭk brĕd/] **81**–28
    rye bread [rī/ brĕd/] **71**–20
    wheat bread [wēt/ brĕd/] **71**–19
    white bread [wīt/ brĕd/] **71**–18
break [brāk] **77**–Q, **116**–P
    break down [brāk/ down/] **162**–D

Breakfast Special [brĕk/fəst spē/shəl] **80**
breasts [brĕsts] **70**–19, **107**–26
breathe [brēdh] **116**–N
breathing [brē/dhĭng] **117**–16
bricklayer [brĭk/lā/ər] **186**–8
bricks [brĭks] **178**–12, **178**–B
briefcase [brēf/kās/] **88**–13
briefs [brēfs] **91**–5, **91**–14
bright blue [brīt/ blōō/] **24**–12
bring [brĭng] **174**–D, **240**–E
broccoli [bräk/ə lē] **69**–13
broiled steak [broyld/ stāk/] **76**–3
broiler [broy/lər] **54**–21
broken [brō/kən] **62**–5, **62**–6, **62**–7, **63**–15, **97**–39
    broken equipment [brō/kən ĭ kwĭp/mənt] **179**–4
broom [brōōm] **61**–16
brother [brŭdh/ər] **34**–6, **35**–28
    brother-in-law [brŭdh/ər ĭn lö/] **34**–17
    stepbrother [stĕp/brŭdh/ər] **35**–30
brown [brown] **24**–17
    brown hair [brown/ hër/] **33**–18
    hash browns [hăsh/ brownz/] **80**–3
browse [browz] **102**–B
bruise [brōōz] **110**–12
brush [brŭsh] **33**–22, **108**–14
    paintbrush [pānt/brŭsh/] **181**–22, **233**–20
    scrub brush [skrŭb/ brŭsh/] **61**–20
    toilet brush [toy/lət brŭsh/] **57**–18
    toothbrush [tōōth/brŭsh/] **109**–22
brush [brŭsh] **108**–I, **109**–J
bubble in [bŭ/bəl ĭn/] **10**–K
bucket [bŭk/ət] **61**–7, **225**–8
buckle [bŭk/əl] **94**–20, **99**–28
buckle up [bŭk/əl ŭp/] **36**–L
bud [bŭd] **211**–7
budget [bŭ jĭt/] **186**–3
buffalo [bŭf/ə lō] **216**–6
buffet [bə fā/] **55**–24, **185**–10
bugs [bŭgz]
    bedbugs [bĕd/bŭgz/] **63**–24
building [bĭl/dĭng] **50**–1, **124**–2
BUILDING SUPPLIES [bĭl/dĭng sə plīz/] **180**–181
bulb [bŭlb] **56** ✦, **211**–2
bulldozer [bŏŏl/dō/zər] **178**–6
bulletin board [bŏŏl/ə tn bōrd/] **7**–14
bump cap [bŭmp/ kăp/] **92**–9
bumper [bŭm/pər] **158**–8
    bumper pad [bŭm/pər păd/] **59**–4
bunch [bŭnch] **68**–29
bunk beds [bŭngk/ bĕdz/] **59**–9
Bunsen burner [bŭn/sən bür/nər] **195**–37
bureau [byŏŏr/ō] **58**–1
burger [bür/gər]
    cheeseburger [chēz/bür/gər] **79**–3
    hamburger [hăm/bür/gər] **79**–1
burglary [bür/glə rē] **142**–2
burn [bürn]
    sunburn [sŭn/bürn/] **110**–14
burn [bürn] **116**–H
burner [bür/nər] **54**–19, **195**–37
burrito [bə rē/tō] **79**–9

bus [bŭs] **128–9, 151–14**
    bus person [bŭs/ pür/sən] **185–13**
    bus route [bŭs/ rōōt/, –rowt/] **152–1**
    bus station [bŭs/ stā/shən] **124–7**
    bus stop [bŭs/ stäp/] **129–16, 151–13**
    miss the bus [mĭs/ dhə bŭs/] **152 ✦**
bus [bŭs] **82–G**
business [bĭz/nəs]
    business owner [bĭz/nəs ō/nər] **166–11**
    businessperson [bĭz/nəs pür/sən] **166–12**
    business suit [bĭz/nəs sōōt/] **88–11**
busser [bŭ/sər] **83–12**
Bus Stop [bŭs/ stäp/] **152**
butcher [bŏŏch/ər] **166–13**
butter [bŭt/ər] **66–6, 83–19**
butterfly [bŭt/ər flī/] **214–19**
buttocks [bŭt/əks] **107–30**
button [bŭt/n] **99–24**
    back button [băk/ bŭt/n] **197–2**
    call button [köl/ bŭt/n] **121–28**
    forward button [för/wərd bŭt/n] **197–3**
buy [bī] **27–G**
    buy a home [bī/ ə hōm/] **41–M**
    buy a snack [bī/ ə snăk/] **11–K**
    buy recycled products
        [bī/ rē sī/kəld präd/ŭkts] **219–D**
Buying a House [bī/ĭng ə hows/] **49**
BUYING AND MAINTAINING A CAR
    [bī/ĭng ən mān tā/nĭng ə kär/] **157**
Buying a Used Car [bī/ĭng ə yōōzd/ kär/] **157**
buzzer [bŭz/ər] **51–31**
cab [kăb] **156–16**
cabbage [kăb/ĭj] **69–2**
Cabinet [kăb/ə nət] **138–10**
cabinet [kăb/ə nət] **54–1**
    file cabinet [fīl/ kăb/ə nət] **182–11**
    medicine cabinet [mĕd/ə sən kăb/ə nət] **57–20**
    supply cabinet [sə plī/ kăb/ə nət] **182–1**
cables [kā/bəlz] **158–21, 196–13**
cactus [kăk/təs] **210–21**
cafeteria [kăf/ə tïr/ē ə] **5–14**
cage [kāj] **107–48**
cake [kāk] **73–39, 81–33**
    cake pan [kāk/ păn/] **78–26**
    cheesecake [chēz/kāk/] **81–34**
    pancakes [păn/kāks/] **80–7**
Cake [kāk] **77**
calculate [kăl/kyə lāt/] **17–B**
calculator [kăl/kyə lā/tər] **17–6, 183–25**
calculus [kăl/kyə ləs] **192–19**
CALENDAR [kăl/ən dər] **20–21**
CALENDAR EVENTS [kăl/ən dər ĭ vĕnts/] **22**
calf [kăf] **106–22**
    calf-length [kăf/ lĕnth/] **96–17**
call [köl]
    call button [köl/ bŭt/n] **121–28**
    international call [ĭn/tər năsh/ə nəl köl/] **15–35**
    Internet phone call [ĭn/tər nĕt/ fōn/ köl/] **14–20**
    local call [lō/kəl köl/] **15–31**
    long distance call [löng/ dĭs/təns köl/] **15–32**
call [köl] **48–A, 147–L**
    call in [köl/ ĭn/] **186–A**

calling card [kö/lĭng kärd/] **14–15**
calm [köm] **42–8**
camcorder [kăm/kör dər] **235–24**
camel [kăm/əl] **217–38**
camera [kăm/rə]
    camera case [kăm/rə kàs/] **235–28**
    digital camera [dĭ/jə təl kăm/rə] **235–19**
    film camera [fĭlm/ kăm/rə] **235–21**
    security camera [sĭ kyōōr/ə tē kăm/rə] **50–19**
    35 mm camera
        [thür/tē fīv/ mĭl/ə mē/tər kăm/rə] **235–21**
camisole [kăm/ə sōl/] **91–21**
campaign [kăm pān/] **139–29**
camper [kăm/pər] **156–9**
campfire [kămp/fīr/] **226–11**
camping [kăm/pĭng] **226–5**
    camping stove [kăm/pĭng stōv/] **226–16**
Campus [kăm/pəs] **5**
can [kăn] **74–3, 74–15**
    can opener [kăn/ ō/pə nər] **78–1, 146–8**
    electric can opener [ĭ lĕk/trĭk/ kăn/ ō/pə nər] **54–14**
    garbage can [gär/bĭj kăn/] **53–24**
cancer [kăn/sər] **111–10**
candle [kăn/dl] **56–20**
    candle holder [kăn/dl hōl/dər] **56–21**
candy [kăn/dē] **239–12**
    candy bar [kăn/dē bär/] **73–37**
    candy cane [kăn/dē kān/] **239–17**
    candy store [kăn/dē stör/] **131–17**
cane [kān] **113–16, 239–17**
canned food [kănd/ fōōd/] **146–9**
Canned Foods [kănd/ fōōdz/] **72**
canoeing [kə nōō/ĭng] **226–3**
can't breathe [kănt/ brēdh/] **116–N**
canteen [kăn tēn/] **226–24**
canvas [kăn/vəs] **233–17**
canyon [kăn/yən] **204–17**
cap [kăp] **88–1, 206–7**
    baseball cap [bās/böl/ kăp/] **86–5**
    bump cap [bŭmp/ kăp/] **92–9**
    shower cap [show/ər kăp/] **108–1**
    surgical cap [sür/jĭ kəl kăp/] **121–37**
    surgical scrub cap [sür/jĭ kəl skrŭb/ kăp/] **93–35**
capital [kă/pət əl] **139–22**
capitalize [kă/pət əl īz/] **190–A, 190–B**
Capitol [kă/pət əl] **138–1**
capris [kə prēz] **88–8**
capsule [kăp/səl] **113–23**
car [kär] **150–1**
    car accident [kär/ ăk/sə dənt] **144–2**
    car dealership [kär/ dē/lər shĭp/] **126–4**
    car safety seat [kär/ sāf/tē sēt/] **37–19**
    4-door car [för/dör/ kär/] **156–1**
    sports car [spörts/kär/] **156–4**
    subway car [sŭb/wā/ kär/] **152–6**
    town car [town/ kär/] **152–20**
    2-door car [tōō/dör/ kär/] **156–2**
Car [kär] **157, 159**
CAR [kär] **156, 157, 158–159**
card [kärd] **239–5**
    ATM card [ā/tē/ĕm/ kärd/] **132–15**
    auto club card [ö tō/ klŭb/ kärd/] **162–4**

baseball cards [bās/böl/ kärdz/] **232–2**
card store [kärd/ stör/] **130–7**
copies of ID and credit cards
    [kä/pēz əv ī/dē/ ən krĕd/ət/ kärdz/] **146–19**
emergency card [ĭ mür/jən sē/ kärd/] **161–23**
fare card [fër/ kärd/] **152–11**
folding card table [fōl/dĭng/ kärd/ tā/bəl] **102–4**
green card [grĕn/ kärd/] **40–2**
greeting card [grē/tĭng kärd/] **134–15**
health insurance card
    [hĕlth/ ĭn shōōr/əns kärd/] **118–3**
memory card [mĕm/ə rē kärd/] **235–20**
post card [pōst/ kärd/] **134–16**
Resident Alien card [rĕz/ə dənt ā/lē ən kärd/] **40–2**
rotary card file [rō/tə rē kärd/ fīl/] **183–44**
Social Security card
    [sō/shəl sĭ kyōōr/ə tē kärd/] **40–5**
Card [kärd] **135**
cardigan sweater [kär/də gən swĕt/ər] **88–2**
Cardinal Numbers [kärd/nəl nŭm/bərz] **16**
cardiologist [kär/dē äl/ə jïst] **120–3**
cardiopulmonary resuscitation (CPR)
    [kär/dē ō pōōl mə nër/ē rĭ sŭs/ə tā/shən] /
    [sē/pē/är/] **117–17**
care [kër] **167–32**
careful worker [kër/fəl wür/kər] **179–2**
careless worker [kër/ləs wür/kər] **179–1**
childcare worker [chīld/kër wür/kər] **166–16**
CARE [kër] **114–115, 118, 119**
Care of Your Car [kër/ əv yər kär/] **157**
career counselor [kə rër/ kown/slər] **172–10**
Career Path [kə rër/ păth/] **172**
CAREER PLANNING [kə rër/ plăn/ĭng] **172**
cargo van [kär/gō văn/] **156–13**
carnation [kär nā/shən] **211–20**
carousel [kär/ə sĕl/] **161–23**
carpenter [kär/pən tər] **62–12, 166–14**
carpet [kär/pət] **56–24**
carpool [kär/pōōl/] **219–I**
carriage [kär/ĭj] **37–20**
carrier [kär/ē ər] **37–17, 134–20**
carrots [kär/əts] **69–3**
carry [kär/ē] **11–F, 82–H**
CARS AND TRUCKS [kärz/ ən trŭks/] **156**
cart [kärt] **72–7, 129–28**
    housekeeping cart [hows/kē/pĭng kärt/] **184–19**
    luggage cart [lŭg/ĭj kärt/] **184–8**
carton [kär/tn] **74–4, 74–16**
cartoon [kär/tōōn] **236–3**
cartridge [kär/trĭj] **183–45**
carving knife [kär/vĭng nīf/] **78–12**
case [kàs] **94–5, 235–28**
cash [kăsh]
    cash and coins [kăsh/ ən koynz/] **146–17**
    cash register [kăsh/ rĕj/ə stər] **27–10, 73–15**
cash [kăsh] **27–F, 132–A**
cashier [kă shïr/] **73–13, 166–15**
cashmere [kăzh/mïr/] **98–4**
Casserole [kăs/ə rōl] **77**
casserole dish [kăs/ə rōl dĭsh/] **78–10**
cassette [kə sĕt/] **234–6**
    videocassette [vĭ/dē ō kə sĕt/] **133–18**

cast [kăst] **113**–20
castle [kă/səl] **225**–12
Casual Clothes [kăzh/ōō əl klōz/] **88**
CASUAL, WORK, AND FORMAL CLOTHES
[kăzh/ōō əl würk/ ən för/məl klōz/] **88**–**89**
cat [kăt] **215**–9
catfish [kăt/fĭsh/] **71**–2
catalog [kăt ə /lög] **133**–11
catch [kăch] **230**–D
catcher's mask [kăch/ərz măsk/] **231**–15
caterer [kā/tər ər] **185**–16
caterpillar [kăt ə pĭl/ər, kăt/ər–] **214**–20
cattle [kăt/l] **177**–21
cauliflower [kö/lĭ flow/ər, kä/–] **69**–14
cave [kāv] **220**–6
caverns [kă/vərnz] **220**–7
cavity [kăv/ə tē] **119**–7
C-clamp [sē/klămp/] **180**–6
CD [sē/dē/] **196**–9, **234**–5
CD boombox [sē/dē/ bōōm/bäks/] **234**–1
CD player [sē/dē/ plā/ər] **159**–38
celebrate [sĕl/ə brāt] **206**–C
celery [sĕl/ə rē] **69**–9
cell [sĕl] **194**–4
cell membrane [sĕl/ mĕm/brān] **194**–6
cell phone holder [sĕl/ fōn/ hōl/dər] **94**–15
cell phone kiosk [sĕl/ fōn/ kē/ösk] **131**–22
cell phone number [sĕl/ fōn/ nŭm/bər] **4**–12
cell wall [sĕl/ wäl/] **194**–5
cello [chĕl/ō] **238**–7
cellular phone [sĕl/yə lər fōn/] **14**–8
Celsius [sĕl/sē əs] **13**–2
cemetery [sĕl/mə tĕr/ē] **127**–15
cent [sĕnt] **26**–1, **26**–2, **26**–3, **26**–4
center [sĕn/tər]
automated postal center (APC)
[ö/tə māt ĭd pōs/təl sĕn/tər] / [ā/pē/sē/] **135**–10
childcare center [chīld/kër/ sĕn/tər] **129**–30
convention center [kən vĕn/shən sĕn/tər] **127**–24
copy center [käp/ē sĕn/tər] **129**–18
entertainment center
[ĕn/tər tān/mənt sĕn/tər] **56**–5
resource center [rē/sörs sĕn/tər] **172**–9
CENTER [sĕn/tər] **208**–**209**
centimeter [cm] [sĕn/tə mē/tər] **17**–14
CENTRAL AMERICA [sĕn/trəl ə mĕr/ə kə] **200**–**201**
Central time [sĕn/trəl tīm/] **19**–31
cereal [sïr/ē əl] **80**–9
ceremony [sĕr/ə mō/nē] **206**–6
certificate [sər tĭf/ə kət] **40**–1, **41**–11
Certificate of Naturalization
[sər tĭf/ə kət əv năch/rə lə zā/shən] **40**–6
certified [sür/tə fīd/]
Certified Mail® [sür/tə fīd/ māl/] **134**–4
certified nursing assistant (CNA)
[sür/tə fīd/ nür/sĭng ə sĭs/tənt] / [sē/ĕn/ā/]
120–12
chain [chān] **51**–33, **95**–33, **180**–41
chair [chër] **7**–11
armchair [ärm/chër] **56**–22
beach chair [bēch/ chër/] **225**–22
dining room chair [dī/nĭng rōōm/chër/] **55**–8

easy chair [ē/zē/ chër/] **56**–22
folding chair [fōld/ĭng chër/] **102**–5
high chair [hī/ chër/] **37**–6, **82**–3
rocking chair [räk/ĭng chër/] **37**–21
wheelchair [wēl/chër/] **113**–9
chalk [chök] **7**–18
chalkboard [chök/börd/] **6**–1
challenged [chăl/əngd] **32**–10
change [chānj] **36**–G, **60**–P, **148**–C
change purse [chānj/ pürs/] **94**–14
changing [chān/jĭng]
changing pad [chān/jĭng păd/] **59**–2
changing table [chān/jĭng tā/bəl] **59**–1
charger [chär/jər] **14**–10, **234**–17, **235**–27
chart [chärt] **121**–24
cheap [chēp] **23**–20
check [chĕk] **132**–13
check book [chĕk/ bōōk/] **132**–12
check-in kiosk [chĕk/ĭn/ kē/ösk] **160**–2
checkstand [chĕk/stănd/] **73**–12
paycheck [pā/chĕk/] **165**–14
check [chĕk]
check blood pressure [chĕk/ blŭd/ prĕsh/ər] **118**–A
check email [chĕk/ ē/ māl/] **39**–W
check in [chĕk/ ĭn/] **160**–A
check Internet job sites
[chĕk/ ĭn/tər nĕt/ jäb/ sīts/] **173**–D
check messages [chĕk/ mĕs/ə jĭz] **171**–R
check out [chĕk/ owt/] **133**–C
check the correct boxes
[chĕk/ dhə kə rĕkt/ bäk/səz] **9**–U
check the oil [chĕk/ dhə oyl/] **157**–H
check the pronunciation
[chĕk/ dhe prə nən sē ā/ shən] **8**–D
check your bags [chĕk/ yər băgz/] **160**–B
check pulse [chĕk/ püls/] **122**–A
check your spelling [chĕk/ yər spĕl/ĭng] **197**–F
check your understanding
[chĕk/ yər ŭn/dər stănd/ĭng] **12**–N
check your work [chĕk/ yər würk/] **10**–L
checked [chĕkt] **96**–24
checkers [chĕk/ərz] **232**–7
checking account number
[chĕk/ĭng ə kownt/ nŭm/bər] **132**–14
checkout [chĕk/owt/] **133**–10
Checkpoint [chĕk/poynt/] **160**
cheddar cheese [chĕd/ər chēz/] **71**–28
cheek [chēk] **106**–3
cheese [chēz] **66**–4
American cheese [ə mĕr/ə kən chēz/] **71**–26
cheddar cheese [chĕd/ər chēz/] **71**–28
cheeseburger [chēz/bür/gər] **79**–3
cheesecake [chēz/kāk/] **81**–34
grilled cheese sandwich
[grĭld/ chēz/ săn/wĭch, –sănd/–] **80**–10
Swiss cheese [swĭs/ chēz/] **71**–27
Cheesy Tofu Vegetable Casserole
[chē/zē tō/fōō vĕj/tə bəl kăs/ə rōl] **77**
chef [shĕf] **83**–16
chef's hat [shĕfs/ hăt/] **93**–28
chef's jacket [shĕfs/ jăk/ət] **93**–29
chef's salad [shĕfs/ săl/ əd] **80**–14

executive chef [ĭg zĕk/yə tĭv shĕf/] **185**–7
head chef [hĕd/ shĕf/] **185**–7
sous chef [sōō/ shĕf/] **185**–6
Chef [shĕf] **93**
chemist [kĕm/ĭst] **195**–25
Chemistry [kĕm/ə strē] **195**
cherries [chĕr/ēz] **68**–11
cherry picker [chĕr/ē pĭk/ər] **178**–5
chess [chĕs] **232**–8
chest [chĕst] **59**–16, **104**–4, **107**–25
chest of drawers [chĕst/ əv drörz/] **59**–6
chicken [chĭk/ən] **66**–3, **70**–16
chicken pox [chĭk/ən päks/] **111**–6
chicken sandwich [chĭk/ən săn/wĭch, –sănd–] **79**–5
fried chicken [frīd/ chĭk/ən] **76**–1
roast chicken [rōst/ chĭk/ən] **81**–22
Chicken [chĭk/ən] **77**
chief justice [chēf/ jŭs/təs] **138**–13
CHILDCARE AND PARENTING
[chīld/kër ən për/ən tĭng] **36**–**37**
child / children [chīld] / [chĭl/ drən]
childcare center [chīld/kër sĕn/tər] **129**–30
childcare worker [chīld/kër wür/kər] **166**–16
children's program [chĭl/drənz prō/grăm] **236**–9
child safety seat [chīld/ sāf/tē sēt/] **159**–53
grandchild [grăn/chīld, grănd/–] **34** ✦
lost child [löst/ chīld/] **144**–1
Childhood Diseases [chīld/hōōd dĭ zē/zəz] **111**
chili peppers [chĭl/ē pĕp/ərz] **69**–29
chill [chĭl] **76**–D
chills [chĭlz] **110**–9
chimney [chĭm/nē] **53**–5
chimpanzee [chĭm/păn zē/] **217**–27
chin [chĭn] **106**–1
chipmunk [chĭp/mŭngk] **215**–20
chips [chĭps] **73**–35
chiropractors [kī/rō prăk/tərz] **120**
chisel [chĭz/əl] **181**–55
choke [chōk] **116**–L
choose [chōōz] **9**–P
chop [chäp] **77**–L
chops [chäps] **70**–10, **70**–15
Christmas [krĭs/məs] **22**–18
Christmas tree [krĭs/məs trē/] **239**–16
chromosome [krō/mə zōm/] **194**–8
chrysanthemum [krĭ săn/thə məm] **211**–21
church [chürch] **127**–14
chute [shōōt] **51**–26
circle [sür/ kəl] **193**–34
circle [sür/ kəl] **9**–Q
circular saw [sür/kyə lər sö/] **180**–9
circulation desk [sür/kyə lā/shən dĕsk/] **133**–2
circumference [sər kŭm/frəns] **193**–36
citizen [sĭt/ə zən] **30**–5
Citizenship Requirements
[sĭt/ə zən shĭp/ rĭ kwīr/mənts] **140**
city [sĭt/ē] **4**–7, **52**–1
city code [sĭt/ē kōd/] **15**–34
city council [sĭt/ē kown/səl] **139**–27
city hall [sĭt/ē häl/] **124**–8
City Government [sĭt/ē gŭ/vərn mənt] **139**
CITY STREETS [sĭt/ē strēts/] **126**–**127**

Index

CIVIC RIGHTS AND RESPONSIBILITIES
[sĭ/vĭk rĭts n rĭ spän/sə bĭl/ə tēz] **140**
Civilizations [sĭ/və lə zā/shenz] **199**
claim [klām] **160**–L
clamp [klämp] **180**–6
clams [klämz] **71**–15
clarinet [klär/ə nĕt/] **238**–2
classical [kla/sĭ kəl] **237**–21
classical concert [kla/sĭ kəl kän/sərt] **223**–14
classified ad [kläs/e fīd] **48**–2
Classmates [kläs/māts/] **8**
classroom [kläs/rōōm] **5**–7
CLASSROOM [kläs/rōōm/] **6**–7
claw [klö] **214**–2
clean [klēn] **101**–16
clean [klēn] **76**–A
clean teeth [klēn/ tēth/] **119**–A
clean the house [klēn/ dhə hows/] **39**–O
clean the lint trap [klēn/ dhə lĭnt/ trăp/] **101**–D
clean the oven [klēn/ dhə ŭv/ən] **60**–C
clean up [klēn/ ŭp/] **147**–M
cleaner [klēn/ər]
dry cleaners [drī/ klēn/ərz] **128**–2
glass cleaner [glăs/ klēn/ər] **61**–14
oven cleaner [ŭv/ən klēn/ər] **61**–3
vacuum cleaner [văk/yōōm klēn/ər] **61**–10
vacuum cleaner attachments
[văk/yōōm klēn/ər ə tăch/mənts] **61**–11
vacuum cleaner bag [văk/yəm klēn/ər băg/] **61**–12
CLEANING SUPPLIES [klē/nĭng sə plīz/] **61**
cleanser [klēn/zər] **61**–18
CLEANUP [klēn/ŭp/] **148**–149
clear [klĭr] **13**–9
clear tape [klĭr/tāp/] **183**–30
clear [klĭr] **82**–G
clear off [klĭr/ äf/] **10**–I
clerk [klŭrk] **5**–13, **182**–2
admissions clerk [əd mĭsh/ənz klŭrk/] **120**–14
desk clerk [dĕsk/ klŭrk/] **184**–11
DMV clerk [dē/ĕm/vē/ klŭrk/] **136**–3
file clerk [fīl/ klŭrk/] **182**–10
grocery clerk [grōs/rē klŭrk/, grōsh/–, grō/sə–] **72**–4
library clerk [lī/brër ē klŭrk/] **133**–1
payroll clerk [pā/rōl/ klŭrk/] **165**–10
postal clerk [pō/stəl klŭrk/] **135**–7
retail clerk [rē/tāl/ klŭrk/] **169**–53
salesclerk [sālz/klŭrk/] **94**–3
shipping clerk [shĭp/ĭng klŭrk/] **175**–16
stock clerk [stäk/ klŭrk/] **169**–59
click [klĭk] **197**–B
climb [klīm] **224**–C
climbing apparatus [klīm/ĭng ă/pə ră/təs] **224**–14
clinic [klĭn/ĭk] **186**–2
clip-on earrings [klĭp/än ĭr/ĭngz, –ön–] **95**–37
clipper [klĭp/ər] **109**–31, **176**–11
clips [klĭps] **108**–19, **183**–31, **194**–24
clock [kläk] **7**–9, **58**–24, **165**–7
clock radio [kläk/ rā/dē ō] **102**–6
close [klōz] **6**–H
closet [kläz/ət] **57** ✦, **58**–5
Closures [klō/zhərz] **99**

cloth [klöth] **181**–54
cloth diaper [klöth/ dī/pərz] **37**–8
tablecloth [tā/bəl klöth/] **55**–12
washcloth [wäsh/klöth/] **57**–4
clothes [klōz] **146**–6
clothesline [klōz/līn/] **101**–9
clothespin [klōz/pĭn/] **101**–10
CLOTHES [klōz] **86**–87, **88**–89, **96**–97, **98**–99
clothing [klō/dhĭng] **102**–2
CLOTHING [klō/dhĭng] **90**, **92**–93
Clothing Problems [klō/dhĭng präb/ləmz] **97**
cloudy [klow/dē] **13**–10
club [klŭb] **162**–4, **223**–12, **231**–1
club sandwich [klŭb săn/wĭch/, –sănd–] **80**–12
clubs [klŭbz] **233**–32
clutch [klŭch] **159**–49
clutch bag [klŭch/ băg/] **89**–19
CNA (certified nursing assistant) [sē/ĕn/ā/] /
[sür/tə tə fīd/ nür/sĭng ə sĭs/tənt] **120**–12
coach [kōch] **5**–20, **229**–2
coal [kōl] **218**–4
coarse adjustment knob
[körs/ ə jŭst/mənt näb/] **194**–22
Coast Guard [kōst/ gärd/] **138**–18
coat [kōt] **90**–2, **216**–19
lab coat [lăb/ kōt/] **93**–33
raincoat [rān/ kōt/] **90**–18
sports coat [spörts/ kōt/] **89**–14
trench coat [trĕnch/ kōt/] **90**–21
cobra [kō/brə] **213**–41
cockpit [käk/pĭt/] **161**–10
cockroaches [käk/rō/chəz] **63**–26
cocktail dress [käk/tāl/ drĕs/] **89**–20
coconuts [kō/kə nŭts/] **68**–24
cod [käd] **71**–8, **212**–5
code [kōd]
area code [ër/ē ə kōd/] **15**–29
bar code [bär/ kōd/] **27**–4
city code [sĭt/ē kōd/] **15**–34
country code [kŭn/trē kōd/] **15**–33
coffee [kö/fē] **73**–33, **81**–37, **81**–38
coffeemaker [kö/fē mā/kər] **54**–11
coffee mug [kö/fē mŭg/] **55**–7
coffee shop [kö/fē shäp/] **126**–11
coffee table [kö/fē tā/bəl] **56**–19
COFFEE SHOP MENU [kö/fē shäp/ mĕn/yōō] **80**–81
coins [koynz] **146**–17
coin purse [koyn/ pürs/] **94**–14
Coins [koynz] **26**
colander [käl/ən dər] **78**–17
cold [kōld] **13**–6, **42**–4, **111**–1
cold tablets [kōld tăb/ləts] **113**–27
cold water [kōld wö/tər] **57**–7
coleslaw [kōl/slö/] **80**–18
collar [käl/ər] **100**–4
collate [kō/lāt/, kə lāt/] **171**–E
collect [kə lĕkt/] **232**–A
college [käl/ĭj] **127**–17, **188**–6, **188**–7
college degree [käl/ĭj də grē/] **41**–7
college dormitory [käl/ĭj dör/mə tör/ē] **52**–8
cologne [kə lōn/] **108**–6
colon [kō/lən] **190**–17

Colonial Period [kə lō/nē əl pïr/ē əd] **198**
colonies [kä/lə nēz] **198**–1
colonists [kä/lə nĭsts] **198**–2
color [kŭl/ər]
watercolor [wö/tər kŭl/ər] **233**–21
color [kŭl/ər] **33**–D
coloring book [kŭl/ə rĭng bōŏk/] **59**–13
Colors [kŭl/ərs] **24**
COLORS [kŭl/ərs] **24**
Columbus Day [kə lŭm/bəs dā/] **22**–15
column [käl/ŭm] **107**–49
comb [kōm] **33**–21, **108**–13
comb [kōm] **108**–G
come [kŭm] **39**–R
comedy [käm/ə dē] **236**–2, **237**–13
comet [käm/ət] **205**–24
comfort [kŭm/fərt] **36**–I
comma [käm/ə] **190**–14
commercial fisher [kə mür/shəl fĭsh/ər] **167**–17
commit a crime [kə mĭt/ ə krīm/] **142** ✦
Common Illnesses and Childhood Diseases
[käm/ən ĭl/nə səz ən chīld/hŏŏd-dĭ zē/zəz] **111**
COMMUNITY CLEANUP
[kə myōō/nə tē klēn/ŭp] **148**–149
community college
[kə myōō/nə tē käl/ĭj] **127**–17, **188**–6
Comparing Clothing [kəm për/ĭng klō/dhĭng] **97**
compartment [kəm pärt/mənt] **159**–44, **161**–13
complaint [kəm plānt/] **97** ✦
Complex [käm/plĕks] **51**
compliment [käm/plə mĕnt/] **12** ✦
compliment [käm/plə mĕnt/] **12**–C
composer [kəm pō/zər] **199**–15
composition [käm/pə zĭsh/ən] **199**–14
compost [käm/pōst/] **219**–M
compost pile [käm/pōst pīl/] **53**–25
computer [kəm pyōō/tər] **7**–15, **183**–17
computer lab [kəm pyōō/tər lăb/] **5**–15
computer software engineer
[kəm pyōō/tər söft/wër/ ĕn/jə nïr/] **167**–18
computer technician [kəm pyōō/tər tĕk nĭsh/ən]
167–19, **182**–12
Computer [kəm pyōō/tər] **196**
COMPUTERS [kəm pyōō/tərz] **196**
conceal [kən sēl/] **143**–C
concert [kän/sərt] **222**–5, **223**–14
concierge [kän/sē ërzh/, kōn/–] **184**–4
conclusion [kən klōō/zhən] **190**–8
concrete [käng/krēt, kän krēt/] **178**–10
conditioner [kən dĭsh/ə nər] **108**–11, **159**–39
Conditions [kən dĭsh/ənz] **13**, **111**
CONDITIONS [kən dĭsh/ənz] **111**
condominium [kän/də mĭn/ē əm] **52**–5
conduct [kən dŭkt/] **238**–C
conductor [kən dŭk/tər] **152**–13
cone [kōn] **79**–13, **193**–40
pinecone [pīn/kōn] **210**–11
conference room [kän/frəns rōōm/] **182**–4
confetti [kən fĕt/ē] **239**–3
confused [kən fyōōzd/] **43**–26
congestion [kən jĕs/chən] **110**–7
Congress [käng/grəs] **138**–2, **198**–6

congressperson [kän/grəs pür/sən] **138**–4
CONSERVATION [kän/sər vā/shən] **218**–**219**
Conserve Energy and Resources
[kən sürv/ ĕn/ər jē ən rē/sörs/əz] **219**
console [kän/söl] **232**–3
constellation [kän/stə lā/shən] **205**–14
Constitution [kän/stə tōō/shən] **198**–19
construction [kən strŭk/shən]
construction paper [kən strŭk/shən pā/pər] **232**–12
construction site [kən strŭk/shən sīt/] **126**–2
construction worker
[kən strŭk/shən wür/kər] **178**–1
CONSTRUCTION [kən strŭk/shən] **178**
Construction Worker [kən strŭk/shən wür/kər] **92**
contact [kän/täkt] **146**–2
contact lenses [kän/täkt lĕn/zəz] **115**–8
container [kən tā/nər] **74**–5, **74**–17, **78**–4
CONTAINERS AND PACKAGING
[kən tā/nərz ən păk/ĭ jĭng] **74**
continental [kän/tə nĕnt/əl] **198**–6
contractor [kän/trăk tər] **186**–5
control [kən tröl/] **121**–27, **232**–4
convenience store [kən vēn/yəns stör/] **128**–3
convention center [kən vĕn/shən sĕn/tər] **127**–24
convert [kən vürt/] **17**–D, **75**–C
convertible [kən vür/tə bəl] **156**–5
conveyer belt [kən vā/ər bĕlt/] **175**–16
convict [kän/vĭkt] **141**–15
convict [kən vĭkt/] **141**–E
cook [kŏŏk] **185**–1, **185** ✦
cook [kŏŏk] **39**–Q, **76**–C, **170**–C
cooked [kŏŏkt] **70**–25
cookies [kŏŏk/ēz] **73**–38
cookie sheet [kŏŏk/ē shĕt/] **78**–27
cool [kōōl] **13**–5
cooler [kōō/lər] **225**–19
co-op [kō/äp/] **52** ✦
copier [kä/pē ər]
photocopier [fō/tō kä/pē ər] **183**–23
copies / copy [kä/pēz] / [kä/pē]
copies of ID and credit cards
[käp/ēz əv ī/dē ən krĕd/ət kärdz/] **146**–19
copies of important papers
[käp/ēz əv ĭm pört/ənt pā/pərz] **146**–20
copy center [käp/ē sĕn/tər] **129**–18
copy [käp/ē] **8**–E
coral [kör/əl] **220**–5
cord [körd] **14**–2
bungee cord [bŭn/jē körd] **181**–15
cordless phone [körd/ləs fōn/] **15**–24
extension cord [ĭk stĕn/shən körd/] **181**–14
frayed cord [frād/ körd/] **179**–5
power cord [pow/ər körd/] **196**–2
corduroy [kör/də roy/] **99**–11
core course [kör/ körs/] **189** ✦
corn [körn] **69**–12, **177**–4
corn rows [körn/ rōz/] **33**–14
corned beef [körnd/ bēf/] **71**–22
corner [kör/nər] **128**–7
coronary disease [kör/ə nĕ/rē dĭ zēz/] **111** ✦
corral [kə răl/] **177**–17
correct [kə rĕkt/] **10**–N

correction [kə rĕk/shən]
correction fluid [kə rĕk/shən flōō/əd] **183**–36
correction tape [kə rĕk/shən tāp/] **183**–37
cost [köst] **27**–7, **122**–1
costume [käs/tōōm] **239**–11
cotton [kät/n] **98**–1, **177**–6
couch [kowch] **56**–18
cough [köf] **110**–A
cough syrup [köf/ sïr/əp, –sür/–] **113**–29
council [kown/səl] **139**–27
councilperson [kown/səl pür/sən] **139**–28
counselor [kown/slər] **5**–6, **172**–10
count [kownt] **84**–A
counter [kown/tər] **54**–22, **113**–18
counterperson [kown/tər pür/sən] **79**–17
Counterperson [kown/tər pür/sən] **93**
country [kŭn/trē] **52**–4, **227**–3, **237**–27
country code [kŭn/trē kōd/] **15**–33
county fair [kown/tē fër/] **223**–13
coupe [kōōp] **156**–2
couple [kŭ/pəl] **35**–20, **35**–21, **239**–4
coupons [kōō/pönz] **67**–15
courier [kür/ē ər, kŏŏr/–] **168**–40
course [körs] **172**–8, **189** ✦
court [kört]
basketball court [băs/kət böl/ kört/] **229**–7
courthouse [kört/hows/] **125**–13
courtroom [kört/rōōm/] **141**–7
court reporter [kört/ rĭ pör/tər] **141**–12
courtyard [kört/yärd/] **51**–21
food court [fōōd/ kört/] **131**–15
Supreme Court [sə prēm/ kört/] **138**–11
tennis court [tĕ/nəs kört/] **224**–6
cousin [kŭz/ən] **34**–9
cover [kŭv/ər] **158**–9, **181**–46
coveralls [kŭv/ər ölz/] **92**–8
cover-up [kŭv/ər ŭp/] **90**–25
cow [kow] **215**–1
cowboy hat [kow/boy/ hăt/] **92**–18
coyote [kī ō/tē, kī/ōt/] **216**–3
CPR (cardiopulmonary resuscitation) [sē/pē/är/] /
[kär/dē ō pŏŏl/mə nër/ē sŭs/ə tā/shən] **117**–17
CPU [sē/pē/yōō/] **196**–4
crab [krăb] **71**–9, **212**–20
cracked [krăkt] **62**–4
cradle [krād/l] **59**–20
crane [krān] **178**–7
crash [krăsh] **144**–3
crayons [krā/änz] **59**–14
cream [krēm] **24**–16, **81**–41, **113**–25
antihistamine cream
[ăn/tī hĭs/tə mēn krēm/] **117**–11
ice-cream [īs/ krēm/] **72**–26
ice-cream cone [īs/ krēm kōn/] **79**–13
ice cream shop [īs/ krēm shäp/] **131**–16
shaving cream [shā/vĭng krēm/] **109**–29
sour cream [sow/ər krēm/] **72**–21
creamer [krē/mər] **55**–15
credit [krĕd/ət] **146**–19
creek [krēk, krĭk] **204** ✦
crescent moon [krĕs/ənt mōōn/] **205**–10

crew [krōō] **176**–1, **176**–4
crewneck [krōō/nĕk] **96**–7
crew socks [krōō/säks/] **91**–8
crib [krĭb] **59**–3
cricket [krĭk/ət] **214**–23
crime [krīm] **142** ✦
CRIME [krīm] **142**
criminal [krĭm/ə nəl] **142** ✦
crocheting [krō shā/ĭng] **233**–25
crocodile [kräk/ə dīl/] **213**–37
crocus [krō/kəs] **211**–17
Crops [kräps] **177**
cross [krös]
cross-country skiing [krös/kŭn/trē skē/ĭng] **227**–3
crosswalk [krös/wök/] **128**–15
cross [krös] **128**–A
cross out [krös/ owt/] **9**–R
crossing [krö/sĭng] **154**–13, **154**–14, **154**–15
crown [krown] **119**–9
crucible tongs [krōō/sə bəl tängz/, –töngz/] **195**–44
crutches [krŭch/əz] **113**–10
cry [krī] **206**–B
cube [kyōōb] **193**–38
cubicle [kyōō/bə kəl] **182**–7
cucumbers [kyōō/kŭm bərz] **69**–10
cuff [kŭf] **100**–9
cup [kŭp] **75**–2, **75**–10, **83**–24
1/2 cup [hăf/ kŭp/] **75**–9
1/4 cup [kwör/tər kŭp/] **75**–8
teacup [tē/kŭp/] **55**–6
curb [kürb] **129**–21
curling iron [kür/lĭng ī/ərn] **108**–17
curly hair [kür/lē hër/] **33**–11
cursor [kür/sər] **197**–14
curtains [kür/tnz] **57**–12, **58**–7
curved line [kürvd/ līn/] **193**–23
cushion [kŏŏ/shən] **56** ✦, **100**–13
customer [kŭs/tə mər] **72**–1, **94**–4, **132**–2, **164**–2
customer service [kŭs/tə mər sür/vəs] **97** ✦
customer service representative
[kŭs/tə mər-sür/vəs rĕ/prə zĕn/tə tĭv] **167**–20
Customs [kŭs/təmz] **161**
customs officer [kŭs/təmz ö/fə sər] **161**–17
cut [kŭt] **91**–10, **110**–13
cut [kŭt] **33**–A, **109**–N
cut up [kŭt/ ŭp/] **77**–I
cute [kyōōt] **32**–14
cutlets [kŭt/ləts] **70**–6
cutter [kut/ər] **183**–22, **232**–16
cutting board [kŭt/ĭng börd/] **54**–27
cycling [sī/klĭng] **228**–5
cyclist [sī/klĭst] **224**–2
cylinder [sĭl/ən dər] **193**–41, **195**–38
cytoplasm [sī/tə plăzm] **194**–9
daffodil [dăf/ə dĭl/] **211**–25
daily [dā/lē] **20**–21
DAILY ROUTINES [dā/lē rōō tēnz/] **38**–39
Dairy [dër/ē] **72**
daisy [dā/zē] **211**–14
dance [dăns] **64**–A
dangerous [dān/jər əs] **186**–1
dark blue [därk/ blōō/] **24**–10

Dashboard and Instrument Panel
[dăsh/bôrd/ ən ĭn/strə mənt păn/əl] **159**
dates [dāts] **20**–1, **68**–28
  date of birth [dāt əv bürth/] **4**–13
  expiration date
    [ĕk/spə rā/shən dāt] **112**–7, **136**–10
daughter [dô/tər] **34**–14
  daughter-in-law [dô/tər ĭn lö/] **34** ✦
  granddaughters [grăn/dô/tərz] **34** ✦
  stepdaughter [stĕp/dô/tər] **35** ✦
day [dā] **20**–2
  birthday [bürth/dā/] **22**–1
  Columbus Day [kə lŭm/bəs dā/] **22**–15
  daylight saving time [dā/līt/ sā/vĭng tīm/] **19**–25
  every day [ĕv/rē dā/] **20**–21
  Independence Day [ĭn/də pĕn/dəns dā/] **22**–13
  Labor Day [lā/bər dā/] **22**–14
  Martin Luther King Jr. Day
    [mär/tən lōō/thər kĭng/ jōōn/yər-dā/] **22**–10
  Memorial Day [mə môr/ē əl dā/] **22**–12
  New Year's Day [nōō/ yirz/ dā/] **22**–9
  Presidents' Day [prĕz/ə dənts dā/] **22**–11
  Veterans Day [vĕt/ər ənz dā/] **22**–16
Day [dā] **18**
DAY AT SCHOOL [dā/ ăt skōōl/] **11**
DAY AT WORK [dā/ ăt würk/] **186**–187
Days of the Week [dāz/ əv dhə wēk/] **20**
dead [dĕd]
  dead-bolt lock [dĕd/bōlt/ läk/] **51**–34
  dead end [dĕd/ĕnd/] **154**–6
deaf [dĕf] **32**–12
Dealer [dē/lər] **158**
dealership [dē/lər shĭp/] **126**–4
death certificate [dĕth/ sər tĭf/ə kət] **41**–11
debate [də bāt/] **139**–B
decaf coffee [dē/kăf/ kö/fē] **81**–38
decay [də kā/] **119**–7
December [dĭ sĕm/bər] **21**–36
decimal point [dĕs/ə məl poynt/] **17**–7
Decimals [dĕs/ə məlz] **17**
deck [dĕk] **240**–2
declaration [dĕk/lə rā/shən]
  declaration form [dĕk/lə rā/shən förm/] **161**–16
  Declaration of Independence
    [dĕk/lə rā/shən əv ĭn/də pĕn/dəns] **198**–5
decline [də klīn/] **12**–J
decorations [dĕk/ə rā/shənz] **240**–1
deductions [də dŭk/shənz] **165**–13
deed [dēd] **41**–9
deer [dir] **216**–14
defendant [dĭ fĕn/dənt] **141**–5
defense attorney [dĭ fĕns/ ə tür/nē] **141**–4
defroster [də frös/tər] **159**–41
degrees [də grēz/] **13**–8, **193**–26
delayed flight [də lād/ flīt/] **161**–30
delete [də lēt/] **196**–C
DELI [dĕl/ē] **71**
deliver [də lĭv/ər] **11**–G, **135**–E
delivery person [də lĭv/ə rē pür/sən] **167**–21
dementia [də mĕn/shə] **111**–18
demonstration [dĕ/mən strā/shən] **122**–6
denim [dĕ/nəm] **99**–7

denominator [də nömə nā/tər] **192**–6
dental [dĕn/təl]
  dental assistant [dĕn/təl ə sĭs/tənt] **119**–2, **167**–22
  dental floss [dĕn/təl flös/, –fläs/] **109**–24
  dental hygienist [dĕn/təl hī jē/nĭst, –jĕ/nĭst] **119**–3
  dental instruments [dĕn/təl ĭn/strə mənts] **119**–4
DENTAL CARE [dĕn/təl kër/] **119**
Dental Problems [dĕn/təl präb/ləmz] **119**
dentist [dĕn/tĭst] **119**–1
Dentistry [dĕn/təs trē/] **119**
dentures [dĕn/chərz] **119**–10
deodorant [dē ō/dər ənt] **108**–5
department [dĭ pärt/mənt] **95**–7, **95**–8
  Department of Motor Vehicles
    [dĭ pärt/mənt əv mō/tər vē/ī kəlz] **124**–4
  department store [dĭ pärt/mənt stör/] **131**–13
DEPARTMENT OF MOTOR VEHICLES (DMV)
    [dĭ pärt/mənt əv mō/tər vē/ī kəlz] / [dē/ĕm/vē/]
    136–137
departure [dĭ pär/chər] **161**–5, **161**–7
deposit [dĭ päz/ət] **132**–3, **132**–7
  deposit slip [dĭ päz/ət slĭp/] **132**–4
depression [də prĕ/shən] **115**–5
depth [dĕpth] **17**–18
DESCRIBING CLOTHES [dĭ skrī/bĭng klōz/] **96**–97
DESCRIBING HAIR [dĭ skrī/bĭng hër/] **33**
DESCRIBING PEOPLE [dĭ skrī/bĭng pē/pəl] **32**
DESCRIBING THINGS [dĭ skrī/bĭng thĭngz/] **23**
desert [dĕz/ərt] **204**–4
design [dĭ zīn/] **175**–A
designated drivers [dĕz/ĭg nā/təd drī/vərz] **143** ✦
designer [dĭ zī/nər] **98** ✦, **167**–30, **175**–2, **176**–5
desk [dĕsk] **6**–7, **182**–9
  circulation desk [sür/kyə lā/shən dĕsk/] **133**–2
  desk clerk [dĕsk klürk/] **184**–11
  front desk [frŭnt/ dĕsk/] **184**–12
Desktop Computer [dĕsk/täp/ kəm pyōō/tər] **196**
Desserts [dĭ zürts/] **81**
dessert tray [dĭ zürt/ trā/] **83**–10
destination [dĕs/tə nā/shən] **161** ✦
detector [dĭ tĕk/tər] **51**–29
detergent [dĭ tür/jənt] **101**–8
device [də vīs/] **225**–20
diabetes [dī/ə bē/tēz, –təs] **111**–12
diagonal [dī ăg/ə nəl, –ăg/nəl] **193**–31
dial [dī/əl] **15**–A, **15**–E
diameter [dī ăm/ə tər] **193**–37
diamonds [dī/məndz] **233**–29
diaper [dī/pər] **37**–8, **37**–10
  diaper pail [dī/pər pāl/] **37**–7
diaphragm [dī/ə frăm/] **194**–19
dice [dīs] **232**–6
dice [dīs] **77**–J
dictate [dĭk/tāt] **8**–N
dictator [dĭk/tā/tər] **199**–6
dictionary [dĭk/shə nër/ē] **7**–30, **7**–31
die [dī] **41**–R
dietician [dī/ə tĭsh/ən] **120**–15
difference [dĭf/rəns] **192**–8
different [dĭ/frənt, dī/fə rənt] **23**–16
DIFFERENT [dĭ/frənt, dī/fə rənt] **28**–29

DIFFERENT PLACES TO LIVE
    [dĭ/frənt plā/səz tə lĭv/, dī/fə rənt] **52**
difficult [dĭf/ĭ kŭlt/] **23**–24
digital [dĭ/jə təl]
  digital camera [dĭ/jə təl kăm/rə] **235**–19
  digital photo album [dĭ/jə təl fō/tō ăl/bəm] **235**–32
dime [dīm] **26**–3
Dimensions [də mĕn/shənz] **17**
diner [dī/nər] **82**–6, **185**–9
dining [dī/nĭng]
  dining area [dī/nĭng ër/ē ə] **46**–7
  dining room [dī/nĭng rōōm/] **82**–1
  dining room chair [dī/nĭng rōōm/ chër/] **55**–8
  dining room table [dī/nĭng rōōm/tā/bəl] **55**–9
Dining [dī/nĭng] **185**
DINING AREA [dī/nĭng ër/ē ə] **55**
dinner [dĭn/ər] **72**–28
  dinner fork [dĭn/ər förk/] **83**–28
  dinner plate [dĭn/ər plāt/] **83**–18
  dinner salad [dĭn/ər săl/əd] **80**–15
Dinner [dĭn/ər] **81**
diploma [də plō/mə] **40**–3
direct flight [də rĕkt/ flīt/, dī–] **161** ✦
Directions [də rĕk/shənz] **9, 155**
DIRECTIONS AND MAPS
    [də rĕk/shənz ən măps/, dī–] **155**
directory [də rĕk/tə rē, dī–] **131**–24
  directory assistance
    [də rĕk/tə rē ə sĭs/təns, dī–] **14**–22
dirty [dür/tē] **101**–15
Disabilities [dĭ/sə bĭ/lə tēz] **32**
disagree [dĭ/sə grē/] **12**–L
disappointed [dĭ/sə poyn/təd] **28**–4
DISASTERS [dĭ/zăs tərz] **144**–145
disc [dĭsk] **231**–27
discipline [dĭs/ə plən] **36**–K
discuss [dĭ skŭs/] **8**–G
disease [dĭ zēz/] **111**–11, **111** ✦, **119**–11
Diseases [dĭ zē/zəz] **111**
disgusted [dĭ skŭs/təd] **42**–7
dish [dĭsh] **55**–1
  casserole dish [kăs/ə rōl dĭsh/] **78**–10
  dish rack [dĭsh/ răk/] **54**–5
  dish room [dĭsh/ rōōm/] **83**–13
  dish towel [dĭsh/ tow/əl] **61**–22
  dishwasher [dĭsh/wä/shər, –wö–]
    54–8, **83**–14, **185**–2
  dishwashing liquid [dĭsh/wä/shĭng lĭk/wəd] **61**–21
  satellite dish [să/tə lit dĭsh/] **53**–6
  soap dish [sōp/ dĭsh/] **57**–25
disinfectant wipes [dĭs/ən fĕk/tənt wīps/] **61**–23
display case [dĭ splā/ kās/] **94**–5
disposable [dĭ spō/zə bəl]
  disposable diaper [dĭ spō/zə bəl dī/pər] **37**–10
  disposable gloves [dĭ spō/zə bəl glŭvz/] **93**–27
disposal [dĭ spō/zəl] **54**–7, **121**–31
dive [dīv] **230**–K
divide [də vīd/] **17**–A, **192**–D
diving [dī/vĭng] **227**–12
  diving mask [dī/vĭng măsk/] **225**–6
divorced couple [də vôrst/ kŭ/pəl] **35**–21
DJ [dē/jā/] **64**–4

DMV [dē/ĕm/vē/]
  DMV clerk [dē/ĕm/vē/ klürk/] **136**–3
  DMV handbook [dē/ĕm/vē/ hănd/bŏŏk/] **136**–1
do [dōō] **39**–T
  do an experiment [dōō ən ĭk spĕr/ə mənt] **195**–B
  do crafts [dōō krăfts/] **232**–D
  do errands [dōō ĕr/əndz] **128** ✦
  do manual labor [dōō măn/yōō əl lā/bər] **170**–D
  do not drink [dōō nät drĭnk/] **112**–F
  do not enter [dōō nät/ ĕn/tər] **154**–2
  do not operate [dōō nät/ äp/ə rāt/] **112**–E
  do not take [dōō nät/ tāk/] **112**–F
  don't be late [dōnt/ bē/ lāt/] **174**–E
  don't litter [dōnt/ lĭ/tər] **219**–L
  don't smoke [dōnt/ smōk/] **114**–G
dock [däk] **175**–15, **234**–3
  dockworker [däk/wür/kər] **167**–23
doctor [däk/tər] **118**–5
DOCUMENTS [dä/kyə mənts] **40**–41
dog [dög] **79**–6, **215**–11, **215**–22
dogwood [dög/wŏŏd/] **210**–15
DOING THE LAUNDRY [dō/ĭng dhə lön/drē] **101**
doll [däl] **59**–21, **233**–28
  dollhouse [däl/hows/] **59**–16
  doll making kit [däl/ mā/kĭng kĭt/] **232**–13
dollar [däl/ər] **26**–7
  dollar coin [däl/ər koyn/] **26**–6
  fifty dollars [fĭf/tē däl/ərz] **26**–11
  five dollars [fīv/ däl/ərz] **26**–8
  half dollar [hăf/ däl/ər] **26**–5
  one hundred dollars
    [wŭn/ hŭn/drəd däl/ərz] **26**–12
  ten dollars [tĕn/ däl/ərz] **26**–9
  twenty dollars [twĕn/tē däl/ərz] **26**–10
dolphin [däl/fən, döl/–] **213**–31
domesticated [də mĕs/tə kā/təd] **215** ✦
DOMESTIC ANIMALS AND RODENTS
    [də mĕs/tĭk ăn/ə məlz ən rōd/nts] **215**
donkey [däng/kē, dŭng/–, döng/–] **215**–3
donut [dō/nŭt] **79**–15
  donut shop [dō/nŭt shäp/] **129**–17
door [dör] **46**–3
  doorbell [dör/bĕl/] **53**–14
  door chain [dör/ chān/] **51**–33
  doorknob [dör/näb/] **53**–12
  door lock [dör/ läk] **159**–25
  doorman [dör/măn/] **184**–1
  4-door car [för/ dör kär/] **156**–1
  front door [frŭnt/ dör/] **53**–11
  garage door [gə räj/ dör/] **53**–7
  revolving door [rĭ väl/vĭng dör/] **184**–2
  screen door [skrēn/ dör/] **53**–15
  sliding glass door [slī/dĭng glăs/dör/] **53**–18
  storm door [störm/ dör/] **53**–10
  2-door car [tōō/ dör kär/] **156**–2
dorm / dormitory [dörm] / [dör/mə tör/ē] **52**–8
dosage [dō/sĭj] **112**–6
double [dŭb/əl]
  double bed [dŭb/əl bĕd/] **184**–14
  double boiler [dŭb/əl boy/lər] **78**–8

down [down]
  break down [brāk/ down/] **162**–D
  downhill skiing [down/hĭl/ skē/ĭng] **227**–1
  down jacket [down jăk/ət] **90**–16
  down vest [down vĕst/] **90**–14
  drop-down menu [drăp/ down/ mĕn/yōō/] **197**–8
  put down [pŏŏt/ down/] **6**–J
  sit down [sĭt down/] **6**–F
  walk down [wäk down/] **153**–D
downstairs [down/stërz/] **51** ✦
DOWNTOWN [down/town/] **124**–125
drain [drān] **57**–5
drama [drä/mə] **236**–12
drapes [drāps] **56**–16
draw [drö] **8**–F, **118**–F, **195**–E
drawer [drör] **54**–23, **58**–2, **59**–6
dress [drĕs] **86**–3, **88**–5, **89**–20
  dressmaker [drĕs/mā/kər] **100**–1
  dressmaker's dummy [drĕs/mā/kərz dŭ/mē] **100**–2
  dress socks [drĕs/ säks/] **91**–9
dress [drĕs] **36**–H, **174**–B
dressed [drĕst] **38**–D
dresser [drĕs/ər] **58**–1
Dressings [drĕs/ĭngz] **80**
dribble [drĭb/əl] **230**–J
drill [drĭl] **178**–9, **180**–8
  drill bit [drĭl bĭt] **180**–28
drill [drĭl] **119**–D
drink [drĭnk] **11**–J
  do not drink alcohol
    [dōō/ nät/ drĭnk/ ăl/kə höl/] **112**–F
  don't drink and drive [dōnt/ drĭnk ən drīv/] **143**–G
  drink fluids [drĭnk flōō/ədz] **114**–C
drip [drĭp] **121**–25
dripping [drĭp/ĭng] **63**–17
drive [drīv] **196**–6, **196**–8, **196**–9
  drive-thru window [drīv/thrōō/ wĭn/dō] **128**–11
  driveway [drīv/wā/] **53**–8
drive [drīv]
  don't drink and drive [dōnt/drĭnk ən drīv/] **143**–G
  drive a truck [drīv ə trŭk/] **170**–E
  drive through [drīv/ thrōō] **153**–K
  drive to work [drīv/ tə würk/] **38**–I
driver [drī/vər] **152**–21, **169**–61
  designated drivers [dĕz/ĭg nā/təd drī/vərz] **143** ✦
  driver's license [drī/vərz lī/səns] **40**–4, **136**–9
  driver's license number
    [drī/vərz lī/səns nŭm/bər] **136**–11
  Phillips screwdriver [fĭl/ĭps skrōō/drī/vər] **180**–31
  screwdriver [skrōō/drī/vər] **180**–30
driving [drī/vĭng] **142**–5
drop [dräp]
  drop cloth [dräp/ klöth/] **181**–54
  drop-down menu [dräp/ down/ mĕn/yōō/] **197**–8
drop off [dräp/ öf/] **38**–G
dropper [dräp/ər] **195**–45
drops [dräps] **113**–31
drought [drowt] **145**–11
drown [drown] **116**–I
drugs [drŭgz] **116**–K, **142**–6
drums [drŭmz] **238**–16
drumsticks [drŭm/stĭks/] **70**–23
drunk driving [drŭngk/ drī/vĭng] **142**–5

dry [drī] **101**–18
  dry cleaners [drī/ klē/nərz] **128**–2
  dry erase marker [drī/ ĭ rās/ mär/kər] **7**–17
  drywall [drī/wöl/] **178**–19
dry [drī] **60**–N, **108**–H
dryer [drī/ər] **50**–13, **101**–4
  blow dryer [blō/ drī/ər] **33**–23, **108**–18
  dryer sheets [drī/ər shēts/] **101**–5
Dry Measures [drī/ mĕzh/ərz] **75**
duck [dŭk] **70**–18, **214**–12
duct tape [dŭkt/ tāp/] **181**–49
dummy [dŭ/mē] **100**–2
dump truck [dŭmp/ trŭk/] **156**–19
dune [dōōn] **204**–5
duplex [dōō/plĕks/] **52** ✦
During an Emergency [dōō/rĭng ən ĭ mür/jən sē] **147**
dust [dŭst]
  dustpan [dŭst/păn/] **61**–17
  dust ruffle [dŭst/ rŭf/əl] **58**–17
  dust storm [dŭst/ störm/] **13**–19
dust [dŭst] **60**–A
duster [dŭs/tər] **61**–1
DVD [dē/vē/dē/] **133**–19, **234**–11
  DVD and CD-ROM drive
    [dē/vē/dē/ ən sē/dē/räm/ drīv/] **196**–9
  DVD player [dē/vē/dē/ plā/ ər] **56**–7, **234**–10
dye [dī] **33**–D
eagle [ē/gəl] **214**–9
ear [ïr] **32**–17, **105**–11
  earache [ïr/āk/] **110**–3
  ear infection [ïr/ ĭn fĕk/shən] **111**–3
  earmuffs [ïr/mŭfs/] **90**–13, **179**–16
  ear plugs [ïr/ plŭgz/] **179**–15
  pierced earrings [pïrst/ ïr/ĭngz] **95**–36
early [ür/lē] **19**–22
Earth [ürth] **205**–3
earthquake [ürth/kwāk/] **144**–5
easel [ē/zəl] **233**–18
east [ēst] **155**–4
Eastern time [ē/stərn tīm/] **19**–32
easy [ē/zē] **23**–23, **76**–11
  easy chair [ē/zē chër/] **56**–22
Easy Chicken Soup [ē/zē chĭk/ən sōōp/] **77**
eat [ēt] **11**–1
  eat a healthy diet [ēt ə hĕl/thē dī/ət] **114**–F
  eat breakfast [ēt brĕk/fəst] **38**–E
  eat dinner [ēt dĭn/ər] **39**–S
  eat out [ēt/ owt/] **82** ✦
eater [ē/tər] **176**–12
eclipse [ĭ klĭps/] **205**–16, **205** ✦
edit [ĕd/ət] **191**–I
education [ĕ jyōō/ kā/shən] **189**–17
eel [ēl] **212**–12
eggplants [ĕg/plănts/] **69**–23
eggs [ĕgz] **66**–7
  eggbeater [ĕg/bē/tər] **78**–20
  eggs over easy [ĕgz ō/vər ē/zē] **76**–11
  eggs sunny-side up [ĕgz sŭn/ē sīd/ ŭp/] **76**–10
  hardboiled eggs [härd/ boyld/ ĕgz/] **76**–8
  poached eggs [pōcht/ ĕgz/] **76**–9
  scrambled eggs [skrăm/bəld ĕgz/] **76**–7
Eggs [ĕgz] **76**

Index

eight [āt] **16**
eighteen [ā/tēn/] **16**
eighteenth [ā/tēnth/] **16**
eighth [ātth, āth] **16**
eightieth [ā/tē/əth] **16**
eighty [ā/tē] **16**
elastic bandage [ĭ lăs/tĭk băn/dĭj] **117**–12
elbow [ĕl/bō] **106**–12
elderly [ĕl/dər lē] **32**–3
elected [ĭ lĕk/təd] **139**–C
    elected official [ĭ lĕk/təd ə fĭ/shəl] **139**–32
Election [ĭ lĕk/shən] **139**
election results [ĭ lĕk/shən rĭ zŭltz/] **139**–31
elective [ĭ lĕk/tĭv] **189** ✦
electric [ĭ lĕk/trĭk] **116**–F
    electric can opener [ĭ lĕk/trĭk kăn/ ō/pə nər] **54**–14
    electric drill [ĭ lĕk/trĭk drĭl/] **180**–8
    electric keyboard [ĭ lĕk/trĭk kē/bōrd] **238**–18
    electric mixer [ĭ lĕk/trĭk mĭk/sər] **54**–25
    electric pencil sharpener
        [ĭ lĕk/trĭk pĕn/səl shär/pə nər] **183**–26
    electric shaver [ĭ lĕk/trĭk shā/vər] **109**–26
electrical [ĭ lĕk/trĭ kəl]
    electrical hazard [ĭ lĕk/trĭ kəl hăz/ərd] **186**–6
    electrical tape [ĭ lĕk/trĭ kəl tāp/] **181**–43
electrician [ĭ lĕk trĭsh/ən] **62**–9
electron [ĭ lĕk/trän] **195**–30
electronics [ĭ lĕk trän/ĭks]
    electronics repair person
        [ĭ lĕk trän/ĭks rĭ pĕr/ pür/sən] **167**–24
    electronics store [ĭ lĕk trän/ĭks stōr/] **131**–20
ELECTRONICS AND PHOTOGRAPHY
    [ĭ lĕk trän/ĭks ən fə tăg/rə fē] **234**–235
elementary school [ĕl/ə mĕn/trē skōōl/] **188**–2
elephant [ĕl/ə fənt] **217**–42
elevator [ĕl/ə vā/tər] **50**–9, **131**–21, **184**–9
eleven [ĭ lĕv/ən] **16**
eleventh [ĭ lĕv/ənth] **16**
elm [ĕlm] **210**–16
Email [ē/māl/] **197**
embarrassed [ĭm băr/əst] **43**–24
embroidery [ĭm broy/də rē] **233**–24
EMERGENCIES [ĭ mür/jən sēz] **116**
EMERGENCIES AND NATURAL DISASTERS
    [ĭ mür/jən sēz ən năch/rəl dĭ zăs/tərz,–năch/ə rəl–]
    144–145
emergency [ĭ mür/jən sē] **117**–3
    emergency card [ĭ mür/jən sē kärd/] **161**–26
    emergency exit
        [ĭ mür/jən sē ĕg/zət,–ĕk/sət] **51**–25, **161**–14
    emergency medical technician (EMT) [ĭ mür/jən sē
        mĕd/ĭ kəl tĕk nĭsh/ən] / [ē/ĕm/tē/] **121**–32
Emergency [ĭ mür/jən sē] **146**–147
Emergency Call [ĭ mür/jən sē köl/] **15**
EMERGENCY PROCEDURES
    [ĭ mür/jən sē prə sē/jərz] **146**–147
Emergency Room Entrance
    [ĭ mür/jən sē rōōm/ ĕn/trəns] **121**
Emergency Worker [ĭ mür/jən sē wür/kər] **93**
emery board [ĕm/ə rē bōrd/, ĕm/rē-] **109**–32
emperor [ĕm/pər ər] **199**–3
employee [ĕm ploy/ē] **165**–9

employer [ĕm ploy/ər] **164**–4
empty [ĕmp/tē] **23**–10
empty [ĕmp/tē] **60**–L
EMT (emergency medical technician) [ē/ĕm/tē/] /
    [ĭ mür/jən sē mĕd/ĭ kəl tĕk nish/ən] **121**–32
end [ĕnd] **154**–6
    endpoint [ĕnd/poynt/] **193**–21
    end table [ĕnd/ tā/bəl] **56**–14
energy [ĕn/ər jē] **218**–1, **218**–7, **218**–8
    bioenergy [bī/ō ĕn/ər jē] **218**–9
ENERGY AND CONSERVATION
    [ĕn/ər jē ən kän/sər vā/shən] **218**–219
Energy and Resources [ĕn/ər jē ən rē/sōr/səz] **219**
Energy Sources [ĕn/ər jē sōr/səz] **218**
engine [ĕn/jən] **158**–18, **197**–6
engineer [ĕn/jə nïr/] **167**–18, **167**–25
ENGLISH COMPOSITION
    [ĭng/glĭsh käm/pə zĭsh/ən] **190**–191
English muffin [ĭng/glĭsh mŭf/ən] **80**–5
enter [ĕn/tər]
    do not **enter** [dōō/ nät/ ĕn/tər] **154**–2
    enter data [ĕn/tər dā/tə] **171**–B
    enter the room [ĕn/tər dhe rōōm/] **11**–A
    enter your PIN [ĕn/tər yər pĭn/] **132**–E
ENTERTAINMENT [ĕn/tər tān/mənt] **236**–237
entertainment center [ĕn/tər tān/mənt sĕn/tər] **56**–5
entrance [ĕn/trəns] **164**–1
Entrance [ĕn/trəns] **50, 121**
entry-level job [ĕn/trē lĕv/əl jäb/] **172**–1
Entryway [ĕn/trē wā/] **51**
envelope [ĕn/və lōp/] **134**–14, **183**–43
equation [ĭ kwā/zhən] **192**–13
equipment [ĭ kwĭp/mənt] **177**–12, **179**–4
Equipment [ĭ kwĭp/mənt] **179, 183**
EQUIPMENT [ĭ kwĭp/mənt] **231**
Equivalencies [ĭ kwĭ/və lən sēz/] **17, 75**
erase [ĭ rās/] **10**–M
eraser [ĭ rā/sər] **7**–19, **7**–21
errands [ĕr/əndz] **128** ✦
eruption [ĭ rŭp/shən] **145**–16
escalator [ĕs/kə lā/tər] **131**–23
escape [ĭs kāp/] **50**–2
    escape route [ĭs kāp/ rōōt/, rowt/] **146**–3
ESL [ē/ĕs/ĕl/] **189**–14
ESOL [ē/ĕs/ō/ĕl/] **189**–14
essay [ĕs/ā] **190**–4
Essay [ĕs/ā] **190**
e-ticket [ē/tĭ kət] **161**–19
evacuate [ĭ văk/yōō/ āt] **147**–K
evacuation route [ĭ văk/yōō/ā shən rōōt/, rowt/] **146**–5
evening [ĕv/nĭng] **18**–19
    evening gown [ĕv/nĭng gown/] **89**–18
even numbers [ē/vən nŭm/bərz] **192**–4
EVENTS [ĭ vĕnts/] **22, 40**–41
every day [ĕv/rē dā/] **20**–21
EVERYDAY CLOTHES [ĕv/rē dā/ klōz] **86**–87
EVERDAY CONVERSATION
    [ĕv/rē dā/ kän/vər sā/shən] **12**
evidence [ĕv/ĭ dəns/] **141**–9
exam [ĭg zăm/] **122**–1, **136**–6
examination table [ĭg zăm/ə nā/shən tā/bəl] **118**–7
examine [ĭg zăm/ən] **118**–D, **118**–E

Examining Room [ĭg zăm/ə nĭng rōōm/] **118**
exchange [ĭks chănj/] **27**–I
excited [ĭk sī/təd] **43**–22
exclamation mark [ĕk/sklə mā/shən märk/] **190**–13
executive [ĭg zĕk/yə tĭv] **182**–5
    executive chef [ĭg zĕk/yə tĭv shĕf/] **185**–7
Executive Branch [ĭg zĕk/yə tĭv brănch/] **138**
exercise [ĕk/sər sīz/] **122**–4
exercise [ĕk/sər sĭz/] **39**–P, **230**–N
Exercise Wear [ĕk/sər sīz/wĕr] **89**
exhausted [ĭg zö/stəd] **43** ✦
ex-husband [ĕks/ hŭz/bənd] **35** ✦
exit [eg/zət, ĕk/sət] **51**–25, **51** ✦, **161**–14
expensive [ĭk spĕn/sĭv] **23**–19, **97**–44
Experiment [ĭk spĕr/ə mənt] **195**
expiration date [ĕk/spə rā/shən dāt/] **112**–7, **136**–10
expire [ĕk/spïr/] **136** ✦
explain [ĭk splān/] **12**–M
exploration [ĕk/splə rā/shən] **199**–8
explorer [ĭk splōr/ər] **199**–9
explosion [ĭk splō/zhən] **144**–4
exposed [ĭk spōzd/]
    overexposed [ō/vər ĭk spōzd/] **235**–34
    underexposed [ŭn/dər ĭk spōzd/] **235**–35
Express Mail® [ĭk sprĕs/ māl/] **134**–2
Extended Family [ĭk stĕn/dəd făm/lē, făm/ə lē] **34**
extension cord [ĭk stĕn/shən kōrd/] **181**–14
exterminate [ĭk stür/mə nāt/] **62** ✦
exterminator [ĭk stür/mə nā/tər] **63**–21
extinguisher [ĭk stĭn/gwə shər] **179**–21
extra [ĕk/strə]
    extra large [ĕk/strə lärj/] **96**–5
    extra small [ĕk/strə smöl/] **96**–1
ex-wife [ĕks/ wif/] **35** ✦
eye [ī] **99**–27, **105**–11
    eyebrow [ī/brow/] **106**–9
    eyebrow pencil [ī/brow/ pĕn/səl] **109**–34
    eye drops [ī/dräps/] **113**–31
    eye hook [ī/hōōk/] **180**–40
    eyelashes [ī/lăsh/əz] **106**–11
    eyelid [ī/lĭd/] **106**–10
    eyeliner [ī/lī/nər] **109**–36
    eyepiece [ī/pēs/] **194**–14
    eye shadow [ī/shă/dō] **109**–35
Eye [ī] **106**
fabric [făb/rĭk] **98**–15
    fabric softener [făb/rĭk sö/fə nər] **101**–6
Fabric Store [făb/rĭk stōr/] **99**
face [fās] **193**–44
    face mask [fās măsk/] **93**–32
    face powder [fās/ pow/dər] **109**–41
Face [fās] **106**
factory [făk/tə rē, –trē] **126**–3
    factory owner [făk/tə rē ō/nər] **175**–1
    factory worker [făk/tə rē wür/kər] **175**–3
Factory [făk/tə rē] **98**
FACTORY [făk/tə rē] **175**
Fahrenheit [făr/ən hīt/] **13**–1
fair [fĕr] **172**–13, **223**–13
    fair trial [fĕr/ trī/əl] **140**–5
FAIR [fĕr] **122**–123
fall [föl] **21**–39

fall [föl] **40**–H, **116**–O
FAMILIES [făm/lēz, făm/ə lēz] **34–35**
Family [făm/lē, făm/ə lē] **34**
FAMILY REUNION
[făm/lē rē yōōn/yən, făm/ə lē] **44–45**
famine [fă/mĭn] **145**–12
fan [făn] **55**–19, **229**–4
fancy [făn/sē] **97**–34
far from [fär/ frŭm/, –frəm/] **25** ✦
fare [fër] **152**–2
fare card [fër kärd/] **152**–11
farm [färm] **52**–9
farm equipment [färm ĭ kwĭp/mənt] **177**–12
farmworker [färm/ wür/kər] **177**–8
Farm Animals [färm/ ăn/ə məlz] **215**
farmer [fär/mər] **177**–13
FARMERS' MARKET [fär/mərz mär/kət] **84–85**
FARMING AND RANCHING
[fär/mĭng ən răn/chĭng] **177**
Farmworker [färm/ wür/kər] **92**
fashion [făsh/ən] **88** ✦
fashion designer [făsh/ən dĭ zi/nər] **98** ✦
fast [făst] **23**–3
fast food restaurant [făst/ fōōd/ rĕs/tə rənt, –ränt]
128–10
fasten [făs/ən] **160**–H
fastener [făs/nər] **99**–29
FAST FOOD RESTAURANT
[făst/ fōōd/ rĕs/tə rənt, –ränt] **79**
fast forward [făst/ för/wərd] **235**–D
fat [făt] **32**–7
father [fä/dhər] **34**–4, **35**–23
father-in-law [fä/dhər ĭn lö/] **34**–11
grandfather [grăn/fä/dhər, grănd/–] **34**–2
stepfather [stĕp/fädhər] **35**–25
faucet [fö/sət] **57**–6
fax [făks] **171**–G
fax machine [făks/ mə shēn/] **183**–21
feast [fēst] **239**–13
feather [fĕdh/ər] **214**–4
feather duster [fĕdh/ər dŭs/tər] **61**–1
February [fĕb/yōō ër/ē, fĕb/rōō–] **21**–26
Federal Government
[fĕ/də rəl gŭ/vərn mənt, fĕ/drəl] **138**
feed [fēd] **36**–C, **176**–D, **177**–D
feed dog / feed bar [fēd/dög/ / fēd/ bär/] **98**–20
feel [fēl] **110**–C, **110**–D
FEELINGS [fē/lĭngz] **42–43**
female [fē/māl/] **4**–18
fence [fĕns] **177**–19
fencing [fĕn/sĭng] **228**–7
ferry [fër/ē] **220**–4
fertilize [fürt/ əl īz/] **176**–D
fever [fē/vər] **110**–8
fiction [fĭk/shən] **237**–18
field [fēld] **5**–2, **177**–7
ball field [böl/ fēld/] **224**–1
track and field [trăk/ ən fēld/] **228**–18
fifteen [fĭf/tēn/] **16**
fifteenth [fĭf/tēnth/] **16**
fifth [fĭfth] **16**
fiftieth [fĭf/tē əth] **16**

fifty [fĭf/tē] **16**
fifty dollars [fĭf/tē däl/ərz] **26**–11
50 percent [fĭf/tē pər sĕnt/] **17**–10
fighter [fi/tər]
firefighter [fir/fi/tər] **144**–9, **167**–26
figs [fĭgz] **68**–27
figure [fĭg/yər] **233**–26
figure skating [fĭg/yər skā/tĭng] **227**–5
figurine [fĭg/yə rēn/] **232**–1
file [fil] **183**–44
file cabinet [fil kăb/ə nət] **182**–11
file clerk [fil klürk/] **182**–10
file folder [fil föl/dər] **183**–50
fill [fil]
fill a cavity [fil/ ə kăv/ə tē] **119**–E
fill prescriptions [fil/ prĭ skrĭp/shənz] **112** ✦
fill in [fil/ ĭn] **9**–O
fill out [fil/ owt/] **173**–J
fill the tank [fil/ dhe tănk/] **157**–G
fill the tires [fil/ dhe tirz/] **157**–L
filling [fil/ĭng] **119**–8
Filling Out a Form [fil/ĭng owt ə förm/] **4**
film [film] **235**–22
film camera [film kăm/rə] **235**–21
find [find] **160**–F
FINDING A HOME [fin/dĭng ə hōm/] **48–49**
fine adjustment knob [fin/ ə jüst/mənt näb/] **194**–23
fingers [fĭng/gərz] **105**–16, **110**–16
fingernail [fĭng/gər nāl/] **106**–18
fingerprint [fĭng/gər prĭnt/] **136**–5
Fingers [fĭng/gərz] **106**
finish [fĭn/ĭsh] **112**–C, **230**–T
fins [fĭnz] **212**–1, **225**–7
fire [fir] **144**–7, **144**–8
campfire [kămp/fir/] **226**–11
fire escape [fir ĭ skāp/] **50**–2
fire exit [fir/ ĕg/zət, –ĕk/sət] **51** ✦
fire extinguisher [fir ĭk stĭng/gwĭ shər] **179**–21
firefighter [fir/fi/tər] **144**–9, **167**–26
fire hydrant [fir hi/drənt] **129**–27
fireplace [fir/plās/] **56**–13
fire screen [fir skrēn/] **56**–12
fire station [fir stā/shən] **125**–12
fire truck [fir trŭk/] **144**–10
fireworks [fir/würks/] **239**–7
first [fürst] **16**
first aid kit [fürst/ ād/ kĭt/] **117**–1, **146**–18
first aid manual [fürst/ ād/ măn/yōō əl] **117**–2
First Continental Congress
[fürst/ kän/tə nĕnt/ əl käng/grəs] **198**–6
first name [fürst/ nām/] **4**–2
first president [fürst/ prĕz/ə dənt] **198**–11
First Aid [fürst/ ād/] **117**
FIRST AID [fürst/ ād/] **117**
First Aid Procedures [fürst/ ād/ prə sē/ jərz] **117**
First Floor [fürst/ flör/] **50**
First License [fürst/ li/səns] **137**
fish [fish] **66**–1, **81**–29, **209**–14
catfish [kăt/fish/] **71**–2
goldfish [gōld/fish/] **215**–16
jellyfish [jĕ/lē fish/] **212**–14
starfish [stär/fish/] **212**–16
swordfish [sörd/fish/] **71**–5

Fish [fish] **71**, **212**
fisher [fish/ər] **167**–17
fishing [fish/ĭng] **226**–4
fishing net [fish/ĭng nĕt/] **226**–17
fishing pole [fish/ĭng pōl/] **226**–18
fitted sheet [fit/əd shēt/] **58**–12
fittings [fit/ĭngz] **181**–18
five [fiv] **16**
five after one [fiv ăf/tər wŭn/] **18**–7
five dollars [fiv däl/ərz] **26**–8
fix [fĭks] **62** ✦, **219**–F
fixture [fĭks/chər] **55**–18
flag [flăg] **239**–8
flammable liquids [flăm/ə bəl lĭk/wədz] **179**–8
flashlight [flăsh/lit/] **146**–14
flat [flăt]
flat panel TV [flăt/ păn/əl tē/vē/] **234**–7
flat screen TV [flăt/ skrēn/ tē/vē/] **234**–7
flat sheet [flăt/ shēt/] **58**–13
have a flat tire [hăv/ ə flăt/ tir/] **162**–F
flats [flăts] **95**–27
fleas [flēz] **63**–25
flea market [flē/ mär/kət] **222**–6
flight [flit] **161**–30, **161** ✦
flight attendant [flit/ ə tĕn/dənt] **161**–12
Flight [flit] **160**
float [flōt/] **239**–2
flood [flŭd] **145**–19
floor [flör] **46**–6, **58**–21, **179**–6
floor lamp [flör lămp/] **56**–15
floor plan [flör plăn/] **186**–4
Floor [flör] **50**
floral [flör/əl] **96**–25
florist [flör/ĭst] **130**–8, **167**–27
floss [flös, fläs] **109**–24
floss [flös, fläs] **109**–K
flounder [flown/dər] **212**–15
flour [flow/ər] **73**–29
Flower [flow/ər] **211**
flowers [flow/ərz] **208**–7
flower bed [flow/ər bĕd/] **53**–20
FLOWERS [flow/ərz] **211**
flu [flōō] **111**–2
fluid [flōō/əd] **183**–36
fluid ounce [flōō/əd owns/] **75**–1
flute [flōōt] **238**–1
fly [fli] **214**–28
fly [fli] **170**–F
flyer [fli/ər] **102**–1
flying disc [fli/ĭng dĭsk/] **231**–27
foam pad [fōm/ păd/] **226**–13
focus [fō/kəs] **235**–33
foggy [fö/gē, fäg/ē] **13**–20
foil [foyl] **72**–23
fold [fōld] **101**–F
folder [fōl/dər] **183**–50
folding [fōl/dĭng]
folding card table [fōl/dĭng kärd/ tā/bəl] **102**–4
folding chair [fōl/dĭng chër/] **102**–5
folk [fōk] **237**–29
follow [fäl/ō] **114**–J, **147**–F
Following Directions [fäl/ō də rek/shənz, –dĭ–] **9**

Index

food [fōōd]
baby food [bā/bē fōōd/] **37**–4
canned food [kănd/ fōōd] **146**–9
fast food restaurant [făst/ fōōd/ rĕs/tə ränt] **128**–10
food court [fōōd/kört] **131**–15
food preparation worker
  [fōōd/ prĕ/pə rā/shən wür/kər] **185**–4
food processor [fōōd/ prä/sĕ sər] **54**–26
packaged food [păk/ĭjd fōōd/] **146**–10
pet food [pĕt/ fōōd/] **72**–5
FOOD [fōōd] **79**
FOOD PREPARATION AND SAFETY
  [fōōd/ prĕ/pə rā/shən ən săf/tē] **76**–77
Food Processor [fōōd/ prä/sĕ sər] **92**
Foods [fōōdz] **72, 73**
Food Safety [fōōd/ săf/tē] **76**
FOOD SERVICE [fōōd/sür/vəs] **185**
foot [fōōt] **104**–8
football [fōōt/böl/] **229**–11, **231**–21
football helmet [fōōt/böl/ hĕl/mət] **231**–19
footnote [fōōt/nōt/] **190**–10
Foot [fōōt] **106**
for [för] **128**–B, **173**–C
forceps [för/səps, –sĕps] **195**–43
forearm [för/ärm/] **106**–13
forehead [för/əd/, –hĕd/, fär/–] **106**–2
forest [för/əst, fär/–] **204**–1, **204**–11
forest fire [för/əst fir/] **144**–7
fork [förk] **55**–3, **83**–27, **83**–28
forklift [förk/lĭft/] **175**–12
Form [förm] **4**
Formal Clothes [förm/əl klōz/] **89**
former husband [för/mər hŭz/bənd] **35** ✦
former wife [för/mər wif/] **35** ✦
forms [förmz] **118**–4, **134**–19, **161**–16
formula [för/myə lə] **37**–3, **195**–34
fortieth [för/tē əth] **16**
forty [för/tē] **16**
forward [för/wərd] **235**–D
forward button [för/wərd bŭt/n] **197**–3
foundation [fown dā/shən] **109**–40
founders [fown/dərz] **198**–7
fountain [fown/tn] **224**–5, **224**–9
four [för] **16**
4-door car [för/dör kär/] **156**–1
2 x 4 (two by four) [tōō/ bi för/] **181**–19
fourteen [för/tēn/] **16**
fourteenth [för/tēnth/] **16**
fourth [förth] **16**
Fourth Floor [förth flör/] **50**
Fourth of July [förth əv jōō li/] **22**–13
fox [fäks] **216**–15
Fractions [frăk/shənz] **192**
Fractions and Decimals [frăk/shənz ən dĕ/sə məlz] **17**
frame [frām] **58**–4, **58**–18
frayed cord [frād/ körd] **179**–5
free [frē] **122**–7
free speech [frē/ spēch/] **140**–2
freedom [frē/dəm]
freedom of religion [frē/dəm əv rĭ lĭ/jən] **140**–3
freedom of the press [frē/dəm əv dhə prĕs/] **140**–4
freezer [frē/zər] **54**–10, **185**–3

freezing [frē/zĭng] **13**–7
French [frĕnch]
french fries [frĕnch/ friz/] **79**–2
French horn [frĕnch/ hörn/] **238**–13
Frequency [frē/kwən sē/] **20**
fresh [frĕsh] **71**–16
Friday [fri/dā, –dē] **20**–13
fried [frid] **76**–6
fried chicken [frid/ chĭk/ən] **76**–1
fringe [frĭnj] **99**–34
frog [frög, fräg] **212**–25
front [frŭnt] **25**–7
front desk [frŭnt/ dĕsk/] **184**–12
front door [frŭnt/ dör/] **53**–11
front seat [frŭnt/ sēt/] **159**–51
front walk [frŭnt/ wök/] **53**–2
Front Porch [frŭnt/ pörch/] **53**
Font Yard and House [frŭnt/ yärd/ en hows/] **53**
frostbite [fräst/bit/] **116**–G
frozen [frō/zən] **63**–16, **71**–17
frozen dinner [frō/zən dĭn/ər] **72**–28
frozen vegetables [frō/zən vĕj/tə bəlz] **72**–27
Frozen Foods [frō/zən fōōdz/] **72**
fruit [frōōt] **67**–9
fruit salad [frōōt săl/əd] **80**–21
FRUIT [frōōt] **68**
frustrated [frŭs/trā/təd] **43**–27
frying pan [fri/ing păn/] **78**–5
fuel injection system
  [fyōō/əl ĭn jĕk/shən sĭs/təm] **158**–17
full [fōōl] **23**–9, **42**–6
full-length mirror [fōōl/lĕnth/ mĭr/ər] **58**–6
full moon [fōōl/ mōōn/] **205**–12
full slip [fōōl/ slĭp/] **91**–22
fumes [fyōōmz] **179**–3
funnel [fŭn/əl] **195**–40
funny photo [fŭn/ē fō/tō] **206**–2
fur [für] **216**–19
furious [fyōōr/ē əs] **43** ✦
furnished apartment [für/nĭsht ə pärt/mənt] **48**–3
furniture [für/nĭ chər] **53**–19
furniture polish [für/nĭ chər päl/ĭsh] **61**–8
furniture store [für/nĭ chər stör/] **126**–8
Furniture and Accessories
  [für/nĭ chər ən ĭk sĕs/ə rēz] **59**
fuse box [fyōōz/ bäks/] **62**–13
fusion [fyōō/zhən] **218**–10
galaxy [găl/ək sē] **205**–15
gallbladder [göl/blăd/ər] **107**–44
gallon [găl/ən] **75**–5
game [gām]
baseball game [bās/böl gām/] **44**–2
board game [börd/ gām/] **232**–5
game show [gām/ shō/] **236**–8
video game console [vĭd/ē ō gām/ kän/sōl] **232**–3
video game control [vĭd/ē ō gām kən tröl/] **232**–4
Games [gāmz] **59**
GAMES [gāmz] **232**–233
gang violence [găng/ vi/ə ləns] **142**–4
garage [gə räzh/, –räj/] **47**–14, **124**–1
garage door [gə räzh/ dör/] **53**–7
Garage [gə räzh/, –räj/] **50**

GARAGE SALE [gə räzh/ säl/] **102**–103
garbage [gär/bĭj]
garbage can [gär/bĭj kăn/] **53**–24
garbage disposal [gär/bĭj dĭ spō/zəl] **54**–7
garbage truck [gär/bĭj trŭk/] **127**–22
garden [gär/dn]
botanical garden [bə tăn/ə kəl gär/dn] **222**–3
roof garden [rōōf/gär/dn] **50**–4
vegetable garden [vĕj/tə bəl gär/dn] **53**–27, **177**–14
garden [gär/dn] **53**–B
gardener [gär/dn er, gärd/nər] **167**–28
gardenia [gär dēn/yə] **211**–18
gardening [gärd/nĭng]
gardening crew [gärd/nĭng krōō/] **176**–1
gardening crew leader
  [gärd/nĭng krōō lēd/ər] **176**–4
GARDENING [gärd/nĭng] **176**
gargle [gär/gəl] **109**–L
garlic [gär/lĭk] **69**–30
garlic bread [gär/lĭk brĕd/] **81**–28
garlic press [gär/lĭk prĕs/] **78**–11
Garment Factory [gär/mənt făk/tə rē, făk/trē] **98**
garment worker [gär/mənt wür/kər] **167**–29
garter [gär/tər]
garter belt [gär/tər bĕlt/] **91**–16
garter snake [gär/tər snāk/] **213**–39
gas [găs] **218**–3
gas gauge [găs/gāj/] **159**–31
gas meter [găs mē/tər] **62**–14
gas pedal [găs pĕd/l] **159**–46
gas shut-off valve [găs/ shŭt/öf välv/] **146**–4
gas station [găs stā/shən] **125**–10
gas station attendant
  [găs stā/shən ə tĕn/dənt] **162**–3
gas tank [găs tăngk/] **158**–10
gate [gāt] **50**–16, **53**–9, **161**–8
Gate [gāt] **161**
gauge [gāj]
blood pressure gauge [blŭd/ prĕsh/ər gāj/] **118**–9
gas gauge [găs/gāj/] **159**–31
oil gauge [oyl/gāj/] **159**–29
temperature gauge [tĕm/prə chər gāj/] **159**–30
gauze [göz] **117**–8
gear shift [gĭr/ shĭft/] **159**–47
gel [jĕl] **108**–2, **108**–16
GEOGRAPHY AND HABITATS
  [jē äg/rə fē ən hă/bə tăts/] **204**
Geometric Solids [jē/ə mĕ/trĭk säl/ədz] **193**
geometry [jē äm/ə trē] **192**–17
geothermal energy [jē/ō thür/məl ĕn/ər jē] **218**–7
get [gĕt]
get a job [gĕt/ ə jäb/] **40**–F
get a learner's permit
  [gĕt/ ə lürn/ərz pür/mĭt] **137**–F
get a library card [gĕt/ ə li/brër ē kärd/] **133**–A
get a loan [gĕt/ ə lōn/] **49**–J
get an electric shock [gĕt/ ən ĭ lĕk/trĭk shäk/] **116**–F
get a speeding ticket [gĕt/ ə spē/dĭng tĭk/ət] **162**–C
get bed rest [gĕt/ bĕd/ rĕst/] **114**–B
get change [gĕt/ chānj/] **26**–A
get dressed [gĕt/ drĕst/] **38**–D
get elected [gĕt/ ĭ lĕk/təd] **139**–C

get engaged [gĕt/ ĭn gājd/] **41**–J
get feedback [gĕt/ fēd/bӑk/] **191**–K
get frostbite [gĕt/ fröst/bīt/] **116**–G
get good grades [gĕt/ good/ grādz/] **10**–H
get hired [gĕt/ hīrd/] **173**–L
get home [gĕt/ hōm/] **39**–R
get immunized [gĕt/ ĭm/yə nīzd/] **114**–I
get into [gĕt/ ĭn/tōo] **153**–E
get lost [gĕt/ löst/] **162**–B
get married [gĕt/ mӑr/ēd] **41**–K
get off [gĕt/ öf/] **153**–J
get on [gĕt/ ӑn, ön/] **153**–I
get out of [gĕt/ owt/ əv/] **153**–F
get the title [gĕt/ dhə tīt/l] **157**–E
get up [gĕt/ ŭp/] **38**–B
get your license [gĕt/ yər lī/səns] **137**–I
Getting Your First License
    [gĕt/ĭng yər fürst/ lī/səns] **137**
Get Well [gĕt/ wĕl/] **114**
gift [gĭft] **94** ✦, **240**–3
gift shop [gĭft/ shӑp/] **130** ✦, **184**–5
gills [gĭlz] **212**–2
giraffe [jə rӑf/] **217**–32
girder [gür/dər] **178**–3
girdle [gür/dl] **91**–15
girl [gürl] **31**–10
give [gĭv] **15**–F, **122**–B, **148**–A,
glad [glӑd] **44**–5
glass [glӑs] **53**–18, **83**–22, **83**–23
    glass cleaner [glӑs klē/nər] **61**–14
glasses [glӑs/əz] **92**–10, **115**–7, **179**–10
    sunglasses [sŭn/glӑs/əz] **90**–27
global positioning system (GPS) [glō/bəl
    pə zĭ/shə nĭng sĭs/təm] / [jē/pē/ĕs/] **155**–11
gloves [glŭvz] **90**–6, **231**–17
    disposable gloves [dĭ spō/ zə bəl glŭvz/] **93**–27
    glove compartment [glŭv/ kəm pärt/mənt] **159**–44
    latex gloves [lā/tĕks glŭvz/] **93**–34
    rubber gloves [rŭb/ər glŭvz/] **61**–4
    surgical gloves [sür/jĭ kəl glŭvz/] **121**–39
    work gloves [würk/ glŭvz/] **92**–17, **179**–17
glue [glōo] **183**–33
    glue stick [glōo/ stĭk/] **232**–11
go [gō]
    go back [gō/ bӑk/] **11**–M
    go for [gō/ fər] **157**–J
    go on [gō/ ӑn] **173**–K
    go over [gō/ ō/vər] **153**–B
    go past [gō/ pӑst/] **155**–E
    go straight [gō/ strāt/] **155**–A
    go through [gō/ throo/] **160**–D
    go to an employment agency
        [gō/ tə ən ĭm ploy/mənt ā/jən sē] **173**–E
    go to bed [gō/ tə bĕd/] **39**–Y
    go to college [gō/ tə kӑl/ĭj] **41**–I
    go to jail [gō/ tə jāl/] **141**–G
    go to prison [gō/ tə prĭz/ən] **141**–G
    go to school [gō/ tə skōol] **38**–J
    go to sleep [gō/ tə slēp/] **39**–Z

go to the grocery store
    [gō/ tə dhə grōs/rē stör/, grösh/rē] **38**–L
go to the next line [gō/ tə dhə nĕkst/ lĭn] **196**–D
go to work [gō/ tə würk/] **38**–I
go under [gō/ ŭn/dər] **153**–A
to-go box [tə gō/ bӑks/] **82**–5
GO [gō] **222**–223
goat [gōt] **215**–5
goggles [gӑg/əlz] **179**–11
goldfish [gōld/fish/] **215**–16
golf [gälf, gölf] **228**–8
    golf club [gälf/ klŭb/] **231**–1
good [good] **23**–17
Goods [goodz] **73**
goose [gōos] **214**–13
gopher [gō/fər] **215**–19
gorilla [gə rĭl/ə] **217**–29
gospel [gäs/pəl] **237**–30
Government [gŭ/ vərn mənt] **138**–139
GOVERNMENT AND MILITARY SERVICE
    [gŭ/ vərn mənt ən mĭ/ lə tër ē sür/vəs] **138**–139
governor [gŭ/ vər nər] **139**–20, **139**–21
gown [gown] **206**–8
    evening gown [ēv/nĭng gown/] **89**–18
    hospital gown [häs/pĭ tl gown/] **121**–19
    nightgown [nīt/gown/] **91**–25
    surgical gown [sür/jə kəl gown/] **93**–37, **121**–38
GPS (global positioning system) [jē/pē/ĕs/] /
    [glō/bəl pə zĭ/shə nĭng sĭs/təm] **155**–11
grab bar [grӑb/ bär/] **57**–9
grades [grādz] **10**–4
graduate [grӑj/ōo ӑt/] **40**–D
graduated cylinder [grӑj/ōo ā/təd sĭl/ən dər] **195**–38
GRADUATION [grӑj/ōo ā/shən] **206**–207
graffiti [grə fēt/tē] **148**–1
grandchild [grӑn/chīld, grӑnd/–] **34** ✦
granddaughters [grӑn/dö/tərz] **34** ✦
grandfather [grӑn/fä/dhər, grӑnd/–] **34**–2
grandmother [grӑn/mŭdh/ər, grӑnd/–] **34**–1
Grandparents [grӑn/për/ənts, grӑnd/–] **34**
grandson [grӑn/sŭn/, grӑnd/–] **34** ✦
grapefruit [grāp/frōot/] **68**–6
grapes [grāps] **68**–3
graph [grӑf] **192**–15
graphic designer [grӑf/ĭk dĭ zi/nər] **167**–30
grasshopper [grӑs/häp/ər] **214**–24
grate [grāt] **77**–G
grater [grā/tər] **78**–2
gray [grā] **24**–15
    gray hair [grā hër/] **33**–13
grease [grēs] **77**–B
green [grēn] **24**–5
    green card [grēn/ kärd/] **40**–2
    green onions [grēn/ ŭn/yənz] **69**–20
greet [grēt] **3**–G, **171**–M, **174**–H
GREETING [grē/tĭng] **2**–3
greeting card [grē/tĭng kärd/] **134**–15
grill [grĭl] **53**–17
grilled [grĭld/]
    grilled cheese sandwich
        [grĭld/ chēz/ sӑn/wĭch, –sӑnd/–] **80**–10

grilled fish [grĭld/ fish/] **81**–29
grilled ribs [grĭld/ rĭbz/] **76**–2
grocery [grōs/rē, grösh/rē]
    grocery bag [grōs/rē bӑg/] **67**–13
    grocery clerk [grōs/rē klürk/] **72**–4
Grocery Products [grōs/rē prӑd/ŭkts] **72**
GROCERY STORE [grōs/ rē stör/] **72**–73
ground [grownd]
    ground beef [grownd/ bēf/] **70**–4
    ground post [grownd/ pōst/] **134**–6
    playground [plā/grownd/] **50**–3
group [grōop] **115**–15
grower [grō/ər] **177**–13
guard [gärd] **141**–3
    Coast Guard [kōst/ gärd/] **138**–18
    lifeguard [līf/gärd/] **225**–19
    lifeguard station [līf/gärd/ stā/shən] **225**–21
    National Guard [nӑ/shə nəl gärd/] **138**–19
    security guard [sĭ kyōor/ə tē gärd/] **132**–5, **169**–55
    shin guards [shĭn/ gärdz/] **231**–13
guest [gĕst] **184**–10
    guest room [gĕst/ rōom] **184**–13
    guest services [gĕst/ sür/vəs əs] **130**–12
    guest speaker [gĕst/ spē/kər] **206**–4
guinea pig [gĭn/ē pĭg/] **215**–14
guitar [gĭ tär/] **238**–9
gums [gŭmz] **106**–6
    gum disease [gŭm/ dĭ zēz/] **119**–11
gun [gŭn] **142**–13, **181**–21
gurney [gür/nē] **121**–33
gutter [gŭt/ər] **53**–4
gym [jĭm] **5**–19, **126**–10, **184**–24
gymnastics [jĭm nӑs/tĭks] **228**–9
gynecologists [gi/nə käl/ə jĭsts] **120** ✦
habitat [hӑ/bə tӑt/] **194**–12
HABITATS [hӑ/bə tӑts/] **204**
hacksaw [hӑk/sö/] **180**–5
hail a taxi [hāl/ ə tӑx/ē/] **152** ✦
hailstorm [hāl/störm/] **13**–21
hair [hër] **104**–2
    black hair [blӑk/ hër/] **33**–16
    blond hair [blӑnd/ hër/] **33**–17
    brown hair [brown/ hër/] **33**–18
    curly hair [kür/lē hër/] **33**–11
    gray hair [grā/ hër/] **33**–13
    hair clip [hër klĭp/] **108**–19
    hairdresser [hër/drĕs/ər] **167**–31
    hair gel [hër jĕl/] **108**–16
    hairnet [hër nĕt/] **93**–25
    hair salon [hër sə län/] **131**–18
    hair spray [hër sprā/] **108**–12
    hair stylist [hër stī/lĭst] **167**–31
    long hair [löng/ hër/] **33**–3
    red hair [rĕd/ hër/] **33**–15
    short hair [shört/hër/] **33**–1
    shoulder-length hair [shōl/dər lĕnth/ hër/] **33**–2
    straight hair [strāt/ hër/] **33**–9
    wavy hair [wā/vē hër/] **33**–10
HAIR [hër] **33**

half [hăf]
  half bath [hăf/ băth/] **57** ✦
  half brother [hăf/ brŭdh/ər] **35**–28
  1/2 cup [hăf/ kŭp] **75**–9
  half dollar [hăf/ däl/ər] **26**–5
  half past one [hăf/ păst/ wŭn] **18**–11
  half sister [hăf/ sĭs/tər] **35**–27
  half slip [hăf/ slĭp/] **91**–23
halibut steak [hăl/ə bət stāk/] **71**–6
hall [höl] **124**–8
  hallway [höl/wā/] **5**–10, **184**–18
Hallway [höl/wā/] **51**
ham [hăm] **70**–9, **76**–5
hamburger [hăm/bür/gər] **79**–1
hammer [hăm/ər] **180**–1
  jackhammer [jăk/hăm/ər] **178**–9
  sledgehammer [slĕj/ hăm/ər] **178**–23
hammer [hăm/ər] **178**–D
hammock [hăm/ək] **53**–23
hamper [hăm/pər] **57**–1
hand [hănd] **105**–15, **177**–20
  DMV handbook [dē/ĕm/vē/ hănd/bŏŏk] **136**–1
  handbag [hănd/băg/] **87**–9, **94**–2
  handbrake [hănd/ brāk/] **59**–48
  handcuffs [hănd/kŭfs/] **141**–2
  handsaw [hănd/sö/] **180**–4
  handset [hănd/sĕt/] **14**–1
  hand towel [hănd tow/əl] **57**–15
  hand truck [hănd trŭk/] **175**–11
Hand [hănd] **106**
handicapped parking [hăn/dē kăpt pär/kĭng]
    128–6, **154**–12
hand in [hănd/ ĭn/] **10**–O
hanger [hăng/gər] **101**–11
hang up [hăng/ ŭp/] **15**–D, **101**–H
happy [hăp/ē] **28**–6, **43**–31
hard [härd] **23**–5, **23**–24
  hardboiled eggs [härd/boyld/ ĕgz/] **76**–8
  hard drive [härd/ drīv/] **196**–6
  hard hat [härd/ hăt/] **92**–1, **179**–9
hardware store [härd/wër/stör/] **148**–4
harmonica [här mä/ nĭ kə] **238**–21
harvest [här/vəst] **177**–B
hash browns [hăsh/ brownz/] **80**–3
hats [hăts] **90**–1, **95**–11
  chef's hat [shĕfs/ hăt/] **93**–28
  cowboy hat [kow/boy/ hăt/] **92**–18
  hard hat [härd/ hăt/] **92**–1, **179**–9
  ski hat [skē/ hăt/] **90**–11
  straw hat [strö/ hăt/] **90**–23
have [hăv]
  have a baby [hăv/ ə bā/bē] **41**–L
  have a conversation [hăv/ ə kän/vər sā/shən] **11**–L
  have a heart attack [hăv/ ə härt/ ə tăk/] **116**–D
  have an allergic reaction
      [hăv/ ən ə lür/jĭk rē ăk/shən] **116**–E
  have a picnic [hăv/ ə pĭk/nĭk] **224**–D
  have dinner [hăv/ dĭn/ər] **39**–S
  have regular checkups
      [hăv/ rĕg/yə lər chĕk/ups] **114**–H
Hawaii-Aleutian time [hə wī/ē ə lŏŏ/shən tīm/] **19**–27

hay [hā] **177**–18
hazard [hăz/ərd] **186**–6
  hazard lights [hăz/ərd līts/] **159**–36
Hazardous Materials [hăz/ər dəs mə tïr/ē əlz] **179**
hazardous waste [hăz/ər dəs wāst/] **218**–12
Hazards [hăz/ərdz] **179**
head [hĕd] **69**–32, **104**–1
  headache [hĕd/āk/] **110**–1
  headband [hĕd/bănd/] **90**–3
  headboard [hĕd/börd/] **58**–10
  head chef [hĕd/ shĕf/] **185**–7
  headlight [hĕd/līt/] **158**–7
  headline [hĕd/līn/] **133**–7
  headphones [hĕd/fōnz/] **6**–8, **234**–4
  headset [hĕd/sĕt/] **14**–13
  headwaiter [hĕd/wā/tər] **185**–12
  headwrap [hĕd/răp/] **90**–7
  letterhead [lĕt/ər hĕd/] **183**–42
  overhead compartment
      [ō/vər hĕd/ kəm pärt/mənt] **161**–13
  overhead projector [ō/vər hĕd/prə jĕk/tər] **7**–16
  wireless headset [wïr/ləs hĕd/sĕt/] **14**–14
health [hĕlth] **167**–32
  health history form [hĕlth/ hĭs/tə rē förm/] **118**–4
  health insurance card
      [hĕlth/ ĭn shŏŏr/əns kärd/] **118**–3
HEALTH [hĕlth] **114**–**115**
HEALTH FAIR [hĕlth/ fër/] **122**–**123**
Health Problems [hĕlth/ präb/ləmz] **115**
hear [hïr] **106**–B
hearing [hïr/ïng]
  hearing aid [hïr/ïng ād/] **115**–10
  hearing impaired [hïr/ïng ĭm përd/] **32**–12
  hearing loss [hïr/ïng lös/] **115**–2
heart [härt] **107**–38, **116**–D, **239**–6
  heart disease [härt/ dĭ zēz/] **111**–11
hearts [härts] **233**–31
heater [hē/tər] **159**–40
heating pad [hē/tïng păd/] **113**–13
heat wave [hēt/ wāv/] **13**–13
heavy [hĕv/ē] **23**–13, **32**–7, **97**–27
hedge clippers [hĕj/ klĭp/ərz] **176**–11
heel [hēl] **94**–22, **106**–24
  high heels [hī/ hēlz/] **89**–21, **95**–25
height [hīt] **17**–16, **32**–5
Height [hīt] **32**
Heimlich maneuver [hīm/lĭk mə nŏŏ/vər] **117**–18
helicopter [hĕl/ə käp/tər] **151**–9
helmet [hĕl/mət] **93**–23, **231**–19
help [hĕlp] **8**–J, **147**–G
Help with Health Problems
    [hĕlp/ wïth/ hĕlth/ präb/ləmz] **115**
hem [hĕm] **100**–8
hen [hĕn] **215**–8
herbal tea [ür/bəl tē/, hür/bəl–] **81**–40
herbs [ürbz, hürbz] **84**–9
hibiscus [hī bĭs/kəs, hĭ–] **211**–12
hide [hīd] **240**–D
high [hī] **91**–12, **97**–32, **188**–3
  high blood pressure [hī/ blŭd/ prĕsh/ər] **111**–14
  high chair [hī/ chër/] **37**–6, **82**–3
  high heels [hī/ hēlz/] **89**–21, **95**–25

high-rise [hī/ rīz/] **127**–13
high school [hī/ skŏŏl] **188**–4
highway [hī/wā] **155**–9
  highway marker [hī/wā mär/kər] **154**–17
hiking [hī/kĭng] **226**–7
  hiking boots [hī/kĭng bŏŏts/] **95**–31
hills [hĭlz] **204**–16
  downhill skiing [down/hĭl/ skē/ĭng] **227**–1
hip hop [hĭp/häp] **237**–26
hippopotamus [hĭp/ə pät/ə məs] **217**–43
hire [hïr] **141**–B
hired hand [hïrd/ hănd/] **177**–20
Historical Terms [hĭs/tör/ə kəl türmz/] **199**
history [hĭs/tə rē] **118**–4, **189**–12
HISTORY [hĭs/tə rē] **198**–**199**
hit [hĭt] **230**–B
HIV (human immunodeficiency virus)
    [āch/ī/vē/] / [hyōō/mən ĭm/yə nō
    dĭ fĭsh/ən sē vī/rəs] **111**–17
Hi-Visibility safety vest [hī/vĭ/zə bĭl/ə tē vĕst/] **92**–4
HOBBIES AND GAMES [häb/ēz ən gāmz/] **232**–**233**
hockey [häk/ē] **229**–13
  hockey stick [häk/ē stĭk/] **231**–11
hold [hōld] **36**–A
holder [hōl/dər]
  candle holder [kăn/dl hōl/dər] **56**–21
  cell phone holder [sĕl/ fōn/ hōld/ər] **94**–15
  magazine holder [măg/ə zēn/ hōld/ər] **56**–23
  pot holders [pät/ hōl/dərz] **78**–29
  toothbrush holder [tōōth/brŭsh/ hōld/ər] **57**–22
holiday [häl/ə dā/] **22**–7, **22**–8
Holidays [häl/ə dāz/] **22**
HOLIDAYS [häl/ə dāz/] **239**
holly [häl/ē] **210**–19
home [hōm] **52**–7, **52**–12
  home health care aide [hōm/ hĕlth/ kër ād/] **167**–32
  home improvement store
      [hōm/ ĭm prōōv/mənt stör/] **127**–20
  homemaker [hōm/mā/kər] **168**–33
  homesick [hōm/sĭk/] **43**–20
HOME [hōm] **46**–**47**, **48**–**49**
honeybee [hŭn/ē bē/] **214**–25
hood [hŏŏd] **158**–4
Hood [hŏŏd] **158**
hoof / hooves [hŏŏf/] / [hŏŏvz/] **216**–17
hook [hŏŏk] **180**–39, **180**–40
  hook and eye [hŏŏk/ ən ī/] **99**–27
  hook and loop fastener
      [hŏŏk/ ən lōōp/ fă/sən ər] **99**–29
horn [hörn] **159**–32, **216**–21, **238**–11
  French horn [frĕnch/ hörn] **238**–13
horror story [hör/ər stör/ē, här/–] **237**–17
horse [hörs] **215**–4
  horseback riding [hörs/băk rī/dĭng] **226**–9
  horse racing [hörs/ rā/sĭng] **228**–19
  seahorse [sē/hörs/] **212**–13
hose [hōz] **53**–21, **91**–18
hospital [häs/pĭ tl] **125**–9, **154**–18
  hospital bed [häs/pĭ tl bĕd/] **121**–22
  hospital gown [häs/pĭ tl gown/] **121**–19
HOSPITAL [häs/pĭ tl] **120**–**121**
Hospital Room [häs/pĭ tl rōōm/] **121**

Hospital Staff [häs/pĭ tl stăf/] **120**
hostess [hō/stəs] **82**–2
hot [hät] **13**–3, **42**–1
  hot cereal [hät sïr/ē əl] **80**–9
  hot dog [hät/ dög/] **79**–6
  hot water [hät/ wö/tər] **57**–8
  hot water bottle [hät/ wö/tər bät/l] **113**–15
hotel [hō tĕl/] **124**–3
A HOTEL [hō tĕl/] **184**
hour [ow/ər] **18**–1
house [hows]
  courthouse [kört/hows/] **125**–13
  dollhouse [däl/hows/] **59**–18
  housekeeper [hows/kē/pər] **168**–34, **184**–20
  housekeeping cart [hows/kē/pǐng kärt/] **184**–19
  House of Representatives
    [hows/ əv rĕp/rǐ zĕn/tə tǐvz] **138**–3
  house painter [hows/ pān/tər] **168**–46
  houseplant [hows/plănt/] **56**–4, **211**–27
  townhouse [town/hows/] **52**–6
  two-story house [tōō/stör/ē hows/] **52** ✦
  warehouse [wĕr/hows/] **175**–7
  White House [wīt/ hows/] **138**–7
House [hows] **49, 53**
A HOUSE AND YARD [hows/ən yärd/] **53**
HOUSEHOLD PROBLEMS AND REPAIRS
  [hows/höld/ präb/ləmz ən rǐ përz/] **62–63**
HOUSEWORK [hows/würk/] **60**
housing [how/zǐng] **52**–11
hubcap [hŭb/kăp/] **158**–9
hug [hŭg] **2**–E
human immunodeficiency virus (HIV)
  [hyōō/mən ǐm/yə nō dǐ fǐsh/ən sē vī/rəs] /
  [āch/ī/vē/] **111**–17
humid [hyōō/məd] **13**–15
humidifier [hyōō mǐd/ə fī/ər] **113**–11
humiliated [hyōō mǐl/ē ā/təd] **43** ✦
hummingbird [hŭm/ǐng bürd/] **214**–10
hump [hŭmp] **217**–51
hungry [hŭng/grē] **42**–5
hurricane [hür/ə kān/] **145**–14
hurt [hürt] **42**–16, **116**–C
husband [hŭz/bənd] **34**–13
  ex-husband [ĕks/ hŭz/bənd] **35** ✦
  former husband [för/mər hŭz/bənd] **35** ✦
hutch [hŭch] **55**–22
hybrid [hy/brǐd] **156**–3
hydrant [hī/drənt] **129**–27
hydroelectric power [hī/drō ĭ lĕk/trǐk pow/ər] **218**–5
hydrogen peroxide [hī/drə jən pə räk/sīd] **117**–9
hyena [hī ē/nə] **217**–30
HYGIENE [hy/jēn] **108–109**
hygienist [hī jē/nǐst, –jĕn/ǐst] **119**–3
hypertension [hī/pər tĕn/shən] **111**–14
hyphen [hy/fən] **190**–20
hypoallergenic [hī/pō ăl/ər jĕn/ĭk] **108** ✦
I beam [ī/ bēm/] **178**–3
ice [īs]
  ice cream [īs/ krēm/] **72**–26
  ice-cream cone [īs/ krēm/ kōn] **79**–13
  ice cream shop [īs/ krēm/ shäp] **131**–16
  ice hockey [īs/ häk/ē] **229**–13

ice pack [īs/ păk/] **117**–13
ice skates [īs/ skāts/] **231**–9
ice skating [īs/ skā/tǐng] **227**–4
iced tea [īst/ tē/] **79**–12
icy [ī/sē] **13**–22
ID [ī/dē/] **146**–19
identity theft [ī dĕn/tə tē thĕft/] **142**–9
ignition [ĭg nĭsh/ən] **159**–33
illegal drugs [ĭ lē/gəl drŭgz/] **142**–6
Illnesses and Childhood Diseases
  [ĭl/nə səz ən chīld/hōōd dĭ zēz/ əz] **111**
ILLNESSES AND MEDICAL CONDITIONS
  [ĭl/nə səz ən mĕd/ĭ kəl kən dĭsh/ənz] **111**
Immediate Family
  [ĭ mē/ dē ət făm/lē, –fă/məlē] **34**
immigrant [ĭm/ə grənt] **199**–19
immigrate [ĭm/ə grāt/] **40**–C
immigration [ĭm/ə grā/shən] **199**–18
immunization [ĭm/yə nə zā/shən] **114** ✦
immunodeficiency [ĭm/yə nō dǐ fĭsh/ən sē] **111**–17
impaired [ĭm përd] **32**–11, **32**–12
important [ĭm pört/ənt] **146**–19
improvement [ĭm prōōv/mənt] **127**–20
in [ĭn] **25**–6
  be in shock [bē/ ĭn shäk/] **116**–B
  bubble in [bŭb/l ĭn/] **10**–K
  call in [käl/ ĭn/] **186**–A
  check in [chĕk/ ĭn/] **160**–A
  check-in kiosk [chĕk/ĭn kē/äsk/] **160**–2
  fall in love [fäl/ ĭn lŭv/] **40**–H
  fill in [fĭl/ ĭn/] **9**–O
  hand in [hănd/ĭn/] **10**–O
  in fashion [ĭn făsh/ən] **88** ✦
  in front of [ĭn frŭnt/ əv] **24**–7
  in love [ĭn lŭv/] **42**–18
  in pain [ĭn pān/] **42**–11
  in style [ĭn stīl/] **88** ✦
  in the middle [ĭn dhə mĭd/l] **24**–2
  look in [lōōk/ ĭn] **173**–B
  move in [mōōv/ ĭn/] **48**–F
  send in [sĕnd/ ĭn/] **173**–H
  take in [tāk/ ĭn/] **100**–D
  turn in [türn/ ĭn/] **191**–M
  walk-in freezer [wäk/ĭn frē/zər] **185**–3
inch [ĭnch] **17**–15
indent [ĭn dĕnt/] **190**–D
independence [ĭn/də pĕn/dəns]
  Declaration of Independence
    [dĕk/lə rā/shən əv ĭn/də pĕn/dəns] **198**–5
  Independence Day [ĭn/də pĕn/dəns dā/] **22**–13
INDIVIDUAL SPORTS [ĭn/də vĭj/ōō əl spörts/] **228**
infant [ĭn/fənt] **31**–6
infection [ĭn fĕk/shən] **111**–3
infectious disease [ĭn fĕk/shəs dǐ zēz/] **111** ✦
influenza [ĭn/flōō ĕn/zə] **111** ✦
INFORMATION [ĭn/fər mā/shən] **4**
inhaler [ĭn hā/lər] **113**–33
injection [ĭn jək/shən] **114** ✦, **158**–17
injured [ĭn/ jərd] **116**–C
INJURIES [ĭn/jə rēz] **110**

ink [ĭnk]
  ink cartridge [ĭnk/ kär/trĭj] **183**–45
  inkjet printer [ĭnk/jĕt prĭn/tər] **183**–18
  ink pad [ĭnk/ păd/] **183**–46
inline [ĭn/lĭn/]
  inline skates [ĭn/lĭn/ skāts/] **231**–10
  inline skating [ĭn/lĭn/ skā/tǐng] **228**–10
inquire about benefits
  [ĭn kwĭr/ ə bowt/bĕn/ə fĭts] **174** ✦
insects [ĭn/sĕkts] **209**–11
  insect bite [ĭn/sĕkt bĭt/] **110**–11
  insect repellent [ĭn/sĕkt rĭ pĕl/ənt] **226**–23
Insects [ĭn/sĕkts] **214**
INSECTS [ĭn/sĕkts] **214**
insert [ĭn sürt/] **132**–D
INSIDE AND OUTSIDE THE BODY
  [ĭn/sīd/ ən owt/sīd/ dhə băd/ē] **106–107**
Inside the Car [ĭn/sīd/ dhə kär/] **159**
Inside the Kit [ĭn/sīd/ dhə kĭt/] **117**
Inside the Trunk [ĭn/sīd/ dhə trŭnk/] **158**
inspect [ĭn spĕkt/] **147**–N
install [ĭn stäl/] **176**–H, **178**–C
instructor [ĭn strŭk/tər] **6**–4
Instrument Panel [ĭn/strə mənt păn/əl] **159**
instruments [ĭn/strə mənts] **119**–4, **238**
insulation [ĭn/sə lā/shən] **178**–14
insurance [ĭn shōōr/əns] **118**–3, **136**–8
integers [ĭn/tə jərz] **192**–1, **192**–2
Integers [ĭn/tə jərz] **192**
intercom [ĭn/tər käm/] **50**–5
interest inventory [ĭn/trəst ĭn/vən tör/ ē] **172**–11
international call [ĭn/tər năsh/ə nəl köl/] **15**–35
Internet [ĭn/tər nĕt/]
  Internet listing [ĭn/tər nĕt/ lĭst/ĭng] **48**–1
  Internet map [ĭn/tər nĕt/ măp/] **155**–12
  Internet phone call [ĭn/tər nĕt/ fōn/ käl] **14**–20
INTERNET [ĭn/tər nĕt/] **197**
internist [ĭn/tür/nĭst] **120**–1
internship [ĭn/türn shĭp/] **172**–6
interpreter [ĭn tür/prə tər] **168**–35
INTERSECTION [ĭn/tər sĕk/shən] **128–129**
INTERVIEW SKILLS [ĭn/tər vyōō/ skĭlz/] **174**
intestinal parasites [ĭn tĕs/tə nəl păr/ə sīts/] **111**–13
intestines [ĭn tĕs/tənz] **107**–42
In the Airline Terminal [ĭn dhə ĕr/lĭn tür/mə nəl] **160**
In the Examining Room
  [ĭn dhə ĭg zăm/ə nĭng rōōm/] **118**
In the Waiting Room [ĭn dhə wā/tĭng rōōm/] **118**
into [ĭn/tōō, –tə] **153**–E
intravenous drip (IV)
  [ĭn/trə vē/nəs drĭp/] / [ī/vē/] **121**–25
introduce [ĭn/trə dōōs/] **2**–C, **3**–I
introduction [ĭn/trə dŭk/shən] **190**–6
invention [ĭn vĕn/shən] **199**–12
inventor [ĭn vĕn/tər] **199**–13
inventory [ĭn/vən tör/ ē] **172**–11, **172**–12
invertebrates [ĭn vür/ tə brəts/] **194**–13
invitation [ĭn və tā/shən] **12**–I, **12**–J, **64**–9
invite [ĭn vīt/] **12**–H
iris [ī/rəs] **211**–16
iron [ī/ərn] **101**–13, **108**–17
iron [ī/ərn] **101**–G

ironed [ī/ərnd] **101**–20
ironing board [ī/ər nĭng börd/] **101**–14
irritated [ĭr/ə tā/təd] **64**–6
island [ī/lənd] **204**–8
IV (intravenous drip)
　　[ī/vē/] / [ĭn/trə vē/nəs drĭp/] **121**–25
ivory [ī/vər ē] **24**–16
ivy [ī/vē] **210**–25
jack [jăk] **158**–24
jacket [jăk/ət] **90**–8
　　chef's jacket [shĕfs/ jăk/ət] **93**–29
　　down jacket [down/ jăk/ət] **90**–16
　　leather jacket [lĕdh/ər jăk/ət] **90**–4
　　sports jacket [spörts/ jăk/ət] **89**–14
jackhammer [jăk/ hăm/ər] **178**–9
jack-o'-lantern [jăk/ə lăn/tərn] **239**–10
janitor [jăn/ĭ tər] **182**–3
January [jăn/yōō ër/ē] **21**–25
jar [jär] **74**–2, **74**–14
jasmine [jăz/mən] **211**–22
jaw [jö] **106**–4
jay [jā] **214**–6
jaywalk [jā/wäk] **128**–C
jazz [jăz] **237**–24
jeans [jēnz] **86**–2, **92**–19
jellyfish [jĕl/ē fĭsh/] **212**–14
jewelry [jōō/əl rē]
　　jewelry department [jōō/əl rē dĭ pärt/mənt] **95**–8
　　jewelry store [jōō/əl rē stör/] **130**–2
jigsaw [jĭg/sö/] **180**–10
job [jäb] **172**–1, **172**–3, **172**–7
　　job fair [jäb/ fër] **172**–13
JOB SAFETY [jäb/ sāf/tē] **179**
JOBS AND OCCUPATIONS
　　[jäbz/ ən äk/yə pā/shənz] **166**–**169**
JOB SEARCH [jäb/ sürch/] **173**
JOB SKILLS [jäb/ skĭlz/] **170**
Job Training [jäb/ trān/ĭng] **172**
jockstrap [jäk/străp/] **91**–6
join [joyn] **143**–L
judge [jŭj] **141**–6
Judicial Branch [jōō dĭ/shəl brănch/] **138**
juice [jōōs] **73**–32
July [jŏŏ lī/] **21**–31
jump [jŭmp] **230**–I
jumper cables [jŭm/pər kā/bəlz] **158**–21
jump rope [jŭmp/ rōp/] **224**–4
jumpsuit [jŭmp/sōōt/] **93**–24
June [jōōn] **21**–30
junior high school [jōōn/yər hī/ skōōl] **188**–3
junk mail [jŭnk/ māl/] **135** ✦
Jupiter [jōō/pə tər] **205**–5
jury [jûr/ē] **141**–8
justices [jŭs/tə səz] **138**–12, **138**–13
kangaroo [kăng/gə rōō/] **217**–44
keep [kēp] **28**–B
ketchup [kĕch/əp, kăch/–] **79**–21
kettle [kĕt/l] **54**–21
key [kē] **51**–30, **155**–9
　　key pad [kē/ păd/] **14**–5
　　pound key [pownd/ kē/] **14**–7
　　star key [stär/ kē/] **14**–6

keyboard [kē/börd/] **196**–14, **238**–18
Keyboarding [kē/börd/ĭng] **196**
kick [kĭk] **230**–E
kidney [kĭd/nē] **107**–43
kids' bedroom [kĭdz/ bĕd/rōōm/] **47**–9
KIDS' BEDROOM [kĭdz/ bĕd/rōōm/] **59**
king-size bed [kĭng/sīz/ bĕd/] **184**–15
kiosk [kē/äsk/] **131**–22, **160**–2
kiss [kĭs] **3**–K, **36**–P
kit [kĭt]
　　doll making kit [däl/ mā/kĭng kĭt/] **232**–13
　　first aid kit [fürst/ ād/ kĭt/] **117**–1, **146**–18
　　model kit [mäd/l kĭt/] **232**–9
　　woodworking kit [wŏŏd/wür/kĭng kĭt/] **232**–14
Kit [kĭt] **117**
kitchen [kĭch/ən] **46**–5, **83**–15
　　kitchen timer [kĭch/ən tī/mər] **78**–18
A KITCHEN [ə kĭch/ən] **54**
Kitchen [kĭch/ən] **185**
KITCHEN UTENSILS [kĭch/ən yōō tĕn/səlz] **78**
kite [kīt] **225**–2
kitten [kĭt/n] **215**–10
kiwi [kē/wē] **68**–22
knee [nē] **106**–20
　　knee highs [nē/hīz/] **91**–12
　　knee pads [nē/pădz/] **179**–19
knife [nīf] **55**–4, **83**–30
　　carving knife [kär/vĭng nīf/] **78**–12
　　multi-use knife [mŭl/tē yōōs/nīf/, mŭl/tī–] **226**–20
　　paring knife [për/ĭng nīf/] **78**–16
　　steak knife [stāk/ nīf/] **83**–29
knit [nĭt] **233**–F
knitting needles [nĭt/ĭng nēd/lz] **233**–23
knit top [nĭt/ täp/] **88**–7
knob [näb] **194**–22, **194**–23
　　doorknob [dör/näb/] **53**–12
knuckle [nŭk/l] **106**–17
koala [kō ä/lə] **217**–45
lab [lăb] **5**–15
　　lab coat [lăb/ kōt/] **93**–33
Lab [lăb] **195**
label [lā/bəl]
　　mailing label [mā/lĭng lā/bəl] **183**–41
　　nutrition label [nōō trĭ/shən lā/bəl] **122**–8
　　prescription label [prĭ skrĭp/shən lā/bəl] **112**–4
　　warning label [wär/nĭng lā/bəl] **112**–8
label [lā/bəl] **9**–V
Labor Day [lā/bər dā/] **22**–14
lace [lās] **99**–9
　　shoelaces [shōō/lā səz] **94**–24
ladder [lăd/ər] **178**–2
ladle [lā/dl] **78**–7
ladybug [lā/dē bŭg/] **214**–26
lake [lāk] **204**–13
lamb [lăm] **70**–14
　　lamb chops [lăm/ chäps/] **70**–15
　　lamb shanks [lăm/ shăngks/] **70**–13
Lamb [lăm] **70**
lamp [lămp] **56**–15, **58**–25
　　lampshade [lămp/shād/] **56** ✦, **58**–26
land [lănd] **160**–K
landlord [lănd/lörd/] **51**–27

landmarks [lănd/märks/] **220**–1
landscape designer [lănd/skāp/ dĭ zī/nər] **176**–5
LANDSCAPING AND GARDENING
　　[lănd/skā/pĭng ən gärd/nĭng] **176**
languages [lăng/gwĭ jəz] **189**–13
　　language arts [lăng/gwĭj ärts/] **189**–9
lantern [lăn/tərn] **226**–22, **239**–10
laptop [lăp/täp/] **196**–16
large [lärj] **96**–4, **96**–5
laser printer [lā/zər prĭn/tər] **183**–19
lashes [lăsh/əz]
　　eyelashes [ī/lăsh/əz] **106**–11
last [lăst]
　　last name [lăst/ nām/] **4**–4
　　last week [lăst/wēk/] **20**–18
late [lāt] **19**–24
latex gloves [lā/tĕks glŭvz/] **93**–34
laugh [lăf] **44**–A
laundromat [lön/drə măt/] **128**–1
laundry [lön/drē] **101**–1
　　laundry basket [lön/drē băs/kət] **101**–2
　　laundry detergent [lön/drē dĭ tür/jənt] **101**–8
LAUNDRY [lön/drē] **101**
Laundry Room [lön/drē rōōm/] **50**
lawn [lön] **53**–26
　　lawn mower [lön/ mō/ər] **176**–6
lawyer [lö/yər] **168**–36
lay [lā] **178**–B
layer cake [lā/ər kāk] **81**–33
LCD projector [ĕl/sē/dē/ prə jĕk/tər] **6**–6, **235**–29
leader [lē/dər] **176**–4
leaf / leaves [lēf] / [lēvz] **210**–6, **211**–6
　　leaf blower [lēf/ blō/ər] **176**–2
leaking [lē/kĭng] **62**–3
learn [lürn] **40**–E
Learning New Words [lür/nĭng nōō/ würdz/] **8**
lease [lēs] **48** ✦, **51**–28
leather [lĕdh/ər] **98**–6
　　leather jacket [lĕdh/ər jăk/ət] **90**–4
leave [lēv] **11**–O, **38**–N, **82**–J, **160**–J, **171**–P
leaves / leaf [lēvz] / [lēf] **210**–6, **211**–6
　　leaf blower [lēf/ blō/ər] **176**–2
lecture [lĕk/chər] **122**–9
left [lĕft] **25**–1, **154**–8, **155**–C
legal [lē/gəl]
　　legal holiday [lē/gəl häl/ə dā/] **22**–8
　　legal pad [lē/gəl păd/] **183**–38
Legal Holidays [lē/gəl häl/ə dāz/] **22**
LEGAL SYSTEM [lē/gəl sĭs/təm] **141**
Leg and Foot [lĕg/ ən fŏŏt/] **106**
leggings [lĕg/ĭngz] **90**–12
Legislature [lĕ/jəs lā/chər] **139**–23
legs [lĕgz] **70**–21, **105**–9
　　leg of lamb [lĕg/ əv lăm/] **70**–14
lemonade [lĕm/ə nād/] **84**–2
lemons [lĕm/ənz] **68**–7
lend [lĕnd] **26**–C
length [lĕngkth] **17**–17, **96**–17
lengthen [lĕngk/thən] **100**–A
lens / lenses [lĕnz] / [lĕnz/əz] **115**–8, **235**–23
leopard [lĕp/ərd] **217**–34
let out [lĕt/ owt/] **100**–C

letter [lĕt/ər] **134**–13
letter carrier [lĕt/ər kăr/ē ər] **134**–20
letterhead [lĕt/ər hĕd/] **183**–42
lettuce [lĕt/əs] **69**–1
level [lĕv/əl] **172**–1, **180**–29
librarian [lī brër/ē ən] **133**–9
library [lī/brër ē] **5**–17, **125**–15
library clerk [lī/brër ē klürk/] **133**–1
library patron [lī/brër ē pā/trən] **133**–3
LIBRARY [lī/brër ē] **133**
license [lī/səns]
driver's license [drī/vərz lī/səns] **40**–4, **136**–9
driver's license number
[drī/vərz lī/səns nŭm/bər] **136**–11
license plate [lī/səns plāt/] **136**–12, **158**–12
marriage license [măr/ĭj lī/səns] **41**–8
renew a license [rĭ nōō/ ə lī/səns, –nyōō/–] **136** ✦
taxi license [tăk/sē lī/səns] **152**–22
License [lī/səns] **137**
licensed practical nurse (LPN)
[lī/sənst prăk/tə kəl nürs/] / [ĕl/pē/ĕn/] **120**–11
lid [lĭd] **78**–24
lieutenant governor [lōō tĕ/nənt gŭ/ vər nər] **139**–21
life [līf]
lifeguard [līf/gärd/] **225**–19
lifeguard station [līf/gärd/ stā/shən] **225**–21
lifesaving device [līf/sā/vĭng dĭ vīs/] **225**–20
life vest [līf/ vĕst/] **161**–25, **226**–14
wildlife [wīld/ līf/] **220**–3
LIFE [līf] **212**–**213**
LIFE EVENTS AND DOCUMENTS
[līf/ ĭ vĕnts/ ən dä/kyə mənts] **40**–**41**
lift [lĭft] **11**–E
light [līt] **23**–14, **97**–28
brake light [brāk/ līt/] **158**–14
daylight saving time [dā/līt/ sā/vĭng tīm/] **19**–25
flashlight [flăsh/līt/] **146**–14
hazard lights [hăz/ərd līts/] **159**–36
headlight [hĕd/ līt/] **158**–7
light blue [līt/ blōō/] **24**–11
light bulb [līt/ bŭlb/] **56** ✦
light fixture [līt/ fĭks/chər] **55**–18
light source [līt/ sörs/] **194**–21
light switch [līt/ swĭch/] **58**–27
night light [nīt/ līt/] **37**–27
porch light [pörch/ līt/] **53**–13
streetlight [strēt/līt/] **148**–3
string lights [strĭng/ lītz/] **239**–18
tail light [tāl/ līt/] **158**–13
traffic light [trăf/ĭk līt/] **128**–8
work light [würk/ līt/] **181**–44
lightning [līt/nĭng] **13**–17
lily [lĭl/ē] **211**–26
limbs [lĭmz] **106** ✦, **210**–3
limes [līmz] **68**–8
limit [lĭ/mət] **154**–4
limo / limousine [lĭ/mō] / [lĭ/mə zēn] **156**–11
line [līn] **73**–11
assembly line [ə sĕm/blē līn] **175**–6
clothesline [klōz/līn/] **101**–9
curved line [kürvd/ līn/] **193**–23
headline [hĕd/līn/] **133**–7

line cook [līn/ kōōk/] **93, 185** ✦
line segment [līn/ sĕg/mənt] **193**–20
line supervisor [līn/ sōō/pər vī zər] **175**–4
parallel lines [pă/rə lĕl līnz/] **193**–25
perpendicular lines
[pür/pən dĭk/yə lər līnz/] **193**–24
straight line [strāt/ līn/] **193**–22
linen [lĭn/ən] **98**–2
linen closet [lĭn/ən kläz/ət] **57** ✦
liner [lī/nər]
eyeliner [ī/lī/nər] **109**–36
Lines [līnz] **193**
lingerie [län/zhə rā/, –jə–] **91** ✦
links [lĭnkz] **197**–10
lion [lī/ən] **213**–33, **216**–2, **217**–36
lip [lĭp] **106**–5
lipstick [lĭp/stĭk/] **109**–38
Liquid Measures [lĭk/wəd mĕzh/ərz] **75**
liquids [lĭk/wədz] **61**–21, **179**–8
list [lĭst] **67**–14
listen [lĭs/ən] **6**–C, **118**–C, **174**–K
listing [lĭst/ĭng] **48**–1
litter [lĭ/tər] **148**–2
litter [lĭ/tər] **219**–L
little [lĭt/l] **23**–1
Little League [lĭt/l lēg/] **229** ✦
live [lĭv] **140**–H
LIVE [lĭv] **52**
live music [lĭv/ myōō/zĭk] **84**–1
liver [lĭv/ər] **70**–7, **107**–40
livestock [lĭv/stäk/] **177**–15
living room [lĭv/ĭng rōōm/] **47**–12
LIVING ROOM [lĭv/ĭng rōōm/] **56**
lizard [lĭz/ərd] **213**–40
llama [lä/mə] **217**–25
load [lōd] **101**–C
loading dock [lō/dĭng däk/] **175**–15
loaf [lōf] **74**–10, **74**–22
meatloaf [mēt/lōf/] **81**–31
loafers [lō/fərz] **95**–30
Lobby [läb/ē] **50**
lobster [läb/stər] **71**–10
local call [lō/kəl köl/] **15**–31
lock [läk] **51**–34, **159**–25
locksmith [läk/smĭth/] **62**–11
lock [läk] **143**–E
locker [lä/kər] **5**–11, **50**–17
locket [läk/ət] **95**–35
Logging on and Sending Email
[lög/ĭng än/ ən sĕnd/ĭng ē/mäl, –ön–] **197**
lonely [lōn/lē] **42**–17
long [löng] **96**–18
long distance call [löng/dĭs/təns köl/] **15**–32
long hair [löng/ hër/] **33**–3
long-sleeved [löng/slēvd/] **96**–14
long underwear [löng/ ŭn/dər wër/] **91**–3
look [lōōk]
look at [lōōk/ ăt/, –ət] **49**–H, **157**–A
look for [lōōk/ för/] / [lōōk/ fər] **133**–B, **173**–C
look in [lōōk/ ĭn] **173**–B
look up [lōōk/ ŭp] **8**–A
loop [lōōp] **99**–29

loose [lōōs] **97**–30
lose [lōōz] **229** ✦
loss [lös] **115**–2
lost child [löst/ chīld/] **144**–1
lotion [lō/shən] **37**–13, **108**–9
loud [lowd] **23**–11
loungewear [lownj/wër/] **91** ✦
love [lŭv] **40**–H, **42**–18
love seat [lŭv sēt/] **56**–1
low [lō] **97**–31
low-cost exam [lō/köst ĭg zăm/] **122**–1
low-cut socks [lō/kŭt/ säks/] **91**–10
low-fat milk [lō/făt/ mĭlk/] **81**–42
lower back [lō/ər băk/] **107**–29
lozenges [läz/ən jəz] **113**–30
LPN (licensed practical nurse) [ĕl/pē/ĕn/] /
[lī/sənst präk/tə kəl nürs/] **120**–11
luggage [lŭg/ĭj] **161**–18
luggage cart [lŭg/ĭj kärt/] **184**–8
lug wrench [lŭg/ rĕnch/] **158**–22
lumber [lŭm/bər] **178**–17
Lunch [lŭnch] **80**
lung [lŭng] **107**–39
machine [mə shēn/]
answering machine [ăn/sər ĭng mə shēn/] **14**–17
ATM (Automated Teller Machine) [ā/tē/ĕm/] /
[ö/tə mät ĭd tĕ/lər mə shēn/] **132**
fax machine [făks/ mə shēn/] **183**–21
machine operator [mə shēn/ äp/ə rā tər] **168**–37
machine screw [mə shēn/ skrōō/] **180**–32
sewing machine [sō/ĭng mə shēn/] **98**–13
sewing machine operator
[sō/ĭng mə shēn/ äp/ə rā/tər] **98**–14
stamp machine [stămp/ mə shēn/] **135**–11
vending machine [vĕnd/ĭng mə shēn/] **152**–9
Machine [mə shēn/] **98, 132**
magazine [măg/ə zēn/, măg/ə zēn/] **133**–5
magazine holder [măg/ə zēn/ hōl/dər] **56**–23
magnet [măg/nət] **195**–36
magnolia [măg nōl/yə] **210**–8
mail
airmail [ër/māl/] **134**–5
Certified Mail® [sür/tə fīd māl/] **134**–4
Express Mail® [ĭk sprĕs/ māl/] **134**–2
junk mail [jŭnk/ māl/] **135** ✦
mailboxes [māl/bäk/səz] **50**–11, **53**–1, **128**–13,
135–12
media mail [mē/dē ə māl/] **134**–3
overnight / next day mail
[ō/vər nīt/ / nĕkst/ dā/ māl/] **135** ✦
Priority Mail® [prī/ör ə tē māl/] **134**–1
mail [māl/] **135**–D
mailer [mā/lər] **183**–40
mailing [mā/lĭng]
mailing address [mā/lĭng ə drĕs/, ă/drĕs/] **134**–22
mailing label [mā/lĭng lā/bəl] **183**–41
main office [mān/ ö/fəs] **5**–12
MAINTAINING A CAR [mān/tā nĭng ə kär/] **157**
maintenance [mān/tn əns] **184**–23
maitre d' [mā/trə dē/] **185**–11
make [māk] **156** ✦

make [māk]
  make a deposit [māk/ ə dĭ pāz/ət] **132**–B
  make a disaster kit [māk/ ə dĭz/ăs tər kĭt/] **146**–B
  make a mortgage payment
    [māk/ ə mör/gəj pā/mənt] **49**–L
  make an offer [māk/ ən ö/fər] **49**–I
  make a wish [māk/ ə wĭsh/] **240**–B
  make copies [māk/ käp/ēz] **171**–D
  make dinner [māk/ dĭn/ər] **39**–Q
  make eye contact [māk/ ī/ kän/tăkt] **174**–J
  make furniture [māk/ für/nĭ chər] **170**–G
  make lunch [māk/ lŭnch/] **38**–F
  make progress [māk/ prä/grəs] **10**–G
  make small talk [māk/ smöl/tök] **12**–B
  make the bed [māk/dhə bĕd/] **60**–F
maker [mā/kər]
  dressmaker [drĕs/mā/kər] **100**–1
  dressmaker's dummy [drĕs/mā/kərz dŭ/mē] **100**–2
  homemaker [hōm/mā/kər] **168**–33
Makeup [māk/ŭp] **109**
makeup remover [māk/ŭp rĭ mōōv/ər] **109**–42
making [mā/kĭng] **232**–13
MAKING ALTERATIONS [māk/ĭng öl/tə rā/shənz] **100**
MAKING CLOTHES [māk/ĭng klōz/] **98**–**99**
Making an Emergency Call
  [mā/kĭng ən ĭ mür/jən sē köl/] **15**
Making a Phone Call [mā/kĭng ə fōn/ köl/] **15**
male [māl] **4**–17
mall [möl] **126**–7
MALL [möl] **130**–**131**
mallet [măl/ət] **180**–2
mammals [măm/əlz] **209**–10
Mammals [măm/əlz] **213**
MAMMALS [măm/əlz] **216**–**217**
manager [măn/ĭ jər] **50**–8, **72**–8
  account manager [ə kownt/ măn/ĭ jər] **132**–9
  office manager [ö/fəs măn/ĭ jər] **182**–8
Manager [măn/ĭ jər] **92**
mane [mān] **217**–49
maneuver [mə nōō/vər] **117**–18
mangoes [măng/gōz] **68**–21
manicurist [măn/ə kyōō/rĭst] **168**–38
man / men [măn] / [mĕn] **30**–1, **30**–4
  doorman [dör/măn/] **184**–1
mantle [măn/təl] **56**–11
manual [măn/yōō əl] **117**–2
Manual Transmission [măn/yōō əl trănz mĭsh/ən] **159**
manufacture [măn/yə făk/chər] **175**–B
map [măp] **7**–12, **155**–12
Map [măp] **13**
maple [mā/pəl] **210**–12
Maps [măps] **155**
MAPS [măps] **155**
March [märch] **21**–27
margarine [mär/jər ən] **72**–20
marigold [măr/ə göld/] **211**–13
MARINE LIFE, AMPHIBIANS, AND REPTILES
  [mə rēn/ līf/ ăm fĭb/ē ənz ən rĕp/tīlz] **212**–**213**
Marines [mə rēnz/] **138**–17
mark [märk] **190**–12, **190**–13, **190**–15
  postmark [pōst/märk/] **134**–24

markers [mär/kərz] **7**–17, **7**–24, **154**–17
market [mär/kət] **222**–6
  supermarket [sōō/pər mar/kət] **127**–18
MARKET [mär/kət] **66**–**67**
marriage license [măr/ĭj lī/səns] **41**–8
married couple [măr/ēd kŭ/pəl] **35**–20
Mars [märz] **205**–4
martial arts [mär/shəl ärts/] **228**–11
Martin Luther King Jr. Day
  [mär/tən lōō/thər-kĭng/ jōōn/yər dā/] **22**–10
mascara [mă skăr/ə] **109**–39
mashed potatoes [măsht/ pə tā/tōz] **81**–23
mask [măsk] **239**–9
  catcher's mask [kăch/ərz măsk/] **231**–15
  diving mask [dī/vĭng măsk/] **225**–6
  face mask [fās/ măsk/] **93**–32
  oxygen mask [äk/sĭ jən măsk/] **161**–24
  particle mask [pär/tĭ kəl măsk/] **179**–14
  ski mask [skē/ măsk/] **90**–15
  surgical mask [sür/jĭ kəl măsk/] **93**–36
  ventilation mask [vĕnt/əl ā/shən măsk/] **92**–7
masking tape [măs/kĭng tāp/] **181**–53
mat [măt] **57**–3, **57**–28
  placemat [plās/măt] **55**–11
match [măch] **9**–T
matches [măch/əz] **146**–16, **226**–21
matching [mă/chĭng] **28**–3
Material [mə tïr/ē əl] **98**
materials [mə tïr/ē əlz] **98** ✦, **179**–7
Materials [mə tïr/ē əlz] **179**
maternity [mə tür/nə tē]
  maternity dress [mə tür/nə tē drĕs/] **88**–5
  maternity store [mə tür/nə tē stör/] **131**–19
math [măth] **189**–10
MATHEMATICS [măth/ə măt/ĭks] **192**–**193**
Math Operations [măth/ äp/ə rā/shənz] **192**
Math Problem [măth/ präb/ləmz] **192**
mattress [mă/trəs] **58**–20
May [mā] **21**–29
mayonnaise [mā/ə nāz/, mā/ə nāz/] **79**–23
mayor [mā/ər] **139**–26
meadow [mĕd/ō] **204**–20
measles [mē/zəlz] **111**–5
measure [mĕzh/ər] **100**–17, **181**–45
measure [mĕzh/ər] **17**–C
Measurement [mĕzh/ər mənt] **17**
MEASUREMENTS [mĕzh/ər mənts] **17, 75**
Measures [mĕzh/ərz] **75**
Measuring Area and Volume
  [mĕ/zhər ĭng ĕr/ē ə ən văl/yəm, –yōōm] **193**
meat [mĕt] **66**–2
  meatballs [mĕt/bölz] **81**–27
  meatloaf [mĕt/löf/] **81**–31
Meat [mĕt] **70, 76**
MEAT AND POULTRY [mĕt/ n pōl/trē] **70**
mechanic [mə kăn/ĭk] **166**–8
Mechanic [mə kăn/ĭk] **158**
media mail [mē/dē ə māl/] **134**–3
medical [mĕd/ĭ kəl] **121**–32
  medical chart [mĕd/ĭ kəl chärt/] **121**–24
  medical emergency bracelet
    [mĕd/ĭ kəl ĭ mür/jən sē brās/lət] **117**–3

medical records technician
  [mĕd/ĭ kəl rĕkərdz tĕk nĭsh/ən] **168**–39
medical waste disposal
  [mĕd/ĭ kəl wāst/ dĭ spō/zəl] **121**–31
MEDICAL CARE [mĕd/ĭ kəl kër/] **118**
MEDICAL CONDITIONS [mĕd/ĭ kəl kən dĭsh/ənz] **111**
MEDICAL EMERGENCIES [mĕd/ĭ kəl ĭ mür/jən sēz] **116**
Medical Procedures [mĕd/ĭ kəl prə se/jərz] **118**
Medical Specialists [mĕd/ĭ kəl spē/shə lĭsts] **120**
Medical Technician [mĕd/ĭ kəl tĕk nĭsh/ən] **93**
Medical Warnings [mĕd/ĭ kəl wör/nĭngz] **112**
medication [mĕd/ə kā/shən] **112**–3, **112** ✦,
  113–18, **121**–20
Medication [mĕd/ə kā/shən] **113**
medicine cabinet [mĕd/ə sən kăb/ə nət] **57**–20
medium [mē/dē əm] **96**–3
meet [mĕt] **222**–6
meet [mĕt] **49**–G, **49**–R
meeting [mē/tĭng]
  meeting place [mē/tĭng plās/] **146**–1
  meeting room [mē/tĭng rōōm/] **184**–25
MEETING AND GREETING [mē/tĭng ən grē/tĭng] **2**–**3**
melons [mĕl/ənz] **68**–19
  watermelons [wö/tər mĕl/ənz] **68**–18
membrane [mĕm/brān] **194**–6
Memorial Day [mə mör/ē əl dā/] **22**–12
memory card [mĕm/ə rē kärd/] **235**–20
men / man [mĕn] / [măn] **30**–1, **30**–4
  doorman [dör/măn/] **184**–1
  men's store [mĕnz/ stör/] **130** ✦
Men's Underwear [mĕnz/ un/dər wër/] **91**
menu [mĕn/yōō] **82**–7, **197**–8
  menu bar [mĕn/yōō bär/] **197**–1
MENU [mĕn/yōō] **80**–**81**
Mercury [mür/kyə rē] **205**–1
merge [mürj] **154**–10
mess [mĕs] **64**–8
message [mĕs/ĭj] **14**–18, **14**–19
messenger [mĕs/ən jər] **168**–40
meter [mē/tər] **62**–14, **129**–25, **152**–23
mice / mouse [mīs] / [mows] **63**–28, **196**–15, **215**–18
microphone [mī/krə fōn/] **234**–18
microprocessor [mī/krō prä/sĕ sər] **196**–4
Microscope [mī/krə skōp/] **194**
microwave [mī/krə wāv/] **77**–T
microwave oven [mī/krə wāv/ ŭv/ən] **54**–13
middle [mĭd/l] **25**–2
  middle-aged [mĭd/l ājd/] **32**–2
  middle initial [mĭd/l ĭ nĭsh/əl] **4**–3
  middle school [mĭd/l skōōl/] **188**–3
mid-length [mĭd/lĕnth] **96**–17
midnight [mĭd/nīt/] **18**–21
Military [mĭ/lə tër ē] **138**
MILITARY SERVICE [mĭ/lə tër ē sür/vəs] **138**–**139**
milk [mĭlk] **66**–5, **81**–42
  milkshake [mĭlk shāk/] **79**–14
milk [mĭlk] **177**–C
mini [mĭn/ē] **96**–15
  mini-blinds [mĭn/ē blīndz/] **58**–8
  minivan [mĭn/ē văn/] **156**–8
minister [mĭ/nə stər] **199**–7

minutes [mǐn/əts] **18**–2
mirror [mǐr/ər] **57**–16
　full-length mirror [fool/lĕnth mǐr/ər] **58**–6
　rearview mirror [rǐr/vyoo/ mǐr/ər] **159**–35
　sideview mirror [sǐd/vyoo/ mǐr/ər] **158**–3
misbehave [mǐs/bǐ hāv/] **44**–B
miss the bus [mǐs dhə bǔs/] **152** ✦
missing [mǐs/ǐng] **97**–40
mittens [mǐt/nz] **90**–10
mix [mǐks] **77**–R
mixed berries [mǐkst/ bĕr/ēz] **81**–36
mixer [mǐk/sər] **54**–25
mixing bowl [mǐk/sǐng bōl/] **54**–28, **78**–31
mobile [mō/bēl] **59**–5
　mobile home [mō/bəl hōm/] **52**–7
model [mäd/l] **156** ✦, **168**–41
　model kit [mäd/l kǐt/] **232**–9
　model trains [mäd/l trānz/] **233**–27
modern [mä/dərn] **199**–2
moist towelettes [moyst/ tow/əl ĕts] **146**–12
moisturizer [moys/chə rī/zər] **108**–9
mole [mōl] **32**–16
molecule [mäl/ĭ kyool/] **195**–27
monarch [mä/nərk, mä/närk/] **199**–4
Monday [mǔn/dā, –dē] **20**–9
MONEY [mǔn/ē] **26**
monitor [män/ə tər] **196**–11
　arrival and departure monitors
　　[ə rī/vəl ən dǐ pär/chər män/ə tərz] **161**–7
　baby monitor [bā/bē män/ə tər] **59**–7
　vital signs monitor [vī/təl sīnz män/ə tər] **121**–26
monkey [mǔng/kē] **217**–26
month [mǔnth] **20**–3
Months of the Year [mǔnths/ əv dhə yǐr/] **21**
moon [moon]
　crescent moon [krĕs/ənt moon/] **205**–10
　full moon [fool/ moon/] **205**–12
　new moon [noo/ moon/] **205**–9
　quarter moon [kwör/tər moon/] **205**–11
Moon [moon] **205**
moose [moos] **216**–1
mop [mäp] **61**–6
mop [mäp] **60**–D
morning [mör/nǐng] **18**–15
mosque [mäsk] **126**–5
mosquito [mə skē/tō] **214**–22
motel [mō tĕl/] **126**–12
moth [möth] **214**–21
mother [mǔdh/ər] **34**–3, **35**–22
　grandmother [grän/mǔdh/ər, gränd/–] **34**–1
　motherboard [mǔdh/ər börd/] **196**–5
　mother-in-law [mǔdh/ər ĭn lö/] **34**–10
　stepmother [stĕp/mǔdh/ər] **35**–26
MOTION [mō/shən] **153**
motor [mō/tər] **124**–4
motorcycle [mō/tər sī/kəl] **150**–4
mountain [mown/tn]
　mountain biking [mown/tn bī/kǐng] **226**–8
　mountain lion [mown/tn lī/ən] **216**–2
　mountain peak [mown/tn pēk/] **204**–14
　mountain range [mown/tn rānj/] **204**–15
　Mountain time [mown/tn tīm/] **19**–30

mouse / mice [mows] / [mīs] **63**–28, **196**–15, **215**–18
mouth [mowth] **104**–7
　mouthwash [mowth/wäsh/, –wösh/] **109**–25
Mouth [mowth] **106**
move in [moov/ ĭn/] **48**–F
move out [moov/ owt/] **48** ✦
movement [moov/mənt] **199**–16
mover [moo/vər] **168**–42
movies [moo/vēz] **222**–2
　movie theater [moo/vē thē/ə tər] **126**–6
Movies [moo/vēz] **237**
Moving In [moo/vǐng ǐn] **49**
moving van [moo/vǐng vän/] **156**–18
mow [mō] **176**–A
mower [mō/ər] **176**–6
mozzarella cheese [möts/ə rĕ lə chēz/] **71**–29
MP3 player [ĕm/pē/thrē/ plā/ər] **234**–2
mudslide [mǔd/slīd] **144**–6
muffin [mǔf/ən] **79**–16, **80**–5
muffler [mǔf/lər] **158**–16
muffs [mǔfs] **179**–16
mug [mǔg] **55**–7
mugging [mǔg/ǐng] **142**–11
multiply [mǔl/tə plī] **192**–C
multi-use knife [mǔl/tē yoos/ nīf/, mǔl/tī–] **226**–20
mumps [mǔmps] **111**–7
murder [mǔr/dər] **142**–12
muscle [mǔs/əl] **107**–32
mushrooms [mǔsh/rōomz/] **69**–27
music [myoo/zĭk] **64**–3, **189**–15
　live music [līv/ myoo/zĭk] **84**–1
　music store [myoo/zĭk stör/] **130**–1
　world music [würld/ myoo/zĭk] **237**–32
Music [myoo/zĭk] **237**
MUSIC [myoo/zĭk] **238**
musician [myoo zĭsh/ən] **168**–43
mussels [mǔs/əlz] **71**–13, **212**–17
mustache [mǔs/täsh] **33**–5
mustard [mǔs/tərd] **79**–22
mystery [mǐs/tə rē] **237**–20
nachos [nä/chōz] **79**–7
nail [nāl] **180**–34
　fingernail [fǐng/gər nāl/] **106**–18
　nail clipper [nāl klǐp/ər] **109**–31
　nail polish [nāl päl/ǐsh] **109**–33
　nail salon [nāl sə län/] **130**–3
　toenail [tō/nāl/] **106** ✦
name [nām] **4**–1, **4**–2, **4**–4
　name tag [nām/ tăg/] **92**–15
napkin [năp/kǐn] **55**–10, **83**–26
narrow [năr/ō] **97**–35
nasal [nā/zəl]
　nasal congestion [nā/zəl kən jĕs/chən] **110**–7
　nasal spray [nā/zəl sprā/] **113**–32
National Guard [nă/shə nəl gärd/] **138**–19
NATIONAL PARKS [nă/shə nəl pärks/] **220**–221
Native Americans [nā/tǐv ə mĕr/ə kənz] **198**–3
natural [năch/rəl, năch/ər əl/]
　natural gas [năch/rəl găs/] **218**–3
　natural materials [năch/rəl mə tǐr/ē əlz] **98** ✦
NATURE CENTER [nā/chər sĕn/tər] **208**–209
nature program [nā/chər prō/grăm] **236**–7

Navigating a Webpage [nă/və gā/tǐng ə wĕb/pāj] **197**
Navy [nā/vē] **138**–15
navy blue [nā/vē bloo/] **28**–5
near [nǐr] **25** ✦
neck [nĕk] **96**–8, **96**–10, **104**–3
　crewneck [kroo/nĕk] **96**–7
　necklaces [nĕk/lə sĕz] **95**–10
　turtleneck [tür/tl nĕk/] **96**–9
needle [nēd/l] **98**–17, **100**–10, **210**–10, **233**–23
　needle plate [nēd/l plāt/] **98**–18
negative integers [nĕ/gə tǐv ǐn/tə jərz] **192**–1
negotiate [nǐ gō/shē āt/] **157**–D
neighborhood [nā/bər hood/] **128** ✦
nephew [nĕf/yoo] **34**–19
Neptune [nĕp/toon] **205**–8
nervous [nür/vəs] **42**–10
nest [nĕst] **209**–12
net [nĕt] **226**–17
　hairnet [hĕr/nĕt/] **93**–25
network [nĕt/würk/] **173**–A
Neutral Colors [noo/trəl kǔl/ərz] **24**
neutron [noo/trän] **195**–32
new [noo]
　new job [noo/ jäb/] **172**–3
　new moon [noo/ moon/] **205**–9
　New Year's Day [noo/ yǐrz/ dā/] **22**–9
Newfoundland time [noo/fən lənd tīm/, –fənd–] **19**–34
news [nooz]
　newspaper [nooz/pā/pər] **133**–6
　news program [nooz prō/grăm] **236**–1
　newsstand [nooz/stănd/] **128**–12
newt [noot] **212**–26
New Words [noo/ würdz/] **8**
next [nĕkst]
　next day mail [nĕkst/ dā/ māl/] **135** ✦
　next to [nĕkst/ too, –tə] **24**–9
　next week [nĕkst/ wēk/] **20**–20
nickel [nĭk/əl] **26**–2
niece [nēs] **34**–18
night [nīt] **18**–20
　nightclub [nīt/klǔb/] **223**–12
　nightgown [nīt/gown/] **91**–25
　night light [nīt/līt/] **37**–27
　nightshirt [nīt/shürt/] **91**–28
　nightstand [nīt/stănd/] **58**–23
　night table [nīt/ tā/bəl] **58**–23
nine [nīn] **16**
nineteen [nīn/tēn/] **16**
nineteenth [nīn/tēnth/] **16**
ninetieth [nīn/tē əth/] **16**
ninety [nīn/tē] **16**
　90° angle [nīn/tē də grē/ ăng/gəl] **193**–26
ninth [nīnth] **16**
nipple [nĭp/əl] **37**–2
no [nō]
　no left turn [nō/ lĕft/ türn] **154**–8
　no outlet [nō/ owt/lĕt, –lət] **154**–6
　no parking [nō/ pär/kǐng] **154**–11
noise [noyz] **64**–5
noisy [noy/zē] **23**–11
noon [noon] **18**–16
　afternoon [ăf/tər noon/] **18**–17

Index

north [nörth] **155**–1
NORTH AMERICA AND CENTRAL AMERICA
[nörth/ ə mĕr/ə kə ən sĕn/trəl ə mĕr/ə kə] **200–201**
nose [nōz] **104**–6, **110**–17
revolving nosepiece [rə väl/vĭng nōz/pēs] **194**–17
not [nät]
can't breathe [kănt/ brēdh/] **116**–N
do not drink [dōō/ nät/ drĭnk] **112**–F
do not enter [dōō/ nät/ ĕn/tər] **154**–2
do not operate [dōō/ nät/ äp/ər āt/] **112**–E
do not take [dōō nät/ tāk/] **112**–D
don't be late [dōnt/ bē/ lāt/] **174**–E
don't litter [dōnt/ lĭt/ər] **219**–L
don't smoke [dōnt/ smōk/] **114**–G
not working [nät/ wür/kĭng] **62**–1
note [nōt] **183**–39
footnote [fōōt/nōt/] **190**–10
notebook [nōt/bōōk/] **7**–27
notebook paper [nōt/bōōk/ pāp/ər] **7**–28
spiral notebook [spī/rəl nōt/bōōk/] **7**–29
novel [nä/vəl] **133**–16
November [nō vĕm/bər] **21**–35
nuclear energy [nōō/klē ər ĕn/ər jē] **218**–8
nucleus [nōō/klē əs] **194**–7, **195**–29
numb [nŭm] **119**–C
number [nŭm/bər]
access number [ăk/sĕs/ nŭm/bər] **14**–16
apartment number [ə pärt/mənt nŭm/bər] **4**–6
cell phone number [sĕl/ fōn/ nŭm/bər] **4**–12
checking account number
[chĕk/ĭng ə kownt/ nŭm/bər] **132**–14
driver's license number
[drī/vərz lī/səns nŭm/bər] **136**–11
even numbers [ēv/ən nŭm/bərz] **192**–4
odd numbers [öd/ nŭm/bərz] **192**–3
phone number [fōn/ nŭm/bər] **4**–11, **15**–30
prescription number
[prĭ skrĭp/shən nŭm/bər] **112**–5
savings account number
[sā/vĭngz ə kownt/ nŭm/bər] **132**–11
SKU number [ĕs/kā/yōō/ nŭm/bər] **27**–5
Social Security number
[sō/shəl sĭ kyōōr/ə tē nŭm/bər] **4**–15
Numbers [nŭm/bərz] **16**
NUMBERS [nŭm/bərz] **16**
Numerals [nōō/mər əlz] **16**
numerator [nōō/mər ā/tər] **192**–5
nurse [nürs] **118**–8, **168**–44
licensed practical nurse (LPN) [lī/sənst
prăk/tə kəl nürs/] / [ĕl/pē/ĕn/] **120**–11
nurse midwives [nürs/ mĭd/wīvz] **120** ✦
nurse practitioners [nürs/ prăk tĭ/shən ərz] **120** ✦
registered nurse (RN) [rĕj/ə stərd nürs/] / [är/ĕn/]
120–10
surgical nurse [sür/jĭ kəl nürs/] **120**–9
nurse [nürs] **36**–B
Nurse [nürs] **93**
nursery [nür/sə rē]
nursery rhymes [nür/sə rē rimz/] **37**–22
nursery school [nür/sə rē skōōl/] **188**–1
nursing [nür/sĭng] **120**–12
nursing home [nür/sĭng hōm/] **52**–12

Nursing Staff [nür/sĭng stăf/] **120**
nutrition label [nōō trĭ/shən lā/bəl] **122**–8
nuts [nŭts] **73**–36, **180**–36
nylon [nī/län] **99**–12
oak [ōk] **210**–17, **210**–24
obey [ō bā/] **140**–C
objective [əb jĕk/tĭv] **194**–18
oboe [ō/bō] **238**–3
observatory [əb zür/və tör/ē] **205**–21
observe [əb zürv/] **195**–C
obstetrician [äb/stə trĭsh/ən] **120**–2
obtuse angle [äb/tōōs ăng/gəl] **193**–27
occupational therapist
[äk/yə pā/shən əl thĕr/ə pĭst] **168**–45
OCCUPATIONS [äk/yə pā/shənz] **166–169**
ocean [ō/shən] **204**–6, **225**–1
o'clock [ə kläk/] **18**–6
October [äk tō/bər] **21**–34
octopus [äk/tə pəs] **212**–9
odd numbers [öd/ nŭm/bərz] **192**–3
odometer [ō däm/ə tər] **159**–28
off [öf]
clear off [klĭr/ öf/] **10**–I
drop off [dräp/ öf/] **38**–G
gas shut-off valve [găs/ shŭt/öf vălv/] **146**–4
get off [gĕt/ öf/] **153**–J
take off [tāk/ öf/] **109**–Q
turn off [türn/ öf/] **11**–P, **160**–I, **174**–G, **219**–G
offer [ö/fər] **12**–D
office [ö/fəs] **164**–3
main office [mān/ ö/fəs] **5**–12
office building [ö/fəs bĭld/ĭng] **124**–2
office manager [ö/fəs măn/ĭ jər] **182**–8
office supply store [ö/fəs sə plī/ stör/] **127**–21
post office [pōst/ ö/fəs] **125**–11
post office box (PO box) [pōst/ ö/fəs bäks/] /
[pē/ō bäks/] **135**–9
run for office [rŭn/ fər ö/fəs] **139**–A
Office [ö/fəs] **51**
OFFICE [ö/fəs] **134–135, 182–183**
Office Equipment [ö/fəs ĭ kwĭp/mənt] **183**
officer [ö/fə sər] **161**–17, **168**–48
Office Skills [ö/fəs skĭlz/] **171**
OFFICE SKILLS [ö/fəs skĭlz/] **171**
Office Supplies [ö/fəs sə plīz/] **183**
Office Visit [ö/fəs vĭ/zət] **119**
official [ə fĭsh/əl] **139**–32, **229**–6
oil [oyl] **73**–31, **218**–6
oil gauge [oyl/ gāj/] **159**–29
oil paint [oyl/ pānt/] **233**–19
oil spill [oyl/ spĭl/] **218**–17
ointment [oynt/mənt] **113**–24, **117**–10
OK [ō kā/] **154**–5
old [ōld] **31**–9, **31**–10
omelet [äm/lət, ä/mə lət] **76**–12
on [än, ön] **25**–11
get on [gĕt/ än, –ön] **153**–I
go on [gō/ än, –ön] **173**–K
on-the-job training [än dhə jäb/ trā/nĭng, –ön]
172–7
on the left [än dhə lĕft/, –ön] **25**–1
on the right [än dhə rīt/, –ön] **25**–3

on time [än tīm/, –ön] **19**–23, **16**–29
overdose on drugs [ō/vər dōs/ än drŭgz/] **116**–K
put on [pŏŏt/ än, –ön] **87**–B, **108**–D, **109**–P
try on [trī/ än, –ön] **95**–C
turn on [türn/ än, –ön] **11**–B
once a week [wŭns/ə wĕk/] **20**–22
oncologist [än/kö lə jĭst/] **120**–5
one [wŭn] **16**
five after one [fīv/ ăf/ tər wŭn/] **18**–7
one billion [wŭn/ bĭl/yən] **16**
one eighth [wŭn/ ātth/, –āth/] **17**–5
one-fifteen [wŭn/fĭf/tēn/] **18**–9
one-forty [wŭn/för/tē] **18**–12
one-forty-five [wŭn/för/tē fīv/] **18**–13
one fourth [wŭn/ förth/] **17**–4
one half [wŭn/ hăf/] **17**–2
one hundred [wŭn/ hŭn/drəd] **16**
one hundred dollars
[wŭn/ hŭn/drəd däl/ərz] **26**–12
one hundred one [wŭn/ hŭn/drəd wŭn/] **16**
100 percent [wŭn/ hŭn/drəd pər sĕnt/] **17**–8
one hundredth [wŭn/ hŭn/drəth] **16**
one hundred thousand
[wŭn/ hŭn/drəd thow/zənd] **16**
one million [wŭn/ mĭl/yən] **16**
one o'clock [wŭn/ ə kläk/] **18**–6
one-oh-five [wŭn/ō fīv/] **18**–7
one-size-fits-all [wŭn/sīz fĭts/äl] **96**–6
one-ten [wŭn/tĕn/] **18**–8
one third [wŭn/ thürd/] **17**–3
one-thirty [wŭn/thür/tē] **18**–11
one thousand [wŭn/ thow/zənd] **16**
one thousandth [wŭn/ thow/zənth] **16**
one-twenty [wŭn/twĕn/tē] **18**–10
one way [wŭn/ wā/] **154**–3
one-way trip [wŭn/wā/ trĭp/] **152**–16
one whole [wŭn/hōl/] **17**–1
quarter after one [kwör/tər ăf/tər wŭn/] **18**–9
ten after one [tĕn/ ăf/tər wŭn/] **18**–8
twenty after one [twĕn/tē ăf/tər wŭn/] **18**–10
onions [ŭn/yənz] **69**–19, **69**–20
onion rings [ŭn/yən rĭngz/] **79**–4
online [än/lĭn/, ön–]
online catalog [än/lĭn/ kä/tə lög, ön–] **133**–11
online course [än/lĭn/ körs/, ön–] **172**–8
only [ōn/lē] **154**–7
On the Airplane [än/ dhe ĕr/plān/] **161**
open [ō/pən] **6**–G, **143**–F
opener [ō/pən ər] **54**–8, **78**–1, **146**–8
Opening an Account [ō/pə nĭng ən ə kownt/] **132**
opera [äp/rə] **223**–11, **236**–5
operate [äp/ə rāt/] **112**–E, **170**–H
Operating Room [äp/ə rā/tĭng rōōm/] **121**
operating table [äp/ə rā/tĭng tā/bəl] **121**–40
Operations [äp/ə rā/shənz] **192**
operator [äp/ə rā/tər] **14**–21, **98**–14, **168**–37
ophthalmologist
[äf/thəl mäl/ə jĭst, –thə mäl/–, äp/–] **120**–7
opinion [ə pĭn/yən] **44**–3
opossum [ə päs/əm, päs/əm] **216**–4
opponent [ə pō/nənt] **139**–30
optician [äp tĭsh/ən] **130**–9

optometrist [äp täm/ə trĭst] **115**–6
orange [ör/ənj, är/–] **24**–4
oranges [ör/ən jəz, är/–] **68**–5
orangutan [ə răng/ə tăng/, –tän/] **217**–39
orchard [ör/chərd] **177**–10
orchid [ör/kĭd] **211**–19
order [ör/dər] **185**–1
    order puller [ör/dər pŏŏl/ər] **175**–10
order [ör/dər] **82**–D
orderly [ör/dər lē] **120**–16
Ordinal Numbers [ör/dn əl nŭm/bərz] **16**
organ [ör/gən] **238**–20
organic [ör gă/nĭk] **84**–2
organisms [ör/gə nĭzmz] **194**–1
organize [ör/gə nīz/] **171**–L, **191**–G
organizer [ör/gə nī/zər] **183**–49
ornament [ör/nə mənt] **239**–15
Orthodontics [ör/thə dän/tĭks] **119**
orthodontist [ör/thə dän/tĭst] **119**–5
orthopedists [ör/thə pē/dĭsts] **120** ✦
Other Instruments [ŭdh/ər ĭn/strə mənts] **238**
otter [ät/ər] **213**–35
ounce [owns] **75**–1, **75**–11
out [owt] **62**–2
    blow out [blō/ owt/] **240**–C
    check out [chĕk/ owt/] **133**–C
    cross out [krös/ owt/] **9**–R
    eat out [ēt/ owt/] **82** ✦
    fill out [fĭl/ owt/] **173**–J
    get out of [gĕt/ owt/ əv] **153**–F
    let out [lĕt/ owt/] **100**–C
    move out [mōōv/ owt/] **48** ✦
    outfit [owt/fĭt] **88** ✦
    out of focus [owt/ əv fō/kəs] **235**–33
    out-of-state contact [owt/əv stāt/ kän/täkt] **146**–2
    run out of gas [rŭn/ owt/ əv găs/] **162**–E
    take out [tāk/ owt/] **9**–Y, **60**–Q, **82** ✦
    work out [würk/ owt/] **230**–N
OUTDOOR RECREATION [owt/dör rĕk/rē ā/shən] **226**
outlet [owt/lĕt, –lət] **58**–28, **154**–6, **159**–42
    outlet cover [owt/lĕt kŭv/ər] **181**–46
OUTSIDE THE BODY [owt/sīd/ dhe bä/dē] **106**–**107**
oven [ŭv/ən] **54**–15, **54**–20
    oven cleaner [ŭv/ən klē/nər] **61**–3
over [ō/vər] **76**–11, **153**–B
    overalls [ō/vər ölz/] **88**–6
    overcoat [ō/vər kōt/] **90**–2
    overexposed [ō/vər ĭk spōzd/] **235**–34
    overflowing [ō/vər flō/ĭng] **63**–17
    overhead compartment
        [ō/vər hĕd/ kəm pärt/mənt] **161**–13
    overhead projector [ō/vər hĕd/ prə jĕk/tər] **7**–16
    overjoyed [ō/vər joyd/] **43** ✦
    overnight mail [ō/vər nīt/ māl/] **135** ✦
    over-the-counter medication
        [ō/vər dhə -kown/tər mĕd/ə kā/shən] **113**–18
overdose [ō/vər dōs/, ō/vər dōs/] **116**–K
Over-the-Counter Medication
    [ō/vər dhə kown/tər mĕd/ə kā/shən] **113**
owl [owl] **214**–5
owner [ō/nər] **166**–11, **175**–1
oxfords [äks/fərdz] **95**–29

oxygen mask [äk/sĭ jən măsk/] **161**–24
oysters [oy/stərz] **71**–14
Pacific time [pə sĭf/ĭk tīm/] **19**–29
pacifier [păs/ə fī/ər] **37**–24
pack [păk] **74**–9, **117**–13, **235**–26
    backpack [băk/păk/] **94**–18, **226**–15
pack [păk] **49**–M, **162**–A
package [păk/ĭj] **74**–8, **74**–20, **134**–17
packaged food [păk/ĭjd fōōd/] **146**–10
PACKAGING [păk/ə jĭng] **74**
packer [păk/ər] **175**–18
packing tape [păk/ĭng tāp/] **183**–32
pad [păd]
    bumper pad [bŭm/pər păd/] **59**–4
    changing pad [chānj/ĭng păd/] **59**–2
    foam pad [fōm/ păd/] **226**–13
    heating pad [hē/tĭng păd/] **113**–13
    ink pad [ĭnk/ păd/] **183**–46
    knee pads [nē/ pădz/] **179**–19
    legal pad [lē/gəl păd/] **183**–38
    shoulder pads [shōl/dər pădz/] **231**–20
    steel-wool soap pads [stēl/wŏŏl/sōp/ pădz/] **61**–5
    sterile pad [stĕr/əl păd/] **117**–6
pail [pāl] **37**–7, **61**–7, **225**–8
pain [pān] **42**–11, **115**–3
    pain reliever [pān rĭ lē/vər] **113**–26
paint [pānt] **181**–25, **232**–10, **233**–19
    paintbrush [pānt/brŭsh/] **181**–22, **233**–20
    paint pan [pānt/ păn/] **181**–51
    paint roller [pānt/ rō/lər] **181**–23
paint [pānt] **49**–P, **178**–A, **233**–E
painter [pān/tər] **168**–46
Painter [pān/tər] **92**
painting [pān/tĭng] **56**–9
pair of scissors [pĕr/ əv sĭz/ərz] **100**–16
paisley [pāz/lē] **96**–26
pajamas [pə jä/məz, –jä/–] **91**–24
pallet [pă/lət] **175**–13
palm [päm] **106**–15, **210**–14
pan [păn] **54**–24
    bed pan [bĕd/ păn/] **121**–28
    cake pan [kāk/ păn/] **78**–26
    dustpan [dŭst/ păn/] **61**–17
    frying pan [frī/ĭng păn/] **78**–5
    paint pan [pānt/ păn/] **181**–51
    pancakes [păn/kāks/] **80**–7
    pie pan [pī/ păn/] **78**–28
    roasting pan [rō/stĭng păn/] **78**–13
    saucepan [sös/păn/] **78**–25
pancreas [păng/krē əs] **107**–45
panda [păn/də] **217**–41
pane [pān] **178**–16
panel [păn/əl] **234**–7
Panel [păn/əl] **159**
panther [păn/thər] **217**–40
panties [păn/tēz] **91**–13
pants [pănts] **87**–12
    security pants [sĭ kyŏŏr/ə tē pănts/] **93**–22
    training pants [trā/nĭng pănts/] **37**–11
    work pants [würk/ pănts/] **92**–5
panty hose [păn/tē hōz/] **91**–18
papayas [pə pī/əz] **68**–20

paper [pā/pər]
    construction paper [kən strŭk/shən pā/pər] **232**–12
    copies of important papers
        [kä/pēz əv ĭm pört/ənt pā/pərz] **146**–20
    newspaper [nōōz/pā/pər] **133**–6
    notebook paper [nōt/bŏŏk/ pā/pər] **7**–28
    paper clip [pā/pər klĭp/] **183**–31
    paper cutter [pā/pər kŭt/ər] **183**–22
    paper dolls [pā/pər dälz/] **233**–28
    paper shredder [pā/pər shrĕd/ər] **183**–24
    paper towels [pā/pər tow/əlz] **54**–3
    sandpaper [sănd/ pā/pər] **181**–56
    toilet paper [toy/lət pā/pər] **57**–17, **146**–13
    wallpaper [wäl/ pā/pər] **59**–8
parade [pə rād/] **239**–1
paragraph [păr/ə grăf/] **190**–3
parakeet [păr/ə kēt/] **215**–15
parallel lines [păr/ə lĕl/ līnz/] **193**–25
parallelogram [păr/ə lĕl/ə grăm/] **193**–33
paramedic [păr/ə mĕ/dĭk] **116**–2
parasites [păr/ə sīts/] **111**–13
parcel post [păr/səl pōst/] **134**–6
parentheses [pə rĕn/thə sēz/] **190**–19
PARENTING [păr/ən tĭng, pĕr/–] **36**–**37**
Parents [păr/ənts, pĕr/–] **34**
parent-teacher conference
    [păr/ənt tē/chər kän/frəns, pĕr/–] **22**–5
paring knife [pĕr/ĭng nīf/] **78**–16
park [pärk] **223**–10
    park ranger [pärk/ rāng/jər] **220**–2
park [pärk] **129**–E
parka [pär/kə] **90**–9
PARK AND PLAYGROUND [pärk/ ən plā/grownd/] **224**
parking [pär/kĭng] **128**–6, **154**–11, **154**–12
    parking attendant [pär/kĭng ə tĕn/dənt] **184**–3
    parking garage [pär/kĭng gə räzh/, –räj/] **124**–1
    parking meter [pär/kĭng mē/tər] **129**–25
    parking space [pär/kĭng spās/] **50**–18, **128**–5
PARKS [pärks] **220**–**221**
parochial school [pə rō/kē əl skōōl/] **5** ✦
parsley [pär/slē] **69**–28
part [pärt] **33**–4
participate [pär tĭ/sə pāt/] **10**–B
particle [pär/tĭ kəl]
    particle board [pär/tĭ kəl börd/] **181**–20
    particle mask [pär/tĭ kəl măsk/] **179**–14
Partner [pärt/nər] **8**
parts [pärts] **175**–5
Parts of a Bird [pärts/ əv ə bürd/] **214**
PARTS OF A CAR [pärts/ əv ə kär/] **158**–**159**
Parts of a Fish [pärts/ əv ə fĭsh/] **212**
Parts of a Flower [pärts/ əv ə flow/ər] **211**
Parts of an Essay [pärts/ əv ən ĕs/ā] **190**
Parts of a Phone [pärts/ əv ə fōn/] **14**
Parts of a Sewing Machine
    [pärts/ əv ə sō/ĭng mə shēn] **98**
Parts of a Tree [pärts/ əv ə trē/] **210**
party [pär/tē] **64**–2
pass [păs] **161**–20
    passbook [păs/bŏŏk/] **132**–10
    passport [păs/pört/] **41**–10
pass [păs] **10**–E, **137**–H, **230**–G

267

passenger [păs/ən jər] **150**–2, **161**–15
past [păst] **155**–E
pasta [päs/tə] **67**–12
    pasta salad [päs/tə săl/əd] **80**–20
paste [pāst]
    toothpaste [tōōth/pāst/] **109**–23
pastrami [pə strä/mē] **71**–23
path [păth] **208**–3, **224**–3
Path [păth] **172**
patient [pā/shənt] **118**–6, **121**–18
patio [păt/ē ō] **53**–16
    patio furniture [păt/ē ō für/nĭ chər] **53**–19
patron [pā/trən] **82**–6, **133**–3
pattern [păt/ərn] **99**–22
PATTERNS [păt/ərnz] **96**
pause [pöz] **235**–E
paw [pö] **216**–20
pay [pā]
    paycheck [pā/chĕk/] **165**–14
    payroll clerk [pā/rōl klürk/] **165**–10
    pay stub [pā/ stŭb/] **165**–11
pay [pā]
    pay a late fine [pā/ ə lāt/ fīn/] **133**–E
    pay attention [pā/ ə tĕn/shən] **147**–D
    pay back [pā/ băk/] **26**–D
    pay cash [pā/ kăsh/] **27**–A
    pay for [pā/ för/, –fər] **27**–G
    pay phone [pā/ fōn] **15**–25, **129**–23
    pay taxes [pā/ tăks/əz] **140**–B
    pay the application fee
        [pā/ dhe ăp/lə kā/shən fē/] **137**–D
    pay the check [pā/ dhe chĕk/] **82**–I
    pay the rent [pā/ dhe rĕnt/] **48**–E
Pay [pā] **27**
PBX [pē/ bē/ ĕks/] **182**–13
peaceful assembly [pēs/fəl ə sĕm/blē] **140**–1
peaches [pē/chəz] **68**–10
peacock [pē/käk/] **214**–14
peak [pēk] **204**–14
pearls [pürlz] **95**–39
pears [pĕrz] **68**–4
peas [pēz] **69**–21
pedal [pĕd/əl] **159**–45, **159**–46
pedestrian [pə dĕs/trē ən] **128**–14
    pedestrian crossing [pə dĕs/trē ən krö/sĭng] **154**–13
pediatrician [pē/dē ə trĭsh/ən] **120**–4
peel [pēl] **77**–K
peeler [pē/lər] **78**–15
peephole [pēp/hōl/] **51**–32
pelvis [pĕl/vəs] **107**–50
pen [pĕn] **7**–22
pencil [pĕn/səl] **7**–20, **109**–34
    pencil eraser [pĕn/səl ĭ rā/sər] **7**–21
    pencil sharpener [pĕn/səl shär/pə nər] **7**–23, **183**–26
penguin [pĕng/wĭn] **214**–11
peninsula [pĕ nĭn/sə lə] **204**–7
penny [pĕn/ē] **26**–1
PEOPLE [pē/pəl] **32**
pepper [pĕp/ər] **55**–13, **69**–7, **69**–29
percent [pər sĕnt/]
    50 percent [fĭf/tē pər sĕnt/] **17**–10
    100 percent [wŭn/ hŭn/drəd pər sĕnt/] **17**–8

75 percent [sĕv/ən tē fīv/ pər sĕnt/] **17**–9
10 percent [tĕn/ pər sĕnt/] **17**–12
25 percent [twĕn/tē fīv/ pər sĕnt/] **17**–11
Percents [pər sĕnts/] **17**
Percussion [pər kŭsh/ən] **238**
perfume [pür/fyōōm/, pər fyōōm/] **108**–6
perimeter [pə rĭ/mə tər] **193**–43
period [pïr/ē əd] **190**–11
Period [pïr/ē əd] **198**
periodicals [pïr/ē äd/ĭ kəlz] **133**–4
periodic table [pïr/ē äd/ĭk tā/bəl] **195**–26
perm [pürm] **33**–B
peroxide [pə räk/ sīd] **117**–9
perpendicular lines [pür/pən dĭk/yə lər līnz/] **193**–24
person [pür/sən]
    appliance repair person
        [ə plī/əns rĭ pĕr/ pür/sən] **166**–4
    assemblyperson [ə sĕm/blē pür/sən] **139**–24
    businessperson [bĭz/nəs pür/sən] **166**–12
    bus person [bŭs/ pür/sən] **185**–13
    congressperson [kän/grəs pür/sən] **138**–4
    councilperson [kown/səl pür/sən] **139**–28
    counterperson [kown/tər pür/sən] **79**–17
    delivery person [də lĭv/ə rē pür/sən] **167**–21
    electronics repair person
        [ĭ lĕk trän/ĭks rĭ pĕr/ pür/sən] **167**–24
    repair person [rĭ pĕr/ pür/sən] **62**–10
personal CD player [pür/sə nəl sē/dē/ plā/ər] **234**–5
PERSONAL HYGIENE [pür/sə nəl hī/jēn] **108**–109
PERSONAL INFORMATION
    [pür/sə nəl ĭn/fər mā/shən] **4**
pesticide poisoning [pĕs/tə sīd/ poy/zə nĭng] **218**–16
pests [pĕsts] **62** ✦
pet [pĕt]
    pet food [pĕt fōōd/] **72**–5
    pet store [pĕt stör/] **130**–6
petals [pĕt/lz] **211**–8
petition [pə tĭ/shən] **148**–5
petroleum [pə trō/lē əm] **218**–6
Pets [pĕts] **215**
pharmacist [fär/mə sĭst] **112**–1
pharmacy [fär/mə sē] **128**–4
PHARMACY [fär/mə sē] **112**–113
Phase of the Moon [fāz/ əf dhə mōōn/] **205**
Phillips screwdriver [fĭl/ĭps skrōō/drī/vər] **180**–31
phlebotomist [flĭ bä/tə mĭst] **121**–29
phone [fōn]
    automated phone system
        [ö/tə mät ĭd fōn/ sĭs/təm] **14**–23
    cell phone holder [sĕl/ fōn/ hōl/dər] **94**–15
    cell phone kiosk [sĕl/ fōn/ kē/ösk] **131**–22
    cell phone number [sĕl/ fōn/ nŭm/bər] **4**–12
    cellular phone [sĕl/yə lər fōn/] **14**–8
    cordless phone [körd/ləs fōn/] **15**–24
    headphones [hĕd/ fōnz/] **6**–8, **234**–4
    Internet phone call [ĭn/tər nĕt/ fōn/ käl/] **14**–20
    microphone [mī/krə fōn/] **234**–18
    pay phone [pā/ fōn/] **15**–25, **129**–23
    phone bill [fōn/ bĭl/] **15**–28
    phone jack [fōn/ jăk/] **14**–3
    phone line [fōn/ lĭn/] **14**–4
    phone number [fōn/ nŭm/bər] **4**–11, **15**–30
    smart phone [smärt/ fōn/] **15**–27

Phone [fōn] **14**
Phone Bill [fōn/ bĭl/] **15**
Phone Call [fōn/ köl/] **15**
photo [fō/tō] **58**–3, **136**–4
    digital photo album [dĭ/jə təl fō/tō ăl/bəm] **235**–32
    funny photo [fŭn/ē fō/tō] **206**–2
    photo album [fō/tō ăl/bəm] **235**–31
    photocopier [fō/tə käp/ē ər] **183**–23
    serious photo [sïr/ē əs fō/tō] **206**–3
photographer [fə täg/rə fər] **206**–1
PHOTOGRAPHY [fə täg/rə fē] **234**–235
photosynthesis [fō/tō sĭn/thə səs] **194**–10
physical [fĭz/ĭ kəl]
    physical education [fĭz/ĭ kəl ĕ jə kā/shən] **189**–17
    physical therapist [fĭz/ĭ kəl thĕr/ə pĭst] **115**–12
    physical therapy [fĭz/ĭ kəl thĕr/ə pē] **115**–11
physically challenged [fĭz/ĭ klē chăl/ənjd] **32**–10
physician assistant [fĭz/ĭ shən ə sĭs/tənt] **168**–47
physicist [fĭz/ĭ sĭst] **195**–33
Physics [fĭz/ĭks] **195**
pi (π) [pī] **193**–46
piano [pē ăn/ō] **238**–14
pick [pĭk] **108**–15
pickax [pĭk/ăks/] **178**–21
picker [pĭ/kər] **178**–5
pickle [pĭk/l] **80**–11
pick up [pĭk/ ŭp/] **6**–I, **11**–E, **38**–M, **112** ✦
pickup truck [pĭk/ŭp trŭk/] **156**–12
picnic [pĭk/nĭk] **224**–D
picnic table [pĭk/nĭk tā/bəl] **224**–8
picture [pĭk/chər]
    picture book [pĭk/chər bōōk/] **133**–12
    picture dictionary [pĭk/chər dĭk/shə nër ē] **7**–31
    picture frame [pĭk/chər frām/] **58**–4
pie [pī] **81**–35
    pie pan [pī/ păn/] **78**–28
pier [pïr] **225**–18
pierced [pïrst]
    pierced ear [pïrst/ ïr/] **32**–17
    pierced earrings [pïrst/ ïr/ĭngz] **95**–36
pig [pĭg] **215**–2, **215**–14
pigeon [pĭj/ən] **214**–15
pile [pīl] **53**–25
pill [pĭl] **113**–21
pillow [pĭl/ō] **56**–2, **58**–11
    pillowcase [pĭl/ō kās/] **58**–14
pilot [pī/lət] **161**–11
pin [pĭn] **95**–38
    bobby pins [bäb/ē pĭnz/] **108**–21
    clothespin [klōz/ pĭn/] **101**–10
    pin cushion [pĭn/ kōōsh/ən] **100**–13
    pushpin [pōōsh/pĭn/] **183**–35
    rolling pin [rō/lĭng pĭn/] **78**–30
    safety pin [sāf/tē pĭn/] **37**–9, **100**–14
    straight pin [strāt pĭn/] **100**–12
pine [pīn] **210**–9
    pinecone [pīn/kōn/] **210**–11
pineapples [pī/năp/əlz] **68**–23
pink [pĭnk] **24**–7
pint [pīnt] **75**–3
pipe [pīp] **158**–15, **181**–17
    pipe wrench [pīp rĕnch/] **181**–47

pitch [pĭch] **230**–A

pizza [pēt′sə] **79**–10

place [plās] **146**–1

  fireplace [fīr′plās′] **56**–13

  placemat [plās′ măt′] **55**–11

  place of birth [plās′ əv bürth′] **4**–14

  place setting [plās′ sĕt′ĭng] **83**–17

PLACES TO GO [plā′səz tə gō′] **222**–223

PLACES TO LIVE [plā′səz tə lĭv′] **52**

plaid [plăd] **96**–22

plain [plān] **97**–33

plains [plānz] **204**–19

plan [plăn] **186**–4

plan [plăn] **146**–A

plane [plān] **144**–3, **150**–8, **181**–57

Planets [plăn′əts] **205**

Planning a Career [plă′nĭng ə kə rēr′] **172**

plant [plănt] **176**–E, **177**–A, **219**–N

plants [plănts] **208**–5

  houseplant [hows′plănt′] **56**–4, **211**–27

Plants [plănts] **210**

PLANTS [plănts] **210**

plaque [plăk] **119**–12

plastic [plăs′tĭk]

  plastic storage bags [plăs′tĭk stör′ĭj băgz] **72**–25

  plastic storage container

    [plăs′tĭk stör′ĭj kən tā′nər] **78**–4

  plastic utensils [plăs′tĭk yōō tĕn′ səlz] **79**–19

  plastic wrap [plăs′tĭk răp′] **72**–24

plate [plāt] **55**–1

  bread-and-butter plate [brĕd′n bŭt′ər plāt′] **83**–19

  dinner plate [dĭn′ər plāt′] **83**–18

  license plate [lī′səns plāt′] **136**–12, **158**–12

  salad plate [săl′əd plāt′] **83**–20

  vanity plate [vă′nə tē plāt′] **136** ✦

platform [plăt′förm′] **152**–7

platter [plăt′ər] **55**–20

platypus [plăt′ĭ pəs, –pŏŏs′] **217**–46

play [plā] **223**–8

  play area [plā′ ĕr′ē ə] **130**–11

  playground [plā′grownd′] **50**–3

play [plā] **235**–B

  play an instrument [plā′ ən ĭn′strə mənt] **238**–A

  play cards [plā′ kärdz′] **233**–H

  play games [plā′ gāmz′] **232**–B

  play with [plā′ wĭth′] **36**–M

player [plā′ər] **229**–5

  CD player [sē′dē plā′ər] **159**–38

  DVD player [dē′vē′dē′ plā′ər] **56**–7, **234**–10

  MP3 player [ĕm′pē′thrē′ plā′ər] **234**–2

  personal CD player [pür′sə nəl sē′dē plā′ər] **234**–5

  portable cassette player

    [pör′tə bəl kə sĕt′ plā′ər] **234**–6

  portable DVD player

    [pör′tə bəl dē′vē′dē′ plā′ər] **234**–11

  video player [vĭd′ē ō plā′ər] **197**–11

PLAYGROUND [plā′grownd′] **224**

pliers [plī′ərz] **180**–7

plugs [plŭgz] **179**–15, **234**–16

plumber [plŭm′ər] **63**–20

plums [plŭmz] **68**–13

plunger [plŭn′jər] **181**–50

plywood [plī′wŏŏd′] **178**–18

p.m. [pē′ĕm′] **18**–5

pneumatic drill [nōō măt′ĭk drĭl′] **178**–9

poached eggs [pōcht′ ĕgz′] **76**–9

PO box (post office box) [pē′ō bäks′] /

  [pōst′ ö′fəs bäks′] **135**–9

pocket [päk′ət] **100**–7

podium [pō′dē əm] **206**–5

poinsettia [poyn sĕt′ē ə, –sĕt′ə] **211**–24

point [poynt] **17**–7,

  endpoint [ĕnd′poynt′] **193**–21

pointer [poyn′tər] **197**–12

poison [poy′zən] **116**–J

  poison ivy [poy′zən ī′vē] **210**–25

  poison oak [poy′zən ōk′] **210**–24

  poison sumac [poy′zən sōō′măk, –shōō′–] **210**–23

poisoning [poy′zən ĭng] **218**–16

poisonous fumes [poy′zən əs fyōōmz′] **179**–3

poles [pōlz] **226**–18, **231**–25

police [pə lēs′]

  police officer [pə lēs′ ö′fə sər] **141**–1, **168**–48

  police station [pə lēs′ stā′shən] **124**–6

polish [päl′ĭsh] **61**–8, **109**–33

polish [päl′ĭsh] **60**–E, **109**–O

political [pə lĭ′tĭ kəl]

  political campaign [pə lĭ′tĭ kəl kăm pān′] **139**–29

  political movement [pə lĭ′tĭ kəl mōōv′mənt] **199**–16

  political party [pə lĭ′tĭ kəl pär′tē] **139** ✦

polka-dotted [pō′kə dät′əd] **96**–21

pollution [pə lōō′shən] **218**–11, **218**–14

Pollution [pə lōō′shən] **218**

polo [pō′lō] **229**–15

  polo shirt [pō′lō shïrt′] **92**–14

poncho [pän′chō] **90**–19

pond [pänd] **204**–21

pool [pōōl] **51**–22, **184**–22, **228**–2

  pool service [pōōl′ sür′vəs] **184**–21

  pool table [pōōl′ tā′bəl] **50**–14

pop [päp] **73**–34, **237**–25

  pop-up ad [päp′ŭp′] **197**–9

porch light [pörch′ līt′] **53**–13

porcupine [pör′kyə pīn′] **216**–10

Pork [pörk] **70**

pork chops [pörk′ chäps′] **70**–10

porpoise [pör′pəs] **213**–30

port [pört] **196**–7

  airport [ĕr′pört′] **151**–10

portable [pör′tə bəl]

  portable cassette player

    [pör′tə bəl kə sĕt′ plā′ər] **234**–6

  portable DVD player

    [pör′tə bəl dē′vē′dē′ plā′ər] **234**–11

  portable TV [pör′tə bəl tē′ vē′] **234**–8

positive integers [pö′zə tiv ĭn′tə jərz] **192**–2

post [pōst] **134**–6

  post card [pōst′kärd′] **134**–16

  postmark [pōst′märk′] **134**–24

  post office [pōst′ ö′fəs] **125**–11

  post office box (PO box) [pōst′ ö′fəs bäks′] /

    [pē′ō bäks′] **135**–9

postage [pō′stĭj] **135** ✦

postal [pō′stəl] **135**–10

  postal clerk [pō′stəl klürk′] **135**–7

  postal forms [pō′stəl förmz′] **134**–19

  postal scale [pō′stəl skāl′] **183**–27

  postal worker [pō′stəl wür′kər] **169**–49

POST OFFICE [pōst′ ö′fəs] **134**–135

pot [pät] **54**–16, **78**–6

  pot holders [pät hōl′dərz] **78**–29

  teapot [tē′pät′] **55**–16

potatoes [pə tā′tōz] **69**–17

  baked potato [bākt′ pə tā′tō] **81**–25

  mashed potatoes [măsht′ pə tā′tōz] **81**–23

  potato chips [pə tā′tō chĭps′] **73**–35

  potato salad [pə tā′tō săl′əd] **80**–19

  sweet potatoes [swĕt′ pə tā′tōz] **69**–18

potty seat [pät′ē sēt′] **37**–12

pouch [powch] **217**–50

Poultry [pōl′trē] **70, 76**

POULTRY [pōl′trē] **70**

pound [pownd] **75**–12

  pound key [pownd′ kē′] **14**–7

pour [pör] **82**–C

powder [pow′dər] **37**–14, **108**–4, **109**–41

power [pow′ər] **218**–2, **218**–5

  power cord [pow′ər körd′] **196**–2

  power outlet [pow′ər owt′lĕt] **159**–42

  power sander [pow′ər săn′dər] **180**–11

pox [pöks] **111**–6

practical [prăk′tə kəl] **120**–11

prairie dog [prër′ē dög′] **215**–22

praise [prāz] **36**–J

pregnant [prĕg′nənt] **32**–15

preheat [prē′hēt′] **77**–A

preparation [prĕ′pə rā′shən] **185**–4

PREPARATION [prĕ′pə rā′shən] **76**–77

prepare [prĭ′për′] **174**–A

PREPOSITIONS [prĕp′ə zĭsh′ənz] **25**

PREPOSITIONS OF MOTION

  [prĕp′ə zĭsh′ənz əv mō′shən] **153**

preschool [prē′skōōl′] **188**–1

prescribe medication [prĭ skrib′mĕd′ə kā′shən] **112** ✦

prescription [prĭ skrĭp′shən] **112**–2

  pick up a prescription

    [pĭk′ ŭp′ə prĭ skrĭp′shən] **112** ✦

  prescription label [prĭ skrĭp′shən lā′bəl] **112**–4

  prescription medication

    [prĭ skrĭp′shən mĕd′ə kā′shən] **112**–3

  prescription number [prĭ skrĭp′shən nŭm′bər]

    112–5

present [prĕz′ənt] **94** ✦, **240**–3

presentation [prĕ′zən tā′shən] **182**–6

president [prĕz′ə dənt] **138**–8, **199**–5

  first president [fürst′ prĕz′ə dənt] **198**–11

  Presidents′ Day [prĕz′ə dənts dā′] **22**–11

  vice president [vīs′ prĕz′ə dənt] **138**–9

press [prĕs] **78**–11, **140**–4

press [prĕs] **15**–B, **15**–D

presser foot [prĕs′ər fŏŏt′] **98**–19

pressure [prĕsh′ər] **111**–14, **118**–9

pretend [prĭ tĕnd′] **233**–G

Prewriting [prē′rī′tĭng] **191**

Index

price [prīs] **27**–2, **27**–3, **27**–7
   price tag [prīs tăg/] **27**–1
prime minister [prīm/ mĭn/ə stər] **199**–7
principal [prĭn/sə pəl] **5**–4
print [prĭnt] **96**–23
   fingerprint [fĭng/gər prĭnt/] **136**–5
print [prĭnt] **4**–C, **171**–I
printer [prĭn/tər] **169**–50, **196**–17
   inkjet printer [ĭnk/jĕt prĭn/tər] **183**–18
   laser printer [lā/zər prĭn/tər] **183**–19
Priority Mail® [prī ör/ə tē māl/, –är/–] **134**–1
prism [prĭz/əm] **195**–35
prisoner [prĭz/nər] **141**–15
private school [prī/vət skool/]**5** ✦
Problem [präb/ləm] **192**
problems [präb/ləmz] **115**–1, **192**–11
Problems [präb/ləmz] **115, 119**
PROBLEMS [präb/ləmz] **62–63**
Procedures [prə sē/jərz] **117, 118**
PROCEDURES [prə sē/jərz] **146–147**
Process [prä/sĕs] **191**
processor [prä/sĕ sər] **54**–26
Processor [prä/sĕ sər] **92**
produce section [prō/doos sĕk/shən] **72**–2
product [präd/ŭkt] **192**–9
Products [präd/ŭkts] **72, 73**
program [prō/grăm]
   children's program [chĭl/drənz prō/grăm] **236**–9
   nature program [nā/chər prō/grăm] **236**–7
   news program [nooz/ prō/grăm] **236**–1
   shopping program [shäp/ĭng prō/grăm] **236**–10
   sports program [spörtz/ prō/grăm] **236**–11
program [prō/grăm] **170**–I
Programs [prō/grămz] **236**
projector [prə jĕk/tər] **6**–6, **7**–16, **235**–29
promotion [prə mō/shən] **172**–4
proof of insurance [proof/ əv/ĭn shoor/əns] **136**–8
proofread [proof/rēd/] **191**–I
prosecuting attorney
   [präs/ĭ kyoo/tĭng ə tür/nē] **141**–10
protect [prə tĕkt/] **143**–D
protector [prə tĕk/tər] **196**–1
proton [prō/tön] **195**–31
proud [prowd] **43**–21
prunes [proonz] **68**–26
pruning shears [proo/nĭng shĭrz/] **176**–11
psychiatrist [sī kī/ə trĭst, sə–] **120**–8
PUBLIC SAFETY [pŭb/lĭk sāf/tē] **143**
public school [pŭb/lĭk skool/] **5** ✦
PUBLIC TRANSPORTATION
   [pŭb/lĭk trăns/pər tā/shən] **152**
pull [pool] **119**–F, **224**–A
puller [pool/ər] **175**–10
pullover sweater [pool/ō/vər swĕt/ər] **88**–3
pulse [pŭls] **122**–A
pumps [pŭmps] **95**–26
Punctuation [pŭngk/choo ā/shən] **190**
puppy [pŭp/ē] **215**–12
purchase [pür/chəs] **94**–A
purifier [pyoo/rə fī/ ər] **113**–13
purple [pür/pəl] **24**–6
purses [pür/səz] **94**–2, **94**–14

push [poosh] **224**–B
pushpin [poosh/pĭn/] **183**–35
put [poot] **9**–X
put away
   [poot/ə wā/] **9**–Z, **60**–G
   put down [poot/ down/] **6**–J
   put in coolant [poot/ ĭn koo/lənt] **157**–I
   put on [poot/ än/, –ön/] **87**–B, **108**–D, **109**–P, **135**–C
   put on hold [poot/ än höld/, –ön] **171**–N
   put the utilities in your name
      [poot/ dhe yoo tĭl/ə tēz ĭn yər nām/] **49**–O
puzzle [pŭz/əl] **59**–17
pyramid [pĭr/ə mĭd] **193**–39
quad [kwäd] **5**–1
quart [kwört] **75**–4
quarter [kwör/tər] **26**–4
   quarter after one [kwör/tər ăf/tər wŭn/] **18**–9
   1/4 cup [kwör/tər kŭp/] **75**–8
   quarter moon [kwör/tər moon/] **205**–11
   quarter to two [kwör/tər tə too/] **18**–13
   3/4 sleeved [thrē/ kwör/tər slēvd/] **96**–13
question mark [kwĕs/chən märk/] **190**–12
Quick and Easy Cake [kwĭk/ ən ē/zē kāk/] **77**
quiet [kwī/ət] **23**–12
quill [kwĭl] **216**–23
quilt [kwĭlt] **58**–16
   quilt block [kwĭlt/ bläk/] **232**–15
quilt [kwĭlt] **232**–C
quotation [kwōt tā/shən] **190**–9
   quotation marks [kwō tā/shən märks/] **190**–15
quotient [kwō /shənt] **192**–10
rabbit [răb/ət] **215**–13
raccoon [ră koon/] **216**–13
race [rās] **230**–S
racing [rā/sĭng] **228**–19
rack [răk] **98**–16
   dish rack [dĭsh/ răk/] **54**–5
   roasting rack [rō/stĭng răk/] **78**–14
   towel rack [tow/əl răk/] **57**–13
racket [răk/ət] **231**–2
racquetball [răk/ət böl/] **228**–12
radiation [rā/dē ā/shən] **218**–15
radiator [rā/dē ā/tər] **158**–19
radio [rā/dē ō] **102**–6, **159**–37, **179**–22
radioactive materials
   [rā/dē ō ăk/tĭv mə tĭr/ē əlz] **179**–7
radiologist [rā/dē äl/ə jĭst] **120**–6
radishes [răd/ĭ shəz] **69**–4
radius [rā/dē əs] **193**–35
rafting [răf/tĭng] **226**–2
rags [răgz] **61**–9
rail [rāl] **59**–10
railroad crossing [rāl/rōd krö/sĭng] **154**–14
rain [rān] **218**–13
   rain boots [rān/ boots/] **90**–20
   raincoat [rān/kōt/] **90**–18
   rain forest [rān/ för/əst, fär/–] **204**–1
raining [rā/nĭng] **13**–11
raise [rāz] **6**–A
raisins [rā/zənz] **68**–25
rake [rāk] **176**–8
rake [rāk] **176**–C

ranch [rănch] **52**–10
rancher [răn/chər] **177**–22
Ranch Hand [rănch hănd/] **92**
RANCHING [răn/chĭng] **177**
R&B [är/n bē/] **237**–28
range [rānj] **204**–15
ranger [rān/jər] **220**–2
rash [răsh] **110**–10
raspberries [răz/bĕr/ēz] **68**–15
rats [răts] **63**–27, **215**–17
rattle [răt/l] **37**–26
   rattlesnake [răt/l snāk/] **213**–38
raw [rö] **70**–24
ray [rā] **212**–11
razor [rā/zər] **109**–27
   razorblade [rā/zər blād/] **109**–28
reaction [rē/ăk shən] **116**–E
read [rēd]
   proofread [proof/rēd/] **191**–I
   read the card [rēd/ dhe kärd/] **135**–G
   read the definition [rēd/ dhe dĕ/fə nĭ/shən] **8**–B
   read the paper [rēd/ dhe pā/pər] **39**–V
   read to [rēd/ too] **36**–N
Reading a Phone Bill [rē/dĭng ə fōn/ bĭl/] **15**
reality show [rē ă lə tē shō/] **236**–6
rearview mirror [rĭr/vyoo/ mĭr/ər] **159**–35
receipt [rĭ sēt/] **27**–6
receive [rĭ sēv/] **135**–F
receiver [rĭ sē/vər] **14**–1
reception area [rĭ sĕp/shən ër/ē ə] **182**–15
receptionist [rĭ sĕp/shə nĭst] **118**–2, **164**–5,
   169–51, **182**–14
reclined seat [rĭ klīnd/ sēt/] **161**–27
record [rĭ körd/] **195**–D, **235**–A
records [rĕk/ərdz] **168**–39
RECREATION [rĕk/rē ā/shən] **226**
recreational vehicle (RV)
   [rĕk/rē ā/shən əl vē/ə kəl] / [är/vē/] **156**–10
Recreation Room [rĕk/rē ā/shən room/] **50**
recruiter [rə kroo/tər] **172**–14
rectangle [rĕk/tăng/gəl] **193**–29
recycle [rē sī/kəl] **60**–B, **219**–C
recycling bin [rē sī/klĭng bĭn/] **61**–2
red [rĕd] **24**–1
   red hair [rĕd/ hër/] **33**–15
   redwood [rĕd/wood/] **210**–18
redecorate [rē dĕk/ə rāt/] **48** ✦
reduce [rĭ doos/] **219**–A
referee [rĕf/ə rē/] **229**–6
reference librarian [rĕf/rəns lī brër/ē ən] **133**–9
refrigerator [rĭ frĭj/ə rā/tər] **54**–9
refund [rē/fŭnd] **97** ✦
reggae [rĕ gā/] **237**–31
register [rĕj/ə stər] **73**–15
register [rĕj/ə stər] **140**–D, **157**–F
registered nurse (RN)
   [rĕj/ə stərd nürs/] / [är/ĕn/] **120**–10
registration [rĕj/ə strā/shən]
   registration sticker
      [rĕj/ə strā/shən stĭk/ər] **136**–13
   registration tag [rĕj/ə strā/shən tăg/] **136**–13
regular price [rĕg/yə lər prĭs/] **27**–2

regulations [rĕ gyə lā/shənz] **164**–6
relatives [rĕ lə tĭvz] **44**–6
relax [rĭ lăks/] **39**–U
relieved [rĭ lēvd/] **42**–15
reliever [rĭ lēv/ər] **113**–26
religious holiday [rĭ lĭj/əs häl/ə dā/] **22**–7
remain [rē/mān] **147**–E
remarried [rē măr/ēd] **35**–24
remote [rĭ mōt/] **234**–9
remove [rĭ mōōv/] **109**–Q, **132**–G
remover [rĭ mōō/vər] **109**–42
renew a license [rĭ nōō/ ə lī/səns, –nyōō/–] **136** ✦
rental agreement [rĕn/təl ə grē/mənt] **51**–28
Rental Office [rĕn/təl ö/fəs] **51**
Renting an Apartment [rĕn/tĭng ən ə pärt/mənt] **48**
repair [rĭ për/] **166**–4, **167**–24
    repair person [rĭ për/ pür/sən] **62**–10
repair [rĭ për/] **170**–J
REPAIRS [rĭ përz/] **62**–63
repellent [rĭ pĕl/ənt] **226**–23
replace [rĭ plās/] **157**–K
report [rĭ pört/] **143**–J, **143**–K
reporter [rĭ pör/tər] **169**–52
representative [rĕ/prĭ zĕn/tə tĭv] **138**–3, **167**–20
Reptiles [rĕp/tĭlz] **213**
REPTILES [rĕp/tĭlz] **212**–213
request [rĭ kwĕst/] **12** ✦
Requirements [rĭ kwīr/mənts] **140**
rescue [rĕs/kyōō] **145**–20
    rescue breathing [rĕs/kyōō brē/dhĭng] **117**–16
Resident Alien card [rĕz/ə dənt ā/lē ən kärd/] **40**–2
resource center [rē/sörs sĕn/tər] **172**–9
Resources [rē/sörs/səz, rĭ sör/səz] **219**
respirator [rĕs/pə rā/tər] **179**–13
Responding [rĭ spän/dĭng] **191**
Responsibilities [rĭ spän/sə bĭl/ə tēz] **140**
RESPONSIBILITIES [rĭ spän/sə bĭl/ə tēz] **140**
restaurant [rĕs/tə rənt, –ränt/] **125**–14, **128**–10
RESTAURANT [rĕs/tə rənt, –ränt/] **79, 82**–83
Restaurant Dining [rĕs/tə rənt dī/nĭng, –ränt/] **185**
Restaurant Kitchen [rĕs/tə rənt kĭ/chən, –ränt/] **185**
restrooms [rĕst/ rōōmz/] **5**–10
results [rĭ zŭltz/] **139**–31
resuscitation [rĭ sə sə tā/shən] **117**–17
retail clerk [rē/tāl/ klürk/] **169**–53
retire [rĭ tīr/] **41**–O
return [rĭtürn/] **73**–16
    return address [rĭ türn/ ə drĕs/, –ă/drĕs] **134**–21
return [rĭ türn/] **27**–H, **133**–D
REUNION [rē yōōn/yən] **44**–45
reuse [rē yōōz/] **219**–B
revise [rĭ vīz/] **191**–J
Revising [rĭ vī/zĭng] **191**
Revolutionary War [rĕ/və lōō/shə nër ē wör/] **198**–8
revolving [rĭ väl/vĭng]
    revolving door [rĭ väl/vĭng dör/] **184**–2
    revolving nosepiece [rĭ väl/vĭng nōz/pēs] **194**–17
rewind [rē wīnd/] **235**–C
rewrite [rē rīt/] **191**–J
rhinoceros [rĭ näs/ər əs] **217**–28
ribbon [rĭ/bən] **99**–30

ribs [rĭbz] **70**–5, **76**–2
    rib cage [rĭb/ kāj/] **107**–48
rice [rīs] **67**–10, **81**–30, **177**–1
ride [rīd] **129**–D
rider [rī/dər] **152**–3
riding [rī/dĭng] **226**–9
right [rīt] **25**–3, **155**–B, **198**–10
    right angle [rīt/ ăng/gəl] **193**–26
    right turn only [rīt/ türn/ ōn/lē] **154**–7
Rights [rīts] **140**
RIGHTS AND RESPONSIBILITIES
    [rīts/ ən rĭ spän/sə bĭl/ə tēz] **140**
ring [rĭng] **37**–25, **79**–4, **95**–40
    clip-on earrings [klĭp/än ïr/ĭngz, –ön–] **95**–37
    pierced earrings [pïrst/ ïr/ĭngz] **95**–36
rinse [rĭns] **108**–F
ripe [rīp] **68**–30
ripped [rĭpt] **97**–41
ripper [rĭ/pər] **100**–18
rise [rīz] **127**–13
    sunrise [sŭn/rīz/] **18**–14
river [rĭv/ər] **155**–10, **204**–3
RN (registered nurse) [är/ĕn/] / [rĕj/ə stərd nürs/]
    120–10
road work [rōd/ würk/] **154**–16
Road Worker [rōd/ wür/kər] **92**
roast [rōst] **70**–1
    roast beef [rōst bēf/] **71**–21
    roast chicken [rōst chĭk/ən] **81**–22
    roasted turkey [rō/stəd tür/kē] **76**–4
    roasting pan [rō/stĭng păn/] **78**–13
    roasting rack [rō/stĭng răk/] **78**–14
robe [rōb] **91**–29
robin [räb/ən] **214**–16
rock [räk] **36**–D
rock concert [räk/ kän/sərt] **222**–5
rocking chair [räk/ĭng chër/] **37**–21
rocks [räks] **208**–6, **237**–23
Rodents [rōd/nts] **215**
RODENTS [rōd/nts] **215**
rollers [rō/lərz] **33**–19, **181**–23
rolling pin [rō/lĭng pĭn/] **78**–30
rolls [rōlz] **74**–11, **74**–23, **80**–17
romance [rō mǎns/, rō/mǎns] **237**–16
Roman Numerals [rō/mən nōō/mər əlz] **16**
roof [rōōf] **46**–1
roof garden [rōōf/ gär/dn] **50**–4
room [rōōm]
    baby's room [bā/bēz rōōm/] **47**–10
    ballroom [böl/ rōōm/] **184**–26
    banquet room [băn/kwət rōōm/] **185**–14
    bathroom [băth/rōōm/] **46**–4
    bedroom [bĕd/rōōm/] **46**–2
    conference room [kän/frəns rōōm/] **182**–4
    dining room [dī/nĭng rōōm/] **82**–1
    dining room chair [dī/nĭng rōōm/ chër/] **55**–8
    dining room table [dī/nĭng rōōm/ tā/bəl] **55**–9
    dish room [dĭsh/ rōōm/] **83**–13
    guest room [gĕst/ rōōm/] **184**–13
    kids' bedroom [kĭdz/ bĕd/rōōm/] **47**–9

living room [lĭv/ĭng rōōm/] **47**–12
meeting room [mē/tĭng rōōm/] **184**–25
roommates [rōōm/māts/] **64**–1
room service [rōōm/ sür/vəs] **184**–17
storeroom [stör/rōōm/] **185**–5
Room [rōōm] **50, 118, 121**
ROOM [rōōm] **56**
rooster [rōō/stər] **215**–7
roots [rōōts] **210**–5, **211**–3
rope [rōp] **224**–4, **226**–19
rose [rōz] **211**–15
rotary [rō/tə rē]
    rotary card file [rō/tə rē kärd/ fīl/] **183**–44
    rotary cutter [rō/tə rē kŭt/ər] **232**–16
rotten [rät/n] **68**–32
round trip [rownd/ trĭp/] **152**–17
route [rōōt] / [rowt]
    bus route [bŭs/ rōōt, –rowt] **152**–1
    escape route [ĕs/kāp rōōt, –rowt] **146**–3
    evacuation route
        [ĭ văk/yōō/ā shən rōōt, –rowt] **146**–5
    U.S. route [yōō/ĕs/ rōōt, –rowt] **154**–17
router [row/tər] **180**–12
ROUTINES [rōō tēnz/] **38**–39
rubber [rŭb/ər]
    rubber band [rŭb/ər bănd/] **183**–34
    rubber gloves [rŭb/ər glŭvz/] **61**–4
    rubber mat [rŭb/ər măt/] **57**–3
ruffle [rŭ/fəl] **58**–17
rug [rŭg] **58**–22
ruler [rōō/lər] **17**–13
rules [rōōlz] **64**–8
Rules [rōōlz] **190**
run [rŭn] **11**–D
    run across [rŭn/ə krös/] **153**–G
    run around [rŭn/ə rownd/] **153**–H
    run for office [rŭn/ fər ö/fəs] **139**–A
    run out [rŭn/owt/] **162**–E
runner [rŭ/nər] **185**–15
rural area [rōōr/əl ër/ē ə] **52**–4
RV (recreational vehicle)
    [är/vē/] / [rĕk/rē ā/shən əl vē/ə kəl] **156**–10
rye bread [rī/ brĕd/] **71**–20
sad [săd] **43**–19
safety [sāf/tē] **37**–19, **92**–4, **159**–53
    safety boots [sāf/tē bōōts/] **179**–20
    safety deposit box [sāf/tē dĭ päz/ət bäks/] **132**–7
    safety glasses [sāf/tē glăs/əz] **92**–10, **179**–10
    safety goggles [sāf/tē gäg/əlz] **179**–11
    safety pin [sāf/tē pĭn/] **37**–9, **100**–14
    safety rail [sāf/tē rāl/] **59**–10
    safety regulations [sāf/tē rĕ/gyə lā/shənz] **164**–6
    safety visor [sāf/tē vī/zər] **179**–12
Safety [sāf/tē] **76**
SAFETY [sāf/tē] **76**–77, **143, 179**
Safety Equipment [sāf/tē ĭ kwĭp/mənt] **179**
Safety Hazards and Hazardous Materials
    [sāf/tē hăz/ərdz ən hăz/ər dəs-mə tïr/ē əlz] **179**
sailboat [sāl/bōt/] **225**–3
sailing [sā/lĭng] **227**–8

Index

salad [săl/əd]
chef's salad [shĕfs/ săl/əd] **80**–14
dinner salad [dĭn/ər săl/əd] **80**–15
fruit salad [frōōt/ săl/əd] **80**–21
pasta salad [päs/tə săl/əd] **80**–20
potato salad [pə tā/tō săl/əd] **80**–19
salad bar [săl/əd bär/] **79**–24
salad fork [săl/əd förk/] **83**–27
salad plate [săl/əd plāt/] **83**–20
spinach salad [spĭ/nĭch săl/əd] **80**–13
Salad Dressings [săl/əd drĕ/sĭngz] **80**
Salads [săl/ədz] **80**
salamander [săl/ə măn/dər] **212**–27
salami [sə lä/mē] **71**–24
SALE [sāl] **102**–**103**
sales [sālz]
sale price [sāl/ prīs/] **27**–3
salesclerk [sālz/klürk/] **94**–3
sales tax [sālz/ tăks/] **27**–8
Salesperson [sālz/pür/sən] **92**
salmon [săm/ən] **71**–3
salmon steak [săm/ən stāk/] **71**–4
salon [sə lön/] **130**–3, **131**–18
salt and pepper shakers
[sölt/ n pĕp/ər shā/kərz] **55**–13
same [sām] **23**–15
SAME AND DIFFERENT
[sām/ ən dĭ/frənt, –dĭ fə rənt] **28**–**29**
samples [săm/pəlz] **84**–5
sand [sănd] **225**–23
sandbox [sănd/bäks/] **224**–15
sand castle [sănd kăs/əl] **225**–12
sand dune [sănd dōōn/] **204**–5
sandpaper [sănd/pā/pər] **181**–56
sandals [săn/dlz] **88**–9
sander [săn/dər] **180**–11
sandwich [săn/wĭch, –sănd/–] **79**–5, **80**–10, **80**–12
sanitation worker [săn/ə tā/shən wür/kər] **169**–54
satellite [săt/əl īt/] **205**–20
satellite dish [săt/əl līt/ dĭsh/] **53**–6
satisfied [săt/ĭs fīd/] **42**–6
Saturday [săt/ər dā/, –dē] **20**–14
Saturn [săt/ərn] **205**–6
saucepan [sös/păn/] **78**–25
saucer [sö/sər] **83**–25
sausage [sö/sĭj] **70**–12, **80**–2
sauté [sö tā/, sö –] **77**–E
save [sāv] **219**–E
saving [sā/vĭng] **19**–25, **225**–20
savings account number
[sā/vĭngz ə kownt/ nŭm/bər] **132**–11
saw [sö] **180**–9
hacksaw [hăk/sö/] **180**–5
jigsaw [jĭg/sö/] **180**–10
saxophone [săk/sə fōn/] **238**–5
say [sā] **2**–A, **3**–L, **4**–A
scaffolding [skăf/əl dĭng] **178**–4
scales [skālz] **57**–27, **72**–3, **135**–8, **155**–7, **195**–41, **212**–3
postal scale [pō/stəl skāl/] **183**–27
scallions [skăl/yənz] **69**–20
scallops [skăl/əps, skäl/–] **71**–12, **212**–19

scan [skăn] **171**–H
scanner [skăn/ər] **183**–20
scared [skërd] **43**–23
scarf / scarves [skärf/] / [skärvz] **95**–12
winter scarf [wĭn/tər skärf/] **90**–5
scenery [sē/ nə rē] / [sēn/rē] **162**–3
schedule [skĕj/ōōl, –ōō əl] **152**–4
schedule [skĕj/ōōl, –ōō əl] **171**–J
school [skōōl] **126**–9
adult school [[ə dŭlt/–, ăd/ŭlt skōōl/] **188**–8
elementary school [ĕl/ə mĕn/trē skōōl/] **188**–2
high school [hī/ skōōl/] **188**–4
junior high school [jōōn/yər hī/ skōōl/] **188**–3
middle school [mĭd/l skōōl/] **188**–3
nursery school [nür/sə rē skōōl/] **188**–1
parochial school [pə rō/kē əl skōōl/] **5** ✦
preschool [prē/skōōl/] **188**–1
private school [prī/vət skōōl/] **5** ✦
public school [pŭb/lĭk skōōl/] **5** ✦
school bus [skōōl/ bŭs/] **156**–21
school crossing [skōōl/ krö/sĭng] **154**–15
technical school [tĕk/nĭ kəl skōōl/] **188**–5
vocational school [vō kā/shə nəl skōōl/] **188**–5
SCHOOL [skōōl] **5, 10, 11**
School Registration Form
[skōōl/ rĕj/ə strā/shən förm/] **4**
SCHOOLS AND SUBJECTS
[skōōz ən sŭb/jĭkts] **188**–**189**
science [sī/əns] **189**–11
SCIENCE [sī/əns] **194**–**195**
Science Lab [sī/əns lăb/] **195**
scissors [sĭz/ərz] **33**–20, **100**–16
scoop neck [skōōp/ nĕk/] **96**–10
score [skör] **10**–3, **229**–1
scorpion [skör/pē ən] **214**–30
scrambled eggs [skrăm/bəld ĕgz/] **76**–7
scraper [skrā/pər] **181**–52
screen [skrēn] **6**–2, **196**–11, **235**–30
big-screen TV [bĭg/skrēn/ tē/ vē/] **50**–15
fire screen [fīr/ skrēn/] **56**–12
flat screen TV [flăt/ skrēn/ tē/vē/] **234**–7
screen door [skrēn/ dör/] **53**–15
sunscreen [sŭn/skrēn/] **108**–7, **225**–10
screener [skrēn/ər] **160**–5
screening area [skrē/nĭng ër/ē ə] **160**–4
screw [skrōō] **180**–32, **180**–33
Phillips screwdriver [fĭl/ĭps skrōō/drī/vər] **180**–31
screwdriver [skrōō/drī/vər] **180**–30
scroll bar [skrōl/bär/] **197**–15
scrub [skrŭb] **60**–K
scrubs [skrŭbz] **93**–31
scrub brush [skrŭb/ brŭsh/] **61**–20
surgical scrub cap [sür/jĭ kəl skrŭb/ kăp/] **93**–35
surgical scrubs [sür/jĭ kəl skrŭbz/] **93**–38
scuba [skōō/bə]
scuba diving [skōō/bə dī/vĭng] **227**–12
scuba tank [skōō/bə tăngk/] **225**–5
sea [sē]
sea anemone [sē/ ə nĕm/ə nē] **212**–24
seahorse [sē/ hörs/] **212**–13
sea lion [sē/ lī/ən] **213**–33
sea otter [sē/ ät/ər] **213**–35

seashell [sē/shĕl/] **225**–24
sea urchin [sē/ ür/chən] **212**–21
seaweed [sē/ wēd/] **225** ✦
Sea Animals [sē/ ăn/ə məlz] **212**
SEAFOOD AND DELI [sē/fōōd/ ən dĕ/lī] **71**
seal [sēl] **213**–34
Sea Mammals [sē/ măm/əlz] **213**
seam ripper [sēm/ rĭp/ər] **100**–18
search [sürch]
search and rescue team
[sürch/ ən rĕs/kyōō tēm/] **145**–20
search box [sürch/ bäks/] **197**–5
search engine [sürch/ ĕn/jən] **197**–6
SEARCH [sürch] **173**
SEASONAL CLOTHING [sē/zə nəl klō/dhĭng] **90**
Seasons [sē/zənz] **21**
seat [sēt]
backseat [băk/ sēt/] **159**–54
car safety seat [kär/ săf/tē sēt/] **37**–19
child safety seat [chīld/ săf/tē sēt/] **159**–53
front seat [frŭnt/ sēt/] **159**–51
love seat [lŭv/ sēt/] **56**–1
potty seat [pät/ē sēt/] **37**–12
reclined seat [rĭ klīnd/ sēt/] **161**–27
seat belt [sēt/ bĕlt/] **159**–52
upright seat [ŭp/rīt/ sēt/] **161**–28
seat [sēt] **82**–B
second [sĕk/ənd] **16**
Second Floor [sĕk/ənd flör/] **50**
seconds [sĕk/əndz] **18**–3
section [sĕk/shən] **72**–2
security [sĭ kyŏŏr/ə tē]
security camera [sĭ kyŏŏr/ə tē kăm/rə] **50**–19
security gate [sĭ kyŏŏr/ə tē gāt/] **50**–16
security guard [sĭ kyŏŏr/ə tē gärd/] **132**–5, **169**–55
security pants [sĭ kyŏŏr/ə tē pănts/] **93**–22
security screener [sĭ kyŏŏr/ə tē skrē/nər] **160**–5
security shirt [sĭ kyŏŏr/ə tē shürt/] **93**–20
Security Checkpoint [sĭ kyŏŏr/ə tē chĕk/poynt/] **160**
Security Guard [sĭ kyŏŏr/ə tē gärd/] **93**
sedan [sə dăn/] **156**–1
see [sē] **106**–A
seed [sēd] **211**–1
seedling [sēd/lĭng] **211**–4
seek [sēk] **114**–A, **147**–H
seesaw [sē/sö/] **224**–16
select [sə lĕkt/] **196**–B
self-checkout [sĕlf/ chĕk/owt/] **73**–10, **133**–10
sell [sĕl] **170**–K
semi [sĕm/ī] **156**–15
semicolon [sĕm/ē kō/lən] **190**–18
Senate [sĕn/ət] **138**–5
senator [sĕn/ə tər] **138**–6
state senator [stāt/ sĕn/ə tər] **139**–25
send [sĕnd] **197**–I
send in [sĕnd/ ĭn] **173**–H
Sending a Card [sĕn/dĭng ə kärd/] **135**
Sending Email [sĕn/dĭng ē/māl/] **197**
senior [sēn/yər]
senior citizen [sēn/yər sĭt/ə zən] **30**–5
senior housing [sēn/yər howz/ĭng] **52**–11
Senses [sĕn/səz] **106**

sentence [sĕn/tns] **190**–2
sentence [sĕn/tns] **141**–E
separate [sĕ/pə rāt/] **76**–B
September [sĕp tĕm/bər] **21**–33
sequins [sē/kwĭnz/] **99**–33
Serious Medical Conditions
   [sïr/ē əs mĕd/ĭ kəl kən dĭsh/ənz] **111**
serious photo [sïr/ē əs fō/tō] **206**–3
serve [sürv] **139**–D, **230**–P
   serve on a jury [sürv/ än ə jōŏr/ē, –ŏn–] **140**–E
   serve the meal [sürv/ dhə mēl/] **82**–F
Serve [sürv] **76**
server [sür/vər] **82**–8, **83**–9, **169**–56, **185**–8
service [sür/vəs]
   customer service [kŭs/tə mər sür/vəs] **97** ✦
   customer service representative
      [kŭs/tə mər-sür/vəs rĕ/prə zĕn/tə tĭv] **167**–20
   guest services [gĕst/ sür/vəs əz] **130**–12
   pool service [pōōl/ sür/vəs] **184**–21
   room service [rōōm/ sür/vəs] **184**–17
SERVICE [sür/vəs] **138**–**139**, **185**
serving bowl [sür/vĭng bōl/] **55**–21
set [sĕt] **10**–A, **33**–C, **82**–A
   set up [sĕt/ ŭp/] **173**–I
   sunset [sŭn/sĕt/] **18**–18
setting [sĕ/tĭng] **83**–17
seven [sĕv/ən] **16**
seventeen [sĕv/ən tēn/] **16**
seventeenth [sĕv/ən tēnth/] **16**
seventh [sĕv/ənth] **16**
seventieth [sĕv/ən tē əth] **16**
seventy [sĕv/ən tē] **16**
   75 percent [sĕv/ən tē fïv/ pər sĕnt/] **17**–9
sew [sō] **98**–A, **98**–B, **170**–L
sewing [sō/ĭng]
   sewing machine [sō/ĭng mə shēn/] **98**–13
   sewing machine operator
      [sō/ĭng mə shēn/ äp/ə rā/ tər] **98**–14
Sewing Machine [sō/ĭng mə shēn/] **98**
Sewing Supplies [sō/ĭng sə plīz/] **100**
sex [sĕks] **4**–16
shade [shād] **225**–13
   lampshade [lămp/shād/] **56** ✦, **58**–26
shadow [shă/dō] **109**–35
shake [shāk]
   milkshake [mĭlk/shāk/] **79**–14
shake [shāk] **3**–J, **174**–I
shakers [shā/kərz] **55**–13
shampoo [shăm pōō/] **108**–10
shanks [shănks] **70**–13
shaper [shā/pər] **91**–15
Shapes [shāps] **193**
share [shĕr] **8**–M
Sharing and Responding
   [shĕr/ĭng ən rĭ spän/dĭng] **191**
shark [shärk] **212**–4
sharpener [shär/pən ər] **183**–26
shave [shāv]
   aftershave [ăf/tər shāv/] **109**–30
shave [shāv] **109**–M
shaver [shā/vər] **109**–26
shaving cream [shā/vĭng krēm/] **109**–29

shears [shïrz] **176**–9
sheep [shēp] **215**–6
sheet [shēt]
   cookie sheet [kŏŏk/ē shēt/] **78**–27
   dryer sheets [drī/ər shēts/] **101**–5
   fitted sheet [fĭt/əd shēt/] **58**–12
   flat sheet [flăt/ shēt/] **58**–13
shelf [shĕlf] **54**–2
shell [shĕl]
   seashell [sē/shĕl/] **225**–24
Shellfish [shĕl/fĭsh/] **71**
shelter [shĕl/tər] **52**–13
shield [shēld]
   windshield [wĭnd/shēld/] **158**–1
   windshield wipers [wĭnd/shēld wī/pərz] **158**–2
shift [shĭft] **159**–49, **159**–50
shin [shĭn] **106**–21
   shin guards [shĭn/ gärdz/] **231**–13
shingles [shĭng/gəlz] **178**–20
ship [shĭp] **175**–D
shipping clerk [shĭp/ĭng klürk/] **175**–14
shirt [shürt] **86**–1
   nightshirt [nīt/shürt/] **91**–28
   polo shirt [pō/lō shürt/] **92**–14
   security shirt [sĭ kyōōr/ə tē shürt/] **93**–20
   sports shirt [spörts/ shürt/] **88**–4
   T-shirt [tē/shürt/] **86**–4
   work shirt [würk/ shürt/] **92**–2
shock [shäk] **116**–B, **116**–F
shoes [shōōz] **86**–7, **87**–13, **95**–32
   shoe department [shōō/ dĭ pärt/mənt] **95**–7
   shoelaces [shōō/lās əz] **94**–24
   shoe store [shōō/ stör/] **130**–10
SHOES AND ACCESSORIES
   [shōōz/ ən ĭk sĕs/ə rēz] **94**–**95**
shoot [shōōt] **211**–5
shoot [shōōt] **230**–H
shop [shäp]
   barbershop [bär/bər shäp/] **129**–19
   beauty shop [byōō/tē shäp/] **130** ✦
   coffee shop [kö/fē shäp/] **126**–11
   donut shop [dō/nŭt shäp/] **129**–17
   gift shop [gĭft/ shäp/] **130** ✦, **184**–5
   ice cream shop [īs/ krēm shäp/] **131**–16
shop [shäp] **28**–A, **143**–H
Shop [shäp] **100**
SHOP [shäp] **80**–**81**
shoplifting [shäp/lĭf/tĭng] **142**–8
shopping [shäp/ĭng]
   shopping basket [shäp/ĭng băs/kət] **73**–9
   shopping list [shäp/ĭng lĭst/] **67**–14
   shopping mall [shäp/ĭng mäl/] **126**–7
   shopping program [shäp/ĭng mäl/] **236**–10
SHOPPING [shäp/ĭng] **27**
shore [shör] **204**–12
short [shört] **32**–6, **96**–16
   short hair [shört/ hĕr/] **33**–1
   short-order cook [shört/ör/dər kŏŏk/] **185**–1
   short-sleeved [shört/slēvd/] **96**–12
shorten [shört/ən] **100**–B
shorts [shörts] **89**–25, **91**–4

shoulder [shōl/dər] **105**–13
   shoulder bag [shōl/dər băg/] **94**–17
   shoulder blade [shōl/dər blād/] **107**–28
   shoulder-length hair [shōl/dər lĕngkth/ hĕr/] **33**–2
   shoulder pads [shōl/dər pădz/] **231**–20
shovel [shŭv/əl] **176**–7, **178**–22
show [shō] **236**–4, **236**–6, **236**–8
show [shō] **137**–C, **160**–C
shower [show/ər]
   shower cap [show/ər kăp/] **108**–1
   shower curtain [show/ər kür/tn] **57**–12
   shower gel [show/ər jĕl/] **108**–2
   showerhead [show/ər hĕd/] **57**–11
   stall shower [stöl/ show/ər] **57** ✦
shredder [shrĕ/dər] **183**–24
shrimp [shrĭmp] **71**–11, **212**–18
shut [shŭt] **146**–4
shuttle [shŭt/l] **152**–19, **205**–19
sick [sĭk] **42**–12
   homesick [hōm/sĭk/] **43**–20
side [sīd] **76**–10
   sideburns [sīd/bürnz/] **33**–7
   sideview mirror [sīd/vyōō/ mïr/ər] **158**–3
Side Salads [sīd/ săl/ədz] **80**
sidewalk [sīd/wök/] **129**–24
sight impaired [sīt/ ĭm pĕrd/] **32**–11
sign [sīn] **4**–D
   street sign [strēt/ sīn/] **129**–26
   vacancy sign [vā/kən sē sīn/] **50**–7
   vital signs monitor [vīt/l sīnz/ män/ə tər] **121**–26
sign [sīn] **48**–D
signal [sĭg/nəl]
   strong signal [ströng/ sĭg/nəl] **14**–11
   turn signal [türn/ sĭg/nəl] **158**–6, **159**–34
   weak signal [wēk/ sĭg/nəl] **14**–12
signature [sĭg/nə chər] **4**–19
SIGNS [sīnz] **154**
silk [sĭlk] **98**–5
simmer [sĭm/ər] **77**–P
sing [sĭng] **36**–O, **238**–B
single [sĭng/gəl]
   single father [sĭng/gəl fä/dhər] **35**–23
   single mother [sĭng/gəl mŭdh/ər] **35**–22
sink [sĭnk] **54**–4, **57**–23
Sirius [sïr/ē əs] **205** ✦
sister [sĭs/tər] **34**–5, **35**–27
   sister-in-law [sĭs/tər ĭn lö/] **34**–16
   stepsister [stĕp/sĭs/tər] **35**–29
sitcom (situation comedy)
   [sĭt/käm/] / [sĭch/ōō ā/shən käm/ə dē] **236**–2
sit down [sĭt/ down/] **6**–F
site [sīt] **126**–2
sitter [sĭt/ər] **166**–9
situation comedy (sitcom)
   [sĭch/ōō ā/shən-käm/ə dē] / [sĭt/käm/] **236**–2
six [sīks] **16**
   six-pack [sīks/păk/] **74**–9, **74**–21
   6-year-old boy [sīks/yïr ōld/boy/] **31**–9
sixteen [sīks/tēn/] **16**
sixteenth [sīks/tēnth/] **16**
sixth [sīksth] **16**
sixtieth [sīks/tē əth] **16**

sixty [sĭks/tē] **16**
Sizes [sī/zəz] **96**
skate [skāt] **230**–U
skates [skāts] **231**–9, **231**–10
skateboard [skāt/börd/] **224**–7
skateboarding [skāt/bör/dĭng] **228**–13
skating [skā/tĭng] **227**–4, **227**–5, **227** ✦, **228**–10
ski [skē] **230**–V
skiing [skē/ĭng] **227**–1, **227**–3
waterskiing [wö/tər skē/ĭng] **227**–7
skill inventory [skĭl/ ĭn/vən tör/ē] **172**–12
Skills [skĭlz] **171**
SKILLS [skĭlz] **170, 171, 174**
skin [skĭn] **107**–31
skinless [skĭn/ləs] **70** ✦
skirt [skürt] **87**–10
skis [skēz] **231**–24
ski boots [skē/ bōōts] **231**–26
ski hat [skē/ hăt/] **90**–11
ski mask [skē/ măsk/] **90**–15
ski poles [skē/ pōlz/] **231**–25
skull [skŭl] **107**–47
skunk [skŭngk] **216**–12
SKU number [ĕs/kā/yōō/ nŭm/bər, skyōō/] **27**–5
sky [skī] **209**–9
skycap [skē/kăp/] **160**–1
skyscraper [skī/skrā/pər] **127**–13
slacks [slăks] **87**–12
slaves [slāvz] **198**–4
sledding [slĕd/ĭng] **227**–6
sledgehammer [slĕj/hăm/ər] **178**–23
sleeper [slē/pər] **91**–27
sleeping bag [slē/pĭng băg/] **226**–12
Sleepwear [slēp/wër] **91**
SLEEPWEAR [slēp/wër] **91**
sleepy [slē/pē] **42**–3
sleeve [slēv] **100**–6
long-sleeved [löng/slēvd/] **96**–14
short-sleeved [shört/slēvd/] **96**–12
sleeveless [slēv/ləs] **96**–11
3/4 sleeved [thrē/kwör/tər slēvd/] **96**–13
slender [slĕn/dər] **32**–9
slice [slīs] **77**–C
slide [slīd] **194**–3, **224**–13
mudslide [mŭd/slīd/] **144**–6
sliding glass door [slī/dĭng glăs/ dör/] **53**–18
sling [slĭng] **113**–19
slip [slĭp] **91**–22, **91**–23, **132**–4
slippers [slĭp/ərz] **91**–26
slippery floor [slĭ/pər ē flör/] **179**–6
slow [slō] **23**–4
small [smöl] **96**–1, **96**–2, **97**–37
small town [smöl/ town/] **52**–3
smart phone [smärt/ fōn/] **15**–27
smell [smĕl] **106**–C
smile [smīl] **2**–D
smock [smŏk] **93**–26
smog [smäg, smög] **218**–11
smoggy [smä/gē, smö/–] **13**–14
smoke [smōk] **114**–G
smoke detector [smōk/ dĭ tĕk/tər] **51**–29
smoked turkey [smōkt/ tür/kē] **71**–25

Snack Foods [snăk/ fōōdz/] **73**
snail [snāl] **212**–22
snake [snāk] **213**–39
rattlesnake [ră/təl snāk/] **213**–38
snap [snăp] **99**–26
sneeze [snēz] **110**–B
snorkeling [snör/kə lĭng] **227**–11
snow [snō]
snowboard [snō/börd/] **231**–23
snowboarding [snō/bör/dĭng] **227**–2
snowstorm [snō/störm/] **13**–23
snowing [snō/ĭng] **13**–12
soap [sōp] **57**–24, **61**–5, **108**–3
soap dish [sōp/ dĭsh/] **57**–25
soap opera [sōp/ äp/rə] **236**–5
sober [sō/ bər] **143** ✦
soccer [säk/ər] **229**–12
soccer ball [säk/ər böl/] **231**–12
social [sō/shəl]
Social Security card
[sō/shəl sĭ kyőōr/ə tē kärd/] **40**–5
Social Security number
[sō/shəl sĭ kyőōr/ə tē nŭm/bər] **4**–15
social worker [sō/shəl wür/kər] **169**–57
socks [säks] **86**–6
ankle socks [ang/kəl säks/] **91**–7
crew socks [krōō/ säks/] **91**–8
dress socks [drĕs/ säks/] **91**–9
low-cut socks [lō/kŭt säks/] **91**–10
Socks [säks] **91**
soda [sō/də] **73**–34, **79**–11
sofa [sō/fə] **56**–18
sofa cushions [sō/fə kōō/shənz] **56** ✦
soft [söft] **23**–6
softball [söft/böl/] **229**–10
softener [sö/fən ər] **101**–6
software [söft/wër/] **167**–18, **196**–10
soil [soyl] **208**–2
solar [sō/lər]
solar eclipse [sō/lər ĭ klĭps/] **205**–16, **205** ✦
solar energy [sō/lər ĕn/ər jē] **218**–1
Solar System and the Planets
[sō/lər sĭs/təm ən dhə plăn/əts] **205**
soldier [sōl/jər] **169**–58
sole [sōl] **94**–21
solid [säl/əd] **96**–19
Solids [säl/ədz] **193**
solution [sə lōō/ shən] **192**–14
solve [sölv] **170**–M
son [sŭn] **34**–15
grandson [grăn/sŭn/, grănd/–] **34** ✦
son-in-law [sŭn/ĭn lö/] **34** ✦
sore throat [sör/ thrōt/] **110**–6
sort [sört] **101**–A
soul [sōl] **237**–28
soup [sōōp] **72**–18, **80**–16
soup bowl [sōōp/ bōl/] **83**–21
soupspoon [sōōp/spōōn/] **83**–32
Soup [sōōp] **77**
sour [söw/ər] **84**–4
sour cream [sow/ər krĕm/] **72**–21
Sources [sör/səz] **218**

sous chef [sōō/ shĕf/] **185**–6
south [sowth] **155**–3
soybeans [soy/bēnz/] **177**–3
space [spās] **50**–18, **128**–5
space shuttle [spās/ shŭt/əl] **205**–19
space station [spās/ stā/shən] **205**–18
Space [spās] **205**
Space Exploration [spās/ ĕk/splə rā/shən] **205**
spades [spādz] **233**–30
spaghetti [spə gĕt/ē] **81**–26
spare tire [spër/ tīr/] **158**–23
sparrow [spăr/ō] **214**–7
spatula [spăch/ə lə] **78**–19
speak [spēk] **170**–N
speakers [spē/kərz] **50**–5, **206**–4, **234**–14
Special [spĕ/shəl] **80**
Specialists [spĕsh/ə lĭsts] **120**
speech [spēch] **140**–2
speed limit [spēd/ lĭm/ət] **154**–4
speedometer [spĭ däm/ə tər] **159**–27
speed skating [spēd/skā/tĭng] **227** ✦
spell [spĕl] **4**–B
sphere [sfīr] **193**–42
spider [spī/dər] **214**–29
spill [spĭl] **218**–17
spinach [spĭn/ĭch] **69**–11
spinach salad [spĭn/ĭch săl/əd] **80**–13
spinal column [spī/nəl käl/əm] **107**–49
splint [splĭnt] **117**–14
spiral notebook [spī/rəl nōt/bōōk/] **7**–29
splint [splĭnt] **117**–14
sponge [spŭnj] **61**–19
sponge mop [spŭnj/ măp/] **61**–6
spoon [spōōn] **55**–5, **78**–9
soupspoon [sōōp/spōōn/] **83**–32
tablespoon [tā/bəl spōōn/] **75**–7
teaspoon [tē/spōōn/] **75**–6, **83**–31
spoon [spōōn] **77**–F
sports [spörts]
sports car [spörts/ kär/] **156**–4
sports coat [spörts/ kōt/] **89**–14
sports jacket [spörts/ jăk/ət] **89**–14
sports program [spörts/ prō/grăm] **236**–11
sports shirt [spörts/ shürt/] **88**–4
sport-utility vehicle (SUV) [spört/
yōō tĭl/ə tē vē/ĭ kəl] / [ĕs/yōō/vē/] **156**–7
SPORTS [spörts] **228, 229, 230, 231**
SPORTS EQUIPMENT [spörts/ ĭ kwĭp/mənt] **231**
SPORTS VERBS [spörts/ vürbz/] **230**
sprained ankle [sprānd/ ăng/kəl] **110**–18
spray [sprā] **108**–12, **113**–32
spray gun [sprā/ gŭn/] **181**–21
spray starch [sprā/ stärch/] **101**–12
spread [sprĕd]
bedspread [bĕd/sprĕd/] **59**–11
spring [sprĭng] **21**–37, **58**–19
sprinkler [sprĭng/klər] **53**–22
square [skwër] **193**–30
squash [skwäsh, skwösh] **69**–24
squeegee [skwē/jē] **61**–15
squid [skwĭd] **212**–7
squirrel [skwür/əl] **215**–21
stadium [stā/dē əm] **126**–1

staff [stăf] **185** ✦
Staff [stăf] **120**
stage [stāj] **194**–16
    stage clips [stāj/ klĭps/] **194**–24
stain [stān] **181**–24
stained [stānd] **97**–42
stairs [stĕrz] **50**–10
stairway [stĕr/ wā/] **50**–10
stall shower [stöl/ show/ər] **57** ✦
stamps [stămps] **134**–18, **134**–23, **183**–47
    stamp machine [stămp/ mə shēn/] **135**–11
stand [stănd] **152**–18
    checkstand [chĕk/ stănd/] **73**–12
    newsstand [nōōz/ stănd/] **128**–12
    nightstand [nīt/ stănd/] **58**–23
stand [stănd] **141**–D
    stand up [stănd/ ŭp/] **6**–D
standard time [stăn/ dərd tīm/] **19**–26
staple [stā/ pəl] **171**–F
stapler [stā/ plər] **183**–28
staples [stā/ pəlz] **183**–29
star [stär] **205**–13
    starfish [stär/ fish/] **212**–16
    star key [stär/ kē/] **14**–6
starch [stärch] **101**–12
start [stärt] **12**–A, **40**–B, **230**–R
starting point [stär/ tĭng poynt/] **162**–1
starving [stär/ vĭng] **43** ✦
state [stāt] **4**–8, **146**–2
    state capital [stāt kă/ pət əl] **139**–22
    state senator [stāt sĕn/ə tər] **139**–25
state [stāt] **15**–G, **195**–A
State Government [stāt gŭ/ vərn mənt] **139**
statement [stāt/ mənt] **132**–16
station [stā/ shən]
    bus station [bus/ stā/ shən] **124**–7
    fire station [fīr/ stā/ shən] **125**–12
    gas station [găs/ stā/ shən] **125**–10
    gas station attendant
        [găs/ stā/ shən ə tĕn/ dənt] **162**–3
    lifeguard station [līf/ gärd/ stā/ shən] **225**–21
    police station [pə lēs/ stā/ shən] **124**–6
    space station [spās/ stā/ shən] **205**–18
    station wagon [stā/ shən wăg/ən] **156**–6
    subway station [sŭb/ wā/ stā/ shən] **151**–11
Station [stā/ shən] **152**
stationery [stā/ shə nĕr/ ē] **183**–42
stay [stā]
    stay away [stā ə wā/] **147**–I
    stay fit [stā fĭt/] **114**–E
    stay on the line [stā ön dhə līn/] **15**–H
    stay on well-lit streets [stā ön wĕl lĭt/ strēts/] **143**–B
Stay Well [stā wĕl/] **114**
steak [stāk] **70**–2, **81**–24
    broiled steak [broyld/ stāk/] **76**–3
    halibut steak [hăl/ə bŭt stāk/] **71**–6
    salmon steak [săm/ən stāk/] **71**–4
    steak knife [stāk/ nīf/] **83**–29
steal [stēl] **142** ✦
steam [stēm] **77**–D
    steamed vegetables [stēmd/ vĕj/tə bəlz] **81**–32
    steamer [stē/ mər] **78**–3

steel [stēl]
    steel toe boots [stēl/ tō/ bōōts/] **92**–6
    steel-wool soap pads [stēl/ wōōl/ sōp/ pădz/] **61**–5
steering wheel [stĭr/ ĭng wēl/] **159**–26
stems [stĕmz] **211**–9
step [stĕp]
    stepbrother [stĕp/ brŭdh/ər] **35**–30
    stepdaughter [stĕp/ dö/ tər] **35** ✦
    stepfather [stĕp/ fä/ dhər] **35**–25
    stepladder [stĕp/ lăd/ər] **61**–13
    stepmother [stĕp/ mŭdh/ər] **35**–26
    steps [stĕps] **53**–3
    stepsister [stĕp/ sĭs/ tər] **35**–29
stereo system [stĕr/ ē ö sĭs/ təm] **56**–8
sterile [stĕr/ əl]
    sterile pad [stĕr/ əl păd/] **117**–6
    sterile tape [stĕr/ əl tāp/] **117**–7
stethoscope [stĕth/ə skōp/] **118**–10
stewing beef [stōō/ ĭng bēf/] **70**–3
stick [stĭk] **231**–11, **232**–11
    drumsticks [drŭm/ stĭks/] **70**–23
    lipstick [lĭp/ stĭk/] **109**–38
    stick shift [stĭk/ shĭft/] **159**–50
    yardstick [yärd/ stĭk/] **181**–16
sticker [stĭk/ər] **102**–3, **136**–13
sticky notes [stĭk/ ē nōts/] **183**–39
stir [stür] **77**–O
    stir-fried beef [stür/ frīd/ bēf/] **76**–6
stitches [stĭch/əz] **117**–15
stock clerk [stäk/ klürk/] **169**–59
stockings [stäk/ ĭngz] **91**–17
stomach [stŭm/ək] **107**–41
    stomachache [stŭm/ək āk/] **110**–4
stop [stäp] **129**–16, **151**–13, **154**–1
    stopover [stäp/ ō/ vər] **161** ✦
stop [stäp] **155**–D
Stop [stäp] **152**
stopped up [stäpt/ ŭp/] **63**–19
storage [stör/ ĭj] **72**–25, **78**–4
    storage locker [stör/ ĭj läk/ər] **50**–17
store [stör]
    bookstore [bŏōk/ stör/] **130**–4
    candy store [kăn/ dē stör/] **131**–17
    card store [kärd/ stör/] **130**–7
    convenience store [kən vēn/ yəns stör/] **128**–3
    department store [dĭ pärt/ mənt stör/] **131**–13
    electronics store [ē lĕk trän/ ĭks stör/] **131**–20
    furniture store [für/ nĭ chər stör/] **126**–8
    hardware store [härd/ wĕr/ stör/] **148**–4
    home improvement store
        [hōm/ ĭm prōōv/ mənt stör/] **127**–20
    jewelry store [jōō/ əl rē stör/] **130**–2
    maternity store [mə tür/ nə tē stör/] **131**–19
    men's store [mĕnz/ stör/] **130** ✦
    music store [myōō/ zĭk stör/] **130**–1
    office supply store [ö/ fəs sə plī/ stör/] **127**–21
    pet store [pĕt/ stör/] **130**–6
    shoe store [shōō/ stör/] **130**–10
    toy store [toy/ stör/] **130**–5
    video store [vĭd/ ē ö stör/] **129**–20
Store [stör] **99**
STORE [stör] **72**–73

storeroom [stör/ rōōm/] **185**–3
storm [störm] **13**–19
    hailstorm [hāl/ störm/] **13**–21
    snowstorm [snō/ störm/] **13**–23
    storm door [störm/ dör/] **53**–10
    thunderstorm [thŭn/ dər störm/] **13**–16
story [stör/ ē]
    action story [ăk/ shən stör/ ē] **237**–19
    adventure story [ăd vĕn/ chər stör/ ē] **237**–19
    horror story [hör/ ər stör/ ē, här/–] **237**–17
    science fiction story [sī/ əns fĭk/ shən stör/ ē] **237**–18
    two-story house [tōō/ stör/ ē hows/] **52** ✦
stove [stōv] **54**–18, **226**–16
stow [stō] **160**–G
straight [strāt] **155**–A
    straight hair [strāt/ hĕr/] **33**–9
    straight line [strāt/ lĭn/] **193**–22
    straight pin [strāt/ pĭn/] **100**–12
strainer [strā/ nər] **78**–22
straw [strö] **79**–18
    strawberries [strö/ bĕr/ ēz] **68**–14
    straw hat [strö/ hăt/] **90**–23
stream [strēm] **204** ✦
street [strēt] **150**–5, **155**–8
    streetlight [strēt/ lĭt/] **148**–3
    street sign [strēt/ sīn/] **129**–26
    street vender [strēt/ vĕn/ dər] **129**–29
STREETS [strēts] **126**–127
strep throat [strĕp/ thrōt/] **111**–4
stress [strĕs] **115**–4
stretch [strĕch] **230**–M
stretcher [strĕch/ər] **121**–33
string [strĭng]
    string beans [strĭng/ bēnz/] **69**–8
    string lights [strĭng/ līts/] **239**–18
    string of pearls [strĭng/ əv pürlz/] **95**–39
Strings [strĭngz] **238**
striped [strīpt] **96**–20
stripper [strĭ/ pər] **181**–42
stroller [strō/ lər] **37**–18
strong signal [sträng/ sĭg/ nəl] **14**–11
stub [stŭb] **165**–11
stucco [stŭk/ ō] **178**–15
student [stōōd/ nt] **6**–5
study [stŭ/ dē] **10**–D, **137**–A
STUDYING [stŭ/ dē ĭng] **8**–9
stuffed animals [stŭft/ ăn/ə məlz] **59**–15
style [stīl/] **88** ✦
Styles [stīlz] **96**
STYLES [stīlz] **96**
stylist [stī/ lĭst] **167**–31
SUBJECTS [sŭb/ jĭkts/] **188**–189
submit [səb mĭt/] **48**–C
substitute [sŭb/ stə tōōt/] **79**–20
subtract [səb trăkt/] **192**–B
suburbs [sŭb/ ürbz] **52**–2
subway [sŭb/ wā/] **151**–12
    subway car [sŭb/ wā/ kär/] **152**–6
    subway station [sŭb/ wā/ stā/ shən] **151**–11
Subway Station [sŭb/ wā/ stā/ shən] **152**
Succeed [sək sēd/] **10**
SUCCEEDING IN SCHOOL [sək sē/ dĭng ən skōōl/] **10**

suede [swād] **99**–8

sugar [shŏŏg/ər] **73**–30
    sugar bowl [shŏŏg/ər bōl/] **55**–14
    sugar-free [shŏŏg/ər frē/] **122**–7
    sugar substitute [shŏŏg/ər sŭb/stə tōōt/] **79**–20

suit [sōōt] **87**–11
    bathing suit [bā/dhĭng sōōt/] **90**–26
    business suit [bĭz/nəs sōōt/] **88**–11
    jumpsuit [jŭmp/sōōt/] **93**–24
    three piece suit [thrē/pēs/ sōōt/] **88** ✦
    wet suit [wĕt/ sōōt/] **225**–4

suite [swēt] **184**–16

sum [sŭm] **192**–7

sumac [sōō/măk] **210**–23

summer [sŭm/ər] **21**–38

sun [sŭn] **209**–8
    sunblock [sŭn/blăk] **108**–8, **225**–0
    sunburn [sŭn/bŭrn/] **110**–14
    sunflower [sŭn/flow/ər] **211**–10
    sunglasses [sŭn/glăs/əz] **90**–27
    sunrise [sŭn/ rīz] **18**–14
    sunscreen [sŭn/skrēn/] **108**–7, **225**–10
    sunset [sŭn/ sĕt] **18**–19

Sunday [sŭn/dā, –dē] **20**–8

sunny [sŭn/ē] **13**–9, **76**–10

superintendent [sōō/prĭn tĕn/dənt, sōō/pər ĭn–] **50**–8

supermarket [sōō/pər/ mär/kət] **127**–18

supervise [sōō/pər vīz/] **170**–O

supervisor [sōō/pər vī/zər] **165**–8, **175**–4

Supplies [sə plīz/] **100, 183**

SUPPLIES [sə plīz/] **61, 180**–**181**

supply [sə plī/] **127**–21
    supply cabinet [sə plī/ kăb/ə nət] **182**–1

support [sə pört/] **179**–18
    support group [sə pört/ grōōp/] **115**–15

supporter [sə pör/tər] **91**–6

Supreme Court [sə prēm/ kört/] **138**–11

surfboard [sürf/börd/] **225**–16

surfer [sür/fər] **225**–15

surfing [sür/fĭng] **227**–9, **227**–10, **227** ✦

surgeon [sür/jən] **121**–36

Surgeon [sür/jən] **93**

surge protector [sürj/ prə tĕk/tər] **196**–1

surgical [sür/jĭ kəl]
    surgical cap [sür/jĭ kəl kăp/] **121**–37
    surgical gloves [sür/jĭ kəl glŭvz/] **121**–39
    surgical gown [sür/jĭ kəl gown/] **93**–37, **121**–38
    surgical mask [sür/jĭ kəl măsk/] **93**–36
    surgical nurse [sür/jĭ kəl nürs/] **120**–9
    surgical scrub cap [sür/jĭ kəl skrŭb/ kăp/] **93**–35
    surgical scrubs [sür/jĭ kəl skrŭbz/] **93**–38

Surgical Assistant [sür/jĭ kəl ə sĭs/tənt] **93**

surprised [sər prīzd/, sə–] **43**–30

suspenders [sə spĕn/dərz] **94**–1

suspense [sŭs/pĕns] **237**–20

SUV (sport-utility vehicle) [ĕs/yōō/vē/] /
    [spört/ yōō tĭl/ə tē vē/ĭ kəl] **156**–7

swallow [swäl/ō] **116**–J

swap meet [swäp/ mēt/] **222**–6

sweat [swĕt]
    sweatpants [swĕt/pănts/] **89**–23
    sweatshirt [swĕt/shürt/] **89**–22

sweater [swĕt/ər] **28**–2, **87**–14
    cardigan sweater [kär/də gən swĕt/ər] **88**–2
    pullover sweater [pŏŏl/ō/vər swĕt/ər] **88**–3

sweep [swēp] **60**–J

sweet potatoes [swēt pə tā/tōz] **69**–18

sweets [swēts] **84**–9

swim [swĭm] **230**–L
    swimsuit [swĭm/sōōt/] **90**–26

swimming [swĭm/ĭng]
    swimming pool [swĭm/ĭng pōōl/] **51**–22
    swimming trunks [swĭm/ĭng trŭngks/] **90**–22

swing [swĭng] **230**–Q

swings [swĭngz] **224**–11

Swiss cheese [swĭs/ chēz/] **71**–27

switch [swĭch] **58**–27

swollen finger [swō/lən fĭng/gər] **110**–16

swordfish [sörd/fĭsh/] **71**–5, **212**–10

symbol [sĭm/bəl] **155**–8

SYMPTOMS AND INJURIES
    [sĭmp/təmz ən ĭn/jə rēz] **110**

synagogue [sĭn/ə gäg/] **127**–16

synthetic materials [sĭn thĕ/tĭk mə tïr/ē əlz] **98** ✦

syringe [sə rĭnj/] **118**–12

syrup [sĭr/əp, sür/–] **113**–29

system [sĭs/təm]
    fuel injection system
        [fyōō/əl ĭn jĕk/shən sĭs/təm] **158**–17
    stereo system [stĕr/ē ō sĭs/təm] **56**–8

SYSTEM [sĭs/təm] **141**

tab [tăb] **197**–7

table [tā/bəl]
    bed table [bĕd/ tā/bəl] **121**–21
    changing table [chān/jĭng tā/bəl] **59**–1
    coffee table [kö/fē tā/bəl] **56**–19
    dining room table [dī/nĭng rōōm/ tā/bəl] **55**–9
    end table [ĕnd/ tā/bəl] **56**–14
    examination table [ĭg zăm/ə nā/shən tā/bəl] **118**–7
    folding card table [fōl/dĭng kärd/ tā/bəl] **102**–4
    night table [nīt/ tā/bəl] **58**–23
    operating table [äp/ə rā/tĭng tā/bəl] **121**–40
    periodic table [pĭr/ē äd/ĭk tā/bəl] **195**–26
    picnic table [pĭk/nĭk tā/bəl] **224**–8
    pool table [pōōl/ tā/bəl] **50**–15
    tablecloth [tā/bəl klöth/] **55**–12
    tablespoon [tā/bəl spōōn/] **75**–7
    table tennis [tā/bəl tĕn/əs] **228**–14
    tray table [trā/ tā/bəl] **161**–21
    turntable [türn/tā/bəl] **234**–12

tablet [tăb/lət] **113**–22, **113**–27

tackle [tăk/əl] **230**–F

taco [tä/kō] **79**–8

tags [tăgz] **92**–15, **136**–13

tail [tāl] **216**–22
    tail light [tāl/ līt/] **158**–13
    tail pipe [tāl/ pīp/] **158**–15

tailor [tā/lər] **100**–3

take [tāk]
    do not take with dairy products
        [dōō nät/ tāk/ wĭth dër/ē prăd/ŭkts] **112**–A
    take a bath [tāk/ ə băth/] **108**–B
    take a break [tāk/ ə brāk/] **11**–H
    take a citizenship test
        [tāk/ ə sĭt/ə zən shĭp tĕst/] **140**–I

take a driver education course
    [tāk/ ə drī/vərz ĕj/ə kā/shən körs/] **137**–B

take a driver's training course
    [tāk/ ə drī/vərz trā/nĭng körs/] **137**–G

take a message [tāk/ ə mĕs/ĭj] **171**–Q

take a nap [tāk/ ə năp/] **53**–A

take a picture [tāk/ ə pĭk/chər] **206**–B

take a seat [tāk/ ə sēt/] **6**–F

take a shower [tāk/ ə show/ər] **38**–C, **108**–A

take a tour [tāk/ ə tōōr/] **220**–A

take a written test [tāk/ ə rĭt/ən tĕst] **137**–E

take care of children [tāk/ kër/ əv chĭl/drən] **170**–P

take cover [tāk/ kŭv/ər] **147**–J

take dictation [tāk/ dĭk/tā shən] **171**–K

take in [tāk/ ĭn] **100**–D

take medicine [tāk/ mĕd/ə sən] **114**–D

take notes [tāk/ nōts/] **10**–C

take off [tāk/ öf/] **109**–Q, **160**–J

take one hour before eating
    [tāk/ wŭn ow/ər bĭ för/ ē/tĭng] **112**–B

take out [tāk/ owt/] **9**–Y, **60**–Q, **82** ✦

take ownership [tāk/ ō/nər shĭp/] **49**–K

take temperature [tāk/ tĕm/prə chər] **118**–B

take the bus to school
    [tāk/ dhə bŭs/ tə skōōl/] **38**–H

take the car to a mechanic
    [tāk/ dhə kär/ tə dhə mə kăn/ĭk] **157**–C

take the children to school
    [tāk/ dhə chĭl/drən tə skōōl/] **38**–G

take the order [tāk/ dhē ör/dər] **82**–E

take with food [tāk/ wĭth fōōd/] **112**–A

take x-rays [tāk/ ĕks/rāz/] **119**–B

Taking a Flight [tā/kĭng ə flīt/] **160**

Taking a Test [tā/kĭng ə tĕst/] **10**

TAKING A TRIP [tā/kĭng ə trĭp/] **162**–**163**

Taking Care of Your Car [tā/kĭng kër/ əv yər kär/] **157**

TAKING CARE OF YOUR HEALTH
    [tā/kĭng kër əv yər hĕlth/] **114**–**115**

talk [tök]
    talk show [tök/ shō/] **236**–4
    talk therapy [tök/ thĕr/ ə pē] **115**–13

talk [tök]
    talk about [tök ə bowt/] **174**–L
    talk on the phone [tök/ ön dhə fōn/] **15**–C
    talk to friends [tök/ tə frĕndz/] **173**–A
    talk to the teacher [tök/ tə dhə tē/chər] **6**–B

tall [töl] **32**–4

tambourine [tăm/bə rēn/] **238**–17

tan [tăn] **24**–18

tangerines [tăn/jə rēnz/] **68**–9

tank [tăngk] **158**–10, **225**–5
    tank top [tăngk/ täp/] **89**–24
    tank truck [tăngk/ trŭk/] **156**–20

tape [tāp]
    clear tape [klēr/ tāp/] **183**–30
    correction tape [kə rĕk/shən tāp/] **183**–37
    duct tape [dŭkt/ tāp/] **181**–49
    electrical tape [ĭ lek/trĭ kəl tāp/] **181**–43
    masking tape [măs/kĭng tāp/] **181**–53
    packing tape [păk/ĭng tāp/] **183**–32
    sterile tape [stĕr/ əl tāp/] **117**–7
    tape measure [tāp mĕzh/ər] **100**–17, **181**–45

target [tär/gət] **231**–7
taste [tāst] **106**–D
tattoo [tă tōō/] **32**–18
tax / taxes [tăks] / [tăks/əz] **27**–8
taxi [tăk/sē] **150**–3
   hail a taxi [hāl/ ə tăk/sē] **152** ✦
   taxi driver [tăk/sē drī/vər] **152**–21
   taxi license [tăk/sē lī/səns] **152**–22
   taxi stand [tăk/sē stănd/] **152**–18
TB (tuberculosis) [tē/bē/] / [tŏō bür/kyə lō/səs] **111**–15
TDD [tē/dē/dē/] **15**–26
tea [tē] **79**–12, **81**–39, **81**–40
   teacup [tē/kŭp] **55**–6
   tea kettle [tē/ kĕt/l] **54**–21
   teapot [tē/pät/] **55**–16
   teaspoon [tē/spōōn/] **75**–6, **83**–31
teach [tēch] **170**–Q
teacher [tē/chər] **5**–8, **6**–4, **22**–5
   teacher's aide [tē/chərz ād/] **5**–16
team [tēm] **145**–20, **229**–3
TEAM SPORTS [tēm/ spörts/] **229**
technical school [tĕk/nĭ kəl skōōl/] **188**–5
technician [tĕk nĭsh/ən]
   computer technician
     [kəm pyōō/tər tĕk nĭsh/ən] **167**–19, **182**–12
   emergency medical technician (EMT)
     [ĭ mür/jən sē mĕd/ĭ kəl tĕk nish/ən] / [ē/ĕm/tē]
     121–32
   medical records technician
     [mĕd/ĭ kəl rĕk/ərdz tĕk nish/ən] **168**–39
Technician [tĕk nĭsh/ən] **93**
teddy bear [tĕd/ē bër/] **37**–23
teen / teenager [tēn] / [tē/nā/jər] **31**–11
teething ring [tē/dhĭng rĭng/] **37**–25
teeth / tooth [tēth] / [tōōth] **106**–7
   toothache [tōōth/āk/] **110**–2
   toothbrush [tōōth/brŭsh/] **57**–21, **109**–22
   toothbrush holder [tōōth/brŭsh/ hōl/dər] **57**–22
   toothpaste [tōōth/pāst/] **109**–23
telemarketer [tĕl/ə mär/kə tər] **169**–60
TELEPHONE [tĕl/ə fōn/] **14**–15
Telephone Skills [tĕl/ə fōn/ skĭlz/] **171**
telescope [tĕl/ə skōp/] **205**–23
television / TV [tĕl/ə vĭzh/ən] / [tē/vē/] **56**–6
   big-screen TV [bĭg/skrēn/ tē/vē/] **50**–14
   flat panel TV [flăt/ păn/əl tē/vē/] **234**–7
   flat screen TV [flăt/ skrēn/ tē/vē/] **234**–7
   portable TV [pör/tə bəl tē/vē/] **234**–8
teller [tĕl/ər] **132**–1
Teller [tĕl/ər] **132**
Telling Time [tĕl/ĭng tīm/] **18**
temperature [tĕm/prə chər] **110**–8
   temperature gauge [tĕm/prə chər gāj/] **159**–30
Temperature [tĕm/prə chər] **13**
ten [tĕn] **16**
   ten after one [tĕn/ ăf/tər wŭn/] **18**–8
   ten dollars [tĕn/ däl/ərz] **26**–9
   10 percent [tĕn/ pər sĕnt/] **17**–12
   ten thousand [tĕn/ thow/zənd] **16**
   10-year-old girl [tĕn/yïr öld/ gürl/] **31**–10
tenant [tĕn/ənt] **50**–6
TENANT MEETING [tĕn/ənt mē/tĭng] **64**–65

tennis [tĕn/əs] **228**–15
   table tennis [tā/bəl tĕn/əs] **228**–14
   tennis court [tĕn/əs kört/] **224**–6
   tennis racket [tĕn/əs răk/ət] **231**–2
   tennis shoes [tĕn/əs shōōz/] **95**–32
tent [tĕnt] **226**–10
tenth [tĕnth] **16**
Terminal [tür/mə nəl] **160**
termites [tür/mīts] **63**–22
term [türm] **139** ✦
Terms [türmz] **199**
terrified [tĕr/ə fīd/] **43** ✦
test [tĕst] **121**–30
   test booklet [tĕst/ bŏŏk/lət] **10**–1
   testing area [tĕs/tĭng ër/ē ə] **136**–2
   test tube [tĕst/ tōōb/] **195**–42
Test [tĕst] **10**
text [tĕkst]
   textbook [tĕkst/bŏŏk/, tĕks/-] **7**–25
   text box [tĕkst/ bäks/, tĕks/-] **197**–13
   text message [tĕkst/ mĕs/ĭj, tĕks/-] **14**–19
thank [thăngk] **12**–E, **174**–N
Thanksgiving [thăngks gĭv/ĭng] **22**–17
theater [thē/ə tər] **126**–6, **127**–23
theft [thĕft] **142**–9
therapist [thĕr/ ə pĭst] **115**–12, **115**–14, **168**–45
therapy [thĕr/ ə pē] **115**–11, **115**–13
thermal undershirt [thür/məl ŭn/dər shürt/] **91**–2
thermometer [thər mäm/ə tər] **118**–11
thick [thĭk] **23**–7
thighs [thīz] **70**–22, **106**–19
thimble [thĭm/bəl] **100**–15
thin [thĭn] **23**–8, **32**–9
THINGS [thĭngz] **23**
think [thĭnk] **191**–E
third [thürd] **16**
Third Floor [thürd/ flör/] **50**
thirsty [thür/stē] **42**–2
thirteen [thür/tēn/] **16**
   thirteen colonies [thür/tēn/ kä/lə nēz] **198**–1
thirteenth [thür/tēnth/] **16**
thirtieth [thür/tē əth] **16**
thirty [thür/tē] **16**
   35 mm camera
     [thür/tē fĭv/ mĭl/ə mē/tər kăm/rə] **235**–21
this week [dhĭs/ wēk/] **20**–19
thorn [thörn] **211**–29
thread [thrĕd] **99**–23, **100**–11
three [thrē] **16**
   three piece suit [thrē/pēs/ sōōt/] **88** ✦
   3-ring binder [thrē/ rĭng/ bīn/dər] **7**–27
   3/4 sleeved [thrē/kwör/tər slēv/] **96**–13
   three times a week [thrē/ tīmz/ ə wēk/] **20**–24
throat [thrōt] **107**–35, **110**–6, **111**–4
   throat lozenges [thrōt/ läz/ən jəz] **113**–30
through [thrōō] **153**–K
throw [thrō] **230**–C
   throw away [thrō/ ə wā/] **11**–N
   throw up [thrō/ ŭp/] **110**–E
throw pillow [thrō/ pĭl/ō] **56**–2
thumb [thŭm] **106**–16
thunderstorm [thŭn/dər störm/] **13**–16

Thursday [thürz/dā, –dē] **20**–12
tick [tĭk] **214**–27
ticket [tĭk/ət] **152**–15, **161**–19
   ticket agent [tĭk/ət ā/jənt] **160**–3
   ticket window [tĭk/ət wĭn/dō] **152**–12
tidal wave [tīd/l wāv/] **145**–17
tide [tīd] **225** ✦
tie [tī] **88**–12, **89**–16, **92**–13, **229** ✦
tie [tī] **86**–A
tiger [tī/gər] **217**–37
tight [tīt] **97**–29
tights [tīts] **91**–19
tile [tīl] **57**–10, **178**–11, **178**–D
time [tīm]
   Alaska time [ə lăs/kə tīm/] **19**–28
   arrival time [ə rī/vəl tīm/] **161** ✦
   Atlantic time [ət lăn/tĭk tīm/] **19**–33
   Central time [sĕn/trəl tīm/] **19**–31
   daylight saving time [dā/līt/ sā/vĭng tīm/] **19**–25
   departure time [dĭ pär/chər tīm/] **161** ✦
   Eastern time [ē/stərn tīm/] **19**–32
   Hawaii-Aleutian time
     [hə wī/ē ə lōō/shən tīm/] **19**–27
   Mountain time [mown/tn tīm/] **19**–30
   Newfoundland time
     [nōō/fən lənd tīm/, –fənd–] **19**–34
   on time [än/ tīm/, ön/ tīm/] **19**–23, **161**–29
   Pacific time [pə sĭf/ĭk tīm/] **19**–29
   standard time [stăn/dərd tīm/] **19**–26
   three times a week [thrē tīmz/ ə wēk/] **20**–24
   time clock [tīm/ kläk/] **165**–7
Time [tīm] **18**
TIME [tīm] **18**–19
timer [tī/mər] **78**–18
Times of Day [tīmz/ əv dā/] **18**
Time Zones [tīm/ zōnz/] **19**
tire [tīr] **158**–5, **158**–23, **162**–F
tired [tīrd] **43**–32
title [tīt/l] **133**–14, **190**–5
toad [tōd] **212**–28
toast [tōst] **80**–4
toaster [tō/stər] **54**–6
   toaster oven [tō/stər ŭv/ən] **54**–15
today [tə dā/] **20**–5
toddler [täd/lər] **31**–8
toe [tō] **92**–6, **94**–23, **105**–10
   toenail [tō/nāl/] **106** ✦
Tofu [tō/fōō/] **77**
toggle bolt [täg/əl bōlt/] **180**–38
to-go box [tə gō/ bäks/] **82**–5
toilet [toy/lət] **57**–19
   toilet brush [toy/lət brŭsh/] **57**–18
   toilet paper [toy/lət pā/pər] **57**–17, **146**–13
token [tō/kən] **152**–10
tomatoes [tə mā/tōz] **69**–6
tomorrow [tə mär/ō, –mör/ō] **20**–6
tongs [tängz, töngz] **78**–23, **195**–44
tongue [tŭng] **106**–8
too [tōō]
   too big [tōō/ bĭg/] **97**–38
   too expensive [tōō/ ĭk spĕn/sĭv/] **97**–44
   too small [tōō/ smöl/] **97**–37

tool belt [tool/ bĕlt/] **92**–3
TOOLS AND BUILDING SUPPLIES
[toolz/ ən bĭl/dĭng sə plīz/] **180–181**
tooth / teeth [tooth] / [tēth] **106**–7
toothache [tooth/āk/] **110**–2
toothbrush [tooth/brŭsh/] **57**–21, **109**–22
toothbrush holder [tooth/brŭsh/ hōl/dər] **57**–22
toothpaste [tooth/pāst/] **109**–23
top [tăp] **88**–7, **89**–24
torn [törn] **97**–41
tornado [tör nā/dō] **145**–15
torso [tör/sō/] **106** ✦
tortoise [tör/təs] **213**–42
total [tōt/l] **27**–9
totebag [tōt/ băg/] **94**–19
touch [tŭch] **106**–E
towel [tow/əl]
bath towel [băth/ tow/əl] **57**–14
dish towel [dĭsh/ tow/əl] **61**–22
hand towel [hănd/ tow/əl] **57**–15
paper towels [pā/pər tow/əlz] **54**–3
towel rack [tow/əl răk/] **57**–13
towelettes [tow/əl ĕts/] **146**–12
tower [tow/ər] **196**–3
town [town] **52**–3
town car [town/ kär/] **152**–20
townhouse [town/hows/] **52**–6
tow truck [tō/ trŭk/] **156**–14
toy [toy]
toy chest [toy/ chĕst/] **59**–16
toy store [toy/ stör/] **130**–5
Toys and Games [toyz/ ən gāmz/] **59**
track [trăk] **5**–21, **152**–14
track and field [trăk/ ən fēld/] **228**–18
tractor [trăk/tər] **177**–9
tractor trailer [trăk/tər trā/lər] **156**–15
traffic light [trăf/ĭk līt/] **128**–8
TRAFFIC SIGNS [trăf/ĭk sīnz/] **154**
tragedy [trăj/ə dē] **237**–14
trailer [trā/lər] **156**–15, **156**–17
train [trān] **150**–7, **233**–27
training [trā/nĭng] **172**–2, **172**–5, **172**–7
training pants [trā/nĭng pănts/] **37**–11
Training [trā/nĭng] **172**
Train Station [trān/ stā/shən] **152**
transcribe [trăn skrīb/] **171**–C
transfer [trăns für/, trăns/fər] **152**–5
transfer [trăns für/, trăns/fər] **171**–O
translate [trănz/lāt] **8**–C
translator [trănz/lā/tər, trăns/–] **168**–35
Transmission [trănz mĭsh/ən, trăns–] **159**
Transportation [trăns/pər tā/shən] **152**
TRANSPORTATION [trăns/pər tā/shən] **150–151, 152**
trash [trăsh]
trash bags [trăsh/ băgz/] **61**–24
trash bin [trăsh/ bĭn/] **51**–23
trash chute [trăsh/ shoot/] **51**–26
travel [trăv/əl] **41**–P
travel agency [trăv/əl ā/jən sē] **131**–14
tray [trā] **55**–17, **83**–10
tray table [trā tā/bəl] **161**–21
Tree [trē] **210**

trees [trēz] **208**–1, **239**–16
TREES AND PLANTS [trēz/ ən plănts/] **210**
trench coat [trĕnch/ kōt/] **90**–21
trial [trī/əl] **140**–5
triangle [trī/ăng/gəl] **193**–32
tricycle [trī/sĭ kəl] **224**–12
trigonometry [trĭg/ə näm/ə trē] **192**–18
trim [trĭm] **176**–B
trip [trĭp] **152**–16, **152**–17
tripe [trīp] **70**–8
tripod [trī/päd] **235**–25
trombone [träm bōn/] **238**–10
trout [trowt] **71**–1
trowel [trow/əl] **176**–10, **178**–13
truck [trŭk] **150**–5
dump truck [dŭmp/trŭk/] **156**–19
fire truck [fīr/ trŭk/] **144**–10
garbage truck [gär/bĭj trŭk/] **127**–22
hand truck [hănd/ trŭk/] **175**–11
pickup truck [pĭk/ŭp trŭk/] **156**–12
tank truck [tăngk/ trŭk/] **156**–20
tow truck [tō/ trŭk/] **156**–14
truck driver [trŭk/ drī/vər] **169**–61
TRUCKS [trŭks] **156**
trumpet [trŭm/pət] **238**–11
Trunk [trŭngk] **158**
trunks [trŭngks] **158**–11, **210**–4, **217**–47
swimming trunks [swĭm/ĭng trŭngks/] **90**–22
try on [trī/ön] **95**–C
TSA agent [tē/ĕs/ā/ ā/jənt] **160**–5
T-shirt [tē/shürt/] **86**–4
tsunami [soo nä/ mē/, tsoo–] **145**–17
tub [tŭb]
bathtub [băth/tŭb/] **57**–2
tuba [too/bə] **238**–12
tube [toob] **74**–12, **74**–24, **195**–42
tuberculosis (TB)
[too bür/kyə lō/səs] / [tē/bē/] **111**–15
Tuesday [tooz/dā, –dē] **20**–10
tulip [too/ləp] **211**–11
tuna [too/nə] **71**–7, **72**–19, **212**–8
tuner [too/nər] **234**–13
turbulence [tür/byə ləns] **161**–22
turkey [tür/kē] **70**–17, **239**–14
roasted turkey [rōs/təd tür/kē] **76**–4
smoked turkey [smōkt/ tür/kē] **71**–25
turn [türn] **154**–5, **154**–7, **154**–8
turn signal [türn/ sĭg/nəl] **158**–6, **159**–34
turnstile [türn/stīl/] **152**–8
turntable [türn/tā/bəl] **234**–12
turn [türn]
turn in [türn/ ĭn/] **191**–M
turn left [türn/ lĕft/] **155**–C
turn off [türn/ öf/] **11**–P, **160**–I, **174**–G, **219**–G
turn on [türn/ ön/, –än/] **11**–B
turn right [türn/ rīt/] **155**–B
turnips [tür/nəps] **69**–16
turquoise [tür/koyz, –kwoyz] **24**–9
turtle [tür/tl] **213**–43
turtleneck [tür/tl nĕk/] **96**–9
tusk [tŭsk] **217**–48
tuxedo [tŭk sē/dō] **89**–17

TV Programs [tē/vē/ prō/grămz] **236**
TV / television [tē/vē/] / [tĕl/ə vĭzh/ən] **56**–6
big-screen TV [bĭg/skrēn/ tē/vē/] **50**–14
flat panel TV [flăt/ păn/əl tē/vē/] **234**–7
flat screen TV [flăt/ skrēn/ tē/ vē/] **234**–7
portable TV [por/tə bəl tē/vē/] **234**–8
tweezers [twē/zərz] **117**–4
twelfth [twĕlfth] **16**
twelve [twĕlv] **16**
twentieth [twĕn/tē əth] **16**
twenty [twĕn/tē] **16**
twenty after one [twĕn/tē ăf/tər wŭn/] **18**–10
twenty dollars [twĕn/tē däl/ərz] **26**–10
twenty-first [twĕn/tē fürst/] **16**
twenty-five [twĕn/tē fīv/] **16**
25 percent [twĕn/fīv/ pər sĕnt/] **17**–11
twenty-four [twĕn/tē för] **16**
twenty-one [twĕn/tē wŭn/] **16**
twenty-three [twĕn/tē thrē/] **16**
twenty to two [twĕn/tē tə too/] **18**–12
twenty-two [twĕn/tē too/] **16**
twice a week [twīs/ ə wēk/] **20**–23
twig [twĭg] **210**–1
twins [twĭnz] **28**–1
two [too] **16**
2-door car [too/dör kär/] **156**–2
two-story house [too/stör/ē hows/] **52** ✦
two-way radio [too/wā rā/dē ō] **179**–22
2 x 4 (two by four) [too/ bī/ för/] **181**–19
type [tīp] **170**–R, **196**–A
type a letter [tīp/ə lĕt/ər] **171**–A
type the message [tīp/ dhə mĕs/ĭj] **197**–E
type the subject [tīp/ dhə sŭb/jĭkt] **197**–D
type your password [tīp/ yər păs/würd/] **197**–A
Types of Health Problems
[tīps/ əv hĕlth/ präb/ləmz] **115**
Types of Job Training [tīps/ əv jäb/ trā/nĭng] **172**
Types of Material [tīps/ əv mə tïr/ē əl] **99**
Types of Math [tīps/ əv măth/] **192**
Types of Medication [tīps/ əv mĕd/ə kā/shən] **113**
Types of Movies [tīps/ əv moo/vēz] **237**
Types of Music [tīps/ əv myoo/zĭk] **237**
Types of TV Programs [tīps/ əv tē/vē/ prō/grămz] **236**
ugly [ŭg/lē] **23**–22
umbrella [ŭm brĕl/ə] **90**–17, **225**–14
umpire [ŭm/pīr] **229** ✦
uncle [ŭng/kəl] **34**–8
uncomfortable [ŭn kŭmf/tə bəl, –tər–] **42**–9
unconscious [ŭn/kän/shəs] **116**–A
under [ŭn/dər] **25**–10, **153**–A
long underwear [löng/ ŭn/dər wër] **91**–3
thermal undershirt [thür/məl ŭn/dər shürt] **91**–2
underexposed [ŭn/dər ĭk spōzd/] **235**–35
underpants [ŭn/dər pănts/] **91**–14
undershirt [ŭn/dər shürt/] **91**–1
underline [ŭn/dər lĭn/] **9**–S
Under the Hood [ŭn/dər dhə hood/] **158**
Underwear [ŭn/dər wër/] **91**
UNDERWEAR AND SLEEPWEAR
[ŭn/dər wër/ ən slēp/wër/] **91**
undress [ən drĕs/] **36**–E

unfurnished apartment
[ŭn/fŭr nĭsht ə pärt/ mənt] **48**–4
uniform [yōō/nə förm/] **88**–10, **231**–16
Unisex Socks [yōō/nə sĕks/ säks/] **91**
Unisex Underwear [yōō/nə sĕks/ ŭn/dər wër] **91**
universal remote [yōō/nə vür/səl rĭ mōt/] **234**–9
UNIVERSE [yōō/nə vürs/] **205**
university [yōō/nə vür/sə tē] **188**–7
unload [ŭn lōd/] **101**–E
unpack [ŭn păk/] **49**–N
unraveling [ŭn răv/əl ĭng] **97**–43
unripe [ŭn rīp/] **68**–31
unscented [ŭn sĕn/təd] **108** ✦
unscramble [ŭn skrăm/bəl] **9**–W
up [ŭp]
  buckle up [bŭk/əl ŭp/] **36**–L
  clean up [klēn/ ŭp/] **147**–M
  cut up [kŭt/ ŭp/] **77**–I
  eggs sunny-side up [ĕgz/ sŭn/ē sīd/ ŭp/] **76**–10
  get up [gĕt/ ŭp/] **38**–B
  hang up [hăng/ ŭp/] **15**–D, **101**–H
  look up [lōōk/ ŭp/] **8**–A
  pick up [pĭk/ ŭp/] **6**–I, **11**–E, **38**–M
  pop-up ad [păp/ ŭp ăd/] **197**–9
  set up [sĕt/ ŭp/] **173**–I
  stand up [stănd/ ŭp/] **6**–D
  stopped up [stäpt/ ŭp/] **63**–19
  throw up [thrō/ ŭp/] **110**–E
  wake up [wāk/ ŭp/] **38**–A
  walk up [wök/ ŭp/] **153**–C
upright seat [ŭp/rīt/ sēt/] **161**–28
upset [ŭp sĕt/] **43**–28
upstairs [ŭp/stërz/] **51** ✦
Uranus [yŏŏr/ə nəs, yŏŏ rā/nəs] **205**–7
urban area [ür/bən ër/ē ə] **52**–1
urchin [ür/chən] **212**–21
URL [yōō/är/ĕl/] **197**–4
U.S. [yōō/ĕs/]
  U.S. Capitol [yōō/ĕs/ kă/pət əl] **138**–1
  U.S. route [yōō/ĕs/ rōōt/, –rowt/] **154**–17
USB port [yōō/ĕs/ bē/ pört/] **196**–7
use [yōōz]
  use a cash register [yōōz/ə kăsh/ rĕj/ə stər] **170**–S
  use a credit card [yōōz/ə krĕ/dət kärd/] **27**–B
  use a debit card [yōōz/ə dĕ/bət kärd/] **27**–C
  use a gift card [yōōz/ ə gĭft/ kärd/] **27**–E
  use deodorant [yōōz/dē ō/dər ənt] **108**–C
  use energy-efficient bulbs
    [yōōz/ ĕn/ər jē ĭ fĭ/shənt bŭlbz] **219**–H
  use punctuation [yōōz/ pŭngk/chōō ā/shən] **190**–C
Used Car [yōōzd/ kär/] **157**
used clothing [yōōzd/ klō/dhĭng] **102**–2
U.S. HISTORY [yōō/ĕs/ hĭs/tə rē] **198**
U.S. NATIONAL PARKS
  [yōō/ĕs năsh/ə nəl pärks/] **220**–**221**
utensils [yōō tĕn/səlz] **79**–19
utility / utilities [yōō tĭl/ə tē] / [yōō tĭl/ə tēz]
  48–5, **156**–7
U-turn [yōō/türn/] **154**–5
vacancy sign [vā/kən sē sīn/] **50**–7
vacation [vā kā/shən] **22**–6
vaccination [văk/sə nā/shən] **114** ✦

vacuum [văk/yōōm]
  vacuum cleaner [văk/yōōm klē/nər] **61**–10
  vacuum cleaner attachments
    [văk/yōōm klē/nər ə tăch/mənts] **61**–11
  vacuum cleaner bag
    [văk/yōōm klē/nər băg/] **61**–12
  vacuum [văk/yōōm] **60**–H
valley [văl/ē] **204**–17
valuables [văl/yə bəlz, –yə wə–] **132**–8
valve [vălv] **146**–4
van [văn] **156**–13, **156**–18
vandalism [văn/də lĭz/əm] **142**–1
vanity plate [vă/nə tē plāt/] **136** ✦
variable [vër/ē ə bəl] **192**–12
vase [vās, văz, väz] **55**–23
vault [völt] **132**–6
VCR [vē/sē/är/] **102**–7
veal cutlets [vēl/ kŭt/ləts] **70**–6
Vegetable [vĕj/tə bəl] **77**
vegetables [vĕj/tə bəlz] **66**–8, **72**–27, **81**–32
  vegetable garden [vĕj/tə bəl gär/dn] **53**–27, **177**–14
  vegetable peeler [vĕj/tə bəl pē/lər] **78**–15
VEGETABLES [vĕj/tə bəlz] **69**
vegetarian [vĕj/ə tër/ē ən] **70** ✦
vehicles [vē/ĭ kəlz] **124**–4, **156**–7, **156**–10
vein [vān] **107**–37
velvet [vĕl/vət] **99**–10
vending machine [vĕn/dĭng mə shēn/] **152**–9
vendors [vĕn/dərz] **84**–7, **129**–29
ventilation mask [vĕnt/əl ā/shən măsk/] **92**–7
Venus [vē/nəs] **205**–2
verdict [vür/dĭkt] **141**–14
vertebrates [vür/ tə brəts] **194**–13
vest [vĕst] **89**–15
  down vest [down/ vĕst] **90**–14
  Hi-Visibility safety vest
    [hī/vĭz/ə bĭl/ə tē sāf/tē vĕst] **92**–6
  life vest [līf/ vĕst/] **161**–25, **226**–14
Veterans Day [vĕt/ər ənz dā/] **22**–16
veterinarian [vĕt/ə ə nër/ē ən] **169**–62
vice president [vīs/ prĕz/ə dənt] **138**–9
victim [vĭk/təm] **142**–10
video [vĭd/ē ō]
  videocassette [vĭd/ē ō kə sĕt/] **133**–18
  video game console [vĭd/ē ō gām/ kän/sōl/] **232**–3
  video game control [vĭd/ē ō gām/ kän trōl/] **232**–4
  video player [vĭd/ē ō plā ər] **197**–11
  video store [vĭd/ē ō stör/] **129**–20
videotape [vĭd/ē ō tāp/] **240**–A
view [vyōō]
  rearview mirror [rïr/vyōō/ mïr/ər] **159**–35
  sideview mirror [sīd/vyōō/ mïr/ər] **158**–3
village [vĭ/lĭj] **52**–3
vine [vīn] **210**–22
vineyard [vĭn/yərd] **177**–16
violence [vī/ləns, vī/ə–] **142**–4
violet [vī/ə lət, vī/lət] **24**–8, **211**–23
violin [vī/ə lĭn/] **238**–6
virus [vī/rəs] **111**–17
vise [vīs] **180**–26
vision [vĭ/zhən]
  vision exam [vĭ/zhən ĭg zăm/] **136**–6
  vision problems [vĭ/zhən präb/ləmz] **115**–1

Visit [vĭ/zət] **119**
visor [vī zər] **179**–12
vital signs monitor [vīt/l sīnz/ män/ə tər] **121**–26
vitamins [vī/tə mənz] **113**–17
v-neck [vē/nĕk/] **96**–8
vocational [vō kā/shə nəl]
  vocational school [vō kā/shə nəl skōōl/] **188**–5
  vocational training [vō kā/shə nəl trā/nĭng] **172**–5
voice message [voys mĕs/ĭj] **14**–18
volcanic eruption [väl kăn/ĭk ĭ rŭp/shən] **145**–16
volleyball [väl/ē böl/] **229**–14, **231**–3
Volume [väl/yəm, –yōōm] **75**, **193**
volunteer [väl/ən tïr/] **121**–17
volunteer [väl/ən tïr/] **41**–Q
vomit [väm/ət] **110**–E
vote [vōt] **140**–A
waffles [wä/fəlz, wö/–] **80**–8
wages [wā/jĭz] **165**–12
wagon [wä/gən] **156**–6
waist [wāst]
  waist apron [wāst/ ā/prən] **93**–30
  waistband [wāst/bănd/] **100**–5
wait [wāt] **94**–B, **128**–B, **170**–T
waiter [wā/tər] **82**–8
  headwaiter [hĕd/wā/tər] **185**–12
waiting area [wā/tĭng ër/ē ə] **182**–16
Waiting Room [wā/tĭng rōōm/] **118**
waitress [wā/trəs] **83**–9
wait staff [wāt/ stăf/] **185** ✦
wake up [wāk/ ŭp/] **38**–A
walk [wök] **53**–2
  crosswalk [krös/wök/] **128**–15
  walk-in freezer [wök/ĭn frē/zər] **185**–3
walk [wök]
  walk a dog [wök ə dög/] **129**–F
  walk down [wök/ down/] **153**–D
  walk to class [wök/ tə kläs/] **11**–C
  walk up [wök/ ŭp/] **153**–C
  walk with a friend [wök/ wïth ə frĕnd/] **143**–A
walker [wö/kər] **113**–11
wall [wöl] **56**–10, **194**–5
  drywall [drī/wöl/] **178**–19
  wallpaper [wöl/pā/pər] **59**–8
wallet [wä/lət, wö/–] **94**–13
walrus [wöl/rəs] **213**–32
war [wör] **199**–10
  Revolutionary War [rĕ/və lōō/shə nër/ē wör/] **198**–8
warehouse [wër/hows/] **175**–7
warm [wörm] **13**–4
  warm clothes [wörm/ klōz/] **146**–6
warning label [wör/nĭng lā/bəl] **112**–8
Warnings [wör/nĭngz] **112**
wash [wäsh, wösh]
  mouthwash [mowth/wäsh/, –wösh/–] **109**–25
  washcloth [wäsh/klöth/, wösh/–] **57**–4
wash [wäsh, wösh]
  wash clothes [wäsh/ klöz/, wösh/–] **219**–K
  wash hair [wäsh/ här/, wösh/–] **108**–E
  wash the dishes [wäsh/ dhə dĭsh/əz, wösh/–] **60**–M
  wash the windows
    [wäsh/ dhə wĭn/dōz, wösh/–] **60**–I
washer [wä/shər, wö/–] **50**–12, **101**–3, **180**–37
  dishwasher [dĭsh/wäsh/ər, –wö–] **54**–8, **185**–2

washing [wä/shǐng, wö/–] **61**–21
wasp [wäsp, wösp] **214**–17
waste [wäst] **121**–31, **218**–12
    wastebasket [wäst/bǎs/kət] **57**–26
watch [wäch, wöch] **94**–16
watch [wäch, wöch] **39**–X, **147**–C
water [wö/tər] **209**–3, **225**–1
    body of water [bäd/ē əv wö/tər] **204** ✦
    bottled water [bät/ld wö/tər] **146**–11
    cold water [kōld/ wö/tər] **57**–7
    hot water [hät/ wö/tər] **57**–8
    hot water bottle [hät/ wö/tər böt/l] **113**–15
    watercolor [wö/tər kül/ər] **233**–21
    waterfall [wä/tər föl/] **204**–2
    water fountain [wö/tər fown/tn] **224**–9
    water glass [wö/tər glǎs/] **83**–22
    watermelons [wö/tər měl/ənz] **68**–18
    water pollution [wö/tər pə lōō/shən] **218**–14
    water polo [wö/tər pō/lō] **229**–15
    waterskiing [wö/tər skē/ǐng] **227**–7
water [wö/tər] **176**–F
WATER SPORTS [wö/tər spörts/] **227**
wave [wāv] **145**–17, **225**–17
wave [wāv] **2**–F
wavy hair [wā/vē hër/] **33**–10
way [wā]
    hallway [häl/wā/] **184**–18
    one way [wŭn/ wā/] **154**–3
    one-way trip [wŭn/wā/ trǐp/] **152**–16
    two-way radio [tōō/wā/ rā/dē ō] **179**–22
    wrong way [röng/ wā/] **154**–2
Ways to Conserve Energy and Resources
    [wāz/ tə kən sürv/ ěn/ər jē n rē/sör/səz,
    –rī sör/səz] **219**
Ways to Get Well [wāz/ tə gět/ wěl/] **114**
Ways to Pay [wāz/ tə pā/] **27**
Ways to Serve Eggs [wāz/ tə sürv/ ěgz/] **76**
Ways to Serve Meat and Poultry
    [wāz/ tə sürv/ mēt/ n pōl/trē] **76**
Ways to Stay Well [wāz/ tə stā/ wěl/] **114**
Ways to Succeed [wāz/tə sək sēd/] **10**
weak signal [wēk/ sǐg/nəl] **14**–12
WEATHER [wědh/ər] **13**
Weather Conditions [wědh/ər kən dǐsh/ənz] **13**
Weather Map [wědh/ər mǎp/] **13**
webcam [wěb/kǎm/] **196**–12
Webpage [wěb/pāg/] **197**
website address [wěb/sīt ə drěs/] **197**–4
wedding [wě/dǐng] **22**–2
Wednesday [wěnz/dā, –dē] **20**–11
weed [wēd]
    seaweed [sē/ wēd/] **225** ✦
    weed eater [wēd/ ē/tər] **176**–12
    weed whacker [wēd/ wǎk/ər] **176**–12
weed [wēd] **176**–G
week [wēk] **20**–15
    last week [lǎst/ wēk/] **20**–18
    next week [někst/ wēk/] **20**–20
    once a week [wŭns/ ə wēk/] **20**–22
    this week [dhǐs/ wēk/] **20**–19
    three times a week [thrē/ tīmz/ ə wēk/] **20**–24
    twice a week [twīs/ ə wēk/] **20**–23

weekdays [wēk/dāz/] **20**–16
weekend [wēk/ěnd/] **20**–17
Week [wēk] **20**
weigh [wā] **75**–B
weight [wāt] **32**–8
Weight [wāt] **32, 75**
weightlifting [wāt/lǐf/tǐng] **228**–16
weights [wāts] **231**–22
WEIGHTS AND MEASUREMENTS
    [wāts/ ən mězh/ər mənts] **75**
welder [wěl/dər] **169**–63
well [wěl] **42**–14
Well [wěl] **114**
west [wěst] **155**–2
western [wěs/tərn] **237**–15
wet [wět] **101**–17
    wet suit [wět/ sōōt/] **225**–4
whacker [wǎk/ər] **176**–12
whale [wāl] **213**–29
wheat [wēt] **177**–2
wheat bread [wēt/ brěd/] **71**–19
wheel [wēl] **159**–26
    wheelbarrow [wēl/bǎr/ō] **176**–3
    wheelchair [wēl/chër/] **113**–9
    wheel cover [wēl/ kŭv/ər] **158**–9
whisk [wǐsk] **78**–21
whiskers [wǐs/kərz] **216**–18
white [wīt] **24**–14
    whiteboard [wīt/börd/] **6**–3
    white bread [wīt/ brěd/] **71**–18
    White House [wīt/ hows/] **138**–7
whole salmon [hōl/ sǎm/ən] **71**–3
wide [wīd] **97**–36
widow [wǐd/ō] **41** ✦
widower [wǐd/ō ər] **41** ✦
width [wǐdth, wǐtth] **17**–19
wife [wīf] **34**–12
    ex-wife [ěks/ wīf/] **35** ✦
    former wife [för/mər wīf/] **35** ✦
wild [wīld] **215** ✦
wildlife [wīld/līf/] **220**–3
willow [wǐl/ō] **210**–13
win [wǐn] **229** ✦
wind [wǐnd]
    windbreaker [wǐnd/brā/kər] **90**–24
    wind power [wǐnd/ pow/ər] **218**–2
    windshield [wǐnd/ shēld/] **158**–1
    windshield wipers [wǐnd/shēld/wǐ/pərz] **158**–2
    windsurfing [wǐnd/sür/fǐng] **227**–10, **227** ✦
window [wǐn/dō] **47**–11, **56**–17, **136**–7
    drive-thru window [drǐv/thrōō/ wǐn/dō] **128**–11
    ticket window [tǐk/ət wǐn/dō] **152**–12
    window pane [wǐn/dō pān/] **178**–16
windy [wǐn/dē] **13**–18
wine glass [wīn/ glǎs/] **83**–23
wing [wǐng] **70**–20, **214**–1
winter [wǐn/tər] **21**–40
    winter scarf [wǐn/tər/skärf/] **90**–5
WINTER AND WATER SPORTS
    [wǐn/tər ən wö/tər spörts/] **227**
wipe [wīp] **60**–O
wipers [wī/pərz] **158**–2

wipes [wīps] **37**–15, **61**–23
wire [wīr] **181**–13
    wire stripper [wīr/ strǐp/ər] **181**–42
wireless headset [wīr/ləs hěd/sět] **14**–14
wiring [wīr/ǐng] **186**–7
withdraw [wǐdh drö/, wǐth–] **132**–F
witness [wǐt/nəs] **141**–11
wolf [wōōlf] **216**–5
woman [wōōm/ən] **30**–2
women [wǐ/mən] **30**–3
Women's Socks [wǐ/mənz säks/] **91**
Women's Underwear [wǐ/mənz ŭn/dər wër/] **91**
wood [wōōd] **178**–18
    plywood [plī/wōōd] **178**–17
    redwood [rěd/wōōd] **210**–18
    wood floor [wōōd/ flör/] **58**–21
    woodpecker [wōōd/pěk/ər] **214**–8
    wood screw [wōōd/ skrōō/] **180**–33
    wood stain [wōōd/ stān/] **181**–24
    woodworking kit [wōōd/wür/kǐng kǐt/] **232**–14
wooden spoon [wōōd/n spōōn/] **78**–9
Woodwinds [wōōd/wǐndz/] **238**
wool [wōōl] **61**–5, **98**–3
word [würd] **190**–1
word problem [würd/ prä/bləm] **192**–11
Words [würdz] **8**
work [würk/] **121**–30, **154**–16
    workbook [würk/bōōk/] **7**–26
    work gloves [würk/ glŭvz/] **92**–17, **179**–17
    work light [würk/ lǐt/] **181**–44
    work pants [würk/ pǎnts/] **92**–5
    work shirt [würk/ shürt/] **92**–2
work [würk] **8**–I, **10**–J, **38**–K
WORK [würk] **186**–187
Work Clothes [würk/ klōz/] **88**
worker [wür/kər]
    careful worker [kër/fəl wür/kər] **179**–2
    careless worker [kër/ləs wür/kər] **179**–1
    childcare worker [chǐld/kër wür/kər] **166**–16
    construction worker
        [kən strŭk/shən wür/kər] **178**–1
    dockworker [däk/wür/kər] **167**–23
    factory worker [fǎk/tə rē wür/kər, –trē] **175**–3
    farmworker [färm/wür/kər] **177**–8
    food preparation worker
        [fōōd/ prěp ə rā/shən wür/kər] **185**–4
    garment worker [gär/mənt wür/kər] **167**–29
    postal worker [pō/stəl wür/kər] **169**–49
    sanitation worker [săn/ə tā/shən wür/kər] **169**–54
    social worker [sō/shəl wür/kər] **169**–57
Worker [wür/kər] **92, 93**
working [wür/kǐng]
    not working [nät/ wür/kǐng] **62**–1
    woodworking kit [wōōd/wür/kǐng kǐt/] **232**–14
Working with a Partner [wür/kǐng wǐth ə pärt/nər] **8**
Working with Your Classmates
    [wür/kǐng wǐth yər klǎs/māts/] **8**
work out [würk/ owt/] **230**–N
WORKPLACE [würk/ plǎs/] **164**–165
WORKPLACE CLOTHING
    [würk/ plǎs/ klō/dhǐng] **92**–93

world [würld]
 world languages [würld/ lăng/gwĭ jəz] **189**–13
 world music [würld/ myōō/zĭk] **237**–32
WORLD MAP [würld/măp/] **202–203**
WORLD HISTORY [würld hĭs/tə rē] **199**
worm [würm] **212**–23
worried [wür/ēd] **42**–13
wrap [răp] **72**–24
wrap [răp] **240**–F
wrench [rĕnch] **158**–22, **181**–47, **181**–48
wrestling [rĕs/lĭng] **228**–17
wrinkled [rĭng/kəld] **101**–19
wrist [rĭst] **106**–14
 wristwatch [rĭst/wäch/, –wöch/] **94**–16
write [rīt]
 write a check [rīt/ ə chĕk/] **27**–D
 write a cover letter [rīt/ ə kŭv/ər lĕt/ər] **173**–G
 write a final draft [rīt/ ə fī/nəl drăft/] **191**–L
 write a first draft [rīt/ ə fürst/ drăft/] **191**–H
 write a note [rīt/ ə nōt/] **135**–A
 write a resume [rīt/ ə rĕ/zə mā/] **173**–F
 write a thank-you note
   [rīt/ ə thăngk/ yōō nōt/] **174**–O
 write back [rīt/ băk/] **135**–H
 write on the board [rīt/ ön dhə börd/] **6**–E
writer [rī/tər] **169**–64
Writing and Revising [rī/tĭng ən rĭ vī/ zĭng] **191**
Writing Process [rī/tĭng prä/sĕs] **191**
Writing Rules [rī/tĭng rōōlz] **190**
wrong way [röng/ wā/] **154**–2
xylophone [zī/lə fōn/] **238**–15
yard [yärd]
 courtyard [kört/ yärd/] **51**–21
 yardstick [yärd/stĭk/] **181**–16
YARD [yärd] **53**
yarn [yärn] **233**–22
year [yĭr] **20**–4, **31**–9, **31**–10
Year [yĭr] **21**
yellow [yĕl/ō] **24**–2
yesterday [yĕs/tər dā/, –dē] **20**–7
yield [yēld] **154**–9
yoga [yō/gə] **122**–4
yogurt [yō/gərt] **72**–22
young [yŭng] **32**–1
Your First License [yər fürst/ lī/səns] **137**
YOUR HEALTH [yər hĕlth/] **114–115**
zebra [zē/brə] **217**–33
zero [zĭr/ō] **16**
ZIP code [zĭp/ kōd/] **4**–9
zipper [zĭp/ər] **99**–25
Zones [zōnz] **19**
zoo [zōō] **222**–1
zoom lens [zōōm/ lĕnz/] **235**–23
zucchini [zōō kē/nē] **69**–25

Geographical Index

Continents

Africa [ăf/rĭ kə] **202–5**
Antarctica [ănt ärk/tĭ kə, –är/tĭ–] **202–7**
Asia [ā/zhə] **202–4**
Australia [ö strāl/yə] **202–6**
Europe [yŏŏr/əp] **202–3**
North America [nörth/ ə mĕr/ə kə] **200–201, 202–1**
South America [sowth/ ə mĕr/ə kə] **202–2**

Countries and other locations

Afghanistan [ăf găn/ə stăn/] **203**
Albania [ăl bā/nē ə] **203**
Aleutian Islands [ə lōō/shən ī/ləndz] **200, 203**
Algeria [ăl jïr/ē ə] **203**
American Samoa [ə mĕr/ə kən sə mō/ə] **202**
Andaman Islands [ăn/də mən ī/ləndz] **203**
Angola [ăng gō/lə] **203**
Argentina [är/jən tē/nə] **202**
Armenia [är mē/nē ə] **203**
Austria [ö/strē ə] **203**
Azerbaijan [ăz/ər bī jän/] **203**
Azores [ā/zörz] **202**
Baffin Island [băf/ən ī/lənd] **200**
Bahamas [bə hä/məz] **200, 202**
Bahrain [bä rān/] **203**
Bangladesh [băng/glə dĕsh/, băng/–] **203**
Banks Island [bănks/ ī/lənd] **200**
Belarus [bē/lə rōōs/, byĕl/ə–] **203**
Belgium [bĕl/jəm] **203**
Belize [bə lēz/] **201, 202**
Benin [bə nĭn/, –nēn/] **203**
Bermuda Islands [bər myōō/də ī/ ləndz] **200, 202**
Bhutan [bōō tän/] **203**
Bolivia [bə lĭv/ē ə] **203**
Bosnia [băz/nē ə] **203**
Botswana [bät swä/nə] **203**
Brazil [brə zĭl/] **202**
Brunei [brōō nī/] **203**
Bulgaria [bŭl gĕr/ē ə] **203**
Burkina Faso [bər kē/nə fä/sō] **203**
Burma [bür/mə] **203**
Burundi [bŏŏ rōōn/dē] **203**
Cambodia [kăm bō/dē ə] **203**
Cameroon [kăm/ə rōōn/] **203**
Canada [kăn/ə də] **200, 202**
Canary Islands [kə nĕr/ē ī/ ləndz] **203**
Cape Verde [kāp/ vürd/] **202**
Central African Republic
   [sĕn/trəl ăf/rĭ kən rĭ pŭb/lĭk] **203**
Chad [chăd] **203**
Chile [chĭl/ē] **202**
China [chī/nə] **203**
Colombia [kə lŭm/bē ə] **202**
Comoros [kăm/ə rōz] **203**
Congo [käng/gō] **203**
Cook Islands [kŏŏk/ ī/ləndz] **202**
Corsica [kör/sĭ kə] **203**
Costa Rica [kōs/tə rē/kə, käs/–] **201, 202**
Croatia [krō ā/shə] **203**
Cuba [kyōō/bə] **201, 202**
Cyprus [sī/prəs] **203**
Czech Republic [chĕk/ rĭ pŭb/lĭk] **203**

Democratic Republic of the Congo
   [dĕm/ə krăt/ĭk rĭ pŭb/lĭk əv dhə käng/gō] **203**
Denmark [dĕn/märk] **203**
Devon Island [dĕv/ən ī/lənd] **200**
Djibouti [jĭ bōō/tē] **203**
Dominican Republic [də mĭn/ĭ kən rĭ pŭb/lĭk] **201, 202**
Ecuador [ĕk/wə dör/] **202**
Egypt [ē/jĭpt] **203**
Ellesmere Island [ĕl/əs mïr/ ī/lənd] **200**
El Salvador [ĕl săl/və dör/] **201, 202**
Equatorial Guinea [ē/kwə tör/ē əl gĭn/ē, ĕk/wə–] **203**
Eritrea [ĕr/ə trē/ə] **203**
Estonia [ĕ stō/nē ə] **203**
Ethiopia [ē/thē ō/pē ə] **203**
Federated States of Micronesia
   [fĕ/də rā/təd stāts/ əv mī/krə nē/zhə] **203**
Fiji [fē/jē] **203**
Finland [fĭn/lənd] **203**
France [frăns] **203**
Franz Josef Land [fränz/ yō/səf länd/] **203**
French Guiana [frĕnch/ gē ăn/ə, –ä/nə] **202**
French Polynesia [frĕnch/ păl/ə nē/zhə] **202**
Gabon [gă bōn/] **203**
Galápagos Islands [gə lä pə gōs ī/ləndz] **202**
Gambia [găm/bē ə] **203**
Georgia [jör/jə] **203**
Germany [jür/mə nē] **203**
Ghana [gä/nə] **203**
Greater Antilles [grā/tər ăn tĭl/ēz] **201**
Greece [grēs] **203**
Greenland [grēn/lənd, –lănd/] **200, 202**
Guam [gwäm] **203**
Guatemala [gwä/tə mä/lə] **201, 202**
Guinea [gĭn/ē] **203**
Guinea-Bissau [gĭn/ē bĭ sow/] **203**
Guyana [gī ăn/ə] **202**
Haiti [hā/tē] **201, 202**
Hawaiian Islands [hə wī/ən ī/lənds] **200, 202**
Hispaniola [hĭs/pən yō/lə] **201**
Honduras [hän dŏŏr/əs] **201, 202**
Hong Kong [häng/ käng/] **203**
Hungary [hŭng/gə rē] **203**
Iceland [īs/lənd] **203**
India [ĭn/dē ə] **203**
Indonesia [ĭn/də nē/zhə] **203**
Iran [ĭ răn/, ĭ rän/] **203**
Iraq [ĭ räk/, ĭ răk/] **203**
Ireland [īr/lənd] **203**
Israel [ĭz/rē əl, –rā–] **203**
Italy [ĭt/l ē] **203**
Ivory Coast [īv/rē kōst/] **203**
Jamaica [jə mā/kə] **201, 202**
Japan [jə păn/] **203**
Jordan [jör/dn] **203**
Kazakhstan [kä/zäk stän/] **203**
Kenya [kĕn/yə, kēn/–] **203**
Kiribati [kïr/ə băs/] **203**
Kuwait [kōō wāt/] **203**
Kyrgyzstan [kïr/gĭ stän/, –stăn/] **203**
Laos [lows, lä/ōs] **203**
Latvia [lăt/vē ə] **203**
Lebanon [lĕb/ə nən, –nän/] **203**

Lesotho [lə sō/tō, –sōō/tōō] **203**
Lesser Antilles [lĕ/sər ăn tĭl/ēz] **201, 202**
Liberia [lī bïr/ē ə] **203**
Libya [lĭb/ē ə] **203**
Lithuania [lĭth/ōō ā/nē ə] **203**
Luxembourg [lŭk/səm bürg/] **203**
Macedonia [măs/ə dō/nē ə] **203**
Madagascar [măd/ə găs/kər] **203**
Madeira Islands [mə dïr/ə ī/ləndz] **203**
Malawi [mə lä/wē] **203**
Malaysia [mə lā/zhə] **203**
Maldives [möl/dēvz, mäl/–] **203**
Mali [mä/lē] **203**
Malta [möl/tə] **203**
Marshall Islands [mär/shəl ī/ləndz] **203**
Mauritania [mör/ə tā/nē ə] **203**
Mauritius [mö rĭsh/əs] **203**
Mexico [mĕk/sĭ kō/] **200, 201, 202**
Moldova [möl dō/və, mäl–] **203**
Monaco [män/ə kō/] **203**
Mongolia [mäng gō/lē ə] **203**
Montenegro [män/tə nē/grō, –nĕ/–] **203**
Morocco [mə räk/ō] **203**
Mozambique [mō/zəm bēk/] **203**
Namibia [nə mĭb/ē ə] **203**
Nepal [nə pöl/, –päl/] **203**
Netherlands [nĕdh/ər ləndz] **203**
New Caledonia [nōō/ kăl/ə dō/nē ə] **203**
New Zealand [nōō/ zē/lənd] **203**
Nicaragua [nĭk/ə rä/gwə] **201, 202**
Niger [nī/jər, nē zhër/] **203**
Nigeria [nī jïr/ē ə] **203**
Northern Mariana Islands
   [nördh/ərn mä/rē ä/nə ī/ləndz] **203**
North Korea [nörth/ kə rē/ə] **203**
Norway [nör/wā] **203**
Oman [ō män/] **203**
Pakistan [păk/ə stăn/] **203**
Palau [pə low/] **203**
Panama [păn/ə mä/] **201, 202**
Papua New Guinea [păp/yŏŏ ə nōō/ gĭn/ē] **203**
Paraguay [păr/ə gwī/, –gwä/] **202**
Peru [pə rōō/] **202**
Philippines [fĭl/ə pēnz/, fĭl/ə pēnz/] **203**
Poland [pō/lənd] **203**
Portugal [pör/chə gəl] **203**
Puerto Rico [pwër/tə rē/kō, pör/tə–] **201, 202**
Qatar [kä/tär, kə tär/] **203**
Romania [rō mā/nē ə, rōō–] **203**
Russia [rŭsh/ə] **203**
Rwanda [rōō än/də] **203**
Samoa [sə mō/ə] **202**
Saudi Arabia [sow/dē ə rā/bē ə, sö/dē–] **203**
Senegal [sĕn/ə göl/, –gäl/] **203**
Serbia [sür/bē ə] **203**
Seychelles [sā shĕlz/, –shĕl/] **203**
Sierra Leone [sē ĕr/ə lē ōn/, –lē ō/nē] **203**
Singapore [sĭng/ə pör/] **203**
Slovakia [slō vä/kē ə] **203**
Slovenia [slō vē/nē ə] **203**
Society Islands [sə sī/ə tē ī/ləndz] **202**
Solomon Islands [säl/ə mən ī/ləndz] **203**

Somalia [sə mä/lē ə] **203**
South Africa [sowth/ ăf/rĭ kə] **203**
South Georgia [sowth/ jör/jə] **202**
South Korea [sowth/ kə rē/ə] **203**
Spain [spān] **203**
Sri Lanka [srē/ läng/kə, shrē/–] **203**
Sudan [sōō dän/] **203**
Suriname [sŏŏr/ə nä/mə] **202**
Svalbard [sväl/bärd] **203**
Swaziland [swä/zē länd/] **203**
Sweden [swēd/n] **203**
Switzerland [swĭt/sər lənd] **203**
Syria [sïr/ē ə] **203**
Tahiti [tə hē/tē] **202**
Taiwan [ti/wän/] **203**
Tajikistan [tä jĭk/ə stän/, –stän/] **203**
Tanzania [tăn/zə nē/ə] **203**
Tasmania [tăz mā/nē ə] **203**
Thailand [ti/länd/, –lənd] **203**
Togo [tō/gō] **203**
Tonga [täng/gə] **202**
Tunisia [tōō nē/zhə] **203**
Turkey [tür/kē] **203**
Turkmenistan [türk mĕn/ə stän/, –stän/] **203**
Uganda [yōō gän/də] **203**
Ukraine [yōō/krān, yōō krän/] **203**
United Arab Emirates [yōō nī/təd är/əb ĕm/ər əts] **203**
United Kingdom [yōō nī/təd kĭng/dəm] **203**
United States of America
  [yōō nī/təd stäts/ əv ə mĕr/ə kə] **200, 202**
Uruguay [yŏŏr/ə gwī/, –gwä/] **202**
Uzbekistan [ŏŏz bĕk/ə stän/, –stän/] **203**
Vanuatu [vä/nōō ä/tōō] **203**
Venezuela [vĕn/ə zwä/lə] **202**
Victoria Island [vĭk/tör ē ə ī/lənd] **200**
Vietnam [vē/ĕt näm/, –näm/] **203**
Wake Island [wāk/ ī/lənd] **203**
Western Sahara [wĕs/tərn sə hăr/ə] **203**
Yemen [yĕm/ən] **203**
Zambia [zăm/bē ə] **203**
Zanzibar [zăn/zə bär] **203**
Zimbabwe [zĭm băb/wā] **203**

Bodies of water
Arctic Ocean [ärk/tĭk ō/shən] **200, 203**
Atlantic Ocean [ət lăn/ tĭk ō/shən] **200, 202–203**
Baffin Bay [băf/ən bā/] **200, 202**
Baltic Sea [böl/tĭk sē/] **203**
Beaufort Sea [bō/fərt sē/] **200**
Bering Sea [bër/ĭng sē/, bïr/–] **200**
Black Sea [blăk/ sē/] **203**
Caribbean Sea [kăr/ə bē/ən sē/, kə rĭb/ē ən–] **201**
Caspian Sea [kăs/pē ən sē/] **203**
Coral Sea [kör/əl sē/] **203**
Gulf of Alaska [gŭlf/ əv ə läs/kə] **200, 202**
Gulf of California [gŭlf/ əv kăl/ə förn/yə] **200**
Gulf of Mexico [gŭlf/ əv mĕk/sĭ kō/] **200, 202**
Hudson Bay [hŭd/sən bā/] **200, 202**
Indian Ocean [ĭn/dē ən ō/shən] **203**
Labrador Sea [lăb/rə dör/ sē/] **200**
Mediterranean Sea [mĕd/ə tə rā/nē ən sē/] **203**

North Atlantic Ocean [nörth/ ət lăn/tĭk ō/shən] **202**
North Pacific Ocean [nörth/ pə sĭf/ĭk ō/shən] **202, 203**
North Sea [nörth/ sē/] **203**
Pacific Ocean [pə sĭf/ĭk ō/shən] **200, 202, 203**
Philippine Sea [fĭl/ə pēn/ sē/] **203**
Red Sea [rĕd/ sē/] **203**
South Atlantic Ocean [sowth/ ət lăn/tĭk ō/shən] **203**
Southern Ocean [sŭdh/ərn ō/shən] **203**
South Pacific Ocean [sowth/ pə sĭf/ĭk ō/shən] **202, 203**

The United States of America
Capital: Washington, D.C. (District of Columbia)
  [wä/shĭng tən dē/sē/, wö/–] **200**

Regions of the United States
Mid-Atlantic States [mĭd/ət lăn/tĭk stäts/] **201-10**
Midwest [mĭd/wĕst/] **201-9**
New England [nōō/ ĭng/glənd] **201-11**
Pacific States [pə sĭf/ĭk stäts/] **201-7**
Rocky Mountain States [räk/ē mown/tn stäts/] **201-8**
South [sowth] **201-13**
Southeast [sowth/ēst/] **201-13**
Southwest [sowth/wĕst/] **201-12**
West Coast [wĕst/ kōst/] **201-7**

States of the United States
Alabama [ăl/ə băm/ə] **200**
Alaska [ə läs/kə] **200, 202**
Arizona [ăr/ə zō/nə] **200**
Arkansas [är/kən sö/] **200**
California [kăl/ə förn/yə] **200**
Colorado [kăl/ə răd/ō, –ra/dō] **200**
Connecticut [kə nĕt/ĭ kət] **200**
Delaware [dĕl/ə wër/] **200**
Florida [flör/ə də, flär/–] **200**
Georgia [jör/jə] **200**
Hawaii [hə wī/ē] **200**
Idaho [ī/də hō/] **200**
Illinois [ĭl/ə noy/] **200**
Indiana [ĭn/dē ăn/ə] **200**
Iowa [ī/ə wə] **200**
Kansas [kăn/zəs] **200**
Kentucky [kən tŭk/ē] **200**
Louisiana [lōō ē/zē ăn/ə] **200**
Maine [mān] **200**
Maryland [mër/ə lənd] **200**
Massachusetts [măs/ə chōō/səts] **200**
Michigan [mĭsh/ĭ gən] **200**
Minnesota [mĭn/ə sō/tə] **200**
Mississippi [mĭs/ə sĭp/ē] **200**
Missouri [mə zŏŏr/ē, –zōōr/ə] **200**
Montana [män tăn/ə] **200**
Nebraska [nə brăs/kə] **200**
Nevada [nə văd/ə, –vä/də] **200**
New Hampshire [nōō/ hămp/shər] **200**
New Jersey [nōō/ jür/zē] **200**
New Mexico [nōō/ mĕk/sĭ kō/] **200**
New York [nōō/ yörk/] **200**
North Carolina [nörth/ kăr/ə lī/nə] **200**
North Dakota [nörth/ də kō/tə] **200**
Ohio [ō hī/ō] **200**
Oklahoma [ō/klə hō/mə] **200**
Oregon [ör/ĭ gən, –gän/, är/–] **200**

Pennsylvania [pĕn/səl vān/yə] **200**
Rhode Island [rōd/ ī/lənd] **200**
South Carolina [sowth/ kăr/ə li/nə] **200**
South Dakota [sowth/ də kō/tə] **200**
Tennessee [tĕn/ə sē/] **200**
Texas [tĕk/səs] **200**
Utah [yōō/tö, –tä] **200**
Vermont [vər mänt/] **200**
Virginia [vər jĭn/yə] **200**
Washington [wä/shĭng tən, wö/–] **200**
West Virginia [wĕst/ vər jĭn/yə] **200**
Wisconsin [wĭs kän/sən] **200**
Wyoming [wī ō/mĭng] **200**

Canada
Capital: Ottawa [ät/ə wə] **201**

Regions of Canada
British Columbia [brĭt/ĭsh kə lŭm/bē ə] **201-2**
Maritime Provinces [mër/ə tïm präv/ən səz] **201-6**
Northern Canada [nör/dhərn kăn/ə də] **201-1**
Ontario [än tër/ē ō/] **201-4**
Prairie Provinces [prër/ē präv/ən səz] **201-3**
Québec [kwĭ bĕk/] **201-5**

Provinces of Canada
Alberta [ăl bür/tə] **200**
British Columbia [brĭt/ĭsh kə lŭm/bē ə] **200**
Manitoba [măn/ə tō/bə] **200**
New Brunswick [nōō/ brŭnz/wĭk] **200**
Newfoundland and Labrador
  [nōō/fən lənd ən lă/brə dör/] **200**
Northwest Territories [nörth/wĕst/ tër/ə tör/ēz] **200**
Nova Scotia [nō/və skō/shə] **200**
Nunavut [nōō/nə vōōt/] **200**
Ontario [än tër/ē ō/] **200**
Prince Edward Island [prĭns/ ĕd/wərd ī/lənd] **200**
Québec [kwĭ bĕk/] **200**
Saskatchewan [să skăch/ə wən, –wän/] **200**
Yukon [yōō/kän] **200**

Mexico
Capital: Mexico (City) [mĕk/sĭ kō/ (sĭt/ē)] **201**

Regions of Mexico
Chiapas Highlands [chē ä/pəs hī/ləndz] **201-18**
Gulf Coastal Plain [gŭlf/ kō/stəl plān/] **201-16**
Pacific Northwest [pə sĭf/ĭk nörth/wĕst] **201-14**
Plateau of Mexico [plă tō/ əv mĕk/sĭ kō/] **201-15**
Southern Uplands [sŭdh/ərn ŭp/ləndz] **201-17**
Yucatan Peninsula
  [yōō/kə tän/ pə nĭn/sə lə, yōō/kə tän/–] **201-19**

States of Mexico
Aguascalientes [ä/gwəs käl yĕn/täs] **201**
Baja California Norte [bä/hä käl/ə förn/yə nör/tä] **200**
Baja California Sur [bä/hä käl/ə förn/yə sŏŏr/] **200**
Campeche [käm pā/chä, käm pē/chē] **201**
Chiapas [chē ä/pəs] **201**
Chihuahua [chĭ wä/wä, –wə] **200**
Coahuila [kō/ə wē/lə] **200**
Colima Michoacán [kə lē/mə mē/chō ə kän/] **201**
Distrito Federal [dĭ strē/tō fĕd/ə räl/] **201**
Durango [dŏŏ răng/gō, –räng/–] **201**

Geographical Index

Guanajuato [gwä'nə hwä'tō] **201**
Guerrero [gə rër'ō] **201**
Hidalgo [hĭ däl'gō, ē dhäl'gō] **201**
Jalisco [hə lĭs'kō, -lēs'-] **201**
México [mĕk'sĭ kō', mĕ'hē kō] **201**
Morelos [mö rĕl'ōs] **201**
Nayarit [nä'yə rēt'] **201**
Nuevo León [nwä'vō lā ôn'] **200**
Oaxaca [wə hä'kə, wä-] **201**
Puebla [pwĕb'lä] **201**
Querétaro [kə rĕt'ə rō'] **201**
Quintana Roo [kēn tä'nə rō'] **201**
San Luis Potosí [sän' lōō ēs' pō'tə sē'] **201**
Sinaloa [sē'nə lō'ə] **200**
Sonora [sə nör'ə] **200**
Tabasco [tə bäs'kō] **201**
Tamaulipas [tä'mow lē'pəs] **201**
Tlaxcala [tlä skä'lə] **201**
Veracruz [vĕr'ə krōōz', -krōōs'] **201**
Yucatán [yōō'kə tän', -tän'] **201**
Zacatecas [zä'kə tä'kəs, sä'-] **201**

"پڑوس پر نظر رکھنے والی جماعت" میں شمولیت کیجیے۔ L-143

"خدا حافظ" کہیے۔ L-3

"سائن ان" پر کلک کیجیے B-197

(دستی)گھڑی 16-94

(ذاتی) چیک لکھیے D-27

(زنانہ جانگیہ) زیر جامہ 13-91

(سیدھی) پن 100-12

(گولف میں) زور کی ضرب لگائیے Q-230

(گھر کی) پتائی کرنے والا 168-46

(ہوائی) جہاز 150-8

0 صفر 16

1 ایک 16

1 بڑا چمچ بھر 75

1 پائنٹ 75

1 پیالی 75

1 چائے کا چمچ بھر 75

1 رقیق اونس 75

1 سینٹ 26-1

1 کوارٹ 75

2\1 پیالی 75

4\1 پیالی 75

1,000 ایک ہزار 16

1,000,000 ایک ملین 16

1,000,000,000 ایک بلین 16

10 دس 16

10 سال کی لڑکی 31-10

10 سنٹس 26-3

10 فیصد 17-12

10,000 دس ہزار 16

100 ایک سو 16

100 فیصد 17-8

100,000 ایک سو ہزار 16

101 ایک سو ایک 16

11 گیارہ 16

12 بارہ 16

13 تیرہ 16

13 سے 19 سال کی عمر کا 31-11

13 سے 19 سال کی عمر 31-11

14 چودہ 16

15 پندرہ 16

16 سولہ 16

17 سترہ 16

18 اٹھارہ 16

18 سال یا زیادہ عمر ہونا G-140

19 انیس 16

1 گیلن 75

2 دو 16

2 × 4 (دو ضرب چار) 181-19

20 بیس 16

21 اکیس 16

22 بائیس 16

23 تئیس 16

24 چوبیس 16

25 پچیس 16

25 سنٹس 26-4

25 فیصد 17-11

2-دروازوں والی کار 156-2

3 تین 16

4\3-آستین والی قمیض 96-13

30 تیس 16

35 ایم ایم کیمرا 235-21

3-کمانی دار جلد 27-7

4 چار 16

40 چالیس 16

4-دروازوں والی کار 156-1

5 پانچ 16

5 سنٹس 26-2

5 منٹ تک برقی تنور میں پکائیے T-77

50 پچاس 16

50 فیصد 17-10

6 چھ 16

6 سال کا بچہ 31-9

60 ساٹھ 16

7 سات 16

70 ستر 16

75 فیصد 17-9

8 آٹھ 16

80 اسی 16

9 نو 16

90 نوے 16

90 ڈگری کا زاویہ 193-26

911 ڈائل کیجیے۔ E-15

C نما شکنجہ 180-6

U-شکل کی گردن والا سوئیٹر 96-8

آئس اسکیٹنگ 227-4

آئس کریم کون 79-13

آئس کریم کی دکان 131-16

آئس کریم 72-26

آئندہ کل 20-6

آئنمیوں کو ملائیے T-9

آئی بیم 178-3

آئین 198-12

آئینہ 57-18

ابتدائی اسکول 188-2

ابر آلود 13-10

ابرو بنانے والی پنسل 109-34

ابعاد 17

ابلتے پانی میں پکائے گئے چھلے انڈے 76-9

ابلی ہوئی سور کی ران کا گوشت 76-5

ابکائی محسوس کرنا D-110

آبی آلودگی 218-14

آبی رنگ 233-21

اپارٹمنٹ میں داخلہ کا راستہ 51

اپارٹمنٹ نمبر 4-6

اپارٹمنٹ والی عمارت 50-1

اپارٹمنٹ کرایہ پر لینا 48

اپارٹمنٹس 50-51

آپریشن کا کمرہ 121

آپریشن کی میز 121-40

اپریل 28-21

آپریٹر 14-21

اپنا اے ٹی ایم کارڈ داخل کیجیے۔ D-132

اپنا بورڈنگ پاس اور شناخت دکھائیے۔ C-160

اپنا پن داخل کیجیے۔ E-132

اپنا پن نمبر چھپائیے۔ C-143

اپنا پہلا لائسنس حاصل کرنا 137

اپنا تعارف کرائیے۔ C-2

اپنا سیل فون بند کر دیجیے۔ G-174، I-160

اپنا لائسنس حاصل کیجیے۔ I-137

اپنا لفظ شناخت ٹائپ کیجیے A-197

اپنا نام بتائیے۔ A-4، A-15، F

اپنا نام بڑے حروف میں لکھیے۔ C-4

اپنا کارڈ نکالیے۔ G-132

اپنا کوائف نامہ اور خط ارسال کیجیے H-173

اپنا کوائف نامہ اور شناخت لائیے۔ D-174

اپنا کوائف نامہ لکھیے F-173

اپنا باتھ اٹھائیے۔ A-6

اپنی شناخت دکھائیے۔ C-137

اپنی صحت کی دیکھ بھال کرنا 114-115

اپنی فہم کی جانچ کیجیے N-12

اپنی نشست تلاش کیجیے۔ F-160

اپنی نشستی پٹی باندھیے۔ H-160

اپنی ڈیسک صاف کیجیے۔ I-10

اپنی کار کی دیکھ بھال کرنا 157

اپنی کتاب بند کیجیے۔ H-6

اپنی کتاب کھولیے۔ G-6

اپنی کتابیں مقررہ جگہ پر رکھیے۔ Z-9

اپنی بجے کی جانچ کیجیے F-197

اپنے آپ کام کیجیے۔ J-10

اپنے آس پاس باخبر رہیے۔ I-143

اپنے امتحان کی جوابی کاپی جمع کیجیے O-10

اپنے پرس یا بٹوے کی حفاظت کیجیے۔ D-143

اپنے تجربے کے بارے میں بات کیجیے۔ L-174

اپنے تھیلوں کی جانچ کرائیے۔ B-160

اپنے خیالات کو منظم کیجیے۔ G-191

اپنے دروازوں میں تالا لگائیے۔ E-143

اپنے سامان کا مطالبہ کیجیے۔ L-160

اپنے شہر میں دیکھنے کے قابل مقامات 222

اپنے مسودے کو واپس کیجیے۔ M-191

اپنے نام کا دستخط کیجیے۔ D-4

اپنے نام کی ہجے کیجیے۔ B-4

اپنے کام کی جانچ کیجیے۔ L-10

اپنے ہم جماعتوں کے ساتھ کام کرنا 8

اتاریے Q-109

اتالیق 20-5، 229-2

اتریے K-160

آتش دان سے بچاؤ کی جالی 56-12

آتش دان کی دیوار 56-11

آتش دان 56-13

آتش زنی 142-7

آتش فشاں کا پھٹ پڑنا 145-16

اتوار 20-8

آج 20-5

آجر 164-4

اجرتیں 165-12

اجزا کو ملائیے۔ R-77

اجزاء کے ملمے کو پھینٹیے۔ S-77

اجلاس کا مرکز 127-24

اجلاس کا کمرہ 182-4

اجنبیوں کو گھر میں نہ آنے دیجیے۔ F-143

اچار 80-11

اچھا کتا 23-17

اچھلیے I-230

اچھی روشنی والی سڑک استعمال کیجیے۔ B-143

اچھے درجات حاصل کیجیے۔ H-10

احاطہ 193-43

احساسات 43-42

اخبار اور رسائل کی دکان 128-12

اخبار پڑھیے U-39

اخبار 133-6

اخبارات کی بازتشکیل کیجیے B-60

اختتام 190-8

اختلاط 218-10

اختلاف کیجیے L-12

آخری مسودہ لکھیے L-191

آخری نام 4-4

ادائیگی کے طریقے 27

اُداس 43-19

اداکار 167-2

آدھا پیالی کشمش 75-9

ادھر سے نہ جائیں 154-2

آدھی آستین کی قمیض 86-4

آدھی رات 18-21

ادیب 169-64

آروبی 237-28

آروی (آرائش و آسائش والی موٹر گاڑی) 156-10

آراستہ اپارٹمنٹ 48-3

آرام کرسی 56-22

آرام کیجیے U-39

آرچڈ 211-19

'ارسال کریں' دبائیں۔ B-15

آرماڈلو 216-8

آرڈر لیجیے E-82

آرکسٹرا کو ہدایت دیجیے C-238

ازالہ یادداشت 111-18

آزمائش کا علاقہ 136-2

اس پر داغ ہے۔ 97-42

اس سے منسلک کیا جانے والا خط لکھیے G-173

اس کی تعریف پڑھیے۔ B-8

اس ہفتے 20-19

آسان مرغ یخنی 77

آسان مسئلہ 23-23

اسپتال کا ایک کمرہ 121

اسپتال کا بستر 121-22

اسپتال کا عملہ 120

اسپتال کا گاؤن 121-19

اسپتال کا مرد ملازم صفائی کرنے والا 120-16

اسپتال 120-121، 125-9

اسپورٹس کار 156-4

اسپونج پونچھا 61-6

اسپیکر 50-5

اسپیکرز 234-14

استاد سے بات کیجیے۔ B-6

استاد کا معاون 5-16

استاد 5-8، 6-4

استری تختہ 101-14

استری کی ہوئی قمیض 101-20

استری 101-13

استعماریت پسند 198-2

استعمال شدہ کپڑا 102-2

استعمال کی گئی چیزوں کا معائنہ کیجیے۔ N-147

استقبال کار 164-5، 182-14

استقبال کرنے والی 169-51

استقبالیہ علاقہ 182-15

استقبالیہ کار 118-2

آستین یا پائنچوں کا سرا 100-9
آستین 100-6
اسطوانہ، بیلن 193-41
اسفنج 19-61
اسمارٹ فون 27-15
آسمان 209-9
اسنوکر کھیلنے کی میز 50-15
آسٹرابیریاں 68-14
آسٹریلیا 202-6
استو بنانے والا گائے کا گوشت 70-3
اسٹوریج لاکر 50-17
اسٹوو 54-18
اسٹیپل کیجیے F-171
اسٹیپلر 183-28
اسٹیپلر 183-29
اسٹیریو سسٹم 56-8
اسٹیشن ویگن 156-6
اسٹیشنری 183-42
اسٹیل کتن کے صفائی گدے 61-5
اسٹیڈیم 126-1
اسکرال بار (صفحے کو ادھر ادھر یا اوپر نیچے حرکت دینے کے لیے) 197-15
اسکرین 196-2، 6-11
اسکنک 216-12
اسکور 229-1
اسکول اور مضامین 188
اسکول بس 156-21
اسکول جانے کی ابتداء B-40
اسکول میں ایک دن 11
اسکول میں کامیابی 10
اسکول میں اندراج فارم 4
اسکول کراسنگ 154-15
اسکول کی بس پکڑیے H-38
اسکول کی تیاری کی درسگاہ 188-1
اسکول 5، 126-9
اسکی بوٹ 231-26
اسکی کرنے کے دوران لگایا جانے والا نقاب 90-15
اسکی کرنے کے دوران لگایا جانے والا ٹوپ 90-11
اسکی کیجیے U-230
اسکینر 183-20
اسکیٹ بورڈ 224-7
اسکیٹ کیجیے U-230
اسی وان 16
اسیکٹنگ بورڈنگ 228-13
اشارہ کنندہ 197-12
اشتہار 148-1
اشیاء کو ناپیے۔ A-75
اضافی حفاظتی دروازہ 53-10
اطالوی پنیر 71-29
اظہار تشکر 22-17
اعداد صحیح 192
اعداد 16
اعشاریہ 17-7
اعلان آزادی 198-5
افراد کے لیے مفت رہائش 52-13
افریقہ 202-5
آفس منتظم 182-8
آفس 164-3
افسر 229-6

افق پیما آلہ 180-29
اقتباس 190-9
اقلیدس 192-17
اقلیدسی ٹھوس شکلیں 193
آگ بجھانے والا فرد 144-9
آگ بجھانے والا ٹرک 144-10
آگ بجھانے والا 167-26
آگ بجھانے کا آلہ 179-21
آگ بجھانے کے لیے پانی حاصل کرنے کا نلکا 129-27
آگ پکڑنے والے سیالات 179-8
آگ لگنے پر بھاگنے کے لیے عقبی زینہ 50-2
آگ 144-8
اگانے والا 177-13
اگست 21-32
اگلی بانہہ 106-13
اگلی سطر پر جائیے D-196
اگلے ہفتے 20-20
آگے بڑھائیے D-235
آگے جانے کا بٹن 197-3
آگے کی سیٹ 159-51
آل 69-20
آلات کی مرمت کا مستری 167-4
آلات کی مرمت کیجیے J-170
الارم گھڑی 58-24
الاسکا وقت 19-28
الجبرا 192-16
الجھن میں گرفتار 43-26
الرجیاں 111-8
الفالفا 177-5
الگ کیجیے B-76
الگنی 101-9
آلو 214-5
الماری 54-2، 58-5، 98-5، 16-16
المونیم کی پنی 72-23
المیہ 237-14
آلو بخارے 68-13
آلو کا بھرتا 81-23
آلو کی سلاد 80-19
آلو کے قتلے 73-35
آلو 69-17
آلودگی 218
الٹی کرنا E-110
الیکٹرونک اشیاء کی دکان 131-20
الیکٹرونک سامانوں کا مستری 167-24
الیکٹرونکس اور فوٹوگرافی 234-235
الیکٹرک پنسل تراش 183-26
آم 68-21
امتحان میں شریک ہونا 10
امتحان میں کامیابی حاصل کیجیے۔ E-10
امتحان کی کاپی 10-1
آمد اور روانگی کے نگراں 161-7
آمد درج کرانے کی جگہ 160-2
امدادی گروپ 115-15
امریکی انقلاب کے زمانے کا فوجی رضاکار 198-10
امریکی پنیر 71-26
امریکی تاریخ 198
امریکی حبشی نژاد باشندوں کا گانا 237-24
امریکی سرخ لکڑی کا پیڑ 210-18

املا لکھیے K-171
آملیٹ 76-12
آموزگار اجازت نامہ حاصل کیجیے۔ F-137
ان لائن اسکیٹس 231-10
ان لائن اسکیٹنگ 228-10
آن لائن بینک کاری کیجیے۔ C-132
اناج سے بنا ناشتے کا ڈبہ 74-18
اناج کوٹھی 177-11
آنت کے اندر قیمہ بھرا مسالے دار کیسہ 70-12
آنت کے اندر مسالے دار قیمہ بھر کر بنایا گیا کیسہ 80-2
انتباہ کا لیبل 112-8
انتباہات پر توجہ دیجیے۔ D-147
انتخاب کے نتائج 139-31
انتخاب 139
انتظار گاہ 182-16
انتظار گاہ میں 118
آنتوں کے طفیلی کیڑے 111-13
آنتیں 107-42
انجن کا خول 158-4
انجن کے خول کے نیچے 158
انجن 158-18
انجکشن لگانے کا آلہ 118-12
انجیر 68-27
انجینئر 167-25
انچ [انچ] 17-15
انخلاء کا راستہ 146-5
اندر رکھنے والا پودا 56-4
اندراج شدہ نرس (آراین) 120-10
اندراج شدہ ڈاک 134-4
اندراج کا اسپیکر 136-13
اندراج کا بلا 136-13
آندھی 145-14
اندھیری بڑی غار 220-7
انفرادی کھیل کود 228
انقلاب پسند 199-17
انقلابی جنگ 198-8
انگریزی دیگر زبان بولنے والوں کی دوسری زبان 189-14
انگریزی زبان کی تالیفی ترکیب 191-190
انگشتانہ 100-15
انگلی پر سوجن 110-16
انگلی کا نشان 136-5
انگلی کے ناخن 106-18
انگلی 105-16
انگلیوں کے جوڑ خصوصاً ہاتھ کے 106-17
آنگن کا فرنیچر 53-19
آنگن 51-21، 53-16
انگور کا باغ 177-16
انگور 68-3، 210-22
انگوٹھا 105-10
انگوٹھا 95-40
اناناس 68-23
انٹارکٹکا 202-7
انٹرنیٹ سے تلاش 48-1
انٹرنیٹ فون کال 14-20
انٹرنیٹ نقشہ 155-12
انٹرنیٹ کی ملازمتی سائٹیں دیکھیں D-173
انٹرنیٹ کے ذریعے نصابی تربیت 172-8

انٹرنیٹ 197
انٹرویو دیجیے K-173
انٹرویو لینے والوں کا استقبال کیجیے۔ H-174
انٹرویو لینے والے کا شکریہ ادا کیجیے۔ N-174
انٹرویو مقرر کیجیے I-173
انٹرویو کی تیاری کیجیے۔ A-174
انٹرویو کی مہارتیں 174
آنٹیریو 201-4
انڈا پھینٹنے کا آلہ 78-20
انڈا پیش کرنے کے طریقے 76
انڈوں کا کارٹن 74-16
انڈے کی زردی، تیل اور سرکے سے تیار چٹنی 79-23
انڈے، آٹے، دودھ سے بنا کیک 80-8
انڈے 66-7
اتک پیڈ 183-46
اتک جیٹ پرنٹر 183-18
اتک کارٹرج 183-45
آنکھ میں ڈالنے کے قطرات 113-31
آنکھ کا نمبر جانچ کر عینک بنانے والا ماہر 115-6
آنکھ کی پتلی پر لگانے والے عدسے 115-8
آنکھ کی تکلیفیں 115-1
آنکھ 105-11، 106
انکھوا 211-4
آنکھوں کا... معاینہ کیجیے D-118
آنکھوں کے گرد آرائشی لکیر بنانے والی پنسل 109-36
آنکھوں کے گرد چھڑکنے والا پاؤڈر 109-35
آنکھیں ملائیے۔ J-174
انیسواں 16
آنے جانے والی بس 152-19
آواز میں ریکارڈ کی گئی کتاب 133-17
اوپر تلے بنے ہوئے بستر 59-9
اوپر چمچ سے چٹنی لگائیے۔F-77
اوپر سامان رکھنے کے خانے 161-13
اوپری پروجیکٹر 7-16
اوپوسم 216-4
اوپیرا 223-11
اود بلاؤ 213-35
اوراق کی تصحیح کیجیے۔ I-191
اورنگٹان 217-39
اوزار اور تعمیر کے سامان 180-181
اوزار بیلٹ 92-3
اوسط قد 32-5
اوسط وزن 32-8
اوضاع 96
اون 233-22
اونچائی 17-16
اونچی ایڑی کے جوتے 89-21، 95-25
اونچی کرسی 37-6
اونچے درجے کا دم الفشار 111-14
اونگھتا ہوا 42-3
اونٹ 217-38
اونی 98-3
اوک اسٹریٹ پر بائیں مڑیے C-155
اوک 210-17
آٹا 73-29
اٹلانٹک وقت 19-33
آٹو کلب کارڈ 162-4
آٹھ پایہ صوفہ 212-9

انٹھ جائیے۔ B-38
انٹھائی گیری 8-142
انٹھارہواں 16
آٹھواں حصہ 5-17
آٹھواں 16
آئے کا تھیلا 74-19
اڈاپٹر 234-15
آڑ میں رہیے۔ J-147
آڑا 193-31
اڑان بھریے J-160
اڑانے والی تشتری 231-27
آڑو 68-10
اکاؤنٹ منیجر 132-9
اکتایا ہوا 43-25
اکتوبر 21-34
آکسفرڈ طرز کے جوتے 95-29
آکسیجن کی نقاب 161-24
آکٹوپس 212-9
اکیسواں 16
اہم علامات کا نگراں 121-26
اہم علامات 220-1
اہم کاغذات کی نقلیں 146-20
ای میل ارسال کیجیے I-197
ای میل کا پتہ لکھیے C-197
ایئر لائن ٹرمنل کے اندر 160
ایئر کنڈیشنر 159-39
ایجاد 199-19
ایچ آئی وی (انسانی قوت مدافعت کم کرنے والا جرثومہ) K-111-17
ایس یو وی (کھیلوں میں مستعمل گاڑی) 156-7
ایشیا 202-4
ایگزیکٹینو باورچی 185-7
ایگزیکٹینو برانچ 138
ایگزیکٹینو 182-5
ایل سی ڈی پروجیکٹر 6-6، 6-29، 235
ایلم اسٹریٹ پر سیدھے جائیے۔ A-155
ایم پی تھری پلیئر 234-2
ایمرجنسی کارڈ 161-26
ای-میل دیکھیے W-39
اینٹ کے پتوں کا سلسلہ 233-29
اینٹینا 14-9
اینیمل بچھائیے B-178
اینیمل 178-12
ایوان نمائندگان 138-3
اینلس 133-8
ایڑی 106-24
ایک آونس پنیر 75-11
ایک بج کر بیس منٹ 18-10
ایک بج کر پانچ منٹ 18-7
ایک بج کر دس منٹ 18-8
ایک بجے 18-6
ایک بنن غائب ہے۔ 97-40
ایک بیس 18-10
ایک پائنٹ جما ہوا دہی 75-3
ایک پاؤنڈ بھنا ہوا گائے کا گوشت 75-12
ایک پانچ 18-7
ایک پندرہ 18-9
ایک پہیہ کی باغبانی کی گاڑی 176-3
ایک پیالی آٹا 75-10

ایک پیالی تیل 75-2
ایک پینتالیس 18-13
ایک پینی 26-1
ایک تجربہ 195
ایک تصویر بنائیے۔ F-8
ایک تیس 18-11
ایک چائے کی چمچ بھر چینی 75-7
ایک چائے کی چمچ بھر نمک 75-6
ایک چالیس 18-12
ایک چوتھائی پیالی کھانڈ 75-8
ایک دس 18-8
ایک 18-8
ایک رقیق آونس دودھ 75-1
ایک زیر زمین اسٹیشن 152
ایک سائز سب کو فٹ ہونے والا 96-6
ایک سائنسی تجربہ گاہ 195
ایک سالگرہ کی تقریب 240
ایک سو ڈالر 26-12
ایک سے زیادہ مرد 30-4
ایک طرف سے تلے ہوئے انڈے 76-10
ایک گاؤں 52-3
ایک گیلن پانی 75-5
ایک ملک سے دوسرے ملک جانا C-40
ایک مکمل 17-1
ایک نکل 26-2
ایک نی کی نفیری 238-2
ایک وقفہ لیجیے H-11
ایک ڈائم 26-3
ایک ڈالر کا سکہ 26-6
ایک ڈالر 26-7
ایک کوارٹ دودھ 75-4
ایک کوارٹر 26-4
ایکریلک رنگ 232-10
ایکس-رے لینا B-119
اے ٹی ایم (خود کار ادائیگی مشین) 132
باؤلنگ کھیلنے کی جگہ 222-4
بائیسن 216-6
بائیسکل چلانا 228-5
بائیں طرف مڑنا منع ہے 154-8
باپ 34-4
بات چیت شروع کیجیے A-12
بات چیت کیجیے۔ L-11
باخبر رہیے F-140
بار کوڈ 27-4
بارانی جنگل 204-1
بارش 13-11
بارہواں 16
بارہ سنگھا 217-35
بارہ سنگھوں کی شاخ 216-16
باز 214-9
بازار سے واپسی 66
بازگردانی کیجیے C-219
بازگردانی کیے گئے سامان خریدیے D-219
بازو 214-20، 70-1
باس 238-8
باسکٹ بال کورٹ 229-7
باسکٹ بال 229-8، 231-4
باغ بانی کیجیے B-53
باغ 177-10
باغبانی عملہ 176-1

باغبانی عملے کا قائد 176-4
باقلا 69-8
باگھ 217-37
بال سکھانے کا آلہ 33-23
بال ہموار کرنے والا مادہ 108-11
بال 104-2
بالغ افراد اور بچے 30
بالغوں کا اسکول 188-8
بالوں پر۔۔ پانی ڈالیے F-108
بالوں میں گھونگر ڈالنے کے رولرز 33-19
بالوں میں لگانے والا جیل 108-16
بالوں میں لگانے کی کلپ 108-19
بالوں میں۔۔ برش کیجیے J-108
بالوں میں۔۔ کنگھا کیجیے G-108
بالوں والی باری جلد 216-19
بالوں کو باندھ کر رکھنے کی بڑی کلپ 108-20
بالوں کو بکھرنے سے روکنے کی پنیں 108-21
بالوں کو ترتیب دیجیے C-33
بالوں کو جمانے والی پھوہار 108-12
بالوں کو رنگیے D-33
بالوں کو گھنگھریالے بنانے کا آلہ 108-17
بالوں کو مستقل گھونگرالا بنائیے B-33
بالوں کی کائیں A-33
بالوں کو۔۔ دھوئیے E-108
بالوں کو۔۔ سکھائیے H-108
بالوں کی آرائش کا سیلون 131-18
بالوں کی آرائش کرنے والا 167-31
بالوں کی جالی 93-25
بالوں کی مانگ 33-4
بالوں کی وضع بنائیے 33
بالوں کی وضع بنانے والا 167-31
بالوں کی وضع قطع 33
بالٹی 61-7، 225-8
بالکل چپے اسکرین کا ٹی وی 234-7
بالکنی 51-20
بام 212-12
باندھیے A-86
بانسری 238-1
بانہوں میں جھلائیے D-36
بانہہ، ہاتھ اور انگلیاں 106
بانہہ 105-14
بانیان 198-7
باورچی خانہ میں برتن دھونے کا حوض 54-4
باورچی خانہ میں وقت شمار گھڑی 78-18
باورچی خانہ 46-5، 54-83، 15
باورچی خانے کے برتن 78
باورچی خانے کی صدری 93-29
باورچی کی ٹوپی 93-28
باورچی 83-16
باڑھ 177-19
بابر سے اندر نہ دیکھ پانی والی چق 58-8
بابر نکلنے کا راستہ نہیں 154-6
باری تفریح 226
بھون 217-31
بجرا چلانا 226-2
بجلی بچانے والے بلب استعمال کیجیے H-219

بجلی مستری 62-9
بجلی نہیں ہے۔ 62-2
بجلی کا بٹن 58-27
بجلی کا پلگ 159-42
بجلی کا جھٹکا لگنا F-116
بجلی کا چمکنا 13-17
بجلی کی فٹنگ کے دوران مستعمل بلب 181-44
بجلی کے پلگ کا خول 181-46
بجلی کے تار 186-7
بحث 186-3
بچ نکلنے کا راستہ 146-3
بچت کھاتے کا نمبر 132-11
بچوں کو اسکول چھوڑیے 38
بچوں کو اسکول لے جائیے G-38
بچوں کو لائیں M-38
بچوں کی خواب گاہ 59
بچوں کی دھکیلنے والی کرسی 37-18
بچوں کی دیکھ بھال کرنے والی 167-9
بچوں کی مالش کا تیل 37-13
بچوں کی نگرانی کرنے والا آلہ 59-7
بچوں کو نگہداشت کیجیے P-170
بچوں کے پروگرام 236-9
بچوں کے سونے کا کمرہ 47-9
بچھو 214-30
بچھڑے کے گوشت کے پارچے 70-6
بچہ پیدا کیجیے L-41
بچے کی اونچی کرسی 82-3
بچے کی حفاظتی سیٹ 159-53
بچے کی غذا 37-4
بچے کی مخصوص غذا 37-3
بچے کی نگہداشت اور پرورش 36-37
بچے کے کپڑے اتاریے E-36
بچے ہوئے کھانے سے کھاد بنائیے M-219
بحث و مباحثہ کیجیے B-139
بحر الکاہل میں پایا جانے والا بحری شیر 213-33
بحر الکاہلی ریاستیں 201-7
بحرالکاہلی شمال مغرب 201-14
بحریہ 138-15
بخار 110-8
بخار پیما 118-11
بخار۔۔ ناپیے B-118
بخشش چھوڑ جائیے J-82
بخیہ کھولنے والی آری 100-18
بد صورت منظر 23-22
بدھ 20-11
براعظم 202
برتن دھونے والا 185-2
برتن دھونے کی مشین 83-14
برتن رکھنے کی جگہ 78-29
برتنوں کا کمرہ 83-13
برتنوں کو دھونے کے بعد ایک کونے میں میز تک پہنچانے والا 185-13
برتنوں کی کھلی الماری 54-5
برساتی بوٹ 90-20
برساتی کوٹ 90-21
برساتی 90-18
برش 33-22، 108-14
برطانوی سپاہی 198-9
برف باری 13-12

برف پر بغیر پھیوں کی گاڑی سے پھسلنا 227-6
برف پر چلنے والے جوتے 231-9
برف پگھلانے والا نظام 159-41
برف رانی والا تختہ 231-23
برف رانی والے لمبے نکیلے تختے 231-24
برف رانی کے ہاتھ سے استعمال کرنے والے ڈنڈے 231-25
برف میں جمی ہوئی مچھلی 71-17
برف کا پیک 117-13
برف کا شدید ٹھنڈا اثر ہونا G-116
برف کا طوفان 13-23
برف کے میدان کا ہاکی کا کھیل 229-13
برفدار 13-22
برفیلی ہواوں کا طوفان 145-13
برقی تار پر لگانے کا ٹیپ 181-43
برقی تختہ کلید 238-18
برقی تنور کے لیے محفوظ پیالی میں 2 انڈے توڑیے۔ Q-77
برقی رو میں اچانک اضافے کو روکنے والا 196-1
برقی طریقے سے اپنی آمد کی جانچ کرائیے۔ A-160
برقی گھنٹی 51-31
برقی لائن سے جوڑنے والا تار 196-2
برقی مخرج 58-28
برقی ٹکٹ 161-19
برقی ڈبہ کھولنے کا آلہ 54-14
برنالہ 53-4
برنجی کنڈلی دار ساز 238-13
برنر 54-19
بروقت 19-23، 164-5
برش کولمبیا 201-2
بری فوج 138-14
بری و بحری فوج کا تربیت یافتہ کارکن 138-17
بریک لگانے پر جلنے والی روشنی 158-14
بریک لگانے والا پیڈل 159-45
بزرگ شہری 30-5
بزرگ 3-32
بزرگوں کی رہائش گاہ 52-11
بس اسٹاپ 129-16، 152
بس اڈا 124-7
بس کا راستہ 152-1
بس کا عارضی کھڑا کرنا 151-13
بس 128-9، 151-14
بستر پر لیٹ جائیے Y-39
بستر سے فرش تک لٹکتی چادر 58-17
بستر سے متصل میز 121-21
بستر ٹھیک کیجیے F-60
بستر کا چوکھٹا 58-18
بستر کا سلفچی 121-23
بستر کو صحیح حالت میں کرنے والا آلہ 121-27
بستر 58-9
بسکٹ 73-38، 80-6
بسکنوں کا پیکٹ 74-20
بطخ خاندان کے آبی پرندے 214-13
بطخ 70-18، 214-12
بطریق 214-11
بغل کے منظر کا آئینہ 158-3
بغلی راستہ 129-24
بغیر آستین کا بنیان 89-24
بغیر تسمے کے جوتے 95-30

بغیر چینی کی 122-7
بغیر ریزڈ والے جانور 194-13
بغیر کالر کا سوئیٹر 96-7
بقایا رقم 132-17
بل ادا کیجیے I-82
بل ڈوزر 178-6
بلانے کا بٹن 121-28
بلدیہ دفاتر 124-8
بلّی کا بچہ 215-10
بلّی 215-9
بلے باز کے پیچھے کھڑے کھلاڑی کا نقاب 231-15
بلے کی طرف گیند پھینکیے A-230
بلڈ پریشر پیما 118-9
بلڈ پریشر... جانچیے A-118
بلیرڈز 228-2
بلیزر 92-12
بلیوں پر چڑھیے C-224
بلیڈ 180-27
بناؤ سنگار 109
بنائی کی سلائیاں 233-23
بنائی کیجیے F-233
بنچ 224-10
بند اشیا 74-8
بند کرنے والی چیزیں 99
بند کرنے والی چین 99-25
بند کیا ہوا غذا کا ڈبہ 146-10
بندر 217-26
بندرگاہ پر کام کرنے والا 167-23
بندوق 142-13
بنسن کا لیمپ 195-37
بنفشہ 211-23
بنفشی سوئیٹر بھورے سوئیٹر کے بعد ہے۔ 25-9
بنفشی 24-8
بنیاد 194-20
بنیادی اعداد 16
بنیادی ذرائع نقل و حمل 150
بوتل بند پانی 146-11
بوتل کی واپسی 73-16
بوتل 37-1
بوتلیں 74-1
بورڈ پر لکھیے۔ E-6
بورڈ گیم 232-5
بوسہ دیجیے۔ K-3
بولٹ 180-35
بولی دار 96-21
بن کی جگہ کف آستین کو بند کرنے والا 99-26
بن 99-24
بنوا 94-13
بنوے 94-2
بڑا بازار (مال) 130-131
بڑا تھیلا 94-19
بڑا کلیدی تختوں پر کلیدوں سے بجایا جانے والا ساز 238-14
بڑا باتھ 23-2
بڑا 96-4
بڑھو 62-12، 167-14
بڑے اسکرین کا ٹی وی 50-14
بڑے سائز کا بیڈ 184-15

بکری 215-5
بکسوا باندھیے L-36
بکسوا 99-28
بکسے کے اندر 117
بھائی 34-6
بھاپ سے پکانے والا برتن 78-3
بھاپ میں ابلی سبزیاں 81-32
بھاری مشینری پر مت کیجیے یا اسے مت چلائیے۔ E-112
بھاری مشینری چلائیے H-170
بھاری وزن اٹھانے والی مشین 178-7
بھاری 32-7
بھانجا، بھتیجا 34-19
بھانجی، بھتیجی 34-18
بھرا ہوا گلاس 23-9
بھرائی 119-8
بھرا ہوا آلو 81-25
بھنا ہوا فیل مرغ 76-4
بھنا ہوا گائے کا گوشت 71-21
بھنا ہوا 70-1
بھنی ہوئی چاپ 76-2
بھوج پتر 210-7
بھورا سوئیٹر نارنجی سوئیٹر کے نیچے ہے۔ 25-10
بھورا 24-15
بھورے بال 33-13، 33-18
بھوسہ 177-18
بھونپو نما باجا 238-12
بھونرا 214-21
بھوننے کا سلاخوں دار خانہ 78-14
بھوننے کا ظرف 78-13
بھوننے کے لیے چولھے پر رکھی جانے والی جالی 54-21
بھوکا 42-5
بھویں 106-9
بھنی ہوئی ہوئی ہے۔ 63-15
بھیڑ 214-17
بھیگی ہوئی قمیض 101-17
بھیگے ہوئے چھوٹے تولیے 146-12
بھینس 216-6
بھیڑ کی چاپ 70-15
بھیڑ کی ٹانگ کا نچلا حصہ 70-13
بھیڑ کی ٹانگ 70-14
بھیڑ 70، 215-6
بھیڑیا 216-5
بہار 21-37
بہت چھوٹا اسکرٹ 96-15
بہرا 32-12
بہرہ پن 115-2
بہن 34-5
بہنوئی 34-17
بیت الخلاء اٹھ گیا ہے۔ 63-19
بیت الخلاء صاف کرنے کا برش 57-20
بیت الخلاء 5-9، 57-21
بیج 211-1
بیچنے والے سے ملکیت کے کاغذات حاصل کیجیے۔ E-157
بیچنے والے سے کار کے بارے میں پوچھیے۔ B-157
بیچنے والے کا ڈیلر کے پاس 158
بید یا بید مجنوں 210-13

بیروں کا سربراہ 185-12
بیری 210-20
بیزار 42-7
بیس بال بلا 231-14
بیس بال ٹوپی 86-5
بیس بال کا کھیل 44-2
بیس بال کارڈ 232-2
بیس بال 229-9، 231-18
بیس ڈالر 26-10
بیساکھیاں 113-10
بیسواں 16
بیگی پتلون 97-30
بیلا 238-6
بیلچہ 176-8، 178-22
بیلن 78-30
بیمار 42-12
بیماروں کو لانے لے جانے والی گاڑی 116-1
بیماری کی فون کال کیجیے A-186
بیماریاں اور صحتی خرابیاں 111
بیمے کا ثبوت 136-8
بین الاقوامی کال 15-35
بینگن 69-23
بینک کا گوشوارہ 132-16
بینک 124-5، 132
بیور 216-9
بیوی 34-12
بینا 34-15
بیٹری پیک 235-26
بیٹری چارجر 235-27
بیٹری کا فون 14-8
بیٹری 158-20
بیڑیاں 146-15
بینھ جائیے۔ F-6
بینھنے کی جگہ 161-9
بینی 34-14
بیڈمنٹن 228-6
بیکر 167-10، 195-39
بیکری مصنوعات 73
بیکری میں بنی اشیاء 73
بیکری 127-19
بے آستین کی قمیض 96-11
بے بی بیگ 37-16
بے بی پاؤڈر 37-14
بے بی کیریر 37-17
بے تار سرفون 14-14
بے تار فون 15-24
بے چین 42-9
بے ہوش ہونا A-116
پانپ جم گئے بیں۔ 63-16
پانپ کسنے کی رینج 181-47
پانپ 181-17
پائندان 98-19
پائن اسپرٹ رکھ دینے مڑیے۔ B-155
پاؤنڈ کے نشان کی کلید 14-7
پابندی سے معائنے کرائیے۔ H-114
چاپ 237-25
پاتر 213-42
پاجامہ 91-24
پارچوں کی صورت میں بھنا قیمہ 81-31

پتیاں 211-6
پتیلی 54، 16، 78-6
پتیوں کو جمع کیجیے 176-C
پچ رنگا یا چار خانے دار 96-22
پچاس ڈالر 26-11
پچاسواں 16
پر اسرار واقعات 237-20
پرتکلف گاڑی (لیمو) 156-11
پرتکلف لباس کے ساتھ پہننے والے جوتے 95-26
پُر سکون اجتماع 140-1
پُر سکون ربیے۔ 147-E
پَر 214-4
پرانی اشیاء کا بازار 222-6
پرانی کار خریدنا 157
پُرجوش 43-22
پرچ 83-25
پرچھتی 47-8
پردہ نما دروازہ 53-15
پردہ 235-30
پردے 56-16، 58-7
پرزے جوڑنے والی لائن 175-6
پرزے جوڑیے 170-A
پرزے لگائیے 175-C
پرزے 175-5
پُرسکون 42-8
پرندے، کیڑے مکوڑے اور مفصل پایہ (چار جوڑی پیر والے کیڑے) 214
پرنسپل 5-4
پرنٹر (چھاپنے والا آلہ) 196-17
پرواز پکڑنا 160
پریری کتّا (کتّے کی سی آواز والا) 215-22
پریری کی ریاستیں 201-3
پریس کی آزادی 140-4
پریشان 43-28
پریڈ 239-1
پستہ قد 32-6
پِستو 63-25
پسلیوں کا ڈھانچہ 107-48
پسندا 81-24
پسندیدہ مشغلے اور کھیل 233-232
پسندے کی چھری 83-29
پسندے 70-2
پسینہ جذب کرنے والی پتلون 89-23
پسینہ جذب کرنے والی 89-22
پسینہ روک پاؤڈر 108-5
پش پن 183-35
پشت یا پنٹھوں کا بنا ہوا گوشت 70-11
پل کے اوپر سے جائیں 153-B
پل کے نیچے سے جائیں 153-A
پلائی وڈ 178-18
پلاس 180-7
پلاسٹک سے بنا لپیٹنے والا لفافہ 72-24
پلاسٹک کا سامان رکھنے والا تھیلا 72-25
پلاسٹک کے برتن 79-19
پلگ 234-16
پَلا 215-12
پلنگ پوش 59-11
پلکوں کو رنگنے والا برش 109-39
پلکیں 106-11

پارسل ڈاک 134-6
پارٹی 64-2
پارک اور کھیل کے میدان 224
پارک رینجر 220-2
پارکنگ چوکیدار 184-3
پارکنگ کی جگہ 128-5
پاس بک 132-10
پاسپورٹ 41-10
پاستا کی سلاد 80-20
پاستا 67-12
پالتو جانور 215
پالتو جانوروں کا کھانا 72-5
پالتو جانوروں کی دکان 130-6
پالتو چوبا 215-14
پالنا 59-3
پالک سلاد 80-13
پالک 69-11
پام 210-14
پان کے پتوں کا سلسلہ 233-31
پانچ ڈالر 26-8
پانچواں 16
پانسہ 232-6
پانڈا 217-41
پانی انڈیلیے 82-C
پانی بجائیے 219-E
پانی چھڑکنے کا آلہ 53-22
پانی چھڑکنے کے نظام کو نصب کیجیے 176-H
پانی سے پیدا کی ہوئی بجلی 218-5
پانی میں چھلانگ لگائیے 230-K
پانی کا پائپ 53-21
پانی کا فوارہ 224-9
پانی کا گلاس 83-22
پانی کا لباس 225-4
پانی کی بوتل 74-13
پانی کے اندر سانس لینے کا ٹینک 225-5
پانی 209-13، 225-1
پانی لگانا 178-4
پپوٹے 106-10
پپیتا 68-20
پت تھیلی 107-44
پت جھڑ / خزاں 21-39
پتلا 32-9
پتلون کو تنگ کیجیے۔ 100-D
پتلون کو چھوٹا کیجیے۔ 100-B
پتلون کو سنبھالنے والی پنی 91-16
پتلون کو لمبا کیجیے۔ 100-A
پتلون کو ڈھیلی کیجیے۔ 100-C
پتلون 87-12
پتلی چونچ 214-3
پتلی نلکی 79-18
پتلی تائی 97-35
پتلی کتاب 23-8
پتنگ 225-2
پتنگا 214-21
پتواری کشتی 225-3
پتھر پھوڑ برما 178-9
پتہ 4-5
پتہ 210-6
پتیاں اڑانے والا 176-2

پنری 152-14
پنہ 51-28
پنی دار 96-20
پنی کا بکسوا 94-20
پڑوسیوں سے ملیے 49-R
پڑھ کر سنائیے 36-N
پڑھائیے 170-Q
پکا ہوا مرغ 70-25
پکنک پر جائیں 224-D
پکنک منائیے 224-D
پکنک کی میز 224-8
پکے کیلے 68-30
پھاٹک پر 161
پھاٹک 53-9، 161-8
پھسلن دار فرش 179-6
پھل 67-9، 68
پھل اور سبزیوں کا سلاد 80-14
پھلوں کی سلاد 80-21
پھلیاں 72-17
پھلیوں کا ٹِن کا ڈبہ 74-15
پھنسنا ہوا رواں صاف کیجیے۔ 101-D
پھول پتی والا 96-25
پھول پودے 84-9
پھول جھاڑو 61-1
پھول گوبھی کو بھاپ دیجیے۔ 77-D
پھول گوبھی کی ایک قسم 69-13
پھول گوبھی 69-14
پھول کے اجزاء 211
پھول کے پتوں کا سلسلہ 233-32
پھول 208-7، 211
پھولوں کی کیاری 53-20
پھونک کر بجانے والا نفیری کی طرز کا ساز 238-5
پھپھڑا 107-39
پھیلائیے 230-M
پھینٹ کرتے ہوئے انڈے 76-7
پھینٹنے والا آلہ 78-21
پھینٹنے کا برقی آلہ 54-25
پھینٹنے کا پیالہ 54-28
پھینکنے والی بال 231-5
پھینکیے 230-C
پھاڑ پر سائیکل چلانا 226-8
پھاڑ سے نیچے کی طرف اسکیٹنگ 227-1
پھاڑ کی چوٹی 204-14
پھاڑوں پر برف کا طوفان 145-18
پھاڑی سلسلہ 204-15
پھاڑی شیر 216-2
پھاڑی علاقوں کا معیاری وقت 19-30
پھاڑیاں 204-16
پھرے دار 141-3
پہلا صدر 198-11
پہلا مسودہ لکھیے۔ 191-H
پہلا نام 4-2
پہلا 16
پہلو تکیہ 56-2
پہلی براعظمی کانگریس 198-6
پہلے اور آخری مہینہ کا کرایہ ادا کیجیے۔ 48-E
پہنچانے والا شخص 167-21
پہنچیے۔ 160-K
پہنیے 87-B

پلیٹ صاف کرنے والا محلول 61-21
پلیٹ فارم 152-7
پلیٹ میں رکھنے کا کاغذی رومال 61-22
پلیٹ 55-1
پلیٹوں کو خشک کیجیے 60-N
پلیٹیں پس 217-46
پلیٹیں اٹھائیے 82-G
پلیٹیں دھوئیے 60-M
پلیٹیں دھونے کی مشین 54-8
پلیٹیں بنائیے 82-G
پن گدی 100-13
پن 95-38
پناہ تلاش کیجیے۔ 147-H
پنجہ 214-2، 214-20
پندرہواں 16
پنسل پکڑیے 6-I
پنسل تراش 7-23
پنسل رکھ دیجیے 6-J
پنسل 7-20
پنگوئن 214-11
پنڈلی تک کی اسکرٹ 96-17
پنڈلی تک کے جوتے 95-28
پنڈلی کے اوپر کا حصہ 106-21
پنڈلی 106-22
پنڈلیوں پر چڑھانے والی پوشش 90-12
پنڈلیوں تک کے موزے 91-9
پنکھ 214-1
پنکھا 55-19
پنکھڑیاں 211-8
پنیر دار ٹوفو (سویابین سے تیار کی گئی پنیھی) سبزی کیسیرول 77
پنیر کو کسیے۔ 77-G
پنیر کیک 81-34
پنیر 66-4
پوچھیے، "آپ کیسے ہیں؟" 2-B
پود لگائیے 177-A
پودوں میں پانی ڈالیے 176-F
پودوں میں غذا 176-D
پودینہ، اجوائن خراسانی 69-28
پودے 208-5، 210
پورا چاند 205-12
پورچ کی روشنی 53-13
پورٹیبل سی ڈی اسٹیریو 234-1
پورٹیبل ویڈیو کیمرہ 235-24
پوری بچھی ہوئی چادر 58-12
پوری طرح ابلی ہوئی انڈے 76-8
پوری طرح بند کرنے کا تالا 51-34
پوری طرح ڈھکنے والا لباس 92-8
پورے جسم کا ایک پارچہ لباس 93-24
پوسٹ آفس باکس (پی او باکس) 135-9
پوسٹ کارڈ 134-16
پول 228-2
پولس افسر 141-1، 168-48
پولس کو جرائم کی اطلاع دیجیے۔ 143-K
پولو قمیض 92-14
پونے دو 18-13
پناخہ 239-7
پنرول کی ٹنکی 158-10
پنرولیم 218-6

تلوا 94-21	تربیتی ملازمت 172-6	پیٹرول پیما آلہ 159-31	پہیہ گاڑی 72-7
تلوار بازی 228-7	تربیتی نیکر 37-11	پہیہ پر سامان لادنا 226-6	پہیہ کرسی 113-9
تلی 193-45	ترتیب سے رکھنے والا 175-10	پہیہ کا نچلا حصہ 107-29	پی بی ایکس 182-13
تلے ہوئے آلو کے قتلے 79-2	ترتیبی اعداد 16	پہیہ 104-5	پیاز چھلے 79-4
تماشہ کیجیے G-233	ترجمان 168-35	پہیاں 94-6	پیاز کے قتلے کیجیے۔ L-77
تمام دوائیں ختم کیجیے۔ C-112	ترجیحی ڈاک 134-1	پیڑ اور پودے 210	پیاز 69-19
تمبو میں استعمال ہونے والا اسنو 226-16	ترقی 172-4	پیڑو کا حصہ 107-50	پیاسا 42-2
تنا 210-4	ترم 238-10، 238-11	پیک کرنے والا 175-8	پیالہ 55-2
تناؤ 115-4	ترمیم کاری کی دکان 100	پیکنگ ٹیپ 183-32	پیالی 83-24
تنخواہ کا چیک 165-14	ترمیم کیجیے I-191	تابکاری والے مواد 179-7	پیپر کلپ 183-31
تنخواہ کلرک 165-10	ترمیمات 100	تاب کاری 218-15	پیتل والے ساز 238
تنخواہ کی پرچی 165-11	ترک وطن 199-12	تاجر 167-12	پیجیے۔ J-11
تندوری مرغ 81-22	تسلی دیجیے I-36	تاخیر سے آنے یا جانے والی پرواز 161-30	پیچ کس 180-30
تنفسی آلہ 179-13	تصحیح کار سیال 183-36	تاخیر سے نہ پہنچیے۔ E-174	پیچھے جانے کا بن 197-2
تنور کو پہلے سے گرم کیجیے۔ A-77	تصحیح کار ٹیپ 183-37	تاخیر سے 19-24	پیچھے جھکی ہوئی سیٹ 161-27
تنور کی صفائی کرنے والا 61-3	تصدیق نامۂ پیدائش 40-1	تاخیر کا جرمانہ ادا کیجیے E-133	پیچھے گھمائیں C-235
تنور کی صفائی کیجیے C-60	تصویر بنانے کا موٹا کپڑا 233-17	تادیب کیجیے K-36	پیچھے کی بتی 158-13
تنور 54-20	تصویر پر لیبل لگائیے۔ U-9	تار کے ربر بنانے کا آلہ 181-42	پیچھے کی سیٹ 159-54
تنکوں کا بنا ٹوپ 90-23	تصویر لیجیے A-206	تار والے ساز 238	پیدائش A-40
تنہا باپ 35-23	تصویر والی لغت 31-7	تار 14-2، 181-13، 196-13	پیدل چلنا 226-7
تنہا ماں 35-22	تصویروں والی کتاب 133-12	تارک وطن 199-13	پیدل چلنے والا 128-14
تنہا 42-17	تصویروں کا فریم 58-4	تاریخ پیدائش (ڈی او بی) 4-13	پیدل چلنے والوں کا راستہ 154-13
تنے 211-9	تصویریں 58-3	تاریخ خاتمہ 112-7	پیر 20-9، 104-8
توانائی اور تحفظ 219-218	تعارف 190-6	تاریخ عالم 199	پیراگراف کے پہلے جملے کا کنارہ خالی
توانائی اور وسائل کو محفوظ رکھنے کے طریقے 219	تعدد 20	تاریخ 20-1، 189-12	چھوڑیے۔ D-190
توانائی کے ذرائع 218	تعدیہ زدہ گلا 111-4	تاریخی اصطلاحات 199	پیراگراف 190-3
تودہ کھسکنا 144-6	تعریف کیجیے J-36، B-148	تاریخی اعتبار سے قدیم مغربی امریکی انداز کی	پیراکیٹ 215-15
توسیعی ڈوری 181-14	تعطیل 22-6	فلمیں 237-15	پیسٹری کی تھوں میں پھرنے والی ڈش تیار کرنے کا
تولیے ٹانگنے کی سلاخ 57-15	تعطیلات 239	تازہ مچھلی 71-16	برتن 78-28
تونا مچھلی 212-8	تعلیم کی تکمیل D-40	تاش کھیلیے H-233	پیسٹری کے لیے تیار کی گئی ڈش 81-35
تکلمی معالجہ 115-13	تعمیر کرنے والا رنگ برنگا کاغذ 232-12	تاشہ 238-16	پیسفک وقت 19-29
تکلیف کی حالت میں 42-11	تعمیر 178	تالا بنانے والا شخص 62-11	پیسے کا حساب لگانے کی مشین 73-15
تکیہ 58-11	تعمیراتی مزدور 178-1	تالا ٹوٹا ہوا ہے۔ 62-6	پیش ادائیگی فون 25-15
تکیے کا غلاف 58-14	تعمیراتی مقام 126-2	تالاب 204-21	پیش ادائیگی فون کارڈ 14-15
تھیٹر 127-23	تغذیہ کا لیبل 122-8	تبادلہ کیجیے I-27	پیش بند 92-11
تھانہ 124-6	تفریح 237-236	تبادلۂ خیال 44-3	پیش تختہ سے کھانے کی میز تک کھانا لانے
تھرموساسٹیٹ ایڈجسٹ کیجیے J-219	تفریح پارک 223-10	تبدیل کیجیے D-17، C-148	والا 185-15
تھن دار جانور 209-10، 216-216، 217	تفریح مرکز 56-5	تتلی کا رینگنے والا بچہ 214-20	پیش تختہ 54-22
تھوڑی دیر تک روشنی پڑنے والی تصویر 235-35	تفویض کے بارے میں سوچیے۔ E-191	تتلی 214-19	پیش رفت کیجیے۔ G-10
تھکا ہوا 43-32	تقرر کار 172-14	تتیا 214-17	پیش کار 141-12
تھیلا 161-18	تقرری پائیے L-173	تجارتی ماہی گیر 167-17	پیش کرنے والی خدمت کار خاتون 83-9
تھیلی 217-50	تقرری 22-4	تجربہ گاہ میں پہنا جانے والا کوٹ 93-33	پیشانی پر بالوں کی جھالر 33-8
تھیلے میں سامان رکھنے والا شخص 73-14	تقریب 206-6	تجربہ گاہ 121	پیشانی 106-2
تھیلے 74-7	تقریر کی آزادی 140-2	تجوری 132-6	پیشکش 182-6
تہ ہو جانے والا اور پھونک کر بجایا جانے والا	تقریر کیجیے A-148	تجویز کردہ دوا 112-3	پیشہ ورانہ تربیتی اسکول 188-5
ساز 238-19	تقسیم کرنا D-192	تحائف کی دکان 184-5	پیشے سے متعلق صلاح کار 172-10
تہائی 17-3	تقسیم کیجیے A-17	تحت جوہری ذرہ 195-32	پیشے کو اپنانے کا طریقہ 172
تہذیب 199	تقویمی تقریبات 22	تحریری امتحان میں شرکت کیجیے۔ E-137	پیشے کی منصوبہ بندی 172
تہنیتی کارڈ 134-15	تل چنا 214-18	تحفظی پن 100-14	پیغام بردار 168-40
تہ خانہ 47-13، 50	تل 32-16	تحفہ 240-3	پیغام ٹائپ کیجیے E-197
تہ دار کیک 81-33	تلا ہوا گائے کا گوشت 76-6	تختۂ سفید 6-3	پیغامات کی جانچ کیجیے R-171
تہ کی جا سکنے والی میز 102-4	تلا ہوا مرغ 76-1	تختۂ سیاہ 6-1	پیمائش 17
تہ کی جا سکنے والی کرسی 102-5	تلاش اور بچاؤ کی ٹیم 145-20	تختۂ کلید کا استعمال 196	پیمائشوں کو تبدیل کیجیے۔ C-75
تیاری غذا کا کارکن 185-4	تلاش میں مدد دینے والی ویب سائٹیں	تختۂ کلید 14-5، 196-14	پیمائشیں 17
تیر اندازی 228-1	(سرچ انجن) 197-6	ترازو 57-27، 72-3، 135-8، 195-41	پیمانہ 155-7، 195-41
تیر 231-8	تلاش و جستجو 199-8	تراشہ 78-16	پینٹ رولر 181-23
تیرنے۔ L-230	تلاش کرنے کا خانہ 197-5	تراش 99	پیٹ بھرا ہوا 42-6
تیراکی لباس کے اوپر پہنا جانے والا پوشش 90-25	تلفظ کی جانچ کیجیے۔ D-8	تربوز 68-18	پیٹ درد 110-4
تیراکی کا پول 184-22	تلنے کی کڑابی 78-5	تربیت 172-2	پیٹ 107-27

چپل 91-26	جوابی مشین 14-17	جرم 142
چپٹی خوردنی 212-15	جوابی معلومات حاصل کیجیے۔ K-191	جزیرہ نما 204-7
چپے پردے کا ٹی وی 234-7	جوتوں کا شعبہ 95-7	جزیرہ 204-8
چپک دار پنی 117-5	جوتے آزمائیے C-95	جسم پر ملنے والا لوشن 108-9
چپکدار نوٹ سلپ 183-39	جوتے اور دیگر اضافی سامان 95-94	جسم میں ہوا پہنچانے کے لیے کثرت 122-5
چپکنے والا لیبل 102-3	جوتے کی اگلی ٹھوکر 94-23	جسم نامیہ 194-1
چتی دار بھونرا 214-26	جوتے کی ایڑی 94-22	جسم کے اندر اور باہر 107-106
چچا زاد، خالہ زاد، ماموں زاد بھائی 34-9	جوتے کی دکان 130-10	جسم 104
چچا زاد، خالہ زاد، ماموں زاد بہن 34-9	جوتے کے فیتے 94-24	جسمانی تعلیم 189-17
چچا، ماموں، خالو 34-8	جوتے 87-13	جسمانی طور پر معذور 32-10
چچی، ممانی، خالہ 34-7	جولائی 21-31	جسمانی معالج 115-12
چراگاہ 204-20	جون 21-30	جسمانی معالجہ 115-11
چراہے کا ٹوپ 92-18	جونیر ہائی اسکول 188-3	جسمانی کرتب بازی 228-9
چست اور پھرتیلی رہیے۔ E-114	جوڑا 239-4	جشن منائیے C-206
چست بڑے کالر والا سوئیٹر 96-9	جوڑنا A-192	جغرافیہ اور مقامات 204
چست پتلون 97-29	جوہر کسی کیمیائی عنصر کا اقل ترین جز 195-28	جفت اعداد 192-4
چست لباس 91-19	جز 210-5، 211-3	جگالی کرنے والے جانور کا قابل خوردنی معدہ 70-8
چسنی 37-24	جزواں 28-1	جگر 107-40
چشمہ 204-2	جھانک کر دیکھنے والا سوراخ 51-32	جلد پر گودا ہوا نقش 32-18
چشمیہ 194-14	جھاڑو 61-16	جلد تیار ہونے والے کھانوں کا باورچی 185-1
چشمے 115-7	جھاڑی کائنات کی قینچی 176-11	جلد کو دھوپ کی تمازت سے بچانے والا 108-8
چقندر 69-5	جھاڑیوں کو چھاننیے B-176	جلد 107-31
چلائیں B-235	جھنجلایا ہوا 64-6	جدی سے پہننے والا مکمل لباس 91-22
چلائیے 77-0	جھنجھنا 37-26	جدی سے پہننے والا نصف لباس 91-23
چلتا پھرتا گھر 52-7	جھنڈا 44-2، 239-8	جدی سے تیار کھانے کا ریستوران 79، 128-10
چلانے والے بچے 23-11	جھولا 59-20	جلسہ گاہ 5-18
چلنا شروع کرنے والا بچہ 31-8	جھولتا ہوا کھلونا 59-5	جما ہوا رات کا کھانا 72-28
چلنے میں مدد کرنے والا 113-11	جھولنے والی کرسی 37-21	جماعت میں کام کیجیے۔ I-8
چمپنزی 217-27	جھولے کو دھکا دیجیے B-224	جماعتی کھیل 229
چمچہ 55-5	جھولے 224-11	جماعتی 237-29
چمگادڑ 216-7	جھوم جھوم کر گانا بجانا 237-23	جمانے والی مشین 54-10
چمنی 53-5	جھکے 230-0	جمانے والی ٹھنڈک 13-7
چمنی جیسا آلہ 195-43	جھیل 204-13	جمعرات 20-12
چمٹی 78-23، 117-4	جھینگا 71-11	جمعہ 20-13
چمڑا 98-6	جھینگر 214-23	جملوں کو ترتیب سے رکھیے۔ X-9
چمڑے کی جیکٹ 90-4	جہازرانی کا کلرک 175-14	جملہ 190-2
چمک دار حفاظتی پنی 92-4	جی پی ایس (کرۂ جاتی مقام بندی نظام) 155-11	جمی ہوئی سبزیاں 72-27
چوبی سنٹر 238-15	جیب 100-7	جمی ہوئی غذائیں 72
چوبی فرش 58-21	جیل میں جائیے G-141	جنس نرگسی کا ذرا بڑا پیلے پھولوں کا پودا 211-25
چوبی بتھوڑا 180-2	جیلی نما جسم کا سمندری مرجانی جانور 212-14	جنس: 4-16
چوتھا 16	جینس 86-2	جنگ 199-10
چوتھائی چاند 205-11	جیوری میں شمولیت کیجیے E-140	جنگل میں آگ 144-7
چوتھائی 17-4	جیوری 141-8	جنگل 204-11
چودھواں 16	جیکٹ 90-8	جنگلہ یا گھیرا 129-21
چورابا 129-128	چائے دانی 55-16	جنگلی چوبا 215-18
چوری 142-2	چائے کا چمچ 83-31	جنگلی زندگی 220-3
چوزا 70-16	چائے کی پیالی 55-6	جنگلی کندر 210-15
چوگوشیہ 5-1	چائے کی کیتلی 54-17	جنوب 155-3، 201-13
چولھے پر بھونا ہوا گوشت 76-3	چائے 81-39	جنوبی امریکا 202-1
چونچ 214-3	چائے 51-30	جنوبی اونچے میدان 201-17
چونگا رکھ دیجیے D-15	چادریں تبدیل کیجیے P-60	جنوبی ساحل 201-7
چونگا 14-1	چار جولائی 22-13	جنوبی مشرق 201-13
چونیاں 63-23	چارا کھلائیے D-177	جنوبی مغرب 201-12
چوٹ لگنا C-116	چارجر 14-10، 234-17	جنوری 21-25
چوڑائی 17-19	چالیسواں 16	جواب پر دائرہ بنائیے Q-9، K-10
چوڑی گردن والا سوئیٹر 96-10	چاول 67-10، 81-30، 177-1	جواب دیجیے H-135
چوڑی ٹائی 97-36	چاک 7-18	جواب نامہ 10-2
چوکی دار 169-55	چبوترہ 240-2	جوابات H-8
چوبا 215-17	چپ منک (زمینی گلہری) 215-20	جوابی پتہ 134-21

چوبی 63-27
چنان 208-6
چڈی بدلیے G-36
چڈی رکھنے کی بالٹی 37-7
چڑھنے والے اوزار 224-14
چڑیا گھر 222-1
چڑیا 208-4
چکوترا 68-6
چکنا D-106
چھ عدد سوڈا (میٹھا مشروب) 74-21
چھ عدد کے پیک 74-9
چھاتہ 90-17
چھاتی 107-26
چھالا 110-15
چھپائیے D-240
چھپانے والا ٹیپ 181-53
چھپکلی 213-40
چھت باغیچہ 50-4
چھت پڑا ہوا بازار 126-7
چھت رس رہی ہے۔ 62-3
چھت مرمت کرنے والا 62-8
چھت کی ٹائلیں 178-20
چھت 46-1
چھتر دار قمیض 89-22
چھچھوندر یا جنگلی چوہیے 63-28
چھری 55، 4-83 30
چھل جانا 110-12
چھلنی 78-22
چھلے آلو کی چاول وغیرہ کے ساتھ بنائی گئی
غذا 80-3
چھلے دار نوٹ بک 29-7
چھلے دار بک 180-40
چھنائی قینچی 176-9
چھونا E-106
چھوٹا اسکرٹ 96-16
چھوٹا بچہ 31-7
چھوٹا بڑا کرنے والا عدسہ 235-23
چھوٹا بیگ 88-13
چھوٹا قصبہ 52-3
چھوٹا ٹی وی 234-8
چھوٹا ڈی وی ڈی پلیئر 234-11
چھوٹا کمرہ 182-7
چھوٹا کیسٹ پلیئر 234-6
چھوٹا باتھ 23-1
چھوٹا 96-2
چھوٹی مورت 232-1
چھوٹی وین 156-8
چھوٹی کشتی چلانا 226-3
چھوٹی-آستین والی قمیض 96-12
چھوٹے بال 33-1
چھوٹے بچے کا کمرہ 47-10
چھونا 16
چھڑکنے والی مشین 181-21
چھڑکنے کا اسٹارچ 101-12
چھید والے دانے 95-34
چھید کرکے لگانے والی بالیاں 95-36
چھید کیے ہوئے دانے 99-32
چھیدا ہوا کان 32-17
چھیلنے والا چاقو 78-16

چھینٹ 96-23
چھینکنا B-110
چھینی 181-55
چہرہ 106
چہرے پر سنگھار و آرائش والی پنسل 109-37
چہرے پر لگایا جانے والا پاؤڈر 109-41
چہرے کا نقاب 93-32
چپاس پہاڑیاں 201-18
چیتھڑے 61-9
چیچڑی 214-27
چیک 111-6
چیخیں B-206
چیری 68-11
چیزوں کو منظم کیجیے L-171
چیزیں جمع کیجیے A-232
چیف جسٹس 138-13
چینی دان 55-14
چینی گوبھی 69-15
چینی کے متبادلات 79-20
چینی 73-30
چیونٹی خور 217-24
چیڈر کا ٹھوس پنیر 71-28
چیڑ کا پھل 210-11
چیڑ 210-9
چیک بک 132-12
چیک بھنائیے۔ A-132
چیک 132-13
حاجتی سیٹ 37-12
حاشیہ 190-10
حاصل تقسیم 192-10
حاصل جمع 192-7
حاصل ضرب 192-9
حافظہ (میموری) کارڈ 235-20
حاملہ 32-15
حجام کی دکان 129-19
حذف کیجیے C-196
حرارت پیما آلہ 159-30
حرارت ربا 158-19
حرارت کا غیر موصل 178-14
حرارت 110-8
حرفتی معالج 168-45
حروف جار 25
حروف کو ترتیب دے کر لفظ بنائیے۔ W-9
حروف ہجاء 13-7
حرکت سے متعلق حروف جار 153
حرکی کھلونا 233-26
حساب لگائیے B-17
حساب کرنے کا کاؤنٹر 73-12
حفاظتی ٹیک لگوائیے I-114
حفاظتی اشیاء کا بکسہ تیار کیجیے B-146
حفاظتی آلات 179
حفاظتی بوٹ 179-20
حفاظتی پتلون 93-22
حفاظتی جانچ سے گذریے D-160
حفاظتی جانچ سے گزرنا 160
حفاظتی جانچ کار 160-5
حفاظتی جمع کرنے کا صندوق 132-7
حفاظتی چشمے 92-10
حفاظتی خطرات اور خطرناک سامان 179

حفاظتی دروازہ 50-16
حفاظتی دستہ کی قمیض 93-20
حفاظتی دھوپ کے چشمے 179-11
حفاظتی صدری 226-14
حفاظتی ضابطے 164-6
حفاظتی عینک 179-10
حفاظتی غبارے 159-43
حفاظتی نقاب 179-12
حفاظتی ٹوپی 92-9
حفاظتی کیمرا 50-19
حفاظتی بتھری 59-10
حقوق کا بل (بل آف رائٹس) 198-13
حقوق 140
حقیقی پروگرام 236-6
حل 192-14
حملہ 142-3
حواس 106
حوالہ جاتی لائبریرین 133-9
حکم کے پتوں کا سلسلہ 233-30
حکمراں 199-4
حیاتیات 194
حیاتیاتی تجمع 218-9
حیاتیاتی توانائی 218-9
حیرت زدہ 43-30
حیرت ناک 237-20
'خاتمہ' دبائیے۔ D-15
خاتمے کی تاریخ 136-10
خاتون میزبان 82-2
خار ماہی 212-6
خالی جگہوں کو بھریے۔ O-9
خالی گلاس 23-10
خالی ہونے کی علامت 50-7
خاموش بچہ 23-12
خاندان کے افراد کا جمع ہونا 44
خاندان 35-34
خانے دار الماری 58-1
خانے دار 96-24
خاکستری 24-18
خبر پہنچانے والا 169-52
خبروں کے پروگرام 236-1
ختم کیجیے T-230
ختم ہفتہ 20-17
خدمت کار 82، 169-8، 56، 185-8
خدمت کیجیے D-139
خراب کٹا 23-18
خربوزہ 68-19
خردہ فروش کلرک 169-53
خردہ فروشی کی خود خدمتی دکان 127-18
خرگوش 215-13
خرید و فروخت کی بڑی دکان 131-13
خرید و فروخت کے پروگرام 236-10
خریداری تھیلوں کو دوبارہ استعمال کیجیے B-219
خریداری کی پرچیاں 67-15
خریداری کی ٹوکری 73-9
خریداری 27
خریداری G-27، A-28، A-94
خریدے جانے والے سامان کی فہرست 67-14
خزانچی 73، 167-13، 15
خزاں 21-39

خسرہ 111-5
خشک چیزوں کی پیمائشیں 75
خشک دیوار 178-19
خشک سالی 145-11
خشک صاف کرنے والے رومال 37-15
خشک منانے والا مارکر 7-17
خشکی اور پانی میں رہنے والے جانور 212
خشکی رفع کرنے والا 108-9
خصوصیات کے بارے میں دریافت کیجیے۔ B-48
خضاب لگائیے D-33
خط مستقیم 193-22
خط منحنی 193-23
خط ٹائپ کیجیے A-171
خط 134-13
خطرناک فضلہ 218-12
خطرناک 186-1
خطرے کی روشنیاں 159-36
خطوط 193
خلا باز 205-17
خلاء روب تھیلا 61-12
خلاء روب منسلکات 61-11
خلاء روب 61-10
خلائی اسٹیشن 205-18
خلائی گاڑی 205-19
خلومایہ 194-9
خلیج ساحلی میدان 201-16
خلیج 204-9
خلیہ 194-4
خلیہ کی جھلی 194-6
خمیدہ تصویروں کے رنگین نقوش والا 96-26
خمیری آٹے میں مکھن ملا کر تیار کیا گیا
کیک 79-16
خواب گاہ 46-2، 58
خوانچہ فروش 129-29
خواہش کا اظہار کیجیے B-240
خوبانی 68-12
خوبصورت منظر 23-21
خوبصورت 32-14
خود جل جانا H-116
خود خدمت چائے کافی خانہ 5-14
خود سامان کی جانچ کرنا 73-10
خود کار ادائیگی مشین کارڈ 132-15
خود کار طور پر اچانک سامنے آنے والے اشتہار 197-9
خود کار ڈاک مرکز (اے پی سی) 135-10
خودکار فون نظام 14-23
خودکار ٹرانسمشن 159
خودکار ٹکٹ مشین 152-9
خوراک 112-6
خوردبین تختی کے کلپ 194-21
خوردبین کی تختی 194-17
خوردبین کے گھومنے والے عدسے 194-15
خوردبین 194
خوردبینی عمل کے دوران باریک بین ردوبدل کرنے کا
پرزہ 194-22
خوردبینی معائنہ کے لیے کسی شئے کو رکھنے کا
شیشہ 194-3
خوش 28، 6-43، 31
خوشبو دار فرحت بخش محلول 108-6
خوف زدہ 43-23

خول دار مچھلی 71
خون بہنا M-116
خون سے متعلق کام 121-30
خون کی جانچ 121-30
خون... نکالیے F-118
خیالات پر غور و خوض کیجیے۔ F-191
خیمہ لگانا 226-5
خیمہ 226-10
دائرہ 193-34
دائرے کے محیط اور قطر کے تناسب کی
علامت 193-46
داخلہ گاہ 50، 164-1
داخلہ کلرک 120-14
داخلی طب کا ماہر 120-1
داخلے کا پاس 161-20
داخلی کی سطح کی ملازمت 172-1
دادا، دادی،نانا، نانی بنیے۔ N-41
دادا، نانا 34-2
دادی،نانی 34-1
دافع بدبو استعمال کیجیے C-108
دافع بدبو پاؤڈر 108-5
دافع تیزابیت 113-28
دافع حرارت سیال ڈالیے۔ I-157
دافع درد دوا 113-26
دافع دیمک وغیرہ 63-21
دانت اکھاڑنا F-119
دانت درد 110-2
دانت صاف کرنے کا برش 109-22
دانت صاف کرنے کا لاس 109-24
دانت میں سوراخ کرنا D-119
دانت میں... برش کیجیے J-109
دانت نکلنے کے دوران منہ میں دبانے والا
چھلا 37-25
دانت کا برش 57-23
دانت کو... لاس سے صاف کیجیے K-109
دانت کے بیماریاں 119
دانت کے ڈاکٹر کا معاون 167-22
دانت... صاف کرنا A-119
دانت 106-7
دانتوں اور جبڑوں کی خرابیوں کے علاج کا ماہر 119-5
دانتوں اور جبڑوں کی خرابیوں کے علاج 119
دانتوں پر جمنے والا جراثیم پرور میل 119-12
دانتوں کا برش رکھنے کا برتن 57-24
دانتوں کو صحیح حالت میں رکھنے کا تار 119-6
دانتوں کی حفاظن صحت کا ماہر 119-3
دانتوں کی دیکھ بھال 119
دانتوں کے اوزار 119-4
داڑھیں بنائیے M-109
داڑھیں بنانے کا برقی آلہ 109-26
داڑھیں بنانے کا محفوظ ریزر 109-27
داڑھیں بنانے کی کریم 109-29
داڑھیں بنانے کے بعد لگانے کا محلول 109-30
داڑھی 33-6
دباؤ سے صاف کرنے کا آلہ 181-50
دبلا 32-9
دبیز سوتی ابھری دھاریوں کا کپڑا 99-11
ددوڑے 110-10
دراز 54، 23-58، 2
درازوں والی الماری 59-6

دربان 184-1
درجات 10-4
درجہ بند سلنڈر 195-38
درجہ حرارت 13
درخت لگائیے E-176 ، N-219
درخت 208-1
درخواست داخل کیجیے۔ C-48
درخواست فارم بھریے J-173
درخواست فیس ادا کیجیے۔ D-137
درد 115-3
درزی کی دکان پر کپڑوں کے نمونے پہنانے کا
پتلا 100-2
درزی 100-3
درست خانوں کی جانچ کیجیے۔ U-9
درسگاہ کا احاطہ 5
درسگاہ کے احاطہ کے اطراف 5
درسی کتاب 25-7
درمیانہ 96-3
درمیانی عمر کا 32-2
درمیانی لمبائی کی اسکرٹ 96-17
درمیانی نام کا پہلا حرف 4-3
دروازہ 46-3
دروازے کا تالا 159-25
دروازے کا لو 53-12
دروازے کی زنجیر 51-33
دروازے کی گھنٹی 53-14
درون ورید (درون ورید دوا کا انجکشن) 121-25
دریا کا کنارہ 204-12
دریائی گھوڑا 217-43
دس پاؤں والا جھینگا 212-18
دس ڈالر 26-9
دستانہ 231-17
دستانے رکھنے کا خانہ 159-44
دستانے 90-6
دستخط 4-19
دستکاری کیجیے D-232
دستی اشتہار 102-1
دستی آلۂ موسیقی 238-20
دستی تولیہ 57-17
دستی تھیلا 87-9
دستی تھیلی 94-2
دستی ٹرانسمشن 159
دسمبر 21-36
دسواں 16
دعوت نامہ قبول کرنے سے انکار کیجیے J-12
دعوت نامہ قبول کیجیے I-12
دعوت نامہ 64-9
دعوت 239-13
دفتر امور کرایہ داری 51
دفتر میں ایک خراب دن 186
دفتر میں ایک ملاقات 119
دفتر کی عمارت 124-2
دفتر کے آلات 183
دفتر 182-183
دفتری سامان کی فراہمی کی دکان 127-21
دفتری سامان 183
دفتری مہارتیں 171
دل کا دورہ پڑنا D-116
دل کا مرض 111-11

دوڑ لگائیے S-230
دوہرا دستانہ، انگلیاں اور انگوٹھا الگ 90-10
دوہری بانسری 238-4
دکھ بھری موسیقی 237-22
دھات کائنے کی آری 180-5
دھاگہ پہنچانے کی چرخی 98-20
دھاگہ پہنچانے کی چھڑ 98-20
دھاگہ لپیٹنے کی چرخی 98-21
دھاگہ 99-100، 23، 11
دھلائی میں استعمال ہونے والا میل کاٹ 101-8
دھلنے والے کپڑوں کی ٹوکری 101-2
دھلنے والے کپڑے 101-1
دھلنے کے کپڑوں کو الگ الگ کیجیے۔ A-101
دھلے کپڑے تہہ کیجیے F-101
دھماکہ 144-4
دھند آلود 13-20
دھند 218-11
دھویں میں بھونا ہوا فیل ہوا مرغ 71-25
دھواں خارج کرنے والی نلکی 158-15
دھواں شناس آلہ 51-29
دھوپ دار 13-9
دھوپ سے بچنے کے لیے اسکرین 225-10
دھوپ سے حفاظت کی کریم لگائیے D-108
دھوپ سے حفاظت کی کریم 108-7
دھوپ میں جھلسنا 110-14
دھوپ کا چشمہ 90-27
دھونے والی مشین میں ڈالیے۔ C-101
دبانے کا عدسہ 194-16
دبرائیں J-191
دبرے تسمے 94-1
دبرے حلقے کی ٹائی 89-16
دبی 72-22
دیسی پنیر کا ڈبہ 74-17
دیگر آلات 238
دیمک 63-22
دیوار خلیہ 194-5
دیوار 56-10
دیواری کاغذ 59-8
دیکھ بھال 184-23
دیکھنا A-106
دیکھنے سے معذور 32-11
دیہات 52-4
دیہاتی علاقے میں اسکیننگ 227-3
دیہی علاقہ 52-4
دیہی 237-27
ذاتی حفظان صحت اور صفائی 108-109
ذاتی سی ڈی پلیئر 234-5
ذاتی معلومات 4
ذخیرہ جمع کرنے کا پلاسٹک کا ڈبہ 78-4
ذخیرہ گاہ 185-5
ذخیرے کا اندراج کرنے والا کلرک 169-59
ذخیرہ کاری فہرست اکائی نمبر 27-5
ذرات سے بچاؤ کا نقاب 179-14
ذمہ داریاں 140
ذیابیطس 111-12
رائی سے بنی چٹپٹی چٹنی 79-22
رائی کی روٹی 71-20
رائبہ مچھلی 212-11
رات میں تمبو کے باہر جلائی گئی آگ 226-11

دل کی دھڑکن ناپنے کا آلہ 118-10
دل کی دھڑکن... سنیے C-118
دل کی روایتی علامت 239-6
دل 107-38
دلچسپی کی فہرست 172-11
دلکش 32-13
دُم 216-22
دماغ 107-34
دمدار ستارہ 205-24
دمہ 111-9
دن کی روشنی کی بچت کا وقت 19-25
دن کے اوقات 18
دن 20-2
دندان سازی کی معاون 119-2
دنیا کا نقشہ 202-203
دنیا کی زبانیں 189-13
دو آدمیوں کے بیٹھنے کا صوفہ 56-1
دو بجنے میں بیس منٹ 18-12
دو پہیہ سائیکل 151-15
دو خانوں کا ابالنے والا ظرف 78-8
دو شاخہ دار مال اٹھانے والی گاڑی 175-12
دو طرفہ ریڈیو 179-22
دو طرفہ سفر 152-17
دوا استعمال کیجیے D-114
دوا خانہ 112-113
دوا دینا 121-20
دوا فروش 112-1
دوا کا نسخہ 112-2
دوا کی الماری 57-22
دوا کی زیادہ خوراک لینا K-116
دواؤں کی اقسام 113
دواؤں کی دکان 128-4
دوبارہ شادی شدہ 24-35
دوبارہ لکھیے J-191
دوپہر بعد 18-5، 17-18
دوپہر سے پہلے 18-4
دوپہر کا کھانا تیار کیجیے F-38
دوپہر 18-16
دودھ سے بنی اشیاء کے ساتھ استعمال نہ
کیجیے۔ D-112
دودھ سے بنی غذائیں 72
دودھ نکالیے C-177
دودھ کا شربت یا لسّی 79-14
دودھ 66-5
دور دراز رابطوں کو فون کیجیے۔ L-147
دور دراز رابطہ 146-2
دوران اڑان معاون 161-12
دوران ملازمت تربیت 172-7
دوربین 205-23
دوست کا تعارف کرائیں۔ I-3
دوستوں سے بات کیجیے A-173
دوسرا 16
دوسری زبان کے طور پر انگریزی 189-14
دوسری گاڑی کو گزرنے دیجیے 154-9
دو صمامی صدفہ 71-14
دو صمامی گھونگھا 71-13، 212-17
دومنہا صدفہ 71-15
دونوں طرف سے تلے ہوئے انڈے 76-11
دوڑ اور دیگر میدانی کھیل 228-18

رات کا کھانا پکائیے 39-Q
رات کا کھانا تیار کیجیے 39-Q
رات کا کھانا لیجیے 39-S
رات کا کھانا کھائیے 39-S
رات کی روشنی 37-27
رات کی قمیض 91-28
رات 20-18
راج درخت بولی 210-19
راستہ بند 154-6
راستہ بھول جانا 162-B
راستہ میں سے سامان اٹھانے والا ٹرک 156-12
راستہ 208-3
رافع مشین 131-21
ران کا گوشت 70-9
ران 106-19
ران 70-22
رانیں 70-22
راک بینڈ میں شمولیت کیجیے 238-D
راک کنسرٹ 222-5
رہبری 10-5، 51-72، 6، 184-18
ربر (پنسل مٹانے والا) 7-21
ربر بینڈ 183-34
ربر کا گدا 226-13
ربر کی چنائی 57-5
ربر کے دستانے 61-4، 93-34
ربط 197-10
رین 99-30
ردوبدل کے قابل رینج 181-48
رس بھریاں 68-15
رسالہ 133-5
رستے ہوئے نلوں کو ٹھیک کیجیے 219-F
رسّہ کودنے والی رسّی 224-4
رسّی 226-19
رسمی لباس 88-11
رسمی کپڑے 89
رسید 27-6
رشتے دار 44-6
رسید 205-21
رصدگاہ 205-21
رضائی بنانے کا بلاک 232-15
رضائی 58-16
رضامندی ظاہر کیجیے 12-K
رضاکار 121-17
رضاکارانہ خدمت کیجیے 41-Q
رفتار بڑھانے والا پیڈل 159-46
رفتار پیما میٹر 159-27
رفتار کی حد 154-4
رقبہ اور مقدار کی پیمائش 193
رقص کا کمرہ 184-26
رقص کیجیے 64-A
رقم ادھار دیجیے 26-C
رقم ادھار لیجیے 26-B
رقم جمع کیجیے 132-B
رقم واپس ادا کیجیے 26-D
رقم 26
رقیق اشیاء پیجیے 114-C
رقیق پیمائشیں 75
رگزنے والا برش 61-20
رموز اوقاف استعمال کیجیے 190-C
رموز اوقاف 190
رندا 181-57

ریشمی 98-5
ریفری 229-6
ریفریجریٹر 54-9
ریگ مال 181-56
ریگستان 204-4
ریل گاڑی کا اسٹیشن 152
ریل گاڑی کا نمونہ 233-27
ریل گاڑی 150-7
ریل کے راستے سے گزرنے والی سڑک 154-14
ریڈیو 159-37
ریژھ والے جانور 194-12
ریژھ کی ہڈی 107-49
ریکارڈ کریں 235-A
ریکون 216-13
ریکٹ بال 228-12
زائد اوقات میں کھلنے والی بڑی دکان 128-3
زانو پوش 55-10
زاویہ منفرجہ 90 ڈگری سے زیادہ 193-27
زاویہ 90 ڈگری سے کم 193-28
زاویۂ قائمہ 193-26
زاویے 193
زبان 106-8
زپ کوڈ 4-9
زپ ٹوٹ گیا ہے۔ 97-39
زچگی کا لباس 88-5
زچگی کے سامان کی دکان 131-19
زحل 205-6
زخمی ہو جانا 116-C
زراعتی فارم مع ریائش 52-9
زرد 24-2
زرد پھول اور گلابی پتیوں کی ایک جھاڑی 211-24
زرد چکتے پھولوں کا درخت میگنولیہ 210-8
زرد سوئٹر بائیں طرف ہے۔ 25-1
زردی آمیز بھورا رنگ 24-18
زعفران 211-17
زلزلہ 144-5
زمرہ بند اشتہارات دیکھیے 173-B
زمرہ بند اشتہارات 48-2
زمین 205-3
زمینی حرارت کی توانائی 218-7
زمینی ڈاک 134-6
زنانہ انگیہ کا مخفف 91-20
زنانہ بالا پوش 87-8
زنانہ چست گاؤدم پتلون 88-8
زنانہ زیر جامہ 91، 91-14، 91-15
زنانہ لمبی جراب 91-17
زنانہ موزے 91
زنانہ کمر سے بندھنے والا لباس 87-10
زنجیر 95-33، 180-41
زندگی بچانے والا محافظ 225-19
زندگی بچانے والی حفاظتی جیکٹ 161-25
زندگی بچانے والے آلات 225-20
زندگی بچانے والے محافظوں کا اسٹیشن 225-21
زندہ آبی جانوروں و پودوں کی نمائش 222-7
زکام 111-2
زیر نگلنا 116-J
زیرہ 205-2
زیریلا آئی وی 210-25
زیریلا اوک 210-24

رنگ وغیرہ سے بچانے کا بچھانے والا کپڑا 181-54
رنگ کا برتن 181-51
رنگ کرنے والی کتاب 59-13
رنگ کرنے کا برش 181-22
رنگ کیجیے 178-A
رنگ 24
رنگ 181-25
رنگ کرنے والا برش 233-20
رنگائی کیجیے 233-E
رنگین چاک یا موم بھری پنسلیں 59-14
رنگین کاغذ کے ٹکڑے 239-3
رونی بھرے جانور 59-15
رونی کو ریشم کے دھاگوں سے بنا 99-9
رونی 177-6
روانہ ہو جائیے۔ 160-J
رواں یا متحرک زینہ 131-23
روچ 63-26
روز مرہ معمولات 38-39
روز مرہ کی بات چیت 12
روزانہ 20-21
روزگاری تربیت 172-5
روزمرہ کے کپڑے 86
روشنی بلب بند کر دیجیے 219-G
روشنی کا انتظار کیجیے 128-B
روشنی کا ماخذ 194-19
روشنی کی تنصیبات 55-18
روشنیاں بند کر دیجیے 11-P
روشنیاں کھولیے۔ 11-B
روم سروس 184-17
رومال 83-26
رومانی 237-16
رومن اعداد 16
روٹی اور مکھن کی قاب 83-19
روٹی کی ٹوکری 83-11
روٹی 67-11
روکی ماؤنٹین ریاستیں 201-8
رکن مجلس انتظامیہ 139-28
رکھیے۔ 28-B
رکیے۔ 154-I
ریائی پائیے۔ 141-H
رینی 142-11
رینی ادائیگی کیجیے۔ 49-L
رہنے کے مختلف مقامات 52
ریاستہائے متحدہ کا خطہ 201
ریاضی کا ایک مسئلہ 192
ریاضی کی قسمیں 192
ریاضی کے اعمال 192
ریاضی کے سوال حل کیجیے 170-M
ریاضی 189-10، 192-193
ریت محل 225-12
ریت کا تودہ 204-5
ریت 225-23
ریچھ 216-11
ریزر میں مستعمل بلیڈ 109-28
ریزگاری رکھنے کا بٹوا 94-14
ریستوران طعام گاہ 185
ریستوران میں کھانے والا 82-6
ریستوران کا باورچی خانہ 185
ریستوراں 82-83، 125-14

زیریلا سماق 210-23
زیریلا کھڑا کھڑیا سانپ 213-38
زہریلے دھوئیں 179-3
زیادہ ایزی 97-32
زیادہ بار بینک سے پیسے نکالنے کا اکاؤنٹ نمبر 132-14
زیادہ دیر تک روشنی پڑنے والی تصویر 235-34
زیبرا 217-33
زیر آب تیرنا 227-11
زیر جامہ اور شب خوابی کا لباس 91
زیر جامے 91-5
زیر زمین اسٹیشن 151-11
زیر زمین چلنے والی گاڑی 152-6
زیر زمین راستہ 151-12
زیریں جانگیہ 91-14
زیریں قمیض 91-1
زینے کا راستہ 50-10
زینے 50-10
زیور 239-15
زیورات کا شعبہ 95-8
زیورات کی دکان 130-2
ژالہ باری 13-21
سانپیں 225-13
سائز، اوضاع اور نمونے 96
سائز 96
سائنس 189-11، 194-195
سائنسی تخیلی کہانی 237-18
سائیکل چلائیے 129-D
سائیکل چلانا 228-5
سائیکل چلانے کا راستہ 224-3
سائیکل سوار 224-2
سائیکل 129-22
ساتواں 16
ساتھ لے جانے والا تھیلا اوپر خانے میں رکھیے۔ 160-G
ساتھ کھیلیے 36-M
ساحل سمندر 204-10، 225
ساحلی چھتری 225-14
ساحلی کرسی 225-22
سادہ بالا پوش 97-33
ساس 34-10
سافٹ بال 229-10
سافٹ ویئر (کمپیوٹر چلانے والے پروگرام) 196-10
ساق بند 231-13
سال کے مہینے 21
سال 20-4
سالا 34-17
سالگرہ 22-1
سالم سالمن 71-3
سالمن کے کباب 71-4
سالمنڈر 212-27
سالمہ 195-27
سالی 34-16
سامان باندھیے۔ 49-M، 162-A
سامان بیچنے والے 84-7
سامان پیک کیے جانے والا بکس 82-5
سامان درست جگہ رکھنا 83-17
سامان رکھنے کی الماری 55-22
سامان رکھنے کی پہیوں کی گاڑی 184-8

سامان رکھنے کی میز 21-161
سامان لائن لے جانے والی گاڑی 19-184
سامان لے جانے والی رواں پٹی 23-161
سامان منتقل کرنے والا 42-168
سامان نقل پذیر تختہ 175-13
سامان کھولیے۔ N-49
سامان کی الماری 182-2
سامان 161-18
سامنے کا پورچ 53
سامنے کا دروازہ 11-53
سامنے کا رخ 193-44
سامنے کا شیشہ 1-158
سامنے کا صحن اور گھر 52
سامنے کی روش 53-2
سامنے کے شیشہ پونچھ بدلیے۔ K-157
سامنے کے شیشے کے پونچھے 2-158
سانپ اور چھپکلی کی نسل کے رینگنے والے جانور 213
سانپ نما مچھلی 12-212
سانچا 113-20
سانس رکنا L-116
سانس لینے کے آلہ کی مدد سے غوطہ لگانا 12-227
سانس نہ لے سکنا N-116
سانس کے ذریعے سونگھنے والی دوائیں 113-33
سانٹھوں 16
ساکر (فٹ بال) 12-229
ساکر بال (فٹ بال) 12-231
سبز جائیے 81-40
سبز سوئیٹر گلابی سوئیٹروں کے درمیان ہے۔ 25-12
سبز 24-5
سبزہ زار 53-26
سبزی باغ 53، 27-177، 14
سبزی چھیلنے کا آلہ 78-15
سبزیاں شامل کیجیے۔ N-77
سبزیاں یا گوشت رکھ کر پکائی گئی موٹی روٹی 79-10
سبزیاں 66-8، 69
سبکدوش ہو جائیے 41-0
سپاہی 169-58
سپرنٹنڈنٹ 50-8
ستاروں کا جھرمٹ 205-14
ستارہ مچھلی 212-16
ستارہ کلید 14-6
ستارہ 99، 33-205، 13
ستاروں 16
ستمبر 21-33
سجاوٹیں 240-1
سخت حفاظتی ٹوپی 179-9
سخت مسئلہ 24-23
سخت ٹوپ 92-1
سخت کرسی 23-5
سر پر باندھنے والی پٹی 90-3
سر پر لپیٹنے والا کپڑا 90-7
سر چکرانا C-110
سر سے پہنا جانے والا سوئیٹر 88-3
سرفون 8-6
سرنامہ 183-42
سرکی حفاظتی ٹوپی 93-23

سر 104-1
سربراہ باورچی 185-7
سربندھن 92-16
سرپرست 82-6
سرخ بال 33-15
سرخ سوئیٹر نیلے سوئیٹروں کے اوپر ہے۔ 25-4
سرخ مرچ 69-29
سرخ 24-1
سرخم کیجیے۔ H-3
سرخی 133-7
سرد خانہ جس میں آنا جانا کر سکتے ہیں 185-3
سرد 13-6
سردرد 110-1
سردی اور پانی کے کھیل 227
سردی کا اسکارف 90-5
سردی 21-40
سرطان 111-10
سرفنگ 227-9
سرفون 14-13
سرنگ سے گاڑی لے جائیے K-153
سرکاری اور فوجی ملازمت 139-138
سرکنے والی پٹی جو سامان پہنچاتی ہے 175-9
سرکنے والے کارڈ کی فائل 183-44
سرہانہ 58-10
سزا یافتہ 141-15
سست رفتار ڈرائیور 23-4
سستی انگوٹھی 23-20
سستی فروخت کاری قیمت 27-3
سر 34-11
سفر میں مدد کرنے والی ایجنسی 131-14
سفر کیجیے۔ P-41، A-220
سفر کے لیے بڑی موٹر گاڑی 156-9
سفید روٹی 71-18
سفید سوئیٹر سیاہ سوئیٹر کے سامنے ہے۔ 25-7
سفید 24-14
سفیدی مائل زرد 24-16
سگریٹ نوشی مت کیجیے۔ G-114
سلائنڈ 224-13
سلائی مشین کا چلانے والا 98-14
سلائی مشین کے حصے 98
سلائی مشین 98-13
سلائی کا سامان 100
سلاد رکھنے کا بڑا ڈبہ 79-24
سلاد کا کانٹا 83-27
سلاد کی قاب 83-20
سلاد کے پتوں والا مونا حصہ 69-32
سلاد کے پتوں کا تھیلا 69-31
سلاد کے چوکور ٹکڑے کاٹیے۔ J-77
سلامی دار ڈھانچہ 224-16
سلووں والی قمیض 101-19
سلیکنو سروس میں اندراج کرائیے D-140
سماجی کارکن 169-57
سماروغ روغن میں بھونیے۔ E-77
سماروغ 69-27
سماعت کا سامنا کیجیے D-141
سماعتی آلہ 115-10
سمتوں اور نقشے 155
سمتیں 155
سمندر 225-1، 204-6

سمندری ارچن 212-21
سمندری تھن دار جانور 213
سمندری حیوانات 212
سمندری زندگی، خشکی و پانی میں رہنے والے حیوانات اور سانپ اور چھپکلی کی نسل کے جانور 212-213
سمندری سیب 225-24
سمندری غذائیں— دکان اور طعام خانہ 71
سمندری نیلا 28-5
سن کے ریشے سے بنا ہوا 98-2
سنترے 68-5
سنجیدہ فوٹو 206-3
سنگار کی بنیادی کریم 109-40
سنگار بنانے والا محلول 109-42
سنگارمیز 58-1
سننا B-106
سننے سے معذور 32-12
سنو بورڈنگ 227-2
سنک سے پانی نکل رہا ہے۔ 63-18
سنک کو گڑیے K-60
سنہرے بال 33-17
سنیچر 20-14
سنیما ہال 126-6
سنیما 222-2
سو جائیے Z-39
سو واں 16
سوئمنگ پول 51-22
سوئٹزرلینڈ کا پنیر 71-27
سوئی نما پتی 210-10
سوئی کی پلیٹ 98-18
سوئی 100-17، 98-10
سوئیوں کے ذریعے چینی طریقۂ علاج 122-2
سوئیٹر 28-2، 87-14
سوا بجے 18-9
سواری کرنے والا 152-3
سوالات پوچھیے۔ M-174
سوالیہ نشان 190-12
سوانح حیات 133-13
سوتی 98-1
سوتیلا باپ 35-25
سوتیلا بھائی 35-30
سوتیلی بہن 35-29
سوتیلی ماں 35-26
سوتے وقت بچوں کا مکمل لباس 91-27
سوتے وقت کی گاؤن 91-25
سور چاپ 70-10
سور کا گوشت 70
سور کی پشت یا پٹھوں کا گوشت 80-1
سور 215-2
سوراخ دار برتن 78-17
سوراخ کرنے والی دھات کی چھڑی 180-28
سورج گرہن 205-16
سورج مکھی 211-10
سورج 209-8
سوسن 211-16
سوشل سکیورٹی کارڈ 40-5
سوشل سکیورٹی نمبر 4-15
سول 237-28
سولہواں 16

سونامی 145-17
سونگھنا C-106
سونڈ 217-47
سونے والے تھیلے 226-12
سونے کے کمرے میں استعمال ہونے والی میز 58-23
سوڈا 73، 34-79، 11
سوکھی قمیض 101-18
سویابین 177-3
سوزن 119-7
سڑک پار کرنے کی جگہ 15-128
سڑک پار کیجیے A-128
سڑک پر لگی علامات 26-129
سڑک پر کام ہو رہا ہے 16-154
سڑک کی روشنی 148-3
سڑک کے آر پار دوڑیے G-153
سڑک 150-5، 155-8
سڑے کیلے 68-32
سکا ہوا پنیر سینڈوچ 80-10
سکا ہوا نان پاؤ 80-4
سکھانے والی پٹیاں 101-5
سکھانے والی مشین سے کپڑے نکالیے۔ E-101
سکھیا ہوا آلو بخارہ 68-26
سکہ ڈال کر بات کرنے والا فون 129-23
سکے رکھنے کا بٹوا 94-14
سکے 26
سہارے کا بٹھا 57-11
سی پی آر (سینے پر دباؤ ڈال کر دل اور پھیپھڑوں کی حرکت بحال کرکے جان بچانا) 117-17
سی پی یو (مرکزی عامل اکائی) 196-4
سی ڈی پلیئر 159-38
سیاسی تحریک 199-16
سیاسی مہم 139-29
سیاف 212-10
سیاہ بال 33-16
سیاہ سوئیٹر سفید سوئیٹر کے پیچھے ہے۔ 25-8
سیاہ 24-13
سیب زمینی 69-22
سیب کا رس 73-32
سیب 68-1
سیدھی کھڑی سیٹ 161-28
سیدھے بال 33-9
سیفٹی پن 37-9
سیل فون رکھنے کا بٹوا 94-15
سیل فون نمبر 4-12
سیل فون کا کھوکا 131-22
سیل 213-34
سیلاب 145-19
سیلز ٹیکس 27-8
سیلسیس 13-2
سیم ماہی 215-16
سیمنٹ کا مسالہ 178-15
سیمی 156-15
سینگ 216-21
سینٹی میٹر [سی ایم] 17-14
سینڈ باکس 224-15
سینڈل 88-9
سینکنے والی بھٹی 53، 17-54، 15
سینکنے والی برتن میں بلکا تیل لگائیے۔ B-77

عام کانٹے دار مچھلی 6-212	صفائی کے سامان - 61	شناخت اور کریڈٹ کارڈوں کی نقلی 19-146	سینکی ہوئی مچھلی 29-81
عبارت میں وقفہ کا نشان 18-190	صلاح کار 5-6	شناخت کی چوری 9-142	سینکی ہوئی 76-2
عبارت 7-190	صندوق 6-74	شور مچانے والے بچے 23-11	سینکیے- H-77
عجائب خانۂ فن 9-223	صوبائی حکومت 139	شور و غل 64-5	سینہ 70-19، 4-104، 25-107
عدالت عظمیٰ 11-138	صوبہ دار الحکومت 22-139	شوربہ 72-18	سینی 55-17
عدالت میں حاضری دیجیے G-141	صوبائی سینیٹ کا ممبر 139-25	شوربے کا پیالہ 83-21	سینیٹ کا ممبر 138-6
عدالت 13-125	صوبہ 4-8	شوربے کا چمچ 83-32	سینیٹ 138-5
عددی (ڈیجیٹل) فوٹو البم 235-32	صوتی پیغام 14-18	شوربہ 34-13	سیٹ پر باندھنے والی پٹی 159-52
عددی (ڈیجیٹل) کیمرا 19-235	صوفہ 56-18	شکر کی ٹکیاں 74-10	سیٹیلائٹ طشتری 53-6
عدسے کے سوراخ کو چھوٹا بڑا کرنے کا پرزہ 18-194	ضائع کی جانے والی چڈی 10-37	شکرخوار 214-10	سیڈان 156-1
عدلیہ برانچ 138	ضابطے 7-64	شکرقند 69-18	سیڑھی 61-13، 178-2
عرشۂ جلوس 2-239	ضرب دینا C-192	شکریے کا نوٹ لکھیے- O-174	سیڑھیاں 53-3
عشائیہ سلاد 15-80	ضرب سے بچانے والے 238	شکلیں 193	سیڑھیوں سے اوپر چڑھیے C-153
عشائیہ کا کانٹا 28-83	ضرب لگائیے B-230	شکنجہ 180-26	سیڑھیوں سے نیچے اتریے D-153
عشق میں گرفتار 18-42	ضروری خدمات کو اپنے نام کرائیے- O-49	شہد کی مکھی 214-25	سیکنڈ 18-3
عضو 3-210	ضروری خدمات 48-5	شہر 52-1	سیہی کا کانٹا 216-23
عطارو 1-205	ضیافت گاہ 185-14	شہر میں ایک دوسرے سے منسلک مکان 52-6	سیہی 216-10
عطر 6-108	ضیافت کا لباس 89-17	شہر کا مرکز 124	شاخ 210-2
عقاب 9-214	طاق اعداد 192-3	شہر کا کوڈ 15-34	شادی 22-2
عقبی صحن 53	طاقت ور اشارہ 14-11	شہر کی سڑکیں 127-126	شادی شدہ جوڑا 35-20
عقبی منظر کا آئینہ 159-35	طالب علم 6-5	شہر 4-7	شادی کا لائسنس 41-8
علاحدہ گوشہ 82-4	طباعت کنندہ 169-50	شہری استعمال کی چھوٹی کار 152-20	شادی کیجیے K-41
علاقہ کا کوڈ 4، 10-15، 29-15	طبی انتخابات 112	شہری حقوق اور ذمہ داریاں 140	شارک مچھلی 212-4
علاقے سے لوگوں کو نکالیے- K-147	طبی تفصیل کا فارم 118-4	شہری حکومت 139	شام کی رسمی گاؤن 89-18
علامات اقتباس 190-15	طبی جدول 121-24	شہری علاقہ 52-1	شام 18-19
علامات اور چوٹیں 110	طبی ریکارڈ ٹکنیشین 168-39	شہری مجلس انتظامیہ 139-27	شاور کا پردہ 57-14
علامتِ استعجاب 190-13	طبی فضلے کی نکاسی 121-31	شہریت سے متعلق امتحان دینا I-140	شاور کا سرا 57-13
علامت اعراب جو اضافت تملکی کے طور پر آتی ہے 190-16	طبی ماہرین 120	شہریت کا حصول G-40	شاور کے دوران استعمال کیا جانے والا جیل 108-2
علامت ربط و الحاق 190-20	طبی مدد حاصل کیجیے- A-114	شہریت کی شرائط 140	شاور کے دوران لگانے کی ٹوپی 108-1
علامت 155-5	طبی مریضوں کی مدد کیجیے B-170	شہنشاہ 199-3	شاہراہ پر آئیے I-153
علامتی بلّا 93-21	طبی مشورہ پر عمل کیجیے- J-114	شیر ببر 217-36	شاہراہ سے نکلیے J-153
علم مثلث 192-18	طبی نگہداشت 118	شیر کی ایال 217-49	شاہراہ کا اشارہ 154-17
عمارت کی کسی منزل کا نقشہ 186-4	طبی کارروائیاں 118	شیشہ صاف 61-14	شاہراہ 155-9
عمر 32	طبی ہنگامی حالات 116	شیشیاں 74-2	شب بخیر کہتے ہوئے بوسہ دیجیے P-36
عمودی خطوط 193-24	طبی ہنگامی حالت کا دست بند 117-3	شیمپو 108-10	شب خوابی کا لباس 91
عنوان 133-14، 190-5	طبیعات 195	صابن دانی 57-3	شجریق 210-16
عوامی حفاظت 143	طربیہ 237-13	صابن 57-4، 108-3	شدید ہوا کے ساتھ برف کا طوفان 23-13
عوامی ذرائع نقل و حمل 152	طریق احصاء 192-19	صاف آدھی آستین کی قمیض 101-16	شراب پی کر گاڑی نہ چلائیے- G-143
عورت 4-18، 30-2	طشت 55-20	صاف ستھرے بنیے- C-174	شراب نہ پیجیے- F-112
عورتیں 30-3	طعام خانے میں سامان رکھنے کی الماری 55-24	صاف کیجیے A-76	شراب کا گلاس 83-23
عہدے کے لیے مقابلہ کیجیے A-139	طعام گاہ کی میز 55-9	صبح 18-15	شراب کی محفلوں میں شام کا ہلکا لباس 89-20
عینک ساز 130-9	طعام گاہ کی کرسی 55-8	صحت بیمہ کارڈ 118-3	شرمندہ 43-24
غار 220-6	طعام گاہ 46-7، 55-82، 1	صحت مند رہنے کے طریقے 114	شروع کیجیے R-230
غبارے 44-4	طلاق شدہ جوڑا 35-21	صحت مند غذا کھائیے- F-114	شریان 107-36
غذا کو تولیے- B-75	طلوع آفتاب 18-14	صحت میلہ 122	شطرنج 232-8
غذا کی تیاری اور حفاظت 76-77	طنبورین 238-17	صحت کے مسائل میں مدد 115	شعاعی تشخیص کا ماہر 120-6
غذا کی حفاظت 76	طہارت کا کاغذ 57-19، 146-13	صحت کے مسائل کی اقسام 115	شفاف ٹیپ 183-30
غذا یا دودھ کے ساتھ استعمال کیجیے- A-112	طیف 195-35	صحت یاب ہونے کے طریقے 114	شلجم 69-16
غذائی اجناس کا حصہ 72-2	ظاہر کنندہ فارم 161-16	صحی شدید خرابیاں اور امراض 111	شمار کنندہ 192-5
غرارہ کیجیے L-109	ظاہری شکل 32	صحیح جواب چنیے- P-9	شمال 155-1
غرب الہندی موسیقی 237-31	عارضی دوکان 122-3	صدر 138-8، 199-5	شمالی امریکا اور وسطی امریکا 201-200
غروب آفتاب 18-18	عارضی گھر 52-7	صدری 89-15	شمالی امریکا 202-2
عالمی موسیقی 237-32	عالمی موسیقی 237-32	صدمے کی حالت میں ہونا B-116	شمالی امریکہ کا پھولے کلُّوں کا چوہا 215-19
غسل خانہ 46-4، 57	عام بیماریاں اور بچپن کے امراض 111	صرف ایک شخص کے گذرنے کا خودکار دروازہ 152-8	شمالی قطبی علاقہ کا فیل البحر 213-32
غسل خانے میں نصب ٹسلہ مع ٹونٹی 57-25	عام ردوبدل کرنے کا پرزہ 194-24	صرف دابنی طرف مڑ سکتے ہیں 154-7	شمالی کناڈا 201-1
غسل خانے کی چھائی 57-28	عام طریقے کے علاوہ کسی اور طریقے سے گاڑی استارٹ کرنے والا تار 158-21	صرف عمارت کے اندر کا فون 50-5	شمسی توانائی 218-1
غسل کیجیے B-108	عام قیمت 27-2	صفائی اور دیکھ بھال کرنے والا 182-3	شمع بجھائیے C-240
غلام 198-4	عام گفتگو کیجیے B-12	صفائی کارکن 169-54	شمع دان 56-21
غلط برتاؤ B-44		صفائی کرنے والی محلول 61-18	شمع 56-20

گابکوں کے لیے کپڑا دھلنے کی خود خدمت	قدیم امریکی باشندے 198-3	فوری طبی امداد کا بدایت نامہ 117-2	غلط راستہ 154-2
جگہ 128-1	قدیم 199-1	فوری طبی امداد کے طریقے 117	غلطیوں کو درست کیجیے۔ N-10
گتے کے ڈبے 74-4	قرض لیجیے۔ J-49	فوری طبی امداد 117	غلطیوں کو منائیے۔ M-10
گدا 56-18، 58-20	قصاب 167-13	فون بل پڑھنا 15	غمگین 42-16
گدھا 215-3	قطار میں انتظار کیجیے B-94	فون بل 15-28	غنڈہ گردی 142-1
گراف 192-15	قطار 73-11	فون پر بات کیجیے۔ C-15	غور سے سنیے۔ K-174
گرج کے ساتھ بارش 13-16	قطر 193-37	فون لائن 14-4	غیر آراستہ اپارٹمنٹ 48-4
گرجا گھر 127-14	قطرہ قطرہ سیال ٹپکانے کا پرزہ 195-45	فون نمبر ڈائل کیجیے A-15	غیر رسمی کپڑے 88
گرد کا طوفان 13-19	قطعہ خط 193-20	فون نمبر 4-11، 15-30	غیر رسمی، کام کے، اور رسمی کپڑے 88-89
گردن 104-3	قلم 7-22	فون کا پلگ 14-3	غیر سنجیدہ تصویر 206-2
گردہ 107-43	قلمیں 33-7	فون کال کرنا 15	غیر قانونی نشیلی دوائیں 142-6
گرم اور مرطوب 13-15	قلی جو سامان کمرے تک پہنچاتا ہے 184-7	فوٹو البم 235-31	غیر محتاط کارکن 179-1
گرم پانی کی بوتل 113-15	قلیوں کا نگراں 184-6	فوٹو گرافر 206-1	غیر معمولی بڑا 96-5
گرم پانی 57-9	قمیض 86-1	فوٹو کاپی کرنے کی دکان 129-18	غیر معمولی چھوٹا سائز 96-1
گرم دلیا 80-9	قوسین (بریکٹ) 190-19	فوٹو کاپیئر 183-23	غیر معمولی فشار خون 111-14
گرم زیریں قمیض 91-2	قید خانے میں جائیے G-141	فوٹو 136-4	غیر ملکی کی شہریت کا تصدیق نامہ 40-6
گرم کاری نظام 159-40	قیدی 141-15	فوکس سے باہر (دھندلی) 235-33	فائر اسٹیشن 125-12
گرم کپڑے 146-6	قیف 195-40	فٹ بال ہیلمٹ 231-19	فائل فولڈر 183-50
گرم کرنے کی گدی 113-13	قیمت ادا کیجیے G-27	فٹ بال 229-11، 231-21	فائل کلرک 182-10
گرم ہوا سے خشک کرنے کا آلہ 108-18	قیمت طے کیجیے۔ D-157	فنگر 181-18	فائل کی الماری 182-11
گرم 13، 42-3، 1	قیمت کا بلا 27-1	فکرمند 42-13	فارم پُر کرنا 4
گرمی کی لہر 13-13	قیمت 27-7	فہرست 82-7	فارمولا 195-34
گرمی 21-38	قیمتی اشیاء 132-8	فہرست پتی 197-1	فاصلہ پیما میٹر 159-28
گرنا 116-0	قیمتی انگوٹھی 23-19	فیرن بائٹ 13-1	فاضل ٹائر 158-23
گرنے سے بچانے کے لیے گدے کی روک 59-4	قیمہ 70-4	فیروزی سوئٹر صندوق میں ہے۔ 25-6	فخرمند 43-21
گروہی تشدد 142-4	قینچی 33-20، 100-16	فیروزی 24-9	فر 216-19
گریجویشن کی ایک تقریب 206	قے کرنا E-110	فیصد 17	فرسٹ اسٹریٹ تک ایک بلاک جائیے۔ F-155
گرین کارڈ 40-2	گاؤن 206-8	فیصلہ 141-14	فرش پونچھنے D-60، J-60
گزشتہ کل 20-7	گائے کا گوشت 70	فیگ اسکیٹنگ 227-5	فرش 46-6
گزشتہ ہفتے 20-18	گائے کی چاپ 70-5	فیل مرغ 70-17، 239-14	فرق 192-8
گفتگو و مباحثے کے پروگرام 236-4	گائے 215-1	فیوز باکس 62-13	فرنٹ ڈیسک 184-12
گفٹ کارڈ استعمال کیجیے E-27	گاجر چھیلیے۔ K-77	فیکس مشین 183-21	فرنیچر اور لوازم 59
گل پنی 113-19	گاجر 69-3	فیکٹری میں تیار کیجیے B-175	فرنیچر بنائیے G-170
گل داؤدی 211-21	گارڈینیا 211-18	فیکٹری کا مالک 175-1	فرنیچر پالش 61-8
گل دار بولٹ 180-38	گال 106-3	فیکٹری کارکن 175-3	فرنیچر کو ترتیب سے رکھیے۔ Q-49
گل دان 55-23	گانٹھ 211-2	فیکٹری 126-3، 175	فرنیچر کی پالش کیجیے E-60
گل دستہ 211-28	گاڑی اسٹارٹ کرنا 159-33	قاب 55-1	فرنیچر کی دکان 126-8
گل سوجا 111-7	گاڑی اٹھانے والا آلہ 158-24	قابل اتلاف دستانے 93-27	فرنیچر کی دھول جھاڑیے A-60
گل فروش 130-8، 167-27	گاڑی چلانا سیکھنا E-40	قابل باز تشکیل اشیاء کی ٹوکری 61-2	فروخت کار کلرک 94-3
گل لحمی 211-20	گاڑی چلانے یا موڑنے کا پہیہ 159-26	قابل تبدیل 156-5	فروری 21-26
گل مچھی 216-18	گاڑی سے کار پر جائیے I-38	قالین کو خلا روب سے صاف کیجیے H-60	فصل کی کٹائی کیجیے B-177
گلا صاف کرنے والی گولیاں 113-30	گاڑی سے بی خریداری کرنے کی کھڑکی 128-11	قالین 56-22، 58-24، 22	فصلیں 177
گلا 107-35	گاڑی لانے کا راستہ 53-8	قانون ساز ادارہ 139-23	فضائیہ 138-16
گلاب 211-15	گاڑی میں خرابی D-162	قانون ساز برانچ 138	فضلہ ادھر ادھر نہ پھیلائیے L-219
گلابی 24-7	گاڑی میں کرین ڈرائیور کی نشست والی	قانون کی تعمیل کیجیے C-140	فلاؤنڈر مچھلی 212-15
گلپھڑا 212-2	جگہ 156-16	قانون تعطیل 22-8	فلپس پیچ کس 180-31
گلو بند 37-5	گاڑی کو مشترک طور پر استعمال کیجیے I-219	قانونی تعطیلات 22	فلم کیمرا 235-21
گلہری 215-21	گاڑی کھڑی کرنا منع ہے 154-11	قانونی نظام 141	فلم 235-22
گلیارا 51-24	گاڑی کھڑی کرنے کا خودکار میٹر 129-25	قبرستان 127-15	فلموں کی قسمیں 237
گلے ملیے E-2	گاڑی کھڑی کرنے کی جگہ 50-18	قتل 142-12	فلک بوس عمارت 127-13
گلے میں خراش 110-6	گاڑی کے اگلے حصے میں گاڑی چلانے اور آلات	قحط 145-12	فلیش ڈرائیو 196-8
گلے میں لٹکانے کا زیور 95-35	وغیرہ رکھنے کا حصہ 159	قد آدم آئینہ 58-6	فنون زبان 189-9
گلے کا... معائنہ کیجیے E-118	گاڑی کے کرایہ کا میٹر 152-23	قد 32	فنون 189-15
گلے کے بار 95-10	گاڑی 37-20	قدرتی گیس 218-3	فنکار 166-6
گم شدہ بچہ 144-1	گاڑیاں پارک کرنے کا گیرج 124-1	قدرتی مرکز 208	فوارہ 224-5
گنتی کیجیے A-84	گابک کو بنھائیے B-82	قدرتی مناظر کے پروگرام 236-7	فوارے سے نہائیے C-38، A-108
گنجا 33-12	گابک کی مدد کیجیے D-95	قدرتی منظر 162-2	فوج 138، 199-11
گنی پگ 215-14	گابک 72-1، 94-4، 132-2، 164-2	قدرتی کھاد کا ڈھیر 53-25	فوری اور آسان کیک 77
گواہ 141-11	گابکوں سے صبر و تحمل کا اظہار کیجیے T-170	قدمچی ٹوٹی ہوئی ہیں۔ 62-7	فوری طبی امداد کا بکسہ 117-1، 146-18

گوبھی 69-2
گود میں لیجیے 36-A
گودام 175-7
گورنر 139-20
گوریا 214-7
گوریلا 217-29
گوشت اور مرغ انڈا وغیرہ پیش کرنے کے طریقے 76
گوشت اور مرغ 70
گوشت 66-2، 107-32
گول آری 180-9
گول چھلے دار روٹی 73-40
گول مرچ 69-7
گول کائنے والی آری 180-10
گولف کلب 231-1
گولف 228-8
گولڈ فش 215-16
گولی 113-21
گوند اسٹک 232-11
گوند 183-33
گوٹ 100-8
گنار 238-9
گنھیا 111-16
گربل 211-12
گڑیا بنانے کا ساز و سامان 232-13
گڑیا گھر 59-18
گڑیا 59-21
گھاس ختم کرنے والا 176-12
گھاس کائنے والا 176-12
گھاس کائنے کی مشین 176-6
گھاس کائنے 176-A
گھاٹ 225-18
گھبرایا ہوا 42-10
گھرآئیے 39-R
گھر اور صحن 53
گھر پر مطالعہ کیجیے۔ 10-D
گھر پہنچیے 39-R
گھر تلاش کرنا 48-49
گھر خریدنا 49
گھر خریدیے 41-M
گھر سے متعلق دشواریاں اور مرمتیں 62-63
گھر میں منتقل ہو جائیں۔ 48-F
گھر میں منتقل ہونا 49
گھر کا کام 60
گھر کی دیکھ بھال کرنے والا 184-20
گھر کی رنگائی کیجیے۔ 49-P
گھر کی صفائی کیجیے 39-O
گھر کی یاد میں رنجیدہ 43-20
گھر کے آرائشی سامان کی دکان 127-20
گھر 46
گھروں کا معائنہ کیجیے۔ 49-H
گھریلو پودا 211-27
گھریلو جانور اور کترنے کے دانتوں والے جانور 215
گھریلو مرغا 215-7
گھریلو معاملات کا انتظام کار 168-34
گھریلو نگہداشت صحت کا معاون 167-32
گھریلو 168-33
گھسی ہوئی تار 179-5
گھمن 178-23
گھنگھرالے بال 33-11

گھنٹہ 18-1
گھنٹی نما مرچ 69-7
گھوم کر دیکھیے 102-B
گھومنے والا دروازہ 184-2
گھونسلا 209-12
گھونگھا کی ایک قسم 212-22
گھونگھا 71-12، 212-19
گھڑ سواری 226-9
گھوڑا مچھلی 212-13
گھوڑا 215-4
گھنانا 192-B
گھنٹا 106-20
گھنٹوں تک کے موزے 91-12
گھٹنے کی گدیاں 179-19
گھڑ دوڑ 228-19
گھڑی ریڈیو 102-6
گھڑی 7-9
گھڑیال 213-36
گھیاتوری 69-25
گہرا نیلا 24-10
گہرائی 17-18
گیر اور کلچ کی دستی منتقلی 159-50
گیر بدلنے والا دستہ 159-47
گیارہواں 16
گیراج میں لگی دکان 102
گیراج کا دروازہ 53-7
گیس اسٹیشن معاون 162-3
گیس اسٹیشن 125-10
گیس بند کرنے کا والو 146-4
گیس پیڈل 159-46
گیس ختم ہو گئی 162-E
گیس میٹر 62-14
گیسٹ روم 184-13
گیند بازی 228-3
گیند پکڑیے 230-D
گیند دوسرے کو دیجیے 230-G
گیند سے کھیل شروع کیجیے 230-P
گیند کو دوسرے کھلاڑی سے بچاتے ہوئے آگے بڑھیے 230-J
گیند کو سنبھالتے ہوئے آگے بڑھیے 230-F
گیند کھیلنے کا میدان 224-1
گیند 59-12
گیندا 211-13
گیندا 217-28
گیہوں کی روٹی 71-19
گیہوں 177-2
لائبریری کا ممبر 133-3
لائبریری کارڈ حاصل کیجیے 133-A
لائبریری کلرک 133-1
لائسنس پلیٹ 136-12
لائسنس یافتہ پریکٹیکل نرس (ایل پی این) 120-11
لائن 68-8
لائن پر موجود رہیے۔ 15-H
لائنے 240-E
لابی 50
لاپرواہی سے سڑک پر چلنا 128-C
لادیے 175-D
لاگت 27-7
لاگ ان اور ای میل ارسال کرنا 197

لالئین 226-22
لالہ 211-11
لاما 217-25
لائری وغیرہ سے متعلق پروگرام 236-8
لاکر 5-11
لباده 91-29
لبادے 88-6
لباس ساز (درزی) 100-1
لباس ساز فیکٹری 98
لباس ساز 167-29
لباس 86-3
لبلبہ جگر 107-45
لمبے (سیریل) پروگرام 236-5
لپٹا ہوا کپڑا 98-15
لپٹی ہوئی اشیاء 74-11
لپٹی ہوئی شکم پور روٹی 79-9
لپیٹیے 240-F
لچکدار پنی 117-12
لچھا سوئیاں 81-26
لغت 7-30
لفافہ 134-14، 183-14، 43-43
لفافی پرتہ لکھیے۔ 135-B
لفظ کا ترجمہ کیجیے۔ 8-C
لفظ کا مسئلہ 192-11
لفظ کو دیکھیے۔ 8-A
لفظ کو کاٹ دیجیے۔ 9-R
لفظ کی نقل کیجیے۔ 8-E
لفظ کے نیچے خط کھینچیے۔ 9-S
لفظ 190-1
لفٹ 184-9، 50-9
لفٹیننٹ گورنر 139-21
لگائیے 109-P
لمبا اسکرٹ 96-18
لمبا آٹھ سرپایہ صدفہ 212-7
لمبا پتلا رینگنے والا جانور 212-23
لمبا زیر جامہ 91-3
لمبا 32-4
لمبائی 17-17
لمبی آستین والی قمیض 96-14
لمبی آستینوں کا سامنے بن لگا سوئیٹر 88-2
لمبی پہیوں والا شمالی امریکی سانپ 213-39
لمبی پیدل دوری طے کرنے کے جوتے 95-31
لمبی جیکٹ 90-16
لمبی چاکلیٹ 73-37
لمبی دم والا طوطا 215-15
لمبی دوری کی کال 15-32
لمبی بال 33-3
لمبے چلنے والے (سیریل) پروگرام 236-5
لوگوں سے اظہار خیر سگلی کیجیے۔ 3-G
لوگوں کی نگرانی کیجیے۔ 170-O
لوگوں کے بارے میں بتانا 32
لومڑی 216-15
لوبیا کا شہنیرہ 178-3
لوبیا کے انگوٹھے والے جوتے 92-6
لڑی دار روشنیاں 239-18
لکچر دیجیے 122-B
لکڑ بگھا 217-30
لکڑ 178-17

لکڑی کا پیچ 180-33
لکڑی کا چمچ 78-9
لکڑی کے برادے سے بنا تختہ 181-20
لکڑی کے کام کا ساز و سامان 232-14
لکڑی 178-17
لکھنے کا عمل 191
لکھنے کی کاپی 7-26
لکھنے کے ضابطے 190
لہر دار بال 33-10
لہر 225-17
لہسن پیسنے کا آلہ 78-11
لہسن ملی روٹی 81-28
لہسن 69-30
لیپ ٹاپ (چھوٹا کمپیوٹر) 196-16
لیزر پرنٹر 183-19
لیمپ کا ٹوپ 58-26
لیمپ 58-25
لیمو کا شربت 84-3
لیمو 68-7
مئی 21-29
ماؤس 196-15
مائکروپروسیسر (مربوط برقی دور) 196-4
مائکروفون 234-18
مائکرویو 54-13
ماچس 146-16، 226-21
مارچ 21-27
مارزنگی 213-38
مارشل آرٹس 228-11
مال ادھر ادھر لے جانے والا ٹرک 156-19
مال بردار گاڑی 156-18
مال لادنے کی گودی 175-15
مالک مکان 51-27
مالک 164-4
مالی 167-28
مانیٹر 196-11
ماں 34-3
ماہر امراض اطفال 120-4
ماہر امراض چشم 120-7
ماہر امراض قلب 120-3
ماہر امراض نسواں 120-2
ماہر تخدیر (جراحت کے لیے بیہوش کرنے کا ماہر) 121-35
ماہر حیاتیات 194-2
ماہر دندان 119-1
ماہر سرطان 120-5
ماہر سمعیات 115-9
ماہر طبیعیات 195-33
ماہر غذائیات 120-15
ماہر فلکیات 205-22
ماہر نفسیاتی امراض 120-8
مایوس 28-4، 43-27
مایوس 115-5
مبادلہ بازار 222-6
مترجم 168-35
متعدد افعال کے لیے ریموٹ 234-9
متغیر 192-12
متفقہ غور و خوض کے بعد حل 8-H
متلاشی 199-9
متن داخل کیجیے 171-B

متن کا خانہ 197-13
متنی پیغام 14-19
متوازی الاضلاع 193-33
متوازی خطوط 193-25
مثانہ 107-46
مثبت اعداد صحیح 192-2
مثلث، تکونہ 193-32
مچھر 214-22
مچھلی پکڑنا 226-4
مچھلی پکڑنے کا جال 226-17
مچھلی پکڑنے کی چھڑ 226-18
مچھلی کی جلد کا کھپرا 212-3
مچھلی کے بازو جیسے پر 225-7
مچھلی کے پنکھ 212-1
مچھلی 66-1، 71، 209-14
محاسب 167-1
محافظ 132-5
محتاط کارکن 179-2
محفوظ ویب سائٹوں سے خریداری کیجیے۔ 143-H
محلول 225-10
محنت کیجیے۔ 230-N
محنت کے کام کیجیے۔ 170-D
محیط 193-36
مخالف امیدوار 139-30
مختلف اشیاء کی تفصیل بیان کرنا 23
مختلف اقسام کی بیریاں 81-36
مختلف رنگ 23-16
مخروط 193-40
مخصوص لباس 239-11
مخلوط اجزاء سے تیار کیک 80-7
مخلوط کار 156-3
مخمل، اونی ریشوں والا 99-10
مدد طلب کیجیے۔ 10-F
مدد مطلوب ہے کی علامات تلاش کیجیے۔ 173-C
مددگار بیرا 83-12
مدربورڈ (برقی دوری نظام کا مجموعہ) 196-5
مدعا علیہ کو سزا سنائیے 141-F
مدعا علیہ کو قصوروار ثابت کیجیے۔ 141-E
مدعا علیہ 141-5
مدغم ٹریفک 154-10
مدوجزر کی لہر 145-17
مذہب کی آزادی 140-3
مذہبی تعطیل 22-7
مذہبی 237-30
مراسلہ بردار 134-20
مربع 193-30
مرد اور عورت دونوں کے استعمال کا زیر جامہ 91
مرد اور عورت دونوں کے استعمال کے موزے 91
مرد کھلاڑیوں کا حفاظتی بند 91-6
مرد 4-17، 30-1
مردانہ زیر جامہ 91
مرصّع بالا پوش 97-34
مرغ انڈا 70
مرغ سینڈوچ 79-5
مرغ کو ابالیے۔ 77-M
مرغ کی ٹانگیں 70-23
مرغ کے ٹکڑے کیجیے۔ 77-I
مرغ 66-3
مرغی 215-8

مرمت کرنے والا شخص 62-10
مرمر پرندہ 214-10
مرکز نگہداشت اطفال 129-30
مرکزہ (ایک خلوی عضو) 194-7
مرکزہ اور خلیہ کی جھلی کے درمیان مادہ 194-9
مرکزہ میں ریشہ نما ساخت 194-8
مرکزہ 195-29
مرکزی دفتر 5-12
مرکزی روشنیاں 158-7
مرکزی وقت 19-31
مریم 113-24
مریخ 205-4
مریض کو لانے لے جانے والی گاڑی 121-34
مریض کو لانے لے جانے کی مخصوص گرنی 121-33
مریض کو لانے لے جانے کی مخصوص ڈولا 121-33
مریض 118-6، 121-18
مزاحیہ صورت حال کا ڈرامہ 236-2
مزدوری کیجیے۔ 170-D
مسافر 150-2، 161-15
مسالے اور پنیر کا مکئی کا کیک 79-7
مسالے دار سلاد 80-18
مسالے دار قیمہ بھرا سموسہ 71-24
مساوات 192-13
مستری کے پاس 158
مستطیل 193-29
مستند نرسنگ معاون (سی این اے) 120-12
مسجد 126-5
مسرور 44-5
مسطر 17-13، 181-16
مسوڑھے کے امراض 119-11
مسوڑھے 106-6
مسکرائیے۔ 2-D
مسکن 194-11
مسیحی 237-30
مشاہدہ کیجیے۔ 195-C
مشترک ماں یا باپ والا بھائی 35-28
مشترک ماں یا باپ والی بہن 35-27
مشتری 205-5
مشرق 155-4
مشرقی وقت 19-32
مشروبات 73
مشکل مسئلہ 23-24
مشکوک پیکٹوں کی اطلاع دیجیے۔ 143-J
مشین آپریٹر 168-37
مشین کا پیچ 180-32
مشین کے ذریعے سلائی 98-A
مشینی ریگ مال 180-11
ملانے والی مشین 174-I
مصف 133-15، 169-64
مصنوعی سیارہ 205-20
مضافات 52-2
مضمون کے اجزاء 190
مضمون 190-4
مطالعہ کرنا 8-9
مطب 186-2
مطلق العنان 199-6
مطمئن 42-6، 42-15
مظاہرہ 122-6
مظلوم 142-10

معائنہ گاہ میں 118
معائنے کی میز 118-7
معالج 115-14
معالجۂ دندان 119
معاون انتظامیہ 167-3
معاون باورچی 185-6
معاون پرنسپل 5-5
معاہدہ 41-9
معاہدہ کرایہ داری 51-28
معدہ 107-41
معذرت قبول کیجیے G-12
معذرت کیجیے F-12
معذور افراد کے لیے پارکنگ 154-12
معذوروں کی پارکنگ 128-6
معذوری سے متاثر لوگوں کی مدد کیجیے۔ G-147
معذوریاں 32
معلم 6-4
معمار 186-8
معمولی خوردہ دوائیں 113
معمہ 59-17
معیاری لیمپ 56-15
معیاری وقت 19-26
مغرب 155-2
مفلر 95-12
مقابلہ کی دوڑ کا راستہ 5-21
مقاصد کا تعین کیجیے۔ A-10
مقام پیدائش 4-14
مقامی لوگوں کے لیے درسگاہ 127-17، 188-6
مقامی کال 15-31
مقدمہ 148-5
مقررہ ملاقات لکھنے کی کاپی 183-48
مقررہ وقت ملاقات 118-1
مقناطیس 195-36
مقیم غیر ملکی کارڈ 40-2
مگمچھ 213-37
ملازم 165-9
ملازمت حاصل کرنا F-40
ملازمت سے متعلق تربیت کی اقسام 172
ملازمت میلہ 172-13
ملازمت کی تلاش 173
ملازمتیں اور پیشے ایچ – پی 168
ملازمتیں اور پیشے اے – سی 166
ملازمتیں اور پیشے پی – ڈبلیو 169
ملازمتیں اور پیشے سی – ایچ 167
ملاقات اور استقبال 2
ملاقات کا کمرہ 184-25
ملانے والی قاب 78-31
ملانے والی مشین 54-12
ملبے کو صاف کیجیے۔ M-147
ملتا جلتا 28-3
ملزم کو گرفتار کیجیے A-141
ملنے کی جگہ 146-1
ملک کا کوڈ 15-33
ملکیت حاصل کیجیے۔ K-49
ملیے P-109
ملے جلے رنگ 24
ممبر اسمبلی 139-24
منبر پر مقرر کے سامنے لمبا بکسہ 206-5
منتخب عہدے دار 139-32

منتخب کیجیے B-196
منتخب ہوجائیے C-139
منتظر بیرا 82-8
منتظم 72-8، 120-13
منتظمین 5
منتقلی ٹکٹ 152-5
منزل 162-5
منصفانہ سماعت 140-5
منصوبہ بندی کی نوٹ بک 183-49
منظر کاری اور باغبانی 176
منظرکاری کرنے والا 176-5
منفی اعداد صحیح 192-1
منفی بار رکھنے کا حامل برقیہ 195-30
منقش پارچہ کاری 99-31
منگل 20-10
منگنی کیجیے J-41
منٹ 18-2
منہ صاف کرنے کا محلول 109-25
منہ کو سن کرنا C-119
منہ 104-7، 106
موت R-41
موت کا تصدیق نامہ 41-11
موتیوں کی لڑی 95-39
موجد 199-18
موجوں پر تیرنے والا 225-15
موجوں پر تیرنے کے لیے لکڑی کا تختہ 225-16
موز 214-14، 216-1
موزوں لباس پہنیے۔ 174-B
موزوں کے ساتھ زنانہ چست پتلون 91-18
موزے 86-6
موسم پر مشاہدہ کیجیے۔ 147-C
موسم کا نقشہ 13
موسم کی حالتیں 13
موسم کی خرابی کی وجہ سے بچکولے 161-22
موسم 13، 21
موسمی لباس 90
موسیقار 168-43
موسیقی ترتیب دینے والا 199-14
موسیقی کی ترتیب دینا 199-15
موسیقی کی دکان 130-1
موسیقی کی قسمیں 237
موسیقی 64-3، 84-1، 189-16، 238
موضوع ٹائپ کیجیے D-197
موقوف کریں E-235
مول بھاؤ کیجیے A-102
مولی 69-4
مونچھ 33-5
مونگا 220-5
موئا 32-7
موٹر سائیکل 150-4
موٹر گاڑی خانہ 47-14
موٹر گاڑی شعبہ کا کلرک 136-3
موٹر گاڑیوں کا شعبہ (ڈی ایم وی) 136-137
موٹر گاڑیوں کا شعبہ 124-4
موٹر گاڑیوں کے شعبہ کا کتابچہ 136-1
موٹر میکینک 167-8
موٹر کی خاموش گرنلکی 158-16
موبل، موٹر گاڑیوں سے سفر کرنے والوں کے لیے ہوٹل 126-12

موٹی جیکٹ 27-97
موٹی کتاب 23-7
موٹی سوتی کپڑے سے بنی چست پتلون 92-19
مویشی بانی کرنے والا 22-177
مویشی باڑا 17-177
مویشی گاہ 52-10
مویشی ڈاکٹر 62-169
مویشی 177-15، 21-177
منانے والا 19-7
مڑ 69-21
منہائی کی گولیوں اور ٹافیوں کی دکان 17-131
منہائیاں 84-8
منی 208-2
مڈل اسکول 188-3
مڑنے کا اشارہ کرنے والی روشنی 34-159
مڑنے کا اشارہ کرنے والی روشنیاں 6-158
مکئی کے دانوں کی طرح بنائے گئے بال 33-14
مکئی 69-12، 177-4
مکعب ٹکڑے 59-19
مکعب 193-38
مکمل آرام کیجیے۔ B-114
مکڑی 214-29
مکھن 66-6
مکھی 214-28
مکے بازی کرنے کے دوران پہنا جانے والا نیکر 91-4
مکے بازی 228-4
مہر 183-47
مہم جوئی کی کہانی 237-19
مہمان مقرر 206-4
مہمان 184-10
مہمانوں کی خدمات 130-12
مہمانوں کی خدمت میں تعینات بیرا 185-11
مہینہ 20-3
مینز 139-26
میپل 210-12
میدان 204-5، 2
میری ٹائم ریاستیں 201-6
میز آراستہ کیجیے۔ A-82
میز پوش 55-12
میگزین رکھنے کا بستہ 56-23
میل کاٹ ڈالیے۔ B-101
میل بنانے والا محلول 101-7
میلر 183-40
میلنگ لیبل 183-41
میلی آدھی آستین کی قمیص 101-15
مین اسٹریٹ سے گذریے E-155
مین لائن سے جوڑنے والا تار 196-2
مینڈک 212-25
مینجر کو فون کیجیے۔ A-48
مینجر 50-8
مینیو سے آرڈر دیجیے D-82
میوہ 73-36
مینہا مشروب 73-34
مینھے آئے کا پیزا 79-15
میڈیا کی ڈاک 134-3
میکسیکو کا پنھار 201-15
میکسیکو کے علاقے 201
نئی ملازمت 172-3
نئے الفاظ سیکھنا 8

نائب صدر 138-9
نائلون 99-12
نائٹ اسٹینڈ 58-23
نابینا 32-11
ناپنے والا فیتہ 100-17
ناپنے کا ٹیپ 181-45
ناپیے C-17
ناخن تراش 109-31
ناخن گھسنے کا آلہ 109-32
ناخن کی آرائش کا سیلون 130-3
ناخن کی آرائش کرنے والا 168-38
ناخن... کائیے N-109
ناخنوں پر پالش کی پالش 109-33
ناخنوں پر... پالش کیجیے 109-0
ناراض 43-29
نارنجی سوئیٹر بھورے سوئیٹر کے اوپر ہے۔ 25-11
نارنجی 24-4
نارنگی کی ایک قسم 68-9
ناریل 68-24
ناشپاتی سے مشابہ ایک وسط امریکی پھل 84-6
ناشپاتی 68-4
ناشتہ کیجیے۔ E-38
ناگ پھنی 210-21
ناگ 213-41
نالی 57-7
نام کا بلّا 92-15
نام: 4-1
ناموں کو بڑے حروف میں لکھیے۔ A-190
نامیاتی مرکب یا الرجی مخالف کریم 117-10
نامیاتی 84-2
نان ختائی کی دکان 129-17
نان کی تہہ میں لپٹا پنیر کا تلا ہوا کباب 79-3
نان کی تہہ میں لپٹا قیمہ کا تلا ہوا کباب 79-1
ناول 133-16
ناک میں جکڑن 110-7
ناک میں چھڑکنے کی دوا 113-32
ناک 104-6
نباتاتی باغ 222-3
نباتی تیلوں اور چربی کا مصنوعی مکھن 72-20
نبض کی... جانچ کیجیے A-122
نیپل 37-2
نتائج کو ریکارڈ کیجیے۔ D-195
نجی ملکیت کے فلینوں کی عمارت 52-5
ندی کے ذریعے بنائی گئی کھائی 204-17
ندی 155-10، 204-3
نرس 118-8، 168-44
نرسری اسکول 188-1
نرسری گیٹ 37-22
نرسلوں والا الفوزہ 238-3
نرسنگ کا عملہ 120
نرسنگ ہوم 52-12
نرگس 211-26
نرم چمڑے سے بنایا گیا جوتا 99-8
نرم کرسی 23-6
نزلہ 111-1
نزلے کی ٹکیاں 113-27
نسب نما 192-6
نسخے کا لیبل 112-4
نسخے کا نمبر 112-5

نشان زد کرنے والا 7-24
نشانہ لگائیے H-230
نشانہ 231-7
نشست سنبھالیے۔ F-6
نشستی کمرہ 47-12، 56
نشے کی حالت میں گاڑی چلانا 142-5
نصف قطر 193-35
نصف ڈالر 26-5
نصف 17-2
نظام الاوقات 152-4
نظام شمسی اور سیارے 205
نظم اور نگرانی کا چھوٹا افسر 141-13
نفیر کنڈلی دار ساز 238-11
نقاب 239-9
نقد ادائیگی کیجیے A-27
نقدی اور سکے 146-17
نقدی جمع کرنا 132-3
نقدی جمع کرنے کی پرچی 132-4
نقدی لینے اور ادا کرنے پر مامور شخص 132-1
نقدی نکالیے۔ F-132
نقشہ نویس 167-5
نقشہ 167-12
نقشے 155
نقطۂ آغاز 162-1
نقطۂ انتہا 193-21
نقل و حمل سے متعلق علامات 154
نقلی دانت 119-10
نقول بنائیے D-171
نگاہ کا معائنہ 136-6
نگرانی کرنے والا 165-8
نگندے دار رضائی بنائیے C-232
نگہداشت اطفال کا کارکن 167-16
نل ٹپک رہا ہے۔ 63-17
نل کار 63-20
نلکی پر ٹیپ لگانے کا ٹیپ 181-49
نمائش دان 94-5
نمبر 10-3
نمبر رسائی 14-16
نمبر کی پلیٹ 158-12
نمونہ 99-22
نمونہ بنانے والا 175-2
نمونہ پیش کرنے والے 168-41
نمونہ تیار کیجیے A-175
نمونہ 84-5، 96.5
نمک اور کالی مرچ دانیاں 55-13
نمکین بڑا گوشت 71-22
نوزائیدہ بچہ 31-6
نوآبادیاتی دور 198
نواں 16
نوجوان 32-1
نوری تالیف 194-10
نومبر 21-35
نوٹ بُک 7-27، 183-38
نوٹ بک پیپر 7-28
نوٹ 26
نوٹس لگانے والا تختہ 7-14
نوے واں 16
نکسیر 110-17
نہانا B-108

نہانے کا تولیہ 57-16
نہانے کا لباس 90-26
نہانے کا ٹب 57-2
نہانے کا کپڑا 57-6
نہانے کی تولیہ 57-16
نہانے کے بعد کا پاؤڈر 108-4
نہلائیے F-36
نیا چاند 205-9
نیپچون 205-8
نیچے تک کی صدری 90-14
نیچے گر دکھائی دینے والی فہرست 197-8
نیشنل گارڈ 138-19
نیلا 24-3
نیلی بہت شور مچانے والی یورپی چڑیا 214-6
نیلی بیریں 68-16
نیلے رنگ کا موٹا پائندار کپڑا 99-7
نیلے سوئیٹر سرخ سوئیٹروں کے نیچے ہیں۔ 25-5
نیم طبی کارکن 116-2
نیم گرم 13-4
نیو انگلینڈ 201-11
نیوفاؤنڈلینڈ وقت 19-34
نیوٹ 212-26
نیوکلیائی توانائی 218-8
نیٹ ورک بنائیے A-173
نیکر 89-25
وائلن کی ایک قسم کا کھرج ساز 238-7
وائلن کی قسموں میں سب سے کمتر سر نکالنے والا ساز 238-8
وائلن 238-6
واپس کیجیے H-27
واپسی گھومنے کی اجازت 154-5
وادی 204-18
واشر 180-37
واشنگٹن کی وہ عمارت جہاں کانگریس کا اجلاس ہوتا ہے 138-1
واقعات زندگی اور دستاویزات 40-41
والدین استاد کی کانفرنس 22-5
والی بال 229-14، 231-3
وائر اسکیننگ 227-7
وائٹر پولو 229-15
وائٹر بیٹر کام نہیں کر رہا ہے۔ 62-1
ورزش گاہ 19-5، 126-10، 184-24
ورزش کا لباس 89
ورزش کیجیے P-39، N-230
ورزش کے جوتے 86-7
ورزش لنگوٹ 91-6
ورید پر نشتر لگانے والا 121-29
ورید 107-37
وزن اور پیمائش 75
وزن اٹھانا 228-16
وزن 32، 75-231، 22
وزنی صندوق 23-13
وزیر اعظم 199-7
وسائل مرکز 172-9
وسط اوقیانوسی ریاستیں 201-10
وسط مغربی 201-9
وضاحت یادداشت کے طور پر لکھیے C-171
وضاحتیں لکھیے۔ C-10
وفاقی حکومت 138

وقت بتانا 18
وقت پر پہنچیے۔ F-174
وقت سے پہلے 22-19
وقت کے منطقے 19
وقت 19-18
وقفہ 190-11
وقفہ 190
ونڈ سرفنگ 227-10
ووٹ دیجیے A-140
ووڈونڈز (منہ سے بجانے والے لکڑی کے ساز) 238
وئمن (حیاتین) 113-17
وکیل استغاثہ 141-10
وکیل دفاع 141-4
وکیل 168-36
وہائٹ باؤس 138-7
وھیل کی نسل کا جانور 213-30
وھیل 213-29
وی سی آر 102-7
ویب سائٹ کا پتہ 197-4
ویب صفحے میں تلاش کرنے کے لیے اسے دیکھنا 197
ویب کیمرہ 196-12
ویگن کو کھینچیے A-224
ویڈیو پلیئر 197-11
ویڈیو گیم کنٹرول 232-4
ویڈیو گیم کھیلنے کا تختہ 232-3
ویڈیو ٹیپ بنائیے A-240
ویڈیو کی دکان 129-20
ویڈیو کیسٹ 133-18
ٹائپ کیجیے R-170، A-196
ٹائر کی ہوا نکل گئی F-162
ٹائر 158-5
ٹائروں میں ہوا بھروائیے۔ L-157
ٹائل چنخی ہوئی ہے۔ 62-4
ٹائل لگائیے C-178
ٹائل 57-12، 178-11
ٹائی 88-12، 13-92
ٹارچ 146-14
ٹافی 239-12
ٹانگ اور پیر 106
ٹانگ 105
ٹانگیں 70-21
ٹانکا کار 169-63
ٹانکے 117-15
ٹاور (بکس جس میں اہم پرزے ہوتے ہیں) 196-3
ٹاکو (مکئی کی روٹی میں لپٹا ہوا قیمہ) 79-8
ٹخنے تک کے موزے 91-7، 11-91
ٹخنے کے اوپر تک کے موزے 91-8
ٹخنے کے نیچے تک کے موزے 91-10
ٹخنہ 106-23
ٹخنے میں موچ 110-18
ٹراؤٹ 71-1
ٹرن ٹیبل 234-12
ٹرک چلائیے E-170
ٹرک ڈرائیور 169-61
ٹرک 150-6
ٹریجڈی 237-14
ٹریفک لائٹ 128-8
ٹریولرز چیک بھنائیے F-27
ٹریکٹر ٹریلر 156-15

ٹریکٹر 177-9
ٹرے لے جائیے H-82
نمائر سرکہ وغیرہ کی چٹنی 79-21
نمائر 69-6
ٹن کے ڈبے 74-3
ٹوپ 90-1
ٹوپی 88-1، 7-206
ٹوپیاں 95-11
ٹوتھ پیسٹ کا ٹیوب 74-24
ٹوتھ پیسٹ 109-23
ٹوسٹر 54-6
ٹوفو کے ٹکڑے کائیے۔ C-77
ٹونا 71-7، 19-72
ٹونئی 57-8
ٹوئی ہوئی بڈی کو جوڑ کر ملانے رکھنے والی پٹی 117-14
ٹوٹے ہوئے اوزار 179-4
ٹوڈ (مینڈک کی ایک قسم) 212-28
ٹوکری 56-3
ٹوکن 152-10
ٹڈی 214-24
ٹکٹ جانچ کرنے والا 160-3
ٹکٹ چپکائیے۔ C-135
ٹکٹ لگانے کی مشین 135
ٹکٹ کھڑکی 152-12
ٹکٹ 134-23، 152-15
ٹکٹوں کی کتاب 134-18
ٹکڑے کرنے کا آلہ 78-2
ٹگر روک 158-8
ٹکیہ 113-22
ٹھنڈا پانی 57-10
ٹھنڈا رکھنے والا 225-9
ٹھنڈا کیجیے D-76
ٹھنڈا 42-4
ٹھنڈی برف والی چائے 79-12
ٹھونکیے D-178
ٹھوڑی 106-1
ٹھوکر لگائیے E-230
ٹھیلا 129-28
ٹھیک 42-14
ٹھیکے دار 186-5
ٹھنی 210-1
ٹی ایس اے ایجنٹ 160-5
ٹی بی (تپ دق) 111-15
ٹی وی (ٹیلی ویژن) 56-6
ٹی وی پروگرام کی قسمیں 236
ٹی وی دیکھیے X-39
ٹی ڈی ڈی (بصری معذور لوگوں کا فون) 15-26
ٹیب 197-7
ٹیبل ٹینس 228-14
ٹیلی فون 14-15
ٹیلیفون سے فروخت کاری کرنے والا 169-60
ٹیلیفون کی مہارتیں 171
ٹیم 229-3
ٹینس کا ریکٹ 231-2
ٹینس کا کورٹ 224-6
ٹینس کھیلنے کے جوتے 95-32
ٹینس 228-15
ٹینک لے جانے والا ٹرک 156-20

ٹیوب 74-12
ٹیونر 234-13
ٹیڈی بیئر 37-23
ٹیکس ادا کیجیے B-140
ٹیکس اسنینڈ 152-18
ٹیکس سے باہر نکلیے F-153
ٹیکسی لائنسنس 152-22
ٹیکسی ڈرائیور 152-21
ٹیکسی کے اندر بیٹھیے E-153
ٹیکسی 150-3
ٹیکنکل اسکول 188-5
ڈائرکٹری مدد 14-22، 24-131
ڈاک ترازو 183-27
ڈاک خانہ 125-11، 135-134
ڈاک صندوق 128-13، 135-12
ڈاک فارم 134-19
ڈاک کا پتہ 134-22
ڈاک کا صندوق 53-1
ڈاک کارکن 169-49
ڈاک کلرک 135-7
ڈاک 234-3
ڈاکٹر (معالج) 118-5
ڈاکٹر کا معاون 168-47
ڈبے اور سامان رکھنے کے طریقے 74
ڈبے 74-5
ڈبل بیڈ 184-14
ڈبل روٹی کا ٹکڑا 74-22
ڈبل روٹی 80-17
ڈبکی لگاتے وقت پہننے والی نقاب 225-6
ڈبہ بند غذا 146-9
ڈبہ بند غذائیں 72
ڈبہ کھولنے کا آلہ 78-1، 146-8
ڈپلوما 40-3
ڈرا ہوا 43-23
ڈراؤنی کھانی 237-17
ڈرائی کلینرز 128-2
ڈرائیور تعلیمی نصاب میں داخلہ لیجیے۔ B-137
ڈرائیور لائنسنس 40-4، 136-9
ڈرائیور کا لائنسنس نمبر 136-11
ڈرائیور کی تربیت کے نصاب میں داخلہ لیجیے۔ G-137
ڈرائیونگ کا امتحان پاس کیجیے۔ H-137
ڈرافٹنگ کا کھیل 232-7
ڈرامہ 223-8، 236-12
ڈسکو کلب 223-12
ڈگریاں 13-8
ڈوبنا I-116
ڈوبنا 52-8
ڈورم 52-8
ڈول 61-7، 225-8
ڈولفن 213-31
ڈکی کے اندر 158
ڈکی 158-11
ڈھانچہ 233-18
ڈھبری 180-36
ڈھبریاں کھولنے کسنے کا اوزار 158-22
ڈھول 238-16
ڈھکن 78-24

ڈھکنے دار پکانے والی طشتری 78-10
ڈھیلا کرتا 93-26
ڈھیلی پتلون 97-30
ڈھیلی چادر 58-13
ڈھیلی ڈھالی 87-12
ڈی جے 64-4
ڈی وی ڈی اور سی روم ڈرائیو 196-9
ڈی وی ڈی پلیئر 56-7، 234-10
ڈی وی ڈی 133-19
ڈیبٹ کارڈ استعمال کیجیے C-27
ڈیزی 211-14
ڈیسک ٹاپ کمپیوٹر 196
ڈیسک کلرک 184-11
ڈیسک 6-2، 182-9
ڈیژم بجے 18-11
کئی زبانیں جاننے والا، سامان، ڈاک، سفری سہولتوں کا منتظم 184-4
کئی کاموں والا چاقو 226-20
کائنات 205
کاؤنٹر پر ملنے والی دوائیں 113-18
کاؤنٹر پر کھڑا شخص 79-17
کاؤنٹر کو پونچھیے O-60
کاؤنٹی میلہ 223-13
کابینہ 54-1، 138-10
کار پارک کیجیے E-129
کار خریدنا اور اس کی دیکھ بھال کرنا 157
کار کا اندراج کرائیے۔ F-157
کار کا حادثہ 144-2
کار کو آلودگی کی جانچ کرانے لے جائیے J-157
کار کو کسی مستری کے پاس لے جائیے۔ C-157
کار کی تجارت 126-4
کار کی حفاظتی سیٹ 37-19
کار کے اندر 159
کار کے پرزے 159-158
کار کے پہیے کا ڈھکنا 158-9
کار کے ٹینک میں گیس بھروائیے۔ G-157
کار 150-1
کارگو وین 156-13
کاروبار کا مالک 167-11
کاروں کے اشتہارات دیکھیے۔ A-157
کارٹون 236-3
کارڈ ارسال کرنا 135
کارڈ پڑھیے۔ G-135
کارڈ حاصل کیجیے۔ F-135
کارڈ میں وضاحت لکھیے۔ A-135
کارڈ و تحائف کی دکان 130-7
کارڈ ڈاک بکس میں پہنچائیے E-135
کارڈ ڈاک میں ڈالیے۔ D-135
کارڈ 239-5
کارکنوں کے وقت کی اندراجی گھڑی 165-7
کاریں اور ٹرک 156
کاریں بیچیے K-170
کاشت کے جانور 215
کاشت کے اندر 158
کاشتکار 177-13
کاشتکاروں کا بازار 84
کاشتکاری اور مویشی بانی 177
کاغذ کا ایک ٹکرا نکالیے۔ Y-9
کاغذ کاٹنے والی مشین 183-22
کاغذ کی گڑیاں 233-28

کاغذ کی کترن کرنے والی مشین 183-24
کاغذ کے رومال 54-3
کاغذ کے رومالوں کا رول 74-23
کاغذات کی ترتیب جانچیے E-171
کافی بنانے والی مشین 54-11
کافی شاپ کا مینیو 81-80
کافی کی پیالی 55-7
کافی کی دکان 126-11
کافی کی میز 56-19
کافی 73-33، 81-37
کال منتقل کیجیے O-171
کال کرنے والے کا استقبال کیجیے M-171
کال کرنے والے کو انتظار کرنے کے لیے کہیے N-171
کالا چیتا 217-40
کالج جائیے I-41
کالج کی سند 41-7
کالج کی مشترکہ اقامت گاہ 52-8
کالج 188-7
کالر 100-4
کالی بیریاں 68-17
کام پر جائیے I-38
کام سے واپس جائیے N-38
کام کی جگہ کا لباس 92-93
کام کی جگہ 164
کام کی مہارتیں 170
کام کیجیے K-38
کام کے دستانے 92-17، 179-17
کام کے دوران پہننے کی پتلون 92-5
کام کے دوران پہننے کی قمیص 92-2
کام کے دوران حفاظت 179
کام کے وقت کا مخصوص لباس 88-10
کام کے کپڑے 88
کاما 190-14
کامیابی کے طریقے 10
کامیڈی 237-13
کان درد 110-3
کان میں تعدیہ 111-3
کان میں لگانے کی ڈاٹ 179-15
کان ڈھکنے کی جالی 179-16
کان 105-12
کانگریس نمائندہ 138-4
کانگریس 138-2
کاننا 55-3، 211-29
کائنے والی چرخی 232-16
کائنے کا تختہ 54-27
کاڈ مچھلی 212-5
کاڈ 71-8
کاکروچ 63-26
کابو کا سلاد 69-1
کبوتر 214-15
کپڑا نرم کرنے والا محلول 101-6
کپڑوں پر استری کیجیے G-101
کپڑوں میں ترمیم کرنا 100
کپڑوں کا موازنہ 97
کپڑوں کو ٹانگیے H-101
کپڑوں کی اقسام 98-99
کپڑوں کی ایک دوکان 99
کپڑوں کی تفصیل 97
کپڑوں کی خرابیاں 97

کپڑوں کی دکان 99
کپڑوں کے اوپر پہننے کا کوٹ 90-2
کپڑے بدلنے کا گدا 59-2
کپڑے بدلنے کی میز 59-1
کپڑے بنانا 99-98
کپڑے پہنائیے H-36
کپڑے پہنئے D-38
کپڑے دھونا 101
کپڑے دھونے والی مشین 50-12، 101-3
کپڑے رکھنے کی قبضہ دار بڑی باسکٹ 57-1
کپڑے سلیے L-170
کپڑے سُکھانے والی مشین 50-13، 101-4
کپڑے لٹکانے کی چٹکیاں 101-10
کپڑے لٹکانے کی لکڑی یا لوہے کی پٹی 101-11
کپڑے ٹھنڈے پانی سے دھوئیے K-219
کپڑے کی چڈی 37-8
کپکپی 110-9
کتاب باہر لے جائیے C-133
کتاب تلاش کیجیے B-133
کتاب واپس کیجیے D-133
کتاب کی الماری 7-10
کتابوں کی آن لائن فہرست 133-11
کتابوں کی خود جانچ کرانا 133-10
کتابوں کی دکان 130-4
کتابیں اٹھائیے E-11
کتابیں پکڑیئے E-11
کتابیں پہنچائیے G-11
کتابیں جاری اور وصول کرنے کا ڈیسک 133-2
کتابیں لائیے F-11
کتب خانہ 5-17، 125-15، 133
کتّا 215-11
کتنے کے دانتوں والے جانور 215
کتھنی سوئیٹر دائیں طرف ہیں۔ 25-3
کتھنی 24-17
کتّے کو ٹہلائیے F-129
کثیر منزلہ 127-13
کچا مرغ 70-24
کچھوا 213-43
کچے کیلے 68-31
کدو کی ایک قسم 69-24
کدو کے خول میں چھید کرکے بنائی انسانی شکل 239-10
کراؤن (خول) 119-9
کرایہ پر رکھا گیا آدمی 177-20
کرایہ دار 50-6
کرایہ داروں کی میٹنگ 64
کرایہ داری معاہدے پر دستخط کیجیے D-48
کرایہ 152-2
کرایہ کا کارڈ 152-11
کرسر 197-14
کرسمس کا پیڑ 239-16
کرسمس 22-18
کرسی 7-11
کرفس، سلاد کے طور پر مستعمل 69-9
کرنی 178-13
کوشیا 233-25
کرہ، گولا 193-42
کریانہ اسٹور جائیے 72-73
کریانہ اسٹور پر جائیے L-38

کریانہ سامان کا تھیلا 67-13
کریانہ کلرک 72-4
کریانہ کے سامان 72
کریم رکھنے کا جگ 55-15
کریم 81-41، 113-25
کرین یا لوگوں کو اوپر اٹھانے والی مشین 178-5
کریڈٹ کارڈ استعمال کیجیے B-27
کستوری 214-16
کسرات اور اعشاریے 17
کسریں 192
کسٹمر افسر 161-17
کسٹمر پر 161
کسی الرجی سے متاثر ہونا E-116
کسی اٹارنی کی خدمات حاصل کیجیے B-141
کسی بات کی وضاحت کیجیے M-12
کسی جائداد فروش سے ملاقات کیجیے G-49
کسی جملے کا پہلا حرف بڑا لکھیے B-190
کسی دوست کے ساتھ ٹھہلیے A-143
کسی روزگار ایجنسی میں جائیے E-173
کسی ساتھی کے ہمراہ کام کرنا 8
کسی سفر پر جانا 162
کسی سوال کا جواب دیجیے L-8
کسی شئے کا بند مجموعہ 134-17
کسی گذشتہ واقعہ کی یاد کی تقریب 22-3
کسی مخصوص کام کا منتظم 175-4
کسی مسئلہ پر گفتگو کیجیے G-8
کسی میٹنگ کا وقت طے کیجیے J-171
کسی وکیل کی خدمات حاصل کیجیے B-141
کسی کا شکریہ ادا کیجیے E-12
کسی کتاب کو ملکر پڑھیے M-8
کسی کو پسند کرنا H-40
کسی کو مدعو کیجیے H-12
کسی کی تعریف کیجیے C-12
کسی بم جماعت کی مدد کیجیے J-8
کسی بنگامی حالت سے پہلے 146
کسی بنگامی حالت کے دوران 147
کشتی رانی 226-1، 227-8
کشتی 220-4، 228-17
کشمش 68-25
کشمیری نرم نفیس اون 98-4
کفچہ 78-19
کفگیر جیسا لمبا چمچہ 78-7
کل پرزے جوڑنے والا 167-7
کل 27-9
کلائی 106-14
کلاس میں جائیے J-38
کلاس میں شرکت کیجیے B-10
کلاس میں واپس جائیے M-11
کلاس کی طرف چلیے C-11
کلاس کی طرف دوڑیے D-11
کلاسیکی موسیقی کی محفل 223-14
کلاسیکی 237-21
کلب البحر 212-4
کلب سپ لگائی جانے والی بالیاں 95-37
کلچ 159-49
کلرک 5-13، 182-3
کلہاڑی 180-3
کلی 211-7
کلیجی 70-7

کلید 155-6
کم ایزی 97-31
کم چکنائی کا دودھ 81-42
کم قیمت جانچ 122-1
کمان 231-6
کمبل نما جنوبی امریکی لبادہ 90-19
کمبل 58-15، 146-7، 225-11
کمپیوٹر پر تصویریں بنانے والا 167-30
کمپیوٹر پروگرام بنائیے I-170
کمپیوٹر تجربہ گاہ 5-15
کمپیوٹر تکنیشین 167-19، 182-12
کمپیوٹر سافٹ ویئر انجینئر 167-18
کمپیوٹر سروس نمائندہ 167-20
کمپیوٹر 7-15، 183-17
کمپیوٹرز 196
کمر بند 100-5
کمر پر لادنے والا تھیلا 226-15
کمر پر لٹکانے والا تھیلا 94-18
کمر پٹکا 91-15
کمرتک کا پیش بند 93-30
کمر درد 110-5
کمر کو سہارا دینے والی پٹی 179-18
کمرہ تدریس 5-5، 7-6
کمرہ عدالت 141-7
کمرے سے باہر جائیے۔ O-11
کمرے میں بکھرا ہوا سامان 64-8
کمرے میں داخل ہوجائیے۔ A-11
کمرے کے ساتھی 64-1
کمزور سگنل 14-12
کمیونٹی کی سطح پر صفائی 148
کناری 99-34
کناڈا کے خطے 201
کندھا 105-13
کندھوں پر لٹکانے والا تھیلا 94-17
کندھے تک کے بال 33-2
کندھے کی گدی 231-20
کندھے کی ہڈی 107-28
کنگارو 217-44
کنگھا 33-21، 108-13
کنگھی 108-15
کنٹوپ 90-13
کنڈلی دار کمانیوں کے گدّے والا بستر 58-19
کنٹکٹر 152-13
کنکریٹ 178-10
کوئلوں پر بھنا ہوا مسالے دار گوشت 71-23
کونٹھہ 218-4
کوئی پیش کش کیجیے۔ I-49
کوئی پیغام چھوڑیے P-171
کوئی پیغام لیجیے Q-171
کوئی تجربہ انجام دیجیے B-195
کوئی تصویر منسلک کیجیے G-197
کوئی جملہ بول کر لکھوائیے۔ N-8
کوئی چیز پیش کیجیے D-12
کوئی دستاویز اسکین کیجیے H-171
کوئی دستاویز چھاپیے I-171
کوئی دستاویز فیکس کیجیے G-171
کوئی دوسری زبان بولیے N-170
کوئی رائے قائم کیجیے۔ E-195
کوئی ساز بجائیے A-238

بتھا 194-23	کھنی 106-12	کھانے سے ایک گھنٹہ پہلے استعمال
بتھوڑا 180-1	کہکشاں 205-15	کیجیے۔ B-112
بتھکڑی 141-2	کھپینے، "بیلو"۔ A-2	کھانے کی اشیاء رکھنے کی پیش تختہ 185-10
بتھ والی کرسی 56-22	کیاریوں میں سے خودرو گھاس چنیے G-176	کھانے کی بڑی قاب 83-18
بتھیلی 106-15	کیپسول 113-23	کھانے کی خدمات 185
بُد بُد 214-8	کیش رجسٹر استعمال کیجیے S-170	کھانے کی دکانوں کا مجموعہ 131-15
ہدایات پر عمل کرنا 9	کیش رجسٹر 27-10	کھانے کی میز پر پلیٹ رکھنے کا تہ پوش 55-11
ہدایات پر عمل کیجیے۔ F-147	کیفین سے خالی کافی 81-38	کھانے کے بعد پیش کی جانے والی ڈش کی
بدیہ 240-3	کیل اکھاڑ کلھاڑی 178-21	سینی 83-10
بر روز 20-21	کیل 180-34	کھجور 68-28
برم (ابرام) 193-39	کیلنڈر 20-21	کھدائی کرنے کی مشین 178-8
برن 216-14	کیلوں کا گچھا 68-29	کھر 216-17
بری پیاز 69-20	کیلکولیٹر 17-6، 183-25	کھرپا 176-7
بزاروں 16	کیلے 68-2	کھرپی 176-10
بفتے 20-15	کیمیا 195	کھرچنی 181-52
بفتے میں ایک بار 20-22	کیمیائی عناصر کی دوری جدول 195-26	کھرچنی کا چاقو 78-12
بفتے میں تین بار 20-24	کیمیاگر 195-25	کھسکانے والا شیشے کا دروازہ 53-18
بفتے میں دو بار 20-23	کین (چھڑ) 113-16	کھلا ہوا 13-9
بفتے کے دن 20، 20-16	کینین 226-24	کھلائی C-36
بلال 205-10	کینڈی کا ڈبہ 239-17	کھلاڑی 229-5
بلکا بھورا گول کیک 80-5	کینڈی 239-12	کھلاڑیوں کی کوٹ 89-14
بلکا صندوق 23-14	کیوبیک 201-5	کھلاڑیوں کی جیکٹ 89-14
بلکا ناشتہ خریدیں۔ K-11	کیوی پھل 68-22	کھلونوں کو دور رکھیے G-60
بلکا نیلا 24-11	کیٹ فش 71-2	کھلونوں کی الماری 59-16
بلکا ٹھنڈا 13-5	کیڑا مار دواوں کے زیریلی اثرات 218-16	کھلونے اور کھیل 59
بلکی آنچ پر پکائیے۔ P-77	کیڑوں کو دور رکھنے والا آلہ 226-23	کھلونے کی دکان 130-5
بلکی جیکٹ 97-28	کیڑے مکوڑے اور مفصل پایہ 214	کھلے پیسے حاصل کیجیے۔ A-26
بلکی نیند لیجیے A-53	کیڑے مکوڑے 209-11	کھوپڑی 107-47
بلکی ناشتے کی غذائیں 73	کیڑے کا کائنا 110-11	کھوکھلا دانت بھرنا E-119
ہموار ایڈی کے جوتے 95-27	کیک بنانے کا برتن 78-26	کھوکھلا 119-7
ہموار 96-19	کیک 73-39	کھوکھلی ڈوری 181-15
بنر کی فہرست 172-12	کیکٹ 71-10	کھنا 84-4
بنس 214-13	کیکڑا 71-9، 212-20	کھنمل 63-24
بنسیے A-44	بانی اسکول 188-4	کھنی کریم 72-21
بنگامی اقدامات 147-146	ہاتھ آرا 180-4	کھڑکی ٹوئی ہونی ہے۔ 62-5
بنگامی حالات اور قدرتی آفات 145-144	ہاتھ سے بنائی تصویر 56-9	کھڑکی کا شیشہ 178-16
بنگامی حالات کے کمرے میں داخلہ 121	ہاتھ سے چلنے والا ٹھیلا 175-11	کھڑکی 47-11، 56-17، 136-7
بنگامی حالت میں نبٹنے کا منصوبہ بنائیے۔ A-146	ہاتھ سے لگانے والا بریک 159-48	کھڑکیاں دھوئیے 60-I
بنگامی حالت کے بعد 147	ہاتھ ملائیے۔ J-3	کھڑکیاں صاف کرنے کا ربر کی دستی آلہ 61-15
بنگامی دروازہ 51-25، 161-14	ہاتھ میں پکڑا جانے والا پرس 89-19	کھڑکیوں سے دور رہیے۔ I-147
بنگامی صورت حال بیان کیجیے۔ G-15	ہاتھ میں پکڑنے والا آلہ 14-1	کھڑے ہو جائیں۔ D-6
بنگامی طبی تکنیشین (ای ایم ٹی) 121-32	ہاتھ کا انگوٹھا 106-16	کھیت پر کام کرنے والا 177-8
بنگامی کال کرنا 15	ہاتھ کے ذریعے سلائی B-98	کھیت 177-7
ہوا سے محفوظ کرنے والی جیکٹ 90-24	ہاتھ بلائیے۔ F-2	کھیتی کے اوزار 177-12
ہوا صاف کرنے والا 113-14	ہاتھ 105-15	کھیرا 69-10
ہوا میں نمی پیدا کرنے والا 113-12	باتھی چوک 69-22	کھیل دیکھنے کا شوقین 229-4
ہوا کے دباؤ سے سخت چنان توزنے کا برما 178-9	باتھی دانت 24-16، 217-48	کھیل کا لباس 231-16
ہوائی آلودگی 218-11	باتھی 217-42	کھیل کا میدان 50-3
ہوائی الوشیان وقت 19-27	بارمونیکا (بڑے سائز کا دھونکنی والا باجا) 238-21	کھیل کود سے متعلق افعال 230
ہوائی اڈہ 151-10، 161-160	بارن 159-32	کھیل کھیلیے۔ B-232
ہوائی اڈے پر تعینات قلی 160-1	بارڈ ڈرائیو (زیادہ معلومات کا ذخیرہ کرنے والی	کھیل کے میدان میں کھلی بیٹھنے کی جگہ 5-3
ہوائی اڈے کے ذرائع نقل و حمل 152	مقناطیسی قرص) 196-6	کھیل 223-8
ہوائی جہاز اڑائیے۔ F-170	بارڈویرر اسٹور 148-4	کھیلنے کا علاقہ 130-11
ہوائی جہاز اڑانے والا 161-11	بالون کا خوردنی ڈنھل 69-26	کھیلنے کی قمیض 88-4
ہوائی جہاز پر سوار ہو جائیے۔ E-160	باٹ ڈاگ (قیمے بھرے گول کلچے) 79-6	کھیلوں کے آلات 231
ہوائی جہاز 161	باڈروجن پراکسائڈ 117-9	کھیلوں کے پروگرام 236-11
ہوائی جہاز میں پائلٹ کا کمرہ 161-10	باکی اسٹک 231-11	کھینچ کر لے جانے والی گاڑی 156-17
ہوائی جہاز کا حادثہ 144-3	بپ باپ 237-26	کھینچنے والا ٹرک 156-14
ہوائی طاقت 218-2		کہر آلود 13-14

کوئی سمندری مرجانی حیویہ 212-24	
کوئی سوال پوچھیے۔ K-8	
کوئی سی ڈی سنیے۔ C-6	
کوئی فائل منسلک کیجیے H-197	
کوئی گانا گائیے B-238	
کوئی لوری گائیے O-36	
کوئی نظریہ بیان کیجیے۔ A-195	
کوئی نمونہ بنانے والا ساز و	
سامان 232-9	
کوالا 217-45	
کوپے 156-2	
کوریئر 168-40	
کوسٹ گارڈ (ساحل محافظ) 138-18	
کوفتہ 81-27	
کولن 190-17	
کولھے 107-30	
کونا 128-7	
کونپل 211-5	
کونڈو 52-5	
کونے پر رکھنے کی تپائی 56-14	
کونے پر رکیے D-155	
کونے کے اطراف دوڑیے H-153	
کوڑا اٹھانے والا ٹرک 127-22	
کوڑا اٹھانے والا 61-17	
کوڑا دان 51-23	
کوڑا رکھنے کے تھیلے 61-24	
کوڑا شگاف 51-26	
کوڑا کرکٹ باہر لے جائیے Q-60	
کوڑا کرکٹ پھینک دیجیے N-11	
کوڑا کرکٹ کم کیجیے A-219	
کوڑا کرکٹ 148-2	
کوڑے دان کو خالی کیجیے L-60	
کوڑے دان 160-6	
کوڑے کی نکاسی 54-7	
کوڑے کی نوکری 53-24، 57-26	
کوکی بنانے کی شیٹ 78-27	
کوبان 217-51	
کویوٹ 216-3	
کنار مچھلی 71-5، 212-10	
کننا 110-13	
کنوٹیاں 165-13	
کنھ پھوڑ 214-8	
کنھالی پکڑنے والی چمنی 195-44	
کرابی 54-24	
کڑھا ہوا انگیہ 91-21	
کڑھائی 233-24	
کڑے 95-9	
کھانئیے۔ I-11	
کھاتھ کھولنا 132	
کھاد ڈالیے D-176	
کھال کا بنا سر ڈھکنے والا کوٹ 90-9	
کھانا بنانے میں مستعمل آلہ 54-26	
کھانا پکائیے C-76, C-170	
کھانا پکانے کا دستے دار برتن 78-25	
کھانا پیش کیجیے F-82	
کھانا فراہم کرنے والا 185-16	
کھانا کھانے والے 185-9	
کھانسا A-110	
کھانسی کی شربت 113-29	

ہوائی ڈاک 134-5
ہوم ورک کیجیے T-40
ہونٹ 106-5
ہونٹوں کی سُرخی 109-38
ہوٹل کا ایک جامع کمرہ 184-16
ہوٹل 124-3، 184
بنائیے Q-109
ہڈی ٹوٹ جانا P-116
ہڈی 107-33
بک اور پھندا 99-27
بک اور ڈوری بند 99-29
بک 180-39
بیلی بٹ کے کباب 71-6
بیلی کاپٹر 151-9
بیملک طریقے سے سانس کی نلی کی رکاوٹ دور
کرنا 117-18
ہینڈبک کا مطالعہ کیجیے۔ A-137
ہیڈفونز 6-8، 234-4
یاسمین 211-22
یخنی شوربہ وغیرہ پیش کرنے کا پیالہ 55-21
یخنی 80-16
یو آر ایل 197-4
یو ایس بی پورٹ 196-7
یو ایس شاہراہ 154-17
یو ایس میں 5 سال یا زیادہ رہنا H-140
یو ایس نیشنل پارکس 220
یورپ 202-3
یورینس 205-7
یوگا 122-4
یوم آزادی 22-13
یوم جنگ دیدہ بزرگان 22-16
یوم سال نو 22-9
یوم صدر 22-11
یوم مارٹن لوتھر کنگ جونیئر 22-10
یوم محنت 22-14
یوم کولمبس 22-15
یوم یاد گار 22-12
یونیورسٹی 188-7
یوکاٹان جزیرہ نما 201-19
یک رنگی زنانہ لباس 87-11
یک رنگی مردانہ لباس 87-11
یک طرفہ راستہ 154-3
یک طرفہ سفر 152-16
یکساں اور مختلف 28
یکساں رنگ 23-15
یہ ادہڑ رہا ہے 97-43
یہ اکھڑ گیا ہے۔ 97-41
یہ بہت بڑا ہے۔ 97-38
یہ بہت چھوٹا ہے۔ 97-37
یہ بہت مہنگا ہے۔ 97-44
یہ پھونڈا ہے۔ 97-43
یہ پھٹ گیا ہے۔ 97-41
یہودی عبادت گاہ 127-16

Research Bibliography

The authors and publisher wish to acknowledge the contribution of the following educators for their research on vocabulary development, which has helped inform the principals underlying OPD.

Burt, M., J. K. Peyton, and R. Adams. *Reading and Adult English Language Learners: A Review of the Research.* Washington, D.C.: Center for Applied Linguistics, 2003.

Coady, J. "Research on ESL/EFL Vocabulary Acquisition: Putting it in Context." In *Second Language Reading and Vocabulary Learning*, edited by T. Huckin, M. Haynes, and J. Coady. Norwood, NJ: Ablex, 1993.

de la Fuente, M. J. "Negotiation and Oral Acquisition of L2 Vocabulary: The Roles of Input and Output in the Receptive and Productive Acquisition of Words." *Studies in Second Language Acquisition* 24 (2002): 81–112.

DeCarrico, J. "Vocabulary learning and teaching." In *Teaching English as a Second or Foreign Language,* edited by M. Celcia-Murcia. 3rd ed. Boston: Heinle & Heinle, 2001.

Ellis, R. *The Study of Second Language Acquisition.* Oxford: Oxford University Press, 1994.

Folse, K. *Vocabulary Myths: Applying Second Language Research to Classroom Teaching.* Ann Arbor, MI: University of Michigan Press, 2004.

Gairns, R. and S. Redman. *Working with Words: A Guide to Teaching and Learning Vocabulary.* Cambridge: Cambridge University Press, 1986.

Gass, S. M. and M.J.A. Torres. "Attention When?: An Investigation Of The Ordering Effect Of Input And Interaction." *Studies in Second Language Acquisition* 27 (Mar 2005): 1–31.

Henriksen, Birgit. "Three Dimensions of Vocabulary Development." *Studies in Second Language Acquisition* 21 (1999): 303–317.

Koprowski, Mark. "Investigating the Usefulness of Lexical Phrases in Contemporary Coursebooks." *Oxford ELT Journal* 59(4) (2005): 322–32.

McCrostie, James. "Examining Learner Vocabulary Notebooks." *Oxford ELT Journal* 61 (July 2007): 246–55.

Nation, P. *Learning Vocabulary in Another Language.* Cambridge: Cambridge University Press, 2001.

National Center for ESL Literacy Education Staff. *Adult English Language Instruction in the 21st Century.* Washington, D.C.: Center for Applied Linguistics, 2003.

National Reading Panel. *Teaching Children to Read: An Evidenced-Based Assessment of the Scientific Research Literature on Reading and its Implications on Reading Instruction.* 2000. http://www.nationalreadingpanel.org/Publications/summary.htm/.

Newton, J. "Options for Vocabulary Learning Through Communication Tasks." *Oxford ELT Journal* 55(1) (2001): 30–37.

Prince, P. "Second Language Vocabulary Learning: The Role of Context Versus Translations as a Function of Proficiency." *Modern Language Journal* 80(4) (1996): 478-93.

Savage, K. L., ed. *Teacher Training Through Video - ESL Techniques: Early Production.* White Plains, NY: Longman Publishing Group, 1992.

Schmitt, N. *Vocabulary in Language Teaching.* Cambridge: Cambridge University Press, 2000.

Smith, C. B. *Vocabulary Instruction and Reading Comprehension.* Bloomington, IN: ERIC Clearinghouse on Reading English and Communication, 1997.

Wood, K. and J. Josefina Tinajero. "Using Pictures to Teach Content to Second Language Learners." *Middle School Journal* 33 (2002): 47–51.